W9-BSY-044

*Sex, Marriage, and Family
in World Religions*

Sex, Marriage, and Family in World Religions

Edited by
Don S. Browning
M. Christian Green
John Witte Jr.

COLUMBIA UNIVERSITY PRESS

NEW YORK

BL
65
54549
2006

Columbia University Press
Publishers Since 1893
New York, Chichester, West Sussex
Copyright © 2006 Columbia University Press

All rights reserved

Library of Congress Cataloging-in-Publication Data
Sex, marriage and family in world religions / edited by Don S. Browning,
M. Christian Green, John Witte Jr.
p.   cm.
Includes bibliographical references and index
ISBN 0-231-13116-X (cloth : alk. paper) — ISBN 0-231-50519-1
1. Sex—religious aspects. 2. Marriage—Religious aspects. 3. Family—Religious aspects.
I. Browning, Don S. II. M. Green, M. Christian (Martha Christian), 1968— .
III. Witte, John, 1959–.
BL65.S4S48 2006
201'.7282—dc22   2005051799

Casebound editions of Columbia University Press books are printed on permanent and
durable acid-free paper.
Printed in the United States of America
c 10 9 8 7 6 5 4 3 2 1

CONTENTS

2. *Christianity*
Luke Timothy Johnson and Mark D. Jordan   77

PREFACE AND ACKNOWLEDGMENTS

This volume is one of a series of new volumes to emerge from the project on Sex, Marriage, and Family and the Religions of the Book, undertaken by the Center for the Study of Law and Religion at Emory University. The project seeks to take stock of the dramatic transformation of marriage and family life in the world today and to craft enduring solutions to the many new problems that transformation has occasioned. The project is interdisciplinary in methodology: It seeks to bring the ancient wisdom of religious traditions and the modern sciences of law, health, public policy, the social sciences, and the humanities into greater conversation and common purpose. The project is interreligious in inspiration: it seeks to understand the lore, law, and life of marriage and family of Judaism, Christianity, and Islam in their genesis and in their exodus, in their origins and in their diasporas. The project is international in orientation: it seeks to place current American debates over sex, marriage, and family within an emerging global conversation. This combination of interdisciplinary, interreligious, and international inquiry featured in our project as a whole is at the heart of the methodology of this volume, but we have deliberately decided to address not only Judaism, Christianity, and Islam but reach further and include the axial religious traditions of Hinduism, Buddhism, and Confucianism.

We wish to express our deep gratitude to our friends at the Pew Charitable Trusts in Philadelphia for their generous support of our Center for the Study of Law and Religion (and its predecessor organizations, the Law and Religion Program and the Center for the Interdisciplinary Study of Religion at Emory University). We are particularly grateful to Pew's president, Rebecca Rimel, and program officers Luis Lugo, Susan Billington Harper, and Diane Winston for masterminding the creation of this center, along with sister centers at ten other American research universities—a bold and visionary act of philanthropy that is helping to transform the study of religion in the American academy.

We also wish to express our deep gratitude to our Emory center colleagues, April Bogle, Eliza Ellison, Anita Mann, Amy Wheeler, and Janice Wiggins, for their extraordinary work. Over the past four years these five colleagues have helped to create a dozen major public forums, an international conference with 80 speakers and 750 participants, and scores of new journal, electronic, and video publications. They are now overseeing the production of 30 new books to come out of this project on Sex, Marriage, and the Family, along with administering a new center project, commenced in the autumn of 2003, on the Child in Law, Religion, and Society. For their editorial and production work on this volume we also wish to express our appreciation to three Emory Law students, Timothy Rybacki, Jonathan Setzer, and Matthew Titus.

We wish to thank Wendy Lochner and her colleagues at Columbia University Press for taking on this volume and working so assiduously to see to its timely publication.

We would also like to thank our friends at Columbia University Press for their permission to reprint excerpts from various of their imprints herein, as well as the authors, editors, and publishers for their permission to reprint herein excerpts from the following texts: Augsburg Fortress Press for permission to reprint Docs. 2-10, 2-17; Baker Books for permission to reprint Docs. 1-17, 2-19; Barnes & Noble Books for permission to reprint Doc. 4-6; Beth Din of America for permission to reprint Doc. 1-58; Broadview Press for permission to reprint Doc. 2-13; Catholic University of America for permission to reprint Doc. 2-11; Central Conference of American Rabbis for permission to reprint Docs. 1-60, 1-61; Clarendon Press for permission to reprint Doc. 6-20; Eastern Book Linkers for permission to reprint Doc. 4-2; Free Press for permission to reprint Doc. 6-11; Harvard University Press for permission to reprint Docs. 2-2, 6-22; Jewish Publication Society for permission to reprint Docs. 1-1, 1-2, 1-3, 1-4, 1-5, 1-6, 1-7, 1-8, 1-9, 1-10, 1-11, 1-12, 1-13, 1-39, 1-40, 1-41, 1-42; Judaica Press (Davka Corp.) for permission to reprint Docs. 1-27, 1-28, 1-29, 1-30, 1-31, 1-32, 1-33, 1-34, 1-35, 1-36; KTAV for permission to reprint Doc. 1-37; Littman Library of Jewish Civilization for permission to reprint Docs. 1-48, 1-49, 1-50, 1-51; Orbis Books for permission to reprint Doc. 2-23; Oxford University Press for permission to reprint Docs. 1-57, 4-4; Pali Text Society for permission to reprint Docs. 5-2, 5-3, 5-4; Paulist Press for permission to reprint Doc. 2-16; Penguin Press UK for permission to reprint Docs. 1-16, 4-1, 4-3; Philadelphia Yearly Meeting of the Religious Society of Friends for permission to reprint Doc. 2-21; B. Porten for permission to reprint Doc. 1-14; Rabbinical Assembly, International Association of Conservative/Masorti Rabbis for permission to reprint Doc. 1-59; Chudamani Raghavan for permission to use "Counting the Flowers," Doc. 4-8, which appeared in the original Tamil as "The Nagalinga Tree"; Random House for permission to reprint Doc. 2-3; St. Vladimir's Seminary Press for permission to reprint Doc. 2-12; Stanford University Press for permission to reprint Doc. 6-13; TAN Books and Publishers for permission to reprint Doc. 2-20; Temple University Press for permission to reprint Doc. 4-5; University of Arizona Press for permission to reprint Doc. 6-21; University of California Press for permission to reprint Docs. 6-10, 6-15; University of Chicago Press for permission to reprint Doc. 1-47; University of Hawaii Press for permission to reprint Docs. 6-1, 6-2, 6-3, 6-4; University of Notre Dame Press for permission to reprint Doc. 2-15; Wadsworth/Thomas Learning for permission to reprint Docs. 5-1, 5-5, 5-6, 5-7, 5-8, 5-9; Westminster John Knox Press for permission to reprint Docs. 2-1, 2-9, 2-22, 2-24; Wheeler Publishing for permission to reprint Doc. 4-7; Wisdom Publications for permission to reprint Doc. 5-10, 5-11; Yale University Press for permission to reprint Doc. 6-24.

ABOUT THE CONTRIBUTORS

Michael S. Berger is associate professor of religion, fellow in the Institute of Jewish Studies, and senior fellow in the Center for the Study of Law and Religion at Emory University.

Don S. Browning is Alexander Campbell Professor of Ethics and the Social Sciences, Emeritus, University of Chicago Divinity School, and Robert W. Woodruff Visiting Professor of Interdisciplinary Religious Studies at Emory University.

Azizah Y. al-Hibri is professor of law at the University of Richmond School of Law.

Alan Cole is associate professor of religious studies and director of East Asian studies at Lewis and Clark College.

Paul B. Courtright is professor of religion and Asian studies and senior fellow in the Center for the Study of Law and Religion at Emory University.

Patricia Buckley Ebrey is professor of history at the University of Washington.

Raja M. El-Habti is director of research at KARAMAH: Muslim Women Lawyers for Human Rights.

M. *Christian Green* is visiting lecturer on ethics at Harvard Divinity School and senior fellow in the Center for the Study of Law and Religion at Emory University.

Luke Timothy Johnson is Robert W. Woodruff Professor of New Testament and Christian Origins and senior fellow in the Center for the Study of Law and Religion at Emory University.

Mark D. Jordan is Asa Griggs Candler Professor of Religion and senior fellow in the Center for the Study of Law and Religion at Emory University.

John Witte Jr. is Jonas Robitscher Professor of Law and director of the Center for the Study of Law and Religion at Emory University.

INTRODUCTION

Social practices involving sex, marriage, and family are undergoing drastic changes throughout the world. These trends raise many questions. Are they real or superficial? Are these changes good, not so good, or positively bad for individuals, societies, and the world? If they are not so good or completely negative, is there anything that can be done to stop these trends and go in another direction? If what we have inherited from the past on sex, marriage, and family needs to be reformed, will the religions that have carried many of our traditional views on these matters have anything to contribute to this process of reformation and reconstruction?

This book does not try to answer whether alterations in sex, marriage, and family are good or bad. Nor does it address what should be done. But it does have a central premise: *we cannot know how to assess these changes or how to think about the future if we do not understand the role of the world religions in shaping attitudes and policies toward sex, marriage, and family in the past.* Can we really go forward if we are totally ignorant of the past? Can we constructively relate to these religious traditions if we are riddled with misunderstandings, false ideas about their teachings, and erroneous views about their complexities and nuances. Furthermore, many of the global conflicts that we face today — conflicts that break out in violent forms of hatred, terrorism, and self-defense — are fueled by misunderstandings that people have about what their own religion and other religions teach about sex, marriage, and family.

The editors of this volume believe that societies cannot form their future on sex, marriage, and family without at least consulting the traditions of the world religions on these matters. The human sciences of law, economics, medicine, psychology, and sociology cannot by themselves shape the future without knowing and listening to the heritage of the great world religions—Judaism, Christianity, Islam, Hinduism, Buddhism, and Confucianism. Furthermore, the peoples of the world cannot get along with each other, appreciate each other, or constructively critique each other without understanding more accurately how their respective traditions have shaped their faithful on these intimate subjects. The great public conflicts of our time are partially shaped by differences over who controls sexuality, who defines marriage, who shapes the family, and what actually constitutes a threat to inherited practices.

MODERNIZATION AND FAMILY CHANGE
AND CONFLICT

During the last several decades a momentous debate has swept across the world over the present health and future prospects of marriages and families. This debate has been especially intense in North America and Europe, but analogous debates have erupted in parts of Latin America, Africa, Asia, Australia, and the Middle East. These debates are about real issues. There are powerful trends affecting both advanced and underdeveloped countries. Some commentators believe these trends are changing marriages and families and undermining their ability to perform customary tasks. These trends are often called the forces of modernization. Theories of modernization are now also being extended by theories of globalization. These processes are having consequences for families in all corners of the earth. Older industrial countries have the wealth to cushion the blows of this disruption, but some experts argue that family decline throws economically fragile countries into even deeper poverty and disarray.[1]

To be sure, there are other sources of family disruption besides the forces of modernization and globalization. Wars, oppression, forced poverty, and discrimination between and among cultures and religions are additional factors. The recent massive family disruptions in Bosnia, Afghanistan, Sudan, Rwanda, Iraq, the Asian tsunami, and before that in Vietnam, Cambodia, Sri Lanka, and apartheid South Africa are still fresh on our minds. Sometimes the abstract yet disruptive forces of modernization get confused with the cultures and religions with which they have been associated historically. Does the West threaten the family codes of Islamic Shari'a? Or is it Christianity that is the threat to Islamic family law? Or is the real threat the modernizing process with which the West and Christianity are thought to be identified? Or, further, is modernization really a threat to families anywhere, especially if wisely understood and appropriately restrained?

Who and what is a threat to a religion's family practices can be asked from a variety of angles. For instance, are the highly pro-family and pro-marriage traditions of not only Islam but also Confucianism and Hinduism a threat to the Western companionate marriage and eventually to Western styles of modernization and democracy? Does a strong pro-family tradition have to be, by definition, patriarchal and oppressive to women or is it possible for a tradition to be both highly pro-marriage and pro-family and still be egalitarian on gender issues? Does marriage in a particular religious tradition have to include sex? Does it have to include children? What, in the first place, is marriage really for? Why are kin relations often, although not always, seen as so vital in several of the major world religions? Under what conditions, however, are kin attachments regarded as an obstacle to spiritual development within a particular religion? And do some religions, in complex and subtle ways, see marriage and family as both a threat to higher levels of spiritual fulfillment while, at the same time, subtly using persons who have attained these higher levels (monks, nuns, gurus) to reinforce and protect the more mundane marriages and families of less accomplished laity?

What are the conditions of divorce in a particular religion, and do women as well as men have the right to divorce? When, and for what reasons, is the practice of annulment used as a substitute for divorce? How were women's rights protected in the past, even in highly patriarchal religious traditions or in religions that practiced polygamy? Why did some religious traditions that practiced polygamy give it up or at least modify the conditions under which it could be practiced? The questions are large in number and overwhelming in complexity. Yet this volume gives insight—sometimes very surprising insights—into these and many other such matters. *And most important of all, we get to hear the answers to the questions straight from the central texts of these religious traditions themselves.*

Most social scientists now acknowledge that modernization, independent of factors such as war, poverty, and terrorism, can by itself be disruptive to families in certain ways. But many distinguished social scientists believe that there is little that can be done to allay these ambiguous consequences. Others are more hopeful that positive steps can be taken. Yet those who are optimistic still quarrel as to whether the religions themselves should have a role to play in the normative clarification, and perhaps reconstruction, of sex, marriage, and family for the future. At the minimum, *the three editors of this volume believe that these religions—all of them to varying degrees—have vital roles to play in the dialogue about the meaning and norms of sex, marriage, and family for the societies of tomorrow.* Hence it is our hope that this volume will serve as a vital resource for students and scholars, religious and political leaders, international and domestic officials alike as they engage in this dialogue.

THE PLAN OF THE VOLUME

This volume provides a number of the essential texts needed to start this dialogue about marriage and the family among the world's main religions and between them and the modern human sciences. We have assembled a group of highly respected and internationally recognized experts on each of these six major world religions. We have asked them to select and introduce the key texts of each tradition. We have invited them to view these axial traditions in their genesis, exodus, and leviticus—describing and documenting the origin, evolution, and institutionalization of their sexual, marital, and familial norms and habits. More specifically, we have asked them to assemble the basic texts—the ur texts, so to speak—that reveal the unfolding of these religions. These texts cover a variety of periods from antiquity to modern times.

These texts also represent several different genres through which religious traditions express themselves . These include classic canonical, theological, liturgical, legal, poetic, and prophetic statements on sex, marriage, and family drawn from the traditions of Judaism, Christianity, Islam, Hinduism, Buddhism, and Confucianism. All of these religions tend to use all of these genres. The reader will notice, however, that some traditions use legal texts more than other genres while still other religions may rely heavily on stories and poetry. Some religions—such as Judaism, Christianity, and Islam—have firm scriptural traditions while other traditions are carried by more loosely associated basic texts of various genres.

The chapter editors were asked to select texts for the various religions that addressed a number of common topics. Religions vary, however, in their directness in speaking to these issues. These topics include a) the purpose of sexuality, b) its relation to pleasure, procreation, and intimacy, c) the nature of family, d) the meaning, purpose, and institutionalization of marriage, e) gender roles in the family, f) the role of fathers, g) the nature of intergenerational obligations, and, when materials exist, h) the place of same-sex relations. At the same time, we hoped that editors would find texts that also would throw light on sex, marriage, and family from the angle of the major stages of the life cycle (birth, childhood, adulthood, aging, and death) and from the perspective of the ritual patterns and meanings governing these transitions.

THE PLACE OF RELIGION IN THE WORLD DIALOGUE ABOUT MARRIAGE AND THE FAMILY

The various religions can sometimes perceive each other as threats to their respective sex, marriage, and family traditions. Increasingly, as we saw above, the religions consider modernization to be a threat as well. Modernization can be defined in a variety of ways. One view defines it as the spread of technical rationality into various spheres of life.[2] Technical rationality tends to reduce life to efficient means of attaining short-term and untested individual satisfactions. The American sociologist Alan Wolfe, building in the insights of the German social theorist Jürgen Habermas, has argued that modernization viewed as the spread of technical rationality can function either in the service of market capitalism, as it does in countries such as the United States, or it can serve more bureaucratic state goals as it did in the Soviet Union and, to lesser degrees, even today in countries such as Norway and Sweden.[3] In either case, as Wolfe has convincingly argued, older patterns of mutual dependencies in families and marriage get transferred to the marketplace, as in capitalism, or to the state, as in more socialist societies. In both cases there is likely to be more divorce, more births out of wedlock, later marriages, more nonmarriage, more cohabitation, and more general belief that marriage and family life are irrelevant to modern societies.[4] Many scholars believe that along with these trends come more poverty for single mothers, more father absence, and for children and youth more crime, emotional difficulties, school problems, obesity, and nonmarital births.[5]

As a further perspective on modernization, English sociologist Anthony Giddens has argued that complex modern societies tend to differentiate their social systems into specialized and relatively autonomous sectors. This leads to social-system differentiations such as the separation between home and work, home and school, the social life of the young from parental supervision, the work life of spouses from the supervision of each other, and, finally, the separation of religious guidance from various sectors of society—especially the sectors of sexuality and intimacy.[6] In addition, modernization in the form of technical rationality leads to more effective contraception and a huge array of reproductive technologies that can, especially in the United States, be used within or outside of marriage, by singles or by couples, and by heterosexuals or by gays.

The processes of modernization are generally thought to lead to many positive values most of us want to retain and enhance, for example, more control over the contingencies of life, better education, more wealth, better health, more equality for both males and females, and more freedom for nearly everyone. However, these same processes also threaten to undermine the power of religious traditions to shape and support family and marital solidarity. In turn, the religious traditions themselves feel threatened, and *in the process of defending themselves, they often end up attacking each other rather than the elusive processes of modernization and their extension into globalization.* So, the question becomes, how do we learn to live with, appreciate, yet constrain and productively guide modernization in matters pertaining to sex, marriage, and family?

This brings us back to our earlier question. What will be the grounds for guiding sex, marriage, and family in the future? Will we abandon the hope of any coherence in sexual and family norms—any common ideals around which modern societies will organize their goals in the sexual field? Will we turn to the human sciences (law, medicine, economics, sociology, and psychology) and them alone? *Or will the religions of the world be a part of the dialogue?* What will be the sources of the cultural work needed to find the guidelines for sex, marriage, and family?

Many perceptive commentators such as social scientists David Popenoe and James Q. Wilson feel that a new *cultural work* is required that will both support and refashion the sexual and marital fields of life.[7] But these scholars tend to bypass the resources of the world religions in their list of resources of the future. Scholars in family law, family economics, family medicine, and family sociology tend to hold the same point of view, that is, that religions can no longer inform our normative social and cultural visions of sex, marriage, and family.

The exclusion of religion may be shortsighted. First, it seems to assume that religious teachings and practices are so diverse, so contradictory, and so incommensurate that they provide no common grounds for social reconstruction. This may not be true. The six religions illustrated below are not *identical* on issues pertaining to sex, marriage, and family. But they are *not completely different* or contradictory. There are positive *analogies* between them that may contain genuine wisdom and stable points of cooperation for social and cultural reconstruction. Second, the strategy that would exclude the voice of the religious traditions overlooks their complexity. For instance, each of the main axial religious traditions adopted and adapted some marital and family patterns from antecedent and analogous cultures. Furthermore, secular and religious institutions and authorities have often worked hand in hand in contributing to and enforcing the preferred sexual, marital, and familial norms and habits carried by these religious traditions. To say it more simply: *a sexual or family pattern carried by a religion may not have been narrowly religious in its origin.* Religious traditions almost always combine in subtle ways naturalistic, legal, moral, and metaphysical levels of thinking and reasoning. Just because an insight or pattern is wrapped in religion does not mean it was exclusively religious in its origin. Nonetheless, a good deal of the genesis, genius, and generativity of viable and lasting marriage and the family norms may lay in the teachings and practices of the axial religions of the world. These teachings and practices may just be something of the genetic code of what marriage and the family have been and can be.

ANALOGIES AND DIFFERENCES

The texts included in this volume provide possible points on the map of these cultural genetic codes on sex, marriage, and the family. These codes differ in important ways, as you will see in reading these chapters, and they have accordingly produced various domestic patterns throughout the world. But there is more convergence than conflict in the teachings on sex, marriage, and family of the six axial world religions. Here are a few points of convergence that are worth considering:

First, each of these religious traditions confirms marriage as a vital and valuable institution and practice that lies at the heart of the family and at the foundation of broader society. To be sure, Confucianism and ancient Judaism permitted powerful men to have concubines. Christianity sometimes idealized the sexually abstinent marriage and, with Buddhism, commanded celibacy for some of its religious leaders. Islam permitted, sometimes encouraged, polygamous marriages, as did Judaism for a time and occasional Christian sects. All six traditions recognized that some adults were not physically, emotionally, or sexually suited for marriage. But all six religious traditions have long celebrated marriage as a public and community-recognized contract and religious commitment to which the vast majority of adults within the community are naturally inclined and religiously called.

Second, each tradition recognizes that marriage has inherent goods that lie beyond the preferences of the couple. One fundamental good of marriage, emphasized by Judaism, Christianity, Hinduism, and Confucianism is that the husband and wife complete each other; indeed, they are transformed through marriage into a new person—a new *one-flesh* reality. Another fundamental good of marriage is the procreation and nurture of children. Children are sacred gifts to a married couple who carry forth not only the family name, lineage, and property but also the community's religion, culture, and language. All these religions thus see a close relation between marriage and children, just as they saw a close relation, although not an identity, between marriage and sexual expression. And all these religions teach that stable marriages and families are essential to the well being of children.

Third, each tradition regards marriage as a special form of promise, oath, or contract. Indeed, these traditions have often made provision for two contracts— betrothals or future promises to marry and spousals or present promises to marry—with a mandatory waiting period between them. The point of this waiting period is to allow couples to weigh the depth and durability of their mutual love. It is also to invite others to weigh in on the maturity and compatibility of the couple, to offer them counsel and commodities, and to prepare for the celebration of their union and their life together thereafter.

Fourth, each tradition eventually came to insist that marriage depended in its essence on the mutual consent of the man and the woman. Even if the man and woman are represented by parents or guardians during the contract negotiation, their own consent is essential to the validity of their marriage. Jewish, Hindu, Confucian, and Muslim writers came to this insight early in the development of marriage. The Christian tradition reached this insight canonically only in the twelfth century, and Buddhism more recently still. All these traditions have long tolerated the practice of arranged marriages and child marriages, and this pattern persists among Hindus and Muslims today, even in diasporic communities. But the theory has always been that both the young man and the young woman reserved the right to dissent from the arrangement upon reaching the age of consent.

Fifth, each tradition emphasizes that persons are not free to marry just anyone. The divine and/or nature set a first limit to the freedom of marital contract. Parties cannot marry relatives by blood or marriage, nor marry parties of the same sex—a tradition that is now being questioned in the liberal wing of some religions. Custom and culture set a second limit. The parties must be of suitable piety and modesty, of comparable social and economic status, and ideally (and, in some communities, indispensably) of the same faith and caste. The general law of contracts sets a third limit. Both parties must have the capacity and freedom to enter contracts and must follow proper contractual forms and ceremonies. Parents and guardians set a fourth limit. A valid marriage, at least for minors, requires the consent of both sets of parents or guardians—and sometimes as well the consent of political and/or spiritual authorities who stand in loco parentis.

Sixth, in most of these traditions marriage promises were accompanied by exchanges of property. The prospective husband gave to his fiancée (and sometimes her father or family as well) a betrothal gift, on occasion a very elaborate and expensive gift. In some cultures husbands followed this by giving a wedding gift to the wife. The wife, in turn, brought into the marriage her dowry, which minimally covered her basic living articles, maximally a great deal more. These property exchanges were not an absolute condition to the validity of a marriage. But breach of a contract to deliver property in consideration of marriage could often result in dissolution at least of the engagement contract.

Seventh, each tradition developed marriage or wedding liturgies to celebrate the formation of a new marriage and the blending of two families. These could be extraordinary visual and verbal symphonies of prayers, oaths, songs, and blessings, sometimes followed by elaborate feasts. Other media complemented the liturgies—the beautiful artwork, iconography, and religious language of the marriage contracts themselves, the elaborate rituals and etiquette of courtship, consent, and communal involvement in establishing the new household, the impressive production of poems, household manuals, and books of etiquette detailing the ethics of love, marriage, and parentage of a faithful religious believer. All these media, and the ample theological and didactic writings on them, helped to confirm and celebrate that marriage was at heart a religious practice—in emulation of the leader of the faith (in the case of Islam), in implementation of moral instruction (in the case of Confucianism and Buddhism), in obedience to divine commandments (in the cases of Judaism, Christianity, and Hinduism).

Eighth, each tradition gave the husband (and sometimes the wife) standing before religious tribunals (or sometimes secular tribunals that implemented religious laws) to press for the vindication of their marital rights. The right to support, protection, sexual intercourse, and care for the couple's children were the most commonly litigated claims. But any number of other conjugal rights stipulated in the marriage contract or guaranteed by general religious law could be litigated. Included in most of these traditions was the right of the parties to seek dissolution of the marriage on discovery of an absolute impediment to its validity (such as incest) or on grounds of a fundamental breach of the marriage commitment (such as adultery).

Ninth, each tradition emphasized family continuity and the strengths of kin altruism, albeit with different forms and emphases. Family continuity, legacy, and connections between ancestors and present and future generations were very pronounced in Judaism, Hinduism, Islam, and Confucianism. These came to particularly poignant expression in the burial and mourning rituals triggered by the deaths of parents, spouses, and children. Honor and exchange between the generations were emphasized as well, rendering intergenerational continuity and filial piety an enormously powerful welfare system with sacred sanction. Providing care and protection to needy children, parents, siblings, and even more extended family members were essential religious obligations in all six of these traditions. Even in Buddhism, which saw the family as a distraction, and in Christianity, which often viewed marriage and family life as a competitor with the Kingdom of God, family continuity and mutual support were still emphazed.

Tenth, most of these traditions drew a distinction between natural and fictive families, though this varied in its articulation. In Buddhism and Christianity monastic groups were also fictive families. In Christianity congregations were fictive families. But, even then, there were often complex ways in which fictive families reinforced natural families. For instance, Buddhist monks would intervene with a natural family's ancestors, praying for merit from ancestors to natural families—natural families that themselves supported the fictive family of the monastery in order to gain merit from monks and through them from their own ancestors. Although congregations could become fictive families in Christianity, they also generally included and reinforced the strength of the conjugal couple, their offspring, extended family, and households.

Eleventh, most of these religions reinforced intergenerational honor and obligations, but they differed in degree and manner of this reinforcement. Confucianism and Hinduism gave special emphasis to this value, and Buddhism, which inherited many of its family values from Hinduism, followed suit, even though it also saw family as a distraction from higher spiritual pursuits. Even though Judaism, Christianity, and Islam all emphasized honoring parents (father and mother), Christianity warned that family obligations could conflict with the will of God and the demands of the kingdom.

Twelfth, these religions differ considerably on their respective views of sexuality and the erotic. Although all of these religions see sexuality as a potentially unruly force in human affairs, all affirm its rightful place when guided by certain constraints. They all viewed marriage, with few exceptions, as one of the most important such constraints, though this was no substitute for personal sexual discipline. Within marriage religions varied with regard to their appreciation for erotic enjoyment, with Islam and perhaps Hinduism being the most forthright in their affirmation, but Judaism, Christianity, Buddhism, and Confucianism never completely losing an understanding of the role of mutual sexual satisfaction in marriage.

Thirteenth, each tradition kept an ample roll of sexual sins or crimes— incest, bestiality, sodomy, rape, and pedophilia being the most commonly prohibited, with more variant treatment of concubinage, prostitution, and mastur-bation. A growing conflict in many religious communities today, particularly in North America and Western Europe, is whether to retain traditional prohibi-tions against homosexuality. Some denominations within western Christianity are now experimenting with the legitimation of same-sex unions, and compa-rable experiments are afoot in small segments of western communities of Ju-daism and Hinduism.

Fourteenth, each tradition draws a distinction between legitimate and ille-gitimate children. Legitimate children are those born to a lawfully married couple. Illegitimate children are those born outside of lawful marriage—prod-ucts of adultery, fornication, concubinage, rape, incest, and in some commu-nities products of illicit relations between parties of different castes, races, or religions. Illegitimate children were historically stigmatized, sometimes se-verely, and formally precluded from holding or inheriting property, gaining various political, religious, or social positions, and attaining a variety of other public or private rights. In western societies, as well as in modern-day Australia, New Zealand, Japan, Korea, and parts of southeast Asia, illegitimate children have gained constitutional protections and state welfare provisions and have benefited from the expansion of adoption. But in some Islamic, Hindu, and Confucian communities illegitimate children and their mothers still suffer am-ple social stigmatization, and they are still sometimes sentenced to "honor kill-ings" or mandatory abortions or infanticide.

Fifteenth, these traditions varied in their handling of sex, marriage, and family depending on whether they perceived themselves to be a majority or minority religion. Judaism since the diaspora has viewed itself as a minority religion, and this affected some of its perspectives on sexual issues, especially in contrast to the official views of the state or the dominant religion. Buddhism has seldom viewed itself as a dominant religion within a particular territory or state. On the other hand, Christianity, Islam, Hinduism, and Confucianism have all perceived their traditions at various times to be dominant religions, and this has affected the range of issues in sex, marriage, and family that they addressed. As majorities these groups have often looked to the state to imple-ment their basic teaching on sex, marriage, and family. In the twentieth century secularism, socialism, and pluralism alike have eroded these state-sanctioned religious understandings of marriage and family. In some communities, such as Europe and Canada, dominant religious communities have largely acqui-esced in these movements or have had insufficient power to resist them. In other communities, such as Latin America, Russia, South Africa, and the Indian subcontinent, once dominant religious communities have developed their own internal religious legal systems to govern the marriage and family affairs of their own voluntary members.

Sixteenth, although the origins of Hinduism, Judaism, and Confucianism are obscure, Christianity, Islam, and Buddhism are more open to historical investigation. Early Christianity and Islam were more progressive in their treatment of gender issues, women, and children than later expressions of the religion, especially as it became more established by the state, closer to powerful political and economic interests, and therefore mirrored some of the hierarchical structures of empires, kings, and caliphs. Studying the origins of a religion is helpful in determining some of its basic impulses, directions, and resources on sex, marriage, and family. At the same time, religions do indeed complicate and mature as time passes. Understanding a religion from the perspective of its more complex later legal and philosophical developments, as in the case of twelfth- and thirteenth-century Judaism, Christianity, and Islam and later developments in Confucianism (neo-Confucianism) is crucial for understanding the wisdom of a religious tradition on sex, marriage, and family.

HOW AND BY WHOM SHOULD THE BOOK BE USED?

We envision this book as a basic textbook for courses in colleges, universities, and professional schools. It should work for both undergraduates and graduates. Of course, the text must be adapted, supplemented, and used selectively depending on the context and purpose of the class where it is used. In addition, the Center for the Study of Law and Religion at Emory University that supported the creation of this text hopes to provide other resources that will help professors and students carry the dialogue more directly into the twenty-first century.[8]

More specifically, we think this text can be used to teach comparative religion and history of religions. Most of the distinctive features of these religions can be discerned through the prism of their teachings on sex, marriage, and family. In addition, what the concepts, symbols, and teachings of these religions really meant can sometimes be seen with vivid clarity when viewed from the perspective of their implications for the sexual and familial field of meaning. This leads to a deeper and more concrete understanding of the religion itself.

But, as we have pointed out in this introduction, the field of sexuality is in and of itself worth studying from the perspective of these religions. There is little doubt that defining and guiding sexuality in marriage, in family, and perhaps outside of marriage and family will be one of the major preoccupations of the twenty-first century. As we have said above, we expect a grand cultural dialogue on these issues. We expect, and hope, that the great world religions will be a part of this dialogue.

We also believe that this text can be used in a variety of more specialized settings. We will list a few of them. We believe that academic programs in the sociology and psychology of the family should introduce courses using this resource. We believe that social work schools preparing students to work with families from increasingly more diverse religious and cultural backgrounds should offer such courses. The field of family law should help its students understand the family codes and legal rationalities within these religious traditions. Psychiatrists, psychotherapists, and school counselors working with diverse families should know much of what is in the volume. For general understanding, for practical work with people, and for preparation for the emerging world dialogue on sex, marriage, and family, we recommend this volume as a resource.

NOTES

1. William Goode, *Changes in Divorce Patterns* (New Haven, CT: Yale University Press, 1993).

2. Max Weber, *The Protestant Ethic and the Spirit of Capitalism* (New York: Scribner's, 1958), 181; Jürgen Habermas, *Theory of Communicative Action I* (Boston: Beacon, 1981), 340–341.

3. Alan Wolfe, *Whose Keeper: Social Science and Moral Obligation* (Berkeley: University of California Press, 1989), 52–60, 133–140.

4. For summaries of studies and statistics supporting these claims on a comparative international basis, see Wolfe, *Whose Keeper*, 56–58; David Popenoe, *Disturbing the Nest: Family Change and Decline in Modern Societies* (New York: Aldine de Gruyter, 1988); David Popenoe, *Life Without Father* (New York: Free, 1996); Linda Waite, ed., *The Ties That Bind: Perspectives on Marriage and Cohabitation* (New York: Aldine de Gruyter, 2000).

5. For the specific effect of these trends on children, see Paul Amato and Alan Booth, *A Generation at Risk: Growing Up in an Era of Family Upheaval* (Cambridge: Harvard University Press, 1997); see also the recent report distributed by the YMCA of the USA, Dartmouth Medical School, and the Institute for American Values, *Hardwired to Connect: The New Scientific Case for Authoritative Communities* (New York: Institute for American Values, 2003).

6. Anthony Giddens, *The Transformation of Intimacy: Sexuality, Love, and Eroticism in Modern Societies* (Cambridge: Polity, 1992).

7. Popenoe, *Life Without Father*, 196–201; James Q. Wilson, *The Problem of Marriage* (New York: HarperCollins, 2002), 207–221.

8. See, e.g., Abdullahi Ahmed An-Na'im et al., *Islamic Family in a Changing World: A Global Resource Book* (London: Zed, 2003); Abdullahi Ahmed An-Na'im, eds., *Interreligious Marriage: Threat or Promise?* (forthcoming); Abdullahi Ahmed An-Na'im, *The Future of Shari'a* (forthcoming); Don S. Browning, *Marriage and Modernization: How Globalization Threatens Marriage and What to Do About it* (Grand Rapids: Eerdmans, 2003); Don S. Browning and David Clairmont, eds., *American Religions and the Family* (New York: Columbia University Press, forthcoming); Michael J. Broyde and Michael S. Berger, eds., *Marriage and Family in the Jewish Tradition* (Lanham, NY: Rowman and Littlefield, 2005); Paul B. Courtright, *Dower and Divorce in Diaspora Hinduism* (New Brunswick, NJ: Rutgers University Press, in press); Robert M. Franklin, *Crisis in the Village: Restoring Hope for Families in African-American Communities*

(forthcoming); M. Christian Green, *Feminism, Fatherhood, and Family Law* (forthcoming); Steven M. Tipton and John Witte Jr., eds., *The Family Transformed: Religion, Values, and Science in American Life* (Washington, DC: Georgetown University Press, 2005); John Witte Jr. and Eliza Ellison, eds., *Covenant Marriage in Comparative Perspective* (Grand Rapids: Eerdmans, 2005); John Witte Jr., *Ishamel's Bane: Illegitimacy Reconsidered* (Cambridge: Cambridge University Press, forthcoming).

Sex, Marriage, and Family
in World Religions

Chapter 1

JUDAISM

Michael S. Berger

INTRODUCTION

Judaism, like other millennia-old world religions, has within it many voices and opinions on such core human subjects as sexuality, marriage, and family. Unlike other world religions, however, Judaism has been, for most of its history, the tradition of a minority—a powerless, stateless, and oftentimes persecuted, minority. To be sure, an early period of independence, roughly coeval with the Bible, produced the literature (or its antecedents) that would become the foundational text of Judaism. But beginning with the destruction of Solomon's Temple in 586 BCE and the consequent exile of Judeans to Babylonia and Egypt, minority status became the norm for Jews, with few exceptions, all the way up to the modern period.

This reality had a profound impact on every facet of Judaism. Survival was the constant call, and the tradition mustered all of its resources—theological, legal, social, and economic—to meet the challenge. The family was, in many cases, the primary vehicle for preserving distinctiveness from the majority culture, and so the tradition used law, custom, and lore to govern its formation and maintenance. Indeed, from the Bible forward the Jewish people is portrayed at its core as a large extended family descended from the patriarch Jacob, and from the Second Temple period forward Jews increasingly insisted on endogamy to ensure a common heritage.

Practically speaking, however, boundaries were far more permeable than was claimed; the forces preserving distinctiveness were always offset by those promoting accommodation. Jews were in regular contact with their neighbors, producing a startling array of Jewish thought and practice in all areas, including marriage and family. Indeed, some of the most significant alterations in the form and content of Jewish marriage, such as the emphasis on documents or the switch to monogamy, can be understood in this light. Therefore, the history of Jewish views on sex, marriage, and family can be most helpfully understood as the oscillation between the two poles of continuity, with the Jewish covenant on the one hand and correlation with one's surroundings on the other.

SEX, MARRIAGE, AND FAMILY
IN THE HEBREW BIBLE

While the majority of the Hebrew Bible, known as *TaNaKh*, recounts the period of Israelite settlement in the land of Canaan, most scholars insist that the majority of canonical texts reached their current form in the Persian period (sixth to fourth century BCE) when Jews lived as a minority population both in the province of Yehud in the Land of Israel and elsewhere in Mesopotamia and Egypt. Out of their minority perspective this collection of texts came to be the main scripture of the Jewish people because virtually all its books are *about* the Jewish people—or, more specifically, its covenant with God.

Given the portrayal of the Jewish people as an extended family, one might think that such a parochial story would begin with, or would quickly reach, the story of the nation's progenitor, Abraham. However, the first eleven chapters of Genesis speak of God's relationship with the world, beginning with the creation of a highly ordered and differentiated world. Each creature is part of a species, a group that is meant to know its place in the world and maintain its boundaries and functions. Man and woman are both informed and blessed to procreate, to "be fruitful and multiply" and assert stewardship over the created order. This state, termed "very good" in divine eyes (Gen. 1:31), is presented somewhat differently in chapter 2, which offers the creation of woman as a response to the first man's loneliness: "Therefore a man leaves his father and mother, clings to his wife, and becomes one flesh" (Gen. 2:24). Thus, between the first two chapters, there emerges a sense that the union of man and woman was inherently good, intended since creation for the purposes of procreation and companionship (whether practical or emotional). But this idyllic state collapses as the first couple eats from forbidden fruit, with the consequence that they sense, for the first time, sexual shame (Gen. 3:7). Painful childbirth, female sexual passion, and male domination of the female are all presented as punishment for the woman's submission to temptation and her insistence that her husband join her in the sin (Doc. 1–1).

Humanity's decline continues until God chooses Abraham, promising him that his descendants would become abundant, great, and would receive the

Land of Canaan as an inheritance (Gen. 12:1–3). This divine blessing, later symbolized through circumcision (Gen. 17), comes to be the reward of a covenant whereby Abraham's descendants must obey God's law as it was revealed to Moses at Sinai and during the wilderness wanderings. The people's status as God's "special treasure among all the nations . . . a kingdom of priests, a holy nation" (Ex. 19:5–6) is predicated on their living according to demanding standards, including a host of sexual norms (Doc. 1–2). These are deemed the idolatrous and abominable practices of the local tribes, and the Jews must maintain their purity and holiness—or suffer a similar fate of displacement and exile.

The *TaNaKh*'s presentation of the history of the Jewish people as that of an extended family—twelve tribes, the descendants of the sons of Jacob, settling on ancestrally allotted land—highlights the text's assumption that the covenant is meant to be lived out in the context of large, agrarian patriarchal families, with very specific division of labor between men, women and children and traditions passed from parents to children. The consequences of this orientation for our subjects cannot be overstated, yet virtually all have a "covenantal overlay" as well. Strict rules of endogamy and exogamy, including the prohibitions against incest mentioned above, controlled marriage with the aim of producing legitimate heirs; yet the text often adds the importance of these rules in maintaining allegiance to God: alien, non-Israelite women will lead men astray (Docs. 1–3, 1–4) unless, like Ruth, they accept the God of Israel. Polygamy is allowed (concubinage seemed to be the preserve of the aristocracy) so long as primogeniture is not disrupted; yet grave spiritual dangers accompany the pursuit of women other than one's wife, and monogamous marriage becomes the metaphor of the God-Israel covenant (Docs. 1–5 to 1–7). The ideal woman, extolled in Proverbs' famous poem in chapter 31, is both a competent manager of the household, overseeing food and cloth production, as well as a God-fearer (Doc. 1–8). To maintain order and preserve tradition in these agrarian hierarchies, respect of parents is demanded in the Decalogue; incorrigibly disobedient children are to be publicly executed. At the same time, parents must educate children and pass on the tale of the nation's birth and Sinaitic covenant with God, so that they may fear the Lord as well (Docs. 1–9 to 1–13).

As we enter the Persian period, during which much of the TaNaKh reached its current form, the process of marriage in particular seems to have undergone greater formalization. Based on the evidence of fragmentary papyri from Elephantine, a Jewish garrison in Egypt, we may conclude that marriage was a multistaged process: the bridegroom first asked the woman's male guardian for the bride and then declared "she is my wife and I am her husband." A dowry was set and a written contract was then drawn up (Doc. 1–14). This contractualizing trend in marriage would continue through the Greco-Roman period and into Rabbinic Judaism.

It is likely that over the course of the Biblical period, as Jews became a dispersed minority and came into close contact with other peoples (even in

Yehud itself), greater emphasis was placed on endogamy as critical to preserving the covenant—as exemplified in the fifth-century BCE account of the expulsion of foreign women and their children by Ezra the Scribe and his renewal of the covenant with the Jews of Jerusalem (Ezra 9–10). A close connection between living the covenant and endogamous marriage, however, may not yet be inferred: the Elephantine papyri attest to exogamous marriage, so we may have here a parallel tradition to that in Jerusalem or a more exceptional situation given the lack of Jewish females in the garrison. In any event, it appears that both the more conservative agricultural society in which Jews lived and the growing sense of Jewish exclusiveness and covenantal status as they carved out a minority identity contributed to emerging Jewish attitudes towards sex, marriage, and family.

SEX, MARRIAGE, AND FAMILY IN THE INTERTESTAMENTAL PERIOD

The establishment of Alexander's empire in the fourth century BCE brought Jews into direct and sustained contact with Hellenism, although the extent of that influence is very hard to gauge and was likely diverse across the empire. Jews generally remained in rural settings, although Jerusalem and other cities in Judea (as the Greek province was now called) grew in size and importance, and had substantial Jewish populations. During this time a substantial Jewish population lived in the "diaspora," the world outside the land of Israel, in contact with local Gentiles and other groups created by the cosmopolitan character of Greek cities. Nevertheless, within the multiethnic environment of the Greco-Roman and Sassanian Babylonian empires, Jews shared several practices—circumcision, dietary restrictions, and Sabbath observance—that they were able to regard themselves, and be regarded by others, as a distinct people.

On the intellectual level the consequences of contact with Hellenism were felt in many circles, but most keenly among Egyptian Jewry. Philosophical ideas penetrated deeply into Jewish self-understanding, producing an entire genre of wisdom literature that emphasized virtuous conduct, including respect for one's parents, the marriage ideal with the proper behavior of husbands and wives, sexual temperance, and the importance of educating and disciplining one's children. The Wisdom of Ben Sira, known more commonly by its apocryphal title Ecclesiasticus, is paradigmatic of this literature (Doc. 1–15). In contrast to the covenantal context of the Biblical sources, these texts linked familiar Jewish values to wisdom as an expression of divine illumination independently worthy of human pursuit. Biblical notions of purity, including restrictions on food and sex, found natural analogues in certain Greek notions of ascetic discipline and moral wisdom and were so interpreted by Jewish philosophers such as the first-century CE Egyptian allegorist Philo of Alexandria. Such efforts were no doubt intended both to strengthen religious observances among Jews and to defend Judaism against its pagan detractors. This literature, all in Greek, entered the legacy of early Christianity, which embraced these ideas and their language of expression as its own.

On the social level, in the absence of a central institution to impose a single pattern of behavior, various types of Jewish communities evolved in this period. As we noted, common custom united "natural communities" of Jews (that is, those born to Jewish parents), who were rather open to "God-fearers" and other non-Jews participating in communal life. At the same time, "intentional Judaic communities" grew up, particularly in Judea but elsewhere as well, that had what they took to be "correct" interpretations of Jewish Scripture and stricter standards of behavior, which helped determine insiders and exclude others. These communities, such as Qumran, which we know from the Dead Sea Scrolls, saw themselves as God's chosen, living the ideal form of the covenant on this earth. Their rigorous, highly structured, and disciplined communal life allowed some members to marry, but only monogamously, and preferred sexual abstinence (Doc. 1–16). This sectarian community, like others in the Land of Israel, was extremely concerned with purity, and emphasized a strict sexual morality. Philo, in his book *On the Contemplative Life*, describes a similar community, the Therapeutae of Egypt, which were separate male and female Jewish communities living simple lives, dedicated to reflection on the Torah and philosophy. Joining husbandless and childless, these women were free to develop their minds and spirits in the ways of Wisdom.

These philosophical or ascetic "elites," however, were not representative of most contemporary Jews, whether in Judea or the diaspora. Generally speaking, Jewish families were virtually identical in their structure and dynamics to those around them. The overwhelming majority lived in what we termed "natural communities," in regular contact with the non-Jewish world yet maintaining practices distinctive to their own ethnic group. By late antiquity intramarriage seemed to be the norm among Jews, with women marrying between the ages of fifteen and twenty, slightly later than the Roman norm of thirteen. Jewish nuptials, which were divided into betrothal and a later wedding ceremony, included a contract that stipulated both a dowry and specific obligations (continuing a trend we noted in the Persian period) and were followed by a wedding feast (Doc. 1–17). While we must be careful not to read Rabbinic views back to earlier times, the general impression we therefore have of the Jewish family in the intertestamental period is that of a monogamous patriarchal family, with children required to obey their parents and continue their family's religious traditions. Marriage and divorce, regulated by increasingly specific law and custom, were affairs arranged almost exclusively by men, although evidence exists of these being initiated by women as well. Sex was only legitimate if performed within marriage, and while its primary purpose was procreation, it also served to appease urges that would otherwise lead to prostitution or adultery. Other Greek attitudes toward sex, such as homosexuality and the representation of the human nude, find no echo in the Jewish material of this period that has survived.

SEX, MARRIAGE, AND FAMILY
IN RABBINIC LITERATURE

The literary legacy of the Rabbinic period, which dates roughly from the destruction of the Second Temple in 70 CE to the rise of Islam in the seventh century, is extraordinary. Hundreds of scholars and tens of thousands of statements attributed to them fill texts of various literary genres, including legal codes and commentary, biblical exegesis, and homiletic advice. Several of the major texts, such as the Babylonian Talmud, are themselves anthologies of many sorts of Rabbinic utterances. As noted, this voluminous legacy came to be the basis of most medieval Jewish reflection on all matters of law and lore, yet we must resist the temptation to use these sources as evidence of contemporary reality. Aside from the literary redaction these texts underwent and the dubious reliability of some of their attributions, we currently lack independent corroboration of the relevance of these texts outside of Rabbinic circles. Indeed, the nature of the texts' evolution, often anonymously redacted over the course of centuries, should make us wary of finding in these sources evidence of widespread contemporary phenomena. No doubt there were social trends and historic realities that underlay the Rabbinic statements, legal or otherwise—certainly within the Rabbinic class itself and possibly within a broader base. However, in ways not dissimilar to the Hebrew Bible, we are on firmer ground if we eschew efforts to describe social reality of the late Roman/Byzantine and Sassanian Babylonian periods and instead seek to outline the views of sex, marriage, and family contained in the literature.

Since marriage was a status-effecting ceremony, it received much attention within Rabbinic circles, centered as it was on law: in the Mishnah (ca. 200 CE), Rabbinic Judaism's earliest text, four of the seven tractates within the Order of Women deal with marriage and divorce. One may say, along with several historians, that the texts of Rabbinic Judaism situated marriage between the strict contractual notion held by Roman society, on the one hand, and the near sacramental, symbolic status that early Christianity gave it, on the other. Marriage was, to be sure, a contract between two individuals that entailed specific obligations and responsibilities one to the other: at that time women were in need of protection and material support, while men were in need of household assistance and a way to fulfill their commandment to procreate. Sex is presented as the husband's conjugal duty to his wife, even to the point of enumerating the accepted frequency of intercourse a woman might insist upon. In discussing marriage, then, the language of the Mishnah rarely strays from the language of a legal arrangement between consenting parties, with the norm highly regulated and every eventuality anticipated and negotiated; similarly, divorce is portrayed as the consequence of one party failing to uphold its "part of the bargain," including the ability to bear children—extending the procreative aspect of marriage we saw in the intertestamental period (Docs. 1–18 to 1–26).

But in the nonlegal Rabbinic material, collected in aggadic compilations and in Talmudic commentary on the Mishnah, we begin to observe appreciation of the broader aspects of marriage. In perhaps explicit response to Christianity's tepid endorsement of marriage as "better . . . than burning with vain desire" (1 Corinthians 7:9), Rabbinic sources elevate the institution to an independent good, an ideal that partakes in the basic foundation of the created order and sees man and woman as "complete" only if married. Marriage and family are part of the "sanctification of Israel," a theme underscored in the liturgy that grew up around the betrothal and marriage ceremonies, which also employed the religious motifs of divine creation and a restoring of destroyed Jerusalem (Docs. 1–27 to 1–29). Indeed, we sense the Rabbinic tradition deliberately made the home the central locus of religious life: most Rabbinic rules of purity revolved around food and sex, Sabbath and holiday celebrations were to include meals with one's family, and respect for one's parents was coupled with the demand that parents—not professional teachers—be responsible for the children's basic religious education. Whether this move was intended to rival other existing institutions, such as the Temple or synagogue, or was only promoted in response to their loss is impossible to know. But the aggadic discussions of marriage and family helped underscore the critical role the traditional family played in ensuring Jewish life in diaspora (Docs. 1–30 to 1–35).

Most interesting, we find in Rabbinic sources a move away from the more ascetic view of sexuality found in Hellenistic Jewish texts that Christianity endorsed and developed. Procreation and conjugal duties aside, the Babylonian Talmud and other texts of that culture speak of romantic sex between a married couple in remarkably frank and uninhibited ways (Doc. 1–36). According to these male-addressing texts, even as physical contact with one's wife had to abide by strict rules of menstrual impurity *(niddah)*, it nevertheless had to be infused with warmth, playfulness, and an appreciation of the woman's desires.

To be sure, Rabbinic views, no different than Jewish views of other periods, were influenced by their environment. For instance, the polygamy allowed by Biblical law was discouraged in the "West" (Palestine and Asia Minor) where first Roman and then Christian insistence on monogamy made this position harder to defend; Babylonian Jews knew of no such pressure, and polygamy was clearly tolerated there. Similarly, in spite of their strong endorsement of marriage, Palestinian sources seem to allow the delay, if not suspension, of marriage in favor of certain higher intellectual goals such as Torah study—a delay never sanctioned by Babylonian sources.

Even as we cite Rabbinic sources on our subjects, we cannot forget their highly crafted, dialogic character. These texts include both multiple genres—

law, folklore, and homiletics—and multiple opinions on all manner of subjects—monogamy and polygyny, ascetic and more indulgent sexuality, strict
and lenient grounds for legitimate divorce—making it difficult to reach firm
historical conclusions based on this literature. Yet it is precisely the multivocal
nature of Rabbinic texts, particularly the Talmuds, that will allow the diverse
schools of the Middle Ages to each claim origins in these canonical sources.

SEX, MARRIAGE, AND FAMILY IN THE POST-TALMUDIC PERIOD

The rise of Islam in the seventh century, politically centered in Baghdad, brings
with it the ascendancy of the Babylonian Talmud for the majority of world
Jewry. Although Jewish communities will rise, flourish, and decline throughout
the Near East, North Africa, and Europe over the course of the next thirteen
centuries, until the modern period most will see their religious practice governed by, or at least rooted in, this Rabbinic text.

In spite of the common Talmudic basis, three factors contributed to the
emergence of variation, at times significant. First, varying traditions of Talmudic
interpretation evolved, often regionally based, leading to different rulings and
applications of Rabbinic dicta. Over time these amalgamated into two general
cultural spheres—Sefardic (Spain and the Mediterranean) and Ashkenazic
(central and eastern European)—that differed in many respects on the full
range of legal and philosophic matters, including sex, marriage, and family.
Second, the structures, rules, and mores of Jewish communities were greatly
influenced by their interactions with the local Muslim or Christian society, be
it open, tolerant, or discriminatory. Local Jewish ordinances and customs were
largely a product of these idiosyncratic realities. Finally, at times major religious
movements, such as the pietistic German Hasidim and the mystical trends
introduced by Kabbalists in Spain and then later throughout Jewry, had considerable impact on Jewish views and practices on family issues. All these
sources of variety were compounded throughout this period by the Jewish mi-
grations (voluntary or forced) that often brought Jews of differing practice and
outlook together.

Actually, the separateness of the Jews in medieval society turned out to be a
boon for the development of Jewish law. The relative autonomy granted Jewish
communities in matters of personal status through most of the Middle Ages
meant Jewish authorities were able to redress serious issues with great effect,
even if these contravened Talmudic law. Thus shortly after the Muslim conquest
the Babylonian academies issued an ordinance, known as *takanta de-metivta*,
allowing a woman to sue for divorce in court by claiming "my husband is
detestable to me" *(ma'is alai)*, undermining the husband's exclusive and unilateral right to divorce granted him in the Talmud (Doc. 1–37). In northern
France and Germany ordinances attributed to the eleventh-century Gershom,

"the Light of the Exiles," prohibited bigamy and would not allow a man to divorce his wife against her will (Doc. 1–38). Ultimately, all of Ashkenaz and even some Sefardic communities would accept Gershom's rulings, but the Babylonian ordinance was no longer normative by the thirteenth century. Other ordinances affecting inheritance, clandestine marriages, and deception were also common during this period. In medieval society common custom could be as effective as the ordinance; although polygyny remained a practice among wealthier Jews in Muslim lands, financial stipulations evolved in near eastern Jewish marriage contracts intended to discourage this practice, and by the eleventh century the clause was standard (Doc. 1–39).

During much of this period Jewish families were relatively stable, with average family size between two and six children (Jews in Arab lands being at the higher end of that range and always preferring sons). First marriages were often arranged by parents, and children usually married in their teens, an option afforded by the concentration of Jews in commercial or financial professions. Motives for unions, especially in the middle classes, were frequently based on family or business considerations, factors that could also destabilize marriage when relations soured. But other factors undermined Jewish family life, as well, including concern for a family's reputation, the extended absences of Jewish traders, persecution and its consequences, and conversion of a spouse to the majority's faith. Furthermore, sexual impropriety, whether with Jews or non-Jews, was not uncommon at different times, especially among the social elite, who also applied their poetic talents to physical pleasures (Docs. 1–40 to 1–42). All in all, though, the married state was the natural one for adults; widowed or divorced individuals remarried, especially if there were smaller children, but even if they were older. We do not find movements among Jews parallel to the strong ascetic communities found among Christians and Muslims, although some ambivalence over marriage occasionally surfaced in Jewish literature.

Owing to its urban setting, Jewish life in both Muslim and Christian societies was intensely communal. Marriage and divorce assumed a public character: weddings moved to the synagogue, and consent of community leaders was at times required for weddings and divorces. Indeed, most family celebrations (births, circumcisions, deaths) became public events, with many local rituals evolving for each. In medieval Europe the involvement of religious authorities grew (as it did among Christians), leading to increased standardization of both practice and contracts in marriage and divorce to ensure the propriety of all such ceremonies. Codification became its own genre, and handbooks for divorce were common in the fourteenth to sixteenth centuries. (Doc. 1–43). The community saw itself responsible as well for the education of youth (i.e., boys), ensuring the transmission of traditional values to another generation.

Both medieval Islam and Christianity were marked by dualistic views of the human being, pitting body and soul in an ongoing struggle for dominance—and not infrequently linking the soul with maleness and body with the feminine. Perhaps as expressions of a common Zeitgeist, from the twelfth century onward ascetic and body-negating trends emerged in Jewish circles in three different contexts. Rationalists, such as Maimonides, associated Judaism's goals with the intellectual perfection found in classic philosophy, and in his legal and philosophical writings one finds an unrelenting effort to limit indulgence of the body through food and particularly sex, except to fulfill the command-ment to procreate or the wife's conjugal right (Docs. 1–44 to 1–47). In Spain, and later throughout the Jewish world, mysticism was becoming much more structured and systematic through the Kabbalah and similarly looked to dampen the body's urges as the soul sought communion (deveikut) with God—although sexual metaphors were constantly used to describe the desired metaphysical state (Docs. 1–48 to 1–51). Finally, German Jewish pietism, perhaps in mimicry of its Christian surroundings, devalued the sexual appetite as a distraction that saps energy for higher purposes (Docs. 1–52 to 1–55). Nevertheless, one does find texts in this period that attempt to infuse sex with sensitivity and spirituality, considering the carnal capable of sanctification (Doc. 1–56).

SEX, MARRIAGE, AND FAMILY IN THE MODERN PERIOD

The relatively segregated character of Jewish society and its traditional mores began to erode over the course of the late Middle Ages. Profound political, economic, and social forces, along with powerful charismatic religious move-ments such as messianism and Hasidism, contributed to fundamental changes in European Jewish family life. Intellectually, the Enlightenment as well began to seep into Jewish thinking in the form of the Haskalah, leading to a more historical thinking and humanism among the elite. The Jews, therefore, who in the late eighteenth to early nineteenth century were being considered for entry into central and western European society as full and equal citizens, were already reimagining themselves and the look of their own society.

From the perspective of the European nation-state, emancipating the Jews came with the expectation of their "normalization," that is, the shedding of their unique customs and their adoption of the norms of civil society, including intermarriage (Doc. 1–57). "Be a Frenchman outside and a Jew at home" be-came the formula for successful integration, granting the family, which had always been central to Jewish life, an even more central role in the preservation of Jewish identity. Thus European and American bourgeois society, which rel-egated women to the home, also elevated the role of women in helping main-tain religious identity, closely linking concern for family with religious ritual. But the husband's acculturation to the larger society, the disintegration of ex-tended kinship networks, and the primacy of the nuclear family all worked against the preservation of Jewish identity along old lines. The modernization of the Jewish family, which took place over two centuries in a variety of contexts, affected sexual mores, family size, women's roles, and parent-child relations everywhere.

In the West an intellectual elite in the nineteenth century articulated a variety of Jewish responses to the dilemma of integration based on radically differing views on the nature of Judaism, including the degree to which change is possible. These divisions, which evolved into denominations, ranged from a humanistic "religion" on the model of liberal Protestantism (Reform), to the distinctive beliefs and practices of a "people" (Conservative), to a divinely revealed set of laws that could not be altered (Orthodox).

Originally, the debates were centered on ritual, including marriage and divorce. Reform Judaism accepted Western legal forms of entering and dissolving the marital state, relegating rabbis to agents of the state and the marriage contract to a formalistic exchange of vows. For Conservative and Orthodox Judaism, however, who preserved Jewish law in this area, Jews were now living under two jurisdictions—the state and that of Jewish law—and the two did not always match up. Divorce was the greater problem, for the state did not recognize the need for a religious divorce prior to remarriage, but Jewish law viewed this second marriage as adulterous, the children illegitimate. With the acceptance of no-fault divorce in most states starting in the 1960s, this situation left many women who observed Jewish law chained to a dead marriage, and each denomination sought a solution. The Conservative movement composed a *ketubah*, the religious marriage contract, that could demand a husband and wife submit to a Jewish court, and many Orthodox organizations endorsed a prenuptial agreement, which contractually binds a husband to pay his wife's maintenance until he divorces her religiously (Docs. 1–58 to 1–60).

As important as ritual matters were, ethnic and familial ties among Jews were still strong, especially as the West received a steady flow of more traditional eastern European Jewish immigrants. After the destruction of European Jewry in World War II, the rise of Israel as a Jewish state served to enhance Jewish identification through the late twentieth century. But as the twenty-first century approached, intermarriage with non-Jews moved above the 50 percent mark; many American Jews saw it as a crisis that threatened Jewish continuity, with books and conferences devoted to seeking solutions. The denominations split over the question of intermarriage and the definition of Jewishness, with Reform and Reconstructionism adopting a standard that incorporated both parentage (either parent Jewish) and how the child was raised (Doc. 1–61). The same sort of division can be seen with respect to same-sex unions or marriages, with the liberal denominations seeking to include these couples within the framework of Jewish marriage and the others maintaining the traditional exclusion.

Zionism, which began in the late 1800s, saw itself as a movement that was at once a continuation of the diaspora dream of return and a rejection of the traditional Judaism that had evolved in Europe. Many secular Jews acknowledged the right of Jewish tradition to regulate life-cycle events, allowing the state to establish an Orthodox chief rabbinate, an institution inherited from the Ottoman and British periods of occupation. Nevertheless, a few groups arrayed themselves into agrarian collectives, which in some cases replaced the traditional nuclear or extended family. As Israeli society became less agrarian and more Western, it reverted to the model of the traditional family. But this Westernization has also opened Israelis to the diversity of American Judaism, and Orthodox hegemony over marriage law and rituals has weakened over the last decade.

Despite heightened assimilation, sociologists and historians observe that American Jews are displaying a simultaneous, albeit inconsistent and paradoxical, move toward greater tradition. Reaffirmation of ritual among liberal Jews is not uncommon, and more Jewish communities have endorsed separate Jewish schooling for children (usually up to middle or high school) during which a Jewish identity could be imprinted. But, except for the Orthodox, American mores on sex, marriage (including late marriage and high divorce rates), and family (small numbers of children) apply equally to American Jews, and increasingly to Israeli Jews via the spread of American culture through technology and globalization. Currently, one may say that among Jews the drive toward integration and accommodation is almost universally ascendant over the preservation of distinctiveness—a trend with profound implications for Jewish life.

THE HEBREW BIBLE

The Hebrew Bible, known as the *TaNaKh—Torah* (Pentateuch), *Nevi'im* (Prophets), and *Ketuvim* (Writings)—is the first major canonical text of Judaism. It is a compendium of books that achieved sacred status in the Jewish community over centuries, reaching its current form in the early Persian period (6th–4th centuries BCE). About half the books are historical, covering time from the creation of the world until the early Second Temple period. The other texts are primarily prophetic or wisdom literature, often in poetic form.

In addition, the Torah contains significant legal portions that the Jewish tradition, since the Persian period and up to the modern period, deemed binding as God's revealed word. Still performed regularly in synagogues and taught in Jewish schools, the Torah is a living, relevant text to most Jews, even if not regarded as revealed. Below are selections of multiple genres that deal with the origins of humans, illicit sexual unions, marriage, and the family's central role in transmitting the covenant.

CREATION

Document 1–1

GENESIS 1–3

[1:1]When God began to create heaven and earth—[2]the earth being unformed and void, with darkness over the surface of the deep and a wind from God sweeping over the water—[3]God said, "Let there be light"; and there was light.

[4]God saw that the light was good, and God separated the light from the darkness. [5]God called the light Day, and the darkness He called Night. And there was evening and there was morning, a first day.

[6]God said, "Let there be an expanse in the midst of the water, that it may separate water from water." . . . [8]God called the expanse Sky. And there was evening and there was morning, a second day.

[9]God said, "Let the water below the sky be gathered into one area, that the dry land may appear." And it was so. [10]God called the dry land Earth, and the gathering of waters He called Seas. And God saw that this was good. [11]And God said, "Let the earth sprout vegetation: seed-bearing plants, fruit trees of every kind on earth that bear fruit with the seed in it." And it was so. . . . [13]And there was evening and there was morning, a third day.

[14]God said, "Let there be lights in the expanse of the sky to separate day from night; they shall serve as signs for the set times—the days and the years; [15]and they shall serve as lights in the expanse of the sky to shine upon the earth." And it was so. . . . [19]And there was evening and there was morning, a fourth day.

[20]God said, "Let the waters bring forth swarms of living creatures, and birds that fly above the earth across the expanse of the sky." . . . [22]God blessed them, saying, "Be fertile and increase, fill the waters in the seas, and let the birds increase on the earth." [23]And there was evening and there was morning, a fifth day.

[24]God said, "Let the earth bring forth every kind of living creature: cattle, creeping things, and wild beasts of every kind." And it was so. [25]God made wild beasts of every kind and cattle of every kind, and all kinds of creeping things of the earth. And God saw that this was good. [26]And God said, "Let us make man in our image, after our likeness. They shall rule the fish of the sea, the birds of the sky, the cattle, the whole earth, and all the creeping things that creep on earth." [27]And God created man in His image, in the image of God He created him; male and female He created them. [28]God blessed them and God said to them, "Be fertile and increase, fill the earth and master it; and rule the fish of the sea, the birds of the sky, and all the living things that creep on earth."

[29]God said, "See, I give you every seed-bearing plant that is upon all the earth, and every tree that has seed-bearing fruit; they shall be yours for food. [30]And to all the animals on land, to all the birds of the sky, and to everything that creeps on earth, in which there is the breath of life, [I give] all the green plants for food." And it was so. [31]And God saw all that He had made, and found it very good. And there was evening and there was morning, the sixth day.

[2:1]The heaven and the earth were finished, and all their array. [2]On the seventh day God finished the work that He had been doing, and He ceased on the seventh day from all the work that He had done. [3]And God blessed the seventh day and declared it holy, because on it God ceased from all the work of creation that He had done. [4]Such is the story of heaven and earth when they were created.

When the Lord God made earth and heaven—⁵when no shrub of the field was yet on earth and no grasses of the field had yet sprouted, because the Lord God had not sent rain upon the earth and there was no man to till the soil, ⁶but a flow would well up from the ground and water the whole surface of the earth—⁷the Lord God formed man from the dust of the earth. He blew into his nostrils the breath of life, and man became a living being.

⁸The Lord God planted a garden in Eden, in the east, and placed there the man whom He had formed. ⁹And from the ground the Lord God caused to grow every tree that was pleasing to the sight and good for food, with the tree of life in the middle of the garden, and the tree of knowledge of good and bad.

¹⁰A river issues from Eden to water the garden, and it then divides and becomes four branches. . . .

¹⁵The Lord God took the man and placed him in the garden of Eden, to till it and tend it. ¹⁶And the Lord God commanded the man, saying, "Of every tree of the garden you are free to eat; ¹⁷but as for the tree of knowledge of good and bad, you must not eat of it; for as soon as you eat of it, you shall die."

¹⁸The Lord God said, "It is not good for man to be alone; I will make a fitting helper for him." ¹⁹And the Lord God formed out of the earth all the wild beasts and all the birds of the sky, and brought them to the man to see what he would call them; and whatever the man called each living creature, that would be its name. ²⁰And the man gave names to all the cattle and to the birds of the sky and to all the wild beasts; but for Adam no fitting helper was found. ²¹So the Lord God cast a deep sleep upon the man; and, while he slept, He took one of his ribs and closed up the flesh at that spot. ²²And the Lord God fashioned the rib that He had taken from the man into a woman; and He brought her to the man. ²³Then the man said, "This one at last is bone of my bones and flesh of my flesh. This one shall be called Woman, for from man was she taken."

²⁴Hence a man leaves his father and mother and clings to his wife, so that they become one flesh.

²⁵The two of them were naked, the man and his wife, yet they felt no shame. ³:¹Now the serpent was the shrewdest of all the wild beasts that the Lord God had made. He said to the woman, "Did God really say: You shall not eat of any tree of the garden?" ²The woman replied to the serpent, "We may eat of the fruit of the other trees of the garden. ³It is only about fruit of the tree in the middle of the garden that God said: 'You shall not eat of it or touch it, lest you die.'" ⁴And the serpent said to the woman, "You are not going to die, ⁵but God knows that as soon as you eat of it your eyes will be opened and you will be like divine beings who know good and bad." ⁶When the woman saw that the tree was good for eating and a delight to the eyes, and that the tree was desirable as a source of wisdom, she took of its fruit and ate. She also gave some to her husband, and he ate. ⁷Then the eyes of both of them were opened and they perceived that they were naked; and they sewed together fig leaves and made themselves loincloths.

⁸They heard the sound of the Lord God moving about in the garden at the breezy time of day; and the man and his wife hid from the Lord God among the trees of the garden. ⁹The Lord God called out to the man and said to him, "Where are you?" ¹⁰He replied, "I heard the sound of You in the garden, and I was afraid because I was naked, so I hid." ¹¹Then He asked, "Who told you that you were naked? Did you eat of the tree from which I had forbidden you to eat?" ¹²The man said, "The woman You put at my side—she gave me of the tree, and I ate." ¹³And the Lord God said to the woman, "What is this you have done!" The woman replied, "The serpent duped me, and I ate." ¹⁴Then the Lord God said to the serpent, "Because you did this, more cursed shall you be than all cattle and all the wild beasts: On your belly shall you crawl and dirt shall you eat all the days of your life. ¹⁵I will put enmity between you and the woman, and between your offspring and hers; they shall strike at your head, and you shall strike at their heel."

¹⁶And to the woman He said, "I will make most severe your pangs in childbearing; in pain shall you bear children. Yet your urge shall be for your husband, and he shall rule over you."

¹⁷To Adam He said, "Because you did as your wife said and ate of the tree about which I commanded you, 'You shall not eat of it,' cursed be the ground because of you; by toil shall you eat of it all the days of your life: ¹⁸Thorns and thistles shall it sprout for you. But your food shall be the grasses of the field; ¹⁹By the sweat of your brow shall you get bread to eat, until you return to the ground—for from it you were taken. For dust you are, and to dust you shall return."

²⁰The man named his wife Eve, because she was the mother of all the living. ²¹And the Lord God made garments of skins for Adam and his wife, and clothed them.

²²And the Lord God said, "Now that the man has become like one of us, knowing good and bad, what if he should stretch out his hand and take also from the tree of life and eat, and live forever!" ²³So the Lord God banished him from the garden of Eden, to till the soil from which he was taken. ²⁴He drove the man out, and stationed east of the garden of Eden the cherubim and the fiery ever-turning sword, to guard the way to the tree of life.

[*JPS Tanakh*, the new Jewish Publication Society translation, 1st ed. (Philadelphia: Jewish Publication Society, 1985)]

ILLICIT SEXUAL UNIONS AND PRACTICES

Document 1–2

LEVITICUS 18

¹The Lord spoke to Moses, saying: ²Speak to the Israelite people and say to them:

I the Lord am your God. ³You shall not copy the practices of the land of Egypt where you dwelt, or of the land of Canaan to which I am taking you; nor shall you follow their laws. ⁴My rules alone shall you observe, and faithfully follow My laws: I the Lord am your God. . . .

⁶None of you shall come near anyone of his own flesh to uncover nakedness: I am the Lord.

⁷Your father's nakedness, that is, the nakedness of your mother, you shall not uncover; she is your mother—you shall not uncover her nakedness. . . .

⁹The nakedness of your sister—your father's daughter or your mother's, whether born into the household or outside—do not uncover their nakedness.

¹⁰The nakedness of your son's daughter, or of your daughter's daughter—do not uncover their nakedness; for their nakedness is yours. . . .

¹⁷Do not uncover the nakedness of a woman and her daughter; nor shall you marry her son's daughter or her daughter's daughter and uncover her nakedness: they are kindred; it is depravity. . . .

¹⁹Do not come near a woman during her period of uncleanness to uncover her nakedness.

²⁰Do not have carnal relations with your neighbor's wife and defile yourself with her. . . .

²²Do not lie with a male as one lies with a woman; it is an abhorrence.

²³Do not have carnal relations with any beast and defile yourself thereby; and let no woman lend herself to a beast to mate with it; it is perversion.

²⁴Do not defile yourselves in any of those ways, for it is by such that the nations that I am casting out before you defiled themselves. ²⁵Thus the land became defiled; and I called it to account for its iniquity, and the land spewed out its inhabitants. . . . ²⁸So let not the land spew you out for defiling it, as it spewed out the nation that came before you. ²⁹All who do any of those abhorrent things—such persons shall be cut off from their people. ³⁰You shall keep My charge not to engage in any of the abhorrent practices that were carried on before you, and you shall not defile yourselves through them: I the Lord am your God.

[New JPS translation]

PROHIBITED MARRIAGES

Document 1–3

DEUTERONOMY 23:2–9

²No one whose testes are crushed or whose member is cut off shall be admitted into the congregation of the Lord.

³No one misbegotten shall be admitted into the congregation of the Lord. . . .

⁴No Ammonite or Moabite shall be admitted into the congregation of the Lord; none of their descendents, even in the tenth generation, shall ever be admitted into the congregation of the Lord, ⁵because they did not meet you with food and water on your journey after you left Egypt, and because they hired Balaam son of Beor, from Pethor of Aramnaharaim, to curse you. . . .

⁸You shall not abhor an Edomite, for he is your kinsman. You shall not abhor an Egyptian, for you were a stranger in his land. ⁹Children born to them may be admitted into the congregation of the Lord in the third generation.

[New JPS translation]

Document 1–4

DEUTERONOMY 7:1–5

¹When the Lord your God brings you to the land that you are about to enter and possess, and He dislodges many nations before you—the Hittites, Girgashites, Amorites, Canaanites, Perizzites, Hivites, and Jebusites, seven nations much larger than you. . . . ³You shall not intermarry with them: do not give your daughters to their sons or take their daughters for your sons. ⁴For they will turn your children away from Me to worship other gods, and the Lord's anger will blaze forth against you and He will promptly wipe you out.

[New JPS translation]

HUSBAND AND WIFE

Document 1–5

DEUTERONOMY 21:15–17

¹⁵If a man has two wives, one loved and the other unloved, and both the loved and the unloved have borne him sons, but the first-born is the son of the unloved one—¹⁶when he wills his property to his sons, he may not treat as first-born the son of the loved one in disregard of the son of the unloved one who is older. ¹⁷Instead, he must accept the first-born, the son of the unloved one, and allot to him a double portion of all he possesses; since he is the first fruit of his vigor, the birthright is his due.

[New JPS translation]

Document 1–6

PROVERBS 5

¹My son, listen to my wisdom;
Incline your ear to my insight. . . .
³For the lips of a forbidden woman drip honey;

Her mouth is smoother than oil;
⁴But in the end she is as bitter as wormwood,
Sharp as a two-edged sword. . . .
⁶She does not chart a path of life;
Her course meanders for lack of knowledge. . . .
⁸Keep yourself far away from her;
Do not come near the doorway of her house
⁹Lest you give up your vigor to others,
Your years to a ruthless one. . . .
¹⁵Drink water from your own cistern,
Running water from your own well.
¹⁶Your springs will gush forth
In streams in the public squares.
¹⁷They will be yours alone,
Others having no part with you.
¹⁸Let your fountain be blessed;
Find joy in the wife of your youth—
¹⁹A loving doe, a graceful mountain goat.
Let her breasts satisfy you at all times;
Be infatuated with love of her always.

[New JPS translation]

Document 1–7

EZEKIEL 16:1–38

¹The word of the Lord came to me: ²O mortal, proclaim Jerusalem's abominations to her, ³and say: Thus said the Lord God to Jerusalem: . . . ⁵on the day
you were born, you were left lying, rejected, in the open field. . . . ⁷I let you
grow like the plants of the field; and you continued to grow up until you attained
to womanhood, until your breasts became firm and your hair sprouted.

You were still naked and bare ⁸when I passed by you [again] and saw that
your time for love had arrived. So I spread My robe over you and covered your
nakedness, and I entered into a covenant with you by oath—declares the Lord
God; thus you became Mine. . . . ¹¹I decked you out in finery and put bracelets
on your arms and a chain around your neck. . . .

¹⁵But confident in your beauty and fame, you played the harlot: you lavished
your favors on every passerby; they were his. . . . ¹⁷You took your beautiful things,
made of the gold and silver that I had given you, and you made yourself phallic
images and fornicated with them. . . . ²⁶You played the whore with your neighbors, the lustful Egyptians—you multiplied your harlotries to anger Me. . . .

²⁸In your insatiable lust you also played the whore with the Assyrians; you
played the whore with them, but were still unsated. ²⁹You multiplied your harlotries with Chaldea, that land of traders; yet even with this you were not

satisfied. . . . ³¹Yet you were not like a prostitute, for you spurned fees; ³²[you were like] the adulterous wife who welcomes strangers instead of her husband. . . . ³⁸I will inflict upon you the punishment of women who commit adultery and murder, and I will direct bloody and impassioned fury against you.

[New JPS translation]

THE IDEAL WIFE

Document 1–8

PROVERBS 31:10–31

¹⁰What a rare find is a capable wife! / Her worth is far beyond that of rubies.

¹¹Her husband puts his confidence in her, / And lacks no good thing.

¹²She is good to him, never bad, / All the days of her life. . . .

¹⁵She rises while it is still night, / And supplies provisions for her household, / The daily fare of her maids. . . .

¹⁷She girds herself with strength, / And performs her tasks with vigor.

¹⁸She sees that her business thrives; / Her lamp never goes out at night.

¹⁹She sets her hand to the distaff; / Her fingers work the spindle.

²⁰She gives generously to the poor; / Her hands are stretched out to the needy. . . .

²³Her husband is prominent in the gates, / As he sits among the elders of the land. . . .

²⁶Her mouth is full of wisdom, / Her tongue with kindly teaching.

²⁷She oversees the activities of her household / And never eats the bread of idleness.

²⁸Her children declare her happy; / Her husband praises her,

²⁹Many women have done well, / But you surpass them all."

³⁰Grace is deceptive, / Beauty is illusory;

It is for her fear of the Lord / That a woman is to be praised.

[New JPS translation]

PARENTS AND CHILDREN

Document 1–9

EXODUS 20:12

¹²Honor your father and your mother, that you may long endure on the land that the Lord your God is assigning to you.

[New JPS translation]

Document 1–10

DEUTERONOMY 21:18–21

[18]If a man has a wayward and defiant son, who does not heed his father or mother and does not obey them. . . . [19]His father and mother shall take hold of him and bring him out to the elders of his town at the public place of his community. [20]They shall say to the elders of his town, "This son of ours is disloyal and defiant; he does not heed us. . . . [21]Thereupon the men of his town shall stone him to death. Thus you will sweep out evil from your midst. . . .

[New JPS translation]

Document 1–11

DEUTERONOMY 4:9–10

[9]But take utmost care and watch yourselves scrupulously, so that you do not forget the things that you saw with your own eyes. . . . And make them known to your children and to your children's children: [10]The day you stood before the Lord your God at Horeb, when the Lord said to me, "Gather the people to Me that I may let them hear My words, in order that they may learn to revere Me as long as they live on earth, and may so teach their children."

[New JPS translation]

Document 1–12

DEUTERONOMY 6:4–7

[4]Hear, O Israel! The Lord is our God, the Lord alone. [5]You shall love the Lord your God with all your heart and with all your soul and with all your might. [6]Take to heart these instructions with which I charge you this day. [7]Impress them upon your children. . . .

[New JPS translation]

Document 1–13

DEUTERONOMY 6:20–21

[20]When, in time to come, your children ask you, "What mean the decrees, laws, and rules that the Lord our God has enjoined upon you?" [21]you shall say to your children, "We were slaves to Pharaoh in Egypt and the Lord freed us from Egypt with a mighty hand. . . . "

[New JPS translation]

THE ELEPHANTINE MARRIAGE CONTRACT

In the Persian period (ca. 536–332 BCE), Jews lived in the small province of Yehud and in other parts of the empire, including a garrison in the southern Egyptian called Elephantine. While they saw themselves as Jews, some of their practices diverged from those developing in Judea, including marriage with Egyptians and worship of other deities in addition to Yahweh.

Excavations at the garrison unearthed a number of papyrii, written in Aramaic, that deal with legal transactions such as marriage, divorce, and property transfer. Taken together, they exemplify the contractualizing trend in Persian society, which clearly affected Jewish practice. In this document we see that marriage is a status achieved after fulfilling several stages involving declarations and payment of a brideprice to the woman's family. Most noteworthy is the right of the woman written into the document to divorce her husband, a practice that would not be normative within Rabbinic Judaism; its prevalence, however, is purely speculative.

Document 1–14

ELEPHANTINE MARRIAGE CONTRACT

On the 26th [of] Tishri, [that is the __]6th month of Epiph, [y]ear [__ of] Kin[g Atraxerx]es,

Eshor, son of Se[ha], a builder of the king, said to Mah[seiah, an A]ramean of Syene of the detachment of Varyazata, saying:

I [c]ame to your house (and asked you) to give me your daughter Mipta(h)iah for wifehood. She is my wife and I am her husband from this day and forever.

I gave you (as) *mohar* for your daughter Miptahiah: [silver], 5 shekels by the stone(-weight)s of [the] king. It came into you and your heart was satisfied herein.

[Your daughter] Miptahiah brought into me in her hand: silver money 1 karsh by the stone(-weight)s of the king, silver 2 (quarters) to the 10.

She brought into me in her hand:

1 new woolen garment, striped with dye doubly-well, worth (in) silver
    2 karsh, shekels by the stone(-weight)s of the king;
1 new shawl, worth (in) silver 8 shekels by the stone(-weight)s of the king;
another woolen garment, finely-woven, worth (in) silver 7 shekels;
1 bronze mirror, worth (in) silver 1 shekel, 2 q(uarters);
1 bronze bowl worth (in) silver 1 shekel, 2 q(uarters);
2 bronze cups, worth (in) silver 2 shekels;
1 bronze jug, worth (in) silver 2 q(uarters).

All the silver and the value of the goods: (in) silver 6 karsh, 5 shekels, 20 hallurs, silver 2 q(uarters) to the 10, by the stone(-weight)s of the king.

Tomorrow or (the) n[ex]t day, should Eshor die not having a child, male or female, by Mipta[h]iah his wife, it is Miptahiah (who) has the right to the house of Eshor and [hi]s goods and his property and all that he has on the face of the whole earth.

Tomorrow or (the) next day, should Miptahiah die not having a child, male or female, by Eshor her husband, it is Eshor (who) shall inherit from her goods and her property.

Tomorrow or (the) next day, should Miptahiah stand up in assembly and say: "I hated Eshor my husband," silver of hatred is on her head. She shall place upon the balance-scale and weigh out to Eshor silver, 6[+1] (= 7) shekels, 2 q(uarters), and all that she bought in in her hand she shall take out, from straw to string, and go away wherever she desires, without suit or without process.

Tomorrow or (the) next day, should Eshor stand up in assembly and say: "I hated my [wif]e Miptahiah," her *mohar* [will be] lost (= forfeit) and all that she brought in in her hand she shall take out, from straw to string, on one day in one stroke, and she shall go away wherever she desires, without suit or without process.

And I shall not be able to re[lease] my goods and my property from Miptahiah.

Nathan son of Ananiah wrote [this document at the instruction of Eshor].

And the witnesses herein: Penuliah son of Jezaniah; [. . .]iah son of Ahio; Menaham son of [Za]ccur; witness *Vyzblw* (endorsement missing)

[B. Porten and A. Yardeni, *Textbook of Aramaic Documents from Ancient Egypt: Contracts* (Jerusalem: Hebrew University, 1989), vol. 2, doc. B2.6.]

HELLENISTIC JEWISH PHILOSOPHY IN THE WISDOM OF BEN SIRACH (ECCLESIASTICUS)

Alexander's conquests of the fourth century BCE brought Jews under the influence of Hellenism. One outgrowth of this encounter was the emergence of a genre known as "wisdom literature," which advised readers on the importance of wisdom and virtue, often expressed in poetic aphoristic form.

Simeon Ben Sira was a second century BCE Judean sage who likely composed this work in Hebrew ca. 170 BCE. Its maxims are very similar to those of the Book of Proverbs and are arranged by subject with headings. In 132 BCE a Greek translation was done that ultimately entered the Christian Apocrypha under the name Ecclesiasticus (by the author known as Jesus ben Sira). While the work did not formally enter the Jewish canon, many of Ben Sira's sayings, both homiletic and legal, are quoted in Rabbinic literature, and Rabbinic liturgy shows the influence of this text.

The selections below warn men of sexual intemperance and stress the importance of the family circle in nurturing virtuous behavior.

Document 1–15

ECCLESIASTICUS 3:1–14, 9:2–9, 23:16–26, 25:13–26:16, 30:1–13

³:¹Children listen to me, for I am your father; do what I tell you, if you wish to be safe. ²It is the Lord's will that a father should be honoured by his children, and a mother's rights recognized by her sons. ³Respect for a father atones for sins, ⁴and to honour your mother is to lay up a fortune. ⁵A son who respects his father will be made happy by his own children; when he prays, he will be heard. ⁶He who honours his father will have a long life, and he who obeys the Lord comforts his mother; ⁷he obeys his parents as though he were their slave. . . . ¹²My son, look after your father in his old age; do nothing to vex him as long as he lives. ¹³Even if his mind fails, make allowances for him, and do not despise him because you are in your prime. ¹⁴If you support your father it will never be forgotten, but be put to your credit against your sins. . . .

⁹:² Do not surrender yourself to a woman and let her trample down your strength. ³Do not go near a loose woman, for fear of falling into her snares. ⁴Do not keep company with a dancing-girl, or you may be caught by her tricks. ⁵Do not let your mind dwell on a virgin, or you may be trapped into paying damages for her. ⁶Never surrender yourself to prostitutes, for fear of losing all you possess, ⁷nor gaze about you in the city streets or saunter in deserted corners. ⁸Do not let your eye linger on a woman's figure or your thoughts dwell on beauty not yours to possess. Many have been seduced by the beauty of a woman, which kindles passion like fire. ⁹Never sit at table with another man's wife or join her in a drinking party, for fear of succumbing to her charms and slipping into fatal disaster. . . .

²³:¹⁶Two kinds of men add sin to sin, and a third brings retribution on himself. Hot lust that blazes like a fire can never be quenched till life is destroyed. A man whose whole body is given to sensuality never stops till the fire consumes him. ¹⁷To a seducer every loaf is as sweet as the last, and he does not weary until he dies. . . . ²¹This man will pay the penalty in the public street, caught where he least expected it. ²²So too with the woman who is unfaithful to her husband, presenting him with an heir by a different father: ²³first, she disobeys the law of the Most High; secondly, she commits an offence against her husband; thirdly, she has prostituted herself by bearing bastard children. . . . ²⁵Her children will not take root, nor will fruit grow on her branches. ²⁶A curse will rest on her memory, and her shame will never be blotted out. . . .

²⁵:¹³Any wound but a wound in the heart! Any spite but a woman's! . . . ¹⁶I would sooner share a home with a lion or a snake than keep house with a spiteful wife. ¹⁷Her spite changes her expression, making her look as surly

as a bear. [18]Her husband goes to a neighbour for his meals and cannot repress a bitter sigh. [19]There is nothing so bad as a bad wife; may the fate of the wicked overtake her! . . . [23]A bad wife brings humiliation, downcast looks, and a wounded heart. . . . [24]Woman is the origin of sin, and it is through her that we all die. [26]If she does not accept your control, divorce her and send her away.

[26:1] A good wife makes a happy husband; she doubles the length of his life. [2]A staunch wife is her husband's joy; he will live out his days in peace. [3]A good wife means a good life; she is one of the Lord's gifts to those who fear him. . . . [13]A wife's charm is the delight of her husband, and her womanly skill puts flesh on his bones. [14]A silent wife is a gift from the Lord; her restraint is more than money can buy. . . . [16]As beautiful as the sunrise in the Lord's heaven is a good wife in a well-ordered home.

[30:1]A man who loves his son will whip him often so that when he grows up he may be a joy to him. [2] He who disciplines his son will find profit in him and take pride in him among his acquaintances. [3]He who gives his son a good education will make his enemy jealous and will boast of him among his friends. [4]When the father dies, it is as if he were still alive, for he has left a copy of himself behind him. . . . [7]A man who spoils his son will bandage every wound and will be on tenterhooks at every cry. . . . [9]Pamper a boy and he will shock you; play with him and he will grieve you. . . . [11]Do not give him freedom while he is young or overlook his errors. [13]Discipline your son and take pains with him or he may offend you by some disgraceful act.

[*The New English Bible with the Apocrypha*, ed. Samuel Sandmel
(New York: Oxford University Press, 1976)]

THE DAMASCUS DOCUMENT OF THE DEAD SEA SCROLLS

The Qumran Community, which existed in the Judean desert from the second century BCE to the first century CE, was a messianic group that led an ascetic communitarian life awaiting the cataclysmic End of Days. Discoveries in Cairo and Qumran over the last one hundred years have yielded a rather complete document regarding the community's code of conduct, known as the "Damascus Document." While it echoes some practices of other Second Temple Jewish groups, most scholars agree this community was extremely small demographically, ceasing to exist by the Jewish Revolt in 70 CE.

The document begins with a biblical view of history, identifying the present age as defiled through sexual impropriety, but redemption being near. Like other Qumran documents, the majority of the text is its prescriptions for proper conduct, with many biblical laws cited. There is an abiding concern with purity, especially related to food and sex, but marriage and procreation are not discouraged.

Document 1–16

THE DAMASCUS DOCUMENT OF THE DEAD SEA SCROLLS

Listen now all you who know righteousness, and consider the works of God; for He has a dispute with all flesh and will condemn all those who despise Him.

For when they were unfaithful and forsook Him, He hid His face from Israel and His Sanctuary and delivered them up to the sword. But remembering the Covenant of the forefathers, He left a remnant to Israel and did not deliver it up to be destroyed. . . .

The *sons of Zadok* are the elect of Israel, the men called by name who shall stand at the end of days. . . .

During all those years Belial shall be unleashed against Israel. . . .

The "builders of the wall" (Ezek. 23:10) who have followed after "Precept" . . . shall be caught in fornication twice by taking a second wife while the first is alive, whereas the principle of creation is, *Male and female created He them* (Gen. 1:27). Also, those who entered the Ark went in two by two. And concerning the prince it is written, *He shall not multiply wives to himself* (Deut. 17:17). . . .

Moreover, they profane the Temple because they do not observe the distinction (between clean and unclean) in accordance with the Law, but lie with a woman who sees her bloody discharge.

And each man marries the daughter of his brother or sister, whereas Moses said, *You shall not approach your mother's sister; she is your mother's near kin* (Lev. 18:13). But although the laws against incest are written for men, they also apply to women. . . .

None of those brought into the Covenant shall enter the Temple to light His altar in vain. They shall bar the door, forasmuch as God said, *Who among you will bar its door?* And, *You shall not light my altar in vain* (Mal. 1:10). They shall take care to act according to the exact interpretation of the Law during the age of wickedness. They shall separate from the sons of the Pit . . . they shall not rob the poor of His people, to make of widows their prey and of the fatherless their victim (Isa. 10:2). They shall distinguish between clean and unclean, and shall proclaim the difference between holy and profane. They shall keep the Sabbath day according to its exact interpretation, and the feasts and the Day of Fasting according to the finding of the members of the New Covenant in the land of Damascus. . . . They shall love each man his brother as himself; they shall succour the poor, the needy, and the stranger.

A man shall seek his brother's well-being and shall not sin against his near kin. They shall keep from fornication according to the statute. They shall rebuke each man his brother according to the commandment and shall bear no rancour from one day to the next. They shall keep apart from every uncleanness according to the statutes relating to each one, and no man shall defile his holy spirit since God has set them apart. For all who walk in these (precepts) in perfect holiness, according to all the teaching of God, the Covenant of God shall be an assurance that they shall live for thousands of generations (MS. B: as it is written, *Keeping the Covenant and grace with those who love me and keep my commandments, to a thousand generations,* Deut. 7:9).

And if they live in camps according to the rule of the Land (MS. B: as it was from ancient times), marrying (MS. B: according to the custom of the Law) and begetting children, they shall walk according to the Law and according to the statute concerning binding vows, according to the rule of the Law which says, *Between a man and his wife and between a father and his son* (Num. 30:17). . . .

And all those who have entered the Covenant, granted to all Israel for ever, shall make their children who have reached the age of enrolment, swear with the oath of the Covenant. And thus shall it be during all the age of wickedness for every man who repents of his corrupted way. On the day that he speaks to the Guardian of the congregation, they shall enroll him with the oath of the Covenant which Moses made with Israel, the Covenant to return to the Law of Moses with a whole heart and soul, to whatever is found should be done at that time. No man shall make known the statutes to him until he has stood before the Guardian, lest when examining him the Guardian be deceived by him. But if he transgresses after swearing to return to the Law of Moses with a whole heart and soul, they (the members) shall be innocent should he transgress. And should he err in any matter that is revealed of the Law to the multitude of the camp, the Guardian shall instruct him and shall issue directions concerning him: he should study for a full year. . . .

And the law concerning a man with a flux. Any man with a flux issuing from his flesh, or one that causes a lewd thought to arise or . . . the woman . . . the man who approaches her will have the sin of menstrual uncleanness on him. And if she sees blood again and this is not during the uncleanness of seven days, she shall not eat sacred food and shall not enter the Sanctuary until the sun has set on the eighth day.

[Geza Vermes, *The Complete Dead Sea Scrolls in English*
(New York: Penguin, 1997), pp. 127–148]

JOSEPHUS ON MARRIAGE LAW

Flavius Josephus was a first-century CE Judean who, having survived the Jewish War of 70 by defecting to the Roman side, wrote several works that are our major testimony to Jewish history and culture of this period. Aside from his voluminous historical works, preserved in Greek, he authored an apologetic work, *Against Apion,* defending Judaism against its Greco-Roman detractors. Originally titled *On the Antiquity of the Jews,* it refutes anti-Jewish contentions among Near Eastern Hellenists and then goes on in part 2 to show the inner value of Judaism and its ethical superiority over Hellenism.

In this selection Josephus emphasizes the procreative function of marriage but also underscores how Jews preserve their character among a Gentile majority by educating their children in the covenant's laws and the nation's history. The family is clearly the unit of survival and distinctiveness, and he ends the section with other familial obligations.

Document 1–17

FLAVIUS JOSEPHUS, ON THE ANTIQUITY OF THE JEWS,
AGAINST APION, BOOK 11

25. But then; what are our laws about marriage? That law owns no other mixture of sexes but that which nature hath appointed, of a man with his wife, and that this be used only for the procreation of children. But it abhors the mixture of a male with a male; and if anyone do that, death is his punishment. It commands us also, when we marry, not to have regard to portion, nor to take a woman by violence, nor to persuade her deceitfully and knavishly; but demand her in marriage of him who hath power to dispose of her, and is fit to give her away by the nearness of his kindred; for, saith the Scripture, "A woman is inferior to her husband in all things."[1] Let her, therefore, be obedient to him; not so, that he should abuse her, but that she may acknowledge her duty to her husband; for God hath given the authority to the husband. A husband, therefore, is to lie only with his wife whom he hath married; but to have to do with another man's wife is a wicked thing; which, if anyone venture upon, death is inevitably his punishment: no more can he avoid the same who forces a virgin betrothed to another man, or entices another man's wife. The law, moreover enjoins us to bring up all our offspring, and forbids women to cause abortion of what is begotten, or to destroy it afterward; and if any woman appears to have so done, she will be a murderer of her child, by destroying a living creature, and diminishing human kind: if anyone, therefore, proceeds to such fornication or murder, he cannot be clean. Moreover, the law enjoins, that after the man and wife have lain together in a regular way, they shall bathe themselves; for there is a defilement contracted thereby, both in soul and body, as if they had gone into another country; for indeed the soul, by being united to the body, is subject to miseries, and is not freed therefrom again but by death; on which. account the law requires this purification to be entirely performed.

26. Nay, indeed, the law does not permit us to make festivals at the births of our children, and thereby afford occasion of drinking to excess; but it ordains that the very beginning of our education should be immediately directed to sobriety. It also commands us to bring those children up in learning and to exercise them in the laws, and make them acquainted with the acts of their predecessors, in order to their imitation of them, and that they may be nourished up in the laws from their infancy, and might neither transgress them, nor yet have any pretence for their ignorance of them.

27. Our law hath also taken care of the decent burial of the dead, but without any extravagant expenses for their funerals, and without the erection of any illustrious monuments for them; but hath ordered that their nearest relations should perform their obsequies; and hath shown it to be regular, that all who pass by when anyone is buried, should accompany the funeral, and join in the lamentation. It also ordains, that the house and its inhabitants should be purified after the funeral is over, that everyone may thence learn to keep at a great distance from the thoughts of being pure, if he hath been once guilty of murder.

28. The law ordains also, that parents should be honored immediately after God himself, and delivers that son who does not requite them for the benefits he hath received from them, but is deficient on any such occasion, to be stoned. It also says, that the young men should pay due respect to every elder, since God is the eldest of all beings.

[*The Works of Flavius Josephus*, trans. William Whiston, 4 vols.
(Grand Rapids: Baker, 1974), vol. 4, pp. 224–225]

MISHNAH ON PROCREATION, MARRIAGE, AND DIVORCE

The Mishnah, Rabbinic Judaism's first text, was redacted by Judah the Patriarch in Sepphoris in the early third century CE. Composed for oral performance in Rabbinic learning communities, it brought together the preserved traditions of two centuries of diverse sages into a coherent, rational system dubbed "the Oral Torah," parallel to the Written Torah of Moses.

Within a short time the Mishnah, with its succinct style and topical organization, became the unchallenged central text of the Rabbis, who were fashioning the most salient form of the Jewish tradition in northern Palestine and Babylonia, Jewry's two main centers. Wide-ranging academic expositions of the Mishnah evolved into the Talmuds of these two communities and ultimately formed the basis of medieval Jewish practice.

The selections below, taken from units called *tractates* within the Order of Women, address how one effects valid marriage or divorce and define conjugal duties and the commandment to procreate in straightforward, legal terms.

Document 1–18

TRACTATE YEVAMOT 6:6 [ON PROCREATION]

A man should not abstain from [the commandment] to procreate unless he already has children. The School of Shammai says: two males. The School of Hillel says: a male and a female, as it is stated "male and female He created them" (Gen. 5:2). . . . If he took a wife and lived with her ten years and she did not bear children, he is not permitted to abstain [from the commandment to procreate, but must take another wife]. . . . And if she miscarried, one counts [the ten years] from the time she miscarried. The man is commanded to procreate, but not the woman. Rabbi Yochanan ben Beroka says, "Of both [men and women] it says "God blessed them, and He said to them, 'Be fruitful and multiply'. . . . " (Gen. 1:28).

> [*The Mishnah*, ed. W. H. Howe (Cambridge: Cambridge University Press, 1883), translated by Michael S. Berger]

Document 1–19

TRACTATE KIDDUSHIN 1:1, 2:1 [ON BETROTHAL]

A woman is acquired in three ways, and acquires her freedom in two ways. She is acquired by means of money, a document, or sexual intercourse. "By money": the School of Shammi say a *dinar* [= half a *shekel*] or an object worth a *dinar*; the School of Hillel say a *perutah* [1/192 of a *dinar*] or an object worth a *perutah*. . . . And she acquires herself through a bill of divorce or by the husband's death. . . .

A man betroths [a woman] personally or through an agent. A woman may accept betrothal personally or through her agent. A man may offer his daughter in marriage while she is still a maiden (younger than 12.5 years). . . .

> [*The Mishnah*, translated by Michael S. Berger]

Document 1–20

TRACTATE KETUBOT 5:5, 5:8 [ON MARITAL OBLIGATIONS]

These are the tasks that a wife carries out for her husband: grinding corn, baking, washing, cooking, suckling her child, making his bed for him, and working in wool. If she brings with her one maidservant [into the marriage], she need not grind, bake, or wash; [if she bring in] two, she need not cook, nor suckle her child; three [maidservants], she need not make his bed, nor work in wool; four [maidservants], she may sit on a high seat [i.e., not work at all]. Rabbi Eliezer says: even if she brought into the marriage one hundred maidservants, he may compel her to work in wool, for idleness leads to lewdness.

If one supported his wife through a third person, he must give her at least 2 *kab* of wheat or four *kab* of barley. . . . He must also give her half a *kab* of peas and half a *log* of oil and a *kab* of dried figs or a *maneh* of fig-cake; and if he has none of these, he gives her the equivalent in other produce. And he gives her a bed [frame], a mat [for sleeping], and a cover. And he gives her a cover for her head and a girdle for her loins, and new shoes every holiday, and new clothing worth 50 *zuz* every year. . . He gives her a silver *ma'ah* for her needs, and she should eat with him every Sabbath evening. If he does not give her the silver *ma'ah*, she keeps her earnings.

> [*The Mishnah*, translated by Michael S. Berger]

Document 1–21

TRACTATE KETUBOT 5:6–7 [ON CONJUGAL DUTIES]

The conjugal duty enjoined in the Torah is: men of independent means—every day; laborers—twice a week; ass-drivers—once a week; camel-drivers—once in thirty days; sailors—once in six months. This is the view of Rabbi Eliezer.

The woman who rebels against her husband [and refuses to copulate], they reduce her marriage settlement seven *dinars* a week. Rabbi Judah says, seven half-dinars. How long does the reduction continue? Until the full amount of the marriage settlement is reached. . . . Rabbi Yose says, he may continue to diminish it, for she might receive an inheritance from another source and he can collect from that. Similarly, the man who rebels against his wife [and refuses to copulate], they add to her marriage settlement three *dinars* a week. Rabbi Judah says, three half-dinars.

[*The Mishnah,* translated by Michael S. Berger]

Document 1–22

TRACTATE KETUBOT 7:6 [ON GROUNDS FOR DIVORCE]

These are the women who are divorced without receiving their marriage settlement: one who transgresses the Law of Moses and "that of Judith" [that is, Jewish custom]. What is meant by the Law of Moses? She serves him food that is not tithed, she has intercourse with him during menstruation, she does not separate the priests'-share from the dough [before serving it], or she vows but does not fulfill the vow. And what is meant by "the Law of Judith"? She goes out and her hair is uncovered, she spins [wool] in the market, or speaks with all people. Abba Saul says, also one who curses his parents in front of him. . . .

[*The Mishnah,* translated by Michael S. Berger]

Document 1–23

TRACTATE GITTIN 9:10 [ON GROUNDS FOR DIVORCE]

The School of Shammai says: A man ought not divorce his wife unless he has found in her unchastity, as it says, "for he found in her an unseemly matter" (Deuteronomy 24:1). And the School of Hillel says: even if she spoiled his food. . . . Rabbi Akiva says: even if he found another woman more pleasant than she. . ..

[*The Mishnah,* translated by Michael S. Berger]

Document 1–24

TRACTATE YEVAMOT 14:1 [ON GROUNDS FOR DIVORCE]

A woman is divorced with her consent or against her will, while the man divorces only willfully.

[*The Mishnah*, translated by Michael S. Berger]

Document 1–25

TRACTATE GITTIN 9:3, 2:5 [ON THE DIVORCE DOCUMENT]

The essence of the divorce document is: "Behold you are permitted to [marry] any man." Rabbi Judah says: [in addition, the divorce document must include] "and this is your divorce document, your letter of separation . . . to go and marry any man you wish."

All are eligible to write the divorce document, even a deaf-mute, a mentally incapacitated person, and a minor. A woman may write her own divorce document . . . for the witnesses' signature is what renders it [a] valid [document].

[*The Mishnah*, translated by Michael S. Berger]

Document 1–26

TRACTATE KIDDUSHIN 1:9 [ON FAMILIAL OBLIGATIONS]

All obligations which devolve upon the father (that is, circumcision; redemption of the firstborn son; teaching Torah, an occupation, and swimming; and arranging marriage) men are obligated to perform, and women are exempt. And all the obligations which devolve upon the child regarding his father (that is, showing awe and respect) both men and women are obligated to perform.

[*The Mishnah*, translated by Michael S. Berger]

THE BABYLONIAN TALMUD

Within the Rabbinic academies of the Land of Israel and Babylonia, the sages' Oral Torah continued to evolve. The Mishnah's terse laws and unresolved debates were closely analyzed and interpreted by scholars, known as *amoraim*, who began to assemble these discussions into formal memorized units. Over time local legal traditions, homiletical insights, and instructions for practice were grafted onto these Mishnah expositions. The resulting corpus of loosely associated oral discussions was redacted into the respective Talmuds of Palestine and Babylonia from the fifth to seventh centuries CE. The selections below, quoted at length, display the associative quality of these discussions, which move seamlessly between legal and nonlegal subject matter.

In contrast to their Palestinian counterparts who suffered under Byzantine rule, the Rabbinic academies of Babylonia thrived, allowing their Talmudic discussions and commentary to continue expanding. The voluminous text became the basis for Rabbinic practice, which under law-centered Islam achieved primacy in most Jewish communities.

Document 1–27

TRACTATE KETHUBOTH 63A–63B

Mishnah: "The woman who rebels against her husband."

GEMARA. Rebels in what [respect]?—Rabbi Huna replied: [In respect] of conjugal union. Rabbi Jose, the son of Rabbi Hanina replied: [In respect] of work.

We learned, similarly if a husband rebels against his wife. Now according to him who said, "[In Respect] of conjugal union" [this ruling] is quite logical and intelligible; but according to him who said, "[In respect] of work," is he [it may be objected] under any obligation [at all to work] for her?—Yes, [rebellion being possible] when he declares "I will neither sustain nor support [my wife]," he must divorce her and pay her the *kethubah*—Is it not necessary to consult him [before ordering him to divorce her]? . . .

[To turn to] the main text. If a wife rebels against her husband, her *kethubah* may be reduced by seven *denarii* a week. Rabbi Judah said: Seven *tropaics*. Our Masters, however, took a second vote [and ordained] that an announcement regarding her shall be made on four consecutive Sabbaths and that then the court shall send her [the following warning]: "Be it known to you that even if your *kethubah* is for a hundred *maneh* you have forfeited it." The same [law is applicable to a woman] betrothed or married, even to a menstruant, even to a sick woman, and even to one who was awaiting the decision of the levir. Said Rabbi Hiyya b. Joseph to Samuel: Is a menstruant capable of conjugal union?— The other replied: One who has bread in his basket is not like one who has a no bread in his basket.[2] . . .

What is to be understood by a "rebellious woman"—Amemar said: [One] who says, "I like him but wish to torment him."[3] If she said, however, "He is repulsive to me," no pressure is to be brought to bear upon her. Mar Zutra ruled: Pressure is to be brought to bear upon her. Such a case once occurred, and Mar Zutra exercised pressure upon the woman and [as a result of the reconciliation that ensued] Rabbi Hanina of Sura was born from the re-union. This, however, was not [the right thing to do].

[*Babylonian Talmud*, Soncino Classics Collection [electronic] (Brooklyn: Judaica, 2001)]

Document 1–28

TRACTATE KETHUBOTH 7B–8A

The Rabbis taught: The benediction of the bridegrooms is said in the house of the bridegroom. Rabbi Judah says: Also in the house of the betrothal it is said. Abaye said: And in [the province of] Judah they taught [the opinion of Rabbi Judah] because [in the province of Judah] he is alone with her.

Another [Baraitha] teaches: The benediction of the bridegrooms is said in the house of the bridegrooms and the benediction of betrothal in the house of betrothal. [As to] the benediction of betrothal—what does one say?—Rabin b. Rabbi Adda and Rabbah son of Rabbi Adda both said in the name of Rab Judah: Blessed art Thou, O Lord our God, King of the Universe, who has sanctified us by his commandments and has commanded us concerning the forbidden relations and has forbidden unto us the betrothed and has allowed unto us the wedded through [the marriage] canopy and betrothal. Rabbi Aha, the son of Raba, concludes it, in the name of Rab Judah, [with the words]: Blessed art Thou, O Lord, who sanctifies Israel through canopy and betrothal. . . . Our Rabbis taught: The blessing of the bridegrooms is said in the presence of ten [persons] all seven days [after the wedding]. Rab Judah said: And that is only if new guests come. What does one say? Rab Judah said: "Blessed art Thou, O Lord our God, King of the Universe, who has created all things to his glory." and "the Creator of man," and "who has created man in his image, in the image of the likeness of his form, and has prepared unto him out of himself a building for ever. Blessed art thou, O Lord, Creator of man." "May the barren greatly rejoice and exult when her children will be gathered in her midst in joy. Blessed art Thou, O Lord, who maketh Zion joyful through her children." "Mayest Thou make the loved companions greatly to rejoice, even as of old Thou didst gladden Thy creature in the Garden of Eden. Blessed art thou, O Lord, who maketh bridegroom and bride to rejoice." "Blessed art Thou, O Lord our King, God of the universe, who has created joy and gladness, bridegroom and bride, rejoicing. song, mirth. and delight, love, and brotherhood, and peace, and friendship." "O Speedily, O Lord our God. may be heard in the cities of Judah, and in the streets of Jerusalem, the voice of joy and the voice of gladness, the voice of the bridegroom and the voice of the bride, the voice of the singing of bridegrooms from their canopies and of youths from their feasts of song. Blessed art Thou, O Lord, who maketh the bridegroom to rejoice with the bride."

[Babylonian Talmud]

Document 1–29

TRACTATE YEBAMOT 62B–64A

Rabbi Tanhum stated in the name of Rabbi Hanilai: Any man who has no wife lives without joy, without blessing, and without goodness. . . .

In the West it was stated: Without Torah and without a [protecting] wall. . . . Raba b. "Ulla said: Without peace. . . . "

Rabbi Joshua b. Levi said: Whosoever knows his wife to be a God-fearing woman and does not duly visit her conjugally is called a sinner; for it is said, "You will know that all is well with your household," etc. [Job 5:24]

Rabbi Joshua b. Levi further stated: It is a man's duty to pay a visit to his wife when he starts on a journey; for it is said, "You will know that all is well with your household, etc." [Job 5:24] Is this deduced from here? Surely it is deduced from the following: "You shall be eager for your husband" [Gen. 3:16] teaches that a woman yearns for her husband when he sets out on a journey!— Rabbi Joseph replied: This was required only in the case where her menstruation period was near. And this applies only [when the journey is] for a secular purpose, but when for a religious purpose [it does not apply, since then] people are in a state of anxiety. . . .

Rabbi Eleazar said: Any man who has no wife is no proper man; for it is said, "He created them male and female, and on the day when he created them, he blessed them and called them man" [Gen. 5:2]. . . .

Rabbi Eleazar further stated: What is the meaning of the Scriptural text, "I will provide a partner for him"? [Gen. 2:18] If he was worthy she is a help to him; if he was not worthy she is against him. . . .

Rabbi Jose met Elijah and asked him: It is written, "I will make him a help"; how does a woman help a man? The other replied: If a man brings wheat, does he chew the wheat? If flax, does he put on the flax? Does she not, then, bring light to his eyes and put him on his feet!

Rabbi Eleazar further stated: What is meant by the Scriptural text, "Now this, at last—bone from my bones, flesh from my flesh!—this shall be called woman, for from man was this taken" [Gen. 2:23]. This teaches that Adam had intercourse with every beast and animal but found no satisfaction until he cohabited with Eve. . . .

Rabbi Hama b. Hanina stated: As soon as a man takes a wife his sins are buried; for it is said: "Whoso findeth a wife findeth a great good and obtaineth favour of the Lord" [Prov. 18:22] . . .

Raba said: [If one has] a bad wife it is a meritorious act to divorce her, for it is said, "Drive out the insolent man, and strife goes with him; if he sits on the bench, he makes a mockery of justice." [Prov. 22:10]

Raba further stated: A bad wife, the amount of whose *kethubah* is large, [should be given] a rival at her side; as people say, "By her partner rather than by a thorn."

Raba further stated: A bad wife is as troublesome as a very rainy day; for it is said, "Endless dripping on a rainy day—that is what a nagging wife is like" [Prov. 27:15]. . . .

It is written in the book of Ben Sira: A good wife is a precious gift; she will be put in the bosom of the God-fearing man. A bad wife is a plague to her husband. What remedy has he?—Let him give her a letter of divorce and be healed.

A beautiful wife is a joy to her husband; the number of his days shall be double. . . .

It was taught: Rabbi Eliezer stated, He who does not engage in propagation of the race is as though he sheds blood; for it is said, "He that sheds the blood of a man, for that man his blood shall be shed" [Gen. 9:6], and this is immediately followed by the text, "But you must be fruitful and increase" [Gen. 9:7]. As though he has diminished the Divine Image; since it is said, "For in the image of God had God made man" [Gen. 9:6], and this is immediately followed by, "But you must be fruitful etc." [Gen. 9:7]. Ben "Azzai said: As though he sheds blood *and* diminishes the Divine Image; since it is said, "But you must be fruitful and increase" [Gen. 9:7].

They said to Ben 'Azzai: Some preach well and act well, others act well but do not preach well; you, however, preach well but do not act well! Ben 'Azzai replied: But what shall I do, seeing that my soul is in love with the Torah; the world can be carried on by others. . . .

[*Babylonian Talmud*]

AGGADIC MIDRASH ON MARRIAGE AND FAMILY

With the Bible's canonization in the Second Temple period, several Jewish groups began to read the sacred text more closely to derive proper practice and belief. This process, known as exegesis (*midrash*), evolved among the post-Temple Rabbis into a more formal set of interpretive strategies that yielded both legal and nonlegal insights. The latter, which expanded biblical stories, linked current and ancient events, and offered homiletical advice, came to be known as *Aggadah*, in contrast to the legal *Halakhah*. Aggadic material was continually produced and compiled into various collections through the early middle ages.

While Aggadah is not formally binding, its elegant style and profound content have gripped the Jewish imagination for centuries. In a sense, it provides the "soul" of Judaism, the sinews to the legal skeleton of the *Halakhah*.

The following passages extol marriage and family, which, in the absence of a Jewish state, came to be the cornerstone of Jewish community and continuity.

Document 1–30

MIDRASH RABBAH, GENESIS 68:4

Rabbi Yehuda b. Simon began a discussion with the verse from Psalms 68: "God makes the solitary dwell in the house."

An important lady once asked Rabbi Yose b. Chalaphta, "For how many days did God create His world?"

"For six days," he replied, "As the verse says (Exodus 31) 'For in six days God made the Heaven and the Earth.'"

"What does He do from the hour He finished to now?" she asked.

"God sits and pairs up couples: The daughter of so-and-so is for so-and-so. The wife of so-and-so is for so-and-so. The money of so-and-so will go to so-and-so."

"That's His job?" she exclaimed, "Even I could do that! I have so many menservants and maidservants, in one hour I could easily pair all of them."

To this Rabbi Yose b. Chalaphta replied, "You say that is so easy for you, for God it is as difficult as the splitting of the Red Sea." And he went away. What did the woman do? She took one thousand menservants and one thousand maidservants and stood them in two lines. She told one servant to marry someone, and one maid to marry a manservant, and she paired them all off in one night. The next day they all returned to her. This one had his brain split open, this one had his eye knocked out, and this one's leg was broken.

She asked them all, "What happened?"

One said, "That man is not for me." Another said, "I am not fitting for that woman." The woman immediately sent for Rabbi Yose b. Chalaphta.

When he was brought before her she said, "There is no God like your God, true is your Torah, pleasant and praiseworthy. You said well."

He responded, "I did not say that. All I said was if it is easy in your eyes, but to God it is as difficult as the splitting of the Red Sea. . . ."

> [*Aggadic Midrash*, in Soncino Classics Collection [electronic]
> (Brooklyn: Judaica, 2001)]

Document 1–31

PIRKEI D'RABBI ELIEZER, 16

A groom is similar to a king. Just like a king does not go out into the marketplace alone, also a groom should not go to the marketplace alone. Just like a king wears clothes of honor, a groom should also wear clothes of honor all his seven days of feasting. Just like a king's face shines like the light of the sun, a groom's face shines like sunlight, as it says in Psalms, "And he is like a groom going out from his wedding canopy" (Psalms 19).

> [*Aggadic Midrash*]

Document 1–32

PIRKEI D'RABBI ELIEZER, 17

Solomon saw that the trait of kindness is held highly before God. When he built the temple he built two special gates: one for grooms and one for mourners. Jews would go on the Sabbath and sit between these two gates, and when one would enter the gate of grooms they would know that he was a groom and they would say to him, "May the One who dwells in this house make you happy with sons and daughters." Once the temple was destroyed the rabbis established that grooms and mourners should enter the synagogues and the study halls, and the people of the place will see them and rejoice with them. This was done in order that all Jews will be easily able to fulfill their obligation to do kindness. On this it was said, "Blessed are You God who pays reward to those who do kindness."

[*Aggadic Midrash*]

Document 1–33

TANNA D'BEI ELIYAHU ZUTA, 3

One who marries a woman for immorality, the end result will come out a rebellious son. One who marries a woman for the sake of heaven will result in having children who will save Israel in their time of trouble, and will increase Torah and religious observance in Israel. One who marries for money will end up needing others. One who marries a woman for greatness, someone from her family will rise up and ultimately reduce his descendants.

[*Aggadic Midrash*]

Document 1–34

PIRKEI D'RABBI ELIEZER, 36

"And Laban said to Jacob, 'Because you are my brother. . . .'" (Genesis 29:15). Was he his brother? Was he not his nephew? To teach that the son of one's sister is called his son and the nephew of someone is like his brother. From where do we learn it—from Abraham, who said to Lot, "Because we are brothers" (Genesis 13:8). And where do we see that one's grandchildren are like his children—from Jacob, who said, "Ephraim and Menasha are like Reuben and Simeon to me" (Genesis 48:5). Aren't Ephraim and Menasha Jacob's grandchildren? To teach that one's son's sons are like his children. And where do we see that one's daughter's sons are also like his sons—from Laban, who said to Jacob, "The sons are my sons, and the daughters are my daughters" (Genesis 31). . . . Are they his children, aren't they his daughter's children? To teach that one's daughter's children are like one's own children.

[*Aggadic Midrash*]

Document 1–35

MIDRASH HAGADOL, LEVITICUS 25:35

["The merciful man does good to his own soul; but he that is cruel troubles his own flesh" (Proverbs 11:17).] Alternatively, ["The merciful man] does good to his own soul," means one who brings close his relatives and does kindness for his relatives, is as if he did kindness for himself, because a person's relatives are seen as a part of himself. "But he that is cruel troubles his own flesh," this refers to one who does not attach himself to his family. From here we derive that one should always involve oneself in acts of kindness with all people, and even more so with one's relatives even if they do not need it.

[*Aggadic Midrash*]

THE BABYLONIAN TALMUD ON MARITAL SEX

This Talmudic passage is the locus classicus of the Rabbis' view of marital sex. Several features of the text are striking. First, the Rabbis' permissive attitude is grounded not in a modern appreciation of sexuality but in the more contractarian view of marriage whereby a husband acquires rights to intercourse with his wife. Nevertheless, the passage ends by warning against abusing this right, manifesting a concern that sex express genuine emotional bonds.

Second, Talmudic culture was comfortable with multiple standards of behavior. Conjugal relations, while a requirement, had to be placed in the broader context of one's religious development, and so Rabbinic scholars were expected to behave differently.

Finally, we must acknowledge the passage's frustrating use of euphemism, a longstanding tradition of Hebrew literature. Unclear phrases required subsequent interpretation, producing debate among medieval jurists.

While the text's thrust is permissive, later commentators, particularly in pietistic circles, circumscribed marital sex—a view that came to dominate medieval legal literature.

Document 1–36

NEDARIM 33B

Rabbi Johanan b. Dahabai said: The Ministering Angels told me four things: People are born lame because they [that is, their parents] "overturned their table"; dumb, because they kiss "that place"; deaf, because they converse during cohabitation; blind, because they look at "that place. . . ."

Rabbi Johanan said: The above is the view of Rabbi Johanan b. Dahabai; but our Sages said: The *halachah* is not as Rabbi Johanan b. Dahabai, but a man may do whatever he pleases with his wife [at intercourse]: A parable; Meat which comes from the abattoir, may be eaten salted, roasted, cooked or seethed; so with fish from the fishmonger.[4] Amemar said: Who are the "Ministering Angels"? The Rabbis. For should you maintain it literally, why did Rabbi Johanan say that the *halachah* is not as Rabbi Johanan b. Dahabai, seeing that the angels know more about the formation of the fetus than we? And why are they designated "Ministering Angels"?—Because they are as distinguished as they.

A woman once came before Rabbi and said, "Rabbi! I set a table before my husband, but he overturned it." Rabbi replied: "My daughter! the Torah has permitted you to him—what then can I do for you?" A woman once came before Rab and complained. "Rabbi! I set a table before my husband, but he overturned it." Rab replied: Wherein does it differ from a fish?

And that ye seek not after your own heart. [Deducing] from this Rabbi taught: One may not drink out of one goblet and think of another.[5] Rabina said: This is necessary only when both are his wives.

[Baylonian Talmud]

THE BABYLONIAN ORDINANCE FROM THE ACADEMY ON DIVORCE

Islam's rapid spread in the seventh and eighth centuries CE brought most of world Jewry under single rule and elevated the authority and prestige of the Babylonian academies and their heads, the *geonim*. These heads established the Babylonian Talmud as the foundation of Jewish practice and instituted ordinances to address severely changed conditions, such as in divorce law.

Talmudic tradition insisted that only the husband could divorce his wife through a unilateral and willful act; any other type of divorce was invalid. Islamic courts, however, perceived their jurisdiction to extend to anyone who would appeal to them and would grant divorces or dissolve marriages for Jewish women who came to them seeking divorce. Fearing widespread invalid divorces, seventh-century geonim instituted that Jewish courts, under certain conditions consistent with Talmudic law, would aid a woman wishing a divorce. The radical ordinance, explained in this tenth-century responsum, was in effect for over four centuries but was rejected by later Rabbinic authorities.

Document 1–37

THE BABYLONIAN ORDINANCE FROM THE ACADEMY ON DIVORCE

And concerning your question: In the case of a woman who is living with her husband and says to him, "Divorce me, I do not wish to live with you," is [her husband] obligated to give her anything from the alimony provided for by the marriage contract, and is she [considered] a rebellious wife or not?

We have seen that the original requirement of the law was that the husband was not obligated to divorce his wife if she demanded a divorce except in those [cases] where the Rabbis said that they can force him to divorce [her]. And when a woman abstains from sexual relations and refuses to perform those household duties she is obligated to do for him, she is a rebellious wife, from whose alimony a weekly sum is deducted, and she requires a warning. Afterwards they enacted another decree, that they make a [public] announcement concerning her for four consecutive weeks, and they send her [a warning] from the Jewish court: "Know that even if the alimony provided for you by your marriage contract is one hundred *maneh*, you shall lose it." They [further add] that Rami bar Hama says, "this [warning] must be sent to her twice: once before the [public] announcement and once after it."

All [the discussion concerning the weekly reduction of alimony] pertains only to those objects which the husband obligated himself to give her but which are not now in existence, and to whatever of her dowry has been destroyed or lost. . . . Subsequently they decreed that they [publicly] announce [concerning] her for four weeks, [at which time] she forfeits everything.

Nevertheless, they did not obligate the husband to give her a bill of divorce, and if he dies, his inheritors are freed from [those obligations] of the marriage contract for which he was responsible. But those objects which remain in existence, either from her dowry or from ornaments [received after her marriage], belong to whoever takes them. . . .

And then they decreed that they cause her to wait without a divorce twelve months, in case she can be reconciled. And after twelve months the husband is forced to write her a bill of divorce.

And afterwards the Sabboraitic sages saw that Jewish women were attaching themselves to the Gentiles to get divorces from their husbands by force, and that there were those [wives] who were satisfied with a "forced" divorce which was not in accordance with Jewish law, and from which ruin emanates. It was therefore decreed in the days of Mar Rav Rabba and Rav Hunai [ca. 670 CE], may they rest in Eden, concerning a rebellious wife who demands a divorce, that he must pay for all the property that she brought with her into the marriage and for which he assumed responsibility; he must even give her restitution for those articles which were destroyed or lost. As for his own objects or property which he had included in the marriage contract as his obligation to her in the event of his death or divorce, [if she divorces him, their status is as follows:] those which are not now in existence he need not give her, and whatever she seizes of those which are in existence, must be taken from her and returned to her husband.

They force him, and he must write her a bill of divorce immediately. She also receives one hundred or two hundred [*zuzim*, the basic alimony sum]. In this manner do we conduct ourselves today, and have done so for three hundred years and more. So should you do too.

> [Shlomo Riskin, *Women and Jewish Divorce: The Rebellious Wife, the Agunah, and the Right of Women to Initiate Divorce in Jewish Law, a Halakhic Solution* (Hoboken, NJ: KTAV, 1989), pp. 57–59.]

THE ORDINANCES OF RABBI GERSHOM
(THE LIGHT OF THE EXILE)

The communities of Ashkenaz, the Jewish cultural sphere of northern Europe, enjoyed considerable sovereignty under Christendom. Restricted by law to financial and some commercial occupations, these Jewish communities achieved economic success, particularly with the opening of trade routes to the east that linked Jewish communities worldwide.

Economic improvement brought with it a rise in the status of women. As part of this enhancement, Rabbi Gershom, the unrivaled eleventh-century rabbinic leader, ordained that women could not be divorced against their will, as the Talmud permitted, and he outlawed polygamy, which both biblical and Rabbinic law allowed. Scholars speculate that economic conditions destabilized marriage and necessitated these ordinances: husbands traveling for trade would divorce their wives while abroad or marry other women and not return for long periods of time. In any event, the combined effect of these ordinances was to create greater balance in marriage by severely limiting the husband's prerogatives.

These two ordinances quickly took hold throughout all of Ashkenazic Jewry and have remained the enforced position ever since.

Document 1–38

ENCYCLOPEDIA TALMUDICA, VOL. 17

Sources that cite the ordinances of R. Gershom regarding marriage and divorce:

Although there are no extant sources from the period of Rabbi Gershom's lifetime (960–1040) that explicitly bear witness to his ordinances or those of the sages of his generation, Rashi (Rabbi Shlomo ben Issac, 1040–1105) and his grandchildren (the Tosafists) refer to R. Gershom as an enactor of decrees and ordinances in various matters.

The first source that refers to R. Gershom's ordinances on marriage and divorce is Rabbi Eliezer b. Nathan (Raavan, one of the first of the Tosafists and a contemporary of Rashi's grandchildren, 1090–1170) in his commentary to Tractate *Ketubot* (65:1): "Nowadays, that the decree upon the community is not to marry an additional wife and not to divorce a woman against her will . . . "

We again find mention of R. Gershom's ordinance as cited by Raavan in the responsa of Maharam bar Baruch (rabbi of 14th-century Austria): "On this Rabbi Eliezer b. Nathan wrote that [the law pertaining to] *Moredet*, a rebellious wife, still applies in our days even though the Enlightener of the Diaspora decreed not to marry two wives and not to force a divorce . . . "

We also find the following by Raavan's grandson, Rabbi Eliezer b. Yoel ha-Levi (Raaviah), in a responsum: "On the matter of a woman who became insane and her husband requested to be absolved of the prohibition of the Exalted Rabbi Light of the Exile (not to divorce a woman against her will or marry another woman simultaneously) and they did not want to permit him. . . . "
And in another responsum [regarding levirate marriage (see Deut. 25:5–10)]: ". . . the widow desired to perform the halizah separation ceremony, while her deceased husband's brothers wanted to perform the levirate marriage, despite the fact that they had wives. The brothers claimed that the commandment to

perform levirate marriage superseded the Exalted Rabbi Light of the Exile's decree against having multiple wives."

[Supplement to Shelomoh Sha'anan, "Herem deRabbenu Gershom,"
in *Encyclopedia Talmudica* (Jerusalem: Talmudic Encyclopedia Institute, 1969),
vol. 17, col. 757ff., translated by Michael J. Broyde]

MEDIEVAL MARRIAGE CONTRACTS FROM THE CAIRO GENIZA

Through the eleventh century the Eastern Mediterranean was the center of world Jewry, with major communities in Palestine, Babylonia, Egypt, and Asia Minor. In 1897 a synagogue storeroom in Cairo was discovered to contain thousands of centuries-old Jewish documents from these regions, ranging from sacred texts to secular forms. Dating from the eleventh through fourteenth centuries, they provide a fascinating snapshot of daily Jewish life at that time.

Many Geniza documents relating to family matters affirm Talmudic practices. In these communities betrothal and marriage were still separated by a significant amount of time, during which the ceremony and the terms of the marriage contract were arranged. The tendency to document every aspect of marriage continued with deeds of betrothal. The selection below, explicitly designated a "ketubah of betrothal," has the groom unconditionally betroth the bride, but makes his obligation for support conditional on her entering the bridal chamber.

Document 1–39

KETUBAH OF BETROTHAL FROM THE CAIRO GENIZA

On the first day of the week, which is the eleventh day of the month Tamuz, year four thousand, seven hundred and sixty-seven A.M., which is year one thousand, three hundred and eighteen of the era by which we are accustomed to count in Fustat, Egypt, which is situated on the Nile river, Israel b. [= son of] Daniel betrothed Sittūna, the virgin, who is of age, daughter of David, represented by her father David b. Abraham, after his agency had been verified by two witnesses—namely David b. Rabbi Sema"ya the elder and Khalaf b. Abraham—with *qinyan* [a formal transaction] (to affirm) that she had consented to his agency to give her in marriage to this Israel. And the witnesses were acquainted with her. This betrothal is for *qiddush* with a marriage gift of 250 good, fully weighted dinars. At the time of her betrothal (*qiddush*), he gave her 100 dinars, which is the total advanced payment. There remain (as a debt) incumbent upon him 150 good, fully weighted dinars, which is the total delayed payment. And this Israel b. Daniel undertook to nourish her, to maintain and esteem (her), when she enters his home. And she undertook, this Sittūna daughter of David, to attend him in purity and cleanness, after she enters the marriage chamber.

With this understanding, the two sides agreed, Israel, the betrothed, b. Daniel and David, the agent, b. Abraham. And this Israel gave to David, his father-in-law, the agent, in our presence, 100 dinars, the advanced *mohar*, and the rings with which he effected the *qiddushin*. This David, the agent, b. Abraham, received them in our presence. And the two of them instructed the scribe to write and the witnesses to testify.

We performed a complete and strict *qinyan* with them, with the consent of both of them, with a proper implement for performing it. Strong and valid.

Jephthah ha-Kohen b. Toviah.

Samuel b. Hanokh (whose) s(oul is at) r(est).

Nehuma b. Wahb.

Mu'ammar, the scribe, b. Isaac (whose) s(oul is at) r(est).

> [Mordecai A. Friedman, *Jewish Marriage in Palestine: A Cairo Genizah Study*,
> 2 vols. (New York: Jewish Theological Seminary of America, 1982),
> vol. 2, pp. 378–380]

LOVE POETRY FROM THE GOLDEN AGE OF SPAIN

In the early middle ages high culture in Islamic Spain was based on the twin pillars of philosophy and poetry. Jews participated fully in this courtly society, in what became known as the Golden Age of Spain. This integration also spawned cultural competition, with Jews developing Hebrew poetry in the same genres their Muslim hosts did in Arabic—including love poetry.

Medieval poetry was highly formalized, and love poems could be either descriptive—celebrating the beauty of a nameless, and often genderless, body of a beloved—or petitionary, where the poet pleads with another to respond to his unrequited love. In both we never learn of the particular circumstances of the individuals involved.

We do not know whether this poetry reflected realities in Jewish society or merely imitated literary conventions. Regardless, these Hebrew poems reflect the spiritualization of love, the Greek notion that beauty points to an ideal beyond itself—a genuine innovation in Jewish literature.

Document 1–40

POETRY OF MOSES IBN EZRA

Caress a lovely woman's breast by night,
And kiss some beauty's lips by morning light.
Silence those who criticize you, those
Officious talkers. Take advice from me:
With beauty's children only can we live.
Kidnapped were they from Paradise to gall
The living; living men are lovers all.
Immerse your heart in pleasure and in joy,

And by the bank a bottle drink of wine,
Enjoy the swallow's chirp and viol's whine.
Laugh, dance, and stamp your feet upon the floor!
Get drunk, and knock at dawn on some girl's door.
This is the joy of life, so take your due.
You too deserve a portion of the Ram
Of Consecration, like your people's chiefs.
To suck the juice of lips do not be shy,
But take what's rightly yours—the breast and thigh!

[Raymond P. Scheindlin, ed., *Wine, Women, and Death: Medieval Hebrew Poems on the Good Life* (Philadelphia: Jewish Publication Society, 1986), poem no. 11]

Document 1–41

POETRY OF MOSES IBN EZRA

These rivers reveal for the world to see
The secret love concealed in me.
You who blame me, Ah! be still.
My love's a stag who's learned to kill,
Arrogant, with stubborn will.
Passion has disheartened me
Cruel of him to part from me.
A fawn is he with slender thighs.
The sun goes dark when it sees him rise.
Darts are flying from his eyes.
Stole my sleep away from me,
Altogether wasted me.
Never will I forget the night
We lay together in delight
Upon my bed till morning light.
All night he made love to me,
At his mouth he suckled me.
Charming even in deceit;
The fruit of his mouth is like candy sweet.
Played me false, that little cheat!
Deceived me, then made fun of me;
I did him no wrong, but he wronged me.
One day when my eyes were filled to the brim
There came to my ears this little hymn,
So I sang my doleful song to him:
"How dear that boy is to me!
Maybe he'll come back to me."

[Scheindlin, *Wine, Women, and Death*, no. 13.]

Document 1–42

POETRY OF JUDAH HALEVI

Bear my greetings, mixed with tears,
Mountains, hills—whoever hears—
To ten lovely fingernails
Painted with blood from my entrails;
To eyes mascaraed with black dye
From the pupil of my eye.
Though she'll never call me dear,
Maybe she'll pity me for my tear.

[Scheindlin, *Wine, Women, and Death*, no. 19.]

THE ORDER OF THE *GET*

Under Jewish law, sex with another man's wife was a sin with high stakes: the child of this union had the status of a *mamzer* (bastard) who may never marry another Jew. It was thus vital to scrutinize each divorce to ensure its validity, freeing the woman to marry another man.

Divorce among medieval European Jews was extremely rare, and only expert scholars conducted them, thus guaranteeing the marriage was truly terminated. Beginning in the fourteenth century, persecution, migration, and conversions to Christianity both destabilized Jewish families and diminished the number of trained scholars to supervise divorce. These conditions produced a new genre— the divorce handbook—that guided rabbis through the complex and detailed process of writing the Jewish divorce. This guaranteed the documents' validity, allowing divorced women to remarry.

The passage below, taken from the sixteenth century *Shulhan Arukh* by Joseph Karo, is one of the final versions of this genre and still guides traditional Jewish divorce.

Document 1–43

JOSEPH KARO, SHULHAN ARUKH

1. Some are careful not to arrange the *get* on the Sabbath eve (Friday).

2. A scribe should be appointed, as well as two witnesses who are not related to one another, nor to the woman.

3. One should take care that the scribe not be one of the witnesses. . . .

5. [The scribe or the sage arranging the *get*] must recognize that he is the specified man and she is the specified woman, unless it is a time of grave danger. . . .

7. If the divorcing husband was on his deathbed, one must take care to ensure that he is lucid both at the time of writing and handing over the *get*.

8. If one wishes to divorce conditionally, he should not mention any condition at all; rather, he should instruct the scribe to write a *get* and the witnesses to sign it, and not mention any condition until the time that he hands it over [to her].

9. All are fit to write a *get*, except for a deaf-mute, an insane person, a minor, a slave, a non-Jew, an apostatized Jew, or one who publicly desecrates the Sabbath.

10. The husband himself should not write the *get*, wherever possible. . . .

13. The scribe shall bestow the parchment, ink, and quill as a gift to the husband, and the husband shall raise them to legally acquire them.

14. The sage shall ask the divorcing husband: "You are giving this *get* of your own volition, without any duress; you have not made any of the various forms of vows or oaths which are forcing you to give it—tell us and we will annul it." The divorcing husband responds: "I have not vowed nor taken an oath, and I have no duress; rather, of my own volition am I giving this *get*, with a full heart, without any duress or conditions."

15. The husband shall extend the parchment, quill, and ink to the scribe before witnesses and say to him in their presence: "Write a *get* for me for the purpose of divorcing my wife—So-and-so, daughter of so-and-so—and for the purpose of ending the marriage. And I give you permission to write the *get* up to one hundred times until one fit draft emerges without any flaws, whether in the writing or in the signatures, in accordance with the sage—Rabbi so-and-so.

16. "And you, so-and-so and so-and-so, be witnesses and sign this *get*, for the purpose of divorcing my wife—So-and-so, daughter of so-and-so—and for the purpose of ending the marriage, and I grant you permission to sign up to one hundred different Gittin until a fit one emerges, in accordance with the sage—Rabbi so-and-so, without any flaws, whether in the writing or in the signatures.". . .

18. The scribe shall not write, and the witnesses shall not sign, until they hear instructions directly from the husband—to the scribe to write and to the witnesses to sign—and not from a messenger-agent; Even if he told three [separate messenger-agents]: Tell so-and-so to write and so-and-so to sign, they shall not write or sign, as they did not hear directly from [the husband].

19. The husband pays the fees of the scribe; and if the wife paid, it is valid.

20. The husband shall say before witnesses: "Behold, I nullify before you any intent to renege on this later. . . . "

21. The husband must appoint the same witnesses before whom he instructed the scribe to write the *get* for his wife, to sign it. And they must stand at the time that the line with the man's name and the woman's name and the date is written, and hear that it is being written specifically for this man and this woman.

22. [The witnesses] must be able to identify that this is the *get* that the scribe wrote specifically for this man and this woman. . . .

23. It is a good idea for the husband to remain with the scribe and the witnesses until the *get* is written, signed, and delivered, so that he will not be able to renege and claim later that he was not intending to follow through on his plans. . . .

36. When the scribe comes to write the *get*, before he begins to write, he should inquire of the divorcing man as to his name and his father's name, and whether his father had multiple names (e.g., a name changed as a result of illness), and whether he or his father have nicknames.

37. So, too, one should inquire about the woman['s name] and her father['s], like the man.

38. The scribe and the witnesses must stand in the same place (at the same time).

39. The parchment should be pre-cut to the size of the *get*, so that it will not be necessary to cut off anything after the *get* is written. . . .

41. The parchment must be longer than it is wide. And the length is determined by how it is read (i.e., vertically) from beginning to end.

42. Thirteen guidelines should be etched into it; and the last line should be divided into two shorter lines, as the witnesses sign there one beneath the other. . . .

54. If a flaw is found in the *get*, and one is required to write another one, if the husband is present, he must re-instruct, as before, the scribe to write a *get* for his wife and the witnesses to sign it.

55. When the scribe comes to write the *get*, he should say before the witnesses, "Behold, I am writing this *get* specifically for so-and-so son of so-and-so, and specifically to divorce his wife so-and-so daughter of so-and-so, so that he divorce her with it, specifically for him and specifically for her, for the purpose of ending the marriage." And he shall [then] write the *get* immediately.

56. The [lettering of the] *get* must be dried before the witnesses sign.

57. After the *get* is dried, the witnesses sign one under the other.

58. The witnesses must sign in the presence of each other.

59. Each witness shall say before he signs: "I am signing this *get* specifically for so-and-so son of so-and-so to divorce his wife so-and-so daughter of so-and-so with it, specifically for him and specifically for her, for the purpose of ending the marriage." And he shall [then] sign immediately. . . .

62. Each of the witnesses must specify his name and his father's name, such that he signs: so-and-so, son of so-and so, witness.

63. The writing of the witnesses shall be clear and legible, so that the letters not be joined to one another, just like the *get* itself.

66–73. The sage and the witnesses shall read the *get*, including the witnesses' signatures. Afterward, the sage shall ask the scribe, "Is this the *get* you wrote—did you write it on the instruction of the husband, specifically for him, and specifically for her, and specifically for the purpose of divorcing his wife so-and-so, daughter of so-and-so?" He shall answer, "Yes." [The sage] then asks one of the witnesses, "Did you hear the husband instruct the scribe to write [a document] specifically for him and specifically for the purpose of divorcing his wife so-and-so daughter of so-and-so? Do you recognize this to be that *get*? Did you sign as per the instructions of the husband? Did you sign specifically for him, specifically for her, and specifically for the purpose of divorcing his wife so-and-so? Do you recognize your signature? Did you sign before your colleague? Do you recognize his signature?" He shall answer, "Yes," to each question. And so, too, shall be done to the second witness.

74. Afterward [the sage] shall give the *get* to the husband. Then he shall repeat and ask him again if he is giving it knowingly and willingly, as mentioned above. . . .

77. [The sage] shall gather a quorum, in order to give the *get* before an assembled group of ten.

78. The sage shall say to all the assembled before the *get* is given, "If there is anyone who knows of any flaw against this *get*, and wishes to object or raise questions, let him speak now before it is given, for after it is handed over, a ban will go into effect to not cast aspersions upon this *get*." . . .

81. [The sage] shall instruct the woman to remove the ring on her hand, and afterward to put out her hands, open them, and bring them together in order for her to accept the *get*. . . .

84. The husband shall place the *get* in her hands and say the following when he gives it to her: "Behold, this is your *get*, and behold, you are divorced—through it—from me and are permitted to all men."

85. After he places the *get* in her hands and removes his hands entirely, she shall then close her hands, grasp the *get*, and raise both hands (containing the *get*) upward. After this, the sage shall take the *get* from her hands and read it a second time in the presence of witnesses. He shall then place a ban upon anyone who will cast aspersions on this *get*.

86. He shall then cut it in a crosswise manner.

87. The sage shall warn the woman not to become engaged to another man until ninety days have elapsed (not including that day). . . .

90. The husband must not be intimate with the woman between the time that the *get* is written and the time that it is given. If he was intimate with her, it becomes a *get yashan* (literally, a *get* that has been slept with), and may not be used to divorce.

91. A messenger-agent who brings a *get* shall give it to her in the presence of two [witnesses]; and if he is a relative or otherwise invalid [to testify], he shall give it to her in the presence of three [witnesses]. He shall say at the time it is handed over: "Behold this is your *get*, which your husband sent to you, and behold, you are divorced—through it—from him and are permitted to all men; and this *get* was written in my presence and signed in my presence." . . .

101. A person should be very careful not to become involved in *get* matters unless one is an expert in the laws of *gittin,* for the minutiae are great and one may easily come to err in them, leading to the proliferation of children with the forbidden status of *mamzer* [which results from inappropriate sexual relationships, especially that of a married woman with another man; married, in this case, because her divorce proceedings were mishandled and thus null and void.] May the Strength of Israel save us from [such] errors, Amen.

[*Shulchan Arukh ha-bahir* [Bar Ilan electronic version 11.01 2003], translated by Michael J. Broyde]

MAIMONIDES ON SEX

Under the conditions of an open and educated Islamic society, Jews seriously engaged Greek philosophy and sought a synthesis with Rabbinic culture. Theology, metaphysics, and science flourished among the Jewish elite. The greatest exemplar of this cultural fusion was the twelfth-century scholar-philosopher, Moses Maimonides.

A systematic thinker and writer, Maimonides organized the first comprehensive code of Jewish law in almost one thousand years. All Talmudic law, even if inapplicable, was included, and classified under appropriate headings. At the same time, Maimonides undertook the most thorough integration of Aristotelian philosophy and Jewish thought, embodied in his *Guide of the Perplexed.* For him, Judaism's goal—to love and perceive the divine—required intellectual perfection, which could be achieved through philosophical study.

This approach provides the context for Maimonides' view of sex, expressed in both his code and philosophical writing. Carnal appetites were base and to be suppressed, an attitude seemingly verified by the Torah's many sexual prohibitions.

Document 1–44

MOSES MAIMONIDES, LAWS OF DE'OTH (CHARACTERISTICS) 3:2

A man must focus all of his thoughts and actions exclusively toward knowing God, blessed be He. His resting, arising, and his speech should all be directed to this end. How so? When he engages in business or does work to earn a wage, he should not have the intention merely to acquire wealth, rather he should engage in these activities in order to gain things that the body needs such as food, drink, shelter, and marriage. So too, when he eats, drinks, or has relations, he should not have in mind merely to gain pleasure from these acts until the point where he eats and drinks only that which is sweet to his cheek and has relations only for pleasure; rather, he should eat and drink only to remain healthy of body and limb. . . . So too, when he has relations, he should only have relations to maintain bodily vigor and in order to procreate.

[Translated by Michael J. Broyde]

Document 1-45

MOSES MAIMONIDES, LAWS OF DE'OTH (CHARACTERISTICS) 5:1, 4:5

Even though a man's wife is always permitted to him, it is fitting for a Torah scholar to behave himself in a holy manner and not to habituate with his wife like barnyard animals, rather from one Sabbath to the next Sabbath, if he has strength. And when he speaks with her, he will not speak with her in the beginning of the night when he is satisfied and his stomach is full, and not at the end of the night when he is hungry, but rather in the middle of the night when his food is digested in his intestines. And he shall not be frivolous, and he shall not pollute his mouth with words of nothingness, even between him and her. . . . And the both shall not be drunk and not lazy and not angry, or even one of them shall not be, and she should not be sleeping, and he should not rape her, and it should not be when she does not have the will, but rather when they both want it, happily. And he will speak and play with her for a while so that her spirit will be calmed and one will have relations modestly and not brazenly, and they should separate immediately.

[Translated by Michael J. Broyde]

Document 1-46

MOSES MAIMONIDES, LAWS OF MARRIAGE 15:1–3

1. A wife who allowed her husband, after the wedding, to hold back on her conjugal rights, this is permitted. When is this applicable? When he has already had sons and fulfilled the commandment of be fruitful and multiply, but if he has not fulfilled this commandment, he must have relations with her with all due frequency until he has sons, since there is a commandment from the Torah to "be fruitful and multiply" (Genesis 1:28).

2. The man is obligated to be fruitful and multiply, and not the woman. And from when is the man obligated by this commandment? From the age of seventeen. And when twenty years have passed and he has not acquired a wife, then behold, he has transgressed and negated a positive commandment, but if he was busy with Torah studies and immersed in them, and was afraid of taking a wife, for fear of having to work for sustenance and then be distracted from Torah, then behold, this is allowed, because one who is fulfilling one commandment is exempt from another commandment, and even more so with Torah studies.

3. One whose soul is drawn to Torah studies and is engrossed in them, like Ben-Azzai, and clings to them [Torah studies] all his days and does not acquire a wife, he does not transgress a commandment, he who does not let his desires overpower him. But he who does let his desires overpower him must take a wife even if he has sons, in case he comes to have forbidden thoughts.

[Translated by Michael J. Broyde]

Document 1–47

THE GUIDE OF THE PERPLEXED

BOOK II: CHAPTER 36

Thereupon that individual desiring perfection would obtain knowledge and wisdom[6] until he passes from potentiality to actuality and acquires a perfect and accomplished human intellect and pure and well-tempered[7] human moral habits. . . . His thought will always go toward noble matters, and he will be interested only in the knowledge of the deity and in reflection on His works and on what ought to be believed with regard to that. By then, he will have detached his thought from, and abolished his desire for, bestial things—I mean the preference for the pleasures of eating, drinking, sexual intercourse, and in general, of the sense of touch, with regard to which Aristotle gave a clear explanation in the "Ethics," saying that this sense is a disgrace to us.[8] How fine is what he said, and how true it is that it is a disgrace! For we have it in so far as we are animals like the other beasts, and nothing that belongs to the notion of humanity pertains to it.

BOOK III: CHAPTER 49

Another important consideration comes in as a reason for the prohibition of *harlots*. This is the prevention of an intense lust for sexual intercourse and for constant preoccupation with it. For lust is increased through the change of the individuals that are *harlots*, for man is not stirred in the same way by an individual to whom he has been continuously accustomed as by individuals who are constantly renewed and who differ in shapes and manners. . . . In order to prevent these great evils and to bring about the common utility—namely, knowledge of the lines of ancestry—*harlots* and *male prostitutes* are prohibited and there is no way to engage in permitted sexual intercourse other than through singling out a woman for oneself and marrying her in public. For if it is sufficed merely to single her out, most men would bring a *harlot* to their house for a certain time, having made an agreement with her about this, and say that she is a wife. Therefore a binding ceremony and a certain act have been prescribed signifying that the woman is allotted to the man; this is the *betrothal*. Then when the act is made in public, it is the ceremony of *marriage*. Sometimes the union of the two may be discordant and matters in their household not in good order. Consequently divorce is permitted. However, if a divorce could become valid merely by means of the utterance of words or through the man's turning the woman out of his house, the woman might watch for some negligence on the part of her husband and then go out and claim to be divorced. Or if some individual had fornicated with her, she and the adulterer might claim that she had been divorced beforehand. Therefore the Law has given to us the ordinance that a divorce can only be made valid by means of a writ attesting it. . . .

Similarly with regard to *circumcision,* one of the reasons for it is, in my opinion, the wish to bring about a decrease in sexual intercourse and a weakening of the organ in question, so that this activity be diminished and the organ be in as quiet a state as possible.

> [Moses Maimonides, *The Guide of the Perplexed,* trans. Shlomo Pines
> (Chicago: University of Chicago Press, 1963), pp. 371, 602]

JEWISH MYSTICISM ON MARRIAGE AND SEX

In thirteenth-century Spain Jewish mysticism flourished, evolving into a systematic understanding of the world, the Bible, and Jewish practice known as Kabbalah. Its main text was the Zohar ("the Shining Light"), attributed pseudonymously to a second-century sage. In it divine metaphysics underlying reality are laid out and the proper intentions to accompany Jewish ritual are emphasized.

Despite Judaism's strict monotheism, Kabbalists maintained that the Godhead was divided into distinct aspects known as *sephirot,* which included male and female aspects. The human soul mirrored this system of divine forces; originally created in the divine image as a male-female combination, it descended into the physical world as "half a soul." Marriage thus restored a soul's original unity; intercourse was a sacred act that reflected and embodied divine unity.

Kabbalah spread widely in the later Middle Ages, most popularly through Hasidism, and seeped into many aspects of Jewish life. Modern Jewish spirituality draws heavily on Kabbalistic ideas.

Document 1–48

ZOHAR I, 85B [ON MALE AND FEMALE SOULS]

"Its fruit is sweet to my taste" (Song of Songs 2:3). These are the souls of the righteous, which are all of them the fruit of the deeds of the Holy One, blessed be He, and they abide with Him in the upper world.

Come and see. All the souls in the world, which are the fruit of the deeds of the Holy One, blessed be He, are all one, and [originate] in a single mystery. When they descend into the world they all become separated into male and female forms, but the male and female are joined together.

Come and see. The desire of the female for the male makes the soul. And the desire of the male for the female and his cleaving to her produce the soul. He encloses the desire of the female and receives it, so that the lower desire is comprised within the desire above, and they become one desire undivided. Then the female receives all, and she is impregnated by the male, the two desires cleaving together. Therefore all is comprised together, one with the other.

When the souls emerge, they emerge as male and female together. After this, when they descend, they become separated, one on one side and one on the other, and the Holy One, blessed be He, unites them subsequently. This union is accomplished by none but the Holy One, blessed be He, since only He knows how to unite them correctly. Happy is the man whose deeds are meritorious and who walks in the true way, so that soul may be joined to soul as at the very beginning. . . .

[*The Wisdom of the Zohar: An Anthology of Texts*, ed. Isaiah Tishby, trans. David Goldstein, 3 vols. (London: Littman Library of Jewish Civilization, 1989), vol. 3, pp. 1381–1382]

Document 1–49

ZOHAR I, 12B–13A [ON THE COMMANDMENT OF PROCREATION]

The sixth commandment is that one should engage in procreation, for whoever engages in procreation causes the river to flow continually, so that its waters never cease, the sea is filled on all sides, new souls come into being and emerge from the tree, and many powers grow in the world above with these souls. This is the meaning of "Let the waters swarm with swarms of living creatures (*nefesh hayyah*) [and let birds fly above the earth. . . .]" (Genesis 1:20). This is the sign of the holy covenant [of circumcision], the river that flows continually, whose waters increase and swarm with swarms of souls for the living creature (*hayyah*). . . .

Whoever refuses to procreate diminishes, as it were, the image that comprises all images, stops the waters of the river from flowing, and damages the holy covenant on all sides. Concerning him it is written "They shall go out and look on the carcasses of the men that have rebelled against Me" (Isaiah 66:24). "Against Me" — specifically. This refers to the body. As for the soul, it does not penetrate the royal curtain at all, but is driven out of that world.

[*The Wisdom of the Zohar*, pp. 1382–1384]

Document 1–50

ZOHAR I, 49A–49B [ON CONJUGAL MANNERS]

"The Lord God made the rib (*zela*), [which He had taken from the man, into a woman, and He brought her to the man]" Genesis 2:22). . . .

This teaches us that the bride's father and mother should bring her into the possession of the bridegroom, as it is said, "I gave my daughter to this man" (Deuteronomy 22:16). . . . Thenceforward her husband goes in to her, for it is her home, as it is written: "And [Jacob] went in to [Leah]" (Genesis 29:23), "And he went in also to Rachel" (ibid., 29:30). First of all, "He brought her to the man," for up to that time it is the duty of the father and mother to act. After this, he goes in to her, for the whole house is hers, and he must obtain permission from her.

This can be substantiated from the verse "[Jacob] approached the place, and lay there, [because the sun had set, and he took of the stones of the place, and put it under his head, and lay down in that place]" (ibid., 28:11). First of all, he obtained permission. This teaches us that when a man wishes to lie with his wife he must first of all coax her and persuade her with words, and if he is unsuccessful he should not lie with her, for they must share the same desire and there must be no compulsion.

"He lay there because the sun had set." This shows that it is forbidden to have sexual intercourse during the day.

"He took of the stones of the place, and put it under his head." This teaches us that even if a king has beds of gold and precious coverlets in which to lie, nevertheless if his consort prepares a bed of stones for him he should leave his own and lie in the bed that she has prepared, as it is written "and he lay down in that place."

Come and see. It is written: "The man said: This is now [bone of my bones, and flesh of my flesh; she shall therefore (le-zot) be called "woman" (ishah) because she was taken out of man (ish)]" (Genesis 2:23). These are pleasant coaxing words, to arouse love in her and to persuade her to share his desire. See how beautiful these words are, how full of love: "Bone of my bones, and flesh of my flesh," to show her that they are one and that there is no separation at all between them. Then he begins to praise her: she shall therefore (le-zot) be called "woman."" This is she who is unparalleled; she is the glory of the home; all women compared with her are like monkeys when compared with men. Indeed, "for this she shall be called "woman""—the perfection of all, "for this" and for no other. These are all words of love, as it is said, "Many daughters have done valiantly but you excel them all" (Proverbs 31:29).

"Therefore, a man should leave his father and his mother and cleave to his wife, and they shall be one flesh" (Genesis 2: 24). This is still intended to persuade her with love, so that he might cleave to her. When he had aroused all these things in her, Scripture then says "The serpent was more cunning [than any other beast of the field]" (Genesis 3:1). The evil inclination bestirred himself in order to take hold of her, to bind her with bodily desires, and arouse in her other things in which the evil inclination could delight. So much so that "when the woman saw that the tree was good for food, and that it was a delight to the eyes, and that the tree was to be desired, [for it could make one wise], she took of its fruit and ate" (ibid., 3:6). She received it willingly. "And she gave some to her husband as well." Her desire for him was aroused, so that she bestowed on him love and desire. This demonstrates that events among men are patterned on the world above.

[*The Wisdom of the Zohar*, 1388–1390]

Document 1–51

ZOHAR HADASH, BERESHIT 11A–11B, MIDRASH HA-NE'ELAM [ON THE SANCTIFICATION OF INTERCOURSE]

Our rabbis have taught: Rabbi Judah ben Jacob said: I sometimes wonder whether most of the men of our generation were procreated in the proper manner. It is written "You shall sanctify yourselves and you shall be holy" (Leviticus 11:44). This teaches that one should sanctify oneself during intercourse.

What is the relevance of sanctification here? Rabbi Judah ben Jacob said: It means that one should not act licentiously or obscenely, or with whorish intentions like animals, for this is how animals act. For we have learned whoever has intercourse for immoral reasons, or with any of the intentions that we have mentioned, and does not pay heed to those matters that are essential, then, as the Mishnah says, the child that is produced will be wicked, licentious, impudent, and shameless, and will not be counted among the seed of truth. But if he has intercourse for the sake of fulfilling the commandment [of procreation], and sanctifies himself, and directs his mind to heaven, he will have worthy children, righteous and pious, holy children, full of the fear of heaven. This is the meaning of "You shall sanctify yourselves and you shall be holy."

Rabbi Judah said: The wicked, because they procreate only for obscene and licentious purposes, possess only the animal soul that is given to beasts, for their conduct is like that of animals. But of the righteous, who know how to sanctify themselves, it is written "I have planted you as a vine, entirely a seed of truth" (Jeremiah 2:21). . . . .

Rabbi Isaac said: "Truth *(emet)*" is an abbreviation for "Truth springs out of the earth" (ibid., 85:12).

What is the implication? Rabbi Isaac said: It refers to the time of intercourse, where there should be truth and uprightness; at the moment when [the child] develops from the earth at the very beginning, and not when he is actually formed. . . .

Rabbi Zeira said: I was once traveling in the desert and I met an Arab who was carrying a load weighing ten *seahs* on his shoulder, although he was old. I told him that such strength should be applied to the Torah. He said: My father and mother did not make me for that, but to do this kind of work. For my father told me that when he begot me his desire was for a son who would be strong enough to bring in produce from the field, and he was thinking of it at the time. And now I am old, and what can I do?

[*The Wisdom of the Zohar*, pp. 1394–1395]

THE BOOK OF THE PIOUS
OF MEDIEVAL GERMANY

In the thirteenth century a pietistic movement known as Hasidism (distinct from the eighteenth-century eastern European movement) emerged among Ashkenazic Jews of Germany that emphasized purity in thought and deed. Sexual temptation was seen to lurk everywhere, and so Hasidim pursued a more thorough separation of the sexes. Penance was critical for the sinner's rehabilitation, demanding at times radical acts of self-deprivation.

Genuine piety was, in fact, a communal affair, and required the support of others. Teachers, friends, and especially spouses had to be carefully chosen; at the same time, educators and even parents were expected to expel the noncompliant child lest others be infected.

Although pietists were instructed to find women from scholarly families, they nevertheless viewed marriage as divinely predetermined. Thus the Hasid in a bad marriage must resign himself to his fate and seek to improve it.

Ashkenazic practice was greatly influenced by this work, whose contents can be found in the traditional legal literature down to the present.

Document 1–52

SEFER HASIDIM, CHS. 9, 99, 168
[ON SEPARATION OF MEN AND WOMEN]

CHAPTER 9

The essence of the fortitude of piety is that a person, despite ridicule, never abandons his piety, and his intentions remain for the sake of Heaven. He does not ever look at women's faces, particularly when amongst other people who all are looking at women; for instance, if he was at a wedding where women are dressed in beautiful clothing and everyone is looking at them, he refrains from looking. . . . Therefore, it is good for a person, when he encounters a woman, whether single or married, Jew or gentile, old or young, to turn his face away from seeing her as we find in Job (31:1), "I made a covenant with my eyes; how then should I look upon a maid?" So too it says in Ben Sira, "Avert your eyes from a woman of grace, lest you be ensnared by her net" (var. of Ecclesiasticus 9:5, cited in BT Yevamoth 63b). . . . And so the sage said, there is no barrier to forbidden desire like the closing of the eyes.

CHAPTER 99

"You shall not covet [your neighbor's] wife" (Exodus 20:14) is written incompletely [without the letter "*vav*"] to indicate that it includes a prohibition against beautifying oneself in order that . . . there shall not be an arousal of desire in your neighbor's wife. Also, the verse "You shall not covet" encompasses the prohibition not to extol the attractiveness of a beautiful woman in front of his neighbor, lest he be drawn after her and encounter sin. . . .

CHAPTER 168

Boys and girls should not mingle together lest they sin: "Then shall the virgin rejoice in the dance"—by themselves—but, "The young men and the old together" (Jeremiah 31:12). Also, "Boys and girls playing in the streets" (Zachariah 8:5)—boys separately from the girls.

> [Judah ben Samuel, *Sefer Hasidim ha-shalem le-rabenu Yehudah he-hasid* (Jerusalem: Netivah, 1984), translated by Michael J. Broyde]

Document 1–53

SEFER HASIDIM, CHAPTER 167
[ON PENANCE FOR SEXUAL TRANSGRESSIONS]

If a man who had relations with a married woman comes to ask how to repent. . . [The Rabbis] said (BT Megillah 7b), "Those deserving of communal excision who received lashes become exempted from the punishment of excision"; therefore, he should do penance in a way equal to lashes or excision. This is appropriate penance: In the winter time, when the river freezes, if he desires [appropriate penance], he should break the ice and sit in the freezing water, and he should continue to do this so long as there is ice in the river. In the summer, he should sit in a disheveled state and have a vessel filled with water to wash with afterward. During the time where there is neither extreme cold nor heat, he should fast, eating only bread and water at night, as it says regarding Reuben that he returned to his sack and his fasting. . . . In the case where she gave birth to an illegitimate child—such an incident occurred and he was advised and he carried out the advice to step on ant-hills during the day and lie on the ground during the summer nights in order that that fleas crawl all over him. . . . If one has sinned repeatedly with [illicit sexuality], he must do for many years as is written here.

> [Translated by Michael J. Broyde]

Document 1–54

SEFER HASIDIM, CHS. 188–189, 306, 313, 685
[ON RAISING AND EDUCATING CHILDREN]

CHAPTER 188

There was a man whose son converted to another religion and went among the gentiles and acted like them. His father and mother attempted to extract him and bring him back to their house, even attempting to bribe him to return. The sage said to them: Desist, lest you come to regret that he do more evil. I have heard that he wanted to take evil council to seduce and attempt to sway his brethren to go among the gentiles, and even more, when he was still a Jew he would place forbidden meat into [kosher] pots. It is better that you leave him among the gentiles and not have him cause others to sin and feed others forbidden things.

CHAPTER 189

If a sage has students and one of them seeks to vex the teacher and his fellow students, it is best to banish the one bad student for the benefit of the others as it says, "Cast out the scorner, and contention will go out" (Proverbs 22:10). . . .

CHAPTER 306

A person should not allow his son to learn from those easily given to anger, for the teacher will hit the son or punish him harshly. . . .

CHAPTER 313

A man is obligated to teach his daughters Jewish law. That which they said (BT Sotah 20a), that one who teaches a woman Torah, it is as though he taught her foolishness—this refers to the depth of Talmud, the reasons behind commandments and the deep wisdom of Torah; these things one must not teach a woman or a child. But the laws of how to keep the commandments one should teach her, because if [, for instance,] she does not know the laws of the Sabbath, how will she be able to observe the Sabbath? And so too about all commandments [one must teach her], in order that she be able to keep the commandments diligently. . . .

CHAPTER 685

If a man has many sons and one among them is a glutton and a drunkard, he should not put out (literally, uproot) himself and his sons on behalf of the one son, because eventually that son will end up rebellious and depraved. Therefore, it is better for him to act as though he never had this son in the first place and not [actually] harm him.

[Translated by Michael J. Broyde]

Document 1–55

SEFER HASIDIM, CHS. 385, 387, 749 [ON PREDESTINED MARRIAGE]

CHAPTER 385

There once was a young maiden who did not adorn herself. They said to her, Whoever sees you unadorned will not desire you [for marriage]. She responded, since the Holy One, Blessed be He, creates couples, I am not worried. It turned out that she married a righteous Torah scholar.

CHAPTER 387

One man fasted for a few days so that the Holy One, blessed be He, should arrange for him as a wife a particular woman he loved, but his fasting and prayers were not answered. He inquired of a sage, Behold I fasted and I cried, but it was to no avail?! The sage replied, Perhaps this particular woman was not decreed [by Heaven] to be your mate. The man further asked, But why are my fasts and tears to no avail, for I also pray and fast that [God] turn my heart from she who was not decreed for me and open it up to love the one who is indeed decreed for me? The sage said, [Your prayers have not been answered] because you leer at women. . . .

CHAPTER 749

If a man hates his wife, he should not ask G-d to give him another wife; rather, if she angers him or is not good in his eyes, he should request from G-d that He influence her heart to love him or that she should find grace and favor in his eyes so he should love her, and so she shall [then] love him.

[Translated by Michael J. Broyde]

"THE EPISTLE ON HOLINESS" ("IGGERET HA-QODESH")

The view that carnal urges were inherently antithetical to the goal of religious perfection (previous selection) was not universally held among Jews. Some took the view that marital sex, like most human actions, could be either sanctifying or demeaning, depending on the person's intentions and behaviors.

An essay dedicated to this position, "The Epistle on Holiness," argued against the Maimonidean view. It is attributed to Nahmanides, the premier authority of thirteenth-century Spanish Jewry, who was both a major jurist and a member of the emerging mystical circle there. The author makes the assumption, common in medieval physiology, that a person's intentions during sex affect the quality of the semen that in turn affects the character of the resulting progeny. Time, food, and temper thus all contribute to the right frame of mind for intercourse, critical for producing proper children. Marital sex thus partakes of *imitatio Dei*, imitating God, who created human beings.

Document 1–56

THE EPISTLE ON HOLINESS

CHAPTER ONE

Know and understand that the nation of Israel is singled out and designated to God. . . . Now God, who is our Master and we His servants, who is Holy like no other holiness, commanded us to be holy as He is holy. . . . And since all our actions are to imitate divine behavior, the result is that whenever we do the right and proper thing we sanctify God's great Name . . . And whenever we do not behave properly and our actions are depraved, we thereby defame the heavenly Name, since we are required to imitate Him. . . .

Now that we have informed you of this, know that since man's nature and material cause him to be good or wicked from the aspect of the balance of humors according to the drop [of semen] from which he came into existence, it follows that human copulation is the cause of sanctifying God or defaming Him according to the children that he will sire. Therefore, God commanded and warned us that we must sanctify ourselves during intercourse. . . . This is divided into five subjects: the essence of copulation, the time of copulation, food intake appropriate for copulation, intentions during intercourse, and the quality of intercourse.

CHAPTER TWO: THE ESSENCE OF COPULATION

Know that intercourse between a man and his wife is a holy and pure matter. Copulation should be engaged in properly, at the proper time, with the proper intentions. And do not think that within proper intercourse there is degradation and ugliness. On the contrary—copulation is called intimacy. . . . And the matter is not like what Maimonides, of blessed memory, theorized in *The Guide of the Perplexed*, when he praised Aristotle for saying that the urge for sexual gratification is shameful. Heaven forbid, the matter is not like the Greek's statement. . . . Those of us under the yolk of the Holy Bible believe that the Holy One, blessed be He, created everything according to how his wisdom dictated, and did not create anything that has within it degradation or ugliness. If we say that intercourse is a thing of degradation, then behold, the sexual organs are instruments of degradation, yet our exalted God created them, as it says, "He made you and intended you" (Deuteronomy 32:6). . . . But the matter is, as it says, that the Holy One, blessed be He, "Has eyes that are too pure to see bad" (Habakkuk 1:13); and He doesn't see before Him the matter of depravity or filth, and He created man and woman, and created all their organs and prepared their framework and He did not create within them any degrading parts. And the clear testimony said in creation, "And the two of them, the man and his wife, were naked, and they were not embarrassed" (Genesis 2:25). All this occurred before they sinned, because they were involved with their pure consciousness, and all of their intentions were for the sake of Heaven. . . . This is how it is with the sexual organ: it is praised and exalted by good deeds, and it is degraded and made ugly by bad deeds. This is what occurred with Adam's sexual organs. If so, it seems that the ways of the Lord, Blessed Be He, are just, pure, and clean, and it seems that the ugliness comes via man's actions. . . .

And this is the deeper meaning of, "Let us make man in our image, after our likeness" (Genesis 1:26). Meaning, I, [God,] am also a partner in the creation of man, and this partnership is that different elements of the body are drawn from the mother and the father, and the Lord, blessed be He, thrusts their soul into them. As it says, "And He breathed in his nostril the breath of life" (Genesis 2:7). And it says, "And he will return the dust to the earth like it had been, and the wind will return to the One who gave it" (Ecclesiastes 12:7). And it is impossible for the perceptive among us to see something degrading in something that the Lord, blessed be He, participated in creating. Therefore, proper intercourse between a man and his wife is the underpinning of the world and its inhabitants, and makes [man] a partner with God in creation.

CHAPTER FIVE: INTENTIONS DURING INTERCOURSE

And behold, when a man is having intercourse with his wife, if his mind is focused on words of wisdom and understanding and proper manners, those very thoughts have the power to influence the drop of sperm and create [in the child], without a doubt, qualities akin to his thoughts during copulation. . . .

And this having been said, the thoughts and intentions [one has during intercourse] cause the fetus to be a righteous or wicked person. If so, every man must strive to cleanse his thoughts and intentions, and to make them meritorious during copulation. He should not think words of sin and decadence, rather he should think only holy and pure thoughts. He should turn away from evil and hasty thoughts; he should think about righteous, pure, and holy people, because those thoughts will have influence on the sperm and will cause it to be created in the mold of his thoughts during intercourse. And so it is fitting for him to settle his wife's thoughts; he should make her happy and prepare her to think thoughts that are pleasing to the heart, in order that she will be receptive to pure and meritorious thoughts. And the two of them should be one in the matter of this commandment, because then their consciousnesses will meld into one, the divine presence will rest with them, and they will have a child created in a pure form.

CHAPTER SIX: THE QUALITY OF INTERCOURSE

It is known that every pious and modest person only speaks with soft words and gentle language and a pleasant spirit; he does not speak with grandeur . . . Therefore, make your head light with regard to woman, and do not engage in excessive idle chatter with her . . . Therefore, you should bring her in with words that draw in her heart, and settle her thoughts, and make her happy in order to meld your consciousness with her consciousness, and your intentions with her intentions. And speak a few words that enhance her love, connection, desire, will, and courtship, and a few that draw her into fearing the heavens, and piety, and modest ways. And talk with her about the ways of modest and pious women, and how from them come children that are fit, suitable, and pure, fitting for the crown of the Almighty, bearers of Torah and fear of the Lord, grand and holy, and doers of good deeds. . . . And so it is fitting for a man to bring in his wife with good words, some of them courting her and some of them dealing with fear of God, and he will converse with her in the middle of the night, or in the pre-dawn hours of the night. And he will not have intercourse with her against her will, and he will not rape her. . . . And it is not fitting to argue with her or hit her about matters of copulation. . . . Rather it is fitting to draw in her heart with charm, seduction, and other proper and settling things, so that their intentions will be one for the sake of heaven. It is also not fitting to have intercourse with one's wife when she is sleeping, because she has not agreed, but one may wake her with words of will and desire. . . .

In conclusion: when you see for yourself that you are fitting to have intercourse, make sure your wife agrees with you; do not hurry to arouse your desires and set aside your arousal in order to settle your wife's thoughts and bring her into the ways of love and will, so that she will be fertilized early, in order that her seed will be like mortar and your seed will be like bricks. . . .

May the Almighty Lord, in His mercy, open our eyes with the light of his Torah, and merit us to connect with the deeper meaning of his Torah, and to bear children who are ready to fear and serve Him. Amen and amen.

[Ch. Chavel, *Kitvei Rabbenu Mosheh ben Nahman* (Jerusalem: Mossad Harav Kook, 1964), vol. 2, pp. 315–337, translated by Michael J. Broyde]

EXCHANGE BETWEEN NAPOLEON AND THE JEWISH "SANHEDRIN" ON ISSUES OF MARRIAGE

In the seventeenth and eighteenth centuries the Enlightenment and the rise of the nation-state allowed Christian society for the first time to imagine Jews as fellow citizens, equal under the law. "Emancipation" of the Jews began in France with the Revolution and spread slowly throughout Europe over the next 130 years.

Christian society, however, was wary of allowing in a group that was so distinctive in language, practice, and belief. Worries persisted whether Jews would truly integrate into the majority culture. In 1806 Napoleon assembled Jewish leaders to answer a set of questions related to the Jews' acculturation. Chief among them were those that concerned marriage and divorce, but they included Jewish obedience to civil law, service in the army, and willingness to engage in all types of work.

In many ways these questions and their answers epitomize the Jews' condition in the modern period. Jews are welcome into the modern state—but usually on the condition they abandon their distinctiveness and assimilate.

Document 1–57

EXCHANGE BETWEEN NAPOLEON AND JEWISH SANHEDRIN OF FRANCE

NAPOLEON'S INSTRUCTIONS TO THE ASSEMBLY OF JEWISH NOTABLES (JULY 29, 1806)

His Majesty, the Emperor and King, having named us Commissioners to transact whatever relates to you, has this day sent us to this assembly to acquaint you with his intentions. Called together from the extremities of this vast empire, no one among you is ignorant of the object for which his Majesty has convened this assembly. . . .

Far from considering the government under which you live as a power against which you should be on your guard, you will assist it with your experience and cooperate with it in all the good it intends; thus you will prove that, following the example of all Frenchmen, you do not seclude yourselves from the rest of mankind.

The laws which have been imposed on individuals of your religion have been different in the several parts of the world: often they have been dictated by the interest of the day. But, as an assembly like the present, has no precedent in the annals of Christianity; so will you be judged, for the first time, with justice, and you will see your fate irrevocably fixed by a Christian Prince. The wish of His Majesty is that you should be Frenchmen; it remains with you to accept the proffered title, without forgetting that, to prove unworthy of it, would be renouncing it altogether.

You will hear the questions submitted to you, your duty is to answer the whole truth on every one of them . . .

Is it lawful for Jews to marry more than one wife?

Is divorce allowed by the Jewish religion? Is divorce valid, when not pronounced by courts of justice, and by virtue of laws in contradiction with the French code?

Can a Jewess marry a Christian, or a Jew a Christian woman? Or has the law ordered that the Jews should only intermarry among themselves?

In the eyes of Jews are Frenchmen considered as brethren or as strangers?

In either case what conduct does their law prescribe towards Frenchmen not of their religion?

THE ASSEMBLY OF JEWISH NOTABLES: ANSWERS TO NAPOLEON (1806)

Resolved, by the French deputies professing the religion of Moses, that the following Declaration shall precede the answers returned to the questions proposed by the Commissioners of His Imperial and Royal Majesty.

The assembly, impressed with a deep sense of gratitude, love, respect, and admiration, for the sacred person of His Imperial and Royal Majesty, declares, in the name of all Frenchmen professing the religion of Moses, that they are fully determined to prove worthy of the favours His Majesty intends for them, by scrupulously conforming to his paternal intentions; that their religion makes it their duty to consider the law of the prince as the supreme law in civil and political matters; that consequently, should their religious code, or its various interpretations, contain civil or political commands, at variance with those of the French code, those commands would, of course, cease to influence and govern them, since they must, above all, acknowledge and obey the laws of the prince.

That, in consequence of this principle, the Jews have, at all times, considered it their duty to obey the laws of the state, and that, since the revolution, they, like all Frenchmen, have acknowledged no others.

First Question: *Is it lawful for Jews to marry more than one wife?*

Answer: It is not lawful for Jews to marry more than one wife: in all European countries they conform to the general practice marrying only one.

Moses does not command expressly to take several, but he does not forbid it. . . . Although this practice still prevails in the East, yet their ancient doctors have enjoined them to restrain from taking more than one wife, except when the man is enabled by his fortune to maintain several.

The case has been different in the West; the wish of adopting the customs of the inhabitants of this part of the world has induced the Jews to renounce polygamy. But as several individuals still indulged in that practice, a synod was convened at Worms in the eleventh century, composed of one hundred Rabbis, with Gershom at their head. This assembly pronounced an anathema against every Israelite who should, in future, take more than one wife. . . .

Second Question: *Is divorce allowed by the Jewish religion? Is divorce valid when not pronounced by courts of justice by virtue of laws in contradiction with those of the French Code?*

Answer: Repudiation is allowed by the law of Moses; but it is not valid if not previously pronounced by the French code.

In the eyes of every Israelite, without exception, submission to the prince is the first of duties. It is a principle generally acknowledged among them, that, in every thing relating to civil or political interests, the law of the state is the supreme law. Before they were admitted in France to share the rights of all citizens . . . they had the ability to divorce their wives; but it was extremely rare to see it put into practice.

Since the revolution, they have acknowledged no other laws on this head but those of the empire. . . .

Third Question: *Can a Jewess marry a Christian, and a Jew a Christian woman? Or does the law allow the Jews to marry only among themselves?*

Answer: The law does not say that a Jewess cannot marry a Christian, nor a Jew a Christian woman; nor does it state that the Jews can only marry among themselves.

The only marriages expressly forbidden by the law, are those with the seven Canaanite nations, with Amon and Moab, and with the Egyptians. . . . The prohibition in general applies only to nations in idolatry. The Talmud declares formally that modern nations are not to be considered as such, since they worship like us, the God of heaven and earth. And, accordingly, there have been, at several periods, intermarriages between Jews and Christians in France, in Spain, and in Germany: these marriages were sometimes tolerated, and sometimes forbidden by the laws of those sovereigns, who had received Jews into their dominions.

Unions of this kind are still found in France; but we cannot deny that the opinion of the Rabbis is against these marriages. According to their doctrine, although the religion of Moses has not forbidden the Jews from intermarrying with nations not of their religion, yet, as marriage, according to the Talmud, requires religious ceremonies called Kiduschin, with the benediction used in such cases, no marriage can be religiously valid unless these ceremonies have been performed. This could not be done towards persons who would not both of them consider these ceremonies as sacred; and in that case the married couple could separate without the religious divorce; they would then be considered as married civilly but not religiously. . . .

Fourth Question: *In the eyes of Jews, are Frenchmen considered as their brethren? Or are they considered as strangers?*

Answer: In the eyes of Jews Frenchmen are their brethren, and are not strangers.

The true spirit of the law of Moses is consonant with this mode of considering Frenchmen.

When the Israelites formed a settled and independent nation, their law made it a rule for them to consider strangers as their brethren. . . .

Respect and benevolence towards strangers are enforced by Moses, not as an exhortation to the practice of social morality only, but as an obligation imposed by God himself.

A religion whose fundamental maxims are such—a religion which makes a duty of loving the stranger—which enforces the practice of social virtues, must surely require that its followers should consider their fellow citizens as brethren . . .

Yes, France is our country; all Frenchmen are our brethren, and this glorious title, by raising us our own esteem, becomes a sure pledge that we shall never cease to be worthy of it.

Fifth Question: *In either case, what line of conduct does their law prescribe towards Frenchmen not of their religion?*

Answer: The line of conduct prescribed towards Frenchmen not of our religion, is the same as that prescribed between Jews themselves; we admit of no difference but that of worshipping the Supreme Being, every one in his own way.

The answer to the preceding question has explained the line of conduct which the law of Moses and the Talmud prescribe towards Frenchmen not of our religion. At the present time, when the Jews no longer form a separate people, but enjoy the advantage of being incorporated with the Great Nation (which privilege they consider as a kind of political redemption), it is impossible that a Jew should treat a Frenchman, not of his religion, in any other manner than he would treat one of his Israelite brethren.

[Paul Mendes-Flohr and Jehuda Reinharz, ed., *The Jew in the Modern World: A Documentary History* (New York: Oxford, 1995), pp. 124–126, 128–131.]

CONTEMPORARY DEVELOPMENTS IN JEWISH MARRIAGE CONTRACTS

As Jews integrated into the state, they naturally came under the jurisdiction of civil law—including marriage and divorce, which traditionally were within the domain of Jewish law. The new reality meant Jews were under dual jurisdiction, inevitably leading to tension between the two. Divorce was the more serious issue, since a marriage not terminated properly had grave consequences (see Doc. 1–43).

Judaism's denominations in America responded differently. Reform Judaism saw civil divorce as sufficient and did not require any religious rite. Conservative Judaism added a clause to the *ketubah* whereby the civilly divorcing couple agrees to have their marriage also terminated in a Jewish court. Orthodoxy, which insisted Jewish law was exclusively normative, recently developed a civil prenuptial agreement that creates financial consequences for the husband if the couple no longer lives together yet remains religiously married. These radically different solutions were not uniformly recognized by all Jews, contributing to denominational strife.

Document 1–58

BETH DIN OF AMERICA, BINDING ARBITRATION AGREEMENT

Instructions for filling out this document may be found on the accompanying sheet.
It is important that the instructions be carefully read and followed in completing the form.
THIS AGREEMENT MADE ON THE _____ DAY OF THE MONTH OF
_____ IN THE YEAR 20__, IN THE CITY/TOWN/VILLAGE OF
_____ STATE OF _____, *between:*
HUSBAND-TO-BE: _____
WIFE-TO-BE: _____
RESIDING   AT: _____
RESIDING   AT: _____

_____

The parties, who intend to be married in the near future, hereby agree as follows:
I. Should a dispute arise between the parties after they are married, so that they do not live together as husband and wife, they agree to refer their marital dispute to an arbitration panel, namely, The Beth Din of the United States of America, Inc. (currently located at 305 Seventh Ave., New York, NY 10001, tel. 212 807–9042, www.bethdin.org) for a binding decision.

II. The decision of the Beth Din of America shall be fully enforceable in any court of competent jurisdiction.

III. The parties agree that the Beth Din of America is authorized to decide all issues relating to a *get* (Jewish divorce) as well as any issues arising from this Agreement or the *ketubah* and *tena'im* (Jewish premarital agreements) entered into by the Husband-to-Be and the Wife-to-Be. Each of the parties agrees to appear in person before the Beth Din of America at the demand of the other party.

IV: The Beth Din of America may consider the respective responsibilities of either or both of the parties for the end of the marriage, is an additional, but not exclusive, factor in determining the distribution of marital property and maintenance, should such a determination be authorized by Section IV:A or Section IV:B.

V. Failure of either party to perform his or her obligations under this Agreement shall make that party liable for all costs awarded by either the Beth Din of America or a court of competent jurisdiction, including reasonable attorney's fees, incurred by one side in order to obtain the other party's performance of the terms of this Agreement.

SECTIONS IV:A & IV:B ARE OPTIONAL
(Unless one of these option is chosen, the Beth Din of America will be without jurisdiction to address matters of general financial and parenting disputes between the parties. For more information, see the instructions.)

IV:A(1). The parties agree that the Beth Din of America is authorized to decide all monetary disputes (including division of property and maintenance) that may arise between them. **We choose to have Paragraph IV:A(1) apply to our arbitration agreement.**
Signature of Husband-to-Be_____
Signature of Wife-to-Be_____

IV:A(2). The parties agree that the Beth Din of America is authorized to decide any monetary disputes (including division of property and maintenance) that may arise between them based on principles of equitable distribution law customarily employed in the United States as found in the Uniform Marriage and Divorce Act.
We choose to have Paragraph IV:A(2) apply to our arbitration agreement.
Signature of Husband-to-Be_____
Signature of Wife-to-Be_____

IV:A(3). The parties agree that the Beth Din of America is authorized to decide any monetary disputes (including division of property and maintenance) that may arise between them based on the principles of community property law customarily employed in the United States as found in the Uniform Marriage and Divorce Act.

We choose to have Paragraph. IV:A(3) apply to our arbitration agreement.
Signature of Husband-to-Be_____
Signature of Wife-to-Be_____

IV:B. The parties agree that the Beth Din of America is authorized to decide all disputes, including child custody, child support, and visitation matters, as well as any other disputes that may arise between them.

We choose to have Section IV:B apply to our arbitration agreement.
Signature of Husband-to-Be_____
Signature of Wife-to-Be_____

VI. The decision of the Beth Din of America shall be made in accordance with Jewish law *(halakha)* or Beth Din ordered settlement in accordance with the principles of Jewish law *(peshara krova la-din)*, except as specifically provided otherwise in this Agreement. The parties waive their right to contest the jurisdiction or procedures of the Beth Din of America or the validity of this Agreement in any other rabbinical court or arbitration forum other than the Beth Din of America. The parties agree to abide by the published Rules and Procedures of the Beth Din of America (which are available at www.bethdin.org, or by calling the Beth Din of America) which are in effect at the time of the arbitration. The Beth Din of America shall follow its rules and procedures, which shall govern this arbitration to the fullest extent permitted by law. Both parties obligate themselves to pay for the services of the Beth Din of America as directed by the Beth Din of America.

VII. The parties agree to appear in person before the Beth Din of America at the demand of the other party, and to cooperate with the adjudication of the Beth Din of America in every way and manner. In the event of the failure of either party to appear before the Beth Din of America upon reasonable notice, the Beth Din of America may issue its decision despite the defaulting party's failure to appear, and may impose costs and other penalties as legally permitted. Furthermore, Husband-to-Be acknowledges that he recites and accepts the following:

I hereby now (me'achshav), *obligate myself to support my Wife-to-Be from the date that our domestic residence together shall cease for whatever reasons, at the rate of $150 per day (calculated as of the date of our marriage, adjusted annually by the Consumer Price Index–All Urban Consumers, as published by the US Department of Labor, Bureau of Labor Statistics) in lieu of my Jewish law obligation of support so long as the two of us remain married according to Jewish law, even if she has another source of income or earnings. Furthermore, I waive my* halakhic *rights to my wife's earnings for the period that she is entitled to the* *above stipulated sum, and I acknowledge, that I shall be deemed to have repeated this waiver at the time of our wedding. I acknowledge that I have effected the above obligation by means of a* kinyan *(formal Jewish transaction) in an esteemed* (chashuv) *Beth Din as prescribed by Jewish law.* However, this support obligation shall terminate if Wife-to-Be refuses to appear upon due notice before the Beth Din of America or in the event that Wife-to-Be fails to abide by the decision or recommendation of the Beth Din of America.

VIII. This Agreement may be signed in one or more duplicates, each one of which shall be considered an original.

IX. This Agreement constitutes a fully enforceable arbitration agreement. Should any provision of this Agreement be deemed unenforceable, all other surviving provisions shall still be deemed fully enforceable; each and every provision of this Agreement shall be severable from the other. As a matter of Jewish law, the parties agree that to effectuate this agreement in full form and purpose, they accept now (through the Jewish law mechanism of *kim li*) whatever minority views determined by the Beth Din of America are needed to effectuate the obligations contained in Section VII and the procedures and jurisdictional mandates found in Sections I, II, III and VI of this Agreement.

X. Each of the parties acknowledges that he or she has been given the opportunity prior to signing this Agreement to consult with his or her own rabbinic advisor and legal advisor. The obligations and conditions contained herein are executed according to all legal and *halachic* requirements. In witness of all the above, the Husband-to-Be and Wife-to-Be have entered into this Agreement.

SIGNATURE OF HUSBAND-TO-BE: _____

SIGNATURE OF WIFE-TO-BE:_____

WITNESS: _____

WITNESS: _____

WITNESS: _____

WITNESS: _____

The paragraphs below allow for easy notarization. For further information, see the Instructions.

ACKNOWLEDGMENT FOR HUSBAND-TO-BE

State of _____

County of _____

On the _____ day of _____ in the year _____ before me, the undersigned, personally appeared _____, personally known to me or proved to me on the basis of satisfactory evidence to be the individual whose name is subscribed to within this agreement and acknowledged to me that he executed the same in his capacity, and that by his signature on the arbitration agreement, the individual executed the agreement.

_____

Notary Public

ACKNOWLEDGMENT FOR WIFE-TO-BE

State of _____

County of _____

On the _____ day of _____ in the year _____ before me, the under-signed, personally appeared _____, person-ally known to me or proved to me on the basis of satisfactory evidence to be the individual whose name is subscribed to within this agreement and acknowl-edged to me that she executed the same in her capacity, and that by her sig-nature on the arbitration agreement, the individual executed the agreement.

_____

Notary Public

[Beth Din of America, "Binding Arbitration Agreement," available at http://ocweb.org/images/uploads/PNA_web_with_instructions.pdf]

Document 1–59

THE LIEBERMAN CLAUSE

In 1953 the Rabbinical Assembly and the Jewish Theological Seminary accepted an additional clause in the *ketubah* proposed by Professor Saul Lieberman. The purpose of the Lieberman *takana* was to help solve the problem of *agunot* (women whose husbands refuse to grant them a religious divorce and who are thus prohibited from remarrying). The bride and groom agree to recognize the authority of the Bet Din of the Rabbinical Assembly and the Jewish Theological Seminary to summon either party at the request of the other to enable the party so requesting to live in accordance with the Torah. The point of this clause is to exert moral suasion upon a recalcitrant spouse already divorced under civil law to agree to a traditional *get*.

In 1991, the Joint Bet Din of the Conservative Movement suggested the couple sign a letter of intent in addition to the clause in the *ketubah*. The wording was worked out in order to ensure its viability in American courts.

The English texts of the Lieberman clause and the letter of intent follow.

LIEBERMAN CLAUSE

This paragraph appears as the penultimate paragraph in the *ketubah:*

_____, the groom, and _____, the bride, further agreed that should either contemplate dissolution of the marriage, or following the dissolution of their marriage in the civil courts, each may summon the other to the Bet Din of the Rabbinical Assembly and the Jewish Theological Semi-nary, or its representative, and that each will abide by its instructions so that throughout life each will be able to live according to the laws of the Torah.

LETTER OF INTENT

Each of us has met with Rabbi _____, who has provided us with a copy of the ketubah (a copy of which is attached) and explained to each of us the provisions contained in the ketubah concerning the dissolution of marriage.

Each of us acknowledges and confirms our understanding that this ketubah is a legal contract and shall be binding under both Jewish and civil law concerning the formation and dissolution of our marriage.

In particular, each of us acknowledges that according to this ketubah, should our marriage be dissolved in the civil courts, each of us is bound to appear before the Joint Bet Din of the Conservative Movement, or such Bet Din as shall be designated by the Joint Bet Din, if so requested by the other, and to abide by its instruction and decision with respect to the dissolution of our marriage under Jewish law. Each of us intends that the undertaking to appear before and to be bound by the directions of the Bet Din may be enforced by the civil court of law. Each of us acknowledges our agreement to the ketubah and our willingness to be bound by its terms.

Dated _____

Signature of Bride _____

Signature of Groom _____

Explained and signed under the supervision of

Rabbi _____

Signature of Rabbi _____

[Saul Lieberman, "Lieberman Clause," available at http://www.ritualwell.org/Rituals/ritual.html?docid = 754.]

Document 1–60

CENTRAL CONFERENCE OF AMERICAN RABBIS, AMERICAN REFORM RESPONSA 162, REFORM JUDAISM AND DIVORCE

Question: What is the traditional Jewish attitude toward divorce? What is the Reform attitude toward divorce? Is a *Get* necessary before remarriage can occur?

Answer: Judaism looks upon divorce with sadness (Git. 90b; San. 22a), but recognizes that it might occur.

As divorce proceedings frequently involve a great deal of bitterness, the husband may not be willing to provide a religious divorce *(Get)* along with the civil divorce unless a large payment or some other concessions are made. Sometimes a religious divorce is stipulated as part of the arrangement in a secular divorce. The Conservative Movement has sought to remove itself from this predicament by including a special statement in its marriage document. It provides for authority of a rabbinic court to grant a divorce in cases where the husband is unwilling to do so or if he becomes unavailable (Isaac Klein, *A Guide to Jewish Religious Practice*, p. 498). This kind of ante-nuptial agreement, as well as other possible solutions, have been suggested by various traditional scholars (Freimann, *Seder Kiddushin Venisuin; Berkovits, Tenai Benisu-in Uveget*), but they have met only strong opposition among other Orthodox authorities.

The Reform Movement has concerned itself with the problems of both marriage and divorce since its inception. The matter was raised at the Paris Sanhedrin in 1806, when it was asked whether divorce was allowed and whether civil divorce would be recognized. It was clearly stated that a religious divorce would only be given if a valid civil divorce had preceded it. This statement weakened the status of religious divorce, although that was not the intent of the respondents. The Brunswick Conference of 1844 appointed a committee to look into all of the questions connected with marriage and divorce. . . . They reaffirmed the Paris statement that marriage and divorce were subject not only to Jewish law, but to the laws of the land in which Jews reside. Although various reports and motions were presented to rabbinic conferences . . . none of these resulted in any definite actions. . . . Holdheim had earlier suggested that divorce be eliminated entirely from the set of Jewish proceedings and that civil divorce simply be accepted. This was the point of view accepted by the Philadelphia Conference of 1869 . . .

The discussion of divorce continued at later rabbinic conferences, but without any formal action being taken. Generally, the civil decree was simply accepted (*CCAR Yearbook*, vol. 23, p. 154; Freehof, *Reform Jewish Practice*, vol. I, p. 106) . . . Kaufmann Kohler, in his discussion of the problem of marriage and divorce and their relationship to civil laws, recommended that civil divorce be recognized as long as the grounds for such divorce were in consonance with those provided by previous rabbinic tradition (*CCAR Yearbook*, vol. 25, pp. 376ff). His recommendations were heard by the Conference, but not accepted in any formal manner.

Technically, of course, the child of a woman (and possibly a man) who has remarried without prior religious divorce would be considered illegitimate (*Mamzer*). Such a child would, according to Orthodox law, be considered unlawful, and akin to one born of incestuous or adulterous relationship (*Mishna*, Kid. III.12; *Yad*, 49a; *Shulchan Aruch*, Even Ha-ezer 4.2). This was the attitude taken toward Karaites until recently. In fact, however, there is nothing that Reform or Conservative Jews can do to avoid this possible predicament. It does not matter to the Orthodox authorities whether we simply recognize civil divorce or proceed to initiate our own form of *Get*. The latter is also not recognized by them . . .

At the present time, the Central Conference of American Rabbis makes no provision for a religious divorce and civil divorce is recognized as dissolving a marriage by most Reform rabbis.

Walter Jacob

[Walter Jacob, 162. Reform Judaism and Divorce (1980), available at http://www.ccarnet.org/cgi-bin/respdisp.pl?file = 162&year = arr]

REFORM OPINION ON PATRILINEAL AND MATRILINEAL DESCENT

Since the rise of the diaspora in Second Temple times, Jews saw a need to define themselves vis-à-vis their surrounding culture. Rabbinic Judaism insisted that having a Jewish mother was sufficient to be deemed a Jew—a position consistent with the view that Jews were a people and transmitted identity genetically.

The modern period, however, viewed religion as a matter of personal choice, challenging the normative "biological" view. With the rise of intermarriage in America and its increased acceptance among Jews, the traditional notion was seriously tested, particularly as these couples sought affiliation in synagogues and temples. Reform Judaism, which sees religion as constantly evolving, therefore redefined Jewishness in 1983 to reflect both nature and nurture: a child is Jewish if either parent is Jewish and the child is raised as a Jew. This significant departure from the traditional definition meant some individuals were not universally recognized as Jews—another cause of internecine Jewish conflict.

Document 1–61

CENTRAL CONFERENCE OF AMERICAN RABBIS, 38. PATRILINEAL
AND MATRILINEAL DESCENT. OCTOBER 1983

Question: What are the origins of matrilineal descent in the Jewish tradition; what *halakhic* justification is there for the recent Central Conference of American Rabbi's resolution on matrilineal and patrilineal descent which also adds various requirements for the establishment of Jewish status?

Answer: . . . These discussions show us that our tradition responded to particular needs. It changed the laws of descent to meet the problems of a specific age and if those problems persisted, then the changes remained in effect.

The previous cited material has dealt with situations entirely different from those which have arisen in the last century and a half. Unions between Jews and non-Jews during earlier times remained rare. Furthermore, the cultural and sociological relationship with the people among whom we lived did not approach the freedom and equality which most Jews in the Western World now enjoy.

We in the twentieth century have been faced with an increasing number of mixed marriages, with changes in the structure of the family, and with the development of a new relationship between men and women . . .

We may elaborate further with the following statements which reflect the previously cited historical background, the introduction to the resolution as well as other concerns. We shall turn first to the question of descent and then to the required "acts of identification."

1. In the Biblical period, till the time of Ezra or beyond, patrilineal descent determined the status of a child, so the children of the kings of Israel married to non-Jewish wives were unquestionably Jewish. This was equally true of other figures. Furthermore, our tradition has generally determined lineage (*yihus*) through the father, i.e., in all valid but originally forbidden marriages. This was also true for priestly, Levitical and Israelite lineage which was and continues to be traced through the paternal line. . . .

Yihus was considered significant, especially in the Biblical period, and long genealogical lines were recorded; an effort was made in the time of Ezra and, subsequently, to guarantee pure lines of descent and precise records were maintained (Ezra 2:59 ff; genealogies of I, II Chronicles). An echo of that practice of recording genealogies remained in the *Mishnah* and *Talmud* despite the difficulties caused by the wars of the first and second century which led to the destruction of many records (M. Kid. 4.1; Kid. 28a, 70a ff). In the Biblical period and in specific later instances, lineage was determined by the father.

2. Mishnaic and Talmudic authorities changed the Biblical laws of descent, as shown earlier in this responsum, as well as many others when social or religious conditions warranted it. Family law was changed in many other ways as demonstrated by the laws of marriage. For example, the Talmudic authorities validated the marriage of Boaz to Ruth, the Moabitess, despite the strict ruling against such marriages (Deut. 23.4); they indicated that the Biblical rule applied only to males, not to females (Yeb. 76b ff). Earlier the *Mishnah* (Yad. 4.4) claimed that the various ethnic groups had been so intermingled by the invasion of Sennacherib that none of the prohibitions against marriage with neighboring people remained valid. In this instance and others similar to them, we are dealing with clear Biblical injunctions which have been revised by the rabbinic tradition. We have followed these examples in our own twentieth century revision.

3. The Reform movement has espoused the equality of men and women, virtually since its inception. As equality has been applied to every facet of Reform Jewish life, it should be applied in this instance.

4. We, and virtually all Jews, recognize a civil marriage between a Jew and a Gentile as a marriage although not *quidushin*, and have done so since the French Sanhedrin of 1807. We are morally obliged to make provisions for the offsprings of such a union when either the father or mother seek to have their children recognized and educated as a Jew . . .

For the reasons cited in the introduction to the Resolution, those stated above and others, we have equated matrilineal and patrilineal descent in the determination of Jewish identity of a child of a mixed marriage.

Now let us turn to the section of the resolution which deals with "positive acts of identification." There are both traditional and modern considerations for requiring such acts and not relying on birth alone.

The clause which deals with the "appropriate and timely acts of identification with the Jewish faith and people. . . . " has gone beyond the traditional requirements for consideration as a Jew. Here we have become stricter than traditional Judaism. We have done so as the normal life of Jews has changed during the last two centuries.

In earlier periods of our history . . . individuals identified themselves and lived as part of the Jewish community. . . . Its entire way of life was Jewish. Emancipation changed this condition. . . . [V]irtually all Jews live in two worlds.

In order to overcome these problems as well as others, we now require "appropriate and timely public and formal acts. . . . " The requirement has been worded to permit some flexibility for individual circumstances. With time and experience, custom will designate certain acts as appropriate and others not. It would be wrong, however, to set limits now at the beginning of the process.

We are aware that we have made more stringent requirements than our tradition. We believe that this will lead to a firmer commitment to Judaism on the part of these individuals and that it will enable them to become fully integrated into the Jewish community. We have taken this step for the following additional reasons:

1. We do not view birth as a determining factor in the religious identification of children of a mixed marriage.

2. We distinguish between descent and identification.

3. The mobility of American Jews has diminished the influence of the extended family upon such a child. This means that a significant informal bond with Judaism which played a role in the past does not exist for our generation.

4. Education has always been a strong factor in Jewish identity. In the recent past we could assume a minimal Jewish education for most children. In our time almost half the American Jewish community remains unaffiliated, and their children receive no Jewish education.

For those reasons the Central Conference of American Rabbis has declared: "The Central Conference of American Rabbis declares that the child of one Jewish parent is under the presumption of Jewish descent. This presumption of the Jewish status of the offspring of any mixed marriage is to be established through appropriate and timely public and formal acts of identification with the Jewish faith and people. The performance of these *mitzvot* serves to commit those who participate in them, both parents and child, to Jewish life.

"Depending on circumstances, *mitzvot* leading toward a positive and exclusive Jewish identity will include entry into the covenant, acquisition of a Hebrew name, *Torah* study, *Bar/Bat Mitzvah*, and *Kabbalat Torah* (Confirmation). For those beyond childhood claiming Jewish identity, other public acts or declarations may be added or substituted after consultation with their rabbi."

[Central Conference of American Rabbis, 233. A Reform Get (July 1988), available at http://www.ccarnet.org/cgi-bin/respdisp.pl?file = 38&year = carr.]

NOTES

1. This text is nowhere in our present copies of the Old Testament.

2. The woman's declared rebellion and the man's knowledge that even during cleanness she will remain forbidden aggravate the pain of the deprivation and entitle him to immediate redress.

3. In this case divorce is delayed in the hope that the weekly reductions of her ketubah and the persuasions used by the court will induce her to change her attitude.

4. This parable serves to express the absence of reserve that may characterize the mutual and intimate relationship of husband and wife without offending the laws of chastity.

5. Whilst cohabitating with one woman to think of another.

6. Or: science and philosophy.

7. I.e., observing the golden mean.

8. Cf. *Nicomachean Ethics* iii.10.1118b2ff. The passage referring to the sense of touch reads as follows in Rackham's translation: "Hence the sense to which profligacy is related is the most universal of the senses; and there appears to be good ground for the disrepute in which it is held, because it belongs to us not as human beings but as animals."

Chapter 2

CHRISTIANITY

Luke Timothy Johnson and Mark D. Jordan

INTRODUCTION

UNEASY EMBODIMENT, SEXUAL AMBIVALENCE, AND THE INCARNATED AND RESURRECTED CHRIST

From the beginning Christianity has had an uneasy relationship with the human body and therefore also to sexuality, marriage, and family. This uneasiness is found in the complex and sometimes contradictory teachings of the New Testament, the collection of first-century CE compositions that Christians have always read, together with the Old Testament, as an inspired Word of God directing humans how to live. The deep ambivalence concerning sexuality finds its roots in classic Christian writings and throughout the history of Christianity.

The distinctive complexity of the New Testament can be approached by means of contrast to the other great monotheistic traditions of the West, Judaism and Islam, each based more or less directly on the Scriptures of ancient Israel. As religious systems they are simple: God creates, reveals his will through law, and rewards or punishes human behavior. Humans, in turn, are free either to obey or disobey God's commands. Equally simple and straightforward are these traditions' views of sex. Both Moses and Muhammad marry, have children, live to an old age, and die naturally. Both Torah and Qur'an are unequivocally in favor of marriage, even while recognizing the reality of divorce. These traditions view family as an unambiguous blessing from God and approve of heterosexual activity within the bounds of marriage, while rejecting sex outside marriage, whether polygamous or monogamous. Sexual love can be celebrated within the sacred text, and the marriage bond between man and woman powerfully symbolizes the covenant between God and humans. Both Judaism and Islam are uncomplicatedly committed to the goodness of sex, marriage, and family.

Why did Christians, who read the same sacred texts—although in the Greek translation called the Septuagint rather than in the Hebrew—come to such complicated and confusing conclusions on the same issues? It is because they read their Scripture from within quite a different set of circumstances and religious experiences. The circumstances were those of the Greco-Roman culture of the first-century Mediterranean. The religious experiences had to do with Jesus of Nazareth.

THE COMPLEX WITNESS OF EARLY CHRISTIAN TEACHING AND PRACTICE

The New Testament compositions were written over a roughly seventy-year period after the death of Jesus and include four narratives about Jesus (Gospels), an account of Christian beginnings (Acts of the Apostles), an apocalyptic writing (Revelation), and a collection of twenty-one letters from Paul and other early leaders. They vary in their social location, literary form, and perspective. But all of them engage already developed forms of moral teaching among Greco-Roman philosophers and Jews who also spoke and thought in Greek—and also interpreted life by means of the Septuagint.

Attitudes toward sex and marriage were considerably less relaxed in the early empire than they had been earlier. Philosophers of classical Greece had thought of sex primarily in terms of health rather than morality. But like the emperor Augustus himself—who introduced stringent laws concerning marriage and divorce—Greco-Roman moralists showed anxiety about sex, especially sexual pleasure. Cicero thought of pleasure and vice as virtually synonymous. Epictetus thought marriage and children an unacceptable distraction for the true philosopher (Doc. 2–4). Musonius Rufus allowed sexual intercourse, even within marriage, only in order to have children (Doc. 2–3). Hellenistic Jews also developed strict views of sex. Philo's ideal contemplatives were celibates. Whereas the Old Testament thought of virginity as a curse or punishment, Philo regarded it positively as a freedom for philosophy. Other Hellenistic Jewish writers worried about desire, especially sexual desire or lust. And Hellenistic Jews all rejected homosexuality as a distinctively Gentile vice.

The New Testament, in short, did not flow directly from the Old Testament. Christians read their Greek version of the Bible in light of changing sexual mores in the world around them. But even more important were four factors that directly affected the shaping of the New Testament's extraordinarily complex, if not inconsistent, teaching on sex, marriage, and the family.

1. The ministry and death of Christianity's founder. In contrast to Moses and Muhammad, Jesus died young and violently. He had neither wife nor children. Jesus is not a model for active sexuality, marriage, or family. The short ministry preceding his death, moreover, most resembled that of a Cynic philosopher or Elijah-like prophet. He was itinerant and demanded that his disciples imitate him. In the Gospels, furthermore, Jesus's teachings are at once nonsystematic and radical.

2. The character of the founding experience. Unlike Judaism and Islam, which formed societies based on the words and exemplary deeds of a prophet, Christianity took its origins from experiences and convictions connected to the death and resurrection of Jesus. The resurrection is the key. Jesus was not resuscitated in order to continue his mortal life, but entered into a full share of God's life and power. Through the Holy Spirit, furthermore, he gave other humans a share in that same life and power, a gift of "eternal life." The resurrection as source of true life marks a real departure from the this-worldly perceptions of Torah. The New Testament interprets the blessing of Abraham, not in terms of many biological descendents and a prosperous and safe life on the land, but in terms of "the promise that is the Holy Spirit." For early Christians, then, fullness of life is not the result of the natural processes of the body but the paradoxical expression of death and resurrection. A split between spirit and body results, but one that is different from Plato's mind-body distinction. Christians meant that there was a gap between natural human capacity (the body) and divine gift (the Holy Spirit).

3. The intense eschatology of early Christians. In one way or another, all New Testament compositions agree with Paul that "the frame of this world is passing away" (1 Cor. 7:31 [Doc. 2–6]), whether they think of this "passing away" in temporal terms—the world will come to an end soon—or in more existential terms as a "new creation" (2 Cor. 5:17; Gal. 6:15). For no early Christian was "this age" a sufficient measure of reality or worth. The death and resurrection of Jesus introduces a new age, which already participates in the "age to come." Jesus is therefore more than a new Moses, a declarer of law; he is the "final Adam," the "new human" into whose image his followers are to be formed. However the eschaton is understood, at the very least it means that the ordinary round of "marrying and giving in marriage" as well as of "buying and selling" is called into question (Luke 17:26–30; 1 Cor. 7:29–31 [Doc. 2–6]).

4. Early Christianity's lack of sociological and cultural definition. The Christian religion did not grow out of a natural kinship group or nation. Christians formed an intentional community whose boundaries required negotiation with both Judaism and Hellenism, with elements from each accepted and rejected. Gentile idolatry was rejected as well as (explicitly) its philosophy—though much crept in—while a number of distinctive Greco-Roman moral values were

embraced. Similarly, they rejected Jewish circumcision and ritual observance, while holding firmly to the covenantal ideals of Law and Prophets. While the founding experience of the new religion was distinctive, it drew eclectically if purposefully from older and more stable traditions within its environment.

Given the extraordinary character of the Christian experience and claims, the perilousness of its early years, the pluralism of the world within which it defined itself, and the haphazard production of its normative texts, it should be no surprise to find the teaching of the New Testament on family, marriage, and sexuality to be less than consistent.

FAMILY, HOUSEHOLD, AND EKKLESIA IN THE NEW TESTAMENT

Family was of obvious importance in Israel: the children of Abraham are less a nation in the political sense than a household *(oikos)*, an extended kinship system. The family was no less significant in Greco-Roman culture: the household *(oikos)* was the basic unit for mapping the social world.

The New Testament itself contains some positive appreciation of the natural family. Two of the Gospels pay positive attention to Jesus's family of origins. In Matthew, Joseph is a heroic protector who preserves the life of the infant Messiah (Matt. 1–2). In Luke's Gospel, Mary exemplifies those who belong to Jesus's true family because they "hear the word of God and keep it" (Luke 1–2; 8:15). During his ministry Jesus is shown sharing the hospitality of households and is considered by foes as overly fond of household celebrations; he is no ascetic like John the Baptist (see Luke 7:31–50). Jesus is also fond of children and makes the manner of receiving children a mark of the rule of God he proclaims (see Mark 9:14–29, 33–37, 42–48; 10:13–16, 35–45).

Households also played an important role in the early mission. The Acts of the Apostles shows the good news spreading through the conversion of entire households (Acts 10:24–48; 16:14–34). Early letters assume the household as the natural place for families as well as the meeting place for the congregations. Leaders of households tend to become leaders of local assemblies or churches *(ekklesiai)*. Parenting skills serve to qualify for leadership in the assembly. Moral instruction for households developed in Greco-Roman philosophy is applied to Christian families, mitigating only slightly the patriarchal structures of ancient households.

But the New Testament has as much by way of direct challenge to the natural family. In the Gospels of Mark and John, Jesus is at odds with his natural family, which does not recognize him (Mark 3:20–35; 6:1–6; John 7:1–9). Jesus says he has nowhere to lay his head (Matt. 8:20; Luke 9:58) and must depend on the hospitality of others (Luke 10:38–42). He calls his disciples to a radical renunciation of natural family: they are to leave parents, spouses, and children in order to follow him (Luke 9:57–62; 14:25–33 [Doc. 2–5]). Jesus's followers form with him a fictive kinship group, a family gathered around the prophet: those who listen to him are his mother and father, sister and brother (Luke 8:15, 19–21; Mark 3:34).

The same challenge to family continued in early Christian communities. The *ekklesia* gathered on the basis of faith, not natural kinship ties. Members were called out of their previous lives to participate in this more public and heterogeneous body. A distinctive feature of this movement was its use of fictive kinship language. The founder of a community was its father (1 Cor. 4:15) and members called each other "brother and sister" (1 Cor. 1:10; Rom. 16:1). Such language strengthened bonds between members and provided an alternative to the natural family. And since the ideals of the assembly were more egalitarian than patriarchal (see Gal. 3:28; Col. 3:10–11), this alternative family also became a source of stress within natural families, especially when the fictive family of the *ekklesia* held its meetings in a household run on conventional lines (see, e.g. 1 Cor. 11:3–16; 1 Tim. 2:11–15; 6:1–2).

SEX AND MARRIAGE IN ESCHATOLOGICAL PERSPECTIVE

On the positive side, Jesus appears to approve of marriages (or at least weddings!) by his miracle at a wedding (John 2:1–12). And he uses traditional biblical language for covenant when he speaks of himself as "the bridegroom" (Luke 5:34). Jesus is also far stricter concerning divorce than any Greco-Roman or Jewish teacher. In the earliest form of his statement on divorce, Jesus forbids it absolutely (Mark 10:2–12; Luke 16:18), a prohibition known, approved, and reported by Paul (Doc. 2–6). In Matthew 5:31 and 19:3–9 a partially modified form of the prohibition is attributed to Jesus: divorce is allowed only on the grounds of the partner's sexual immorality *(porneia)*.

In the more radical form of the prohibition, Jesus calls Moses's allowance of divorce (see Deut. 24:1–4) a concession to human hardness of heart. He bases his demand of absolute fidelity on the original state of humanity in Eden. Mark has Jesus quote the first creation account in Genesis 1:27 (Doc. 1–1 in chapter 1: God "made them male and female") in direct connection with the second in Gen. 2:24 (Doc. 2–1: "for this reason a man shall leave his father and mother and be joined to his wife and the two shall become one flesh," Mark 10:6–7). Since they are one flesh, God has joined them, and humans should not separate them (Mark 10:8–9). If either husband or wife divorce and marry again, they commit adultery (Mark 10:11–12), and if anyone marries a divorced person, he or she commits adultery (Luke 16:18).

Paul is sometimes considered an opponent of marriage, but the majority of statements in his letters support it strongly. He tells the Thessalonians to "abstain from fornication, that each one of you know how to take a wife in holiness and honor, not with lustful passion like the Gentiles who do not know God"

(1 Thess. 4:4–5; see also the positive statements in Heb. 13:4 and 1 Pet. 3:1–7). Paul approves of community leaders who have been faithful to one wife (1 Tim. 3:2, 12) and widows who have been married to but one husband (1 Tim. 5:9). Paul includes marriage with food and drink among "all the things that God has created good" and considers those who forbid marriage to be "liars whose consciences are seared" (1 Tim. 4:3). He wants younger widows to "marry, bear children, and manage their households" rather than be a burden on the community's meager financial resources (1 Tim. 5:14). He tells his delegate Titus that older women should instruct younger women to love their husbands and children and be good managers of households (Titus 2:4).

In his first letter to the Corinthians (Doc. 2–6) Paul repeats Jesus's prohibition of divorce even when partners do not share the faith. Couples who separate should seek reconciliation. Marriage is a way that partners and even their children can be sanctified. Yet if an unbeliever chooses to leave a marriage, the believer in that case is not still bound. In his letter to the Ephesians (Doc. 2–7) Paul gives particular attention to the marriage relationship. Once more the Genesis account is invoked, but now the marriage between man and woman is configured to the relationship between Christ and the church. Just as Christ gave himself for the church, so should the husband love the wife, and as the church obeys Christ so should the wife obey the husband. Marriage is now more than an analogy to covenant. It is a *mysterion* that expresses the covenant between God and humans: "This is a great mystery. I speak it with regard to Christ and the church. But you also, each of you, thus should love his own wife as himself, and the wife should reverence the husband" (Eph. 5:32–33).

Ephesians is the high-water mark of a positive view of marriage in early Christianity. But such intense Christological symbolism can actually serve as a solvent of the actual human bond. If Jesus is the bridegroom, and one's relationship with the Lord Jesus renders relative all other relationships—as Paul argues to the Corinthians (Doc. 2–6)—then cannot marriage as a sign or symbol be transcended by an even more dramatic form of embodied commitment? Would not a direct relationship with the bridegroom be more impressive than the marriage of man and woman? Similarly, if marriage and its indissolubility are based in the order of creation, what happens when there is a new creation, initiated by the resurrection? Which creation counts the most?

Paul's own struggle with this tension is poignantly shown in 1 Cor. 11:2–16. In his discussion of women praying or prophesying without traditional headwear, he argues for the subordination of women based on the order of creation in Genesis 2. But he can't do so consistently because of the new creation found "in the Lord" (1 Cor. 11:11–12). And in 1 Corinthians 7 (Doc. 2–8) Paul finally chooses celibacy as preferable in the present eschatological circumstances, because it allows an undistracted devotion to the Lord. Those who are married are conflicted by anxiety for their loved ones. In such circumstances, Paul says, "even those who have wives [should] be as though they had none." In this new creation virgins and widows do not need to be attached to a man to have worth. They are under no compulsion to marry. Eschatology calls all human institutions into question. Resurrection gives a life biology can't supply. Jesus is reported as telling the Sadducees, "Those who belong to this age marry and are given in marriage, but those who are considered worthy of a place in that age and in the resurrection of the dead neither marry nor are given in marriage" (Luke 20:24–38 [Doc. 2–5]; Doc. 2–7).

Despite demanding that the married stay married forever, Jesus himself is unfettered by spouse; he is the "bridegroom" of his followers (Matt. 9:15; John 3:29). And when his followers complain of the difficulty of staying married forever, Jesus holds out as an (implicitly) higher state being a "eunuch for the sake of the kingdom of heaven," adding, "Let anyone accept this who can" (Matt. 19:10–12 [Doc. 2–6]). Nor does Jesus support the institution of marriage when he demands of his disciples that they abandon parents, spouses, and children (Luke 14:26; Doc. 2–7). Just as the New Testament offers some support for the natural family while at the same time undercutting its significance, so it praises marriage even while proposing celibacy as a legitimate and perhaps superior alternative.

The New Testament is also remarkable for its lack of interest in aesthetics, pleasure, or the erotic. Yet the sexual body is a cause of considerable concern, most notably in Paul's complex discussion of the dangers of *porneia* (Doc. 2–6). In Jesus's teaching, desire and lust are equivalent to actual fornication and adultery (Matt. 5:27–28). The sexual drive appears as dangerous (1 Cor. 7:9 [Doc. 2–6]; 1 Thess. 4:5; 1 Pet. 2:11). The concept of *porneia* includes a catalogue of sexual sins from adultery to homosexuality (see Rom. 1:18–32). On this whole side of things the New Testament is emphatically Jewish. Sex is to take place only in marriage, and marriage must be faithfully monogamous. Sex is not a matter of health or recreation. It is viewed entirely within the framework of moral and religious commitment. Sex is serious.

Sex is serious rather than playful because the sexual body is regarded as powerful, both negatively and positively. Against those who would regard sexual intercourse as no more significant than eating, Paul insists that sexual intercourse engages personal and even cosmic powers (Doc. 2–8). Negatively, therefore, sex with a prostitute damages the social body of the church. Positively, sexual intercourse between husband and wife can sanctify both partners and their children and should therefore be relinquished only by mutual consent and for a short time, in order to pray. Human sexuality is located within the context of the resurrection body of Jesus and the "body of Christ" that is the church. Thus, virginity can be a symbol of dedication to the resurrected Lord (Acts 21:9; 1 Cor. 7:34 [Doc. 2–6]; Rev. 14:4), and marriage can be a symbol of the relationship between Christ and the church.

HISTORICAL DEVELOPMENT OF SEX, MARRIAGE, AND FAMILY DOCTRINE IN CHRISTIANITY

In the historical elaboration of various versions of Christianity, family norms depend in part on the writings compiled as the New Testament—but only in part. The teachings and practices were determined by the engagement of church beliefs and practices with other competing religious prescriptions, civil laws, family customs, and community expectations. The conditions under which Christianity first spread increased the range and complication of these engagements. Christianity began as a minority within a minority: it was a persecuted sect of Judaism, which was itself increasingly under suspicion by Roman authorities. Christian communities decided early on to spread beyond the Jewish homeland. They translated Jesus's teachings into Greek, one of the international languages of the time, and they relaxed the expectation that one should live as a Jew in order to be a Christian. These decisions and others encouraged the growth of Christian communities around the Roman Empire, but they also underscored some salient facts: Christians did not have a national homeland with laws or even uniform customs regulating human relations. During the churches' first centuries, converts to the new religious way brought their own marriage customs or rituals. Outside the churches imperial and local laws regulated sex, marriage, and family. Christianity did not have detailed rules for marrying, and it did not need them.

For reasons of their own, Christian communities were happy to stand back from the business of regulating marriages. To many believers the "good news" of Christianity implied separation so far as possible from the demands of pagan governments and decadent societies. Conversion could easily require separation from one's birth family, at least for a time, and especially when they disapproved. Without a sharp skepticism about family obligations, Christianity could never have separated from Judaism or sought converts from other religions. The church was offered as a new family, with its Father and its founder in heaven and a growing number of new brothers and sisters here on earth. The church family was unbounded by biological connection. In fact, it was often quite suspicious of the demands of reproduction and the bodily pleasures they implied. So even after Christianity was tolerated and then adopted by the imperial government, it was slow to develop marriage liturgy or theology. In the western churches there is no solid evidence of marriage rites performed in church before the fourth century CE and no surviving wedding liturgy earlier than the seventh or eighth century. To elaborate a theology that counted marriage a sacrament of the same genus as Eucharist and baptism took until the thirteenth century. Then theology and liturgy had to be redone from the sixteenth century on, in the course of the Protestant Reformation and the Catholic Counter-Reformation, not to mention the challenges of modernity.

Telling the story of Christian marriage as a sequence of developments and reforms can make it seem that there was only a single story to be told. Yet one of the hardest things to decide for the historian is who should be counted into the story. The definition of Christianity is a topic of endless dispute for Christians. The disputes sometimes concern matters of high doctrine, like the "nature" of God or Jesus Christ, but they often center on morals or church organization. Sex has figured in a surprisingly large number of these debates, either as the main topic or as a supplementary accusation. In many Christian communities deviation from the prevailing sexual norms (that is, ideals) has often been counted both the cause and effect of heresy. To preach alternative sexual arrangements makes one a heretic. All heretics, whatever they preach, are often accused of committing sexual indecencies. Some Christian individuals and groups did teach radical alternatives for marriage (such as polygyny) or sex (such as ritual promiscuity), but then they were immediately declared not to be Christians. Before efforts at ecumenical reconciliation, similar declarations would be made across the largest divisions in Christianity. Eastern Orthodox, Protestant, Anglican, and Roman Catholic Christians have often traded charges of heresy around issues of marriage and sex. Even today, some of the sharpest denominational boundaries are set by these issues.

When Christians rehearse these old disagreements among themselves, they often forget how much has changed since the disagreements began. The changes are hardest to see when the parties in dispute take them for granted. For example, many Christians assume that when the Christian Bible and other ancient authorities speak of marriage and family, they mean something like the "nuclear family" of the American Dream: Dad, Mom, and their children living in their own house. The truth is very different. Domestic arrangements and definitions of "family" have changed markedly across time and place in the history of Christianity. Christian teaching and practice have changed with them. In medieval European Christianity, for example, great importance was given to "spiritual kinship," that is, to family relations created by the performance of Christian rites other than marriage. A woman who stood as sponsor or God-mother at an infant's baptism became kin to that child. She took on the serious duties and severe prohibitions of being family. Christian churches have also recognized choices about spiritual kinship with rites that most Christians have now forgotten. Until fairly recent times, to take another example, Greek and Slavic churches performed a rite for blessing "spiritual" brotherhood or sisterhood. The rite was typically used to bless vows between friends of the same sex who wanted to become family to each other. It should also be remembered that many Christians have long fostered and praised single-sex religious "families," whether monasteries or religious orders or devotional organizations. The history of Christian marriage cannot be understood without remembering these networks of alternate kinship.

FIVE THEMES IN CHRISTIAN TEACHING ON SEX, MARRIAGE, AND FAMILY

Can anything be said about Christian teaching on sex, marriage, and family across this complex history of (often neglected) disagreements and changes? Some principles or professions do run through the teaching of most churches, at least until very recent times. The most important of these is the claim that sexual activity can only be justified within marriage. The principle can be argued on different grounds. Some Christians hold that sexual organs or capacities were made for having children and that children can only be cared for properly within a marriage. The nature of sex implies marriage. Other Christians contend that sexual desire has been essentially disordered since human beings fell into sin and that it can only be excused now when ordered to the greater good of procreation or community. The sinfulness of sex requires the remedy of marriage. Our suggestion is that the great principle that marriage justifies sex is really the product of other convictions and concerns that reappear regularly in Christian thinking. Without pretending to be exhaustive, we identify five of these themes or commitments: fidelity, reproduction, mutual giving, self-control, and social order. The five have often played against each other; they have certainly received different emphases over the centuries. Yet each persists as a motif in Christian thinking.

The first theme, *fidelity*, still means sexual exclusivity in common English usage. To be unfaithful to a spouse or partner is to have sex with someone else. This is a remnant of a much fuller Christian notion of fidelity. It specified monogamy or sexual exclusivity, to be sure, but also uniqueness or permanence of the couple's bond and solemn commitment to it by a vow or promise. The Hebrew Scriptures use marital faithfulness as an image for God's commitment to Israel or (in Christian eyes) the church. Christian churches have invoked God's singular commitment to believers in Christ as the high ideal of earthly marriage. In the early centuries this was expressed in the maxim "one husband" or "one wife." The maxim not only excluded polyandry or polygyny, it prohibited remarriage even after the death of a spouse. Over time the maxim proved too severe and a series of mitigations were introduced to allow not only exit from a marriage but also remarriage after the death of a spouse or if there had been an essential defect in the first marriage (such as fraud, coercion, or incest). While denominations disagreed over what to count as an essential defect, they continued to endorse the ideal of Christian marriage as a serious, exclusive, and enduring commitment.

The endorsement became more emphatic when linked to the second motif of *reproduction* and the idea that sexual relations are for the sake of having and raising children. Historically this notion is more ambivalent than the first, and Christian churches have qualified it in various ways. Some theologians have held that sexual activity was not required for a marriage. Couples have been urged to abstain from sex in order to have a more spiritual relation. Some couples might have a marriage without ever having "consummated" it sexually—as some believed of Jesus's parents, Mary and Joseph. Still, theologians assumed that most marriages would include sexual activity, at least in their early years, and so they counted having children as one of the goods of marriage. In consequence, they taught that attempts to interfere with conception were sinful. Contraception, whether "natural" or artificial, was regarded as a serious breach of marriage in the great majority of churches. There could be marriages without sexual intercourse, but any intercourse had to be left open to the good of children.

The third motif, *mutual self-giving*, enters here. Christian teachers have typically held that wife and husband give themselves to each other wholly, generously, as body and soul. Spouses should treat each other lovingly, of course, but that is no more than all Christians are called to do for any human being. Married Christians further pledge their bodies to each other in something like an exchange of ownership. Spouses "owe" physical intimacy to each other, unless they should together make a religious decision to refrain. The mutual gift of bodies becomes a sign and cause of more complete union between them. Christian writers have often praised the vowed friendship between spouses. Indeed, they have counted it among the goods of marriage alongside having children. They have understood marital intimacy as a figure for the union between Christ and the church. Christian marriage, especially with children, is often pictured as the church in miniature.

The exchange of bodies is a splendid sign of union, but it can also be a fearful temptation. Sexual temptation calls forth the fourth theme of *self-control*. In a religion generally skittish about sexual pleasure, the lascivious possibilities of the marriage bed had to be curtailed—and they were, by a commitment to self-control or chastity in marriage. The goods of marriage could justify sex, but not of any kind in any quantity. Christian spouses were to be moderate in their sexual relations. They were not to seek them mainly for pleasure, but for other goods, like children or friendship. This was another reason for prohibiting sexual practices that appeared only to offer pleasure rather than procreation. It can further explain the absence of anything like a Christian "erotic" teaching, much less any Christian pornography. Only married believers are permitted sex, and their concern with it is precisely not to refine or manipulate pleasures. Even Christian marriage manuals describe sexual matters mainly to warn and restrict. The only place Christian traditions have regularly offered for erotic writing is in descriptions of the soul's relation to God. Until recently, Christians did not publish workbooks on having better sex. Christian depictions of the techniques of passionate love are written by mystics aflame with God.

For Christians marriage has been a more worldly matter, as the final theme of concern for the *social order* suggests. Most Christian writers have recognized the importance of well-regulated marriage for a stable society, just as they have condemned unbridled sex as contrary to the common good. Yet there is an old uncertainty about how much Christian marriage belongs to the churches and how much to civil authority. In western Christendom, the collapse of imperial government encouraged churches to assert more and more jurisdiction over marriage. They were to devise not only its rites, but its regulations. Once marriage was declared a sacrament, it became by definition a matter essentially subject to church teaching and church courts—in the same way that the Eucharist or baptism would be. But there was still uncertainty, because permanent, monogamous unions outside the church were also considered marriage according to the "law" of nature. Many Protestant reformers rejected the tangle of medieval marriage law and the corrupt proceedings of church courts, especially in regard to separations or dissolutions. They tried in various ways to rethink the balance of jurisdiction between church and civil government. At the same time, the Reformation gave increased importance to marriage as a Christian vocation, thus reasserting the moral or spiritual stake of the churches in good marriages. The distinction between church and civil government was also blurred as rulers or governments adopted principles of reformed Christianity. What could it mean to insist the marriage belong to the state when the state itself was intent on enforcing denominational policies?

CONTEMPORARY CHRISTIAN DEBATES

The latter half of the twentieth century saw significant and even startling changes in the position of the churches on sex, marriage, and family. Many contemporary Christians in the developed nations, both "liberal" and "conservative," hold views on sex or marriage that earlier churches would have instantly pronounced unChristian. The most obvious changes concern contraception and divorce. Around 1900 the huge majority of European, Canadian, and American Christians stood with the tradition in considering contraception mostly immoral and divorce an unusual, unhappy remedy for extreme situations. By the year 2000 it is much easier—and much quicker—to enumerate Christian bodies that still do reject contraception or divorce. More diffuse changes, but in some ways more profound, have affected women's roles in marriage and family. As women have gained their civil rights, and then more of their share as full members of Christian churches, they have been less willing to accept a view of marriage in which they are treated as perpetually incomplete or immature human beings. The claims of women to be equal members in church and, for that matter, in the writing of Christian theology have hardly been settled. Even where women have been allowed into ordained ministry or denominational leadership, the theological implications of women's equality are only just beginning to be worked through. For the longest time Christian teaching on marriage has been written by men on behalf of women. Now women can teach in their own voices.

Most recently, Christian teachings have been challenged by blunt questions about their old denigration of sexual pleasure. A few decades ago the challenge was posed by "premarital" sex: Should a man and a woman who would soon be married have sex with each other before the wedding day? In retrospect that question seems charmingly naive. The fiercest fights now rage around the sexual activity of avowedly lesbian or gay Christians, some of whom want not only approval of their embodied loves but a full share in Christian marriage. The controversies have already divided some denominations in fact, and they may shortly divide them constitutionally into separate churches. This would be unfortunate, but also misleading. Both extramarital sex and same-sex unions are proxies for a much larger controversy that will prove decisive for future Christian teaching, whether it considers itself progressive or traditionalist. It is a controversy about the fundamental logic of justifying sex through marriage. Indeed, it threatens to undo the original compact that gave marriage a place in church thinking and ritual. At the heart of this controversy is this question: can Christians approve sexual pleasure that is not subordinated to procreation or contained within the marriage of one man and one woman?

CREATION AND FALL IN THE BOOK OF GENESIS

In the first century CE Christianity emerged as a sect of Judaism and interacted with Hellenistic culture. The New Testament constantly reinterprets the scriptures shared with Judaism in light of the experience of Jesus, the crucified and resurrected Messiah. But earliest Christian attitudes toward sexuality, marriage, and family were also affected by stringent sexual teaching developed by Greco-Roman and Hellenistic Jewish moral teachers. While Jewish interpreters were drawn to legal texts, early Christian writers focused on the narrative parts of Scripture, above all the creation stories. On one side, Jesus points to the union of Adam and Eve as the ideal for marriage. On the other side, the story of the fall of humanity suggests the shattering of that ideal. Finally, Paul considers the resurrection of Jesus to be a "new creation" and Jesus to be the "last Adam," which creates some tension with the "first creation." Ancient writers did not consider the two distinct creation accounts to be from two different sources (as critical scholars do), but read them continuously as a single account. Thus the ideal conception of humanity is the image of God reflected in both male and female. But in the actual flesh, woman is secondary, created to be a "fit helper" for the man. When Adam and Eve transgressed God's command and ate from the tree of the knowledge of good and evil, they ruptured not only their relationship with God but also their relationship with each other and to the earth itself. (See Doc. 1-1 in chapter 1.)

THE GRECO-ROMAN CONTEXT

There is no evidence that the writers of the New Testament knew or made direct use of the Greco-Roman writings presented here. We include them to indicate the cultural context within which the New Testament was composed. The popular perception of the Roman Empire is as a cauldron of sexual license—and there is ample support for that portrayal in ancient historians, novelists, and satirists. But a countercurrent of strict sexual ethics was found among some philosophers, especially those of the Stoic-Cynic tradition, such as Musonius Rufus and Epictetus. Musonius (b. ca. 30 CE) is notable for the stringency of his sexual teaching. Epictetus (ca. 55–135 CE) calls for a "functional celibacy" for the Cynic philosopher like that advocated by Paul in 1 Cor. 7:25–35.

Document 2–1

MUSONIUS RUFUS, ON SEXUAL INDULGENCE

Not the least significant part of the life of luxury and self-indulgence lies also in sexual excess; for example those who lead such a life crave a variety of loves not only lawful but unlawful ones as well, not women alone but also men; sometimes they pursue one love and sometimes another, and not being satisfied with those which are available, pursue those which are rare and inaccessible, and invent shameful intimacies, all of which constitute a grave indictment of manhood.

   Men who are not wantons or immoral are bound to consider sexual intercourse justified only when it occurs in marriage and is indulged in for the purpose of begetting children, since that is lawful, but unjust and unlawful when it is mere pleasure-seeking, even in marriage. But of all sexual relations those involving adultery are the most unlawful, and no more tolerable are those of men with men, because it is a monstrous thing and contrary to nature. But, furthermore, leaving out of consideration adultery, all intercourse with women which is without lawful character is shameful and is practiced from lack of self-restraint.

   [Musonius Rufus, "On Sexual Indulgence" (Fragment 12), in *Moral Exhortation,*
A Greco-Roman Sourcebook, ed. A. J. Malherbe, Library of Early Christianity
(Philadelphia: Westminster, 1986), pp. 152–153]

Document 2–2

EPICTETUS, ON THE CALLING OF A CYNIC

But, said the young man, will marriage and children be undertaken by the Cynic as a matter of prime importance?—If, replied Epictetus, you grant me a city of wise men, it might very well be that no one will lightly adopt the Cynic's profession. For in whose interest would he take on this style of life? If, nevertheless, we assume that he does so act, there will be nothing to prevent him from both marrying and having children; for his wife will be another person like himself, and so will his father-in-law, and his children will be brought up in the same fashion. But in such an order of things as the present, which is like that of a battle-field, it is a question, perhaps, if the Cynic ought not to be free from distraction, wholly devoted to the service of God, free to go about among men, not tied down by the private duties of men, nor involved with relationships which he cannot violate and still maintain his role as a good and excellent man, whereas, on the other hand, if he observes them, he will destroy the messenger, the scout, the herald of the gods, that he is . . . from this point of view, we do not find that marriage, under present conditions, is a matter of prime importance for the Cynic.

[Epictetus, "On the Calling of a Cynic" (Discourse III, 22, 67–77), in *Epictetus, the Discourses*, trans. W. A. Oldfather, Loeb Classical Library (Cambridge: Harvard University Press, 1928), vol. 2, pp. 153–155]

HELLENISTIC JEWISH MORAL INSTRUCTION

Jewish authors writing in Greek interpreted the traditions of Scripture in ways strongly influenced by Greco-Roman philosophy. Philo of Alexandria was typically strict in his condemnation of pleasure-seeking and sensuality. In the following passage an anonymous Jewish author, called Pseudo-Phocylides, writing in the first century CE, camouflages Jewish ideas within a literary form (gnomic wisdom) and style that are entirely Greek.

Document 2–3

PSEUDO-PHOCYLIDES ON DOMESTIC ETHICS

[175]Do not remain unmarried, lest you die nameless. [176]Give nature her due, you also, beget in your turn as you were begotten. [177]Do not prostitute your wife, defiling your children. [178]For the adulterous bed brings not sons in (your) likeness. [179]Do not touch your stepmother, your father's second wife, [180]but honor her as a mother, because she follows the footsteps of your mother. [181]Do not have intercourse with the concubines of (your) father. [182]Do not approach the bed of (your) sister, (a bed) to turn away from. [183]Nor go to bed with the wives of your brothers. [184]Do not let a woman destroy the unborn baby in her belly, [185]nor after its birth throw it before the dogs and the vultures as a prey. [186]Do not lay your hand upon your wife when she is pregnant. [187]Do not cut a youth's masculine procreative faculty. [188]Do not seek sexual union with irrational animals. [189]Do not outrage (your) wife by shameful ways of intercourse. [190]Do not transgress with unlawful sex the limits set by nature. [191]For even animals are not pleased by intercourse of male with male. [192]And let women not imitate the

sexual role of men. [193]Do not surrender wholly to unbridled sensuality toward
your wife. [194]For eros is not a god, but a passion destructive of all.

> ["The Sentences of Pseudo-Phocylides," trans. P. W. van der Horst,
> in *Old Testament Pseudepigrapha*, ed. J. H. Charlesworth
> (New York: Doubleday, 1985), vol. 2, pp. 580–581]

GOSPELS OF MATTHEW AND LUKE

The canonical Gospels (written between 70–90 CE) contain four versions of
Jesus's teaching regarding divorce: Luke 16:16 is a simple prohibition. Mark
10:1–10 contains Jesus's teaching within the context of a controversy with Pharisees, and makes the prohibition of divorce without exception. Matthew has
two versions. The first is in the Sermon on the Mount, as one of the "antitheses"
that contrast Jesus's teaching to Moses and the oral tradition (5:31–32). Jesus
here allows a man to divorce his wife in the case of *porneia* (sexual immorality).
The second Matthew passage (19:1–12) parallels the controversy in Mark 10:1–
10. Again, Jesus allows divorce for *porneia*, and adds a saying that appears to
suggest celibacy as a higher state for those who can follow it.

Document 2–4

THE GOSPEL OF MATTHEW 19:1–12

[19:1]Now when Jesus had finished these sayings, he went away from Galilee and
entered the region of Judea beyond the Jordan; [2]and large crowds followed him,
and he healed them there. [3]And Pharisees came up to him and tested him by
asking, "Is it lawful to divorce one's wife for any cause?" [4]He answered, "Have
you not read that he who made them from the beginning made them male and
female," [5]and said, "For this reason a man shall leave his father and mother
and be joined to his wife, and the two shall become one flesh?" [6]So they are
no longer two but one flesh. What, therefore God has joined together, let not
man put asunder." [7]They said to him, "Why then did Moses command one to
give a certificate of divorce, and to put her away?" [8]He said to them, "For your
hardness of heart Moses allowed you to divorce your wives, but from the beginning it was not so. [9]And I say to you: whoever divorces his wife, except for
unchastity, and marries another, commits adultery." [10]The disciples said to him,
"If such is the case of a man with his wife, it is not expedient to marry." [11]But
he said to them, "Not all men can receive this saying, but only those to whom
it is given. [12]For there are eunuchs who have been so from birth, and there are
eunuchs who have been made eunuchs by men, and there are eunuchs who
have made themselves eunuchs for the sake of the kingdom of heaven. He who
is able to receive this, let him receive it." . . .

> [*The Holy Bible with the Apocrypha*, Revised Standard Version
> (New York: Oxford University Press, 2002)]

At the same time that the Gospels report Jesus as demanding absolute fidelity in marriage, they also contain sayings that demand of Jesus's followers that they leave all human ties and possessions behind.

Document 2–5

THE GOSPEL OF LUKE 14:25–33, 18:18–30, 20:27–38

14:25Now great multitudes accompanied him; and he turned and said to them, 26"If any one comes to me and does not hate his own father and mother and wife and children and brothers and sisters, yes, and even his own life, he cannot be my disciple. . . . 33So therefore, whoever of you does not renounce all that he has cannot be my disciple." . . .

18:18And a ruler asked him, "Good Teacher, what shall I do to inherit eternal life?" 19And Jesus said to him, "Why do you call me good? No one is good but God alone. 20You know the commandments: 'Do not commit adultery, Do not kill, Do not steal, Do not bear false witness, Honor your father and mother.'" 21And he said, "All these I have observed from my youth." 22And when Jesus heard it, he said to him, "One thing you still lack. Sell all that you have and distribute to the poor, and you will have treasure in heaven; and come, follow me." 23But when he heard this, he became sad, for he was very rich. 24Jesus, looking at him, said, "How hard it is for those who have riches to enter the kingdom of God! 25For it is easier for a camel to pass through the eye of a needle than for a rich man to enter the kingdom of God." 26Then those who heard it said, "Then who can be saved?" 27But he said, "What is impossible with men is possible with God." 28And Peter said, "Lo, we have left our homes and followed you." 29And he said to them, "Truly, I say to you, there is no man who has left house or wife or brothers or parents or children, for the sake of the kingdom of God, 30who will not receive manifold more in this time, and in the age to come eternal life." . . .

[The Gospels also report Jesus in controversy with the Sadducees on the issue of levirate marriage, in which a brother was obliged to marry his brother's widow (Gen. 38:8; Deut. 25:5–10). Jesus's response to the reductio ad absurdum reveals the Christian sense of sharp discontinuity between natural life and the resurrection life.]

20:27There came to him some Sadducees, those who say that there is no resurrection, 28and they asked him a question, saying, "Teacher, Moses wrote for us that if a man's brother dies, having a wife but no children, the man must take the wife and raise up children for his brother. 29Now there were seven brothers; the first took a wife, and died without children; 30and the second 31and the third took her, and likewise all seven left no children and died. 32Afterward the woman also died. 33In the resurrection, therefore, whose wife will the woman be? For the seven had her as wife." 34And Jesus said to them, "The sons of this age marry and are given in marriage; 35but those who are accounted worthy to attain to that age and to the resurrection from the dead neither marry nor are given in marriage, ³⁶for they cannot die any more, because they are equal to angels and are sons of God, being sons of the resurrection. ³⁷But that the dead are raised, even Moses showed, in the passage about the bush, where he calls the Lord the God of Abraham and the God of Isaac and the God of Jacob. ³⁸Now he is not the God of the dead, but the God of the living, for all live to him." . . .

[Revised Standard Version]

PAUL'S LETTERS TO THE CORINTHIANS AND EPHESIANS

Paul was the first and most important interpreter of the Christian experience. In his letters, between 49–68 CE, we find him struggling to think through the implications of the "new creation" that was the resurrection of Jesus for specific moral behavior. The status of sex, marriage, and family were obviously in question. It is not surprising to find in Paul's letters elements that do not entirely agree. We provide here three passages that have probably had the greatest effect on Christian thinking concerning these issues. The first is a long section of 1 Corinthians, which touches on sexual immorality, marriage, divorce, and virginity. The second is Paul's most powerful affirmation of marriage in his letter to the Ephesians as a "mystery" pointing to the relationship between Christ and the church. The third is another passage from 1 Corinthians that does not mention marriage but whose exalted conception of love *(agape,* not *eros)* has caused it to be read at countless Christian weddings and provide a moral ideal for enduring Christian marriages.

Document 2–6

1 CORINTHIANS 5:1–7:40

⁵·¹It is actually reported that there is immorality *(porneia)* among you and of a kind that is not found even among pagans; for a man is living with his father's wife. ²And you are arrogant! Ought you not rather to mourn? Let him who has done this be removed from among you. ³For though absent in body I am present in spirit, and as if present, I have already pronounced judgment ⁴in the name of the Lord Jesus on the man who has done such a thing. When you are assembled, and my spirit is present, with the power of our Lord Jesus, ⁵you are to deliver this man to Satan for the destruction of the flesh, that his spirit may be saved in the day of the Lord Jesus. ⁶Your boasting is not good. Do you not know that a little leaven leavens the whole lump? ⁷Cleanse out the old leaven that you may be a new lump, as you really are unleavened. For Christ, our paschal lamb, has been sacrificed. ⁸Let us, therefore, celebrate the festival, not with the old leaven, the leaven of malice and evil, but with the unleavened

bread of sincerity and truth. [9]I wrote to you in my letter not to associate with immoral men *(pornoi)*; [10]not at all meaning the immoral of this world, or the greedy and robbers, or idolaters, since then you would need to go out of the world. [11]But rather I wrote you not to associate with anyone who bears the name of brother if he is guilty of immorality *(porneia)* or greed, or is an idolater, reviler, drunkard, or robber—not even to eat with such a one. [12]For what have I to do with judging outsiders? Is it not those inside the church whom you are to judge? [13]God judges those outside. "Drive out the wicked person from among you." . . .

[6:9]Do you not know that the unrighteous will not inherit the kingdom of God? Do not be deceived; neither the immoral *(pornoi)* nor idolaters, nor adulterers, nor sexual perverts, [10]nor thieves, nor the greedy, nor drunkards, nor revilers, nor robbers will inherit the kingdom of God. [11]And such were some of you. But you were washed, you were sanctified, you were justified in the name of the Lord Jesus Christ and in the Spirit of our God. [12]"All things are lawful for me," but not all things are helpful. "All things are lawful for me," but I will not be enslaved by anything. [13]"Food is meant for the stomach and the stomach for food"—and God will destroy both one and the other. The body is not meant for immorality *(porneia)* but for the Lord, and the Lord for the body. [14]And God raised the Lord and will raise us up by his power. [15]Do you not know that your bodies are members of Christ? Shall I therefore take the members of Christ and make them members of a prostitute *(porne)*? Never! [16]Do you not know that he who joins himself to a prostitute becomes one body with her? For, as it is written, "The two shall become one flesh" [Gen. 2:24]. [17]But he who is united to the Lord becomes one spirit with him. [18]Shun immorality *(porneia)*. Every other sin which a man commits is outside the body; but the immoral man *(pornos)* sins against his own body. [19]Do you not know that your body is a temple of the Holy Spirit within you, which you have from God? You are not your own; [20]you were bought with a price. So glorify God in your body.

[7:1]Now concerning the matters about which you wrote. It is well for a man not to touch a woman. [2]But because of the temptation to immorality *(porneia)*, each man should have his own wife and each woman her own husband. [3]The husband should give his wife her conjugal rights, and likewise the wife to her husband. [4]For the wife does not rule over her own body, but the husband does; likewise the husband does not rule over his own body, but the wife does. [5]Do not refuse one another except perhaps by agreement for a season, that you may devote yourselves to prayer; but then come together again, lest Satan tempt you through lack of self-control. [6]I say this by way of concession, not of command. [7]I wish that all were as I myself am. But each has his own special gift from God, one of one kind, and one of another.

[8]To the unmarried and the widows I say that it is well for them to remain single as I do. [9]But if they cannot exercise self-control, they should marry. For it is better to marry than to be aflame with passion.

[10]To the married I give charge, not I but the Lord, that the wife should not separate from the husband [11](but if she does, let her remain single or else be reconciled to her husband)—and that the husband should not divorce his wife.

[12]To the rest I say, not the Lord, that if any brother has a wife who is an unbeliever, and she consents to live with him, he should not divorce her. [13]If any woman has a husband who is an unbeliever, and he consents to live with her, she should not divorce him. [14]For the unbelieving husband is consecrated through his wife, and the unbelieving wife is consecrated through her husband. Otherwise, your children would be unclean, but as it is they are holy. [15]But if the unbelieving partner desires to separate, let it be so; in such a case, the brother or sister is not bound. For God called us to peace. [16]Wife, how do you know whether you will save your husband? Husband, how do you know you will save your wife?

[17]Only, let everyone lead the life which the Lord has assigned to him, and in which God has called him. This is my rule in all the churches. [18]Was anyone at the time of his call already circumcised? Let him not seek to remove the marks of circumcision. [19]For neither circumcision counts for anything nor un-circumcision, but keeping the commandments of God. [20]Everyone should remain in the state in which he was called. [21]Were you a slave when called? Never mind. But if you can gain your freedom, avail yourself of the opportunity. [22]For he who was called in the Lord as a slave is a freedman of the Lord. Likewise he who was free when called is a slave of Christ. [23]You were bought with a price; do not become slaves of men. [24]So, brethren, in whatever state each was called, there let him remain with God.

[25]Now concerning the unmarried, I have no command of the Lord, but I give my opinion as one who by the Lord's mercy is trustworthy. [26]I think that in view of the present distress, it is well for a person to remain as he is. [27]Are you bound to a wife? Do not seek to be free. Are you free from a wife? Do not seek marriage. [28]But if you marry, you do not sin, and if a girl marries she does not sin. Yet those who marry will have worldly troubles, and I would spare you that. [29]I mean, brethren, the appointed time has grown very short; from now on, let those who have wives live as though they had none, [30]and those who mourn as though they were not mourning, and those who rejoice as though they were not rejoicing, and those who buy as though they had no goods, [31]and those who deal with the world as though they had no dealings with it. For the form of this world is passing away.

[32]I want you to be free from anxieties. The unmarried man is anxious about the affairs of the Lord, how to please the Lord; [33]but the married man is anxious about worldly affairs, how to please his wife, [34]and his interests are divided. And the unmarried woman or girl is anxious about the affairs of the Lord, how to be holy in body and spirit; but the married woman is anxious about worldly affairs, how to please her husband. [35]I say this for your own benefit, not to lay any restraint upon you, but to promote good order and to secure your undivided devotion to the Lord.

[36]If any one thinks that he is not behaving properly toward his betrothed, if his passions are strong, and it has to be, let him do as he wishes: let them marry—it is no sin. [37]But whoever is firmly established in his heart, being under no necessity but having his desire under control, and has determined this in his heart, to keep her as his betrothed, he will do well. [38]So that he who marries his betrothed does well; and he who will refrain from marriage will do better.

[39]A wife is bound to her husband as long as he lives. If the husband dies, she is free to be married to whom she wishes, only in the Lord. [40]But in my judgment she is happier if she remains as she is. And I think that I have the Spirit of God.

[Revised Standard Version]

Document 2–7

EPHESIANS 5:21–6:4

[5:21]Be subject to one another out of reverence for Christ. [22]Wives, be subject to your husbands, as to the Lord. [23]For the husband is the head of the wife as Christ is head of the church, his body, and is himself its savior. [24]As the church is subject to Christ, so let wives also be subject in everything to their husbands. [25]Husbands, love your wives, as Christ loved the church and gave himself up for her, [26]that he might sanctify her, having cleansed her by the washing of water with the word, [27]that he might present the church to himself in splendor, without spot or wrinkle or any such thing, that she might be holy and without blemish. [28]Even so husbands should love their wives as their own bodies. He who loves his wife loves himself. [29]For no man ever hates his own flesh, but nourishes and cherishes it, as Christ does the church, [30]because we are members of his body. [31]"For this reason a man shall leave his father and mother and be joined to his wife, and the two shall become one flesh." [32]This mystery is a profound one, and I am saying that it refers to Christ and the church; [33]however, let each one of you love his wife as himself, and let the wife see that she respects her husband.

[6:1]Children, obey your parents in the Lord, for this is right. [2]"Honor your mother and your father" (this is the first commandment with a promise), [3]"that it may be well with you and that you may live long on the earth." [4]Fathers, do not provoke your children to anger, but bring them up in the discipline and instruction of the Lord.

[Revised Standard Version]

Document 2–8

1 CORINTHIANS 13:1–13

[1]If I speak in the tongues of men and of angels, but have not love (*agape*), I am a noisy gong or a clanging cymbal. [2]And if I have prophetic powers, and un-

derstand all mysteries and all knowledge, and if I have all faith, so as to remove mountains, but have no love, I am nothing. [3]If I give away all I have, and if I deliver my body to be burned, but have not love, I gain nothing. [4]Love is patient and kind; love is not jealous or boastful; [5]it is not arrogant or rude. Love does not insist on its own way; it is not irritable or resentful; [6]it does not rejoice at wrong, but rejoices in the right. [7]Love bears all things, believes all things, hopes all things, endures all things. [8]Love never ends; as for prophecies, they will pass away; as for tongues, they will cease; as for knowledge, it will pass away. [9]For our knowledge is imperfect and our prophecy is imperfect; [10]but when the perfect comes, the imperfect will pass away. [11]When I was a child, I spoke like a child, I thought like a child, I reasoned like a child; when I became a man, I gave up childish ways. [12]For now we see in a mirror dimly, but then face to face. Now I know in part; then I shall understand fully, even as I have been fully understood. [13]So faith, hope, love abide, these three; but the greatest of these is love.

[Revised Standard Version]

APOCRYPHAL CHRISTIAN TEXTS

Already by the mid-second century Christians wrote and read religious literature outside the canonical Scripture. Some of these writings claimed divine authority, and some of them enjoyed wide popularity. Many of them contained views of marriage, family, and sexuality that were even more stringent than those in the New Testament. Some apocryphal writings came from more or less organized parties, like the Gnostics, and were rejected by their orthodox opponents. Others entered quietly into popular piety without much attention or fuss. But in all these writings—in contrast to Paul—we find a genuine "body/spirit" dualism that evaluates the body (especially the sexual body) negatively We cannot accurately assess the impact of such writings on Christian consciousness, but it is clear that the failure to develop a truly positive theology of marriage within the Christian tradition owes something to them. We here provide short excerpts from two apocryphal writings from the second century. In The Acts of Paul and Thecla we see Paul recasting the beatitudes in a form that virtually equates faith with virginity. And in The Gospel of James the simple report of the canonical Gospels that Mary was a virgin (Matt 1:23; Luke 1:26–35) is elaborated into an extensive legend concerning Jesus's mother in which even natural bodily processes are regarded as dangerous and polluting.

Document 2–9

THE ACTS OF PAUL AND THECLA

And when Paul was entered into the house of Onesiphorus there was great joy, and bowing of knees and breaking of bread, and the word of God concerning continence and the resurrection, as Paul said: "Blessed are the pure of heart, for they shall see God. Blessed are they who have kept the flesh pure, for they shall become a temple of God. Blessed are the continent, for to them God will speak. Blessed are they who have renounced this world, for they shall be well pleasing unto God. Blessed are they who have wives as though they had them not, for they shall inherit God. Blessed are they who have fear of God, for they shall become angels of God. Blessed are they who tremble at the words of God, for they shall be comforted. Blessed are they who have received the wisdom of Jesus Christ, for they shall be called sons of the Most High. Blessed are they who have kept their baptisms secure, for they shall rest with the Father and the Son. Blessed are they who have laid hold on the understanding of Jesus Christ, for they shall be in light. Blessed are they who through love of God have departed from the form of this world, for they shall judge angels and at the right hand of the Father they shall be blessed. Blessed are the merciful, for they shall obtain mercy, and shall not see the bitter day of judgment. Blessed are the bodies of the virgins, for they shall be well pleasing to God, and shall not lose the reward of their purity. For the word of the Father shall be for them a work of salvation in the day of his Son, and they shall have rest for ever and ever."

> ["The Acts of Paul and Thecla," trans. R. McL. Wilson, in E. Hennecke,
> *New Testament Apocrypha*, ed. W. Schneemelcher
> (Philadelphia: Westminster, 1964), vol. 2, pp. 354–355]

Document 2–10

THE GOSPEL OF JAMES

8.2. Now Mary was in the Temple of the Lord like a dove being fed, and she received food from the hand of an angel. 3. When she was twelve years old there took place a conference of the priests, saying, "Behold, Mary has become twelve years old in the Temple of the Lord our God. 4. What, therefore, shall we do with her, lest she defile the sanctuary of the Lord?" 5. The High Priests said to Zacharias, "You stand at the altar of the Lord. Enter and pray concerning her; and whatever the Lord God may reveal to you, this let us do." 6. The priest entered the Holy of Holies, taking the vestment with the twelve bells, and he prayed concerning her. 7. And behold, an angel of the Lord appeared, saying, "Zacharias, Zacharias, go out and call together the widowers of the people, and let each of them bring a rod; and to whomever the Lord God shows a sign, to this one shall she be wife." 8. The heralds therefore went forth through the whole Jewish countryside and sounded the trumpet of the Lord, and all came running.

9.1. Now Joseph, casting down his adze, came himself into their meeting. When they all were gathered together, they came to the priest, taking the rods. 2. He, having received the rods of all of them, went into the Temple and prayed. When he finished the prayer he took the rods and came out and returned them;

and there was no sign on them. 3. Joseph received the last rod, and behold, a dove came forth from the rod and settled on Joseph's head. 4. Then the priest said, "Joseph, Joseph, you has been designated by lot to· receive the virgin of the Lord as your ward." 5. Joseph refused, saying, "I have sons and I am an old man, but she is a young maiden—lest I be a laughing stock to the children of Israel." . . . Joseph, frightened, received her as his ward. . . .

[When it is time for Mary to give birth, Joseph places her in a cave and goes out in search of a Jewish midwife] 19.1. Finding a midwife, he brought her. They came down from the mountain, and Joseph said to the midwife, 2. "Mary is the one who was betrothed to me, but she, having been brought up in the Temple of the Lord, has conceived by the Holy Spirit." And she went with him. 3. They stood in the place of the cave, and a dark [bright] cloud was overshadowing the cave. The midwife said, "My soul is magnified today, for my eyes have seen a mystery: a Savior has been born to Israel!" 4. And immediately the cloud withdrew from the cave, and a great light appeared in the cave so that their eyes could not bear it. 5. After a while, the light withdrew, until the baby appeared. It came and took the breast of its mother Mary; and the midwife cried out, "How great is this day, for I have seen this new wonder!" 20.1. The midwife went in and placed Mary in position, and Salome examined her virginal nature; and Salome cried aloud that she had tempted the living God— "and behold, my hand falls away from me in fire." Then she prayed to the Lord.

["The Gospel of James" in *Documents for the Study of the Gospels*, ed. D. R. Cartlidge and D. L. Dungan (Philadelphia: Fortress, 1994), pp. 104–105, 108]

AUGUSTINE OF HIPPO

Augustine of Hippo (354–430 CE) is rightly regarded as the most influential theologian for the western Christian churches after the authors of the New Testament. The story of his slow conversion to Christianity in the *Confessions* is most famous, but he wrote a small library of other books that fixed the terms of theological debate on many central topics, including sex and marriage. The selection here is from one of Augustine's shorter treatises, *On the Good of Marriage* or *On the Marital Good*, written around 401 CE. Augustine composed it in response to those who claimed that serious Christians should not marry. He offers a limited defense of the goods that Christians can expect from marriage if they seek it with the right motives and sufficient self-control.

Document 2–11

AUGUSTINE, ON THE GOOD OF MARRIAGE

3. This is what we now say, that according to the present condition of birth and death, which we know and in which we were created, the marriage of male and female is something good. This union divine Scripture so commands that

it is not permitted a woman who has been dismissed by her husband to marry again, as long as her husband lives, nor is it permitted a man who has been dismissed by his wife to marry again, unless she who left has died. Therefore, regarding the good of marriage, which even the Lord confirmed in the Gospel [Matt. 19:9], not only because He forbade the dismissal of a wife except for fornication, but also because He came to the marriage when invited [John 2], there is merit in inquiring why it is a good.

This does not seem to me to be a good solely because of the procreation of children, but also because of the natural companionship between the two sexes. Otherwise, we could not speak of marriage in the case of old people, especially if they had either lost their children or had begotten none at all. But, in a good marriage, although one of many years, even if the ardor of youths has cooled between man and woman, the order of charity still flourishes between husband and wife. They are better in proportion as they begin. the earlier to refrain by mutual consent from sexual intercourse, not that it would afterwards happen of necessity that they would not be able to do what they wished, but that it would be a matter of praise that they had refused beforehand what they were able to do. If, then, there is observed that promise of respect and of services due to each other by either sex, even though both members weaken in health and become almost corpse-like, the chastity of souls rightly joined together continues the purer, the more it has been proved, and the more secure, the more it has been calmed.

Marriage has also this good, that carnal or youthful incontinence, even if it is bad, is turned to the honorable task of begetting children, so that marital intercourse makes something good out of the evil of lust. Finally, the concupiscence of the flesh, which parental affection tempers, is repressed and becomes inflamed more modestly. For a kind of dignity prevails when, as husband and wife they unite in the marriage act, they think of themselves as mother and father.

4. There is the added fact that, in the very debt which married persons owe each other, even if they demand its payment somewhat intemperately and incontinently, they owe fidelity equally to each other. And to this fidelity the Apostle has attributed so much right that he called it power, when he said: "The wife has not authority over her body, but the husband; the husband likewise has not authority over his body, but the wife" [1 Cor. 7:4]. But the violation of this fidelity is called adultery, when, either by the instigation of one's own lust or by consent to the lust of another, there is intercourse with another contrary to the marriage compact. And so the fidelity is broken which even in material and base things is a great good of the soul; and so it is certain that it ought to be preferred even to the health of the body wherein his life is contained. For, although a small amount of straw as compared to much gold is as nothing, fidelity, when it is kept pure in a matter of straw, as in a matter of gold, is not of less importance on this account because it is kept in a matter of less value.

But, when fidelity is employed to commit sin, we wonder whether it ought to be called fidelity. However, whatever its nature may be, if even against this something is done, it has an added malice; except when this is abandoned with the view that there might be a return to the true and lawful fidelity, that is, that the sin might be amended by correcting the depravity of the will.

For example, if anyone, when he is unable to rob a man by himself, finds an accomplice for his crime and makes an agreement with him to perform the act together and share the loot, and, after the crime has been committed, he runs off with everything, the other naturally grieves and complains that fidelity had not been observed in his regard. In his very complaint he ought to consider that he should have observed his fidelity to human society by means of a good life, so that he would not rob a man unjustly, if he feels how wickedly fidelity was not kept with him in an association of sin. His partner, faithless on both counts, is certainly to be judged the more wicked. But, if he had been displeased with the wickedness which they had committed and so had refused to divide the spoils with his partner in crime on this account, that he could return them to the man from whom they were taken, not even the faithless man would call him faithless.

So, in the case of a woman who has broken her marriage fidelity but remains faithful to her adulterer, she is surely wicked, but, if she is not faithful even to her adulterer, she is worse. On the contrary, if she repents of her gross sin and returns to conjugal chastity and breaks off all adulterous unions and purposes, I cannot conceive of even the adulterer himself thinking of her as a violator of fidelity. . . .

While continence is of greater merit, it is no sin to render the conjugal debt, but to exact it beyond the need for generation is a venial sin; furthermore, to commit fornication or adultery is a crime that must be punished. Conjugal charity should be on its guard lest, while it seeks for itself the means of being honored more, it creates for the spouse the means of damnation. "Everyone who puts away his wife, save on account of immorality, causes her to commit adultery" [Matt. 5:32]. To such a degree is that nuptial pact which has been entered upon a kind of sacrament that it is not nullified by separation, since, as long as the husband, by whom she has been abandoned, is alive, she commits adultery if she marries another, and he who abandoned her is the cause of the evil.

7. I wonder if, as it is permitted to put away an adulterous wife, it is accordingly permitted, after she has been put away, to marry another. Holy Scripture creates a difficult problem in this matter, since the Apostle says that according to the command of the Lord a wife is not to depart from her husband, but, if she departs, she ought to remain unmarried or be reconciled to her husband [1 Cor. 7:10–11]. She surely ought not to withdraw and remain unmarried except in the case of an adulterous husband, lest, by withdrawing from him who is not an adulterer, she causes him to commit adultery. But, perhaps she can justly be reconciled with her husband either by tolerating him, if she on

her own part cannot contain herself, or after he has been corrected. But I do not see how a man can have freedom to marry another if he leaves an adulteress, since a woman does not have freedom to marry another if she leaves an adulterer.

If this is so, that bond of fellowship between married couples is so strong that, although it is tied for the purpose of procreation, it is not loosed for the purpose of procreation. For, a man might be able to dismiss a wife who is barren and marry someone by whom he might have children, yet in our times and according to Roman law it is not permissible to marry a second wife as long as he has another wife living. Surely, when an adulteress or adulterer is abandoned, more human beings could be born if either the woman were wed to another or the man married another. But, if this is not permitted, as divine Law seems to prescribe, who will not be eager to learn what the meaning of such a strong conjugal bond is? I do not think that this bond could by any means have been so strong, unless a symbol, as it were, of something greater than that which could arise from our weak mortality were applied, something that would remain unshaken for the punishment of men when they abandon and attempt to dissolve this bond, inasmuch as, when divorce intervenes, that nuptial contract is not destroyed, so that the parties of the compact are wedded persons even though separated. Moreover, they commit adultery with those with whom they have intercourse even after their repudiation, whether she with a man, or he with a woman. Yet, except "in the city of our God, His holy mountain" [Ps. 47:2], such is not the case with a woman. . . .

9. Surely we must see that God gives us some goods which are to be sought for their own sake, such as wisdom, health, friendship; others, which are necessary for something else, such as learning, food, drink, sleep, marriage, sexual intercourse. Certain of these are necessary for the sake of wisdom, such as learning; others for the sake of health, such as food and drink and sleep; others for the sake of friendship, such as marriage or intercourse, for from this comes the propagation of the human race in which friendly association is a great good. So, whoever does not use these goods, which are necessary for something else, for the purpose for which they are given does well. As for him for whom they are not necessary, if he does not use them, he does better. In like manner, we wish for these goods rightly when we have need, but we are better off not wishing for them than wishing for them, since we possess them in a better way when we possess them as not necessary.

For this reason it is a good to marry, since it is a good to beget children, to be the mother of a family; but it is better not to marry, since it is better for human society itself not to have need of marriage. For, such is the present state of the human race that not only some who do not check themselves are taken up with marriage, but many are wanton and given over to illicit intercourse. Since the good Creator draws good out of their evils, there is no lack of numerous progeny and an abundance of generation whence holy friendships might be sought out.

In this regard it is gathered that in the earliest times of the human race, especially to propagate the people of God, through whom the Prince and Savior of all peoples might both be prophesied and be born, the saints were obliged to make use of this good of marriage, to be sought not for its own sake but as necessary for something else. But now, since the opportunity for spiritual relationship abounds on all sides and for all peoples for entering into a holy and pure association, even they who wish to contract marriage only to have children are to be admonished that they practice the greater good of continence.

10. But I know what they murmur. 'What if,' they say, 'all men should be willing to restrain themselves from all intercourse, how would the human race survive?' Would that all men had this wish, if only in "charity, from a pure heart and a good conscience and faith unfeigned" [I Tim. 1:5]. Much more quickly would the City of God be filled and the end of time be hastened. What else does it appear that the Apostle is encouraging when he says, in speaking of this: "For I would that you all were as I am myself" [1 Cor. 7:7]? Or, in another place: "But this I say, brethren, the time is short; it remains that those who have wives be as if they had none; and those who weep, as though not weeping; and those who rejoice, as though not rejoicing; and those who buy, as though not buying; and those who use this world, as though not using it, for this world as we see it is passing away. I would have you free from care." Then he adds: "He who is unmarried thinks about the things of the Lord, how he may please the Lord. Whereas he who is married thinks about the things of the world, how he may please his wife, and he is divided. And the unmarried woman and the virgin, who is unmarried, is concerned about the things of the Lord, that she may be holy in body and in spirit. Whereas she who is married is concerned about the things of the world, how she may please her husband" [1 Cor. 7:29–34].

And so it seems to, me that at this time only those who do not restrain themselves ought to be married in accord with this saying of the same Apostle: "But if they do not have self-control, let them marry, for it is better to marry than to burn" [7:9].

11. Such marriage is not a sin. If it were chosen in preference to fornication, it would be a lesser sin than fornication, but still a sin. But now what are we to say in answer to that very clear statement of the Apostle when he says: "Let him do what he will; he does not sin if she should marry" [7:36] and "But if thou takest a wife, thou hast not sinned. And if a virgin marries, she does not sin" [7:28]. Certainly from this it is not right to doubt that marriage is not a sin. And so it is not the marriage that the Apostle grants as a pardon—for who would doubt that it is most absurd to say that they have not sinned to whom a pardon is granted—but it is that sexual intercourse that comes about through incontinence, not for the sake of procreation and at the time with no thought of procreation, that he grants as a pardon. Marriage does not force this type of intercourse to come about, but asks that it be pardoned, provided it is not so great as to encroach on the times that ought to be set aside for prayer, and does not degenerate into that practice that is against nature, which the Apostle was

not able to pass over in silence when he spoke of the extreme depravities of impure and impious men [Rom. 1:26].

The intercourse necessary for generation is without fault and it alone belongs to marriage. The intercourse that goes beyond this necessity no longer obeys reason but passion. Still, not to demand this intercourse but to render it to a spouse, lest he sin mortally by fornication, concerns the married person. But, if both are subject to such concupiscence, they do something that manifestly does not belong to marriage. However, if in their union they love what is proper rather than what is improper, that is, what belongs to marriage rather than that which does not, this is granted to them with the Apostle as an authority. They do not have a marriage that encourages this crime, but one that intercedes for them, if they do not turn away from themselves the mercy of God, either by not abstaining on certain days so as to be free for prayers, and by this abstinence as by their fasts they put their prayers in a favorable light, or by changing the natural use into that use which is contrary to nature, which is all the more damnable in a spouse.

12. For, although the natural use, when it goes beyond the marriage rights, that is, beyond the need for procreation, is pardonable in a wife but damnable in a prostitute, that use which is against nature is abominable in a prostitute but more abominable in a wife. For, the decree of the Creator and the right order of the creature are of such force that, even though there is an excess in the things that have been granted to be used, this is much more tolerable than a single or rare deviation in those things which have not been granted. Therefore, the immoderation of a spouse in a matter that is permitted is to be tolerated lest lust may break forth into something that has not been granted. So it is that, however demanding one is as regards his wife, he sins much less than one who commits fornication even most rarely.

But, when the husband wishes to use the member of his wife which has not been given for this purpose, the wife is more shameful if she permits this to take place with herself rather than with another woman. The crown of marriage, then, is the chastity of procreation and faithfulness in rendering the carnal debt. This is the province of marriage, this is what the Apostle defended from all blame by saying: "But if thou takest a wife, thou hast not sinned. And if a virgin marries, she does not sin" [1 Cor. 7:28] and "Let him do what he will; he does not sin, if she should marry" [7:36]. The somewhat immoderate departure in demanding the debt from the one or the other sex is given as a concession because of those things which he mentioned before.

[Augustine of Hippo, "On the Good of Marriage (De bono conjugali)," trans. Roy J. Deferrari, in *Saint Augustine: Treatises on Marriage and Other Subjects* (New York: Fathers of the Church, 1955), pp. 12–14, 17–19, 21–26]

JOHN CHRYSOSTOM

John Chrysostom (347–407 CE) earned his second name, which means "Golden Mouth," for the power of his preaching during decades in Antioch. One of the most influential scriptural exegetes and spiritual teachers in the eastern churches, John was traditionally credited with the authorship of the most frequently used Greek Eucharistic liturgy. A powerful advocate of the values of monastic life, John called his hearers out of their urban complacency and into the radical demands of Christian life. The selection here is from one of many homilies that he gave on the letters of Paul.

Document 2–12

JOHN CHRYSOSTOM, HOMILY 20 ON EPHESIANS 5:22–33

"Wives, be subject to your husbands, as to the Lord. For the husband is the head of the wife as Christ is the head of the Church, His Body, and is Himself its Savior. As the Church is subject to Christ, so let wives also be subject in everything to their husbands" [Eph. 5:22–24].

A certain wise man, when enumerating which blessings are most important included "a wife and husband who live in harmony" [Sir. 25:1]. In another place he emphasized this: "A friend or a companion never meets one amiss, but a wife with her husband is better than both" [Sir. 40:23]. From the beginning God in His providence has planned this union of man and woman, and has spoken of the two as one: "male and female He created them" [Gen. 1:27] and "there is neither male nor female, for you are all one *in Christ Jesus*" [Gal. 3:28]. There is no relationship between human beings so close as that of husband and wife, if they are united as they ought to be. When blessed David was mourning for Jonathan, who was of one soul with him, what comparison did he use to describe the loftiness of their love? "Your love to me was wonderful, passing the love of women" [2 Sam 1:26]. The power of this love is truly stronger than any passion; other desires may be strong, but this one alone never fades. This love (eros) is deeply planted within our inmost being. Unnoticed by us, it attracts the bodies of men and women to each other, because in the beginning woman came forth from man, and from man and woman other men and women proceed. Can you see now how close this union is, and how God providentially created it from a single nature? He permitted Adam to marry Eve, who was more than sister or daughter; she was his own flesh! God caused the entire human race to proceed from this one point of origin. He did not, on the one hand, fashion woman independently from man; otherwise man would think of her as essentially different from himself. Nor did He enable woman to bear children without man; if this were the case she would be self-sufficient. Instead, just as the branches of a tree proceed from a single trunk, He made the one man Adam to be the origin of all mankind, both male and female, and made it impossible for men and women to be self-sufficient. Later, He forbade men to marry their sisters or daughters, so that our love would not be limited to members of our families, and withdrawn from the rest of the human race.

All of this is implied in Christ's words: "He who made them from the beginning made them male and female" [Matt. 19:4].

The love of husband and wife is the force that welds society together. Men will take up arms and even sacrifice their lives for the sake of this love. St Paul would not speak so earnestly about this subject without serious reason; why else would he say, "Wives, be subject to your husbands, as to the Lord"? Because when harmony prevails, the children are raised well, the household is kept in order, and neighbors, friends and relatives praise the result. Great benefits, both for families and states, are thus produced. When it is otherwise, however, everything is thrown into confusion and turned upside-down. When the generals of an army are at peace with each other, everything proceeds in an orderly fashion, and when they are not, everything is in disarray. It is the same here. For the sake of harmony, then, he said, "Wives, be subject to your husbands as to the Lord." What? How can He say elsewhere, "Whoever does not renounce wife or husband cannot follow Me"? [cf. Lk. 14:33, 18:29] If a wife must be subject to her husband as to the Lord, how can He tell her to separate herself for the Lord's sake? Indeed she must be subject, but the word "as" does not always express equivalence. Either Paul means "as knowing that you are serving the Lord" (which indeed he says elsewhere, that even if the wife does not obey for her husband's sake, she must do so primarily for the Lord's sake); or else he means, "When you yield to your husband, consider that you are obeying him as part of your service to the Lord." If "he who resists the authorities (governments) resists what God has appointed, and those who resist will incur judgment" [Rom. 13:2], how much more severely will God judge someone who resists not an external authority, but that of her own husband, which God has willed from the beginning?

Let us assume, then, that the husband is to occupy the place of the head, and the wife that of the body, and listen to what "headship" means: "For the husband is the head of the wife as Christ is the head of the Church, His Body, and is Himself its Savior. As the Church is subject to Christ, so let wives also be subject in everything to their husbands" [Eph. 5:23–24]. Notice that after saying "the husband is the head of the wife as Christ is the head of the Church," he immediately says that the Church is His Body, and He is Himself its Savior. It is the head that upholds the wellbeing of the body. In his other epistles Paul has already laid the foundations of marital love, and has assigned to husband and wife each his proper place: to the husband one of leader and provider, and to the wife one of submission. Therefore as the Church is subject to Christ— and the Church, remember, consists of both husbands and wives—so let wives also be subject in everything to their husbands, as to God.

"Husbands, love your wives, just as Christ also loved the Church" [Eph. 5:25]. You have heard how important obedience is; you have praised and marveled at Paul, how he welds our whole life together, as we would expect from an admirable and spiritual man. You have done well. But now listen to what else he requires from you; he has not finished with his example. "Husbands," he says, "love your wives, as Christ loved the Church." You have seen the amount of obedience necessary; now hear about the amount of love necessary. Do you want your wife to be obedient to you, as the Church is to Christ? Then be responsible for the same providential care of her, as Christ is for the Church. And even if it becomes necessary for you to give your life for her, yes, and even to endure and undergo suffering of any kind, do not refuse. Even though you undergo all this, you will never have done anything equal to what Christ has done. You are sacrificing yourself for someone to whom you are already joined, but He offered Himself up for one who turned her back on Him and hated Him. In the same way, then, as He honored her by putting at His feet one who turned her back on Him, who hated, rejected, and disdained Him, as He accomplished this not with threats, or violence, or terror, or anything else like that, but through His untiring love; so also you should behave toward your wife. Even if you see her belittling you, or despising and mocking you, still you will be able to subject her to yourself, through affection, kindness, and your great regard for her. There is no influence more powerful than the bond of love, especially for husband and wife. A servant can be taught submission through fear; but even he, if provoked too much, will soon seek his escape. But one's partner for life, the mother of one's children, the source of one's every joy, should never be fettered with fear and threats, but with love and patience. What kind of marriage can there be when the wife is afraid of her husband? What sort of satisfaction could a husband himself have, if he lives with his wife as if she were a slave, and not with a woman by her own free will? Suffer anything for her sake, but never disgrace her, for Christ never did this with the Church. . . .

A wife should never nag her husband: "You lazy coward, you have no ambition! Look at our relatives and neighbors; they have plenty of money. Their wives have far more than I do." Let no wife say any such thing; she is her husband's body, and it is not for her to dictate to her head, but to submit and obey. "But why should she endure poverty?" some will ask. If she is poor, let her console herself by thinking of those who are much poorer still. If she really loved her husband, she would never speak to him like that, but would value having him close to her more than all the gold in the world. Likewise, if a husband has a wife who behaves this way, he must never exercise his authority by insulting and abusing her. Instead, he should show true nobility of spirit, and patiently remind her that in the wisdom of heaven, poverty is no evil. Then she will stop complaining. But he must not teach her only by words, but by deeds. He should teach her to be detached from high social position. If he is so himself, she will imitate him. Beginning on their wedding night, let him be an example of gentleness, temperance, and self-control; and she will be likewise. He should advise her not to decorate herself with golden earrings, necklaces, or other jewelry, or to accumulate expensive clothes. Instead, her appearance should be dignified, and dignity is never served by theatrical excess. Furnish your house neatly and soberly. If the bridegroom shows his wife that he takes no pleasure in worldly excess, and will not stand for it, their marriage will remain free from the evil influences that are so popular these days. Let them shun the immodest music and dancing that are currently so fashionable. I am aware that many people think me ridiculous for giving such advice; but if you listen to me, you will understand the advantages of a sober life-style more and more as time goes on. You will no longer laugh at me, but will laugh instead at the way people live now like silly children or drunken men. What is our duty, then? Remove from your lives shameful, immodest, and Satanic music, and don't associate with people who enjoy such profligate entertainment. When your bride sees your manner of life, she will say to herself, "Wonderful! What a wise man my husband is! He regards this passing life as nothing; he has married me to be a good mother for his children and a prudent manager of his household." Will this sort of life be distasteful for a young bride? Only perhaps for the shortest time, and soon she will discover how delightful it is to live this way. She will retain her modesty if you retain yours. Don't engage in idle conversations; it never profits anyone to talk too much. Whenever you give your wife advice, always begin by telling her how much you love her. Nothing will persuade her so well to admit the wisdom of your words as her assurance that you are speaking to her with sincere affection. Tell her that you are convinced that money is not important, that only thieves thirst for it constantly, that you love her more than gold; and indeed an intelligent, discreet, and pious young woman is worth more than all the money in the world. Tell her that you love her more than your own life, because this present life is nothing, and that your only hope is that the two of you pass through this life in such a way that in the world to come you will be united in perfect love. Say to her, "Our time here is brief and fleeting, but if we are pleasing to God, we can exchange this life for the Kingdom to come. Then we will be perfectly one both with Christ and each other, and our pleasure will know no bounds. I value your love above all things, and nothing would be so bitter or painful to me as our being at odds with each other. Even if I lose everything, any affliction is tolerable if you will be true to me." Show her that you value her company, and prefer being at home to being out. Esteem her in the presence of your friends and children. Praise and show admiration for her good acts; and if she ever does anything foolish, advise her patiently. Pray together at home and go to Church; when you come back home, let each ask the other the meaning of the readings and the prayers. If you are overtaken by poverty, remember Peter and Paul, who were more honored than kings or rich men, though they spent their lives in hunger and thirst. Remind one another that nothing in life is to be feared, except offending God. If your marriage is like this, your perfection will rival the holiest of monks.

[John Chrysostom, Homily 20 on Ephesians 5:22–33, in On Marriage and Family Life by St. John Chrysostom, trans. and ed. Catharine P. Roth and David Anderson (Crestwood, NY: St. Vladimir's Seminary Press, 1986), pp. 43–47, 58–62]

PETER LOMBARD

Peter Lombard (ca. 1000–1160) was for a very short time bishop of Paris, but he is important as a theological codifier. His *Four Books of Sentences* (compiled 1148–1151) became the standard textbook of Latin theology for several centuries. In the *Sentences* Peter Lombard arranges opinions *(sententiae)* from earlier authorities under a system of topics based on the Christian creeds or professions of faith. He then offers coherent models for clarifying and resolving any points of dispute. Peter's models for the sacraments or central rites of Christian liturgy, including marriage, proved particularly influential, as did his emphasis on spousal consent.

Document 2–13

PETER LOMBARD, BOOK OF SENTENCES, BOOK 4. DISTINCTION 26

1.1. *Concerning the sacrament of marriage: the institution and cause of which is shown.* Although the other sacraments began after sin and on account of sin, it is read that the sacrament of marriage rather was instituted by the Lord, even before sin, not as a remedy but as an office. . . .

2.1. *Concerning the twofold institution of marriage.* Moreover, the institution of marriage is twofold. The first was created in paradise, before sin, as an office, where the bed was unstained and marriages were honorable, from which Adam and Eve conceived without passion, gave birth without pain. The second was created outside paradise, after sin, as a remedy, in order to avoid illicit passions. The first was so that nature would be multiplied, the second so that nature might be excused and sin avoided. For, before sin, God said: "Go forth and multiply" (Gen. 1.28) and also, after sin, when almost every human being had perished in the flood (Gen. 9.1). . . .

2.3. If the first human beings had not sinned, they and their progeny would have joined without the urging of the flesh and the heat of lust. Just as some good deed is worthy of a reward, so their coitus would have been good and worthy of a reward. But, because of sin, the deadly law of concupiscence is inherent in our members, without which there is no carnal union. Their coitus is reprehensible and evil, unless it is excused by the goods of marriage. . . .

5.2. That marriage is a good thing is shown not only by the fact that the Lord is said to have instituted marriage between our first parents, but also because Christ was present at a marriage at Cana in Galilee, and he commended it with a miracle, turning the water into wine (John 2.2–10). Also, afterwards, he forbade a husband to dismiss his wife, except for the reason of fornication (Matt. 5.32, Mark 10.11, Luke 16.18). Also, the Apostle Paul said: "A virgin does not sin if she marries" (1 Cor. 7.28). Therefore, it is established that marriage is a good thing. Otherwise it would not be a sacrament, for a sacrament is a holy sign.

BOOK 4. DISTINCTION 27

2. *What marriage is.* Therefore, nuptials or marriage is the marital union of a man and a woman, between lawful persons, maintaining an indivisible mode of life. "An indivisible mode of life" means that neither is able to profess continence or withdraw for prayer without the consent of the other, and that while they are alive, a conjugal bond endures between them, so that it is not licit for them to join with another, and each shall offer to the other that which belongs to each. Moreover, in this description only the marriage of lawful and faithful persons is included.

3.1. *Concerning the consent which makes marriage.* Moreover, the efficient cause of marriage is consent, not any kind but that expressed by words, not in the future tense but in the present tense. For if they consent in the future tense, saying I will take you as my husband, and I will take you as my wife, this consent does not make marriage. Likewise, if they consent in their minds and do not express it by words or by other sure signs, neither does such consent make marriage. Moreover, if consent were expressed in words, even though they did not will it in their heart, then that bond of the words with which they consented, saying I take you as my husband and I take you as my wife, makes marriage, provided that there was no coercion or deceit there. . . .

4.1. *When marriage begins to exist.* But, in fact, they are spouses from that promise in which the marital agreement is expressed. . . .

5.1. *According to some there is no marriage before sexual intercourse, but rather they are betrothed persons.* Some, nevertheless, assert that true marriage is not contracted before the bride is handed over and sexual intercourse occurs, nor are they truly spouses before sexual union occurs, but rather that from the first promise of betrothal the man is a bridegroom and the woman a bride, not a spouse. Moreover, they say that betrothed men and women are frequently called "spouses" not because they are but because they will be, since they have made a solemn promise between them concerning this matter. And on this account they claim that the words of the previous authorities must be understood in this way.

5.2 *On what reason they depend.* But they argue further that there is a great difference between a bride and a wife from this, that although a bride is allowed to choose to enter a convent before consummation, without consulting her bridegroom or even when he is unwilling, this done, the bridegroom is also allowed to marry another. But a married man or a married woman cannot preserve continence, except by mutual consent, nor enter monastic life, unless both of them equally profess continence. . . .

BOOK 4. DISTINCTION 28

2.1. *Those things which pertain to the necessity and those to the propriety of the sacrament.* For in celebration of this sacrament, just as in others, there are certain things pertinent to the substance of the sacrament, such as present consent, which alone is sufficient to contract marriage. But there are certain things that are pertinent to the propriety and solemnity of the sacrament, such as the handing over of the bride by her parents, the blessing of the priest, and such like, without which the marriage occurs lawfully as to its power but not as to the propriety of the sacrament.

2.2. Therefore, without these things, they do not come together as lawful spouses but as adulterers and fornicators. So, too, those who marry in secret, they especially are fornicators, unless consent expressed in words of the present tense should support them, which consent makes a lawful marriage. For secret consent, expressed in words of the present tense, also makes marriage, although there it is not an honest contract. But consent does not ratify a marriage which was made in secret. For if one should dismiss the other, he or she is not forced to return and remain with his or her spouse by the judgment of the church, because a contract which was made in secret cannot be proved by witnesses. But if they, themselves, who consented to each other in secret, should voluntarily declare that same consent in public, then the proper consent supports them and lawful vows help them to ratify the marriage which previously had been contracted secretly. Therefore, consent expressed secretly by words supports them that a marriage occurred, but expressed publicly supports them to sanction and strengthen the marriage, and makes *it* possible for the church to judge concerning this, if need be.

3.1. *Concerning the very nature of that consent, whether it is to sexual intercourse, to cohabitation, or to something else.* This is asked since present consent makes marriage, of what nature that consent is, whether it is to sexual intercourse or to cohabitation or to both. If consent to cohabitation makes marriage, then a brother is able to contract marriage with his sister, a father with his daughter. If it is to sexual intercourse, then there was no marriage between Mary and Joseph. For Mary proposed to remain a virgin unless God ordered her to do otherwise, according to that which she is seen to have said to the angel: "How can this be since I do not know a man?" (Luke 1.34). That is, I have decided that I will not know a man. For it was not necessary for her to ask how she could have a son because she did not then know a man but because she had decided she would never do so. Bede, in his Commentary on Luke, said that she intended to remain a virgin. Therefore, if she afterwards consented to sexual intercourse, contrary to her intention, it would seem that she would have been guilty concerning the vow, even if it was not violated in deed.

3.2. *Behold what that consent was to.* Therefore, let us say that consent to cohabitation or to sexual intercourse does not make marriage, but rather consent to conjugal partnership, expressed according to words *in* the present tense, as when a man says, "I take you as my wife," not mistress, not servant, but spouse.

BOOK 4. DISTINCTION 29

1.3. From this it appears that marriage is to be made between persons consenting voluntarily, not between those resisting and unwilling. Nevertheless, those who are unwilling and forced to marry, if afterwards they cohabited for some length of time, without objection and complaint, with the ability to separate and the disposition to protest, they would seem to consent and that consequent consent supplies that which the preceding coercion took away. . . .

BOOK 4. DISTINCTION 30

3.2. Therefore, the final cause [goal, purpose] for contracting marriage is principally the procreation of children. For, on account of this, God instituted marriage between the first parents, to whom He said: "Go forth and multiply." The second reason, after the sin of Adam, is to avoid fornication. Whence the Apostle Paul said: "On account of fornication let each man have his own wife and each woman her own husband" (1 Cor. 7.2). And there are other honest reasons such as the reconciliation of enemies and the reestablishment of peace. There are also other less honest reasons, on account of which it is sometimes contracted, such as the beauty of a man or woman which frequently impels souls inflamed by love to enter into marriage, so that they are able to satisfy their desire. Also, profit and the possession of riches is frequently a reason for marriage; and there are many others which it is easy for the diligent reader to discern. . . .

BOOK 4. DISTINCTION 31

5.1. *Concerning the excusing of intercourse which happens for the sake of these goods.* Therefore, when these three goods [faithfulness, sacrament, children] occur together in any marriage they can excuse sexual intercourse. For when spouses join for the sake of conceiving children, preserving the faithfulness of the marriage bed, intercourse is thus excused so that it has no blame. But when they come together because of incontinence, with the good of offspring lacking, even though marital faithfulness is preserved, the intercourse is not thus excused so that it bears no blame, but the fault is venial. Whence Augustine wrote in his book, *On the Good of Marriage*: "Marital intercourse for the sake of procreation has no guilt, however, marital intercourse for the sake of satisfying concupiscence, even though with one's spouse, on account of the faithfulness of the marriage bed, has venial guilt." Likewise: "The fact that married people, conquered by lust, use each other beyond what is necessary for procreating children, I count among those things for which we say each day: 'forgive us our trespasses.'"

[Translated in Love, Marriage, and Family in the Middle Ages: A Reader, ed. and trans. Jacqueline Murray (Peterborough: Broadview, 2001), pp. 171–176]

THE FOURTH LATERAN COUNCIL

The Fourth Lateran Council (1215) is counted by Roman Catholics an ecumenical or churchwide council (and the fourth held at the Lateran Palace in Rome). Unlike some of its predecessors, it did indeed bring together hundreds of bishops and heads of religious houses, not to say representatives of sovereign rulers. The Council was convened by Pope Innocent III with the twin purposes of reconquering the Holy Land and reforming the western churches, especially in matters of pastoral practice. The two canons or individual pieces of legislation given here are only a small sample of the council's decisions.

Document 2–14

FOURTH LATERAN COUNCIL, CANONS 50–51

CANON 50

Summary. The prohibitions against marriage in the second and third degrees of affinity and against the union of the offspring from second marriages to a relative of the first husband, are removed. This prohibition does not apply beyond the fourth degree of consanguinity and affinity.

Text. It must not be deemed reprehensible if human statutes change sometimes with the change of time, especially when urgent necessity or common interest demands it, since God himself has changed in the New Testament some things that He had decreed in the Old. Since, therefore, the prohibition against the contracting of marriage in the second and third kind of affinity [or degree of familial relation] and that against the union of the offspring from second marriages to a relative of the first husband, frequently constitute a source of difficulty and sometimes are a cause of danger to souls, that by a cessation of the prohibition the effect may cease also, we, with the approval of the holy council, revoking previous enactments in this matter, decree in the present statute that such persons may in the future contract marriage without hindrance. The prohibition also is not in the future to affect marriages beyond the fourth degree of consanguinity and affinity; since in degrees beyond the fourth a prohibition of this kind cannot be generally observed without grave inconvenience. This quaternary number agrees well with the prohibition of corporal wedlock of which the Apostle says that "the wife hath not power of her own body, but the husband; and in like manner the husband also hath not power of his own body, but the wife" (1 Cor. 7:4); because there are four humors in the body, which consists of four elements. Since therefore the prohibition of conjugal union is restricted to the fourth degree, we wish that it remain so in perpetuity, notwithstanding the decrees already issued relative to this matter either by others or by ourselves, and should anyone presume to contract marriage contrary to this prohibition, no number of years shall excuse him, since duration of time does not palliate the gravity of sin but rather aggravates it, and his crimes are the graver the longer he holds his unhappy soul in bondage.

CANON 51

Summary. Clandestine marriages and witness to them by a priest are forbidden. Marriages to be contracted must be published in the churches by the priests so that, if legitimate impediments exist, they may be made known. If doubt exists, let the contemplated marriage be forbidden till the matter is cleared up.

Text. Since the prohibition of the conjugal union in the three last degrees has been revoked, we wish that it be strictly observed in the other degrees. Whence, following in the footsteps of our predecessors, we absolutely forbid clandestine marriages; and we forbid also that a priest presume to witness such. Wherefore, extending to other localities generally the particular custom that prevails in some, we decree that when marriages are to be contracted they must be announced publicly in the churches by the priests during a suitable and fixed time, so that if legitimate impediments exist, they may be made known. Let the priests nevertheless investigate whether any impediments exist. But when there is ground for doubt concerning the contemplated union, let the marriage be expressly forbidden until it is evident from reliable sources what ought to be done in regard to it. But if anyone should presume to contract a clandestine or forbidden marriage of this kind within a prohibited degree, even through ignorance, the children from such a union shall be considered illegitimate, nor shall the ignorance of the parents bc pleaded as an extenuating circumstance in their behalf, since they by contracting such marriages appear not as wanting in knowledge but rather as affecting ignorance. In like manner the children shall be considered illegitimate if both parents, knowing that a legitimate impediment exists, presume to contract such a marriage before the church in disregard of every prohibition. The parochial priest who deliberately neglects to forbid such unions, or any regular priest who presumes to witness them, let them be suspended from office for a period of three years and, if the nature of their offense demands it, let them be punished more severely. On those also who presume to contract such marriages in a lawful degree, a condign punishment is to be imposed. If anyone maliciously presents an impediment for the purpose of frustrating a legitimate marriage, let him not escape ecclesiastical punishment.

[*Disciplinary Decrees of the General Councils: Text, Translation, and Commentary,* trans. and ed. H. J. Schroeder (St. Louis: Herder, 1937), pp. 279–281]

THOMAS AQUINAS

During the last four or five centuries Thomas Aquinas (1224/25–1274) has been firmly established as a leading authority for Roman Catholic theology. In his own lifetime he was regarded as brilliant and controversial, especially in his appropriation of non-Christian philosophy and natural science. The selection here is drawn from his *Summa "Against the Gentiles"* (1261–1265) in which Thomas explores how far philosophic argument can reach in understanding God, the world, and human beings. In it he reasons from human nature to secure basic moral principles for marriage.

Document 2–15

THOMAS AQUINAS, SUMMA CONTRA GENTILES, BOOK 3, CHAPTER 122

The Reason Why Simple Fornication Is a Sin according to Divine Law, and That Matrimony is Natural

1. From the foregoing we can see the futility of the argument of certain people who say that simple fornication is not a sin. For they say: Suppose there is a woman who is not married, or under the control of any man, either her father or another man. Now, if a man performs the sexual act with her, and she is willing, he does not injure her, because she favors the action and she has control over her own body. Nor does he injure any other person, because she is understood to be under no other person's control. So, this does not seem to be a sin.

2. Now, to say that he injures God would not seem to be an adequate answer. For we do not offend God except by doing something contrary to our own good, as has been said [in chapter 121]. But this does not appear contrary to man's good. Hence, on this basis, no injury seems to be done to God.

3. Likewise, it also would seem an inadequate answer to say that some injury is done to one's neighbor by this action, inasmuch as he may be scandalized. Indeed, it is possible for him to be scandalized by something which is not in itself a sin. In this event, the act would be accidentally sinful. But our problem is not whether simple fornication is accidentally a sin, but whether it is so essentially.

4. Hence, we must look for a solution in our earlier considerations. We have said [in chapters 112 and following] that God exercises care over every person on the basis of what is good for him. Now, it is good for each person to attain his end, whereas it is bad for him to swerve away from his proper end. Now, this should be considered applicable to the parts, just as it is to the whole being; for instance, each and every part of man, and every one of his acts, should attain the proper end. Now, though the male semen is superfluous in regard to the preservation of the individual, it is nevertheless necessary in regard to the propagation of the species. Other superfluous things, such as excrement, urine, sweat, and such things, are not at all necessary; hence, their emission contributes to man's good. Now, this is not what is sought in the case of semen, but, rather, to emit it for the purpose of generation, to which purpose the sexual act

is directed. But man's generative process would be frustrated unless it were followed by proper nutrition, because the offspring would not survive if proper nutrition were withheld. Therefore, the emission of semen ought to be so ordered that it will result in both the production of the proper offspring and in the upbringing of this offspring.

5. It is evident from this that every emission of semen, in such a way that generation cannot follow, is contrary to the good for man. And if this be done deliberately, it must be a sin. Now, I am speaking of a way from which, *in itself*, generation could not result: such would be any emission of semen apart from the natural union of male and female. For which reason, sins of this type are called contrary to nature. But, if by accident generation cannot result from the emission of semen, then this is not a reason for it being against nature, or a sin; as for instance, if the woman happens to be sterile.

6. Likewise, it must also be contrary to the good for man if the semen be emitted under conditions such that generation could result but the proper upbringing would be prevented. We should take into consideration the fact that, among some animals where the female is able to take care of the upbringing of offspring, male and female do not remain together for any time after the act of generation. This is obviously the case with dogs. But in the case of animals of which the female is not able to provide for the upbringing of offspring, the male and female do stay together after the act of generation as long as is necessary for the upbringing and instruction of the offspring. Examples are found among certain species of birds whose young are not able to seek out food for themselves immediately after hatching. In fact, since a bird does not nourish its young with milk, made available by nature as it were, as occurs in the case of quadrupeds, but the bird must look elsewhere for food for its young, and since besides this it must protect them by sitting on them, the female is not able to do this by herself. So, as a result of divine providence, there is naturally implanted in the male of these animals a tendency to remain with the female in order to bring up the young. Now, it is abundantly evident that the female in the human species is not at all able to take care of the upbringing of offspring by herself, since the needs of human life demand many things which cannot be provided by one person alone. Therefore, it is appropriate to human nature that a man remain together with a woman after the generative act, and not leave her immediately to have such relations with another woman, as is the practice with fornicators.

7. Nor, indeed, is the fact that a woman may be able by means of her own wealth to care for the child by herself an obstacle to this argument. For natural rectitude in human acts is not dependent on things accidentally possible in the case of one individual, but, rather, on those conditions which accompany the entire species.

8. Again, we must consider that in the human species offspring require not only nourishment for the body, as in the case of other animals, but also edu-

cation for the soul. For other animals naturally possess their own kinds of prudence whereby they are enabled to take care of themselves. But a man lives by reason, which he must develop by lengthy, temporal experience so that he may achieve prudence. Hence, children must be instructed by parents who are already experienced people. Nor are they able to receive such instruction as soon as they are born, but after a long time, and especially after they have reached the age of discretion. Moreover, a long time is needed for this instruction. Then, too, because of the impulsion of the passions, through which prudent judgment is vitiated, they require not merely instruction but correction. Now, a woman alone is not adequate to this task; rather, this demands the work of a husband, in whom reason is more developed for giving instruction and strength is more available for giving punishment. Therefore, in the human species, it is not enough, as in the case of birds, to devote a small amount of time to bringing up offspring, for a long period of life is required. Hence, since among all animals it is necessary for male and female to remain together as long as the work of the father is needed by the offspring, it is natural to the human being for the man to establish a lasting association with a designated woman, over no short period of time. Now, we call this society *matrimony*. Therefore, matrimony is natural for man, and promiscuous performance of the sexual act, outside matrimony, is contrary to man's good. For this reason, it must be a sin.

9. Nor, in fact, should it be deemed a slight sin for a man to arrange for the emission of semen apart from the proper purpose of generating and bringing up children, on the argument that it is either a slight sin, or none at all, for a person to use a part of the body for a different use than that to which it is directed by nature (say, for instance, one chose to walk on his hands, or to use his feet for something usually done with the hands) because man's good is not much opposed by such inordinate use. However, the inordinate emission of semen is incompatible with the natural good; namely, the preservation of the species. Hence, after the sin of homicide whereby a human nature already in existence is destroyed, this type of sin appears to take next place, for by it the generation of human nature is precluded.

10. Moreover, these views which have just been given have a solid basis in divine authority. That the emission of semen under conditions in which offspring cannot follow is illicit is quite clear. There is the text of Leviticus (18:22–23): "thou shalt not lie with mankind as with womankind . . . and thou shalt not copulate with any beast." And in 1 Corinthians (6:10): "Nor the effeminate, nor liers with mankind . . . shall possess the kingdom of God."

11. Also, that fornication and every performance of the act of reproduction with a person other than one's wife are illicit is evident. For it is said: "There shall be no whore among the daughters of Israel, nor whoremonger among the sons of Israel" (Deut. 23:17); and in Tobias (4:13): "Take heed to keep thyself

from all fornication, and beside thy wife never endure to know a crime"; and in 1 Corinthians (6:18): "Fly fornication."

12. By this conclusion we refute the error of those who say that there is no more sin in the emission of semen than in the emission of any other superfluous matter, and also of those who state that fornication is not a sin.

[Thomas Aquinas, *Summa Contra Gentiles*, trans. Vernon Bourke (Garden City, NY: Image/Doubleday, 1956), pp. 52–57]

MECHTHILD OF MAGDEBURG

Mechthild of Magdeburg (ca. 1210–ca. 1282) was a contemplative nun who recorded and interpreted her ongoing visions in a book known as *The Flowing Light of the Godhead* (begun around 1250). She was nurtured by one of the many medieval networks that served as "invisible colleges" for religious women. Mechthild's writing, marked by bold poetry, falls into a long line of works that appropriate the languages of erotic passion and marriage to describe the soul's encounters with God.

Document 2–16

MECHTHILD OF MAGDEBURG, *THE FLOWING LIGHT OF THE GODHEAD*

12. How a Bride Who Is United with God Rejects Consolation from All Creatures Except for That from God Alone, and How She Sinks Into Pain

So speaks God's bride who has taken her rest in the sealed treasury of the holy complete Trinity: "Oh, get up and depart from me, all you creatures! You cause me pain and you are not able to console me."

The creatures say: "Why?"

The bride says: "My Love left me as I slept, as I was resting in oneness with him."

"Can't this beautiful world and all the good it contains console you?"

"No, I see the snake of deceit and how treacherous cunning slithers into all the pleasures of this world. I also see the hook of lust in the carcass of base sweetness with which she catches many."

"Can the kingdom of heaven console you at all?"

"No, in itself it would be dead if the living God were not there."

"Well then, Lady Bride, can't the saints console you?"

"No, if they were to be separated from the living God flowing through them, they would weep more bitterly than I; for they have ascended above me and dwell deeper in God."

"Can God's Son ever console you?"

"Yes, I certainly ask him when we stroll through the flowers of holy knowledge, and I beg him full of longing that he open up for me the playful flood flowing in the Holy Trinity from which alone the soul lives.

> If I am to be consoled in proportion to my nobility,
> God's breath must draw me effortlessly into itself,
> For the sparkling sun of the living Godhead
> Shines through the bright water of cheerful humanity,
> And the sweet pleasure of the Holy Spirit
> Who proceeds from them both
> Has taken from me everything
> That dwells beneath the Godhead.
> Nothing tastes good to me but God alone;
> I am wondrously dead.
> I am freely willing to give up this taste
> So that he be wonderfully praised.
> For when I, a worthless human being, cannot praise God with my powers,
> I send all creatures to court
> And bid them that they praise God for me
> With all their wisdom,
> With all their love,
> With all their beauty,
> And with all their longing,
> Just as they were created by God in innocence,
> And also with all their voices
> As they now sing.
> When I look upon this great praising,
> I feel no pain.

"I cannot endure that a single consolation touch me except my Lover. I love my earthly friends in the company of heaven and I love my enemies in holy aching for their happiness. God has enough of everything; caressing souls is the only thing he cannot get enough of."

[Mechthild of Magdeburg, *The Flowing Light of the Godhead*, trans. Frank Tobin (Mahwah, N.J.: Paulist, 1998), pp. 152–156]

MARTIN LUTHER

Martin Luther (1483–1546) stands astride western church history as the great reformer. There were Christian reform movements before his, inside and outside the churches, but none had succeeded either in establishing a separate institution or in articulating a full, alternate theology. Formed as a friar and drilled in scholastic teaching, Luther became convinced over years that church doctrine and practice had departed from scriptural revelation and the example of the early church. He condemned with particular severity the exaltation of vowed celibacy over marriage and the needless complexities in canon law for betrothal, marriage, and divorce. The selection here is an early sermon (1519) written before Luther had published his great reforming treatises or been excommunicated by the pope.

Document 2–17

MARTIN LUTHER, A SERMON ON THE ESTATE OF MARRIAGE

1. God created Adam and brought all the animals before him. Adam did not find a proper companion among them suitable for marriage, so God then said, "It is not good that Adam should be alone. I will create a helpmeet for him to be with him always." And he sent a deep sleep upon Adam, and took a rib from him, and closed his side up again. And out of this very rib taken from Adam, God created a woman and brought her to him. Then Adam said, "This is bone of my bone, and flesh of my flesh. She shall be called a woman, because she was taken from her man. This is why a man shall leave his father and mother and cleave to his wife, and the two shall be one flesh" [Gen. 2:18–24].

All of this is from God's word. These words teach us where man and woman come from, how they were given to one another, for what purpose a wife was created, and what kind of love there should be in the estate of marriage.

2. If God himself does not give the wife or the husband, anything can happen. For the truth indicated here is that Adam found no marriageable partner for himself, but as soon as God had created Eve and brought her to him, he felt a real married love toward her, and recognized that she was his wife. Those who want to enter into the estate of marriage should learn from this that they should earnestly pray to God for a spouse. For the sage says that parents provide goods and houses for their children, but a wife is given by God alone [Prov. 19:14], everyone according to his need, just as Eve was given to Adam by God alone. And true though it is that because of excessive lust of the flesh light-hearted youth pays scant attention to these matters, marriage is nevertheless a weighty matter in the sight of God. For it was not by accident that Almighty God instituted the estate of matrimony only for man and above all animals, and gave such forethought and consideration to marriage. To the other animals God says quite simply, "Be fruitful and multiply" [Gen. 1:22]. It is not written that he brings the female to the male. Therefore, there is no such thing as marriage among animals. But in the case of Adam, God creates for him a unique, special kind of wife out of his own flesh. He brings her to him, he gives her to him, and Adam agrees to accept her. Therefore, that is what marriage is.

3. A woman is created to be a companionable helpmeet to the man in everything, particularly to bear children. And that still holds good, except that since the fall marriage has been adulterated with wicked lust. And now [i.e.,

after the human fall into sin] the desire of the man for the woman, and vice versa, is sought after not only for companionship and children, for which purposes alone marriage was instituted, but also for the pursuance of wicked lust, which is almost as strong a motive.

4. God makes distinctions between the different kinds of love, and shows that the love of a man and woman is (or should be) the greatest and purest of all loves. For he says, "A man shall leave his father and mother and cleave to his wife" [Gen. 2:24], and the wife does the same, as we see happening around us every day. Now there are three kinds of love: false love, natural love, and married love. False love is that which seeks its own, as a man loves money, possessions, honor, and women taken outside of marriage and against God's command. Natural love is that between father and child, brother and sister, friend and relative, and similar relationships. But over and above all these is married love, that is, a bride's love, which glows like a fire and desires nothing but the husband. She says, "It is you I want, not what is yours: I want neither your silver nor your gold; I want neither. I want only you. I want you in your entirety, or not at all." All other kinds of love seek something other than the loved one: this kind wants only to have the beloved's own self completely. If Adam had not fallen, the love of bride and groom would have been the loveliest thing. Now this love is not pure either, for admittedly a married partner desires to have the other, yet each seeks to satisfy his desire with the other, and it is this desire which corrupts this kind of love. Therefore, the married state is now no longer pure and free from sin. The temptation of the flesh has become so strong and consuming that marriage may be likened to a hospital for incurables which prevents inmates from falling into graver sin. Before Adam fell it was a simple matter to remain virgin and chaste, but now it is hardly possible, and without special grace from God, quite impossible. For this very reason neither Christ nor the apostles sought to make chastity a matter of obligation. It is true that Christ counseled chastity, and he left it up to each one to test himself, so that if he could not be continent he was free to marry, but if by the grace of God he could be continent, then chastity is better.

Thus the doctors [that is, church theologians] have found three good and useful things about the married estate, by means of which the sin of lust, which flows beneath the surface, is counteracted and ceases to be a cause of damnation.

First, [the doctors say] that it is a sacrament. A sacrament is a sacred sign of something spiritual, holy, heavenly, and eternal, just as the water of baptism, when the priest pours it over the child, means that the holy, divine, eternal grace is poured into the soul and body of that child at the same time, and cleanses him from his original sin. This also means that the kingdom of God, which is an inestimable benefit, in fact immeasurably greater than the water which conveys this meaning, is within him. In the same way the estate of marriage is a sacrament. It is an outward and spiritual sign of the greatest, holiest, worthiest, and noblest thing that has ever existed or ever will exist: the union of the divine and human natures in Christ. The holy apostle Paul says that as man and wife united in the estate of matrimony are two in one flesh, so God and man are united in the one person Christ, and so Christ and Christendom are one body. It is indeed a wonderful sacrament, as Paul says [Eph. 5:32], that the estate of marriage truly signifies such a great reality. Is it not a wonderful thing that God is man and that he gives himself to man and will be his, just as the husband gives himself to his wife and is hers? But if God is ours, then everything is ours.

Consider this matter with the respect it deserves. Because the union of man and woman signifies such a great mystery, the estate of marriage has to have this special significance. This means that the wicked lust of the flesh, which nobody is without, is a conjugal obligation and is not reprehensible when expressed within marriage, but in all other cases outside the bond of marriage, it is mortal sin. In a parallel way the holy manhood of God covers the shame of the wicked lust of the flesh. Therefore, a married man should have regard for such a sacrament, honor it as sacred, and behave properly in marital obligations, so that those things which originate in the lust of the flesh do not occur [among us] as they do in the world of brute beasts.

Second, [the doctors say] that marriage is a covenant of fidelity. The whole basis and essence of marriage is that each gives himself or herself to the other, and they promise to remain faithful to each other and not give themselves to any other. By binding themselves to each other, and surrendering themselves to each other, the way is barred to the body of anyone else, and they content themselves in the marriage bed with their one companion. In this way God sees to it that the flesh is subdued so as not to rage wherever and however it pleases, and, within this plighted troth, permits even more occasion than is necessary for the begetting of children. But, of course, a man has to control himself and not make a filthy sow's sty of his marriage. . . .

Third, [the doctors say] that marriage produces offspring, for that is the end and chief purpose of marriage. It is not enough, however, merely for children to be born, and so what they say about marriage excusing sin does not apply in this case. Heathen, too, bear offspring. But unfortunately it seldom happens that we bring up children to serve God, to praise and honor him, and want nothing else of them. People seek only heirs in their children, or pleasure in them; the serving of God finds what place it can. You also see people rush into marriage and become mothers and fathers before they know what the commandments are or can pray.

But this at least all married people should know. They can do no better work and do nothing more valuable either for God, for Christendom, for all the world, for themselves, and for their children than to bring up their children well. In comparison with this one work, that married people should bring up their children properly, there is nothing at all in pilgrimages to Rome, Jerusalem, or Compostella [in Spain], nothing at all in building churches, endowing masses, or whatever good works could be named. For bringing up their children properly is their shortest road to heaven. In fact, heaven itself could not be made nearer or achieved more easily than by doing this work. It is also their appointed work. Where parents are not conscientious about this, it is as if everything were the wrong way around, like fire that will not burn or water that is not wet.

By the same token, hell is no more easily earned than with respect to one's own children. You could do no more disastrous work than to spoil the children, let them curse and swear, let them learn profane words and vulgar songs, and just let them do as they please. What is more, some parents use enticements to be more alluring to meet the dictates of the world of fashion, so that they may please only the world, get ahead, and become rich, all the time giving more attention to the care of the body than to the due care of the soul. There is no greater tragedy in Christendom than spoiling children. If we want to help Christendom, we most certainly have to start with the children, as happened in earlier times.

This third point seems to me to be the most important of all, as well as being the most useful. For without a shadow of doubt it is not only a matter of marital obligation, but can completely eclipse all other sins. False natural love blinds parents so that they have more regard for the bodies of their children than they have for their souls. It was because of this that the sage said, "He who spares the rod hates his son, but he who loves him is diligent to discipline him" [Prov. 13:24]. Again, "Folly is bound up in the heart of a child, but the rod of discipline drives it far from him" [Prov. 22:15]. Or again, "If you beat him with the rod you will save his life from hell" [Prov. 23:14]. Therefore, it is of the greatest importance for every married man to pay closer, more thorough, and continuous attention to the health of his child's soul than to the body which he has begotten, and to regard his child as nothing else but an eternal treasure God has commanded him to protect, and so prevent the world, the flesh, and the devil from stealing the child away and bringing him to destruction. For at his death and on the day of judgment he will be asked about his child and will have to give a most solemn account. For what do you think is the cause of the horrible wailing and howling of those who will cry, "O blessed are the wombs which have not bore children, and the breasts which have never suckled" [Luke 23:29]? There is not the slightest doubt that it is because they have failed to restore their children to God, from whom they received them to take care of them.

O what a truly noble, important, and blessed condition the estate of marriage is if it is properly regarded! O what a truly pitiable, horrible, and dangerous condition it is if it is not properly regarded! And to him who bears these things in mind the desire of the flesh may well pass away, and perhaps he could just as well take on chastity as the married state. The young people take a poor view of this and follow only their desires, but God will consider it important and wait on him who is in the right.

Finally, if you really want to atone for all your sins, if you want to obtain the fullest remission [or indulgence] of them on earth as well as in heaven, if you want to see many generations of your children, then look but at this third point with all the seriousness you can muster and bring up your children properly. If you cannot do so, seek out other people who can and ask them to do it. Spare yourself neither money nor expense, neither trouble nor effort, for your children are the churches, the altar, the testament, the vigils and masses for the dead for which you make provision in your will. It is they who will lighten you in your hour of death, and to your journey's end.

> [Martin Luther, "A Sermon on the Estate of Marriage," trans. James Atkinson, in *Luther's Works*, ed. Jaroslav Pelikan and Helmut Lehman (St. Louis: Fortress, 1955–76), vol. 44, pp. 7–14]

ANGLICAN *BOOK OF COMMON PRAYER* (1549)

Thomas Cranmer (1489–1556) is sometimes described as the first engineer of the separation between the Church of England and the papacy. An academic theologian attracted early to the ideas of Luther, Cranmer was propelled to prominence by King Henry VIII, who ended by making him Archbishop of Canterbury—even though he was married. In that office Cranmer undertook systematic reform. He put English Bibles into the churches and oversaw the compilation of an English *Book of Common Prayer* (first edition, 1549). A team of theologians gathered material for the book, but Cranmer's liturgical sensibilities can be felt throughout it. In these selections the spelling and some punctuation has been modernized, but the distinctive language has been left, especially because it still echoes in many English-speaking weddings.

Document 2–18

ANGLICAN *BOOK OF COMMON PRAYER*, THE FORM OF
SOLEMNIZATION OF MATRIMONY

At the day appointed for Solemnization of Matrimony, the persons to be married shall come into the body of the church, with their friends and neighbors. And there the priest shall thus say.

Dearly beloved friends, we are gathered together here in the sight of God, and in the face of his congregation, to join together this man and this woman in holy matrimony, which is an honorable estate instituted of God in paradise, in the time of man's innocence, signifying unto us the mystical union that is between Christ and his Church: which holy estate, Christ adorned and beautified with his presence, and first miracle that he wrought in Cana of Galilee, and is commended of Saint Paul to be honorable among all men; and therefore is not to be enterprised, nor taken in hand unadvisedly, lightly, or wantonly, to satisfy men's carnal lusts and appetites, like brute beasts that have no understanding, but reverently, discretely, advisedly, soberly, and in the fear of God. Duly considering the causes for the which matrimony was ordained. One cause was the procreation of children, to be brought up in the fear and nurture of the Lord, and praise of God. Secondly it was ordained for a remedy against sin, and to avoid fornication, that such persons as be married, might live chastely in matrimony, and keep themselves undefiled members of Christ's body. Thirdly for the mutual society, help, and comfort, that the one ought to have of the other, both in prosperity and adversity. Into the which holy estate these two persons present come now to be joined. Therefore if any man can show any just cause why they may not lawfully be joined so together: Let him now speak, or else hereafter forever hold his peace.

And also speaking to the persons that shall be married, he shall say.
I require and charge you (as you will answer at the dreadful day of judgment, when the secrets of all hearts shall be disclosed) that if either of you do know any impediment, why ye may not be lawfully joined together in matrimony, that ye confess it. For be ye well assured, that so many as be coupled together otherwise than God's word doth allow, are not joined of God, neither is their matrimony lawful. . . .

If no impediment be alleged, then shall the Curate say unto the man.
[Name] wilt thou have this woman to thy wedded wife, to live together after God's ordinance in the holy estate of matrimony? Wilt thou love her, comfort her, honor, and keep her in sickness and in health? And forsaking all others keep thee only to her, so long as you both shall live?
The man shall answer,
I will.

Then shall the priest say to the woman.
[Name] wilt thou have this man to thy wedded husband, to live together after God's ordinance, in the holy estate of matrimony? Will thou obey him, and serve him, love, honor, and keep him in sickness and in health? And forsaking all others keep thee only to him, so long as you both shall live?
The woman shall answer,
I will.

Then shall the Minister say,
Who giveth this woman to be married to this man?
And the minister receiving the woman at her father or friend's hands, shall cause the man to take the woman by the right hand, and so both to give their troth to the other, the man first saying.
I [name] take thee [name] to my wedded wife, to have and to hold from this day forward, for better, for worse, for richer, for poorer, in sickness, and in health, to love and to cherish, till death us depart: according to God's holy ordinance: And thereto I plight thee my troth.

Then shall they loose their hands, and the woman taking again the man by the right hand shall say,

I [name] take thee [name] to my wedded husband, to have and to hold from this day forward, for better, for worse, for richer, for poorer, in sickness, and in health, to love, cherish, and to obey, till death us depart: according to God's holy ordinance: And thereto I give thee my troth.

Then shall they again loose their hands, and the man shall give unto the woman a ring, and other tokens of spousage, as gold or silver, laying the same upon the book, and the Priest taking the ring shall deliver it unto the man, to put it upon the fourth finger of the woman's left hand.

And the man taught by the priest, shall say.

With this ring I thee wed: This gold and silver I thee give: with my body I thee worship: and with all my worldly Goods I thee endow. In the name of the Father, and of the Son, and of the Holy Ghost. Amen.

Then the man leaving the ring upon the fourth finger of the woman's left hand, the minister shall say,

Let us pray. O eternal God creator and preserver of all mankind, giver of all spiritual grace, the author of everlasting life: Send thy blessing upon these thy servants, this man, and this woman, whom we bless in thy name, that as Isaac and Rebecca (after bracelets and jewels of gold given of the one to the other for tokens of their matrimony) lived faithfully together. So these persons may surely perform and keep the vow and covenant between them made, whereof this ring given, and received, is a token and pledge. And may ever remain in perfect love and peace together; And live according to thy laws; through Jesus Christ our lord. Amen.

Then shall the priest join their right hands together, and say.

Those whom god hath joined together: let no man put asunder.

Then shall the minister speak unto the people.

Forasmuch as [name] and [name] have consented together in holy wedlock, and have witnessed the same here before god and this company; and thereto have given and pledged their troth to each other, and have declared the same by giving and receiving gold and silver, and by joining of hands: I pronounce that they be man and wife together. In the name of the Father, of the Son, and of the Holy Ghost. Amen.

And the minister shall add this blessing.

God the Father bless you. God the Son keep you. God the Holy Ghost enlighten your understanding: The Lord mercifully with his favor look upon you, and so fill you with all spiritual benediction, and grace, that you may have remission of your sins in this life, and in the world to come life everlasting. Amen. . . .

The Minister.

Let us pray. O God of Abraham, God of Isaac, God of Jacob, bless these thy servants, and sow the seed of eternal life in their minds, that whatsoever in thy holy word they shall profitably learn: they may in deed fulfill the same. Look,

O Lord, mercifully upon them from heaven, and bless them: And as thou didst send thy Angel Raphael to Tobias, and Sarah, the daughter of Raguel, to their great comfort; so vouchsafe to send thy blessing upon these thy servants, that they obeying thy will, and always being in safety under thy protection: may abide in thy love unto their lives' end: through Jesus Christ our Lord. Amen.

This prayer following shall be omitted where the woman is past childbirth.

O Merciful Lord, and heavenly father, by whose gracious gift mankind is increased: We beseech thee assist with thy blessing these two persons, that they may both be fruitful in procreation of children; and also live together so long in godly love and honesty, that they may see their children's children, unto the third and fourth generation, unto thy praise and honor: through Jesus Christ our Lord. Amen.

O God who by thy mighty power hast made all things out of nothing, who also after other things set in order didst appoint that out of man (created after thine own image and similitude) woman should take her beginning: and, knitting them together, didst teach, that it should never be lawful to put asunder those, whom thou by matrimony hast made one: O God, who hast consecrated the state of matrimony to such an excellent mystery, that in it is signified and represented the spiritual marriage and unity between Christ and his church: Look mercifully upon these thy servants, that both this man may love his wife, according to thy word, as Christ did love his spouse the church, who gave himself for it, loving and cherishing it even as his own flesh. And also that this woman may be loving and amiable to her husband as Rachel, wise as Rebecca, faithful and obedient as Sarah; And in all quietness, sobriety, and peace, be a follower of holy and godly matrons. O Lord, bless them both, and grant them to inherit thy everlasting kingdom, through Jesus Christ our Lord. Amen.

Then shall the priest bless the man and the woman, saying

Almighty God, who at the beginning did create our first parents Adam and Eve, and did sanctify and join them together in marriage: Pour upon you the riches of his grace, sanctify and bless you, that ye may please him both in body and soul; and live together in holy love unto your lives end. Amen. . . .

[There follows a prescribed sermon in which the priest instructs the married couple and all those listening on scriptural teaching about the duties of married life.]

[Thomas Cranmer, comp., *Book of Common Prayer* (1549), in *The First and Second Prayer Books of Edward VI*, intro. Douglas Harrison (London: Dent; New York: Dutton, 1910), pp. 252–258]

JOHN CALVIN

John Calvin (1509–1564) was the leading figure of the generation of reformers after Luther. As systematic theologian, scriptural exegete, legal theorist, and community leader, Calvin effectively opened up a second wing of the reformation. His masterpiece, the *Institutes of Christian Religion,* was first published in 1536, but he continued to revise it periodically. Calvin also wrote extensive scriptural commentaries, substantial sermons, and innumerable church documents or other legal opinions. His views on marriage, while more austere than those of Luther, emphasized that it was a fully Christian vocation and so a serious call to moral growth. The selection here is taken from a sermon on Deuteronomy 5:18 that Calvin delivered on the occasion of a wedding (1555).

Document 2–19

JOHN CALVIN, SERMON ON DEUTERONOMY 5:18

Now we know that if anything ought to be holy in all of human life, it's the faith that a husband has in his wife and her faith in him. In truth, all contracts and all promises that we make ought to be faithfully upheld. But if we should make a comparison, it is not without cause that marriage is called [a] covenant with God. By this word, Solomon [cf. Prov. 2:17] shows that God presides over marriages, and for this reason, whenever a husband breaks his promise which he has made to his wife, he has not only perjured himself with respect to her, but also with respect to God. The same is true of the wife. She not only wrongs her husband, but the living God, for it is to him that she is obligated. More especially, God himself wants to maintain marriage, since he has ordained it and is its author. Therefore when we hear the word *adultery*, it ought to be detestable to us, as if men deliberately wanted to despise God, and like raging beasts wanted to break the sacred bond that he has established in marriage.

Now we understand how he regards uprightness. Why? When he wants us to be sober, chaste, [and] modest, he says to us: "If you are not virtuous and sober, you are like adulterers, that is to say, whatever excuse you might be able to feign before men, regardless of how little and inconsequential your faults, I will hold you with hate; you are stinking to me; your entire life is foul as far as I am concerned."

We see therefore (as I have already touched on) that this is a strict commandment designed to hold us in honesty and modesty. And by means of it we see how frivolous is the excuse of those who say that they wrong no one when they indulge themselves and are full of shocking misdeeds. For our Lord well knows why he used such language; it isn't because he was a stammerer, [or] wasn't able to direct things, but because he wanted to show that if men want to turn a small incident into a profligate matter, there is another side to it, which is that he condemns and curses all adulterers, all who indulge in shamelessness and unchastity. Thus all the more gravely must we weigh this word which is couched here when he says, *You shall not be an adulterer.*

In any event, we ought to follow the points that are contained under this precept. In the first place (as I have already mentioned), let us understand that God wants holy marriage to be preserved. For just as our lives and our persons are precious to him, so also he wills that that faith and mutual loyalty which ought to exist between a husband and wife should be held in its proper esteem and that a thing as holy as marriage should not be exposed to villainy and shame. That is why no one is to look upon his neighbor's wife with lustful eyes. And why? Because our Lord has already united her with her husband; he wants the husband to put her in the shade. And when we think of any evil or shameful desire, he wants us to regard with horror what has been shown us, that is, that God himself will take vengeance on those who have violated the sacred intimacy which he has dedicated in his name. The same holds true for wives with regard to husbands, that is to say, a wife must not surrender herself to lascivious thoughts when she looks upon a married man. Why? Because God has assigned her her own spouse. It is imperative [then] that if we do not want to make war against our creator, that each man should live in his [own] home—provided he has a spouse—and that this order should be maintained inviolable, because God is its author. That is one point.

Furthermore, we must continually return to the nature of God, realizing that he is not an earthly lawgiver who only forbids the external act while permitting us to indulge evil affections, for God has no desire to be served with the eye, nor is he like us. Men are satisfied when they cannot perceive their faults, but God who fathoms our hearts sees the truth, as Jeremiah explains [see Jer. 5:3]. He not merely wanted to restrain our bodies in his law, but above all he considered our souls. Consequently let us note that God has not simply forbidden the act that would in effect violate marriage or break it, but he has forbidden all lasciviousness and wicked intentions. And that is why our Lord Jesus Christ says that when a man looks upon another man's wife with lust, he is an adulterer in God's eyes [see Matt. 5:28]. Although he is not guilty according to human laws and cannot be chastised for having acted promiscuously, nevertheless in God's sight he is already condemned as having transgressed this commandment here.

Therefore when we hear the word *adulterer*, a condition thusly condemned, let us not only learn to restrain ourselves in effect from all promiscuity, but also to maintain our senses chaste that we might be chaste in both eyes and heart. For that is how Saint Paul defined true chastity when he says that those who are not married must be careful how they obey God in keeping themselves pure and clean in body and mind [see 1 Cor. 7:34]. He does not say that those who have not defiled their bodies in adultery are those who are chaste, but those who have taken the trouble to preserve both their bodies and minds from corruption.

Now once we have considered how God curses and detests all adulterers, we need to go further and apply and extend this to all promiscuity. It is true that whosoever breaks the marriage vow commits a double offense and is intensely guilty as I have said. But nevertheless we need to come back to this [and emphasize] that God not only wills for no one to act against marriage, but he does not want men to lead an animal existence, for adultery to be in vogue, or for those who are not married to stray about yielding themselves here and there the way dumb animals do whenever they meet. For it is said that not only our souls, but also our bodies are temples of the Holy Spirit [1 Cor. 6:19], as was just a few moments ago mentioned [in the wedding service]. And those are Saint Paul's words when he admonished the Corinthians that it was too shameful and infamous a thing for them to permit promiscuity, as they were doing. He says: "Do you not know that your bodies are temples of the Holy Spirit?" [1 Cor. 6:19] So it is God who has bestowed this honor upon us, who has chosen these poor bodies which are not only fragile vessels, but [at best] only carrion, made of dirt and corruption. Nevertheless God has honored them to the extent that he wills to make them into temples for his Holy Spirit to indwell. Yet we are going to wallow them in every [kind of] stench? We are going to turn them into sties for swine? What a sacrilege! And that is not all. Let us see where Saint Paul takes us. Our bodies are members of Jesus Christ [1 Cor. 6:15]. Therefore when a man indulges in prostitution, it's the same as if he were to rape the body of Jesus Christ. For we certainly cannot mix the Son of God with our filth and abominations, he who is the fountain of all purity. Therefore when a man throws himself into fornication, it's as much as if he breaks the body of our Lord Jesus Christ into as many pieces as he can. Not that we can actually do that, for the Son of God is not subject to us to be dishonored in that way, but in any event we are guilty of having committed such a blasphemy and offense.

Therefore, in light of that, let us learn that God not only wills for each of us to maintain faith and loyalty with our partner in marriage, but in general that we should be chaste in order to walk in purity of life so that we do not give up the reins at every moral morass and turpitude. And why [do that]? The reasons which I have traced ought sufficiently to motivate us to that end. Moreover with respect to what has already been discussed about adultery, let us also apply it in this way: that we control our senses with such moderation that whenever the devil solicits any lasciviousness within us, he shall always be repulsed and find no access to us. . . .

Now someone may argue at this point: "And just how are we supposed to be able to restrain ourselves from every corruption, seeing our flesh is so fragile?" For [in all honesty] we are aware of the incontinence that exists in men and by means of it are shown, better than anywhere else, how vicious their nature is. Moreover, it is true that men cannot be chaste, for our Lord, thereby, through such intemperance of the flesh, wants us to be conscious of the curse against Adam's sin—unless, as it is written, we possess a special grace not given to everyone [see 1 Cor. 7:7]. Still it is crucial for each to consider what God has given him and to use the gift he has, knowing well that he is all the more obligated to God. But in any event, there is the remedy of marriage for those who cannot restrain themselves. Therefore God, although he wants to leave this mark of weakness in us, nevertheless grants us an appropriate remedy for it. [And so we return to the argument.] Is a man's flesh weak? Is a woman's equally? The matter is certainly a vice, and although it may appear to be an inclination derived from nature, it is from that broken nature which we have incurred from Adam; thus in itself it is condemned, for all such intemperance is far from that excellent dignity that God set in the human race, that we should bear its signs and become like angels [cf. Ps. 8].

Therefore all immoderation of the flesh is wrong, but insofar as our Lord supports us, he has ordained such a means whereby this weakness will not be imputed as a vice. Therefore, if the mantle of marriage is worn, then immoderation of the flesh, which is vicious and damnable in itself, will not be imputed in God's sight. And when a man, having prayed to God and cast himself upon him, sees that he cannot refrain, let him take a wife in order not to lead an immoral life, or behave like a dog, or a bull, or some wild beast. Thus when he marries, as ordained by God, that is how vice is covered, and hidden, and not brought into judgment. And herein we see the inestimable goodness of our God, that although he leaves this vice in us, which indeed ought to make us feel ashamed, he nevertheless ordains a helpful means by which it may be overcome. And although men might be immoderate, they are not indicted before him and his judicial seat, provided they contain themselves within the confines of marriage. For all immoderation is unlawful. For example, when a man wants to enjoy too much license, and a wife the same with her husband, there is no reason for them to make their home into a bordello. But when a man lives honorably with his wife in the fear of God, although their lawful intimate relationship might be disgraceful, nevertheless neither before God nor his angels is such a relationship shameful. And why [is that]? The mantle of marriage exists to sanctify what is defiled and profane; it serves to cleanse what used to be soiled and dirty in itself. Therefore when we see that our Lord is that benign and has ordained such a remedy, are we not that much more malicious and ungrateful if we do not use it and if all the excuses which men put forth are not rejected? Indeed, has God not provided for their needs and made available to us a good physician to heal what is wrong with us? Has he not gone on ahead, as we see [?] Therefore let us reject all [those] subterfuges [based on] our fragile nature, inasmuch as our Lord wanted to relieve us from that matter and has ordained holy marriage in order that those who do not have the gift of continence may nevertheless not succumb to every turpitude. That is what we have to observe.

Now with respect to this subject, let us carefully note what the apostle says about the marriage bed, for when men and women keep themselves within the bounds of the fear of God and complete modesty, the bed is honorable. Instead of there being shame (as indeed there should be), our Lord turns all of that into honor. What the apostle calls honorable in God's sight is hardly a mere trifle; for what should be shameful even in men's eyes, God has forgiven. But he pronounces a curse and vengeance on all adulterers. When we hear such advice, let us learn to cover ourselves with this honorable shadow (wherever we have such need), in order that our ignominies may not be cursed and condemned before God and his angels. And at the same time let us fear this dreadful judgment which is made against all adulterers and fornicators. Indeed, let even those who are able to abstain from marriage be careful to abstain from it for [only] a time, in such a way that they do not reject the remedy which God has assigned them, unless they know that God is holding them back. Thus let those who live outside of marriage be ready overnight to submit to God if he calls them to that estate.

> [*John Calvin's Sermons on the Ten Commandments*, trans. and ed. Benjamin W. Farley (Grand Rapids: Baker, 2000), pp. 169–173, 178–180]

THE COUNCIL OF TRENT

The Council of Trent (1545–1563) refers to a series of meetings over two decades in which representatives loyal to the pope attempted to work out a response to the cascading events of the Protestant Reformation. Some hoped that the council would devote itself to repairing the split in western Christendom, while others wanted it systematize Catholic teaching against the Protestants. In the end, the council did motivate significant church reforms, but it also hardened teaching on a number of disputed points, including marriage and sexual ethics. The selection here comes from the Decree Tametsi, issued in the council's last year, when it was preoccupied with sacramental and liturgical matters.

Document 2–20

COUNCIL OF TRENT, 24TH SESSION, DECREE TAMETSI

DOCTRINE ON THE SACRAMENT OF MATRIMONY

The perpetual and indissoluble bond of matrimony was expressed by the first parent of the human race, when, under the influence of the divine Spirit, he said: "This now is bone of my bones and flesh of my flesh. Wherefore a man shall leave father and mother and shall cleave to his wife, and they shall be two in one flesh" [Gen 2:23–24]. But that by this bond two only are united and joined together, Christ the Lord taught more plainly when referring to those last words as having been spoken by God, He said: "Therefore now they are not two, but one flesh" [Matt. 19:6; Mark 10:8], and immediately ratified the firmness of the bond so long ago proclaimed by Adam with these words: "What therefore God has joined together, let no man put asunder" [Matt. 19:6; Mark 10:9].

But the grace which was to perfect that natural love, and confirm that indissoluble union, and sanctify the persons married, Christ Himself, the instituter and perfecter of the venerable sacraments, merited for us by His passion, which Paul the Apostle intimates when he says: "Husbands love your wives, as Christ also loved the Church, and delivered himself up for it" [Eph. 5:25], adding immediately: "This is a great sacrament, but I speak in Christ and in the Church" [Eph. 5:32].

Since therefore matrimony in the evangelical law surpasses in grace through Christ the ancient marriages, our holy Fathers, the councils, and the tradition of the universal Church, have with good reason always taught that it is to be numbered among the sacraments of the New Law; and since with regard to this teaching ungodly men of this age, raving madly, have not only formed false ideas concerning this venerable sacrament, but, introducing in conformity with their habit under the pretext of the Gospel a carnal liberty, have by word and writing asserted, not without great harm to the faithful of Christ, many things that are foreign to the teaching of the Catholic Church and to the usage approved of since the times of the Apostles, this holy and general council, desiring to restrain their boldness, has thought it proper, lest their pernicious contagion should attract more, that the principal heresies and errors of the aforesaid schismatics be destroyed by directing against those heretics and their errors the following anathemas.

CANONS ON THE SACRAMENT OF MATRIMONY

Canon 1. If anyone says that matrimony is not truly and properly one of the seven sacraments of the evangelical law, instituted by Christ the Lord, but has been devised by men in the Church and does not confer grace, let him be anathema.

Can. 2. If anyone says that it is lawful for Christians to have several wives at the same time and that this is not forbidden by any divine law, let him be anathema.

Can. 3. If anyone says that only those degrees of consanguinity and affinity which are expressed in Leviticus [18:6ff.] can hinder matrimony from being contracted and dissolve it when contracted, and that the Church cannot dispense in some of them or declare that others hinder and dissolve it, let him be anathema.

Can. 4. If anyone says that the Church cannot establish impediments dissolving marriage, or that she has erred in establishing them, let him be anathema.

Can. 5. If anyone says that the bond of matrimony can be dissolved on account of heresy, or irksome cohabitation, or by reason of the voluntary absence of one of the parties, let him be anathema.

Can. 6. If anyone says that matrimony contracted but not consummated is not dissolved by the solemn religious profession of one of the parties, let him be anathema.

Can. 7. If anyone says that the Church errs in that she taught and teaches that in accordance with evangelical and apostolic doctrine the bond of matrimony cannot be dissolved by reason of adultery on the part of one of the parties, and that both, or even the innocent party who gave no occasion for adultery, cannot contract another marriage during the lifetime of the other, and that he is guilty of adultery who, having put away the adulteress, shall marry another, and she also who, having put away the adulterer, shall marry another, let him be anathema.

Can. 8. If anyone says that the Church errs when she declares that for many reasons a separation may take place between husband and wife with regard to bed and with regard to cohabitation for a determinate or indeterminate period, let him be anathema.

Can. 9. If anyone says that clerics constituted in sacred orders or regulars who have made solemn profession of chastity can contract marriage, and that the one contracted is valid notwithstanding the ecclesiastical law or the vow, and that the contrary is nothing else than a condemnation of marriage, and that all who feel that they have not the gift of chastity, even though they have made such a vow, can contract marriage, let him be anathema, since God does not refuse that gift to those who ask for it rightly, neither does "he suffer us to be tempted above that which we are able" [1 Cor. 10:13].

Can. 10. If anyone says that the married state excels the state of virginity or celibacy, and that it is better and happier to be united in matrimony than to remain in virginity or celibacy, let him be anathema.

Can. 11. If anyone says that the prohibition of the solemnization of marriages at certain times of the year is a tyrannical superstition derived from the superstition of the heathen, or condemns the blessings and other ceremonies which the Church makes use of therein, let him be anathema.

Can. 12. If anyone says that matrimonial causes do not belong to ecclesiastical judges, let him be anathema.

DECREE CONCERNING THE REFORM OF MATRIMONY, CHAPTER 1

The form prescribed in the Lateran Council for solemnly contracting marriage is renewed; bishops may dispense with the publication of the banns; whoever contracts marriage otherwise than in the presence of the pastor and of two or three witnesses does so invalidly.

Although it is not to be doubted that clandestine marriages made with the free consent of the contracting parties are valid and true marriages so long as the Church has not declared them invalid, and consequently that those persons are justly to be condemned, as the holy council does condemn them with anathema, who deny that they are true and valid, and those also who falsely assert that marriages contracted by children [minors] without the consent of the parents are invalid, nevertheless the holy Church of God has for very just reasons at all times detested and forbidden them. But while the holy council recognizes that by reason of man's disobedience those prohibitions are no longer of any avail, and considers the grave sins which arise from clandestine marriages, especially the sins of those who continue in the state of damnation, when having left the first wife with whom they contracted secretly, they publicly marry another and live with her in continual adultery, and since the Church which does not judge what is hidden, cannot correct this evil unless a more efficacious remedy is applied, therefore, following in the footsteps of the holy Lateran Council celebrated under Innocent III, it commands that in the future, before a marriage is contracted, the proper pastor of the contracting parties shall publicly announce three times in the church, during the celebration of the mass on three successive festival days, between whom marriage is to be contracted; after which publications, if no legitimate impediment is revealed, the marriage may be proceeded with in the presence of the people, where the parish priest, after having questioned the man and the woman and heard their mutual consent, shall either say: "I join you together in matrimony, in the name of the Father, and of the Son, and of the Holy Ghost," or he may use other words, according to the accepted rite of each province. But if at some time there should a probable suspicion that a marriage might be maliciously hindered if so many publications precede it, then either one publication only may be made or the marriage may be celebrated forthwith in the presence of the parish priest and of two or three witnesses. Then before its consummation that publications shall be made in the church, so that if any impediments exist they may be the more easily discovered, unless the ordinary shall deem it advisable to dispense with the publications which the holy council leaves to his prudence and judgment. Those who shall attempt to contract marriage otherwise than in the presence of the parish priest or of another priest authorized by the parish priest or by the ordinary and in the presence of two or three witnesses, the holy council renders absolutely incapable of thus contracting marriage and declares such contracts invalid and null, as by the present decree it invalidates and annuls them. Moreover, it commands that the parish priest or another priest who shall have been present at a contract of this kind with less than the prescribed number of witnesses, also the witnesses who shall have been present without the parish priest or another priest, and also the contracting parties themselves, shall at the discretion of the ordinary be severely punished. Furthermore, the same holy council exhorts the betrothed parties not to live together in the same house until they have received the sacerdotal blessing in the church; and it decrees that the blessing is to be given by their own parish priest, and permission to impart it cannot be granted to any other priest except by the parish priest himself or by the ordinary, any custom, even though immemorial, which ought rather to be called a corruption, or any privilege notwithstanding. But if any parish priest or any other priest, whether regular or secular, should attempt to unite in marriage or bless the betrothed of another parish without the permission of their parish priest, he shall, even though he may plead that his action was based on a privilege or immemorial custom, remain *ipso jure* suspended until absolved by the ordinary of that parish priest who ought to have been present at the marriage or from whom the blessing ought to have been received. The parish priest shall have a book in which he shall record the names of the persons united in marriage and of the witnesses, and also the day on which and the place where the marriage was contracted, and this book he shall carefully preserve. Finally, the holy council exhorts the betrothed that before they contract marriage, or at least three days before its consummation, they carefully confess their sins and approach devoutly the most holy sacrament of the Eucharist. If any provinces have in this matter other laudable customs and ceremonies in addition to the aforesaid, the holy council wishes earnestly that they be by all means retained. And that these so salutary regulations may not remain unknown to anyone, it commands all ordinaries that they as soon as possible see to it that this decree be published and explained to the people in all the parish churches and dioceses, and that this be done very often during the first year and after that as often as they shall deem it advisable. It decrees, moreover, that this decree shall begin to take effect in every parish at the expiration of thirty days, to be reckoned from the day of its first publication in that church.

[*Canons and Decrees of the Council of Trent*, trans. and ed. H. J. Schroeder (St. Louis: Herder, 1955), pp. 180–185]

GEORGE FOX

George Fox (1624–1691) is the founder of the Religious Society of Friends or Quakers. Raised as a Puritan with strong suspicions of church-state connections and liturgical formalism, Fox spent his life as a preacher and missionary to marginalized Christian groups, including (from the 1650s on) the first Quakers. Always traveling, and often enough in prison for his views, Fox did not marry until he was in his late forties. This description of his wedding is taken from his journal, which he dictated five years afterward (1675).

Document 2–21

JOURNAL OF GEORGE FOX

I had seen from the Lord a considerable time before that I should take Margaret Fell to be my wife. And when I first mentioned it to her, she felt the answer of life from God thereunto. But though the Lord had opened this thing unto me, yet I had not received a command from the Lord for the accomplishment of it then. Wherefore I let the thing rest, and went on in the work and service of the Lord as before, according as the Lord led me, traveling up and down in this nation and through the nation of Ireland. But now, after I was come back from Ireland and was come to Bristol and found Margaret Fell there, it opened in me from the Lord that the thing should be now accomplished.

And after we had discoursed the thing together I told her if she also was satisfied with the accomplishing of it now she should first send for her children, which she did. And when the rest of her daughters were come, I was moved to ask the children (and her sons-in-law) whether they were all satisfied and whether Margaret had answered them according to her husband's will to her children, she being a widow, and if her husband had left anything to her for the assistance of her children, in which if she married they might suffer loss, whether she had answered them in lieu of that and all other things. And the children made answer and said she had doubled it, and would not have me to speak of those things. (I told them I was plain and would have all things done plainly, for I sought not any outward advantage to myself.)

And so when I had thus acquainted the children with it, and when it had been laid before several meetings both of the men and women, assembled together for that purpose, and all were satisfied, there was a large meeting appointed of purpose (in the meeting house at Broad Mead in Bristol, the Lord joining us together in the honorable marriage in the everlasting covenant and immortal Seed of life, where there were several large testimonies borne by Friends [October 27, 1669]. (Then was a certificate, relating both the proceedings and the marriage, openly read and signed by the relations and by most of the ancient Friends of that city, besides many other Friends from divers[e] parts of the nation.)

And before we were married I was moved to write forth a paper to all the meetings in England both of men and woman and elsewhere, for all meetings of Friends which were begotten to the Lord were but as one meeting to me.

After this I stayed in Bristol about a week and then passed with Margaret into the country to Olveston, where Margaret passed homewards towards the north and I passed on in the work of the Lord into Wiltshire, where I had many large and precious meetings.

And from thence I passed into Berkshire, where I had many large precious meetings, and so from thence till I came into Oxfordshire and Buckinghamshire, where I had many precious meetings all along till I came to London.

[*The Journal of George Fox*, ed. John L. Nickalls
(Cambridge: University Press, 1952), pp. 554–555]

A CONTEMPORARY CRITIQUE OF SEXUAL ETHICS

Joseph Fletcher (1905–1991) is remembered as a radical Christian advocate of "situation ethics," especially in sexual matters. In fact, his advocacy of social reform ranged more widely. Early works on the church and property brought unwelcome attention from anti-Communist crusaders, including Joseph McCarthy. A commitment to biomedical ethics led him to help establish the group Planned Parenthood. The selection here, in which Fletcher criticizes older Christian sexual ethics, is taken from *Moral Responsibility* (1967).

Document 2–22

JOSEPH FLETCHER, MORAL RESPONSIBILITY

THE PROBLEM

In terms of ethical analysis we have, so to speak, *two* problem areas. The first one is the problem of premarital sex for those whose moral standards are in the classical religious tradition, based on a faith commitment to a divine sanction— usually, in America, some persuasion or other of the Judeo-Christian kind. The second area is the "secular" one, in which people's moral standards are broadly humanistic, based on a value commitment to human welfare and happiness. It is difficult, if not impossible, to say what proportion of our people falls in either area, but they exist certainly, and the "secular" area is growing all the time.

As a matter of fact, there is by no means a set or unchanging viewpoint in the religious camp. Some Christians are challenging the old morality of the marital monopoly of sex. . . .

Over against this situation ethics or religious relativism stands the legalistic ethics of universal absolutes (usually negatives and prohibitions), condemning every form of sexual expression except horizontal coitus eyeball-to-eyeball solely between the parties to a monogamous marriage contract. Thus one editorial writer in a semifundamentalist magazine said recently, and correctly enough: "The new moralists do not believe that the biblical moral laws are really given by God. Moral laws are not regarded as the products of revelation." A growing company of church people are challenging fixed moral principles or rules about sex or anything else.

The idea in the past has been that the ideal fulfillment of our sex potential lies in a monogamous marriage. But there is no reason to regard this ideal as a legal absolute. For example, if the sex ratio were to be overthrown by disaster, polygamy could well become the ideal or standard. Jesus showed more concern about pride and hypocrisy than about sex. In the story of the woman taken in adultery, her accusers were guiltier than she. Among the seven deadly sins, lust is listed but not sex, and lust can exist in marriage as well as out. But even so, lust is not so grave a sin as pride. As Dorothy Sayers points out scornfully, "A man may be greedy and selfish; spiteful, cruel, jealous and unjust; violent and brutal; grasping, unscrupulous and a liar; stubborn and arrogant; stupid, morose and dead to every noble instinct" and yet, if he practices his sinfulness within the marriage bond, he is not thought by some Christians to be immoral!

The Bible clearly affirms sex as a high-order value, at the same time sanctioning marriage (although not always monogamy), but any claim that the Bible requires that sex be expressed solely within marriage is only an inference. There is nothing explicitly forbidding premarital acts. Only extramarital acts, i.e., adultery, are forbidden. Those Christians who are situational, refusing to absolutize any moral principle except "love thy neighbor," cannot absolutize Paul's one flesh *(henōsis)* theory of marriage in 1 Cor., ch. 6. Paul Ramsey of Princeton has tried to defend premarital intercourse by engaged couples on the ground that they become married thereby. But marriages are not made by the act itself; sexual congress doesn't create a marriage. Marriage is a mutual commitment, willed and purposed interpersonally. Besides, all such "ontological" or "naturalistic" reasoning fails completely to meet the moral question of nonmarital sex acts between *un*engaged couples, since it presumably condemns them all universally as unjustifiable simply because they are nonmarital. It is still the old marital monopoly theory, only one step relaxed.

The humanists in our "secular" society draw close to the nonlegalists, the nonabsolutists among Christians, when they choose concern for personal values as their ethical norm, for this is very close to the Biblical "love thy neighbor as thyself." . . .

On this view, sarcasm and graft are immoral, but not sexual intercourse unless it is malicious or callous or cruel. On this basis, an act is not wrong because of the act itself but because of its *meaning*—its motive and message. . . .

Both religious and secular moralists, in America's plural society, need to remember that freedom *of* religion includes freedom *from* religion. There is no ethical basis for compelling noncreedalists to follow any creedal codes of behavior, Christian or non-Christian. A "sin" is an act against God's will, but if the agent does not believe in God he cannot commit sin, and even those who do believe in God disagree radically as to what God's will is. Speaking to the issue over birth control law, Cardinal Cushing of Boston says, "Catholics do not need the support of civil law to be faithful to their own religious convictions, and they do not need to impose their moral views on other members of society. . . . " What the cardinal says about birth control applies just as much to premarital intercourse. . . .

Nothing we do is truly moral unless we are free to do otherwise. We must be free to decide what to do before any of our actions even begin to be moral. No discipline but self-discipline has any moral significance. This applies to sex, politics, or anything else. A moral act is a free act, done because we want to.

Incidentally, but not insignificantly, let me remark that this freedom which is so essential to moral acts can mean freedom *from* premarital sex as well as freedom for it. Not everybody would choose to engage in it. Some will not because it would endanger the sense of personal integrity. Value sentiments or "morals" may be changing (they *are*, obviously), but we are still "living in the overlap" and a sensitive, imaginative person might both well and wisely decide against it. . . .

Many will oppose premarital sex for reasons of the social welfare, others for relationship reasons, and some for simply egoistic reasons. We may rate these reasons differently in our ethical value systems, but the main point morally is to respect the freedom to choose. And short of coitus, young couples can pet each other at all levels up to orgasm, just so they are honest enough to recognize that merely technical virgins are no better morally than those who go the whole way. . . .

THE SOLUTION

Just as there are two ethical orientations, theistic and humanistic, so there are two distinct questions to ask ourselves. One is: Should we prohibit and condemn premarital sex? The other is: Should we approve of it? To the first one I promptly reply in the negative. To the second I propose an equivocal answer, "Yes and no—depending on each particular situation."

The most solid basis for any ethical approach is on the ground common to both the religiously oriented and the humanistically oriented—namely, the concern both feel for persons. They are alike *personalistically* oriented. For example, both Christians and non-Christians can accept the normative principle, "We ought to love people and use things; immorality only occurs when we love things and use people." They can agree also on a companion maxim: "We ought to love people, not rules or principles; what counts is not any hard and fast moral law but doing what we can for the good of others in every situation."

The first principle means that no sexual act is ethical if it hurts or exploits others. This is the difference between lust and love: lust treats a sexual partner as an object, love as a subject. Charity is more important than chastity, but there is no such thing as "free love." There must be some care and commitment in premarital sex acts or they are immoral. Hugh Hefner, the whipping boy of the stuffies, has readily acknowledged in *Playboy* that "personal" sex relations are to be preferred to impersonal. Even though he denies that mutual commitment needs to go the radical lengths of marriage, he sees at least the difference between casual sex and straight callous congress.

The second principle is one of situation ethics—making a moral decision hangs on the particular case. How, here and now, can I act with the most certain concern for the happiness and welfare of those involved—myself and others? Legalistic moralism, with its absolutes and universals, always thou-shalt-nots, cuts out the middle ground between being a virgin and a sexual profligate. This is an absurd failure to see that morality has to be acted out on a continuum of relativity, like life itself, from situation to situation.

The only independent variable is concern for people; love thy neighbor as thyself. Christians, whether legalistic or situational about their ethics, are agreed that the *ideal* sexually is the combination of marriage and sex. But the ideal gives no reason to demand that others should adopt that ideal or to try to impose it by law, nor is it even any reason to absolutize the ideal in practice for all Christians in all situations. Sex is not always wrong outside marriage, even for Christians; as Paul said, "I know . . . that nothing is unclean in itself" (Rom.

14:14). Another way to put it is to say that character shapes sex conduct, sex does not shape character.

As I proposed some years ago in a paper in *Law and Contemporary Problems,* the Duke University law journal, there are only three proper limitations to guide both the civil law and morality on sexual acts. No sexual act between persons competent to give mutual consent should be prohibited, except when it involves either the seduction of minors or an offense against the public order. These are the principles of the Wolfenden Report to the English Parliament, adopted by that body and endorsed by the Anglican and Roman Catholic archbishops. It is time we acknowledged the difference between "sins" (a private judgment) and "crimes" against the public conscience and social consensus.

Therefore, we can welcome the recent decision of the federal Department of Health, Education, and Welfare to provide birth control assistance to un-married women who desire it. It is a policy that puts into effect the principles of the President's Health Message to Congress of March 1, 1966. If the motive is a truly moral one, it will be concerned not only with relief budgets but with the welfare of the women and a concern to prevent unwanted babies. Why wait for even *one* illegitimate child to be born? . . .

[Joseph Fletcher, *Moral Responsibility* (Philadelphia: Westminster, 1967), pp. 132–140]

A WOMANIST CRITIQUE OF FAMILY THEOLOGY

Delores S. Williams stands in the forefront of "womanist" theology, which seeks to articulate and foster the experience in faith of African American women. Her *Sisters in the Wilderness* (1993) is regularly cited as one of the works that defined the movement's concerns, especially in its biblical reinterpretations of marriage, child rearing, and extended family. Womanist theology intends to supplement and to critique feminist theology so far as feminists unknowingly presume that the experience of women of certain races or classes are universal.

Document 2–23

DELORES WILLIAMS, SISTERS IN THE WILDERNESS

Where would I begin in order to construct Christian theology (or god-talk) from the point of view of African-American women? I pondered this question for over a year. Then one day my professor responded to my complaint about the absence of black women's experience from *all* Christian theology (black liberation and feminist theologies included). He suggested that my anxiety might lessen if my exploration of African-American cultural sources was con-sciously informed by the statement "I am a black WOMAN." He was right. I had not realized before that I read African-American sources from a black male perspective. I assumed black women were included. I had not noticed that what the sources presented as "black experience" was really black male experience. . . .

Nevertheless, when I began reading available black female and black male sources with my female identity fixed firmly in my consciousness, I made a startling discovery. I discovered that even though black liberation theologians used biblical paradigms supporting an androcentric bias in their theological statements, the African-American community had used the Bible quite differently. For over a hundred years, the community had appropriated the Bible in such a way that black women's experience figured just as eminently as black men's in the community's memory, in its self-understanding and in its understanding of God's relation to its life. As I read deeper in black American sources from my female perspective, I began to see that it was possible to identify at least two traditions of African-American biblical appropriation that were useful for the construction of black theology in North America.

One of these traditions of biblical appropriation emphasized liberation of the oppressed and showed God relating to men in the liberation struggles. . . .

My discovery of the second tradition of African-American biblical appropriation excited me greatly. This tradition emphasized female activity and de-emphasized male authority. It lifted up from the Bible the story of a female slave of African descent who was forced to be a surrogate mother, reproducing a child by her slave master because the slave master's wife was barren. For more than a hundred years Hagar—the African slave of the Hebrew woman Sarah—has appeared in the deposits of African-American culture. Sculptors, writers, poets, scholars, preachers and just plain folks have passed along the biblical figure Hagar to generation after generation of black folks.

As I encountered Hagar again and again in African-American sources, I reread her story in the Hebrew testament and Paul's reference to her in the Christian testament. I slowly realized there were striking similarities between Hagar's story and the story of African-American women. Hagar's heritage was African as was black women's. Hagar was a slave. Black American women had emerged from a slave heritage and still lived in light of it. Hagar was brutalized by her slave owner, the Hebrew woman Sarah. The slave narratives of African-American women and some of the narratives of contemporary day-workers tell of the brutal or cruel treatment black women have received from the wives of slave masters and from contemporary white female employers. Hagar had no control over her body. It belonged to her slave owner, whose husband, Abraham, ravished Hagar. A child Ishmael was born; mother and child were eventually cast out of Abraham's and Sarah's home without resources for survival. The bodies of African-American slave women were owned by their masters. Time after time they were raped by their owners and bore children whom the masters seldom claimed—children who were slaves—children and their mothers whom slave-master fathers often cast out by selling them to other slave holders. Hagar resisted the brutalities of slavery by running away. Black American women have a long resistance history that includes running away from slavery in the antebellum era. Like Hagar and her child Ishmael, African-American female slaves and their children, after slavery, were expelled from the homes of many slave holders and given no resources for survival. Hagar, like many women throughout African-American women's history, was a single parent. But she had serious personal and salvific encounters with God—encounters which aided Hagar in the survival struggle of herself and her son. Over and over again, black women in the churches have testified about their serious personal and salvific encounters with God, encounters that helped them and their families survive.

I realized I had stumbled upon the beginning of an answer to my question: Where was I to begin in my effort to construct theology from the point of view of black women's experience? I was to begin with the black community (composed of females and males) and its understanding of God's historic relation to black female life. And, inasmuch as Hagar's story had been appropriated so extensively and for such a long time by the African-American community, I reasoned that her story must be the community's analogue for African-American women's historic experience. My reasoning was supported, I thought, by the striking similarities between Hagar's story and African-American women's history in North America. But what would I name this Hagar-centered tradition of African-American biblical appropriation? I did not feel that it belonged to the liberation tradition of African-American biblical appropriation. My exposure to feminist studies had convinced me that women must claim their experience, which has for so long been submerged by the overlay of oppressive, patriarchal cultural forms. And one way to claim experience is to name it. Naming also establishes some permanence and visibility for women's experience in history.

At this point, my effort to name the women-centered tradition was facilitated by the work of anthropologist Lawrence Levine. He concluded that African Americans (especially during slavery) did not accommodate themselves to the Bible. Rather, they accommodated the Bible to the urgent necessities of their lives. But in this business of accommodating the Bible to life, I knew that the black American religious community had not traditionally put final emphasis upon the hopelessness of the painful aspects of black history, whether paralleled in the Bible or not. Rather, black people used the Bible to put primary emphasis upon God's response to the community's situations of pain and bondage. So I asked myself: What was God's response to Hagar's predicament? Were her pain and God's response to it congruent with African-American women's predicament and their understanding of God's response to black women's suffering? Perhaps by answering these questions I could arrive at a name for this Hagar-centered tradition of African-American biblical appropriation.

A very superficial reading of Genesis 16:1–16 and 21:9–21 in the Hebrew testament revealed that Hagar's predicament involved slavery, poverty, ethnicity, sexual and economic exploitation, surrogacy, rape, domestic violence, homelessness, motherhood, single-parenting and radical encounters with God. Another aspect of Hagar's predicament was made clear in the Christian testament when Paul (Galatians 4:21–5:1) relegated her and her progeny to a position outside of and antagonistic to the great promise Paul says Christ brought to humankind. Thus in Paul's text Hagar bears only negative relation to the new creation Christ represents. In the Christian context of Paul, then, Hagar and her descendants represent the outsider position par excellence. So alienation is also part of the predicament of Hagar and her progeny.

God's response to Hagar's story in the Hebrew testament is not liberation. Rather, God participates in Hagar's and her child's survival on two occasions. When she was a run-away slave, God met her in the wilderness and told her to resubmit herself to her oppressor Sarah, that is, to return to bondage. Latin American biblical scholar Elsa Tamez may be correct when she interprets God's action here to be on behalf of the survival of Hagar and child. Hagar could not give birth in the wilderness. Perhaps neither she nor the child could survive such an ordeal. Perhaps the best resources for assuring the life of mother and child were in the home of Abraham and Sarah. Then, when Hagar and her child were finally cast out of the home of their oppressors and were not given proper resources for survival, God provided Hagar with a resource. God gave her new vision to see survival resources where she had seen none before. Liberation in the Hagar stories is not given by God; it finds its source in human initiative. Finally, in Hagar's story there is the suggestion that God will be instrumental in the development of Ishmael's and Hagar's quality of life, for "God was with the boy. He grew up and made his home in the desert [wilderness], and he became an archer" (Genesis 21:20).

Thus it seemed to me that God's response to Hagar's (and her child's) situation was survival and involvement in their development of an appropriate quality of life, that is, appropriate to their situation and their heritage. Because they would finally live in the wilderness without the protection of a larger social unit, it was perhaps to their advantage that Ishmael be skillful with the bow. He could protect himself and his mother. The fact that Hagar took a wife for Ishmael "from the land of Egypt" suggests that Hagar wanted to perpetuate her own cultural heritage, which was Egyptian, and not that of her oppressors Abraham and Sarah.

Even today, most of Hagar's situation is congruent with many African-American women's predicament of poverty, sexual and economic exploitation, surrogacy, domestic violence, homelessness, rape, motherhood, single-parenting, ethnicity and meetings with God. Many black women have testified that "God helped them make a way out of no way." They believe God is involved not only in their survival struggle, but that God also supports their struggle for quality of life, which "making a way" suggests.

I concluded, then, that the female-centered tradition of African-American biblical appropriation could be named the *survival/quality-of-life tradition of*

African-American biblical appropriation. This naming was consistent with the black American community's way of appropriating the Bible so that emphasis is put upon God's response to black people's situation rather than upon what would appear to be hopeless aspects of African-American people's existence in North America. In black consciousness, God's response of survival and quality of life to Hagar is God's response of survival and quality of life to African-American women and mothers of slave descent struggling to sustain their families with God's help.

[Delores S. Williams, *Sisters in the Wilderness*
(Maryknoll, NY: Orbis, 1993), pp. 1–6]

A CONTEMPORARY LITURGY FOR
SAME-SEX UNIONS

Eleanor L. McLaughlin—Episcopal priest, church historian, and spiritual director—has long been active on behalf of lesbian and gay members of Christian churches. McLaughlin put this liturgy into final form and fixed its theological emphasis on friendship, but parts of it were originally composed by her colleagues Richard Valantasis and Jennifer Phillips at a church in Boston during the years around 1990. The rite underscores the liturgical and pastoral needs that are often obscured in current Christian debates over homosexuality.

Document 2–24

CELEBRATION AND BLESSING OF A COVENANTED UNION

The Address to the Community

CELEBRANT: We gather here, a community of friends, before the Holy One and in the presence of the Holy in each other, to witness, celebrate, and support the covenant of [name] and [name] to live together in lifelong love, friendship, and mutual service with the larger human family. The calling to a covenanted life of faithful and self-giving love is a grace and gift from God, in whose image we are created and by whom we are called to love and reason, work and play, to be still and to know ecstasy, to risk and to trust, to receive and to act. Before God we acknowledge our response to this invitation to live in union and harmony with God, with each other, and with all of creation. In celebrating this covenant, we are reminded of and experience our highest vocation: to love God, to love ourselves, and to love neighbor and stranger as ourselves.

God has given us a sign and promise of everlasting love in the rainbow after the flood; in the loyal affection of Jonathan and David; in the steadfast loyalty of Ruth and Naomi; in the recognition that it is God within who unites us, as Elizabeth and Mary were united; in the promise of God's friendship seen in Jesus's embrace of John, the beloved disciple at the Last Supper; and in the promises of baptism, by which we are made a people, one with each other, in Jesus Christ. So we discern here God-With-Us, in the union of these loving and faithful partners, God sealing in hope their vow and covenant with each other as lovers, and with the world, as justice-makers.

Now [name] and [name] come to stand with each other, surrounded and supported by their family and friends in this community, that in this spring of seasons bright, they may make vows of faithful life together. This covenant and union is intended to be for them a mutual joy, a support in hard times, a comfort in their shared delights. From this union of love and friendship emerges a new family, source of care for the world, the lonely, the lost; a sign for all who see them, that faithfulness and mutual affection triumph over selfishness, egotism, greed, and violence.

We celebrate with them this new family, a "Little Commonwealth," haven and mission of good energy for the healing of the world. Therefore, these mutual promises are to be undertaken and affirmed seriously, reverently, and in accordance with the patterns of truth, beauty, and goodness that enable each to say to the other, "I will you to be." In their commitment, we see the very face of God, a sign of hope and wholeness for all of creation.

[Name] and [name], what do you seek?

COUPLE: We seek a blessing of God, each other, our friends and family, and this community upon our covenant.

Reading
From *Our Passion for Justice: Images of Power, Sexuality and Liberation* by
Carter Heyward
Presentation and Witness of Friends and Family

CELEBRANT: Let us hear the Witness and story of those who present and support [name] and [name] in this commitment.

(*Friends and members of the two families share anecdotes from the past that connect to the present experience of [name] and [name] and point toward their future.*)

Readings
Song of Solomon and 1 Corinthians 13:1–13
Homily
Statement of Intention

CELEBRANT (*addressing each separately*): Do you, [name], choose [name] as lifelong partner in this covenanted union?

Do you, [name], seek to love [name] with all your heart and soul and mind and body?

Will you, [name], be for [name] a loyal, trustworthy, and faithful partner?

Will you, [name], risk in vulnerability to love [name] as *she/he* is, to will *her/him* to be *her/his* best self?

Will you, [name], give your whole and true self to this relationship, that it may become a growing, healthy, and expansive source of love for yourselves and all who know you?

If you both will make this your intention before this community and before God, respond with a wholehearted, "We will and we do."

The Exchange of Vows

(*Vows are written by the couple and said facing each other with hands clasped and bound by a stole or other symbolic cord.*)

The Blessing and Exchange of Rings

(*The rings are presented and the celebrant blesses them.*)

CELEBRANT: Bless, O Holy God, these rings to be a symbol and reminder of the vows by which these *women/men* pledge themselves to be for and with each other a new family in the midst of the human family. May the Spirit fill [name] and [name], who wear these rings with the splendor of growing love, and embody their act of faith, hope, and love in a unity of mind, body, and spirit. Amen.

The Ring Words

(*The ring words are composed by the couple. [name] takes [name]'s ring, puts it on her/his finger and repeats the words of commitment symbolized by the ring. These actions are then repeated by the other partner.*)

The Pronouncement

(*Gathered family and friends may lay their hands on the couple's shoulders. The celebrant may lay her/his hands on their heads.*)

CELEBRANT: Now that [name] and [name] have given themselves to each other by solemn vows, with the joining and binding of hands and the giving and receiving of rings, may the holy God who indwells in the heavens, the earth, and seas, and the heart and spirit of every creature bless this union in the presence of this community. May God be seen in their life together; may the love between them grow and flourish; and may they be a unity at peace with themselves and with all of creation, for the sake of the world. Those whom God has joined and blessed, let no one put asunder.

Prayer

CELEBRANT: Let us be at prayer.

O Holy One, creator and life-fire of all that is, giver of all healing and wholeness, grace and power. Look with favor upon the world you have made and loved, and for which you pour out your God-life, and look especially upon these two *women/men* whom you join together as one flesh, one mind, one heart. Amen.

Give them wisdom and devotion in the ordering of their common life, that each may be to the other a strength in need, a counselor in perplexity, a comfort in sorrow, and a companion in joy. Amen.

Give them grace, when they hurt each other, to recognize and acknowledge their fault and to seek each other's forgiveness and yours. Amen.

Give them such fulfillment of their mutual affection that they may reach out in love and concern for others. Amen.

Grant that all of us, who in hope and faith live in the freedom and responsibility of vowed life together, may find our lives strengthened and our loyalties confirmed. Amen.

Music or Poem

The Blessing of the Covenanted Union

CELEBRANT: Creator God, hovering and indwelling Spirit, you made us not for loneliness but to dwell together in mutual and faithful affection. Bless and keep [name] and [name] that they may honor each other in all times and places. Let the sacred fire of friendship burn brighter between them. Let their love deepen and widen and be as a rich garden bed of every flower and fruit. Let forgiveness end any disputes, humor unburden them in the midst of difficulty, and holy service to the world be the true riches they seek. Now, O Holy Wisdom, give your grace and nurture to [name] and [name] May your birth-giving be a blessing of light and warmth in their lives that they continue to grow in joy with each other and as a reconciling presence in your world. Amen.

Candle Ceremony

(*Celebrant presents [name] and [name] each with a lighted candle. [name] and [name] together light a single larger candle from which the assembly takes individual lights.*)

CELEBRANT: From every human being there rises a light reaching out toward heaven.

When two souls that are called to become one flesh choose each other, their streams of light flow together and a single brighter light goes forth from their united being.

Dismissal

CELEBRANT: Let us dance as David danced, laugh as Sarah laughed, and go in peace and light to set the world on fire. Alleluia, alleluia, alleluia.

[Eleanor L. McLaughlin, "Celebration and Blessing of a Covenanted Union,"
in *Equal Rites: Lesbian and Gay Worship, Ceremonies, and Celebrations,*
ed. Kittredge Cherry and Zalmon Sherwood (Louisville:
Westminster John Knox, 1995), pp. 100–104]

Chapter 3

ISLAM

Azizah Y. Al-Hibri and Raja' M. El Habti

INTRODUCTION

PROPHET MUHAMMAD: THE LAST PROPHET OF ISLAM

Islam is the youngest of the three Abrahamic religions and views itself as the final reiteration and elaboration of the same message that was revealed to Abraham, Moses, Jesus, and other prophets of Christianity and Judaism. The holy book of Islam is the Qur'an, which is viewed by Muslims as the literal word of God revealed to Prophet Muhammad through the Archangel Gabriel.

Muhammad, a disadvantaged orphan, was born in sixth-century Makkah (Mecca) of noble descent to the tribe of Quraysh. This is the same tribe that would, after the revelation, wage ruthless attacks against him and his followers until they migrated from Makkah to Madinah (Medina) upon the invitation of its inhabitants. Because of his modest means and existing social conditions, the Prophet was illiterate, but soon developed a reputation for hard work, wisdom, and trustworthiness. Thus he was known as "al-Amin" (the Trustworthy One), even before he received the revelation.

Ancient biographical sources about the Prophet tell us that his reputation earned him the trust of Khadijah Bint Khuwailid, a rich Makkan businesswoman who hired him to run her trade to Damascus. Impressed by his com-

petence, moral values, and demeanor, she proposed to him in marriage, and
he accepted. She was twenty years his senior but the marriage was highly successful. It was monogamous, and lasted twenty-five years until her death. It gave
the Prophet the only progeny he had. The Prophet's relationship with Khadijah
affected his view of women as equal human beings (see, for example, his statements in section 2, "Creation and the Identity of Origin of Women and Men").
At home he cut meat, mended his shoes, and played with his children. When
faced with a crisis affecting the new Muslim community, he sought and took
the advice of a woman. In his farewell address the Prophet repeatedly enjoined
Muslim men to treat Muslim women kindly.

THE REVELATION

According to Islamic history books, when the Prophet was about forty years of
age, he took a trip to the wilderness, as was his habit, to think and reflect. While
in Cave Hira', the Archangel Gabriel appeared to him and spoke the first word
of the Qur'an: "Read!"[1] The illiterate prophet was taken aback, and Gabriel
repeated his order: "Read in the name of your God, the Creator." The experience shook up the Prophet who broke into sweat and returned to Khadijah
asking her to cover him up. When he recounted his experience in the cave to
her, she assured him that he had received a revelation. Khadijah soon embraced
that revelation and became the first Muslim. This marked a trend in the life of
the early Muslim community, in which women played a leadership role in
various parts of community life, including religious and political leadership.

The Qur'an was revealed over a period of twenty-three years.[2] The central
point of that revelation was deep monotheism that rejected any partnership
with God. The Qur'an is clear in asserting that Jesus is a prophet, not a divinity,
who was born to the Virgin Mary (19:16–35). According to the Qur'an, Mary
was a pious woman who "guarded her chastity," and Jesus was born to her after
Gabriel "breathed into her of Our Spirit" (21:91). The Qur'an attributes various
miracles to Jesus (5:109), including that of speaking in the cradle to quell suspicions about his mother Mary (19:27–33).

SEX, MARRIAGE, AND FAMILY IN THE QUR'AN

The Qur'an states that God created all humanity from a single *nafs* (soul or
spirit), created from like nature its mate, and from the two made humanity into
nations and tribes so that they may get to know each other, that is, to enjoy and
learn from each other's diversity (4:1; 49:13). The only proper criterion for preference among people is that of piety, a quality achievable by anyone (49:13).
The Prophet himself stated, in a famous reported *hadith*, that women are the
twin halves of men. Absent from the Qur'an is the view that woman was created
from Adam's rib.

The Qur'an defines the marriage relationship as one based on tranquillity, mercy, and affection (30:21). It states very clearly that in a marriage the couple must live together amicably or part in kindness (2:229). For this reason, traditional Muslim jurists considered abuse (whether verbal or physical) as adequate justification for divorce. This view is reflected in the personal status codes (family laws) of some Muslim countries, such as Kuwait and Jordan.

Other passages in the Qur'an, however, appear to paint a different picture of gender and family relations. For example, one verse states that men have a "degree" over women (2:228), while another appears to sanction wife beating (4:34). This has led some writers to argue that the Qur'an itself contains patriarchal views. But this view of the Qur'an contradicts the one we described earlier. Since the Qur'an is believed by Muslims to be the divine revelation of an All-Knowing God, jurists have asserted that the revelation cannot be contradictory. Therefore, for pious Muslims, it becomes important to find a serious interpretation of all these verses of the Qur'an that makes them mutually consistent. This fact underlines the importance of thoughtful juristic interpretation in Islam. Our selections are designed to give the reader a glimpse of this effort.

FOUNDATIONS OF ISLAMIC JURISPRUDENCE

QUR'AN

There are four major sources of Islamic jurisprudence; of these the Qur'an is the primary one. The Qur'an was recorded by the Companions of the Prophet at the time of its revelation. In the days of the third *khalifah* (caliph), 'Uthman, all the recorded passages were gathered and organized into a certain (nonchronological) order that has become the standard. Every verse, word, and letter in the collected passages was attested to by the Companions of the Prophet. Hence, there are no substantive disagreements among Muslims about the text of the revelation itself. Disagreements arise only from interpretive efforts. For this reason a Muslim espouses the revelation as a whole. There is no room to pick and choose among verses, since all of them are considered the Word of God.

The Qur'an consists of various elements, such as parables, ethical pronouncements, general legal rules and specific ones, as well as spiritual guidance. Many of the revealed verses addressed certain circumstances or events at the time and must be understood in their light. These events or circumstances are called *asbab al-nuzul*, that is, reasons for the revelation. They shed light on the true meaning of the revelation, even if that revelation has significance beyond those special circumstances. For example, the verse "And when the girl-child who was buried alive is asked [on the Day of Judgment]: 'For what sin was she slain?'" addressed the pre-Islamic custom of female infanticide and prohibited it utterly and completely (see section 3.1). Its significance, however, is not limited to that pre-Islamic practice, but reaches other practices that deny life on the basis of gender, such as gender-based abortion.

SUNNAH

Because the Qur'an is viewed by Muslims as the revealed word of God, it ranks as the highest source and final arbiter. But the second major source in Islamic jurisprudence is the *sunnah* of the Prophet (his example), including his *hadith* (statements). Where a Qur'anic verse is capable of different interpretations, the *sunnah* of the Prophet is consulted whenever possible to shed light on the proper application or interpretation of the verse. This approach is rooted in the belief that the Prophet was the ideal Muslim, and hence he offered the best guidance.

The Qur'an itself states that "if you differ in anything among yourselves, refer it to God and His Messenger" (4:59). Thus this verse emphasizes the importance of the Prophet's *sunnah*. But the *sunnah* is different from the revelation. It represents the words of the Prophet, a human being. Furthermore, the Prophet himself prevented his companions from recording his words during the early days of the revelation in order to keep the revelation distinct from them. When the words of the Prophet were finally recorded, this was done either during the latter part of his life or after his death. Some of the later reports about the Prophet suffered from errors caused by lapses in memory, inaccurate reporting, or even biased or interested reporting. Thus, determining the reliability, accuracy, and authenticity of reported precedents or incidents in *sunnah* or *hadith* became a matter of paramount importance.

A good example of the pitfalls of reported *hadith* is a story recounted by 'A'ishah, the woman the Prophet married after the death of Khadijah. She heard that Abu Hurayrah (d. 677), a Companion of the Prophet, was quoting the Prophet as having stated that "bad omens lie with women, horses, and houses." 'A'ishah then got very upset and protested about these reports, saying: "May God forgive Abu Hurayrah. He [the Prophet] never said that; he said, 'People of *Jahiliyyah* [pre-Islamic period] used to say that bad omens lie with women, horses, and houses.'"[3] By missing the first part of the *hadith*, the reporter totally reversed its meaning. For this reason the study of *hadith* requires a great deal of care and training. So, as to the substance of a *hadith*, a good rule of thumb is that if it contradicts the Qur'an or common sense, then it cannot be true (or we are misinterpreting it).

IJTIHAD

This is the third source of Islamic jurisprudence and is subordinate to both the Qur'an and *sunnah*. The word *ijtihad* means literally "to exert an effort." It is used to refer generally to the jurisprudential activity in which scholars engage either to interpret the Qur'an and *sunnah*, where an interpretation is required, or to reach a ruling involving no clear Qur'anic pronouncement or prophetic precedent. For example, in today's world a Muslim must answer questions about the religious permissibility of cloning or organ transplantation. To reach an answer the Muslim must refer to relevant general principles in the Qur'an and relevant incidents or sayings in the *sunnah* that could, perhaps by the use of analogical reasoning, shed light on the issue. Over the centuries Muslim jurists have engaged in extensive *ijtihad* and have accumulated a very rich tradition. During his lifetime the Prophet encouraged this sort of activity so long as it was based on serious and objective effort.

IJMA'

A fourth source of Islamic law is *ijma'* or consensus. The Prophet is reported to have said that Muslims would not reach consensus on an error. Thus where consensus exists Muslims have become bound by it. The only remaining question becomes, What counts as consensus? For example, would the consensus of scholars suffice, or should the consensus include the general public? Would that include women as well? Does the consensus of an earlier society bind those after it? Muslim jurists have grappled with these sorts of questions and provided different answers.

THE STRUCTURE OF RELIGIOUS AUTHORITY

Muslims do not have either a clergy or a religious structure similar to a church hierarchy. The Qur'an is available to every Muslim to read and think about. Muslims pray to God directly five times a day, and there is no need for a mediator between them and Him. More specifically, Shi'is as well as Sunnis do not have clergy, despite the fact that the American media has fallen into the habit of calling some Shi'i religious figures "clerics." So-called clerics are either religious community leaders or scholarly imams. Modern Shi'i imams are simply serious religious scholars. A select few among them achieve over time such level of Islamic knowledge, wisdom, and piety that their peers view them as worthy of emulation *(muqallad)*. These imams then develop a following. No follower, however, is bound automatically by the choices of another, even the *muqallad* imam. In the final analysis each Muslim is responsible before God for his or her own choices.

It is clear from the above discussion that, while for Muslims the Qur'an is pure divine revelation, the commentators and interpreters are human. Further, the *hadith* itself is reported by humans capable of error who happened to be with the Prophet. Thus it is quite important in Islam to delineate the boundaries between divinely revealed and human statements. The first is indubitable and final for Muslims; the second is subject to a great deal of examination and even refutation. To guard against error, Muslim jurists resorted to an extensive use of reason through historical as well as logical analysis.

EXTRA-QUR'ANIC INFLUENCES ON IJTIHAD

As human activity, *ijtihad* was subject to influences surrounding the jurists themselves. To the extent these influences sway the jurists' interpretations, Muslims are not bound by them. Muslims are only bound by the revelation, not the patriarchal or cultural assumptions of jurists. Further, Muslims in different countries would want to develop their own jurisprudence that takes into account local cultural assumptions, so long as these assumptions do not contradict Qur'anic principles. For example, a society used to making offerings to idols cannot continue such practice if it chooses Islam, because Islam rejects all forms of idol worship. On the other hand, there is no one "decreed" Islamic dress. All Muslims may follow their countries' dress customs, so long as the dress is modest.

There were three major extraneous influences on Muslim jurists throughout history: religious, patriarchal, and cultural. While religious and patriarchal influences can be viewed as part of cultural influences in a society, they transcend any one culture and deserve to be treated separately.

RELIGIOUS INFLUENCES

Islam was revealed in a society that was familiar with the other two Abrahamic revelations, Christianity and Judaism. As mentioned, Islam embraced these earlier messages rather than rejecting them. It also accorded their followers a special status as the People of the Book. This state of affairs has had consequences in various areas, ranging from the acceptance of interfaith marriages with non-Muslim women to the inclusion of some Judeo-Christian ideas in Islamic jurisprudence. For example, the traditional biblical version of the fall of Adam in Genesis was echoed by some Muslim jurists, despite the differences between it and the Qur'anic version (see Docs. 3–1 and 3–2).

PATRIARCHAL INFLUENCES

Patriarchal influences were rampant in the Arabian Penninsula, where Islam was revealed. True, there were some pockets, such as the Madinan society, which treated women more favorably, but Islam came to reverse the dominant patriarchal trend. It did so in many ways, not the least of which was protecting female children from infanticide, guaranteeing women their right to inherit a specified share of their family's wealth, and protecting them economically by giving women both the right to work and education as well as the right to demand maintenance from the closest capable male in their family (or society, in the absence of family).

Patriarchal thinking found expression within Islamic jurisprudence at various levels, including interpretation of the Qur'an, validation and interpretation of *hadith*, and selective adoption of cultural customs. In all these cases the influence is at times subtle, at others flagrant. To purge Islamic jurisprudence of this cultural patriarchal tradition, some Muslim jurists have embarked on a gender-sensitive reading of the Qur'an and are reexamining the tradition with fresh eyes that are not beholden to the distorted vision of an ancient patriarchy.

CULTURAL INFLUENCES

Based on Qur'an 49:13, which is viewed by Muslims as celebrating diversity, Muslim scholars permitted Muslims in various countries to import into their laws cultural norms and customs that do not contradict Islamic law. Thus, there are custom-based legal differences among Muslim countries. Some of these differences are reflected in Islamic jurisprudence itself. It is a well-known story about Imam al-Shafi'i that when he migrated from Iraq to Egypt he revised his school of thought to accommodate the Egyptian society. This fact is generally captured by the Islamic juristic principle that "laws change with the change of time and place." Clearly this principle does not encompass basic Islamic principles that are unchangeable *(thawabit)*, but derivative ones that are capable of adaptation.

Unfortunately, many patriarchal cultural influences seeped into Islamic jurisprudence but were not recognized as inconsistent with the Islamic worldview. These cultural elements, having been mixed with pure Islamic law, were in time mistaken by Muslims to be part of it.

More recently, various Muslim jurists and Islamic countries have come together to reexamine pressing issues and reenergize scholarly activity. As a result, there is currently a movement to produce fresh Islamic jurisprudence that abides by the best of the traditional methodologies yet incorporates in its interpretation the realities of our modern societies and times.

The selections in this chapter were chosen to inform the reader about the basics of Islam as well as the vast diversity of juristic views within it, which range from the misogynist to the feminist. The introduction explains some of the roots of this diversity. The rich tradition of *ijtihad* in Islam opened the door for later jurists, male and female, to review the work of earlier jurists, keep what is suitable, and dispense with what is not, relying mainly on the Qur'an as the leading and final arbiter. This means that this critical period of Islamic history can be very exciting for those who want to lead change. It is a period of struggle of ideas, old versus new, and authentic versus opportunistic or apologetic.

CREATION AND THE IDENTITY OF ORIGIN OF WOMEN AND MEN

The Islamic worldview is based on the fundamental concept of *tawhid*, or the unicity of God as Creator and Supreme Will. Any denial of this unicity constitutes *shirk* (the opposite of *tawhid*), which denial is a sin God tells us He will not forgive. As the Creator, "There is nothing Whatever like unto Him" (Q. 42:11). So, it is inappropriate to ask about the gender of the Creator; for he created genders. While the Qur'anic story of creation is basically similar to that in the Bible, there are some important differences. Most significantly, there is nothing in the Qur'an to suggest that Eve was created from Adam's rib. All the verses related to creation in the Qur'anic passages below state flatly that men and women have the same essence and were created from a "single soul," or *nafs*. Men and women enjoy mutual rights and responsibilities, and they are expected to dwell with their mates in love, mercy, and tranquillity. The Qur'an goes to great lengths to emphasize the essential "sameness" of men and women, while at the same time acknowledging the different challenges and responsibilities they face in their lifecycles and the ongoing lifecycles of their families and communities.

The texts below include Qur'anic passages on the original equality of the sexes in creation and a reported *hadith* that already reflects the incorporation into the Islamic tradition of the biblical "Adam's rib" account in which Eve was created secondarily from Adam. These are followed by several commentaries, some of which seek to reconcile these apparently divergent creation accounts. The traditional commentary of al-Tabari (838–923) in the ninth century emphasizes the relation of tranquillity between the sexes. The modern commentary of Rida in the nineteenth century acknowledges both creation accounts to emphasize gender sameness and difference as the basis for complementarity and cooperation between the sexes. The contemporary interpretations of Amuli (b. 1933), a religious scholar, and Nasseef (b. 1944), a Saudi woman activist, squarely reject the *hadithic* accounts of Eve as being created from Adam's "crooked rib." They return to the Qur'anic principle of sameness of origin and gender equality based on being created from a "single soul." We close with a passage from a recent speech by the King of Morocco in which he used the prophetic *hadith* about women being the split halves of men to call for modernization of the family code and improvement of the status of women in his country.

Document 3–1

QUR'AN 4:1

O humankind! Reverence your Guardian-Lord, who created you from a single soul,[+] created, of like nature, his mate, and from them twain scattered (like seeds) countless men and women; reverence God, through whom you demand your mutual (rights), and (reverence) the wombs (that bore you): for God ever watches over you.

[Al-Nisa', The Women, Abdullah Yusuf 'Ali, *The Meaning of the Holy Qu'ran* (MD: Amana, 1991)]

Document 3–2

QUR'AN 7:189

It is He Who created you from a single soul *(nafs)*, and made of her a mate of like nature, so that he [the mate] might dwell with her in tranquillity.[5]

> [Al-a'raf, The Heights, Abdullah Yusuf 'Ali, *The Meaning of the Holy Qu'ran* (MD: Amana, 1991)]

Document 3–3

QUR'AN 35:11

And God did create you from dust; then from a sperm-drop; then He made you in pairs.

> [Fatir, The Originator of Creation, Abdullah Yusuf 'Ali, *The Meaning of the Holy Qu'ran* (MD: Amana, 1991)]

Document 3–4

HADITH

Women are but *shaqa'iq* (the split halves) of men.

> [Hadith, narrated by `A'ishah in Abu-Dawud, *Sunan Abu Dawud*, bk. 1, Taharah (ablation) no. 236 (9th century CE)]

Document 3–5

HADITH

The Prophet said, "Act kindly towards woman, for they were created from a rib and the most crooked part of a rib is its top. If you attempt to straighten it you will break it, and if you leave it alone it will remain crooked; so act kindly towards women.

> [Hadith narrated by Abu Hurayrah, in al-Bukhari, *Abu Abdillah Muhammad Ibn Ismail* (810–870 CE), *Al-Jami' al-Sahih* (The Sound Comprehensive Collection of Hadiths), known as *Sahih al-Bukhari*, al-Bukhari, *Sahih al-Bukhari*, vol. 7, bk. 62, Nikah (Marriage), no. 114 (Beirut: Dar al-Ma'rifah, n.d.; 9th century CE)]

Document 3–6

ABU JA'FAR MUHAMMAD IBN JARIR AL-TABARI

Our view regarding the verse: "O people! Reverence your Guardian-Lord, who created you from a single soul" is that God described Himself as the sole creator of all humankind, from a single being. He also made known to His subjects the process of genesis as it sprung out from a single being or soul. He draws their attention to the fact that they are the progeny of one single father and one single mother and that they all relate to each other. Therefore, their rights upon each other are established in the same way as the right of a person upon his/her own brother, for they all come from the same father and the same mother. In fact, their responsibility to take care of each other involved by the distant relationship to the same father is similar to the one involved by close familial relationships. And since they are all related, they have to be just with each other and not to commit injustices towards each other, so that the stronger among them protects the weaker as God ordered. . . .

When God gave Adam his dwelling in heaven, he was walking amidst it lonely and without a mate with whom he could find tranquility. Adam then fell asleep for a little while, and when he woke up he found, sitting by his head, a woman who was created from of his own ribs. He asked her what she was and she answered: "A Woman!" He then asked her why she was created, and she said, "so that you might find tranquility with me."

From what we learned from the people of the Book and specifically from the people of the Torah, and from others people of Knowledge . . . God sent Adam into a state of sleep, he then took one rib from his left side and then mended his body—all this while Adam was asleep—till God the Almighty created Adam's mate, Eve, from that same rib. He then made her into a woman so that Adam finds tranquility with her. And when God lifted Adam from his state of sleep, Adam saw her by his side and said,—as the People of the book narrate but God knows better—"My flesh! My blood! My mate!" And he found tranquility in her. . . .

[Abu Ja'far Muhammad Ibn Jarir Al-Tabari, *Jami' al-Bayane fi Tafsir al-Qur'an* (The Exhaustive Commentary on the Qur'an), 23 vols. (Beirut: Dar al-Ma'rifah, 1978), 4:149 (9th century CE)]

Document 3–7

MUHAMMAD RASHID RIDA

And it is He who created you from a single *nafs* [soul or being] from the same kind and essence. He perfected its image to make a perfect human being. "And then He made from its own kind its mate to find quiet of mind in it." . . . They were a pair, male and female, as stated in the verse: "O people, We created you from a male and a female," as He has created the species from pairs, males and females. . . . We also see that each cell from which our bodies develop encloses two nuclei, male and female. Once joined together, they yield a new cell and so on. One also notices that the creation of human beings comes from joining two elements of a complementary nature, together as a pair. God says: "And He truly created the pair, male and female, from the small life-germ [sperm] when it is adapted." But we do not know how the first being doubled to yield the male and female genders. God says: "I made them not witness the creation of heavens and earth, nor their own creation."

And in the Torah of the people of the Book, it is said that Eve was created from one of Adam's ribs. . . . We, therefore, use the *hadith* of our Prophet in this context, which reads: "take good care of women, for woman was created from a crooked rib, and that the most crooked part of the rib is its higher end. If you, therefore, try to redress it you might break it. But if you leave it as it is, it stays crooked. You, hence, shall treat women well." . . . The common meaning that comes to mind from the interpretations of different *hadith* experts is that women were created differently from men. They have their own flaws and differences. So are men indeed. They also have their own flaws and differences. This is why when Ibn Hibban [d. 965] narrated the *hadith*, according to Abu Hurayrah, "woman was created from a crooked rib," he explained that it is similar to God's saying: "man was created from hastiness," which underlines the inherent flaw of human beings known as impatience.

[Muhammad Rashid Rida, *Tafsir al-Qur'an al Hakim* (Commentary on the Wise Qur'an) (known as *Tafsir al-Manar*), 20 vols. (Beirut: Dar al-Ma'rifah, n.d), 9:517
(19th century CE)]

Document 3–8

JAVAADI AMULI

The meaning of the verse is, first, that all human beings, from either gender, be it women or men (for the term *people*[6] includes everybody,) were created from a single essence and entity, and the principle of potential life emanates from the single source. Second, that the first woman was the wife of the first man, and that she was created from the same essence and entity and not from a different essence, she was not part of a man or an auxiliary or a parasitical being or anything similar to that. Nay, God created the first woman from the same essence and origin and then created all men and women from these two humans. . . . These issues mentioned above could be found in the verse: "It is He Who created you from a single soul *(nafs)* and made its mate of like nature [7:189] and the verse: "He created you (all) from a single soul *(nafs)*, then created, of like nature, its mate. . . . " [39:6]. These verses, which deal with the origin of creation, state the sameness of the essence of the principle of potential life from which both men and women were created, as were created the first man and woman from which came all human beings. There are also *hadiths*[7] that refer to the principle of potential life. . . . "Abu Abdillah . . . was asked about the creation of Eve, and why some people say she was created from one of Adam's left flank's ribs, he said, "God be exalted and glorified above all what they claim. Does he who says this believe that God was not able to create a mate for Adam from something else but Adam's rib? . . . And he who says this opens the door for the ill-hearted people to say that Adam was copulating with himself if Eve was a part of his own body." He then said, "He created Eve for him. . . . And Adam — peace be upon him — said, "O Lord! What is this beautiful creation whose presence has comforted me and pleased my eyes?" God said,

"O Adam! This is my subject Eve; do you wish that she be with you, keeps you company, talks to you and follows you?" Adam said, "Yes, O Lord! And all praise be unto you for it forever." And God said, "Then seek her in marriage from me for she is my subject. She could also be your wife for sexual desires." He stirred sexual desire in him. Adam then said, "O Lord! I seek her from you, so what would make you agree to it?" And God said, "I would give you my blessing if you teach her the principles of my faith."

This *hadith* . . . sheds light on important issues, first, that the creation of Eve from Adam's left rib is not true, and second, that the creation of Eve was a wonderful and separate event exactly like Adam's creation. . . . "[8]

[Javaadi Amuli, *Jamal al-Mar'ah wa Jalaluha* (Woman's Beauty and Magnificence) (Beirut: Dar al-Hadi, 1994), pp. 25–26]

Document 3–9

FATIMA NASEEF

"From" does not imply that Eve is necessarily a part of Adam. However, it indicates that the creation of Adam took precedence. Therefore, God (SWT)[9] says, " . . . Created you from a single soul." Sheikh Abdulkareem al-Khateeb [*sic*], says, "It means that He created from this soul, from the same kind and the same substance, a spouse to that one soul, which does not refer to Adam as human being. It refers to a substance set in readiness for the creation of mankind [*sic*]. From this substance Adam has been created, and from this same substance his wife Eve has been created. . . . "

I personally favor the . . . [above] interpretation for the following reasons:

1. The interpretation based on the creation of Eve from Adam's rib originates from the Torah and it is not mentioned in our prophetic narrations;
2. There is nothing in the verse which clearly suggests that "this soul" refers to Adam himself as a person;
3. The narration which describes woman as "a rib which is crooked" is metaphorical, "with the intention to urge men to be kind to their wives and to be patient in dealing with and tolerating their imperfections."

[Fatima Umar Naseef, *Women in Islam: A Discourse in Rights and Obligations* (Cairo: International Islamic Committee for Women and Child, 1999), pp. 51–52]

Document 3–10

KING MOHAMED VI OF MOROCCO

With regards to the issue of the family and the improvement of the status of women, I raised the fundamental problems related to this issue . . . by asking the following question in my address of 20 August 1999: "how can society achieve progress, while the rights of women, who represent half of it, are violated and while they are subject to injustice, violence and marginalization, notwithstanding the dignity and justice granted them by our glorious religion? . . .

Through the instructions I issued and the opinion I expressed regarding the proposed Family Law, I wanted to see to it that the following fundamental reforms be introduced:

Adopt a modern form of wording instead of concepts that undermine the dignity of women as human beings and make husband and wife jointly responsible for the family, in keeping with the words of my ancestor the Prophet Mohammad, peace and blessings be upon Him, who said, "women are the split halves (shaqa'iq) of men [before the law]," and also with the saying: "Only an honorable man will honor them; and only an ignoble man will humiliate them."

[King Mohamed VI of Morocco, excerpt from his speech at the opening of the Parliament fall session, October 10, 2003, introducing the Reform of the Family Code, known as Mudawwanat al-'Usrah[10]]

THE FALL FROM THE GARDEN AND GENDER EQUALITY

The Qur'anic account of the fall from the Garden also differs from the biblical one. For example, the forbidden tree was not that of (carnal) knowledge, but of immortality and an eternal kingdom (Q. 20:120). Both Adam and Eve were equally susceptible to the temptation. The Qur'an does not assign blame to Eve for eating from the forbidden tree and then tempting Adam. According to the Qur'an, Eve was neither the first to succumb to temptation, nor did she seduce Adam. Both shared the responsibility equally, and both received blame equally. Significantly, while the Qur'an recognizes the pain and travails of childbearing, nowhere does it state that God cursed Eve for her disobedience by "increasing her pains in childbearing," as narrated in Genesis 3:16. Nevertheless, in some of the passages below, Muslim exegetes of the Qur'an were clearly influenced by the Judeo-Christian account of the fall in developing their tafasir, or interpretations. This is evident in the interpretation espoused by a group of traditional scholars discussed by al-Suyuti (1445–1505) in the fifteenth century. Such interpretations influenced later attitudes about women, procreation, and gender and marital relationships in Muslim communities. But, as we see in Fatima Naseef's late twentieth-century account, the incorporation of the idea of Eve's responsibility for the fall is being revisited and questioned today even by some conservative Muslim women activists.

The Qur'anic view of gender—both in creation and in the fall—is based on ontological equality and social equity between men and women. Men and women are considered to possess the same dignity in the world and the same value before God. Neither gender has superiority over the other. God judges individuals, male and female, in light of their degree of piety and righteousness. The Qur'an informs us that the most honored in the sight of God are those who are most righteous, regardless of their gender (49:130). The Qur'an also informs us that there will be no guilt by association. The act of every person is his own and no one else will be accountable for it (6:164). On this basis a woman who exhibits in words and deeds a high degree of piety is superior to men who have not reached such an advanced level. In fact, neither gender nor race, wealth, class, or power define a person's true position with respect to others; righteousness does.

Document 3–11

QUR'AN 2:35–36

We said, "O Adam! Dwell thou and thy wife in the Garden; and eat of the bountiful things therein as (where and when) ye will; but approach not this tree, or ye run into harm and transgression."

Then did Satan make them slip from the (Garden), and get them out of the state (of felicity) in which they had been.

[Al-Baqarah, The Cow, Abdullah Yusuf 'Ali, *The Meaning of the Holy Qu'ran* (MD: Amana, 1991)]

Document 3–12

QUR'AN 7:19–20

"O Adam! Dwell thou and thy wife in the Garden, and enjoy (its good things) as ye wish: but approach not this tree, or ye run into harm and transgression.

Then began Satan to whisper suggestions to them, bringing openly before their minds all their shame that was hidden from them (before): he said, "Your Lord only forbade you this tree, lest ye should become angels or such beings as live for ever."

[Al-a'raf, The Heights]

Document 3–13

QUR'AN 20:117–124

"Then We said, "O Adam! Verily, this is an enemy to thee and thy wife: so let him not get you both out of the Garden, so that thou art landed in misery.

There is therein (enough provision) for thee not to go hungry nor to go naked, Nor to suffer from thirst, nor from the sun's heat. But Satan whispered evil to him: he said, "O Adam! Shall I lead thee to the Tree of Eternity and to a kingdom that never decays?"

In the result, they both ate of the tree, and so their nakedness appeared to them: they began to sew together, for their covering, leaves from the Garden: thus did Adam disobey his Lord, and allow himself to be seduced.

But his Lord chose him (for His Grace): He turned to him, and gave him Guidance. He said, "Get ye down, both of you,- all together, from the Garden, with enmity one to another: but if, as is sure, there comes to you Guidance from Me, whosoever follows My Guidance, will not lose his way, nor fall into misery."

[Ta Ha, Abdullah Yusuf 'Ali, *The Meaning
of the Holy Qu'ran* (MD: Amana, 1991)]

Document 3–14

QUR'AN 4:124

"If any do deeds of righteousness—be they male or female—and have faith, they will enter Heaven, and not the least injustice will be done to them."

[Al-Nisa', The Women]

Document 3–15

ABU JA'FAR MUHAMMAD IBN JARIR AL-TABARI

God (may His name be exalted) says that Adam and Eve ate from the tree he had forbidden to them. They obeyed the devil [instead] and disobeyed their Lord. Therefore, they were exposed, which means that their private parts were uncovered. . . .

Satan intended by his saying "do you want me to show you the tree of immortality and eternal prosperity?" to make them exposed to each other and show them what they didn't see of each other, and that Satan knew about their intimate body parts, as he was reading on the sly from the books. Adam was not aware of this, so he refused to eat from it [the tree]. Eve then stepped forward and ate from it and then said, "O Adam! Do eat, for I have eaten from it and no evil befell me." So he ate from it and they were exposed.

[Al-Tabari, *Jami' al-Bayan fi Tafsir al-Qur'an*, 16:163]

Document 3–16

JALAL AL-DIN ABD AL-RAHMAN IBN ABI BAKR AL-SUYUTI

Wahb Ibn Munabbih [654/655–728?] said, when God gave Adam and his wife their abode in Paradise, and after God forbade him to eat from the tree, Adam noticed that the tree branches were intertwined and that it had fruits from which the angels ate regularly, for they were immortal. It was the fruit that was forbidden to him and to his wife.

When the devil decided to lead them astray, he hid inside the beast. The said beast had four legs and a domed back. It was among God's most beautiful creatures. When the beast entered the garden of heaven, the devil jumped out of it, picked some of the tree's fruits and brought them to Eve. The devil said unto her, "Look at this tree, how a soothing fragrance it has! A great taste it has! A beautiful color it has!" Eve then took it from him and brought it to Adam. She said to him, "Look at this tree's fruit! How great a fragrance, taste and color it has!" Adam then ate from it "and they were exposed."

Adam then hid inside the tree. When his Lord called upon him, "O Adam! Where are you?" Adam replied, "Right here my Lord!" God said to him, "Don't you want to get out?" Adam said, "I am too ashamed Lord!" God said, "Descend to earth!" He then said, "O Eve! Did you tempt my servant? For this reason, you shall never bear a child without pain and suffering and you shall never give birth without nearing death many times."

[Jalal al-Din Abd al-Rahman Ibn Abi Bakr Al-Suyuti, *Al-Durr al-Manthur
fi al-Tafsir bi al-Ma'thur* (The Scattered Pearls: A Commentary on the Qur'an
Based on Transmitted Narrations) 7 vols. (Beirut: Dar al-Kutub al 'Ilmiyyah, 2000),
4:555–556 (15th century CE)]

Document 3–17

MUHAMMAD RASHID RIDA

"If any do deeds of righteousness—be they male or female—and have faith, they will enter Heaven, and not the least injustice will be done to them."

This encompasses any one who does all he/she could of righteous deeds, which elevate the soul in its moral, ethical, individual, or social endeavors— either being a male or a female—contrary to some people who look down on women to the point they make them equal to animals. . . .

[Rida, *Tafsir al-Manar*, 2:436 (19th century CE)]

Document 3–18

FATIMA NASEEF

Was not Eve the one who—as they say—tempted Adam and led him to eat from the forbidden tree as mentioned in Genesis? The noble Qur'an denies this false accusation and makes it clear that both Adam and Eve were responsible for their ejection from Paradise. The prohibition was directed to both of them. . . . Both of them disobeyed God (SWT) and together were tempted by Satan. He whispered to both of them, contrary to the biblical version in which Satan whispered to Eve and Eve tempted Adam. . . . Hence Islam exonerates woman [*sic*] from the sin that has been attributed to her, denying that she was responsible for Adam's ejection from Paradise.

[Naseef, *Women in Islam*, pp. 56–57]

THE MARRIAGE CONTRACT

The Qur'an does not refer to the marriage contract as a mere contract based on offer and acceptance. Rather, it describes it as a solemn covenant *(mithaqan ghalithan)*, which is carefully regulated by a body of laws. The term *mithaqan*, which means "covenant," appears in a number of places in the Qur'an. In each place it refers to a momentous context, such as the covenant between God and the children of Israel, or those with whom Muslims have concluded a treaty. Furthermore, Egyptian jurist Malakah Zirar notes that God has placed marriage within the category of *'ibadat*, which relate to God's worship, and not within *mu'amalat*, where contracts are usually placed. This makes the marriage contract radically different from and superior to all other contracts. The *sunnah* of the Prophet is no less emphatic.[11] The Prophet said that the marriage contract is the contract most worthy of fulfillment. In other words, he, too, viewed the marriage contract as superior to all other contracts. He is also reported as saying, "Marriage is my *sunnah*, so the one who turns away from my *sunnah*, turns away from me."[11] After all, marriage concerns human happiness and progeny. Ideally, it brings into being a relationship of affection, tranquillity and mercy, and usually results in offspring, which is not only very dear to the parents' hearts but also very critical to the future of the community. Yet, despite the importance of marriage, jurists disagreed as to whether it was a duty upon a Muslim to marry or whether it was simply a desirable or just permissible act. Some argued that marriage in Islam was not obligatory except to avoid sin. Nevertheless, even jurists who viewed marriage as a duty prohibited a prospective husband from getting married in the presence of evidence that he was abusive. The prohibition is based on the fact that abusive marriages do not fulfill the Qur'anic standard of "Either hold together on equitable terms, or separate with kindness" (2:229).

Document 3–19

QUR'AN 4:21

And they have taken from you a solemn covenant.

[Al-Nisa', The Women]

Document 3–20

ABU JA'FAR MUHAMMAD IBN JARIR AL-TABARI

Opinion in interpreting His saying: "And they have taken from you a solemn covenant". . . this refers to the binding obligations you took before them, those acts you promised and accepted to do, namely to hold together on equitable terms or separate from them with kindness. Muslims used to say to the man

who is getting married: "By God, either you live with her on equitable terms
or you leave her in kindness."

[Al-Tabari, *Jami' al-Bayan Fi Tafsir al-Qur'an* 3:657–658 (9th century CE)]

Document 3–21

MALAKAH ZIRAR

Marriage in Islam has a distinctive characteristic. It is distinguished from other
contracts, so that it does not follow their model nor can it be analogized to
them. For, marriage in the judgment and Law of God and the text of the Noble
Qur'an is a solemn covenant. God Almighty says: "But if you decide to take
one wife in place of another, even if you have given the latter a whole treasure
(as marital gift), take not the least bit of it back: Would you take it by slander
and a manifest wrong? And how could you take it when you have gone into
each other, and they have taken from you a solemn covenant? (Al-Nisa' 4:20–
21) and with this covenant which is recognized by Islamic law, the Law Giver
attached marriage to *ibadat* [matters of worship]. For, the one who follows the
word "covenant" in the Qur'an and its placements in the text, would likely not
find it except (in passages) where God orders His worship, the recognition of
His unicity, and the adoption of his laws.

["Malakah Zirar, Mawsu'at al-Zawaj Wa al'alaaqah al-Zawjiyyah Fi al-Islam Wa
al-Shara'i' al-Ukhra" (Encyclopedia of Marriage and Conjugal Relationship in
Islam and Other Legislations) (Unpublished MS, Cairo, 2002), 1:134]

Document 3–22

WAHBAH AL-ZUHAYLI

Marriage is a civil contract (*'aqd*) that has no formalities. *'Aqd* means tying the
parts of the arrangements, which legally means offering and accepting.

[Wahbah Al-Zuhayli, *Al-Fiqh al-Islami wa Adillatuh* (The Islamic Jurisprudence
and Its Evidences), 4th ed. (Beirut: Dar al-Fikr al-Mu'sair, 1997),
9:6522 (20th century CE)]

Document 3–23

MUHAMMAD ʿABDUH

I have seen that, in the books of Islamic jurisprudence, the definition of the
marital contract is "The contract by means of which the husband owns the
private parts of his wife." I have not seen, however, any reference to anything
other than the physical satisfaction between the spouses. All of those books fail
to value the moral and legal duties expected from one civilized party toward
another. There is, to my knowledge, no other civilized law on earth that brought

more civility into the marital relationship than the verse: "and among his signs is this, that He created for you mates from among yourselves, that ye may dwell in tranquillity with them, and He has put love and mercy between your (hearts)" [30:21].

Whoever draws a comparison between the jurisprudential definition of marriage and the one revealed in the abovementioned verse would realize that the ill treatment of women has started from the scholars of Islamic jurisprudence and spread to the general public. One would not then wonder as to the low levels to which the concept of marriage has descended. Marriage, nowadays, has become a pure carnal relationship, in which men enjoy the body of women and disregard any subsequent responsibilities or duties.

[Muhammad 'Abduh, *Al-a'mal al-Kamilah* (Complete Works) (Beirut: al-Mu'assasah al-'Arabiyah li d–Dirasat wa n-Nashr, 1905), 2:72 (19th century CE)]

CONSENT TO MARRIAGE

Consensual relationships are a hallmark of Islamic law, whether in the family, society, or the state. In the realm of the family no spousal relationship may be formed without the proper consent of the prospective spouses. This means that the consent must be based on proper disclosure of the prospective spouses' health, wealth, marital status, and other relevant matters. It should not be coerced by a father or another person, explicitly or implicitly. This condition was made clear by the prophetic precedent that permitted a Muslim woman to annul her marriage into which she was forced by her father. The wisdom behind this requirement is that marriage relationships should be very special ones that are surrounded with affection, mercy, and tranquillity. When one is married against his or her will, it is harder to come by such relationships. Yet, determining the existence of free consent is not always an easy matter. Informed by his wife 'A'ishah that the virgins of Arabia were too modest at that time to express explicitly their acceptance of a marriage offer, the Prophet allowed for their silence as an indication of acceptance. If, however, such a woman objects, the assumption would be rebutted.

Muslim jurists generally agree, with some exceptions, that a woman's marriage cannot be contracted without her consent, though unfortunately not all require that a virgin be informed that her silence constitutes consent. Most have permitted the father, referred to as the "wali" or guardian of the prospective bride, to execute her marriage contract on her behalf as a protective measure against designing men. The guardian requirement was historically defended as a protective measure for women who might be swept away by their emotions and for the family's honor in cases where women might elect to marry ineligible males. For these reasons even those schools of Islamic law that recognize the right of the adult woman to contract her own marriage without a guardian express their preference for the woman's delegation of that right to a guardian. This paternalistic approach may have been suitable for societies where women were sequestered from public life and could be easily deceived, but Islam does not require such sequestering. Khadijah (d. c. 619), For example, the first love and wife of the Prophet, was a successful businesswoman, and she chose him.

Such considerations prompted the famous jurist Abu Hanifah (d. 767 or 768) to leave with the prospective bride her right to execute her own marriage contract without a wali. He argued that if God has entrusted women fully with control over their financial assets, then certainly their lives are more worthy of being entrusted to them.

Document 3–24

HADITH

The Prophet said, "A matron/widow should not be given in marriage except after consulting her, she should give her permission explicitly; and a virgin should not be given in marriage except with her permission."

[Hadith narrated by Abu Hurayrah, in al-Bukhari, *Sahih al-Bukhari*, bk. 62, Kitab al-Nikah, no. 67 (9th century CE)]

Document 3–25

HADITH

'A'ishah, the Prophet's wife, said, "O God's Apostle! A virgin feels shy to give permission." He said, "Then, her consent is expressed by her silence."

[Hadith narrated by `A'ishah, in al-Bukhari, *Sahih al-Bukhari*, bk. 62, Kitab al-Nikah, no. 68]

Document 3–26

HADITH

The Prophet said, "Consult women about the marriage of their daughters."

[Hadith narrated by Abdullah Ibn Umar, in Abu Dawud, *Sunan Abu Dawud*, bk. 11, Kitab al-Nikah, no. 2095 (9th century CE)]

Document 3–27

HADITH

A young woman came to the Prophet and said, "Prophet of God! My father gave me in marriage to his nephew to elevate his social status. What should I do?" The Prophet gave her the choice to accept or reject that marriage. She then answered, "I condone what my father has done, but I wanted women to know that fathers have no such right."

[Hadith narrated by the father of Ibn Buraydah, in Ibn Majah, *Sunan Ibn Majah*, Kitab al-Nikah, no. 1874 (9th century CE]

Document 3–28

MUHAMMAD IBN AHMAD AL-SARAKHASI

When a father consults his virgin daughter about his intentions of giving her away in marriage and she remains silent about it, marriage is then valid. But if she responds by rejecting the idea, the contract is invalid according to our school of thought. . . . For the divine law made her silence a sign of her consent, due to her shyness that prevents her from expressing her consent.

[Muhammad ibn Ahmad Al-Sarakhasi (d. 1090), *Kitab al-Mabsut*, 30 vols. (Beirut: Dar al-Ma'rifah, 1968), 5:2–3 (11th century CE)]

Document 3–29

MUHAMMAD IBN AHMAD AL-SARAKHASI

It has been reported to us that the Messenger of God separated a couple because the woman was forced into marriage by her father, although she wanted to marry the paternal uncle of her children [her brother-in-law after her husband died]. He separated them and allowed her to marry the man she wanted to marry at first. This is proof that forcing a previously married woman into marriage makes the marriage invalid. This is a subject of consensus among scholars. . . .

It is also evidence that it is up to her to choose a husband and not to her father or guardian, for she is the one who is going to live with her husband. Success is more likely to happen when she chooses her husband.

[Al-Sarakhasi, *Kitab al-Mabsut*, 2:9–10 (11th century CE)]

Document 3–30

IBN HAJAR AL-'ASQALANI

A chapter on: "A father cannot give away in marriage either his virgin *(bikr)* or his nonvirgin daughter except with her consent."

In this title there are four concepts to be discussed; A father giving away in marriage his virgin daughter or his nonvirgin daughter, a nonfather giving away in marriage a virgin, or a nonfather giving away in marriage a nonvirgin one. By adding the age factor more cases come up. A non-virgin, of legal age, cannot be given away in marriage by her father, save with her consent. This case is a matter of agreement among most scholars except those who are extreme. A very young virgin, below legal age *(sagheerah)* can be given away in marriage by her father without her consent. This is a case of agreement among most except those who are extreme. A nonvirgin girl who is below legal age is subject of disagreement among scholars. Malik and Abu Hanifah said that the father can give her away in marriage in the same manner he does for a very young virgin. Al-Shafi'i, Abu Yusuf and Muhammad[12] said that the father cannot force his nonvirgin daughter into marriage whether she lost her virginity as a result of sexual intercourse or otherwise. The rationale of this view is the belief that her having lost her virginity makes her less inhibited. As to the virgin who is of legal age, they differed in their views over her being forced into marriage. The *hadith* suggests that the father or guardian must seek her consent, and that they cannot force her. This is reported by al-Tirmidhi [d. 892] as the view of the majority of scholars.

[Ibn Hajar Al-'Asqalani (1372–1451), *Fath al-Bari Sharh Sahih al-Bukhari* (Victory of the Creator, Explanation of Hadiths Authenticated by al-Bukhari), 13 vols. (Beirut: Dar al-Kutub al 'Ilmiyah, 1989), 9:239–240 (15th century CE)]

Document 3–31

KING MOHAMED VI OF MOROCCO

Through the instructions we issued and the opinion we expressed regarding the proposed Family Law, we aimed to make sure that the following fundamental reforms are introduced. . . . Entitle the mature woman to guardianship if she so chooses or if it best serves her interest, in accordance with one of the interpretations of the Qur'anic verse which stipulates that a woman shall not be forced to marry against her free will. . . . "Do not prevent them from marrying their former husbands, if they mutually agree on equitable terms."[13] . . . A woman may, of her own free will, entrust guardianship to her father or to a relative if she so chooses.

[King Mohamed VI of Morocco, speech to the Parliament fall session, October 10, 2003]

MAHR: THE OBLIGATORY MARITAL GIFT

The Qur'an enjoins prospective husbands to give their wives a *mahr* at the time of marriage as an expression of their affection and serious intent and commitment to married life. *Mahr*, which means a marital gift, is variously referred to in the Qur'an as *saduqat* (pl.) or *nuhl* (sing.), And in some modern Islamic societies as *sadaq* (sing.). All these words have the meaning of gifting. *Mahr* is the analogue of the Western tradition of gifting a diamond ring to the betrothed, but a proper *mahr* may consist of teaching the Qur'an to the prospective bride or a simple iron wedding ring. On the other hand, it may consist of a diamond ring, or a whole fortune, depending on the wish of the betrothed woman. Early Islamic tradition has established that the state may not interfere and impose an upper limit on the *mahr*, as is now the case in some Muslim countries, for Qur'anically that is the pure right of the woman. The amount of *mahr* is usually specified as a stipulation in the marriage contract. The Qur'an made the *mahr* an obligatory gift upon the prospective husband, which he may not demand back if he decides to divorce his wife.

Despite the clear Qur'anic pronouncements on *mahr*, Muslim jurists affected by their cultural surroundings have viewed *mahr* in different ways, some of which are repugnant to the Qur'anic spirit of marital and gender relations. The Hanbali view is most consistent with the Qur'an. Hanbali jurists did not formally define the concept of *mahr*, but their discussions suggest that they consider it an asset—whether money or property, tangible or intangible—that the husband is required to give the wife as a free marital gift. Some Hanafi jurists, on the other hand, view *mahr* as part of an exchange due to the wife for staying at home and is akin to maintenance. Some Shafi'i and Maliki jurists view *mahr* as part of an exchange for sexual enjoyment with the wife. All "exchange" views suffer from the same deficiency: They depart from the Qur'anic ideal of *mahr* as a free gift *(nihlah)* that is not in exchange for anything else. Rather, it is an obligatory gift from the man to his intended wife to express his affection, sincerity, and serious intentions. The modern jurist Malakah Zirar joins a line of distinguished jurists in rejecting this "commodity" view of women's body and sexuality, calling *mahr* instead "one of the most important divine guarantees" to women.

Document 3–32

QUR'AN 4:4

And give the women (on marriage) their dower as a free gift; but if they, of their own good pleasure, remit any part of it to you, take it and enjoy it with right good cheer.

[Al-Nisa', The Women]

Document 3–33

ABU JA'FAR MUHAMMAD IBN JARIR AL-TABARI

Interpretation of His saying "And give the women (on marriage) their dower as a free gift." He, God Almighty, means "give women their *mahr* as a due donation and a prescribed duty."

[Al-Tabari, *Jami' al-Bayan fi Tafsir al-Qur'an*, 3:583 (9th century CE)]

Document 3–34

ABU AL-WALID MUHAMMAD IBN AHMAD IBN RUSHD

They agreed that *mahr* is a requirement for the validity of the marriage contract, and that it is not lawful to consensually eliminate it, because God said, "Give the women their *saduqat* as a free gift *(nihlah)*. . . . " As to its amount, they agreed on the fact that it has no maximum. However, they differed on its minimum, al-Shafi'i, Ahmad, Ishaq, Abu Thawr, and the Tabi'in scholars from

Madinah,[14] said it has no minimum, for anything that could be a price or a compensation for something could also be *mahr*. This is also the view of Ibn Wahb [742/3–812/3] from the Maliki School. Others said that its minimum has to be determined. . . .

The reasons for their divergence are two: first, it is not clear whether the *mahr* is compensation like other compensations, in which the amount, be it big or small, is determined by the concerned parties as is the case in financial transactions; or whether it is a religious duty and worship, and therefore has to be of a determined amount. Indeed, the fact that it allows men to permanently appropriate the women's private parts makes it similar to compensation. But the fact that it is not lawful to agree on eliminating it makes it similar to religious duties and worship.

[Abu al-Walid Muhammad Ibn Ahmad (known in the West as Averroes), *Bidayat al-Mujtahid wa Nihayat al-Muqtasid* (The Distinguished Jurist's Primer), 4 vols. (Beirut: Dar Ibn Hazm, 1995), 3:966–967 (12th century CE)]

Document 3–35

MUHAMMAD AL-TAHER IBN ʿASHUR

Two parties were oppressed in *Jahiliyyah* (the pre-Islamic world): orphans and women. And two rights were violated: orphans' wealth and women's wealth. Thus, the Qur'an highly protected them. . . .

The injunction addresses husbands first so that they do not take advantage of women's shyness and weakness and their eagerness to please them in order to deny them their rights and take their *mahr* from them. . . . If they do so, then rulers must intervene and force men to specify the *mahr*. . . .

Saduqat were called "free gift" *(nihlah)* in order to distinguish them from any kind of payment in exchange for something, and to assimilate it to gifts. For the *mahr* is not a price in exchange for women's services, because the marriage is a contract between the man and the woman in order to live together in kindness *(mu'asharah)*, to establish a strong bond, and to exchange rights between spouses. And this is too valuable a relationship to estimate a monetary payment in exchange for it. If it were possible to do so, the price should be very high and renewed as the services evolve and last, like any other payment for services. Rather, God made it an obligatory gift from husbands in order to prove their respect and commitment to their wives, and also God made it compulsory because it makes the difference between marriage and concubinage and illicit sex.

[Muhammad al-Taher Ibn ʿAshur, Tafsir al-Tahrir wa al-Tanwir (Commentary of Liberation and Illumination) (Tunis: Dar Sahnoon, 1997), pp. 229–231 (20th century CE)]

Document 3–36

MALAKAH ZIRAR

Sadaq is the first Islamic legal rule that results, by God's will, from the covenant of marriage. The Almighty made it compulsory upon the husband and singled him out to undertake the burden of fulfilling this duty, without any responsibility in return from the wife's side and her family members. For it is a God-given gift. It was made so by texts that are beyond any doubt in terms of validity and are also clear-cut in their meanings. It is one of the most important divine legal assurances to the wife and it does not reflect by any means a purchase price or a financial compensation to buy the wife or make her a property of her husband. The *mahr* is not a price for the woman's private parts nor is it in exchange for enjoying them as alleged in many jurisprudential books and subscribed to by a large number of traditional Islamic legal scholars. This point of view was widely adopted to the extent that average Muslims, and even some well-educated ones, became certain that a *mahr* is a means to acquire the wife and appropriate her. These erroneous views resulted in the inferences of rulings that are in total contradiction with some divine rules stated by the Qur'an and the honorable prophetic tradition. . . .

In fact, *mahr* is one of the most important divine guarantees that were imposed by the Qur'an and the honorable prophetic tradition. . . . Therefore, there is no way to exempt the husband from it, even if the parties did not agree about it or did not specify it in the marriage contract. If the parties agree on marriage without *mahr*, then this agreement is null and void, because it eliminates what God has stated and violates the rulings of the Islamic law. In such cases the husband must be forced to pay it, unless the wife gives it up after her right in it is clearly stated. Nevertheless, the act of forgiving the *mahr* cannot be considered valid until it is proven to be a willful act without coercion, misleading, or deception from the husband. The legal proofs about the *mahr* are clear-cut and there is no way to suspend or eliminate it

[Zirar, *Mawsu'at al-Zawaj wa al-'Alaqah al-Zawjiyyah fi al-Islam wa al-Shara'i' al-Ukhra*, pp. 75–80 (21st century CE)]

OTHER STIPULATIONS IN THE MARRIAGE CONTRACT

The marriage contract is a contract between two rational and consenting adults. These adults are permitted to define their special relationship in advance by agreeing on certain stipulations placed in their marriage contract. For example, a young wife may stipulate that her husband may not interrupt her education after marriage, or that he would finance it, or even defer having children until her graduation. In the past some women stipulated that their husbands do not remove them from their hometowns or take second wives. Muslim jurists, however, disagreed about the effect of violating a stipulation in the marriage contract, some taking such violations less seriously than others. These positions often ran contrary to the prophetic *hadith*, which states that Muslims must fulfill their promises, especially those made in the marriage contract. Today some religious clerics who conduct marriage ceremonies tend to discourage the inclusion of stipulations. But they are a legitimate mechanism by which the Muslim woman may negotiate and define her marital life and relations in advance.

Document 3–37

QUR'AN 5:1

O ye who believe! Fulfill (all) obligations.[15]

[Al-Ma'idah, The Table]

Document 3–38

HADITH

The Prophet said, "The conditions which are most worthy of fulfilling are those with which you legitimize sexual relations."

[Hadith narrated by 'Uqbah, in al-Bukhari, *Sahih al-Bukhari*, vol. 7, bk. 62, Kitab al-Nikah, no. 81]

Document 3–39

IBN HAJAR AL-'ASQALANI

'Umar [d. 644][16] said, "Rights are determined by the stipulations set in contracts." Abdu al-Rahman Ibn Ghunm said, "I was sitting close to 'Umar, when a man came and asked him: O Leader of the faithful, I married a woman on the condition not to move her out of her town. However, I am getting ready to move to another country." 'Umar said, "The condition still stands." The man then said, "Woe to men! A woman can divorce her husband whenever she wants then!" 'Umar again said, "People of faith are bound by their stipulations; these define the boundaries of their rights." . . .

His saying "those with which you legitimize sexual relations" means that the stipulations of the marital contract are the most urgent ones to fulfill. Al-Khattabi said, "stipulations in marital contracts are diverse. Some are undisputable and have to be fulfilled such as good companionship or kind parting. To this refers the aforementioned *hadith*. . . . Some other terms and conditions are subject to disagreement." . . .

Al-Tirmidhi, after reviewing this *hadith*, said, "Some knowledgeable Companions of the Prophets applied the rule which suggests that if one agrees with his wife not to move her from her location, as a marriage contract stipulation, he is bound to fulfill his promise and cannot move her." This is also the view of al-Shafi'i, Ahmad and Ishaq.[17]

[Al-'Asqalani, *Fath al-Bari Sharh Sahih al-Bukhari*, 9:271–72 (15th century CE)]

Document 3–40

SAMPLE ELEVENTH-CENTURY MARITAL CONTRACT

This is the *mahr* which [husband's name and surname] offered to [woman's name and surname] at the amount of [sum] Dinars and Dirhams, forty per unit of current currency, in cash advance and delayed credit, in Cordoba at the time of this contract's drafting. The cash amount is [sum] Dinars and Dirhams, and was received on behalf of the spouse by her father [father's name and surname] as she is a maiden, under her father's supervision and guardianship. The cash advance is to serve for preparing her for her husband's home and from which he is relieved of any liability. The delayed credit amounts at [sum] Dinars and Dirhams of the same currency value, and is delayed for [number of] years starting from the wedding date. The first installment shall take effect on [date in month and years].

[Husband's name and surname] voluntarily and willfully—seeking her love and aiming at her pleasure—committed to his wife that he shall not take a second spouse [while married to her] nor shall he hold a relationship with a female slave, nor shall he have a child with any of the female slaves. And that in case he fails any of the aforementioned conditions the wife reserves the full rights and prerogatives to terminate their marriage or that of him with his concubine and also to free the slave with whom he had a child as well as to sell, keep or free any other slave he had a relationship with.

Furthermore, he shall not stay away from her, be it in a short or a long trip, except for pilgrimage on his own behalf. For that reason only he has the right to an absence of three years, if he advises her beforehand of his departure time and destination, while maintaining her expenses, clothing and lodging needs. Anything exceeding this period of time shall entitle her, after swearing before two reliable witnesses that he has been absent for more than the period of time he committed to, to take matters in her own hands. She reserves the rights however, to blame him and her blaming him does not affect this stipulation.

Moreover, he cannot move her from her residence in the city of [name of city and county] save with her consent. In case he moves her against her will, she shall be free to decide. But if she agrees to follow him, but changes her mind and wants to return, she shall again be granted the right to decide after the lapse of thirty days from the day she asked him to go back, and in this case he has to provide for her the full round trip.

He cannot deny her the right to visit any of her female or direct male relatives, nor can he deny them the right to visit her. All this is in a context of common mutual family visits that sustain good relationships. If he denies her any of the abovementioned, she shall be entitled to take the fate of their marriage in her own hands. He shall also treat her well, and keep her good company as God commanded, and in reward of that she shall treat him well and keep him good company in light of the verse, "And men have a degree over women."
. . .

And [husband's name and surname] has been made aware that his wife [her name] is a woman who does not serve herself. She is rather to be served as per her social status. He acknowledged this and agreed to provide her with servants and he stated his capability of doing so.

He wedded her in God's words and according to the tradition of His Prophet Muhammad—peace be upon him—to be a trust in his care, according to the privileges cited in God's book that men live with their wives on equitable terms or let them go in kindness. Her father [name and surname] gave her away to him as a virgin under his care and guardianship, in good physical health, to be his lawful wife as per the marital contract, and as witnessed by [name and surname] from the husband's side and [name and surname] from the wife's side whose names are recorded in this contract, both in good legal standing on the date of [day-month-year]."

> [Muhammed Ibn Amhad Ibn al-'Aththar Al-Umawi, "Kitab al-Watha'iq wa al-Sijillat," in Nasr Hamed Abu Zayd, *Dawa'r al-Khawf, Qira'ah fi Khitab al-Mar'ah* (Circles of Fear, an Approach to the Discourse on Women) (Casablanca: al-Thaqafi al-'Arabi, 2000), pp. 7–9]

MARITAL RELATIONS

The Qur'an describes the ideal of marital relations as characterized by tranquillity, mercy, and affection. The marital relation is supposed to be so close that the Qur'an describes each spouse as being the "garment" of the other, that is, one who covers the other's shortcomings and protects his or her privacy. If that ideal fails, then the Islamic standard for married couples is to "either hold together on equitable terms, or separate with kindness."

Because the goal of marriage as defined by the Qur'an is to create a relation of tranquillity, mercy, and affection, traditional jurists concluded that the marriage contract is a contract for friendship and companionship, not service. Therefore, they concluded that the woman is not obligated to perform housework, cook, or even nurse her baby except for humanitarian reasons. Further, unless she volunteers, the Muslim woman is entitled to compensation for her housework and maintenance from her husband, even if she were richer than him.

The Qur'an limits the ability of a man to interfere in a woman's affairs by 1. requiring two prerequisite conditions and 2. limiting the interference to a *qi-*

wamah, function, a word whose meaning involves the concepts of caretaking and service.

The verse in which the word *qawwamun* (sing. *qawwam*, that is, a man who exercises *qiwamah*) is used recognizes a male's *qiwamah* over a woman only if he 1. is supporting her financially and 2. has been favored by God in certain aspects over her that are relevant (at the time) to the woman's concerns about which he is providing advice and guidance. (An example of the aspects referred to in the second requirement would be business acumen, in a situation where the woman is not herself at that time a knowledgeable business woman, or physical strength, where that particular woman needs at that time physical assistance.) Otherwise, the man cannot assert his *qiwamah* over the woman. Hence this verse functions as a limitation over patriarchal men who would like to interfere in women's lives unjustifiably, solely because of their gender or because they support them financially.

Unfortunately, many male jurists simply missed the significance of the Qur'anic choice of the word *qiwamah*. Their interpretations tended to reflect a patriarchal worldview of authoritarian leadership roles within the family. In fact, the word *qawwam* in the Arabic language has different connotations. For example, the "*qawwam* over the mosque" is the one who serves it, and the "*qawwam* over the plants *(al-zar')*" is the one who tends them. In neither context is there a sense of superiority or domination, but rather one of service.

The limitations on *qiwamah* were interpreted as justifications for gender superiority by adopting a specific linguistic reading of the word *bima* in the Qur'anic verse. This word is a connective. It conditions the first part of the verse on the second two parts. Traditionalists interpreted it to mean *because*. But the word *bima* has a richer and more complex meaning than, for example, the words *lima* or *li'anna*, which are better translated as because but significantly were not used in this verse. *Bima* is better understood to mean "to the extent" or "in circumstances where." These differences in linguistic interpretations may appear slight, but in the context of the verse can make significant difference.

To illustrate this point we have provided two alternative translations of the verse. The traditional one (alternative A), combined with the patriarchal claim that men are always in a more favorable position vis-à-vis women because of their physical strength and superior intellect, provide the basis for the claim of gender superiority. Furthermore, by restricting the woman to the home, patriarchal society made women financially (and otherwise) dependent on men. This approach ensured that both limitations specified in the verse were always satisfied. Alternative B offers a different approach more consistent with the overall Qur'anic view of gender relations.

Another verse in the Qur'an states in part that "men have a degree over women." Taken out of context and combined with the other verse, it was used to develop an overarching interpretation of male supremacy in society and the family. This interpretation, however, encouraged oppressive males to move away from the Islamic ideal of marital relationships and affected the development of healthy gender relations in society.

Document 3–41

QUR'AN 4:34

ALTERNATIVE TRANSLATIONS OF QUR'ANIC VERSE 4:34
(AL-NISA', THE WOMEN):

Alternative A. "Men are the protectors and maintainers of women, because God has given the one more (strength) than the other and because they support them from their means."

[Translation by Yusuf Ali]

Alternative B. "Men are *qawwamun* (caretakers) over women, *bima* (to the extent, in circumstances where) God has given some of them more than others, and *bima* they support them from their means."

[Translation by Azizah Al-Hibri]

Document 3–42

QUR'AN, 2:228–232

And women shall have rights similar to the rights against them, according to what is equitable; but men have a degree (of advantage) over them.[18]

[Al-Baqarah, The Cow]

Document 3–43

QUR'AN 2:187

They are your garments *(libas)* and you are their garments.

[Al-Baqarah, The Cow]

Document 3–44

QUR'AN 9:71

The believers, men and women, are *walis* (protectors), one of another.

[at-Tawbah, Repentance]

Document 3–45

HADITH

The Prophet said, "Every one of you is a shepherd and every one of you is responsible for his flock. A ruler is in charge of his subjects and is responsible for them; a man is in charge of his household and responsible for those in his charge; a wife is in charge of her husband's household and she is responsible for those in her charge. . . . "

[Hadith narrated by 'Abdullah Ibn 'Umar, in al-Bukhari, *Sahih al-Bukhari*, vol. 7, bk. 62, *Kitab al-Nikah* (marriage), 116 and Muslim, *Sahih Muslim*, bk. 20, Kitab al-Imarah, hadith no. 4496 (9th century CE)]

Document 3–46

MUHAMMAD IBN AHMAD AL-ANSARI AL-QURTUBI

"And you are their garments" the term garment *(libas)* refers to all kind of clothes. The fusion of each one of the spouses with the other was analogized to a garment because they blend with each other when they hug and their bodies come close, fuse, and stay together like a garment. . . . "

[Muhammad Ibn Ahmad al-Ansari Al-Qurtubi, *al-Jami' li Ahkam al-Qur'an* (The Compendium of Legal Rulings of the Qur'an), 4 vols. (Beirut: Dar Ihya' al-Turath al-'Arabi, 1985), 2:316 (12th century CE)]

Document 3–47

ABU HAMID AL-GHAZALI

[A] husband is a shepherd in his family and is accountable about his flock. The Prophet said, "It is a blameworthy sin for a man to fail to provide for his co-dependents."

It is also reported that a person who deserts his family is like a fugitive slave. Neither his prayer nor his fasting will be accepted till he returns to them. Similarly, a person who fails to fulfill their rights, even if he were present, would be considered a deserter, for God says, "Shield yourselves and your family from hellfire." God ordered us to protect them from hellfire like we would protect ourselves. One may not be able to fulfill even his own needs, and once married that burden doubles as somebody else's needs become his responsibility. . . . That's why some people decide not to marry altogether . . . That's the excuse Ibrahim Ibn Adham [d. C. 777] gave for his celibate life. He said, "I cannot mislead a woman, and I have no desire in them." He meant that he cannot fulfill her rights, needs, and desires. Also, Bishr [d. 841] said, "What prevents me from marriage is God's saying "and women have rights similar to those against them in a just manner."

[Abu Hamid Al-Ghazali, 'Ihya' 'Ulum al-Din (The Revival of Sciences of Religion), 4 vols. (Egypt: Mustafa al-Babi al Halabi, 1939), 2:43–46 (11th century CE)]

Document 3–48

ABU JA'FAR MUHAMMAD IBN JARIR AL-TABARI

"Men are *qawwamun* over women" means that men are in charge of their women in chastising them, stopping them from doing what they want to do in those matters where the women have obligations towards God and [the husbands]. . . .

It means [men are] princes over women. She has to obey him in matters that God ordered her to obey him, such as being kind to his family, and preserving his wealth. His preference over her is in his maintenance and generosity. . . . It is said the man is *qa'im* [another form for *qawwam*] [meaning] he orders her to obey him, and if she refuses, he may beat her lightly. . .

[Al-Tabari, Jami' al-Bayan fi Tafsir al-Qur'an, 5:37 (9th century CE)]

Document 3–49

MUHAMMAD FAKHR AL-DIN AL-RAZI

You should know that this verse ["Men are *qawwamun* over women"] follows the previous one that reads "And in nowise covet those things in which God hath bestowed His gifts more freely on some of you than on others." We have mentioned that the reason for the revelation of this verse is the fact that some women insinuated that men have a preferential treatment in matters of inheritance. In this verse God reminded them that the rationale of this preferential treatment was due to the fact that men have the duty to financially maintain women. Despite the fact that both of them enjoy each other, men have the duty to provide *mahr* and full maintenance. So that the preference or addition on one side is compensated by additional responsibilities on the other side, which comes to say that there is no preference at all.

[Muhammad Fakhr al-Din al-Razi (1149–1209), *Tafsir al-Fakhr al-Razi* (al-Razi's Commentary on the Qur'an) [the real title is *Mafatih al-Ghayb* (The Keys to the Unknown], 32 vols. (Beirut: Dar al-Fikr, 1985), 10:90 (12th century CE)]

Document 3–50

MUHAMMAD RASHID RIDA

["Men are *qawwamun* over women"] means that it is customary that they [men] take charge of their women, by protecting them, taking care of them, guarding them, or providing for them. . . . The meaning of *qiyam* [noun from *qawwamun*] here is in reference to leadership where the governed can act upon his or her will and choice, rather than being oppressed, deprived of will, and unable to do anything but what he or she is told to do."

[Rida, *Tafsir al-Manar*, 5:67 (19th century CE)]

Document 3–51

MUHAMMAD 'AKLAH

Joint leadership between the man and the woman is not acceptable because it leads to corruption and chaos; . . . it is also unsuitable to place *qiwamah* in the hands of the wife for the following reasons:

1.   The woman does not possess a reserve of nerves or a psychological reserve that would make her capable of carrying the burdens of leadership. . . .
2.   Giving *qiwamah* to the woman is unfair to the man, to his maintenance efforts, and his shouldering of heavy family responsibilities. It means that the man would become subject to the woman's will. This causes his personality to dissolve, and his dignity within the family to disappear.

But the man is capable of shouldering this responsibility [of *qiwamah*] . . . because of his emotional balance and ability to fight and bear the consequences of the fight. This is especially true because woman's housework and huge responsibilities within the home require all her time and exhaust all her energies.

[Muhammad 'Aklah, *Nitham al-Usrah fi al-Islam*
(Amman: Maktabat al-Risala al-Haditha, 1983), pp. 18–19]

Document 3–52

SHEIKH MUHAMMAD MUTAWALLI SHA'RAWI

The duty of *qiwamah* is not an absolute *fadl*[19] (preference) given to the man, it is rather a responsibility or assignment. Therefore "men are *qawwamun* over women" means that men are responsible for taking care of women, providing for them, and serving them. . . . And assuming every other duty that is required by this responsibility. The meaning of "some over the others" is not that God has given a preference to men over women as some people believe. . . . For if God meant this, He would have said, "God has preferred men over women." . . . However, He—the Almighty—said, "God has preferred some over some others." He used the word "some" twice in a vague and general way, which means that *qiwamah* requires a *fadl* of effort, action, and work from the man's side. . . . And this is equated from the other side by qualities that the woman has and the man cannot have. She, therefore, has a preference over him, for he cannot bear children and cannot menstruate. This is the reason why God says in another verse, "And do not covet each other in what God has preferred some of you over some others." This injunction is addressed to everybody and again the word "some" is used so that it shows that some has a preference in one matter and does not have it in other matters. . . . There is, therefore, no point in establishing a comparison between two persons who have different tasks and responsibilities."

[Sheikh Muhammad Mutawalli Sha'rawi (1911–1998) (former minister of Islamic Affairs and Affairs of al-Azhar Institute, Cairo, Egypt), interview with *Al-Anba'* (Kuwaiti newspaper), 4 November 1988, p. 6]

Document 3–53

ABU BAKR MUHAMMAD IBN ABDILLAH IBN AL-ʿARABI AL MALIKI

This verse, "And men have a degree over them (women)," is a clear-cut statement that the man is preferred over her and that he is over her with regard to conjugal rights. However, the term *degree* here is a general term and its meaning is not detailed. It was taken from other evidential texts other than this verse. So in this verse God made women aware that men are superior to them but the details were left to his messenger to explain.

Scholars, however, disagreed as to the true meaning of this verse. They expressed a multitude of views. . . .

No intelligent person could ignore the superiority of men to women. Suffice it to say that the woman was created from man, and in that he is her origin. Nonetheless, the verse did not come to reveal an absolute state of superiority that could be detailed by enumerating the virtues of men over women.

Therefore, it was essential to look at it [the degree] in the context of marital rights, and we found that they could be categorized into seven sections:

The first: the duty of obedience by women, and this is a general right.

The second: the right for men to be served by their wives, and this is a specific right further discussed in matters related to branches of Islamic law *(Furu')*.

The third: the right to oversee her financial dealings, so that she deals not but with his consent.

The fourth: that she puts her obedience to him before that of God in matters related to auxiliary worship,[20] so that she cannot fast without his permission nor can she perform the pilgrimage to Makkah but with him.

The fifth: paying the *mahr*.

The sixth: maintaining her continuously.

The seventh: The permissibility of chastising her, which is stated in God's saying, "Men are the maintainers of women."

[Abu Bakr Muhammad Ibn Abdillah Ibn al-ʿArabi al Maliki, *Ahkam al-Qur'an*, 1:188 (12th century CE)]

Document 3–54

JALAL AL-DIN ABD AL-RAHMAN IBN ABI BAKR AL-SUYUTI

"And they have the same rights as those against them in a just manner." . . . The Almighty said that if women obey their God and their husbands; the man should address her with kindness, not harm her and maintain her from his own wealth.

In a *hadith* narrated by al-Tirmidhi [d. 892] . . . The Messenger of God—peace be upon him—said, "Truly, you have rights against your wives, and your wives have rights against you. As to your rights against them, they shall not allow in your beds people whom you dislike, and they shall not allow into your homes people of whose presence you disapprove. As to their rights, you shall treat them with kindness and maintain them."

And in a *hadith* narrated by . . . Mu'awiyah Ibn Haydah al-Qushayri, that he asked the Prophet—peace be upon him—about the rights of the wife against her husband. The Prophet answered, "To feed her from whatever you eat, to cloth her whenever you buy clothes for yourself, never hit her face, never insult her, and never abandon her except within the confines of the (spousal) home." . . .

The messenger of God—peace be upon him—said, "Whenever one of you has intercourse with his wife, he shall not rush her until she satisfies her needs, in the same way he likes his needs satisfied." . . .

Ibn Abbas . . . said, "I do like to groom myself for my wife as I like her to groom herself for me, for God says 'and they have the same rights as those against them,' but I do not like to claim all my rights against her for God also says 'and men have a degree over them.'"

[Al-Suyuti, *al-Durr al-Manthur fi al-Tafsir bi al-Ma'thur*, 1:393 (15th century CE)]

Document 3–55

MUHAMMAD RASHID RIDA

["And men have a degree over them (women)"] is a sanctified word. . . . It is a general rule attesting to the state of equality of women to men in all rights except one single matter expressed by God's saying, "and men have a degree over them." . . . God referred the details of women's rights and duties to what is customary amongst people in terms of their lifestyles and ways of dealing with their families. In fact, whatever customs exist in societies emanates from people's laws, beliefs, ethics, and dealings. This sentence gives the man a standard for measuring his attitudes towards his wife in all matters of life. So that whenever he is about to claim one of his rights against her, he will remember that she has a similar right against him. This is why Ibn Abbas said, "I do groom myself for my wife in the same way I like my wife to groom herself for me" in accordance with this verse.

The word *similar* does not mean the same in kind and genre. Rather, rights and duties between spouses are shared and they are equals. Indeed, for every duty the wife performs for her husband the husband performs an equivalent duty for her, if not in kind then in genre. For they are alike in rights and duties in the same way they are alike in their essence, their feelings, emotions, and intellect. Each of them is a full human being with a mind that has concerns about his/her interests and a heart that loves what it likes, and hates what does not suit him/her and turns away from it. It is therefore unjust to have one gender in control over the other, making the wives slaves to husbands, humiliating them, and using them for services, especially after tying the knots of marriage and inaugurating a shared life that would not be happy without mutual respect and shared rights. . . .

Furthermore, the verse stresses the position of customs in delineating respective rights to each spouse against the other, except for matters that contradict Islamic law as stated by clear-cut evidence. Customs may vary in time and geographical areas, but the majority of scholars from different schools of thought agree that it is a man's right to have intercourse with his wife; she should not refuse this right to her husband without a legitimate excuse. Likewise, she has the right to maintenance, housing, and other related matters. They say that she is not required to bake, cook, or do any housework or any kind of work in his house, commerce, or property. . . .

As to God's saying "and men have a degree over them," the verse assigns some duties to women and others to men. For this degree is a degree of leadership and taking care of interests as stated in the verse "Men are *qawwamun* over women because God has given the one more (strength) than the other, and because they support them from their means." Conjugal life is a social relationship that requires, like any other congregation, leadership. Because the members of the congregation may diverge in their views and wills, their social life cannot therefore be held together without a leader to whom they refer their conflicts, so that they avoid chaos, disunity, and anarchy. In this respect the man is more qualified to lead because he has greater knowledge of (the family's) interests. He is also more capable of realizing things through his strength of character and financial influence. Thus, he is the one required religiously to protect the woman and maintain her, whereas she is required to obey him to the extent of her abilities. . . .

[Rida, *Tafsir al-Manar*, 2:375, 2:380 (19th century CE)]

POLYGAMY

The Qur'an was revealed to a culture steeped in polygamy. It is reported that in Jahiliyyah some men married more than a hundred women at a time. It was therefore unrealistic to prohibit polygamous behavior abruptly. The Islamic approach to this situation as in other matters was to limit the practice severely, designate avenues for ending it, and provide a prescription/description of the ideal state of affairs that excludes the practice. There are only two Qur'anic verses on polygamy. The first is a conditional permission arising within a very specific context, namely, the treatment of orphaned girls whose guardians may want to marry them in order to appropriate their wealth. The verse limits this practice, which was prevalent at the time. The second verse imposes difficult conditions of fairness and justice on men who want to marry more than one woman, essentially making polygamy impossible for a righteous man. Still, the Qur'anic statement on polygamy is more complex than some scholars are willing to admit. For example, the permission to marry up to four wives is premised upon concerns about the oppression of the orphan girls discussed earlier and appears only within that context. The significance of the full context of the verse has been overlooked by many scholars. Yet it clearly links the permission to marry more than one wife to the specific situation of orphan girls and a specific practice concerning them that existed at the time of the Prophet. Further, the Qur'an states that if men feared being unjust toward orphans these men may marry up to four wives of other (nonorphan) women so long as they treat them equitably and fairly. Yet the Qur'an states in the same chapter that it is not possible to be equitable and fair among wives, even if it were one's ardent desire. Although it is not possible to understand this verse about polygamy in all its complexity without understanding fully the social practice it was revealed to avoid, one thing is nevertheless clear: the Qur'an expressly states that polygamy results in injustice. Consequently, it is not an optimal way of arranging marital relations. As the selections from the nineteenth-century Egyptian scholars Muhammad 'Abduh and Rashid Rida illustrate, many pious men understood the verse on polygamy as a restriction, a regulation, and a limitation of the practice, not as an obligation or even a recommendation. So, they abandoned polygamy in the hope of achieving the ideal of marital relations, described in the Qur'an, namely, that of the state of tranquillity, mercy, and affection. The Prophet himself exhibited preference for monogamy in his long-lasting relationship with Khadijah, who was twenty years his senior, and in his refusal to allow his cousin Ali, who was married to the Prophet's daughter, to take a second wife.[21] Others opted for self-serving conduct by engaging in polygamy without honoring the Qur'anic restrictions. As a result, women and children often suffered, leading to the interference of the state to regulate this practice, as the speech of the King of Morocco illustrates.

Document 3–56

QUR'AN 4:3

If you fear that you shall not be able to deal justly with the orphans, marry women of your choice, two or three or four; but if you fear that you shall not be able to deal justly (with them), then only one. . . .

[Al-Nisa', The Women]

Document 3–57

QUR'AN 4:129

You are never able to be fair and just as between women, even if it is your ardent desire. But turn not away (from a woman) altogether, so as to leave her (as it were) hanging (in the air). If you come to a friendly understanding, and practice self-restraint, God is Oft-forgiving, Most Merciful.

[Al-Nisa', The Women]

Document 3–58

HADITH

I heard the Prophet saying while on the pulpit, "the family of Hisham Ibn al-Mughirah have asked me to allow them to marry their daughter to 'Ali Ibn Abi Talib;[22] but I do not give permission, I do not give permission, and I do not give permission [sic], unless ['Ali] Ibn Abi Talib divorces my daughter in order to marry their daughter. For Fatimah is part of me; whatever hurts her hurts me and whatever harms her harms me."

[Hadith narrated by al-Miswar Ibn Makhramah and reported in al-Bukhari, Sahih Al-Bukhari, bk. 62, Kitab al-Nikah (marriage), No. 157; and Al-Asqalani, *Fath Al-Bari Sharh Sahih al-Bukhari*, 9:408, no. 5230 (9th century CE)]

Document 3–59

ABU JA'FAR MUHAMMAD IBN JARIR AL-TABARI

The verse restricts the number of wives a man may marry at one time to four. It is known that before Islam men used to have more than ten wives at the same time. It warned men that if they fear they cannot do justice among their wives they must be content with one.

[Al- Tabari, *Jami' al-Bayan fi Tafsir al-Qur'an*, 4:157 (9th century CE)]

Document 3–60

MUHAMMAD 'ABDUH

The amount of humiliation to women is self evident in the phenomenon of polygamy. Therefore, God intended to bring his compassion unto women in his law by affirming their rights, elevating their status, and restoring their dignity. For that reason He linked the permissibility of taking more than one wife to justice and equity. Whenever there is an occurrence of injustice or inequity no man is permitted to marry more than one woman. This makes it clear that Islam aims at discouraging the practice of polygamy and not at encouraging it. . . . For Islam restricted the number of permissible wives to four and then questioned the good judgment of polygamous people by stating that if they were reasonable enough they would be content with a single spouse.

The permissibility of abolishing this practice is beyond doubt; first, due to the requirement of justice in the equation. Perhaps that element exists in one case out of a million, but not in the remaining cases. Second, bad treatment of women from men in polygamous relationships is common. This could be seen in cases where women are denied some basic rights, such as maintenance expenses. In cases where injustice prevails in polygamous relationships it is permissible for the ruler or the judge to put an end to the practice. Third, it has become common knowledge that animosity among children originates sometimes from the fact that they have different mothers. That hatred and loathing between them grows in intensity as they grow up and leads in most cases to destructive results. A ruler or a judge may reserve the discretion to end the practice of polygamy to safeguard households from the phenomenon of self-destruction resulting from internal hostilities. It is, however, permissible for the husband of a barren wife to take a second wife for the purpose of having children. In this case the husband should not be prevented from his right to a second wife if he can prove his case before a judge. Religion is not against forbidding this practice; it is rather tradition and customs that are.

['Abduh, Al-a'mal al-Kamilah, 2:84–95 (19th century CE)]

Document 3–61

MUHAMMAD RASHID RIDA

There are three clear-cut matters in here related to polygamy:

The first one: Islam did not make polygamy compulsory and did not recommend it either. It merely mentioned it in the context of stating that most of those who practice it do not escape from committing the forbidden injustice. The wisdom and the reason of this are to make one moderate his impulsive desires and think about the much more serious responsibilities of justice and equity ahead of him.

The second one: Islam did not completely prohibit it, for it took into consideration the nature of men and their inherited customs all over the world in not restricting themselves to enjoying the company of one sole spouse. Some others wish to have progeny but their barren, old, or sick wives cannot. It also took into account the fact that sometimes women populations outnumber those of men in some parts of the world, especially in time of war, and that those widowed women cannot find loving and supportive men but only married ones who can still be just and financially capable.

The third one: for the earlier and the latter reasons God has left polygamy permissible. However, He limited it in number and restricted it by conditions of justice and fairness as previously mentioned so that its harm is avoided and its benefit is kept if the concerned man observes all the requirements we have cited, moral, ethical, and legal.

We have, indeed, seen with our own eyes and heard with our ears some contemporary religious and righteous men, who were not fortunate with their first wives in having children, and those first wives were indeed the ones who encouraged them to take second wives, and that both wives lived in harmony like true sisters. This was the state of most Muslims in early Islam. However, this phenomenon has diminished due to what happened in most Muslim communities, namely, ignorance of Islam, its teachings, rulings, and ethics with regard to marriage. The education of Muslims deteriorated as their governments declined, to the point where polygamy has become in many countries a source of numerous types of corruption *(mafasid)* for couples, children, and their families. The values of the conjugal relationship as described in the Qur'an—namely love, affection, and mercy—were then turned into their opposites. Our sheikh the professor and imam ['Abduh], waged in the course of his interpretation of this verse in al-Azhar[23] an all-out war on this corruption in Egypt and concluded that the nation cannot be properly educated while these corrupt practices of polygamy continue. He then concluded that polygamy should be banned based on the rule "No harming and no harm," stated clearly in the *hadith*, and on the jurisprudential rule that states that preventing harm prevails over bringing about benefits."

[Muhammad Rashid Rida, *Huquq al-Nisa' fi al-Islam* (Women's Rights in Islam) (Beirut: al-Maktab al-Islami, 1975), pp. 66–68 (19th century CE)]

Document 3–62

KING MOHAMED VI OF MOROCCO

Regarding polygamy, we have seen to it that the true, tolerant intentions *(maqasid)* of Islam with respect to justice are duly taken into account. In this regard Almighty God allowed polygamy, but subject to compliance with strict conditions; He said, " . . . And if you fear that you shall not be able to deal justly (with women), then only one."

Then the Almighty ruled out the possibility for man to do justice in this particular case, He said, "You are never able to be fair and just as between women, even if it is your ardent desire." We also have sought guidance from the pristine wisdom of Islam which makes it legally possible for a man to take a second wife, but only in circumstances beyond his control, under strict limitations and with a judge's permission. Failure to allow for such exceptions by outlawing polygamy may result in men being tempted to engage in unlawful polygamy.

Hence, polygamy shall be allowed solely in the following cases and under the legal conditions below:

The judge shall not allow polygamy unless he ascertains that the husband will treat his second wife and her children on an equal footing with the first, that he will provide the same living conditions for all, and that there is an exceptional and objective justification for polygamy;

The woman may, and has the right to, include a stipulation in the marriage contract whereby her husband will refrain from taking a second wife. . . . If no such condition has been stipulated, the judge shall summon the first wife to secure her consent to her husband's second marriage. Similarly, the second wife must be informed that her husband-to-be is already married. Her consent must also be secured. The first wife shall have the right to seek divorce for harm if she so chooses."

[King Mohamed VI of Morocco, speech to the Parliament fall session, October 10, 2003]

MARITAL CONFLICT

The Qur'an encourages couples to resolve marital conflict privately in a spirit of fairness and kindness. Indeed, the Prophet's own behavior with his wives, whom he always treated with respect and affection, is understood by most Muslims to exemplify the ideal relationship between spouses. If a dispute cannot be solved equitably between the spouses, the Qur'an prescribes mediation, based on a principle of family intervention in which both families of the couple are assigned equal roles. Some have argued that a passage in verse 4:34 of the Qur'an, which addresses the "chastisement" of wives, authorizes husbands to hit their wives. But the passage is grammatically quite complicated and exhibits a similar structure as the verse on polygamy. It is conditional and not absolute. It severely restricts and alters the act of hitting, which was rampant in that society, rather than condones it. After all, hitting is diametrically opposed to the ideal marital relationship of tranquillity, mercy, and affection. As with many other societal ills, such as polygamy and drinking alcohol, the Qur'an adopts a gradualist philosophy of change that would make it possible for society to reform. In the so-called chastisement passage the Qur'an reminds men that God is greater and that they have no right to chastise righteous women. But chastisement itself in the Qur'an, as exemplified in the story of Job who took an oath to chastise his wife, has been altered into a thoroughly symbolic act. It allows the husband to express his anger and frustration without harming the woman. Job, for example, was ordered to "hit" his wife with a bunch of basil to satisfy his oath to strike her. This is why Muslim scholars have recognized the Muslim woman's right to take her husband to court , whether for criminal prosecution or for divorce, if he harms her in any way. For example, Jordanian and Kuwaiti Islamic family laws allow an action for divorce if the husband verbally abused his wife. Even medieval jurists permitted a man to "hit" his wife only symbolically with a *miswak* (a soft little twig used as a toothbrush), or handkerchief, and allowed the wife the right to seek punitive action if the husband transgresses beyond these limits. Thus the chastisement passage is truly a passage about anger management for men, not about chastising women. As proof is the fact that, despite all these limitations on the act of hitting in a world where beating women was the norm, a man is not even permitted to reach this stage of symbolic "hitting" until he has first tried to communicate with his wife and then abandoned her in bed without success. Further, the Qur'an makes clear that no husband has the right to express his anger towards a righteous and God-fearing wife. This behavior may only take place when the wife is *nashiz*. Some male jurists have defined this notion broadly to mean a "disobedient" woman. More specifically, they meant a woman who is "disobedient to the husband," as opposed to being disobedient to God. Under this definition, even an act of minor "disobedience" to the husband was used to justify domestic violence. Other jurists, however, defined this word more properly, in part because of the statement made by the Prophet in his farewell address that tied the act of hitting only to cases where the husband fears that the wife is about to commit *fahishah mubayyinah* (an act of adultery clear and evident to all). So these jurists limited the word *nashiz* to this context, just as they limited the act of "hitting" to its symbolic context. Many commentators insist that the prophetic tradition, or *sunnah*, surrounding this passage is very explicit in forbidding violence against wives and women in general and that both the Qur'an and the Prophet exhort Muslims to treat their wives kindly or to part amicably. In light of the Qur'anic ideal of marital relations, the majority of Muslim scholars over the centuries have concluded that while the act of "hitting" is permissible in Islam, abandoning it is preferable and more graceful.

Document 3–63

QUR'AN 4:19

O you who believe! You are forbidden to inherit women against their will. Nor should ye treat them with harshness, that ye may take away part of the dower you have given them, except where they have been guilty of open lewdness; on the contrary live with them on a footing of kindness and equity. If you take a dislike to them it may be that you dislike a thing, and God brings about through it a great deal of good.

[Al-Nisa', The Women]

Document 3–64

QUR'AN 4:128

If a wife fears cruelty or desertion on her husband's part, there is no blame on them if they arrange an amicable settlement between themselves; and such settlement is best; even though men's souls are swayed by greed. But if you do well and practice self-restraint, God is well-acquainted with all that you do.

[Al-Nisa', The Women]

Document 3–65

QUR'AN 4:34

As to those women on whose part you fear disloyalty and ill-conduct [*nushuz*],[24] admonish them (first), (next,) refuse to share their beds, (and last,) beat them (lightly), but if they return to obedience, seek not against them means (of annoyance).

[Al-Nisa', The Women]

Document 3–66

QUR'AN 4:35

If you fear a breach between them twain, appoint (two) arbiters, one from his family, and the other from hers; if they wish peace, God will cause their reconciliation.

[Al-Nisa', The Women]

Document 3–67

HADITH

Be good to women; for they are powerless captives (*'awan*) in your households. You took them in God's trust, and legitimated your sexual relations with the word of God, so come to your senses people, and hear my words.

[Hadith narrated by the father of Ja'far Ibn Muhammad, in Abu Dawud, *Sunan Abu Dawud, Kitab al-Manasik*, no. 1905, vol. 2, p. 455; and al-Tirmidhi in *Sunan al-Tirmidhi, Kitab al-Nikah*, no. 1173 (9th century CE)]

Document 3–68

HADITH

Mu'awiyah al-Qushayri asked, "God's Apostle, what is the right of the wife of one of us over him?" He answered, "Her right is to feed her as you feed yourself, to clothe her as you clothe yourself; do not hit her on the face, do not use insulting language, and do not abandon her except in the house."

[Hadith reported in Abu-Dawud, *Sunan Abu-Dawud*, bk. 11, *Kitab al-Nikah*, no. 2142 (9th century CE)][25]

Document 3–69

HADITH

The Prophet said, "Let not one of you whip his wife like a slave, then have sexual intercourse with her at the end of the day."

[Hadith narrated by 'Abdullah Ibn Zam'a, in Al-Bukhari, *Sahih al-Bukhari*, vol. 7, bk. 62, *Kitab al-Nikah*, no. 132 (9th century CE)]

Document 3-70

HADITH

A believing man should not hate a believing woman; if he dislikes one of her characteristics, he will be pleased with another.

> [Hadith narrated by Abu Hurayrah, in Muslim, *Sahih Muslim*,
> bk. 08, no. 3469. (9th century CE)]

Document 3-71

HADITH

The Prophet said, "The most perfect of the believers in faith is the one who has the best morals, and the best of you are the kindest of you to their wives."

> [Hadith narrated by Abu Hurayrah in al-Tirmidhi, *Sunan al-Tirmidhi*,
> *Kitab al-Nikah*, no. 1172. (9th century CE)]

Document 3-72

HADITH

The Prophet said, "A woman is usually taken in marriage for four qualities, her wealth, her family status, her beauty and her religiosity. So get hold of the religious one, and you will be blessed."

> [Hadith narrated by Abu Hurayrah, in al-Bukhari, *Sahih al-Bukhari*,
> vol. 7, bk. 62, *Kitab al-Nikah*, no. 27 (9th century CE)]

Document 3-73

ABU JA'FAR MUHAMMAD IBN JARIR AL-TABARI

The meaning of the verse, "As to those women on whose part you fear disloyalty and ill-conduct": Expert exegetes of the Qur'an diverged in their views over the meaning of this verse. Some said that the meaning of the verb *fear* here is not but sure knowledge. . . .

A group of other scholars suggested that the meaning of *fear* here is fear that is the opposite of hope. They said this means when you start observing things that make you fear that your wives will turn against you, such as looking at other men or leaving homes frequently, and you become suspicious, you may then admonish them and leave them alone. . . .

As to His saying *nushuz*, it means for wives showing contempt to their husbands, refusing to join them in their conjugal bed, and disobeying them in matters where their obedience is required; all this out of dislike and despise. . . . "Admonish them" means remind them of God's wrath because of their disobedience to their spouses in matters where God ordered them to obey. . . .

[Al-Tabari, *Jami' al-Bayan fi Tafsir al-Qur'an*, 5:39–40 (9th century CE)]

Document 3–74

ABU HAMID AL-GHAZALI

The second quality [among those required for marriage]: treating women well and bearing their ill treatment. . . . God said, "keep them good company." He also said, underlining the gravity of their rights, "they have taken from you a solemn covenant. . . . " The last things the Messenger recommended were three things he kept repeating till his voice faded away: "Uphold the daily prayers, take good care of your slaves, do not burden them with things beyond their capacity, and observe God's exhortations relating to your wives, for they are like slaves in your hands. You took them in trust from God and made them your wives by His words."

The Prophet also said, "Whoever shows patience towards his wife's ill-treatment, God will give him the same reward he gave to Job (Ayyub), and whoever shows patience toward her husband's ill-treatment, God will give her the same reward he gave to Asiyah the wife of Pharaoh." One should also know that treating one's wife well does not only mean not harming her; rather, it means to endure ill treatment and be patient when she gets angry and loses her temper, as the Messenger used to forgive his wives who used to argue with him and turn away from him for the whole day. . . .

'A'ishah once got angry and said to the Prophet, " . . . You, who claims to be Prophet of God!" The Messenger of God smiled and tolerated her in the spirit of forgiveness and generosity. He told her once, "I can tell when you are happy and when you are angry!" She asked, "How?" And he said, "When you are happy you swear by Mohammad's God and when you are angry you swear by Abraham's God." She then said, "You are right, I avoid mentioning your name then!"

It is believed that the first love story in Islam was that of Prophet Muhammad and 'A'ishah.[26] The Prophet used to say to his other wives: "Do not upset me by saying bad things about 'A'ishah, for she is the only woman in whose company I have received the revelation!" Anas reported that the Prophet was the most compassionate person in matters concerning women and children. . . .

Third: respond to their harshness by teasing them, joking and kidding with them, for it is certain this softens women's hearts. The Prophet . . . said, "The people with the most perfect faith are those with the best ethics and who are the kindest toward their families." He also said, "The best among you are those who are the kindest toward their family, and I am the kindest toward my family." 'Umar, despite his toughness, once said, "One should always be like a child with his family, but when they need him they should find a man." Lukman said, "One should be like a child with his family, but once in the community he should behave like a man. . . . "

[Al-Ghazali (1058–1111), *Ihya' 'Ulum al-Din*, 2:34–35 (11th century CE)]

Document 3–75

ABU BAKR MUHAMMAD IBN ABDILLAH IBN AL-'ARABI AL MALIKI

Al-Tabari . . . Choose that the meaning of the verb *hajara*[27] . . . is to tie wives with a rope *(hijar)* in their homes. . . .

Ibn al-'Arabi then said, "What a huge slip from a great scholar! I cannot stop wondering about this view. . . . It is so surprising from him, for he is known to be a knowledgeable linguist, how far from the truth he is and how mistaken he is. Given the situation, it became necessary for us to look at these two matters carefully to uncover the truth. I looked into the Arabic language at the root verb *ha-ja-ra*. . . .

I looked into all these meanings and found out that they all evolve around the same basic episteme, that of keeping away from something. . . . If all this is true, and if all the meanings of this word refer to being far away from something, then the meaning of the verse would be to keep away from them in bed. There is no need to that twisted argument from this scholar. . . . How could al-Tabari have chosen it? . . .

It is reported that the Prophet—peace be upon him—said, "O people, verily, you have rights against your wives and your wives have rights against you. As to your rights, they shall not allow in your conjugal beds someone you hate, they shall not commit clear and evident adultery *(fahishah)*; if they do, then God has allowed you to abandon them in bed and hit them lightly, and if they change their behavior they have the right to their maintenance and clothing in kindness." . . .

Among the best things I heard in interpreting this verse was the interpretation of Sa'id Ibn Jubayr [665 or 6–713 or 714]. He said that the husband should admonish her first; if she does not accept he may then abandon her, if she persists he may then hit her. If she still persists he may send an arbiter from her relatives and one from his. They should find out whose fault it is, and then the *khul'*[28] may proceed. . . .

'Ata'[d. 732][29] said, "He should not hit her even if he orders her and she disobeys, he may only get angry with her."

Al-Qadi[30] said, "This is from 'Ata's extensive knowledge *(fiqh)*, his understanding of Islamic law, and his comprehension of the paths of interpretation, for he understood that the Qur'an command for chastisement is merely a permission, and he realized that it is hateful to do so from other sources—namely, the *hadith* in which the Messenger of God says, "I do hate for a man to hit his woman in anger and he might sleep with her at the end of the day."

. . . The Messenger of God—peace be upon him—was asked for a permission to hit women, he said, "You may do so. But the best of you will not chastise." So he allowed it but recommended against resorting to it.

[Ibn al-'Arabi al-Maliki, *Ahkam al-Qur'an*, 1:418–420 (12th century CE)]

Document 3–76

ABU BAKR MUHAMMAD IBN ABDILLAH IBN AL-'ARABI AL MALIKI

God's saying, "And live with them with kindness. . . . " The real meaning . . . is completeness and perfection. . . . God ordered men if they marry women to make their relationship and companionship with them based on completeness and perfection, for it provides peace of mind, serenity, and comfort. . . .

God says, "And if you hate them, then you may dislike a thing in which God may have placed abundant good." Meaning: If a man finds himself hating his wife, turning away from her, and not having any desire for her even if she did not commit a sin or *nushuz*, then it is recommended that he be patient with her and tolerate her ill treatment and injustice, for it might be for his own good to stay with her. . . .

Sheikh Abu Muhammad Ibn Abi Zayd was a distinguished scholar and a devout worshipper. He had a wife who treated him very badly, failing to fulfill her duties toward him, while subjecting him to her bitter tongue all the time. People would often advise him to let her go, but he preferred patience toward her. He used to say, "I am a man who is blessed with good health and knowledge. . . . Maybe she was sent to me because of some shortcomings in my faith. I do fear if I divorce her I might be subjected to worse punishment than her."

[Ibn al-'Arabi al-Maliki, *Ahkam al-Qur'an*, 1:13 (9th century CE)]

Document 3–77

MUHAMMAD FAKHR AL-DIN AL-RAZI

And God said, "And among His Signs is this that He created for you mates from among yourselves, that you may dwell in tranquillity with them, and He has put love and mercy between your (hearts). Verily in that are Signs for those who reflect." . . .

Some scholars said that His saying "from among yourselves" means that Eve was created from the body of Adam. But the truth of the matter is that she was created from the same kind as men, in the same way God said, "Came unto you a Messenger from among yourselves." This meaning is further reinforced by the phrase "so that you may dwell in tranquillity with them," for two different kinds of being cannot find tranquillity in each other, which means that they would not feel secure one with the other or love each other. . . .

There are many views about His saying: "and put love and mercy between you." Some suggested that *love* comes from sexual pleasure while *mercy* comes through having children. . . . Some, on the other hand, suggested that the term *love* refers to a person's need for his/her mate while the term *mercy* refers to how this same person acts when his/her mate needs him/her. . . . God mentioned two things here, one leads to the other. First, love occurs then it leads to mercy. Therefore, a wife may no more be the subject of sexual desire once she falls sick or grows old, but her husband would still take care of her and vice versa. . . .

Indeed, human beings might find in terms of mutual mercy from their mates what they might not find from close relatives, and this is not due to mere desire, for sexual desires might fade away as time goes by, but mercy lasts, for it is from God. If desire were all that unites spouses, then when anger occurs it kills desire. Desire is not eternal in itself, and therefore there would be separation and divorce each time a quarrel between spouses occurs. Mercy that makes humans protect their families from all harm is from God and this cannot be understood without meditation.

[Al-Razi, *Tafsir al-Fakhr al-Razi*, 25:111 (12th century CE)]

Document 3–78

MUHAMMAD FAKHR AL-DIN AL-RAZI

Al-Shafi'i said that chastisement is permissible but to refrain from it is better. It is narrated that 'Umar said, "We, people of Quraysh, were in command of our women. When we arrived in Madinah we found that Madinan women were in command of their men. Then, our women started mixing with theirs and they started rebelling against their husbands. I then went to the Prophet and told him that our women have become rebellious toward their men. He allowed chastising them. Soon after that, a large crowd of women besieged the Prophet's residence complaining about their husbands. He—peace be upon him—then said, "seventy women came to Muhammad's family tonight all complaining about their husbands; those husbands are not the best of you." Meaning that those who chastised their wives are not better than those who didn't. Al-Shafi'i said, "This *hadith* is clear evidence that it is preferred to refrain from chastising."

[Al-Razi, *Tafsir al-Fakhr al-Razi*, 10:92–93]

Document 3–79

IBN HAJAR AL-'ASQALANI

There has been an absolute ban on beating women. According to Ahmad, Abu Dawud, and al-Nasa'i . . . the Prophet said, "Do not beat God's female subjects." 'Umar then came and said, "Women are rebelling against their men." Men were then allowed to chastise their wives. Following that, more that seventy women surrounded the Prophet's residence protesting against this practice, so the Prophet said, "I have been besieged by seventy women, all complaining from their husbands, those husbands are not the best of you." . . .

Al-Shafi'i said, "There is a possibility that the prophetic ban was optional . . . or that it was said before the revelation of the Qur'anic verse, he then allowed for it after the revelation." The Prophet's saying, "The best among you will not beat their wives" is evidence that chastising is overall permissible, which means that he can beat her to discipline her if she does something he hates in matters where she is required to obey him. . . . Al-Nasa'i reported in this regard `A'ishah's *hadith*, "The messenger of God never chastised a woman or a slave and never raised his hand on anybody except to enforce God's law."

[Al-'Asqalani, *Fath Al-Bari Sharh Sahih Al-Bukhari*, 9:379]

Document 3–80

MUHAMMAD AL-TAHER IBN 'ASHUR

God's saying, "As to those on whose part you fear disloyalty . . . " refers to some states that are opposite to righteousness. . . . The majority of scholars have said disloyalty *(nushuz)* is when the wife disobeys her husband, despises him and shows dislike to him. . . . They linked the permission to admonish, leave, and hit her to this disobedience, and they cited the *hadiths* that allow the husband to hit his disobedient wife. . . . However, I believe that in giving such a permission, those narrations and traditions took into consideration the customs of particular social classes and tribes; for people are different, and rural people do not consider hitting women a form of violence, nor do their women consider it violence against them. . . .

Hitting is grave, and regulating it is very hard; it was only allowed in cases of flagrant corruption, when the woman violated the law. Limits, however, have to be established and explained in jurisprudence; for if we leave it to the husbands' discretion as a way to relieve their anger, this would lead to transgression of limits . . . And the principles of the Shari'a do not allow people to take justice by themselves except in emergency cases. . . . We, therefore, say: if governing powers know that husbands fail to keep the legal punishments in context and to observe the required limitations, then it is possible for them to prohibit husbands from using this permission and to state that whoever hits his wife will be punished so that the situation between spouses does not deteriorate especially knowing that the morality of husbands has weakened.

[Ibn 'Ashur (d. 1867/8), *Tafsir al-Tahrir wa al-Tanwir*, pp. 41–44 (19th century CE)]

Document 3–81

ABU SULAYMAN ABDUL HAMID AHMAD

If we look into the nature of the Qur'anic measures that relates to "beating" or "chastisement," we find that it aims at motivating the reconciliation efforts of the couple. It is another step toward the eradication of discord, using the best available means that would help recover the feelings of love, affection, and intimate communication between the spouses. . . .

If violence, harm, and oppression have no place in a marital relationship and in solving its problems, what is the meaning of "beating" *(darb)* here in the context of resolving conflicts between spouses? Is it a concrete meaning implying the infliction of physical pain, or is it a figurative one? . . .

If we take the interpretation of Ibn Abbas into consideration, chastisement or beating will mean nothing but a slight tap with a *miswak*,[31] and this surely does not constitute a punishment or harm that would inflict physical or psychological pain. It means, rather, a concrete expression by a movement or a tap of the *miswak* so as to denote seriousness and discontent, a state of anger and disappointment toward the wife that keeps her away from the soul of the abandoning husband. It is the opposite of the caress that expresses love and affection. This interpretation is rather acceptable, for it does not destroy the relationship of dignity and due respect between the spouses, who are united by bonds of tenderness and companionship. This understanding leaves no room for a beating that inflicts pain, suffering, humiliation, and oppression—to the contrary of what some jurists said! . . .

Despite this mild interpretation, there remain shadows, insinuations, excuses, and loopholes that were exploited, misunderstood, and used as an excuse in the past. And a lot of men will not abstain from doing the same in the future, leading to physical violence in the name of religion. . . . Therefore, it is crucial that our understanding and solution leave no room for misuse and leave no open doors for mistreatment and ill judgment; an understanding that would be in line with the objectives of Islamic Shari'ah, which aims to build families on principles of love, mercy, and dignity. . . .

If we look at the previously mentioned verses of the Qur'an,[32] we find that, whether used in a transitive or intransitive way, the term *darb* was mostly used in a figurative sense that implies separating, abandoning, withdrawing, and leaving. . . . Hence, the general meaning of the term *darb* in the context of different Qur'anic texts refers to separating, abandoning, withdrawing, and leaving. Therefore, what is the most relevant meaning of the term *darb*, in the context of conflict resolution between the spouses, and in the hope of recovering their love and communication, in the verse? . . .

If we take into consideration both the nature of the context of the verse and the nature of the situation and the objectives of the stated measures of reconciliation and appeasement; and if we consider also the Islamic values of giving dignity to all humans and preserving their self-respect and their right to self-determination; and, finally considering the consensual nature of the marital relationship and the ability of both parties to end it whenever they are not satisfied or if one party does not respect the other party's rights within it, and the fact that nobody can force or coerce a person to stay in it; it becomes clear to us that the meaning of the word *darb* cannot involve inflicting pain or humiliation. The relevant meaning is the general meaning common to all uses of this word in the Qur'an, namely, that of keeping distance, staying away, and abandoning. Indeed, keeping distance from the wife, abandoning her, and leaving the home are all required steps in rehabilitating the marital relationship; for deserting the marital bed and home forces the rebelling wife to confront the consequences of her rebellion, disobedience, and discord with her husband, which could be separation and divorce. . . . She then might consider whether divorce is what she wants . . . or whether her actions were just a moment of anger and stubbornness. . . .

Thus, the primary meaning of *darb*, which is relevant to redressing the conjugal relationship . . . is . . . leaving the conjugal residence, separating from the wife, and abandoning her as a . . . message to the wife and as a last resort in the private effort to save the marital relationship and preserve the family unit.

[Abu Sulayman Abdul Hamid Ahmad, *Darb al-Mar'ah Wasilah li Halli al-Khilaafaat al-Zawjiyah!* (Chastising Wives: A Solution for Conjugal Conflicts!) (Virginia: International Institute of Islamic Thought, 2002), pp. 21–28 (20th century CE)]

DIVORCE

Divorce is a last resort for spouses who cannot live in kindness with each other. It is permissible but not encouraged; for the Muslim marriage is intended to last. In fact, the Muslim marriage contract is described in the Qur'an as a "solemn covenant" (4:21). However, the Qur'an informs us that if spouses are no longer able to live in kindness with each other, they should part amicably. Divorce can be initiated in five ways: (a) through the husband's initiative, (b) through a derivative initiative by the wife if the husband has delegated his right to divorce to her through a stipulation in their marriage contract, (c) through the wife's independent initiative, (d) by mutual agreement between the two, and (e) through a judicial form of divorce, usually initiated by the wife. Each of these forms has different procedures and legal and financial consequences.

For example, if the husband initiates the divorce, the consequences depend on how many times he has done so. If he has done it once or twice, Islamic law provides a "cooling down" period of three *quru'* (menstrual cycles or months) called *iddah* or "waiting period" during which the wife cannot be removed from her marital home and the husband may return to bed and board without a new marriage contract. If he does, the divorce disappears altogether legally; if he does not, the divorce becomes effective automatically at the end of the waiting period. In that case the woman is paid immediately any deferred amount of her *mahr* and usually keeps the custody of her children if they are young. The children's age or other criteria that determine a transfer in that custody differ from one country to the other.

There are important issues relating to this form of divorce, as exemplified by the selection from al-Razi below. There are also some important protections

for the woman under this form of divorce. For example, if a divorce pronouncement is uttered by an angry or drunken husband, it has no legal effect. Further,
if during the waiting period it is discovered that the wife is pregnant, the *iddah*
period does not end until she delivers. This means that the divorce will not
take place while she is pregnant. If the husband divorces his wife three times,
then the situation becomes much more complicated. For this reason, jurists
disagree whether three pronouncements of divorce uttered in one sitting would
count as one or three divorces. After the third divorce the husband is barred
from remarrying his former wife, regardless of how sorry he may become for
his actions. The wife becomes *ba'in*, that is, the husband may no longer remarry
her unless she marries another person and becomes divorced or widowed. In
other words, the third divorce makes the two parties strangers to each other.
Thus, while the "cooling down" period is a device to address constructively
actions taken rashly by angry males who would later regret their actions and
the destruction of their family unit, the Qur'an places a limit. For the preservation of the dignity of the woman, every man knows that on the third divorce
he will lose his wife forever.

Where the divorce action by the wife is based on a delegation by the husband
of his right to divorce, the rules remain substantially the same. The wife can
initiate this form of divorce without the consent of her husband, because such
consent was given at the delegation stage when the stipulation was placed in
the marriage contract. But where the wife initiates an independent undelegated
action for divorce, the rules change drastically. This independent action by the
wife is called *khul'*. *Khul'* allows the wife who has strong feelings of aversion
toward her husband through no fault of his own to leave him, provided that
she returns to him the *mahr* he gave her. In this case the woman informs the
judge that she has such strong aversion toward her husband and that she is
concerned about her ability to observe the limits ordained by God while living
with him. The judge would then try to reconcile the couple within a period of
few months, and if that effort fails he is required to grant the woman her divorce.
In this scenario the husband will not have the option of returning to the wife
within the *iddah* period and resuming their marital relations. Further, traditional jurists, such as Ibn Qudamah who is cited below, have imposed the
requirement of the consent of the husband to such action before it can be
lodged. This point of view, however, is contrary to the clear *sunnah* of the
Prophet as exhibited below in the story about the wife of Thabit ibn Qays. But
until recently Muslim countries required the consent of the husband in this
divorce action. A few years ago, however, the Egyptian al-Azhar which is a major
source of Islamic law and jurisprudence in the Muslim world recognized the
fact that the prophetic tradition does not require the consent of the husband in
a *khul'* form of divorce. As a result, first Egyptian then Jordanian laws were
changed to reflect this jurisprudence. Now, women in these countries are no
longer expected to gain their husband's consent in a *khul'* action. Previously,

women had to buy such consent at a high price to them and their families. The selection from the Moroccan king's speech shows that the Moroccan government opted to equalize divorce rights within the family by decreeing that, as a matter of public policy, the delegation of the man's right to divorce to the woman will no longer be a matter of private negotiations, but rather a matter of law. Thus, women in Morocco will now automatically have the delegated right to divorce as part of their marriage contract.

Finally, if the husband has harmed his wife, then the preferred form of divorce should be the judicial one. If harm is shown, the wife is then entitled to both divorce from her husband and her *mahr* as well.

Document 3–82

QUR'AN 2:228–230

Divorced women shall wait concerning themselves for three monthly periods. Nor is it lawful for them to hide what God Has created in their wombs, if they have faith in God and the Last Day. And their husbands have the better right to take them back in that period, if they wish for reconciliation. And women shall have rights similar to the rights against them, according to what is equitable; but men have a degree (of advantage) over them. And God is Exalted in Power, Wise.

A divorce is only permissible twice: after that, the parties should either hold together on equitable terms, or separate with kindness. It is not lawful for you, (men), to take back any of your gifts (from your wives), except when both parties fear that they would be unable to keep the limits ordained by God. If ye (judges) do indeed fear that they would be unable to keep the limits ordained by God, there is no blame on either of them if she gives something away for her freedom. These are the limits ordained by God; so do not transgress them. If any do transgress the limits ordained by God, such persons wrong (themselves as well as others).

So if a husband divorces his wife (irrevocably), he cannot, after that, remarry her until after she has married another husband and he has divorced her. In that case there is no blame on either of them if they reunite; provided they feel that they can keep the limits ordained by God. Such are the limits ordained by God, which he makes plain to those who understand.

[Al-Baqarah, The Cow]

Document 3–83

QUR'AN 65:1–2

O Prophet! When you do divorce women, divorce them at their prescribed periods, and count (accurately) their prescribed periods: And fear God your

Lord and turn them not out of their houses, nor shall they (themselves) leave, except in case they are guilty of some open lewdness, those are limits set by God.

[Al-Talaq, Divorce]

Document 3–84

QUR'AN 4:20

But if you decide to take one wife in place of another, even if you had given the latter a whole treasure for dower, take not the least bit of it back: Would you take it back by slander and manifest wrong?

[Al-Nisa', The Women]

Document 3–85

HADITH

The Prophet said, "Verily, the most hateful to God of lawful things is divorce."

[Hadith narrated by Ibn 'Umar in Abu Dawud, *Sunan Abu Dawud*, bk. Talaq (Divorce) nos. 2177 and 2178[33] by Ibn Majah in *Sunan Ibn Majah*, bk. Talaq (divorce), no. 2018. (9th century CE)]

Document 3–86

HADITH

The wife of Thabit Ibn Qays came to the Prophet and said, "O God's Apostle! I do not blame Thabit for defects in his character or his religion, but I am afraid I will violate God's law if I remain with him." On that God's Apostle said to her, "Would you give him back the garden he has given you as *mahr*?" She said, "Yes." Then the Prophet said to Thabit, "Take the garden and divorce her at once."

[Hadith narrated by Ibn Abbas, in Al-Bukhari, *Sahih Al-Bukhari*, bk. 63, Talaq (divorce), no. 198 (9th century CE)]

Document 3–87

ABU BAKR MUHAMMAD IBN ABDILLAH IBN AL-'ARABI AL MALIKI

"And it is not lawful to you to take any part of what you gave them."

Some scholars said that this verse refers to the *mahr*, but to me it includes everything he gave her. Although the dower *(mahr)* is a free marital gift, anything else given during the marriage is similar to it, because it is an intentional gift. This is a general rule in all marriages and divorces. . . .

This verse has been subject to many interpretations that are false altogether. It refers to the conviction of each of the concerned parties that they may not be able to fulfill the marital rights of the other party because of some feeling of dislike. In this case there is no harm or blame upon her for paying her way out of the marital contract or for him to take back the returned gift.

God made it clear, however, that the husband cannot touch the divorced wife's wealth in cases in which he was the one who instigated the divorce process, as in the verse "and if you decide to take one in place of another . . ." because it is an instance in which people get greedy and the husband wants to take back what he has given his wife as a marital gift. You might think that whatever you gave her was for having her as wife, and since you are leaving her, then it is fully legitimate to take it back. God therefore prohibited it. . . .

[Ibn al-'Arabi al-Maliki, *Ahkam al-Qur'an*, 1:193–194 (12th century CE)]

Document 3–88

MUHAMMAD FAKHR AL-DIN AL-RAZI

"O Prophet! When you do divorce women divorce them at their prescribed period and count (accurately) their prescribed period." . . .

There are several issues in this verse:

First: What is the difference between a *sunnah* divorce and a *bid'a*[34] divorce? We say that it was called a *bid'a* divorce because, if she had her period, here menstruation days were not to be counted in her waiting period, which would otherwise exceed then the three cycles she is required to observe. It will become more like four cycles. During this whole time she was suspended, so much so she was neither married nor divorced, and this was harmful to her. Also if she was divorced while not menstruating, but after having had intercourse with her husband, she could be pregnant, and the husband would not have divorced her if he knew and might regret divorcing her while she is bearing his child. Divorce during menstrual periods is harmful to the woman; for it makes her waiting period longer. Divorce after having intercourse, with the possibility of pregnancy for the woman, could be harmful to the husband; for he might regret it. Therefore it is always recommended to divorce her after the menstrual period and before any new intercourse. In this case she will uncompromisingly count three cycles and he will have the assurance that she bears him no child.

Second: does the divorce that is contrary to *sunnah* have legal effect? We say that it actually does, despite being sinful. The evidence is in the *hadith* that suggests that a man divorced his wife thrice in the presence of the Prophet, so the Prophet asked him, "Are you playing with the book of God while I am still amongst you?" . . .

"And turn them not out" means that the divorced woman shall not be chased out of her house during her three-cycle waiting period. If the house was rented and the lease has ended, it is obligatory upon the husband to buy or rent another suitable house for this purpose. This is also binding on the wife. She shall not leave the premises of the house at day or at night without a valid reason till the waiting period is fully completed as God recommended, but, if she does, her waiting period is still valid.

Of the verse "unless they come up with an evidenced sin *(fahishah),*" Ibn Abbas said, "If they are proven guilty of adultery, then they should leave."

[Al-Razi, *Tafsir al-Fakhr al-Razi,* 30:31 (12th century CE)]

Document 3–89

MUWAFFAQ AL-DIN IBN QUDAMAH

Overall, if a woman dislikes her husband for his physical appearance, moral behavior, lack of religiosity, age, or weakness, or any other matter of the sort, and in that she fears that she will not be able to fulfill her duties as a wife, she may seek *khul'* by buying her way out of the marital relationship as stated in the verse "and if you fear that they will not uphold God's commands." There is no blame on them in what she gives up to free herself.

[Muwaffaq al-Din Ibn Qudamah (d. 1223), *Al-Mughni* (The Enricher)
(Beirut: Dar al-Kitab al-'Arabi, n.d), 18:173 (12th century CE)]

Document 3–90

MOHAMED SALIM EL-AWA

I would like to point out that the divergence in opinions between supporters of the new reform[35] and its opponents does not revolve around the legitimacy of *khul',* for everybody agrees on it, and all jurisprudential books have dealt with it. The divergence is rather on whether it is permissible to force the husband to accept this divorce or not, or whether it is acceptable to give the judge the authority to pronounce it, and finally on the consequences of a *khul'* sentence as stated by the aforementioned legislation.

Giving the judge the authority of imposing *khul'* is a controversial matter in Islamic jurisprudence. The opinion of the majority of scholars including the four imams[36] is that *khul'* occurs between the spouses without the judge's intervention. The second opinion, which states that the judge can intervene, is that of . . . (various) noble Successors *(Tabi'in)*[37] . . .

Stating that *khul'* occurs without the judge's intervention means that spouses have to reach an agreement. The question is, what happens when they fail to do so? In this case there is no other solution for the women who dislikes her husband but to go to court, this is why the *Tabi'in* said, "The judge has the authority to impose *khul'*" . . .

When a man hates his wife, he can divorce her, although most men do not do so, and when a woman hates her husband she can use *khul'* to leave him. If the husband accepts *khul',* then so be it, but if he does not the judge may intervene and pronounce a one-time final *(ba'in)* divorce against the husband's will. This divorce is final *(ba'in)* because the wife gives back to her husband the *mahr* he had given her so that she can leave him. Therefore, the husband does not have the right to revoke this divorce, otherwise it becomes pointless.

[El-Awa, The Project of the Personal Status Legislation, *al-Ahram*,
no. 41314, January 17, 2000]

Document 3–91

KING MOHAMED VI OF MOROCCO

Divorce, defined as the dissolution of marriage, shall be a prerogative that can be exercised equally by the husband as by the wife, in accordance with Islamic legal rulings for each party, and under judicial supervision. Thus, the husband's misuse of repudiation shall be limited by specific restrictions and conditions. This will be in conformity with the *hadith* of the Prophet, peace and blessings upon him, which says, "The most hateful to God, of all lawful things, is divorce." For this purpose, mechanisms for reconciliation and mediation, through the family and the judge, shall be strengthened.

If divorce is in the husband's hands, the wife has also the right to it through *tamleek* (the right of option).[38] Whatever the case, and before the divorce is authorized, it shall be ascertained that the divorced woman gets all the rights to which she is entitled.

A new procedure for divorce has been established, requiring the court's prior authorization. Divorce cannot be duly registered until it is established that the husband has paid in full all alimonies owed to his previous wife and children. Verbal repudiation, in exceptional cases, shall not be considered valid.

[King Mohamed VI of Morocco, speech to the Parliament fall session,
10 October 2003]

SEXUAL ETHICS

The Islamic view of sexuality is based on the ideal of establishing equilibrium between spirituality and the fulfillment of earthly desires and needs. This goal is achieved through a complex moral and legal system aimed at both sexes, which manages the community's sexual needs and social interaction. Sexuality is based on the concept of harmony of the sexes and aims at achieving a state of completeness of the spouses.[39] When the sexual act occurs within legitimate bonds, pleasure becomes a recognized right for both spouses and does not generate any guilt. This also means that the satisfaction of physical desires and procreation may take place only within the framework of legitimate marriage.

Chastity is highly praised in the Qur'an (17:32) and rules are set to prevent natural desires from leading to unlawful behavior.[40] However, some zealous jurists went very far in establishing strict and hermetic boundaries between the two sexes, severely restricting their interaction, and turning the general principle of modesty into a requirement of almost total seclusion for women. In this regard there are extensive debates in Islamic jurisprudence over the appropriate boundaries for female presence in the public sphere, the extent to which the female body may be revealed, and whether the female voice is '*awrah*[41] or not.

In this same spirit, premarital as well as extramarital sex *(zina)* are considered grave sins, are subject to condemnation, and both men and women are severely and equally punished for engaging in them (Q. 24:2–9). In this Islam shares the same views as other Abrahamic religions. The rather harsh treatment of *zina* in Islam should be considered in light of the moral system articulated by the Islamic faith. It must also be understood within the context of the Islamic social system based among other things on relationships of blood and kinship (as reflected for example in laws of inheritance and marriage). We also need to bear in mind that the punishment for *zina* cannot be meted out unless highly demanding due process requirements are met. For example, the establishment of guilt requires the testimony of four reliable eyewitnesses, all of whom saw the actual act of intercourse at the same time and in the same place between two clearly identifiable parties. This strict due process requirement is quite challenging because of the privacy rule, which is stated in the same chapter as the ruling on *zina*, and because of the fact that if any of the witnesses recant prior to the verdict, all four witnesses will become severely punishable for slandering the accused couple.[42] It is important to note that the Qur'anic evidentiary requirements for *zina* were initially intended to protect women from frivolous charges, even when those charges come from their own husbands (Qur'an, 24:4–9). Needless to say, husbands or other relatives who kill women for engaging in *zina* (honor killings) commit acts of murder punishable under Islamic law.

The Islamic position toward homosexuality is similar to that of the other Abrahamic religions. It is based on the story of Lut, which also appears in the Qur'an (see below). Because of the wording of the verse, many jurists concluded that the punishment for *zina* applied to male homosexuals, but not to lesbians who were assigned a lesser punishment. Again, homosexual acts are subject to the same due process requirements of *zina* and are entitled to the same privacy protections. Thus it would be almost impossible to establish a sex-related violation short of committing a prohibited act in the public square or insisting on a public confession feely and knowingly.

Finally, the great importance given to regulating sexuality in the Muslim world expresses a legitimate concern to apply as faithfully as possible the commands of God. However, cultural and patriarchal influences that look down at women and consider them the ultimate source of temptation for men and a potential source of shame for their families have had disastrous repercussions on women's lives, as is the case in honor killings and female circumcision, which are practices that are unfortunately widespread in some Muslim as well as non-Muslim countries.

Document 3–92

QUR'AN 33:35

For Muslim men and women, for believing men and women, for devout men and women, for true men and women, for men and women who are patient and constant, for men and women who humble themselves, for men and women who give in charity, for men and women who fast (and deny themselves), for men and women who guard their chastity, and for men and women who engage much in God's praise—for [all of] them has God prepared forgiveness and great reward.

[Al-Ahzab, The Coalition, Abdullah Yusuf 'Ali, *The Meaning of the Holy Qu'ran* (MD: Amana, 1991)]

Document 3–93

QUR'AN 17:32

Nor come nigh to adultery: for it is a shameful (deed) and an evil, opening the road (to other evils).

[Al-Isra', The Night Journey, Abdullah Yusuf 'Ali, *The Meaning of the Holy Qu'ran* (MD: Amana, 1991)]

Document 3–94

QUR'AN 24:2–9

The woman and the man guilty of adultery or fornication, flog each of them with a hundred stripes: Let not compassion move you in their case, in a matter prescribed by God, if you believe in God and the Last Day: and let a party of the Believers witness their punishment. . . .

And those who launch a charge against chaste women, and produce not four witnesses (to support their allegations), flog them with eighty stripes and reject their evidence ever after: for such men are wicked transgressors unless they repent thereafter and mend (their conduct); for God is Oft-Forgiving, Most Merciful.

And for those who launch a charge against their spouses, and have (in support) no evidence but their own, their solitary evidence (can be received) if they bear witness four times (with an oath) by God that they are solemnly telling the truth.

And the fifth (oath) (should be) that they solemnly invoke the curse of God upon themselves if they tell a lie.

But it would avert the punishment of the wife, if she bears witness four times (with an oath) By God, that (her husband) is telling a lie.

And the fifth (oath) should be that she solemnly invokes the wrath of God on herself if (her accuser) is telling the truth.

[Al-Noor, The Light, Abdullah Yusuf 'Ali, *The Meaning of the Holy Qu'ran* (MD: Amana, 1991)]

Document 3–95

QUR'AN 4:34

Therefore the righteous women are devoutly obedient,[43] and guard in (the husband's) absence what God would have them guard.

[Al-Nisa, The Women]

Document 3–96

QUR'AN 7:80–81

We also (sent) Lut; He said to his people "Do you commit lewdness such as no people in creation (ever) committed before you? For you practice your lusts on men in preference to women; you are indeed a people transgressing beyond bounds."

[Al-'Araf, The Heights]

Document 3–97

HADITH

A man came to the Prophet, and said, "My wife does not repel the hand of any man who touches her." He said, "Divorce her." The man then said, "I love her." He said, "Then enjoy her."

[Hadith narrated by Abdullah Ibn Abbas, in Abu Dawud, *Sunan Abu-Dawud*, bk. 11, *Kitab al-Nikah*, no. 2044 (9th century CE)]

Document 3–98

HADITH

Sa'd ibn Ubadah asked, "Messenger of God, if I found my wife with a man, should I wait until I bring four witnesses?" The Prophet said, "Yes."

[Hadith narrated by Abu Hurayrah, in Muslim, *Sahih Muslim*, bk. 009, no. 3570 (9th century CE)]

Document 3–99

HADITH

A man from Banu Fazarah came to the Holy Prophet and said, "O God's Apostle! A black child has been born to me." The Prophet asked him, "Have you got camels?" The man said, "Yes." The Prophet asked him, "What color are they?" The man replied, "Red." The Prophet said, "Is there a gray one among them?" The man replied, "Yes." The Prophet said, "Whence comes that?" He said, "Maybe it is because of heredity." The Prophet said, "Maybe your latest son has this color because of heredity."

[Hadith narrated by Abu Hurayrah, in Muslim, *Sahih Muslim*, bk. 9, *Kitab al-Talaq*, no. 3574 (9th century CE)]

Document 3–100

HADITH

The Prophet said, "The most wicked among the people in the sight of God on the Day of Judgment is the man who goes to his wife and she comes to him, they have intercourse, and then he divulges her secrets by describing what they did in their intimacy."

[Hadith reported by Abu Sa'id al-Khudari in Muslim, *Sahih Muslim*, bk. 8, *Kitab al-Nikah*, no. 3369 (9th century CE)]

Document 3–101

HADITH

The Prophet said, "God does not look at a man who has anal sex with his wife."

[Hadith narrated Abu Hurayrah, in Ibn Majah, *Sunan Ibn Majah*, bk. *Al-Nikah* (marriage), no. 1923 (9th century CE)]

Document 3–102

ABU HAMID AL-GHAZALI

He should always start by sweet talk and a lot of kissing, for the Prophet said, "One should not approach his wife the same way a dumb beast does. Let there be an emissary between them." They asked: "What is an emissary here?" He said, "Kissing and soft-speaking." He also said, "Three matters are clear signs of social ineptitude of a man. The first is to meet a good person and to leave him before knowing his name and inquiring about his family. The second is to reject a gift, and the third is to have sex with his wife or female-slave before talking to her or kissing her and to withdraw before she is satisfied."

[Al-Ghazali, 'Ihya' 'Ulum al-Din, 2:51–52 (11th century CE)]

Document 3–103

MUWAFFAQ AL-DIN IBN QUDAMAH

It is reported that 'Umar Ibn Abdul-Aziz related to the Prophet his saying "Do not have intercourse with your wife unless she has the same level of desire that you have, so that you do not reach orgasm before her." He was then asked, "How do we know?" The Prophet said, "Well! You kiss her, touch her and caress her, till you notice that she has the same desire that you have, and then you engage in sex with her." In case he reaches orgasm before her, he must not withdraw before she is satisfied. Anas reported that the Prophet said, "When one of you has sexual intercourse with his wife, he must always be conscious of her needs. If he finishes before her he then must not rush her and must wait for her until she is satisfied, because that frustrates her and prevents her from enjoying her sexuality."

[Ibn Qudamah, *Al-Mughni*, 8:136 (12th century CE)]

RIGHTS WITHIN THE FAMILY

From the early days of Islam the rights of women within the family were carefully articulated. After all, Islam was revealed in a patriarchal society where women's rights were minimal. Sons inherited their father's wives, and fathers practiced female infanticide. Muslim converts came to regret their actions in pre-Islamic times, and Khalifah 'Umar is often quoted as saying that in his society women were not accorded any importance until Islam articulated their rights. Muslim women themselves were actively involved in the articulation of these rights. For example, complaining about men dominating meetings, women asked the Prophet to assign a special day to them where they could ask him questions reflecting their own concerns. In many of these meetings the women asked highly specific and intimate questions. At times the Prophet whispered the answers to his wife `A'ishah, who spoke to the women. Most of the time, however, he answered himself, for it is an established fact in Islam that there is no embarrassment in discussing matters of religion, regardless of how intimate the facts are. Thus, a good part of Islamic jurisprudence discusses various matters of sexuality that would have been unthinkable in a Victorian society, for example, Islam took the position that sexuality is a blessing from God that should be enjoyed, so long as it is within the proper marital framework. But these were only part of the issues discussed in Islam. A whole chapter of the Qur'an is named after a woman who argued with the Prophet about the proper ruling in a certain familial situation. When she disagreed with the Prophet, she asked him to seek a revelation, and he did. A significant part of the Qur'an, *hadith*, and subsequent jurisprudence have all addressed relations within the family, such as the relation of husbands and wives, their duties to each other and to their children, and the children's duties to their parents. In choosing the topics in this section, we were severely limited by consideration of space. So we balanced the emphasis placed by Islamic jurisprudence on certain topics with current debates in our American society, the Islamic American Muslim community, and even Muslim societies around the world. For example, Muslim societies generally do not reflect in their laws the Islamic view of domestic responsibilities. Instead, they reflect customary views that regard housework as the responsibility of the wife. The Islamic view of motherhood is also significantly different from that of Muslim and modern Western societies. While according the mother a great deal of respect for the suffering she undergoes in pregnancy and delivery, it recognizes her right to a respite. So, after delivery, the mother has no legal obligation to nurse the child or take care of her. It is the turn of the husband to take care of both mother and child. That includes hiring a wet nurse or, in today's world, purchasing and preparing the bottle, if the mother opts not to nurse. Other issues discussed in this section, such as the right to education and economic and inheritance rights of Muslim women, are also important not only in Muslim-Western debates, as evidenced by discussions in the United Nation's Fourth World Conference on Women, held in Beijing in 1995, but also in the global outcry against the reported prohibition of women's education in Afghanistan in the late 1990s. While these events are now past, the related debates remain current and unresolved in the minds of many, including some Muslims. These selections should help both Muslims and non-Muslims alike to reach a better understanding of the proper Islamic approach to these matters, untainted by either politics or patriarchal custom.

RESPONSIBILITIES OF PARENTS

Islam places kindness to parents next to the worship of God. In general, parenthood is an extension of the Qur'anic view of ideal marital relations. These relationships, which are to be based on mercy, affection, and tranquillity, result in a cooperative, not hierarchically oppressive, family life. As a result, children are to be raised by both parents, who consult each other on important matters. Mothers, in particular, are highly honored, because of their special role in giving birth. The Qur'an views pregnancy as an arduous experience. Partially for this reason, Muslim jurists do not obligate the mother to nurse her baby, except as a last resort. Nevertheless, in today's Muslim societies Muslim women are obligated by social pressure to nurse their children and be the primary caretakers. These custom-based legal obligations often affect the human development of mothers, especially with respect to their education and career, and need to be reexamined in light of the Islamic view of family relations. After all, even the Prophet participated in caring for his children and in household chores. As to general parental responsibilities, Islamic jurisprudence recognized a host of mutual responsibilities between parents and children that are not mentioned in this short selection. For example, not only is the child entitled to financial support, she is also entitled to a good name. Thus a criminal not only violates society's norms and laws but also his child's right to a good name, and thus his parenting duties. Similarly, parents are entitled to be cared for by their children in their old age, as they took care of their children when they were young. If children ignore this obligation, an Islamic court can enforce it.

Document 3–104

QUR'AN 31:14

And We have enjoined the human being (to be good) to his parents: in travail upon travail did his mother bear him, and in years twain was his weaning: (hear the command), "Show gratitude to Me and to thy parents: to Me is (thy final) goal."

[Luqman, The Wise, Abdullah Yusuf 'Ali, *The Meaning of the Holy Qu'ran* (MD: Amana, 1991)]

Document 3–105

QUR'AN 46:15

We have enjoined the human being kindness to his parents: In pain did his mother bear him, and in pain did she give him birth. The carrying of the (child) to his weaning is (a period of) thirty months. At length, when he reaches the age of full strength and attains forty years, he says, "O my Lord! Grant me that I may be grateful for the favor which You have bestowed upon me, and upon both my parents. . . . "

[Al-Ahqaf, The Dunes, Abdullah Yusuf 'Ali, *The Meaning of the Holy Qu'ran* (MD: Amana, 1991)]

Document 3–106

QUR'AN 2:233

The mothers shall suckle their offspring for two whole years, for those who wish to complete the term. But he [the father] shall bear the cost of their food and clothing on equitable terms. No soul shall have a burden laid on it greater than it can bear. No mother shall be treated unfairly on account of her child; nor father on account of his child; an heir shall be chargeable in the same way. If they both decide on weaning, by mutual consent, and after due consultation, there is no blame on them. If ye decide on wet nurses for your offspring, there is no blame on you, provided ye pay (the mother) what ye offered, on equitable terms. But fear God and know that God sees well what ye do.

[Al-Baqarah, The Cow]

Document 3–107

HADITH

God's Apostle mentioned the greatest sins or he was asked about the greatest sins. He said, "To join partners in worship with God; to kill a soul which God has forbidden to kill; and to be undutiful or unkind to one's parents."

[Hadith narrated by Anas Ibn Malik in al-Bukhari, *Sahih al-Bukhari*, bk. 73, Adab, no. 8]

Document 3–108

HADITH

The prophet told a man, "Go and stay by your mother's feet for paradise lies under them."

[Hadith narrated by Mu'awiyah Ibn Jahimah al-Salami and reported by Ibn Majah in *Sunan Ibn Majah, Kitab Al-Jihad*, no. 2781 (9th century CE)]

Document 3–109

HADITH

A man came to The Prophet and asked him, "O Prophet of God! Who is the person who has the greatest right on me with regards to kindness and attention?" The Prophet replied, "Your mother." The man asked again, "Then who?" The Prophet replied, "Your mother." "Then who?" He replied, "Your mother." "Then who?" He replied, "Then, your father."

[Hadith narrated by Abu Hurayrah in al-Bukhari, *Sahih Al-Bukhari*, bk. 73, Adab, no. 2; and in *Sahih Muslim*, bk. 32, Birr: 1. no. 6180. (9th century CE)]

Document 3–110

MUHAMMAD FAKHR AL-DIN AL-RAZI

"In pain did his mother bear him and in pain did she give him birth." The Qur'an exegesis experts said, she did bear him with hardship and so did she give birth to him. And He did not mean the early pregnancy, which is not a hardship, for He says, "And when they are united she bears a light burden and carries it about," meaning the start of pregnancy, for it is not painful due to the fact that it starts as a sperm, a blood clot, and then a fetus. Only when she becomes heavy that she "bears him in hardship and gives birth to him in hardship." . . .

The verse underlines the fact that the rights of a mother are greater than those of the father, for God mentions both parents together by saying, "We have enjoined on the human being kindness to his parents," he then specifically mentions the mother, "she did bear him in pain and gave him birth in pain," therefore, her rights are greater because the hardships she undergoes are greater. Many *hadiths* are known on this subject.

[Al-Razi, *Tafsir al-Fakhr al-Razi,* 28:14 (12th century CE)]

Document 3–111

MUHAMMAD FAKHR AL-DIN AL-RAZI

As to God's saying, "and mothers shall suckle their children. . . . " This command is not binding. This is evidenced by two facts. The first is God's saying, "And if they suckle (the children) for you, you shall then compensate them [for it if divorced]," so she would not have been eligible for monetary compensation if it were obligatory upon her to suckle her child. The second one: God says, "And if you disagree (on compensation terms) another woman (wet nurse) will suckle for him," and this is a clear-cut text. . . .

If she were required to suckle her child, the husband would not have to compensate her. . . .

One must know that the two-year term is not a binding limitation. . . . [T]he objective of mentioning the two-year term was to settle disputes between the parents with regard to the length of the suckling period. So if the father wanted to wean the child off before the completion of the two-year term and the mother did not, the mother's position prevails and vice versa. But if they both agree on terminating the suckling process before the completion of the two-year period they may do so at their own discretion.

[Al Razi, *Tafsir al-Fakhr al-Razi,* 6:126–27 (12th century CE)]

Document 3–112

MUWAFFAQ AL-DIN IBN QUDAMAH

It is recommended for the father to seek the mother's permission in marrying off her daughter. For the Prophet said, "Consult with the mothers in their daughters' affairs!" This is because she shares responsibilities with the father in looking after her children's interests and also because consulting with her assures her approval and good will.

[Ibn Qudamah, *al-Mughni* 7:383 (12th century CE)]

Document 3–113

MUHAMMED RASHID RIDA

As to God saying: "and mothers shall suckle their children," it appears that the command implies an absolute binding order, because originally the mother must suckle her child. This is the view chosen by the professor and imam 'Abduh. But he recognizes an exception when the mother has a valid reason not to suckle, such as illness. However, this order does not forbid appointing a wet nurse for the purpose of breast-feeding the child if that is not harmful for the child. The rationale for this argument is that the command in this verse is for the benefit *(maslahah)* of the child and is not a religious duty. . . .

By the same token, while it was made a duty upon the mother to suckle her child, she also has a right to do so. This means that the father cannot prevent her. It is indeed more likely that the father prevents his divorcée from suckling her child, if he is allowed to do so, than for the mother to abstain from suckling her child. . . . "

[Rida, *Tafsir al-Manar*, 2:409–410 (19th century CE)]

DOMESTIC RESPONSIBILITIES

In an Islamic marriage, while fostering a deep loving relationship between them, both husband and wife maintain their identity and their independence. The woman keeps her own name and financial independence, remaining an independent legal entity capable of transacting her own business and other affairs. Thus marriage in Islam is a true partnership, not one where the two spouses become one, namely the husband. Further, the wife has no obligation to perform housework. Based on the Qur'anic view that marriage is a relationship of mercy, affection, and tranquillity, jurists have concluded that the marriage contract is a contract of companionship, not service. Therefore, if the husband wants his housework to be done, he must do it himself or arrange for it to be done by another. But he cannot look to the wife to do it, unless she volunteers. For this reason, the Iranian parliament promulgated a law in the 1990s[44] that permitted a divorced woman to demand compensation for all the housework she performed during her marriage. This approach rectified a sad situation, prevalent throughout much of the Islamic world, where women receive a very small settlement upon divorce. Other solutions are being studied in various Muslim countries and by the editors of this section. But the problem of defining properly the financial rights of the Muslim woman upon divorce remains quite urgent as well as important. Patriarchal jurisprudence ignored these rights in order to force the divorced woman to return to her family. As a result, some divorced Muslim women in the United States and other countries have at times suffered hardship and even indignities, especially when they did not have families capable of caring for them.

Document 3–114

HADITH

I asked 'A'ishah, "What did the Prophet use to do at home?" She said, "He used to work for his family, and when he heard the call for the prayer (Adhan), he would go out."

[Hadith narrated by al-Aswad Ibn Yazid in al-Bukhari, *Sahih al-Bukhari*, Bk. 64, no. 276]

Document 3–115

ABU MUHAMMAD ALI IBN SA'ID IBN HAZM

It is not obligatory for the wife to serve her husband in anything, be it kneading the dough, baking it, cooking, tidying up, sweeping the floor, or anything related to household work. But it would be kind of her to do that. It is obligatory for the husband to bring her ready-to-wear clothes and fully cooked meals.

[Abu Muhammad Ali Ibn Sa'id Ibn Hazm, *al-Muhalla bi al-Athar* (The Gilded or Ornamented with Revelation and Tradition), 12 vols. (Beirut: Dar al-Kutub al-'Ilmiyyah, 1988), 9:227–228 (11th century CE)]

Document 3–116

IBN HAJAR AL-'ASQALANI

There is no evidence that permits the coercion of women to serve their husbands in any way. The consensus of scholars is such that he caters to all her needs. Al-Tahawi also reported that the husband is not permitted to dismiss the wife's servant. On the contrary, he has even to provide for that servant, too.

[Al-'Asqalani, *Fath al-Bari Sharh Sahih al-Bukhari*, 9:633]

Document 3–117

SHAYKH SYED MUTAWALLI AD-DARSH

Q: Generally, women look after the home and men go out to work and look after the women. However, in today's society, when it is often essential for a wife to work outside to help support the family, shouldn't a man also do his share of the housework? I know a lot of Muslim women who work and then face household chores whereas their husbands come home and then go off to study circles and so on. The women do not get the chance to study, and the husbands are the first to complain if they get no share of their wife's income and if the house is not clean and tidy. What is your advice? Please do not say, "Give up working outside the home" because we need the money.

A: The Islamic attitude is this: even if the woman is not working, is she under any obligation to do the housework or not? Look at the concept of marriage, at the marriage contract; the Fuqaha'—legalists—define this contract as *Aqdu Istimtaa*'—an agreement allowing all [sic] parties to enjoy themselves in that intimate relationship. It is not an agreement of servitude or anything like that. So when it comes to the legality and everyone says, "Where are my rights?" this contract relieves the woman from cleaning or doing anything like that. In the words of Ibn Hazm, one of the great literalist scholars, it is the duty of the husband to bring the food ready-cooked to his wife. And the *Fuqaha'* (jurists) generally say that if the woman is one of those who are used to being served—

upper class—it is the duty of the husband to provide her with a servant to look after her.[45]

However, it is said that good manners require a woman to look after what is inside the house, and the man to look after what is outside, common courtesy dictates that the husband lend the wife a hand. This was the ruling of the Prophet . . . When he ruled on Fatimah and 'Ali. . . . when 'A'ishah . . . was asked about the manner of the Prophet . . . at home, she said he used to be involved in the work of his family; he would repair his clothes and shoes, look after his bed, and so on. Now, in the situation where a woman is working to earn a living, we are not saying that the husband should necessarily look after the house, but good manners say she [sic] should help in the home and share the duties. This is what I do and what the Prophet . . . did. It is the husband's duty to care for his family and home, not just sit in front of the television for hours on end while his wife does the cooking and looks after the children. This is simply unfair.

[Shaykh Syed Mutawalli Ad-Darsh (1930–1997), *Answers to Questions Ranging from Contemporary to Family Issues*, in http://ireland.iol.ie/˜afifi/Ad-Darsh/27.9.96.htm]

EDUCATION

The Qur'an exhorts Muslims, men and women, to seek education and knowledge. In particular, the prophetic tradition in the matter is rich and clear about women's right to knowledge and education. There is a general agreement among Muslim scholars that educating women is a duty, not just an option or luxury. It is also a consequence of the equal religious duties and obligations incumbent upon both males and females. Since understanding one's religion is *fardh ayn* (a duty that is incumbent on each Muslim), as al-Ghazali put it, Muslim women, just like men, require full access to religious education. Indeed, history makes clear that the religious education of women in early Islam proceeded hand in hand with that of men. Women entered into debates with men about the proper interpretation of the Qur'an and the *hadith* as well as the significance of events in the world around them. Women also were major reporters of *hadith*. As a result, many prominent men came to them for religious education and guidance. This trend continued for several centuries after the death of the Prophet.

Document 3–118

QUR'AN 96:1

Read in the name of thy Lord. . . .

[al-'Alaq, The Clinging Clot]

Document 3–119

QUR'AN 39:9

Are those equal, those who know and those who do not know? It is those who are endowed with understanding that receive admonition.

[Al-Zumar, The Crowds]

Document 3–120

HADITH

Education is a duty *(faridah)* upon all Muslims.

[Hadith narrated by Anas Ibn Malik and reported by Ibn Majah in
Sunan Ibn Majah, bk. 1, *Muqaddimah*, no. 224 (9th century CE)]

Document 3–121

HUSSEIN IBN FAYD AL-HAMDANI

One of the most prominent religious authorities, al-Sultan al Khattab Ibn al-Hasan al- Hujuri al-Hamdani, while responding to the opposing view suggesting that women do not deserve the position of upper religious leadership *(Hujjiyah)*, said, "Garments[46] cannot be a basis for inferring rules or enacting them. . . . On the one hand, we do find some, who happen to be wearing women's garments, to be in most prominent and respected positions, such as al-Zahra' al-Batul . . . Khadija bint Khuwaylid . . . and Maryam daughter of Imran.[47] On the other hand, we find others who have the worst repute. Male or female garments do have little impact upon the character of whoever wears them. It is, rather, the qualities of actions of those who wear them that are of substantial significance. Therefore, when good deeds prevail over evil ones, submission in matters of worship rules over defiance. When sainthood is unblemished by arrogance and acceptance is not frustrated by rejection, a person is likely to receive enlightenment that points at his/her being deeply rooted in knowledge. Only through this way may one distinguish between a genuine believer and a sinful disbeliever. If the person, wearing female garments, has acquired all the good qualities, she should be given the same stature of her male counterparts. . . . And if the one wearing male garments does not have all the necessary qualities he should be treated as equal to his female counterparts. . . . Human bodies, male or female, do not have any significance in this respect. It is the capability of acquiring knowledge that matters.[48]

[Hussein Ibn Fayd Al-Hamdani, Al-Sulhiyun wa al-Harakah al-Fatimiyyah
fi al-Yemen (The Sulayhids and the Fatimid Movement in Yemen) (San'a':
Manshuraat al-Madinah, 1986), pp.144–145 (20th century CE)]

Document 3–122

FATIMA NASEEF

The female companions knew and understood the importance of knowledge in Islam. They passionately competed among themselves and endeavored to gain sound knowledge. The Prophet (S)[49] . . . encouraged their enthusiasm and allowed them to attend his study circle. How could he not after his Lord taught him to say, "Lord, increase my knowledge." (20:114). When the female companions heard the Prophet (S) saying, "When Allah wants to do good for a person; He gives him sound knowledge in religion," they understood this narration to be directed to both male and female Muslims, and not exclusively to men, as some people seem to believe. . . .

'A'ishah (R)[50] said, "How excellent the women of the Ansaar! They do not feel shy while learning sound knowledge in religion." The women persevered in doing so and regularly attended study circles. There they asked the Prophet (S) various questions, some general, some related to women's issues. In a narration by Abu Sa'eed Al-Khudri [sic] we learned that some women requested that the Prophet (S) even set aside a day for them because the men were taking all the time. In response to their request he promised them one day for religious lessons and commandments.

[Naseef, *Women in Islam*, pp. 82–83 (20th century CE)]

ECONOMIC

Islam sees a woman, whether single or married, as an economically independent legal entity, with the right to manage her own affairs, enter into contracts and dissolve them, and own and dispose of her property without any guardianship or control over her, whether by her father, husband, or anyone else. Unfortunately, later patriarchal jurisprudence has tried to erode these rights by giving the husband a say over the disposition of at least part of the wife's property. It has also attempted to expand the authority of the husband over the wife in other areas so as to interfere with her economic independence. For example, many laws in Muslim countries require the wife to obtain her husband's permission before she accepts a job or leaves her home or country. If she does not, she risks losing her maintenance. This type of law clearly interferes with the wife's ability to enter the field of employment or conduct business. Furthermore, laws in some Muslim countries that severely restrict the interaction of the two genders has made the presence of the woman in the marketplace awkward and led in some cases to the establishment of "women's banks." These developments would have appeared incomprehensible to Khadijah, the wealthy businesswoman who married the Prophet, or to al-Shifaa', the woman appointed by Khalifah 'Umar to audit the commercial markets against fraud and irregularities *(hisbah)*. Today Muslim women cannot fully enjoy their economic rights without changing such laws. Some Muslim countries, like Morocco, have started the process, but a great deal still needs to be done by modern Muslim jurists.

Document 3–123

QUR'AN 4:32

To men is allotted what they earn, and to women what they earn: But ask God of His bounty. For God hath full knowledge of all things.

[Al-Nisa', The Women]

Document 3–124

QUR'AN 4:6

Make trial of orphans until they reach the age of marriage; if then you find sound judgment in them release their property to them.

[Al-Nisa', The Women]

Document 3–125

MUHAMMAD IBN IDRIS AL-SHAFI'I

Reaching the age of liability for both genders is defined by their ability to handle their own financial affairs. . . . Reaching the age is completing fifteen years for both genders equally. . . . Both male and female are equal in this regard. . . . The capability of handling financial affairs is known through testing the orphan. . . .

Testing the woman's capability of handling her financial matters, while she is likely to be away from public life, is a little more extensive. Her close relatives should give her a limited amount. If she handles it well then she is ready to handle bigger amounts such as her *mahr* before or after marriage. Marriage does not increase or decrease her mental capacity, as it does not affect her male counterpart. . . . For God has ordered to hand him out his money as soon as he comes of age, and God did not link it to his marital status. Similarly, there should be no condition of marriage for a woman to be given command over her financial matters. A husband does not have the right to interfere in his wife's financial affairs. So whenever a boy or a girl comes of age he or she should be given his/her money to manage, as they deem fit. . . .

When a woman is given her money, as in the case of a man, married or divorced, she has the full right to manage her wealth as she deems right in the same way a man has the power of overseeing his interests. There is no difference between the two of them whatsoever. This is God's ruling and is supported by the Prophet's tradition.

> [Muhammad Ibn Idris Al-Shafi'i (767–820), *Kitab al-Umm* (The Mother Book), 8 vols. (Cairo: Maktabat al-Kuliyyah al-Azhariyyah, 1961), 3:215–216, 219 (9th century CE)]

Document 3–126

ABU BAKR MUHAMMAD IBN ABDILLAH IBN AL-'ARABI AL MALIKI

God says, "To men is allotted what they earn, and to women what they earn." Our scholars have said that their share in terms of religious reward is equal. . . . Each good deed is rewarded tenfold. Man and woman are equal. . . . As to their shares in worldly wealth, according to what God knows is good for humans and what He inspired to people in judging and managing their affairs, He decided their shares. . . .

> [Ibn al-'Arabi al Maliki, *Ahkam al-Qur'an*, 5:31 (12th century CE)]

Document 3–127

ABDEL KABIR AL-ALAOUI AL-MDAGHRI

Among these decrees *(fatawa)*, is one that was written under the title "A woman is entitled to take what is of right to her from her and her husband's earnings" in the book titled *Fatawa Tatahadda al-Ihmal fi Chafchaoun wa ma Hawlaha min Al Jibaal*[51] by Muhammad El-Habti Al-Mawahibi. Here is its text:

And from al-Qal'a,[52] here is a decree signed by its author and his ruling is the following:

Praise be to God, the author was asked about the case of a man and his wife who acquired cattle and money during their marriage.

So he replied, seeking God's guidance, that the woman is entitled to a share in proportion to her work from whatever they have acquired since the day of their wedding. This is what more than one imam has said. The author of the *Al Ajwibah Al Nasiriyyah* said, "She may take a share in proportion to the amount of her labor." . . . Imam Malik and his companions said, "She is entitled to a share from their wealth, whether from the capital or the earnings, in proportion to her labor."

The custom in this land is such that if the wife does handcrafted objects and her husband buys any capital with that, she is entitled to one quarter of those acquisitions. . . . This is enough said about this matter, and there is no need for more. God is all-knowing. This is said and recorded by the humble servant of God Abd al-Salam Ibn Abd al-Salam Ashghaf al-Wathili. . . .

> [Abdel Kabir al-Alaoui Al-Mdaghri, *Al-Mar'ah Bayna Ahkam al-Fiqh wa al-Da'wah ila al-Taghyir* (Woman Between the Legal Ruling of Islamic Jurisprudence and the Calls for Change) (Morocco: Matba'at Fdalah, 1999), pp. 203–204 (20th century CE)]

NOTES

1. Yusuf Ali translates the Arabic word *'iqra'* as "Proclaim! (or read)" But Arabic dictionaries and literature surrounding the incident make the parenthetical translation more accurate. This word is now the opening word in chapter 96 of the Qur'an, entitled *'Alaq* (Clot).

2. The majority of scholars agree that the Qur'an was revealed over a period of twenty-three years. However, some say twenty, and others twenty-five years.

3. Al-'Asqalani, *Fath Al-Bari Sharh Sahih Al-Bukhari*, 6:76–77.

4. Yusuf Ali translates the Qur'anic word *nafs* as "person," in this verse and others. For purposes of accuracy, we have changed the translation to "soul."

5. This is the editor's literal translation. Yusuf Ali's translation reverses the genders in the original text. This reversal may be significant in light of the fact that the verse continues, "When they were united, she bore a light burden." The continuation indicates that the gender attributed to the soul in this verse may not be simply a matter of linguistics.

6. The Arabic word used in the verse for people is *nas*, which is gender neutral and refers to a group of people.

7. The term *hadith* is used in the Shi'i tradition to refer not only to the prophetic tradition but also to the sayings of the Shi'i imams (spiritual leaders), as is the case in this text.

8. This text is from the Shi'i tradition, which is considered the fifth school of thought in Islam. This school is still followed in many parts of the world, particularly in Iran, Iraq, Bahrain, and Lebanon.

9. Abbreviation for *Subhanahu Wa Ta'ala*, which means "the Most Exalted One."

10. The reform of the Moroccan family code, *Mudawwanat al-'Usrah*, has been since approved and the legislation passed by the parliament on January 23, 2004.

11. The word *sunnah* refers to the example set by the life of the Prophet. See Muhammad Mustafa Azami, *Studies in Hadith Methodology and Literature* (Indianapolis: American Trust, 1977), pp. 3–4.

12. *Hadith* narrated by Anas Ibn Malik, in al-Bukhari, *Sahih al-Bukhari*, bk. 62, *Kitab al-Nikah*, no. 67, N. 1 (9th century CE).

13. Al-Shafi'i (767 or 8–820) is the founder of the Shafi'i school, one of the four major Sunni schools of thought; the person named Muhammad is a medieval jurist. Abu Yusuf is Ya'qub Ibn Ibrahim al-Ansari (731 or 2–798), a medieval scholar who was the student and disciple of Abu Hanifah.

14. Qur'an 2:232.

15. All the individuals named are famous medieval scholars. *Tabi'in* refers to the generation of Muslim scholars that followed the Companions of the Prophet.

16. The word *obligations* is used in Y. Ali's translation for *'uqud* (sing. *'aqd*), which means contracts and commitments in Arabic as well, as in *'aqd al-zawaj*, "the marriage contract."

17. 'Umar Ibn al-Khattab, a Companion of the Prophet and the second *khalifah* (caliph) of Islam.

18. Al-Shafi'i is Muhammad Ibn Idriss (767 or 8–820), leader of the Shafi'i school

of thought, one of the four major Sunni schools of thought; Ahamd is Ibn Hanbal, (780–855) leader of the Hanbali school; the two other leaders of Sunni schools of thought are Malik ibn Anas (d. 795) and Abu Hanifah al-Nu'man (d. 767 or 768). Finally, Ishaq Ibn Ibrahim al- Nisaburi (d. 888 or 889) is a Hanbali scholar.

19. This verse is a part of a longer verse that explains the rights and duties of women in the very specific case of divorce. However it has always been taken out of context and its meaning extended to include every woman and every man in all circumstances. See the whole verse and related discussion below in the next section.

20. *Fadl* is a general word that means "preference," "remainder," or "excess in degree or quality."

21. This does not include required religious duties, such as prayers and fasting, because when God's rights are involved they transcend all human rights and privileges, including obedience to humans, whether they are rulers, parents, spouses, or others.

22. It is known that after the death of Khadijah, the Prophet married more than one wife. The Qur'an and the Prophet both viewed the Prophet's situation as exceptional and did not hold it up as the norm.

23. 'Ali Ibn Abi Talib was the cousin of the Prophet and his son-in-law.

24. The prominent religious and educational Egyptian institution in Cairo.

25. Yusuf Ali's translation of the Arabic word *nushuz* as "disloyalty and ill-conduct" is overly broad. See the introduction to this section.

26. This *hadith* has a different number, namely no. 2137, in the online connection.

27. This is al-Ghazali's opinion; there are, however, other indications that the Prophet loved Khadijah, his first wife, with whom he stayed in a monogamous marital relationship until she died. He also was very faithful to her memory and once became very angry at 'A'ishah when she spoke about Khadijah in condescending terms.

28. In the verse 4:34.

29. Divorce initiated by the wife, see the section on divorce.

30. 'Ata' Ibn Abi Rabah is a Tabi'i, from the second generation after the Prophet; he was a great scholar and a narrator of *hadith*.

31. *Al-Qadi* is the Arabic word for judge, it refers here to the author Ibn al-'Arabi. It was common for jurists to refer to themselves in the third person.

32. A small twig used as a toothbrush.

33. Verses where the Arabic verb *daraba* or one of its variations were used.

34. Bk. 12, no. 2173 in the online collection.

35. A *sunnah* divorce is one that takes place according to the *sunnah* of the Prophet. This means, among other things, that the woman may not be divorced during her menstrual cycle or after it, if the couple engages in sexual intercourse during that subsequent period. A *bid'a* divorce deviates from these regulations.

36. The legislation project referred to in this excerpt is the Egyptian reform project of the *khul'* law. It abolished the requirement of the consent of the husband in this form of divorce. See the introduction to this section.

37. The imams are the four Sunni imams: Malik, al-Shafi'i, Abu Hanifah, and Ahmad Ibn Hanbal; see note 22.

38. The author lists Sa'id Ibn Jubayr, al-Hasan al-Basri, Ibn Sirin, and Ziad Ibn Ubayd al-Taqafi (Ziad Ibn Abih). The term *Tabi'in*, meaning "successors," refers to the second generation of the *hadith*'s narrators and jurists who were taught by the Companions of the Prophet.

39. Under Maliki school of thought *tamleek* is when the husband agrees in the marriage contract to give his wife the right to divorce him.

40. See, e.g., Qur'an 2:187 and 9:71.

41. Those rules include, among others: lowering one's gaze before the opposite sex, modesty in dress, and holding to chastity and family values (Q. 24:30–33).

42. An Arabic word that applies to any intimate part of the body that should be concealed, veiled, or lowered, in this case, from the sight or ears of strangers.

43. "O you who believe! Enter not houses other than your own, until you have asked permission and saluted those in them: that is best for you, in order that you may heed (what is seemly). If you find no one in the house, enter not until permission is given to you: if you are asked to go back, go back. That makes for greater purity for yourselves" (Q 24:27–28).

44. There is disagreement as to whether the obedience mentioned here is to God or to the husband. Some jurists circumvented the issue by arguing that obeying one's husband is part of obeying God.

45. Divorce Regulation Amendment Act Approved on March 11, 1992, by the Islamic Parliament and November 19, 1992, by the council for the determination of the suitability of orders, note 6, a.

46. See, e.g., Ibn Hazm, *Al-Muhalla bi al-Athar* (Beirut: Dar al-Kutub al-'Ilmiyyah, 1988), 9:227–228, and Ibn Qudamah, Muwaffaq al-Din (d. 1223), *Al-Mughni* (The Enricher) (Beirut: Dar al-Kitab al-'Arabi, n.d.), 8:130.

47. The word *garment* is used by the author in a metaphoric sense that refers to the gendered body.

48. The three references here are to Fatimah, the Prophet's daughter, Khadijah, the Prophet's first wife, and the Virgin Mary.

49. The author here is originally defending Queen 'Arwa of Yemen, who marked Yemeni history by her strong personality, her knowledge, and sense of justice.

50. An abbreviation meaning "Peace be upon him."

51. Abreviation for *radiya allah 'anha*: "May God be pleased with her."

52. "Decrees Defying Negligence in Chafchaouen and Its Surrounding Mountains."

53. A small town in Northern Morocco.

Chapter 4

HINDUISM

Paul B. Courtright

INTRODUCTION

In the nineteenth century, as the major European powers were extending their empires to various parts of the world, scholars developed categories for organizing the vast amount of new information about the practices and beliefs of the societies over which they were exercising increasing dominance. One of the key categories that emerged during this time was religion. The notion emerged that all human beings conducted their lives in one way or another in relation to higher or supernatural beings and powers. The work of religion, mainly through rituals and sacred stories, gave human beings definition and orientation. As scholars and travelers gained better knowledge of these "religions," the idea of "world" religions emerged. World religions were those that had complex literary traditions, classes of ritual specialists (priests and monks), and an overarching set of ideas and beliefs of how the world ultimately is put together and how humans should act while they are here. The model for such a construction of the concept of religion was, inevitably, Christianity as both the tradition of the dominant group and as the one most familiar to scholars. When we turn to Hinduism as one of the world religions, we see that it does not fit into the model of religion developed in European traditions. Indeed, the very term, Hinduism itself derived from foreigners, first Islamic, then European, who settled in India and attempted to make sense out of what people in India were doing in their ceremonies and shrines.

With this historical background in mind it is useful at the outset to identify some categories that may be instinctively associated with the word, religion, that in a Western context are noticeably absent in the Hindu tradition. Hinduism has no founding figure, such as Jesus, the Buddha, or Mohammed; no single ultimate deity (mono-theism) who rules over the universe. It has no single sacred textual tradition, such as the Bible or Qur'an. It has no comprehensive ecclesiastical organization, such as a church; no single ethical code or commandments.

The Hindu tradition has its own categories and practices, which reveal its foundational understanding of the world and humans' place in it. First, generally speaking, Hinduism does not see a firm boundary separating the human from the divine. Related to this porousness between human and divine is the importance of images and multiple visual representations of deities. Just as humans come in many sizes, genders, colors, and dispositions, so gods, goddesses, saints, and demons populate the Hindu universe. This robust polytheism with its multiple deities, many with multiple arms and faces, is one of the distinctive features of this tradition. If the Abrahamic religions are "religions of the Book," Hinduism may be said to be the "religion of the image." Given the Western tradition's instinctive suspicion of "idols," deriving from the biblical tradition, it is crucial in looking at Hinduism to appreciate that it comes from a very different tradition and relationship to visual images.

Constructing a history of Hinduism in general, or its views on sex, marriage, and family in particular, presents important challenges. While Hinduism is arguably the oldest continuing religion in the world, dating back to at least 1500 BCE, it has developed in many directions while maintaining a core identity. One scholar, Axel Michaels, *Hinduism: Past and Present* (Princeton: Princeton University Press, 2004), has organized the Hindu tradition into six epochs, each one adding a layer of literature:

1. Pre-Vedic, (to 1750 BCE), with inscriptions on seals not yet deciphered
2. Vedic, (1750–900 BCE), Vedas, ritual instructions
3. Ascetic Reformism, (500–200 BCE), Upanisads, *gṛhya* and *dharma sūtras*, Buddhist texts
4. Classical Hinduism (200 BCE–1100 CE), epics, collections of stories (*purāṇas*) treatises on poetry, dance, politics, *dharma*, court literatures, commentaries
5. Sectarian Hinduism, (1100–1850 CE), hagiographies, commentaries, digests, sectarian theologies
6. Modern Hinduism, (from 1850), reform movements, vernacular religious literatures, modern media, religious nationalism, diaspora traditions

In the light of these above-mentioned challenges and the extraordinarily long period of accumulation of religious tradition, it is useful to get a sense of some of the enduring orientations that we might call religious that distinguish Hinduism from other religious and nonreligious worldviews. Rather than look at Hinduism chronologically, it is more useful to think about it thematically.

Several enduring themes may be seen as constituting a "core" set of attitudes, practices, and values that give Hinduism its distinctive identity: 1. A *sense of connection* to and obligation to one's ancestors from whom one has descended, the deities who oversee and protect one's life, and descendents who follow after. This set of three connections serves to locate Hindus within a network that extends horizontally backward and forward in time and vertically between earth and the upper world of the deities and the lower world of the demons. 2. A basic *belief in or orientation toward* the general notion that one's embodied form and situation in the world is the result of actions performed in the past of one's present or previous life, one's *karma*—action—and that all the actions of all beings are woven together into a flowing web, called *samsāra*—that which moves along together. 3. A set of *ritual practices* that may include ascetically oriented mental-physical exercises, yoga, forms of devotion to one or several deities ranging from worship in the forms of images, fasting, prayer, devotional singing, pilgrimages to sacred places, and participating in festivals celebrating episodes in the stories of deities. 4. Veneration of particular texts, stories, or persons who embody the core values of the tradition. 5. A set of social relationships based on kinship, ritual purity, and occupation, *jāti* or caste, which locates persons in an ideal hierarchical arrangement with priests and scholars at the top and descending through political leadership groups, merchants and cultivators, and laborers at the bottom. 6. A view that one's life moves through a series of ideal life stages called *āśrama*s: childhood, studentship, householder, retiree, and ascetic. 7. Related to the life stages are a set of goals or orientations (*puruṣārtha*) toward life, each of which is appropriate in its own context: pleasure (*kāma*), achievement (*artha*), virtue (*dharma*), and release from worldly attachments (*mokṣa*). A general orientation toward asceticism and release from attachment to the ordinary world, *mokṣa*, is seen as a desirable goal even if not attainable in one's present lifetime.

These themes may be gathered up into a framework called *dharma*, a term that, among its many meanings, includes the notion of holding together. *Dharma* includes duties, practices, and attitudes appropriate to one's life circumstances. While there are many virtues that have general application, such as compassion, noninjury, truthfulness, and generosity, *dharma* is not a fixed set of rules or universal commandments but guidelines that give instruction and direction to one's life. Stage of life, social position, occupation, and gender shape what *dharma* is appropriate at a particular moment. For example, the *dharma* of a warrior is different than the *dharma* of an ascetic. The Hindu moral life is context specific: doing the right thing requires a clear wisdom of the situation in which it takes place.

At the most encompassing level the Hindu universe is one of perpetual change and renewal. Vast cycles of time provide the context for matter and consciousness to pass through many variant forms. At the human level each individual appears in the world in a body—bones, muscles, and social identity from the father; soft organs and blood from the mother, according to ancient medical texts—and a set of tendencies or dispositions that have been passed down from actions undertaken in previous forms *(karma)*. At the core of the human situation is the desire or attachment to sensations, objects, relationships, and life itself.

In part because of this vast time frame and the notion of multiple life forms that take place according to *karma,* there emerged from at least the second epoch a split vision between embracing the world of sex, marriage, and family or renouncing the world in favor of nonattachment or asceticism. This split is reflected in the formation of the Buddhist and Jain traditions as well. Classical Hindu texts attempt to reconcile these alternatives by placing renunciation as a sequel to the world of the household rather than as alternative to it. A complex relationship of interdependence arose between those who embraced the world and those who renounced it. The householder provides food and veneration to the ascetic and the ascetic provides a perspective on the world from its margins.

If life in the world of body and society is driven by desire and action as its inevitable condition, then which actions are most conducive to well-being in the immediate context and liberation later on? It is in response to this question that we might begin to look for Hindu notions about family, marriage, and sex. Actions that are most transformative and enduring are those directed away from selfish satisfactions. The enduring core model for these is the sacrifice (Sanskrit: *yajña*; Hindi: *yagya*), offerings into the sacred fire to the gods attended by perfected speech *(mantra)*. As the fire transforms and perfects the gifts of food and transmits them to the gods, the union of male and female in marriage transforms them and those around them. When it comes to question of sex, marriage, and the family in the Hindu context, it would be more appropriate to reverse the order. Family, its continuity and well-being, is the most encompassing framework, then marriage as the primary relationship that makes family possible, and, finally, sex as the embodied difference between human beings as male and female that finds physical pleasure, companionship, and duration in the context of family and society. As a religiously informed orientation to life's actions and obligations, *dharma* gives guidelines to how husbands, wives, children, and parents should conduct themselves. Many of the selections from sources included here advise their audiences on the roles proper for various situations and consider some of the complexities and ambiguities that arise in living according to their discipline.

From a very early period in the tradition marriage has been understood as the foundational transformative event, called a *saṃskāra*, literally, a perfection or completion. Through the ritual of marriage the separate persons of husband and wife become merged together, indissolubly. The wife becomes the "half-body" *(ardhanārīśvara)* of the husband. She is given by her father, through the intermediary of the priest, to her husband. She becomes part of his lineage, lives in his home, and, ideally, provides a son for his (and now her) lineage. In the context of India's agricultural traditions, the wife is often compared to the field and the husband to the seed, with sexual procreation analogous to the plow and the furrow. It is the seed, the male's contribution, that determines the offspring.

Deeply embedded in Hindu notions of marriage is a disposition toward protection. It is the husband's obligation to protect his wife from external predators and temptations and to invest in a relationship that will sustain her commitment to him and his world. At the same time, it is the obligation of the wife to protect her husband by feeding, caring for him, and investing in a relationship that will sustain his commitment. In the context of family lineages and social identity passed through males, the female's capacities and powers in shaping marriage are often more difficult for outsiders to see. Traditionally, the outer world of field, commerce, sacrifice, and battle has been the locale of men; the inner world of the home, food, children, and health has been the province of women.

Given these longitudinal concerns of family lineage, the process of marriage in the Hindu tradition has had an extraordinary continuity. Unlike marriage patterns in modern industrialized societies in which husbands and wives find each other in a marketplace of possibilities, most Hindus have followed highly systematic patterns of locating suitable marriage partners. While individual love and attraction are worthwhile, one of the goals of life, they are subordinate to the larger concerns of the family and lineage. Therefore, when children reach marriageable age, or even before in premodern India, the parents of the bride and groom have the obligation to arrange the marriage on behalf of the family, a family that includes ancestors long deceased and descendants yet unborn.

The chief criterion for such a selection is compatibility or coherence. That is, the husband and wife need to be from similar backgrounds so far as caste and community are concerned, but they need to be from sufficiently different lineages so as to avoid incest. The definition of how close is too close varies to some extent from north to south. In south India cross-cousin (for example, a son marries a mother's brother's daughter) is a preferred practice. In the north such unions have been considered too close.

The process of locating the optimal mate has generally been initiated by the bride's family. A daughter is often seen as a visitor in her natal family, for she will one day be offered as a "gift" to the husband's family, just as food is offered to the gods in sacrifice. A son, on the other hand, remains in his natal family, accepting the gift of the wife with the obligation to protect or guard her, enabling himself to prosper through progeny, and enabling her to care for him and their lineage together. This is the basic logic of the so-called arranged marriage tradition.

SELECTION OF TEXTS

The textual sources for appreciating family, marriage, and sex in Hinduism may be found in many places, and any selection will be arbitrary to some extent. At the core of Hinduism as a religion is ritual. It is through the complex sequences of ceremonial life that the Hindu tradition has most densely and enduringly articulated its understandings of marriage. Hence the sources to which we turn are centered around the wedding ritual as the context for human transformation or completion (saṃskāra).

DOCUMENT 4–1: *RIG VEDA* 10.85

Beginning with a hymn from the ancient Vedas, from the second epoch and earliest textual tradition, a collection of ritual chants much venerated by many Hindus, we see that human marriage is patterned after divine marriage. The daughter of the sun god, Sūrya, and the moon, Soma, form the divine model, just as the sun and moon interact in the world to bring day and night. Hence society and cosmology are linked through ceremony. This Vedic marriage hymn has been recited, in full or in part, in wedding ceremonies for centuries, down to the present day.

DOCUMENT 4–2: AŚVALĀYANA GṚHYA SŪTRA

Moving forward chronologically, the next selection is drawn from ritual manuals used by priests in conducting marriage ceremonies, the *gṛhya sūtras*, and gives a general idea of the process of transformation that takes place in marriage.

DOCUMENTS 4–3 AND 4–4: *MANU* AND THE *KĀMASŪTRA*

The next two selections shift the focus from ritual to general advice on how husbands and wives should conduct themselves in relation to one another and to the larger family and social systems in which they live. The *Laws of Manu* and the *Kāmasūtra*, both from the fourth epic of classical Hinduism, provide two windows into how Hindus who lived according to the traditions taught by the Brahmin elite were advised to conduct themselves. *Manu* takes a more conservative position with respect to marital behaviors.

DOCUMENTS 4–5 AND 4–6: NARRATIVE TRADITIONS OF THE *PURĀṆAS*

From the genre of the teacher's advice the next two selections focus on stories having to do with marriage, both also from the classical period. As mentioned earlier, human marriage is modeled after divine marriage. The story of the marriage of Śiva and Pārvatī both resembles and differs from human practices. Śiva is, after all, the paradigmatic ascetic who remains outside the realm of family. Yet, in this story, he enters the matrimonial world with full enthusiasm. The second story presents a complex telling of the foolishness of kings and wisdom of Brahmins with respect to marriage. The story also provides a framework for teachings that connect with some of the themes addressed in *Manu* as well.

DOCUMENT 4–7: A CONTEMPORARY MARRIAGE CEREMONY

The next selection comes from a text, written by a Hindu living in the United States, designed for English-reading Hindus in middle-class India and abroad. Drawing upon widely followed practices among high-caste Hindus, the author provides extensive instructions on how the wedding arrangements should be conducted, how participants should comport themselves, and what sacred texts are to be recited by the priest and the bride and groom. This contemporary text draws extensively upon traditions that go back very far in Hindu history, including the marriage hymn, or part of it, that began the selections.

DOCUMENT 4–8: "COUNTING THE FLOWERS," A SHORT STORY BY CHUDAMANI RAGHAVAN, TRANSLATED FROM THE TAMIL BY THE AUTHOR

The last selection takes us in a different direction, through the medium of fiction by a contemporary woman writer, into the life world of a young woman in contemporary south India who is witnessing her parents negotiate a marriage on her behalf. The author takes us inside the thoughts and feelings of the bride to be and emphasizes the darker side of arranged marriage in the contemporary context, a context brought under serious critique by Hindu feminists. This story gives an important glimpse of marriage negotiations and the ways in which financial and status issues complicate this most important of human relationships.

For many centuries, as far back as textual sources take us, marriage has been a central concern in the Hindu tradition. It is the cornerstone of society, the link between the past and the future, the source of well-being and children, and the pivot of social life. It is not surprising, therefore, that even in the context of contemporary global pressures that bring dramatic changes in ways of life for Hindus, both in India and abroad, it is marriage that continues to be the most sustaining center of gravity for Hindu life.

RIG VEDA 10.85: THE MARRIAGE HYMN

This ancient hymn (ca. 1200 BCE) is one of the most enduring of all Hindu texts. It contains a story of the divine marriage of Sūryā and Soma as the model for human marriage, a set of instructions for the priest performing the wedding ceremony, the procession from the place of the ceremony to the husband's house, and the sexual consummation of the bridal couple. Verses 1–20 invoke the story of the marriage of Sūryā, daughter of the sun god, Sūrya, and Soma, the moon. The meters of the chants and the chariot bringing the bride to the place of the wedding are linked to parts of the cosmos. The Aśvin twins came there as suitors for the bride but are sent away. The Vedic tradition associated the bride and groom at the human level with the relationship between the sun and moon at the cosmological level. The remainder of the hymn addresses the human couple, invoking divine protection, happiness, and progeny. Verses 28–30, 34–35 refers to the blood of defloration that stains the bridal gown. The blood is auspicious, in that it displays the sacrifice of the bride's virginity to enable the marriage to prosper; at the same time, it is dangerous. Thus, the hymn directs the priest to cut the gown to pieces, a gesture similar to sacrifice itself. Hence marriage is understood to be a transformation or perfection *(sam-skāra)*. This hymn has been recited at Hindu weddings for centuries. Seven verses of this hymn are incorporated in the wedding ceremony as prescribed in the tradition in contemporary India and among many Hindus living abroad.

Document 4–1

RIG VEDA, THE MARRIAGE HYMN

1. The earth is propped up by truth; the sky is propped up by the sun. Through the Law the ādityas stand firm and Soma is placed in the sky.

2. Through Soma the ādityas are mighty; through Soma the earth is great. And in the lap of these constellations Soma has been set.

3. One thinks he has drunk Soma when they press the plant. But the Soma that the Brahmins know—no one ever eats that.

4. Hidden by those charged with veiling you, protected by those who live on high, O Soma, you stand listening to the pressing-stones. No earthling eats you.

5. When they drink you who are a god, then you are filled up again. Vāyu is the guardian of Soma; the moon is the one that shapes the years.

6. The Raibhi metre was the woman who gave her away; the Nārāśāmāī metre was the girl who accompanied her. The fine dress of Sūryā was adorned by the songs.

7. Intelligence was the pillow; sight was the balm. Heaven and Earth were the hope-chest when Sūryā went to her husband.

8. The hymns of praise were the shafts [of the chariot bringing the bride to the groom] and metre was the diadem and coiffure. The Aśvins [divine twins] were the suitors of Sūryā, and Agni was the one who went in front [of the procession].

9. Soma became the bridegroom and the two Aśvins were the suitors, as Savitṛ [Sūrya, father of the bride] gave Sūryā to her husband and she said "Yes" in her heart.

10. Thought was her chariot and the sky was its canopy. The two luminaries [sun and moon of the two months of the marriage season] were the two carriage animals when Sūryā went to the house.

11. Your two cattle, yoked with the verse and the chant, went with the same accord. You had hearing for your two wheels. In the sky the path stretched on and on.

12. The two luminaries were your wheels as you journeyed; the outward breath was made into the axle. Sūryā mounted a chariot made of thought as she went to her husband.

13. The wedding procession of Sūryā went forward as Savitṛ [Sūrya, her father] sent it off. When the sun is in Aghā [the two constellations of the months of the wedding season] they kill the cattle [for the wedding feast], and when it is in Arjunā she is brought home.

14. When you Asvins came to the wedding in your three wheeled chariot, asking for Sūryā for yourselves, all the gods gave you their consent, and Pūṣan, the son, chose you as his two fathers.

15. When you two husbands of beauty came as suitors for Sūryā, where was your single wheel? Where did you two stand to point the way [to the groom's house]?

16. Your two wheels, Sūryā, the Brahmins know in their measured rounds. But the one wheel that is hidden, only the inspired know that.

17. To Sūryā, to the gods, to Mitra and Varuṇa, who are provident for all creation, to them I have bowed down.

18. These two [sun and moon] change places through their power of illusion, now forward, now backward. Like two children at play they circle the sacrificial ground. The one gazes upon all creatures, and the other is born again and again marking the order of the seasons.

19. He [the moon] becomes new and again new as he is born, going in front of the dawns as the banner of the days. As he arrives he apportions to the gods their share. The moon stretches out the long span of life.

20. Mount the world of immortality, O Sūryā, that is adorned with red flowers and made of fragrant wood, carved with many forms and painted with gold, rolling smoothly on its fine wheels. Prepare an exquisite wedding voyage for your husband.

21. "Go away from here! For this woman has a husband." Thus I implore Viśvāsas [the heavenly being, *gandharva*, who distracts brides from their intended husbands] with words of praise as I bow to him. "Look for another girl who is ripe and still lives in her father's house. That is your birthright; find it."

22. "Go away from here, Viśvāsu, we implore you as we bow. Look for another girl, willing and ready. Leave the wife to unite with her husband."

23. May the roads be straight and thornless on which our friends [the rejected suitors] go courting. May Aryaman and Bhaga united lead us together. O Gods, may the united household be easy to manage.

24. I free you from Varuṇa's snare, with which the gentle Savitṛ bound you. In the seat of Law, in the world of good action, I place you unharmed with your husband.

25. I free her from here [her father's house], but not from there [her husband's house]. I have bound her firmly there, so that through the grace of Indra she will have fine sons and be fortunate in her husband's love.

26. Let Pūṣan lead you from here, taking you by the hand; let the Aśvins carry you in their chariot. Go home to be mistress of the house with the right to speak commands to the gathered people [in the village assembly or in her new home].

27. May happiness be fated for you here [the groom's house] through your progeny. Watch over this house as mistress of the house. Mingle your body with that of your husband, and even when you are grey with age you will have the right to speak to the gathered people.

28. The purple and red appears [in the defloration of the bride's first intercourse], a magic spirit; the stain is imprinted. Her family prospers, and her husband is bound in the bonds [of marriage].

29. Throw away the gown, and distribute wealth to the priests. It becomes a magic spirit walking on feet, and like the wife it draws near the husband.

30. The [husband's] body becomes ugly and sinisterly pale if the husband with evil desire covers his sexual limb with his wife's robe.

31. The diseases that come from her own people and follow after the glorious bridal procession, may the gods who receive sacrifices lead them back whence they have come.

32. Let no highwaymen, lying in ambush, fall upon the wedding couple. Let the two of them on good paths avoid the dangerous path. Let all demonic powers run away.

33. This bride has auspicious signs; come and look at her. Wish her the good fortune of her husband's love, and depart, each to your own house.

34. It [the bridal robe] burns, it bites, and it has claws, as dangerous as poison is to eat. Only the priest who knows the Sūryā hymn is able to receive the bridal gown.

35. Cutting, carving, and chopping into pieces—see the colours of Sūryā, which the priest alone purifies.

36. I take your hand for good fortune, so that with me as your husband you will attain a ripe old age. Bhaga, Aryaman, Savitṛ, Purandhi [protector of marriage]—the gods have given you to me to be mistress of the house.

37. Pūṣan [protector of journeys] rouse her to be most eager to please, the woman in whom men sow their seed, so that she will spread her thighs in her desire for us and we, in our desire, will plant our penis in her.

38. To you [the gods] first of all they led Sūryā, circling with the bridal procession. Give her back to her husband, Agni, now as a wife with progeny.

39. Agni has given the wife back again, together with long life and beauty.

Let her have a long life-span, and let her husband live for a hundred autumns.

40. Soma first possessed her, and the Gandharva possessed her second. Agni was your third husband, and the fourth was the son of a man.

41. Soma gave her to the Gandharva, and the Gandharva gave her to Agni. Agni gave me wealth and sons—and her.

42. Stay here and do not separate. Enjoy your whole life-span playing with sons and grandsons and rejoicing in your own home.

43. Let Prajāpati create progeny for us; let Aryaman anoint us into old age. Free from evil signs, enter the world of your husband. Be good luck for our two-legged creatures and good luck for our four-legged creatures.

44. Have no evil eye; do not be a husband-killer. Be friendly to animals, good-tempered and glowing with beauty. Bringing forth strong sons, prosper as one beloved of the gods and eager to please. Be good luck for our two-legged creatures and good luck for our four-legged creatures.

45. Generous Indra, give this woman fine sons and the good fortune of her husband's love. Place ten sons in her and make her husband the eleventh.

46. Be an empress over your husband's father, an empress over your husband's mother; be an empress over your husband's sister and an empress over your husband's brothers.

47. Let all the gods and the waters together anoint our two hearts together. Let [the goddess] Mātariśvan together with the Creator and together with her who shows the way join the two of us together.

[Rig Veda: 10.85, The Marriage Hymn, in *The Rig Veda*, trans. Wendy Doniger (London: Penguin, 1981)]

THE *GṚHYA-SUTRAS*: THE WEDDING CEREMONY

The *Gṛhyasūtras*, Verses Regarding the Household (ca. 500–200 BCE) are a collection of texts from the late Vedic period used by lineages of priests for instructions about various rituals and practices appropriate to life in the household. They were in contrast to the *Śrautasūtras*, Verses for Public Ceremonies, which gave instruction for performing the major sacrifices of the religious year and for special occasions such as installation of kings. Within the collection of instructions on household or domestic rituals, there are chapters dealing with marriage. These abbreviated instructions guided priests in performing their duties in reciting mantras, making offerings, conferring blessings, and offering general instructions for how the families of the bride and groom should conduct themselves, according to their social positions. It also delineates eight types of marriage and which ones are appropriate to which classes. There are some variations in the wedding ritual in the various *gṛhyasūtras* texts, reflecting differences between lineages of priests and their communities. The selection is from the *Aśvalāyana Gṛhyasūtra* (chap. I.5–9).

Document 4–2

AŚVALĀYANA GṚHYASŪTRA, THE WEDDING CEREMONY

I.5.1. He [the priest] should examine the family first, as stated previously: "Those who are from the mother's and the father's side."

2. The father should give the girl to an intelligent young man.

3. He (the bridegroom) should marry a girl of intelligence, beauty, moral conduct and one who is free from disease.

4. It is difficult to discern the character of the intended bridegroom,

5. He should prepare eight lumps of earth and murmur over the lumps the following verse: "In the beginning the right was established; on the right is founded truth. For what this girl is born, may she attain that here. What is true may be revealed here." Then he should speak to the girl to take one of the lumps.

6. If the girl selects the lump of earth from the field that produces two crops in a year, he may know that her children will prosper in food. If she chooses the lump of earth from a cow-stable, her offspring will be rich in cattle. If she chooses the lump of earth from an altar she will be prosperous in holy attainments. If she chooses the lump of earth from a pool that never dries up, she will be rich in everything. If she chooses the lump of earth from a gambling place, she will be addicted to gambling. If she chooses the lump of earth from a place where four roads meet, she will not be faithful to her husband. If she chooses the lump of earth from a barren land, she will be poor. If she chooses the lump of earth from a burial place, she will cause death of her husband.

I.6.1. The father may give away his daughter (to the bridegroom) with a libation of water, after adorning her with ornaments. Such a marriage is called *Brahmā*. A son born of this marriage purifies twelve descendants and twelve ancestors on both sides. The father may give away his daughter to a priest, having adorned her with ornaments, while a sacrifice with the three *śrauta* fires is going on. This marriage is called *Daiva*. The son born of this marriage purifies seven descendants and seven ancestors on both sides. If the bride and bridegroom observe the nuptial rites together, the marriage is called *Prajāpatya*. The son born of this marriage purifies eight descendants and eight ancestors on both sides.

If the father of the girl receives a bull and a cow from the bride-groom, for giving away the girl, the marriage is called *Ārṣa*. A son born of this marriage purifies seven descendants and seven ancestors on both sides.

If the bridegroom marries her after entering into mutual contract it is called *Gāndharva* marriage. If the bridegroom marries her after satisfying her father with money this sort of marriage is called *Āsura*.

If he carries off the girl while her kinsmen are asleep or inattentive, the marriage is called *Paiścāca*. If he carries off the girl after killing her relatives, cutting their heads, while she weeps and they weep, the sort of marriage is called *Rākṣasa*.

I.7.1. Now, indeed, different are the customs of different countries and villages. He should observe those at the wedding.

2. What, however, is common to all the countries and villages we shall state.

3. He should place to the west of fire a stone and a water-vessel to the north-east. He should sacrifice while the bride takes hold of him. He should stand with his face turned to the west, while she sits with her face turned to the east. With the formula, "I take hold of thy hand for the sake of pleasure," he should grasp her thumb if he longs that only male issues be born to him.

4. If he desires only female issues he should catch hold of her fingers alone.

5. If he desires both male and female issues, he should seize her hand on the hair-side, together with the thumb.

6. He should lead her thrice round the nuptial fire and the water-jar so that their right sides are turned to the fire. He should murmur: "This am I, that art thou. That art thou, this am I; the heaven I, the earth thou; the Sāman [song] I, the Ṛk [chant] thou. We shall marry here; we shall produce children. Loving, bright, and kind-hearted, may we live a hundred years."

7. Each time after he has taken the bride round the fire, he makes her ascend the stone reciting the formula: "Ascend on this stone; be firm like a stone, suppress the enemies, tread the enemies down."

8. The bridegroom should pour butter over the hands of the bride while either her brother or a substitute for her brother should pour fried grain twice over the joined hands of the bride.

9. Thrice, as it is customary among the descendants of Jamadagni.

10. He should pour butter again over the sacrificial food.

11. And over what has been cut off.

12. This is the rule about the portions to be cut off.

13. "For god Aryaman the girls have offered oblations to Agni. May he, god Aryaman, release her from this and not from that place, Svāhā.

For god Varuṇa the girls have offered oblations to Agni. May he, god Varuṇa, release her from this and not from that place, Svāhā.

For god Pūṣan the girls have offered oblations to Agni. May he, god Pūṣan, release her from this and not from that place, Svāhā!"

With these verses she should offer the fried grain without opening her joined hands as if she did so with the spoon—śruk.

14. Without taking her round the fire, she offers grain from the neb [tip] of a basket towards herself, silently a fourth time.

15. Some take the bride round the fire each time after the fried grain has been poured out. Thus, the two last oblations do not immediately succeed each other.

16. He then unties two locks of her hair if they are made.

17. If the two tufts of wool are tied round her hair on the two sides, he should release the right tuff first with the following: "I release thee from the noose of Varuna."

18. Next he should release the left tuft with the following: ["I release thee from the noose of Varuna."]

19. He then makes her walk seven steps in the north-eastern direction with the following formula: "For food with one step, for juice with two steps, for the increase of wealth with three steps, for comfort and welfare with four steps, for offspring with five steps, for the seasons with six steps. Be friend with seven steps. Be thou devoted to me. May we acquire many sons who may reach old age."

20. The priest then joins their heads together and sprinkles them with water from the water-jar.

21. The bride should live that night in the house of an aged Brāhmana woman whose husband is alive and whose children are alive.

22. When she sees the polar star, the star Arundhatī and the seven sages (ursha major) she should break silence and say: "May my husband live long and may I get children."

I.8.1. When the newly-wedded couple set out on journey, let the bridegroom help her ascend the chariot with the verse, "May Pūṣan take thee from here grasping thy hand."

2. With the hemistich, "carrying stones, the river flows, hold fast together" he should make her ascend a ship.

3. With the following hemistich [half-line] let him make her descend from it.

4. If she weeps, he should speak the verse, "the living one they lament."

5. They carry the wedding fire in front always.

6. At auspicious places, trees and cross-ways he should murmur: "May no robbers meet us."

7. At each and every abode on the way he should look at the seers and murmur the following verse: "Good fortune brings this woman."

8. He should make her enter the house with the verse: "Here may thy pleasure increase along with offspring."

9. He should set up the nuptial fire (at his dwelling place) and then spread, to the west of it, a hide of the bull with its neck to the east, with the hair outside. He should then offer oblations to the fire while she sits on that hide and takes hold of him. He should murmur the following four verses: "May Prajapati create offering to us" and after each verse offer oblations. And with the verse "May all the gods unite" he partakes of curds and gives a portion thereof to her, or he besmears his as well as her heart with the rest of the *Ājya*.

10. From that time onward, they should not eat saline food, they should observe chastity, decorate their person and sleep on the ground.

11. They should observe this rule for three nights or twelve nights after the performance of sacrifice on entering the house.

12. Or for one year, according to some teachers. Thus a sage will be born to them.

13. When he has fulfilled this vow, he should give the bridal dress to the Bāhmana who knows the Sūryā hymn [*Rig Veda* 10.85 above].

14. He should give food to the Brāhmanas.

15. He should cause the Brāhmanas to recite *svastyayana* hymn.

I.9.1. Beginning from the wedding he should worship the domestic fire himself, or his wife or also his son or his daughter or his pupil.

2. The fire should be kept without break.

3. If it goes out, the wife should fast. Thus say some teachers.

4. The rules in regard to this are the same as in the Agni-hotra.

5. The time for blazing the fire and for sacrificing in it has already been explained.

6. The sacrificial food should not contain meat.

7. If he likes he may perform the sacrifice with rice, barley, and sesamum.

8. He should sacrifice in the evening with the formula "To Agni, Svāhā"; in the morning with the formula "To Sūrya, Svāhā." He should offer the second oblation both times.

[Aśvalāyana Gṛhyasūtra I.5–9, The Wedding Ceremony, in *Asvalayana Grhyasutram*, trans. Narendra Nath Sharma (Delhi: Eastern Book Linkers, 1976), pp. 148–153]

LAWS OF MANU

The *Laws of Manu* (ca. 100 BCE–200 CE) has been a preeminent authority on *dharma* from as early as the third century CE. The text is presented as the teachings received by Manu from the Creator on what actions are appropriate under a vast number of circumstances, with particular instructions for persons of various classes, stages of life, family relations, occupations, and genders in both normal and extraordinary situations. Manu's treatise is not a set of commandments, but rather a description of various actions and their consequences. It reflects the perspective of the Brahmin class and attends primarily to the actions appropriate to twice-born Hindus. Manu takes up the subject of marriage at considerable length, addressing the duties of husbands and wives, how marriage arrangements should be conducted, and the benefits and distresses marriage brings when its obligations are followed or neglected.

Document 4–3

LAWS OF MANU, ON THE DUTIES OF HUSBANDS AND WIVES

[3.1] The vow for studying the three Vedas with a guru is for thirty-six years, or half of that, or a quarter of that, or whenever the undertaking comes to an end. [2] When, unswerving in his chastity, he has learned the Vedas, or two Vedas, or even one Veda, in the proper order, he should enter the householder stage of life. [3] When he is recognized as one who has, by fulfilling his own duties, received the legacy of the Veda from his father, he should first be seated on a couch, adorned with garlands, and honoured with (an offering made from the milk of) a cow.

[4] When he has received his guru's permission and bathed and performed the ritual for homecoming according to the rules, a twice-born man should marry a wife who is of the same class and has the right marks [physical characteristics]. [5] A woman who is neither a co-feeding relative on her mother's side nor belongs to the same lineage (of the sages) on her father's side, and who is a virgin, is recommended for marriage to twice-born men. [6] When a man connects himself with a woman, he should avoid the ten following families, even if they are great, or rich in cows, goats, sheep, property, or grain: [7] a family that has abandoned the rites, or does not have male children, or does not chant the Veda; and those families in which they have hairy bodies, piles, consumption, weak digestion, epilepsy, white leprosy, or black leprosy.

[8] A man should not marry a girl who is a redhead or has an extra limb or is sickly or has no body hair or too much body hair or talks too much or is sallow; [9] or who is named after a constellation, a tree, or a river, or who has a low-caste name, or is named after a mountain, a bird, a snake, or has a menial or frightening name. [10] He should marry a woman who does not lack any part of her body and who has a pleasant name, who walks like a goose or an elephant [that is, gracefully], whose body hair and hair on the head is fine, whose teeth are not big, and who has delicate limbs. [11] A wise man will not marry a woman who has no brother or whose father is unknown, for fear that she may be an appointed daughter or that he may act wrongly.

[12] A woman of the same class is recommended to twice-born men for the first marriage; but for men who are driven by desire, these are the women, in progressively descending order: [13] According to tradition, only a servant woman can be the wife of a servant; she and one of his own class can be the wife of a commoner; these two and one of his own class for a king; and these three and one of his own class for a priest. [14] Not a single story mentions a servant woman as the wife of a priest or a ruler, even in extremity. [15] Twice-born men who are so infatuated as to marry women of low caste quickly reduce their families, including the descendants, to the status of servants. [16] A man falls when he weds a servant woman, according to Atri and to (Gautama) the son of Utathya, or when he has a son by her, according to Śaunaka, or when he has any children by her, according to Bhṛgu [other authorities on *dharma*]. [17] A priest who climbs into bed with a servant woman goes to hell; if he begets a son in her, he loses the status of priest. [18] The ancestors and the gods do not eat the offerings to the gods, to the ancestors, and to guests that such a man makes with her, and so he does not go to heaven. [19] No redemption is prescribed for a man who drinks the saliva from the lips of a servant woman or is tainted by her breath or begets a son in her. . . .

[45] A man should have sex with his wife during her fertile season, and always find his satisfaction in his own wife; when he desires sexual pleasure he should

go to her to whom he is vowed, except on the days at the (lunar) junctures [when abstinence is required]. [46] The natural fertile season of women is traditionally said to last for sixteen nights, though these include four special days [of the menstrual period] that good people despise. [47] Among these (nights), the first four, the eleventh, and the thirteenth are disapproved; the other ten nights are approved. [48] On the even nights, sons are conceived, and on the uneven nights, daughters; therefore a man who wants sons should unite with his wife during her fertile season on the even nights. [49] A male child is born when the semen of the man is greater (than that of the woman), and a female child when (the semen) of the woman is greater (than that of the man); if both are equal, a hermaphrodite is born, or a boy and a girl; and if (the semen) is weak or scanty, the opposite will occur. [50] A man who avoids women on the (six) disapproved nights and on eight other nights is regarded as chaste, no matter which of the four stages of life he is in.

[51] No learned father should take a bride-price for his daughter, no matter how small, for a man who, out of greed, exacts a bride-price would be selling his child like a pimp. [52] And those deluded relatives who live off a woman's property—her carriages, her clothes, and so on—are evil and go to hell. [53] Some say that the cow and bull (given) during the (wedding) of the sages is a bride-price, but it is not so. No matter how great or small (the price), the sale amounts to prostitution. [54] Girls whose relatives do not take the bride-price for themselves are not prostituted; that (gift) is merely honorific and a mercy to maidens.

[55] Fathers, brothers, husbands, and brothers-in-law who wish for great good fortune should revere these women and adorn them. [56] The deities delight in places where women are revered, but where women are not revered all rites are fruitless. [57] Where the women of the family are miserable, the family is soon destroyed, but it always thrives where the women are not miserable. [58] Homes that are cursed by women of the family who have not been treated with due reverence are completely destroyed, as if struck down by witchcraft. [59] Therefore men who wish to prosper should always revere these women with ornaments, clothes, and food at celebrations and festivals.

[60] There is unwavering good fortune in a family where the husband is always satisfied by the wife, and the wife by the husband. [61] If the wife is not radiant she does not stimulate the man; and because the man is unstimulated the making of children does not happen. [62] If the woman is radiant, the whole family is radiant, but if she is not radiant the whole family is not radiant. [63] Through bad marriages, the neglect of rites, failure to study the Veda, and transgressing against priests, families cease to be families. . . .

[5.147] A girl, a young woman, or even an old woman should not do anything independently, even in (her own) house. [148] In childhood a woman should be under her father's control, in youth under her husband's, and when her husband is dead, under her sons'. She should not have independence. [149] A woman should not try to separate herself from her father, her husband, or her sons, for her separation from them would make both (her own and her husband's) families contemptible. [150] She should always be cheerful, and clever at household affairs; she should keep her utensils well polished and not have too free a hand in spending. [151] When her father, or her brother with her father's permission, gives her to someone, she should obey that man while he is alive and not violate her vow to him when he is dead.

[152] Benedictory verses are recited and a sacrifice to the Lord of Creatures is performed at weddings to make them auspicious, but it is the act of giving away (the bride) that makes (the groom) her master. [153] A husband who performs the transformative ritual (of marriage) with Vedic verses always makes his woman happy, both when she is in her fertile season and when she is not, both here on earth and in the world beyond. [154] A virtuous wife should constantly serve her husband like a god, even if he behaves badly, freely indulges his lust, and is devoid of any good qualities.

[155] Apart (from their husbands), women cannot sacrifice or undertake a vow or fast; it is because a wife obeys her husband that she is exalted in heaven. [156] A virtuous wife should never do anything displeasing to the husband who took her hand in marriage, when he is alive or dead, if she longs for her husband's world (after death). [157] When her husband is dead she may fast as much as she likes, (living) on auspicious flowers, roots, and fruits, but she should not even mention the name of another man. [158] She should be long-suffering until death, self-restrained, and chaste, striving (to fulfill) the unsurpassed duty of women who have one husband. [159] Many thousands of priests who were chaste from their youth have gone to heaven without begetting offspring to continue the family.

[160] A virtuous wife who remains chaste when her husband has died goes to heaven just like those chaste men, even if she has no sons. [161] But a woman who violates her (vow to her dead) husband because she is greedy for progeny is the object of reproach here on earth and loses the world beyond. [162] No (legal) progeny are begotten here by another man or in another man's wife; nor is a second husband ever prescribed for virtuous women. [163] A woman who abandons her own inferior husband and lives with a superior man becomes an object of reproach in this world; she is said to be "previously had by another man." [164] A woman who is unfaithful to her husband is an object of reproach in this world; (then) she is reborn in the womb of a jackal and is tormented by the diseases born of her evil.

[165] The woman who is not unfaithful to her husband and who restrains her mind, speech, and body reaches her husband's worlds (after death), and good people call her a virtuous woman. [166] The woman who restrains her mind-and-heart, speech, and body through this behaviour wins the foremost renown here on earth and her husband's world in the hereafter. [167] A twice-born man who knows the law should burn a wife of the same class who behaves

in this way and dies before him, using the (fire of the) daily fire sacrifice and the sacrificial vessels. [168] When he has given the (sacrificial) fires in the final ritual to the wife who has died before him, he may marry again and kindle the fires again. [169] He must never neglect the five (great) sacrifices, but should take a wife and live in his house, in accordance with this rule, for the second part of his life. . . .

[9.1] I will tell the eternal duties of a man and wife who stay on the path of duty both in union and in separation. [2] Men must make their women dependent day and night, and keep under their own control those who are attached to sensory objects. [3] Her father guards her in childhood, her husband guards her in youth, and her sons guard her in old age. A woman is not fit for independence. [4] A father who does not give her away at the proper time should be blamed, and a husband who does not have sex with her at the proper time should be blamed; and the son who does not guard his mother when her husband is dead should be blamed.

[5] Women should especially be guarded against addictions, even trifling ones, for unguarded (women) would bring sorrow upon both families. [6] Regarding this as the supreme duty of all the classes, husbands, even weak ones, try to guard their wives. [7] For by zealously guarding his wife he guards his own descendants, practices, family, and himself, as well as his own duty. [8] The husband enters the wife, becomes an embryo, and is born here on earth. That is why a wife is called a wife (jāyā), because he is born (jāyate) again in her. [9] The wife brings forth a son who is just like the man she makes love with; that is why he should guard his wife zealously, in order to keep his progeny clean.

[10] No man is able to guard women entirely by force, but they can be entirely guarded by using these means: [11] he should keep her busy amassing and spending money, engaging in purification, attending to her duty, cooking food, and looking after the furniture. [12] Women are not guarded when they are confined in a house by men who can be trusted to do their jobs well; but women who guard themselves by themselves are well guarded. [13] Drinking, associating with bad people, being separated from their husbands, wandering about, sleeping, and living in other people's houses are the six things that corrupt women. [14] Good looks do not matter to them, nor do they care about youth.

[15] By running after men like whores, by their fickle minds, and by their natural lack of affection, these women are unfaithful to their husbands even when they are zealously guarded here. [16] Knowing that their very own nature is like this, as it was born at the creation by the Lord of Creatures, a man should make the utmost effort to guard them. [17] The bed and the seat, jewelry, lust, anger, crookedness, a malicious nature, and bad conduct are what Manu assigned to women. [18] There is no ritual with Vedic verses for women; this is a firmly established point of law. For women, who have no virile strength and no

Vedic verses, are falsehood; this is well established. [19] There are many revealed canonical texts to this effect that are sung even in treatises on the meaning of the Vedas, so that women's distinctive traits may be carefully inspected. Now listen to the redemptions for their (errors).

[20] "If my mother has given in to her desire, going astray and violating her vow to her husband, let my father keep that semen away from me." This is a canonical example. [21] If in her mind she thinks of anything that the man that married her would not wish, this is said as a complete reparation for that infidelity. [22] When a woman is joined with a husband in accordance with the rules, she takes on the very same qualities that he has, just like a river flowing down into the ocean. [23] When Aṣamālā, who was born of the lowest womb, united with Vasiṣṭha, and Sārangī, the bird-woman, with Mandapāla, they became worthy of honour. [24] These and other women of vile birth in this world were pulled up through the particular auspicious qualities of their own husbands.

[25] The ordinary life of a husband and wife, which is always auspicious, has thus been described. Now learn the duties regarding progeny, which lead to future happiness, both here on earth and after death. [26] There is no difference at all between the goddesses of good fortune (*śriyas*) who live in houses and women (*striyas*) who are the lamps of their houses, worthy of reverence and greatly blessed because of their progeny). [27] The wife is the visible form of what holds together the begetting of children, the caring for them when they are born, and the ordinary business of every day. [28] Children, the fulfillment of duties, obedience, and the ultimate sexual pleasure depend upon a wife, and so does heaven, for oneself and one's ancestors. [29] The woman who is not unfaithful to her husband but restrains her mind-and-heart, speech, and body reaches her husband's worlds (after death), and good people call her a virtuous woman.

[30] But a woman who is unfaithful to her husband is an object of reproach in this world; (then) she is reborn in the womb of a jackal and is tormented by the diseases (born) of (her) evil. [31] The following discussion about a son was held by good men and great sages born long ago; listen to it, for it has merit and applies to all people.

[32] They say that a son belongs to the husband, but the revealed canon is divided in two about who the "husband" is: some say that he is the begetter, others that he is the one who owns the field. [33] The woman is traditionally said to be the field, and the man is traditionally said to be the seed; all creatures with bodies reborn from the union of the field and the seed. [34] Sometimes the seed prevails, and sometimes the woman's womb; but the offspring are regarded as best when both are equal.

[35] Of the seed and the womb, the seed is said to be more important, for the offspring of all living beings are marked by the mark of the seed. [36] Whatever sort of seed is sown in a field prepared at the right season, precisely

that sort of seed grows in it, manifesting its own particular qualities. [37] For this earth is said to be the eternal womb of creatures, but the seed develops none of the qualities of the womb in the things it grows. [38] For here on earth when farmers at the right season sow seeds of various forms in the earth, even in one single field, they grow up each according to its own nature. [39] Rice, red rice, mung beans, sesame, pulse beans, and barley grow up according to their seed, and so do leeks and sugar-cane.

[40] It never happens that one seed is sown and another grown; for whatever seed is sown, that is precisely the one that grows . [41] A well-educated man who understands this and who has knowledge and understanding will never sow in another man's wife, if he wants to live a long life. [42] People who know the past recite some songs about this sung by the wind god, which say that a man must not sow his seed on another man's property. [43] Just as an arrow is wasted if it is shot into the wound of an animal already wounded by another shot, even so seed is immediately wasted on another man's property. [44] Those who know the past know that the earth (pṛthivī) is still the wife of Pṛthu; they say that a field belongs to the man who clears it of timber, and the deer to the man who owns the arrow.

[45] "A man is only as much as his wife, himself, and his progeny," the priests say, and also this: "The wife is traditionally said to be what the husband is." [46] A wife is not freed from her husband by sale or rejection; we recognize this as the law formulated by the Lord of Creatures long ago. [47] The division (of inheritance) is made once, and the daughter is given (in marriage) once, and a man says "I will give" once; good people do these three things once. [48] Just as the stud is not the one who owns the progeny born in cows, mares, female camels, and slave girls, in buffalo-cows, she-goats, and ewes, so it is too (with progeny born) in other men's wives. [49] People who have no field but have seed and sow it in other men's fields are never the ones who get the fruit of the crop that appears.

[50] If (one man's) bull were to beget a hundred calves in other men's cows, those calves would belong to the owners of the cows, and the bull's seed would be shed in vain. [51] In the very same way, men who have no field but sow their seed in other men's fields are acting for the benefit of the men who own the fields, and the man whose seed it is does not get the fruit. [52] If no agreement about the fruit is made between the owners of the fields and the owners of the seed, it is obvious that, the profit belongs to the owners of the fields; the womb is more important than the seed. [53] But if this (field) is given over for seeding by means of an agreed contract, then in this case both the owner of the seed and the owner of the field are regarded as (equal) sharers of that (crop). [54] Seed that is carried by a flood or a wind into someone's field and grows there belongs to the owner of the field, and the man who sowed the seed does not get the fruit.

[55] This is the law for the offspring of cows and mares, slave girls, female camels, and she-goats, and birds, and female buffalo. [56] The significance and

insignificance of the seed and the womb have thus been proclaimed to you. After that I will explain the law for dealing with women when one is in extremity. [57] The wife of the elder brother is the guru's wife to the younger brother; but the wife of the younger brother is traditionally regarded as the daughter-in-law to the elder brother. [58] If, when he is not in extremity, an elder brother has sex with the wife of a younger brother, or a younger brother with the wife of an elder brother, both of them fall even if they have been appointed (to have a child). [59] When the line of descendants dies out, a woman who has been properly appointed should get the desired children from a brother-in-law or a co-feeding relative.

[60] The appointed man, silent and smeared with clarified butter, should beget one son upon the widow in the night, but never a second. [61] Some people who know about this approve of a second begetting on (such) women, for they consider the purpose of the appointment of the couple incomplete in terms of duty. [62] But when the purpose of the appointment with the widow has been completed in accordance with the rules, the two of them should behave towards one another like a guru and a daughter-in-law. [63] If the appointed couple dispense with the rule and behave lustfully, then they both fall as violators of the bed of a daughter-in-law and a guru.

[64] Twice-born men should not appoint a widow woman to (have a child with) another man, for when they appoint her to another man they destroy the eternal religion.

[65] The appointment of widows is never sanctioned in the Vedic verses about marriage, nor is the remarriage of widows mentioned in the marriage rules. [66] For learned twice-born men despise this as the way of animals, which was prescribed for humans as well when Vena was ruling the kingdom. [67] Formerly, he was a pre-eminent royal sage who enjoyed the whole earth, but his thinking was ruined by lust and he brought about a confusion of the classes. [68] Since that time, virtuous men despise any man who is so deluded as to appoint a woman to have children when her husband has died. [69] If the (intended) husband of a girl dies when their promises have been given verbally, her own brother-in-law should take possession of her, according to this rule: [70] when she is wearing a white dress and has made an unpolluted vow, he should have sex with her in accordance with the rule, and he should make love with her once during each of her fertile seasons, until there is a child. [71] An intelligent man who has given his daughter to someone should not give her again, for a man who gives and then give again is lying to someone. [72] Even if a man has accepted a girl in accordance with the rules, he may reject her if she is despised, ill, or corrupted, or if she was given with something concealed. [73] If anyone gives away a daughter with a flaw and does not mention it, that (gift) from the evil-hearted daughter-giver may be annulled. [74] A man may go away on a journey on business only after he has established a. livelihood for his wife; for even a steady woman could be corrupted if she is starving for lack of livelihood.

[75] If he goes away on a journey after providing a livelihood, she should subject herself to restraints in her life; but if he goes away on a journey without providing for her, she may make her living by crafts that are not disapproved of. [76] If the man has gone away on a journey to fulfill some duty, (she) should wait for him for eight years; (if he has gone) for learning or fame, six; for pleasure, three years. [77] A husband should wait for one year for a wife who hates him; but after a year, he should take away her inheritance and not live with her. [78] If she transgresses against a husband who is infatuated, a drunk, or ill, he may deprive her of her jewelry and personal property and desert her for three months. [79] But if she hates him because he is insane, fallen, impotent, without seed, or suffering from a disease caused by his evil, she should not be deserted or deprived of her inheritance.

[80] A wife who drinks wine, behaves dishonestly, or is rebellious, ill, violent, or wasteful of money may be superseded at any time. [81] A barren wife may be superseded in the eighth year; one whose children have died, in the tenth; one who bears (only) daughters, in the eleventh; but one who says unpleasant things (may be superseded) immediately. [82] But if a woman who is kind and well-behaved becomes ill, she should be superseded (only) when she has been asked for her consent, and she should never be dishonoured. [83] And if a woman who has been superseded should leave the house in fury, she should be locked up immediately or deserted in the presence of the family. [84] But if she drinks wine at celebrations, even when she has been forbidden, or goes to public spectacles or crowded festivals, she should be punished by a fine of six "berries."

[85] If twice-born men take women of their own and other (classes), their seniority, reverence, and dwelling place should be (established) according to the order of their class. [86] For all husbands, a woman of his own (class), and never a woman of his own caste, should care for his body and perform the obligatory daily duties. [87] But if man is so deluded as to have this done by a woman other than the one that he has of his own caste, he is just like someone that people in ancient times regarded as a "Fierce" Untouchable priest. [88] A man should give his daughter, in accordance with the rules, to a distinguished, handsome suitor who is like her, even if she has not reached (the right age). [89] But it would be better for a daughter, even after she has reached puberty, to stay in the house until she dies than for him ever to give her to a man who has no good qualities.

[90] When a girl has reached puberty she should wait for three years, but after that period she should find a husband like her. [91] If she herself approaches a husband when she has not been given one, she commits no error, nor does the man whom she approaches. [92] A girl who chooses her own bridegroom should not take with her the jewelry given to her by her father, mother, or brothers; if she took that away, she would be a thief. [93] Nor should

a man who takes away a girl when she has reached puberty give a bride-price to her father; for (the father) would have neglected his charge over her by impeding (the fulfillment of) her fertile seasons. [94] A thirty-year-old man should marry a twelve-year-old girl who charms his heart, and a man of twenty-four an eight-year-old girl; and if duty is threatened, (he should marry) in haste.

[95] A husband takes his wife as a gift from the gods, not by his own wish; he should always support a virtuous woman, thus pleasing the gods. [96] Women were created to bear children, and men to carry on the line; that is why the revealed canon prescribes a joint duty (for a man) together with his wife. [97] If the man who gave the bride-price should die after the bride-price has been given for the girl, the girl should be given to the brother-in-law, if she consents. [98] Not even a servant should accept a bride-price when he gives his daughter, for a man who takes a bride-price is covertly selling his daughter. [99] Neither in the ancient past nor in recent times did good men ever promise (a girl) to one man and then give her to another; [100] nor have we heard that, even in former aeons, a daughter was ever covertly sold for a sum of money that was called a bride-price. [101] "Let there be mutual absence of infidelity until death"; this should be known as the supreme duty of a man and a woman, in a nutshell. [102] A man and woman who have performed the (wedding) ritual should always try not to become separated and unfaithful to one another. [103] The duty of a man and a woman, which is intimately connected with sexual pleasure, has thus been described to you, as well as the way to obtain children in extremity. Now learn about the division of inheritance. [104] After the father and mother (are dead), the brothers should assemble and divide the paternal estate equally, for they have no power over the two of them while they are alive.

[105] But the eldest brother may take the paternal property without leaving anything, and the rest live off him as if he were their father. [106] As soon as his eldest son is born a man becomes a man with a son, and no longer owes a debt to his ancestors; that is why the (the eldest) deserves to have the whole (estate). [107] The son to whom he transfers his debt and by whom he wins eternity is the one born out of duty; people know that the others are born out of desire. [108] The eldest brother should support his younger brothers as a father (supports) his sons, and in duty they should also behave like sons to their eldest brother. [109] The eldest (brother) makes the family thrive, or else he destroys it; the eldest is most worthy of reverence among people; the eldest is not held in contempt by good men.

[110] An eldest (brother) who behaves like an eldest (brother) is like a mother, like a father; but if he does not behave like an eldest (brother) he should be revered like a relative.

[Laws of Manu 3.1–19, 3.45–63, 5.147–169, 9.1–110, On the Duties of Husbands and Wives, in *The Laws of Manu*, trans. Wendy Doniger and Brian K. Smith (London: Penguin, 1991), pp. 43–45, 47–49, 115–116, 197–210]

THE KĀMASŪTRA

The *Kāmasūtra*, treatise regarding erotic love, was composed in Sanskrit in the third century of the common era, in Northwest India, reputedly by one Vatsyāyana Mallanāga. The text opens with a discussion of how the aims of life, pleasure, success, and virtue, may be achieved. It then focuses on pleasure (*kāma*) with sexual positions, types of women, lovers, wives, co-wives, and courtesans. The *Kāmasūtra* reflects an urbane and sophisticated culture. Like Manu, the *Kāmasūtra* discusses marriage, but from a more secular perspective.

Document 4–4

KĀMASŪTRA, ON HUSBANDS, WIVES AND LOVERS

[4.1.1] An only wife, with deep, intimate trust, treats her husband like a god and always acts in ways compatible with him. [2] Following his thinking, she takes on herself his cares about the household. [3] She keeps the house clean and heart-warming to look at, with well-polished surfaces, all sorts of floral arrangements, and smooth and shiny floors, and she makes sure that offerings are made three times a day and that the gods in the family shrine are properly honoured. [4] For, Gonardiya says, "Nothing holds the heart of householders like this." [5] She treats the man's older relatives, servants, sisters, and sisters' husbands according to their merits. . . .

[11] When she hears his voice outside as he approaches the house, she stands ready in the centre of the house and says, "What should be done?" [12] Pushing aside the female servant, she herself washes his feet. [13] She does not let the man see her alone when she is not wearing make-up and jewellery. [14] If he has spent too much or spent the wrong amount, she tells him in private. [15] Only with his permission does she go to a betrothal, a wedding, or a sacrifice, or get together with her girlfriends, or visit the gods. [16] In any game, she follows his lead. [17] She lies down after him, gets up before him, and never wakes him up when he is asleep. [18] She keeps the kitchen well guarded and well lit. [19] Mildly offended by the man's infidelities, she does not accuse him too much, [20] but she scolds him with abusive language when he is alone or among friends. She does not, however, use love-sorcery worked with roots, [21] for, Gonardiya says, "Nothing destroys trust like that." [22] She refrains from bad language, nasty looks, talking while avoiding his gaze, standing at the doorway or gazing from it, chatting in the park, and lingering in deserted places. [23] She guards against her own sweat, dirty teeth, and bad body odour, for these cool his passion. [24] When she goes to him to make love, she wears gorgeous jewellery, a variety of flowers and scented oils, and a dress dazzling with many different tints. [25] Her everyday dress is made of delicate, smooth, thin silk, with a modest amount of jewellery, good perfume but not too much of scented oils, and flowers both white and of other colours. [26] When the

man fasts or follows a vow, she herself also undertakes this for her own purpose; if he tries to stop her, she refutes his arguments, saying, "I am not going to be thwarted in this matter."

[27] When the price is right, at the right time, she buys household goods made of clay, bamboo, wood, leather, and iron. [28] She lays in a stock of salt and oil as well as hard-to-get perfumes, spices, and medicines, and keeps them hidden within the house. [29] And she buys, and sows at the proper season, the seeds of all sorts of edible plants, such as radishes, arrowroot, ginger, wormwood, mangoes, melons, cucumbers, eggplants, pumpkins, squashes, round yams, trumpet flowers, horse-eye beans, sesame, sandalwood, glory-tree, garlic, and onions. [30] She does not tell other people about her own assets or about her husband's counsels. [31] She surpasses all the women of her group in her skill, her dazzling appearance, her cooking, her pride, and her services. [32] She calculates the year's income and adjusts the expenditure to it. [33] She makes butter from the milk left over from meals, and also from sesame oil and molasses. She spins threads from cotton balls and then weaves cloth with those threads. She collects string-bags, cords, ropes, and bark-fibres; she oversees the grinding and pounding; when rice is boiled, she makes use, afterwards, of the water, the froth, the husks, the uncooked kernels, and the coals. She knows the servants' wages and maintenance. She sees to the tilling of the fields, the care of the cattle, and the upkeep of the carriages. She looks after the rams, cocks, quails, parrots, pheasants, cuckoos, peacocks, monkeys, and deer. And she prepares the daily portions of income and expenditures.

[34] She collects the man's discarded, worn-out clothes, both many-coloured and pure white, and gives them as a favour to servants who have done good work, and as gifts that bestow honour, or she uses them for something else. [35] She sees to the stocking and use of pots of wines and liquors, and to selling and buying them, and she keeps track of the income and expenditure from them. [36] She welcomes and honours the man's friends in the proper way, with gifts of garlands, scented oils, and betel. [37] She serves her father-in-law and mother-in-law, remaining dependent on them; she does not answer back to them, but makes brief, never harsh conversation, not laughing too loud, and treats those who are dear and not dear to them as if they were dear and not dear to her. [38] She is moderate in her enjoyments. [39] She is considerate to servants, [40] but never gives anything to anyone without telling the man. [41] She instructs each servant in the limits of his own work and honours him on festival days. That is the life of an only wife. [42] When he is away on a journey, she wears only jewellery that has religious meaning and power, devotes herself to fasts dedicated to the gods, waits for news, and manages the household. [43] She sleeps at the feet of older relatives and their people, and accomplishes her tasks with their approval. She goes to great pains to acquire and look after things that the man wants. [44] She spends the usual amount on undertakings for daily tasks and special occasions. She also sets her mind on accomplishing those

undertakings that he has begun. [45] She does not go to the family of her own relatives except on occasions of disaster or celebration. And even there she is chaperoned by the man's servants, she does not stay too long, and she does not change out of the clothing that she wears when the man is absent. [46] She fasts with the permission of older relatives. She increases capital and decreases expenditures as much as possible, by authorizing buying and selling to be accomplished by incorruptible servants carrying out orders. [47] When he returns, she appears to him first in her ordinary clothes, and she honours the gods and brings gifts. That is her life during his absence. [48] And there are two verses about this:

> An only wife who wishes for her man's welfare
> adapts herself to his behaviour,
> whether she is a woman of good family,
> a second-hand woman, or even a courtesan.
> Women of good behaviour
> achieve the goals of religion, power, and pleasure,
> a firm position, and
> a husband without a co-wife.

[4.2.1] If his wife is frigid or promiscuous or unlucky in love, or if she continually fails to bear a child or gives birth only to daughters, or if the man is fickle, he supplants her with a co-wife. [2] Therefore, from the very start, a woman tries to avoid this by making known her devotion, good character, and cleverness. And if she does not have children, she herself is the one to urge him to take a co-wife. [3] And when she is being supplanted, by applying all her powers she establishes her own position as higher.

[4] She looks upon the newly arrived woman as a sister. Making an extraordinary effort, she helps her dress and make herself up in the evening, and she makes sure that the man knows about this. She pays no attention if the other woman becomes hostile or haughty as a result of her luck in love. [5] She disregards it if the other woman makes a mistake with her husband. Then, if she thinks, "This is a mistake that she herself will also mend," she advises her carefully about it. [6] But she reveals further particulars about it to the man, privately. [7] She treats the other woman's children in no special way, treats her servants with great sympathy and her girlfriends with affection. She does not care too much for her own relatives, and makes an extra fuss over the other woman's relatives. [8] But if she is supplanted by many co-wives, she allies herself with the one just below her. [9] She provokes quarrels between the woman whom the man wishes to promote to the favourite and the woman who used to be lucky in love, [10] a woman for whom she then shows sympathy. [11] By uniting the other co-wives, without actually getting into the argument herself she maligns the one he wants to promote to the favourite. [12] But she encour-

ages the other woman to quarrel with the man, egging her on by taking her side. [13] And she makes the quarrel grow. [14] Or, if she notes that the quarrel is dying down, she herself fans the flames. [15] But if she realizes, "The man even now inclines to her," then she herself makes peace between them. That is the life of the senior wife.

[16] The junior wife, however, regards her co-wife like a mother. [17] She does not even give anything to her relatives without the other woman's knowledge. [18] She reports her own experiences to her. [19] With her permission, she sleeps with the husband. [20] She never reports to any other woman what the other woman says. [21] She has more regard for the other woman's children than for her own. [22] But privately, she serves the husband more. [23] And she does not tell him how she herself suffers from the hostility of the co-wives. [24] She tries to get some special secret token of her husband's esteem, [25] and she says, "I will live on this, as if it were food to last me on a journey." [26] But she never talks in public about that, either in boast or in passion, [27] for a woman who betrays a secret wins her husband's loathing. [28] Gonardiya says, "Out of fear of the senior wife, she seeks only a secret love-token." [29] If the senior wife is unlucky in love and has no children, the junior wife pities her and urges the man to pity her. [30] But if the junior wife is able to dislodge the senior wife, she assumes the role of the only wife. That is the life of the junior wife.

[31] A second-hand woman, however, is a widow who is tormented by the weakness of the senses and so finds, again, a man who enjoys life and is well endowed with good qualities. [32] But the followers of Babhravya say, "Since she may at will go away again from him too, thinking, 'He is *not* well endowed with good qualities,' she will then want yet another man." [33] It is in search of physical pleasure that she tries, again, to find yet another man. [34] Gonardiya says, "Complete pleasure comes from men's endowments and capacity for enjoyments; therefore one man differs from another." [35] Vatsyāyana says: It is because his mind is compatible with hers. [36] With her relatives, she gets the man to provide sufficient funds to cover the cost of such things as drinking parties, picnics, faith offerings, and gifts to honour friends. [37] Or she may pay for his jewellery and her own out of her own capital. [38] There is no rule about love-gifts. [39] If she leaves the man of her own accord, she gives back everything he has given her except for his love-gifts. But if he throws her out, she does not give anything back. [40] She takes over his house as if she were the woman in charge, [41] but she acts with affection to women of good families, [42] with consideration to the servants, always joking, and with great respect for his friends. In the arts, she has skill and greater knowledge. [43]When there are occasions for a quarrel, she herself scolds the man. [44] She practises the sixty-four arts of love in private. And she herself does favours for the co-wives. She gives jewellery to their children and makes little ornaments for them, and clothing, with care, but she expects those children to serve her as if she were their master. She gives even more things to his entourage and his crowd of friends.

And she is always in the mood for company, for drinking parties, picnics, festivals, and amusements. That is the life of the second-hand woman.

[45] But a woman who is unlucky in love and oppressed by rivalry with her co-wives seeks support from the wife who seems to be chosen most often by their husband. She shows that chosen wife the knowledge of the arts that can be revealed. Because she is unlucky in love, she has no secrets. [46] She performs the functions of a nurse for the man's children. [47] She wins over his friends and then gets them to tell him about her devotion to him. [48] She leads the way in religious duties and in vows and fasts. She is considerate to the servants and has no more regard for herself than for them. [50] In bed, she requites the man's passion in a way that suits him. [51] She does not scold him or show him any contrariness. [52] She restores his desire for any woman with whom he may have quarrelled. [53] If he desires some woman who must remain concealed, she brings the other woman to him and hides her. [54] She takes pains to make the man regard her as a chaste and undeceiving wife. That is the life of the wife unlucky in love.

[55] The life of the women of the harem, too, can be surmised from the preceding sections. [56] The woman chamberlain or bodyguard brings their garlands, scented oils, and clothes to the king, saying, "The queens have sent these." [57] The king takes these and gives them back to the queens as a gift, like the leftover of a deity. [58] In the afternoon, he goes, carefully dressed, to see, all together, all the women of the harem, who are also well dressed. [59] He chats and jokes with them, giving to each one the place and honour due to the time she has served in the harem and her worth. [60] Immediately after that, he sees, in exactly the same way, the second-hand women, [61] and then the courtesans and the dancing girls who belong to the harem. [62] Their places are in the inner rooms assigned to them.

[63] Now, when the king arises from his afternoon siesta, the women attendants who keep track of the roster come to him followed by the servants of the woman whose turn it is to spend the night with the king, of the woman who has been passed over on her night, and of the woman who is in her fertile season. And they present the king with scented oils, each marked with the stamp of the woman's seal ring, and tell him whose turn it is to sleep with him that night and who is in her fertile season. [64] Whichever one among these oils the king takes, he announces that the woman who owns it will sleep with him that night.

[65] At festivals, and at concerts and plays, all of the women of the harem are appropriately honoured and served with drinks. [66] They do not go out, nor do women from outside enter, except for those whose purity is well known. And so the work is carried out undisturbed. Those are the women of the harem.

[67] And there are verses about this:

> But a man who has collected many wives
> must treat them equally.
> He should not treat them with contempt,
> nor put up with their deceptions.

[68] Whatever sort of love-play one woman favours,
or whatever peculiarity her body may have,
or whatever reproach she lets slip in pillow talk—
he must not tell that to the other women.
[69] He should never give women their head
in a cause against a co-wife,
and if one woman begins to slander another in this way,
he should charge her herself with those faults.
[70] He should keep his women happy,
one by confiding in her privately,
another by honouring her in public,
yet another with gifts as tokens of his esteem.
[71] He should enchant each one individually,
with picnics, luxuries, gifts,
honours to her family, and with
the pleasures of love in bed.
[72] A young woman who controls her temper
and behaves according to the textbook
puts her husband in her power
and lords it over her co-wives.

[Vatsyāyana Mallanāga, Kāmasūtra 4.1–2, On Husbands, Wives, and
Lovers, in *Kamasutra*, trans. Wendy Doniger and Sudhir Kakar
(New York: Oxford University Press, 2002), pp. 94–103]

DIVINE MARRIAGE: ŚIVA AND PĀRVATĪ

From the *Rig Veda* forward, Hindu tradition has seen a close connection between divine and human marriage. The marriages of Viṣṇu and Lakṣmī, Rāma and Sītā, and Śiva and Pārvatī are well known. In many versions of the story, as the archetypal ascetic, Śiva was not inclined to marriage and the life of the household. He much preferred his hermitage in the Himalayas. It was only after some strenuous persuasion by the gods and Pārvatī's own capacity for asceticism as rigorous as his own did Śiva reluctantly at first and then wholeheartedly embrace Pārvatī and the idea of marriage. In this version, upon learning that his first wife Satī, who immolated her body in his defense when her father insulted Śiva, had been reborn as Pārvatī, he dispatched the sages to find her and ask her father for her hand in marriage. This is a reversal of the usual marriage pattern on the human level where it is the bride's family that initiates the search for a marriage partner. This delightful telling of the story of the marriage of Śiva and Pārvatī is from the *Vāmana Purāṇa* (ca. 900–1100 CE), chapters 26–27 (condensed), reflecting a devotional perspective toward these deities. Śiva is also called Rudra, Śarva, Śaṅkara, Śambhu and Hara; Pārvatī is also called Kālā and Ūmā.

Document 4–5

VĀMANA PURĀNA, THE BETROTHAL AND WEDDING
OF ŚIVA AND PĀRVĀTI

Rudra, pleased to be so honored by the mountain, called to mind the great seers and Arundhatī [wife of the sage, Vasiṣṭha]. Upon this call of the great-souled Śaṅkara, these seers gathered on mighty Mt. Mandara with its lovely caverns. When the god who destroyed Tripura saw them coming, he rose to greet them, and honoring them, said this, "This fine mountain, worthy of honor and praise by the gods, is most fortunate to be released from evil by the touch of your lotus feet! Please stay here on the mountain, on the wide and beautiful flat plateau whose lotus colored rocks are soft and smooth!" Thus addressed by the god Śaṅkara, the great sages, along with Arundhatī, sat down on the table.

When the sages were seated, Nandin, leader of the *ganas* [attendants] of the god, greeted them with *arghya* [offering of water to a guest] and other offerings and stood before them with his mind intent on devotion. Then the lord of the gods, for the increase of his own glory, spoke righteous and beneficent words to the gods and to the seven seers who were full of self-control.

"Listen, Kaśyapa, Atri and Vasiṣṭha, son of Varuṇa; Viśvāmitra, Gādhi's son, and Gautama, mark my words; listen, Bharadvāja, and you, Angiras, hear what I say! My beloved Satī, Dakṣa's daughter, who (so they say) out of anger with Dakṣa gave up her life long ago through the insight of Yoga, has now been reborn as Ūmā, daughter of the king of the mountains. Go, excellent brahmins, and ask the mountain for her hand on my behalf!" When they were asked to do this, the seven peers replied, "by all means!" And saying, "OM! Praise be to Śaṅkara!" they went to the Himalaya.

Śarva spoke also to Arundhatī, saying, "You go too, lovely woman, for married women know the way of women's duty." When she had been reminded of this inviolable worldly custom, she said, "Praise be to you, O Rudra!" and departed with her husband.

When they reached the plain of herbs on the highest peak of Mt. Hima[laya], they saw the city of the mountain king that looked like the city of the gods. There after being ardently and respectfully worshiped by the mountain women and by Sunābha and the other mountains, by Gandharvas, Kinnaras, Yakṣas [heavenly beings] and others in attendance, they approached the delightful palace of Mt. Hima, which was ablaze with gold. All those great-souled seers, their taints purified by *tapas*, gathered in front of the great gate and stood there waiting for the gate-keeper.

Mt. Gandhamādana, the door-keeper, came at once holding in his hand a great staff studded with rubies. The assembled seers said to him, "We are here to see the great lord of the mountains. We have come with a weighty purpose. Announce our arrival!" Thus addressed by the sages; the chief mountain Gandhamādana went to where the mountain king was sitting surrounded by his fellow mountains. The door-keeper fell to his knees on the ground, tucked his staff under his arm and put his hands up to his forehead. Then he said, "O mountain king; some sages have come to you with a purpose. They are standing at the gate eager to see you on business."

When he heard the door-keeper's words, the lord of the mountain arose and went to the gate himself, carrying the finest *arghya*. After leading them to the assembly hall with *arcya* [guest gift] and *arghya* and other offerings, and they had taken their seats, the mountain spoke to them eloquently. "What is this rain that has fallen from a cloudless sky? This fruit that has ripened without a flower? This visit of yours is so unexpected as to be unbelievable! Today I am rich! Today I am truly the king of the mountains, excellent ones! My body is cleansed now that you have come to court! O best of brahmins, I am made pure by contact with all of you, just as one is purified by the sight of the Sarasvatī when one goes there on foot. I am your servant, O brahmins, who gains merit by your very presence! Tell me why you have come! I stand before you as your servant, O immortals, along with my wife, grandsons and attendants. Tell me what I can do for you!"

When they heard the words of the mountain king, the vow-keeping-sages said to Angiras, the elder, "Tell the mountain why we are here." Thus directed, by Kaśyapa and the other seers, Angiras addressed the king of the mountain with this fine speech: "Hear, excellent, mountain, the purpose which has brought us to your place; along with Arundhatī O mountain. We have been sent by the great-souled Śankara, the universal soul, the destroyer of Daksa's sacrifice, Śarva the trident-bearer, the three-eyed god who rides the bull, Jīmūtaketu, enemy-slayer, enjoyer of sacrifices, the lord called Śiva Sthāṇu, Bhava, Hara, the terrible and violent great lord Mahādeva; the master of animals. By him have we been sent into your presence; O lord of the mountain.

"The lord of the gods wants to marry your daughter Kālā [Pārvatī], the loveliest woman in all the world. Please give her to him! It is a fortunate father indeed whose daughter wins a handsome husband fully endowed with beauty and good family, excellent mountain. This goddess will be the mother of the four kinds of moving and unmoving beings, O mountain, since Hara is called their father. Let the gods who bow down to Śankara also worship your daughter! And so put your ash-covered foot on the head of your enemy!

"We are the suitors, Śarva the groom; your daughter Ūmā [Pārvatī], mother of the whole world, is the bride. Do this for your own benefit!"

When she heard Angiras's words, Kālā hung her head, alternating between hope and despair. And the lord of the mountains said to Gandhamādana, "Go and summon all the mountains, then return." That swift mountain then went rapidly from house to house inviting Meru and the other excellent mountains on all sides. They came in a hurry, realizing this was a task of great importance. These major mountains and other lesser hills prostrated themselves before the seers and took their seats in the assembly hall.

Then the lord of the mountains summoned his wife Menā, and that beautiful, auspicious woman came, along with her child. Saluting the feet of the sages with respect, that ascetic woman greeted all her kin and entered the hall with her daughter. Then when the mountains were seated, O Nārada, the eloquent mountain addressed them all mellifluously, "I must tell you that these seven virtuous seers have requested my little daughter for Maheśvara. Speak to me out of your wisdom. You are my relatives and I shall not give her away against your wishes. Tell me what I should do."

When they had heard the words of Himavat, Meru and the other mighty mountains spoke as follows as they sat there in their seats, "The seers are the suitors and Hara, slayer of Tripura, the groom. Give little Kālā to him, O mountain, for we find him to be a suitable son-in-law!"

Menā, too, spoke to her husband, saying, "Hear my word, chief mountain. It was for this very purpose that the gods worshiped the Fathers and gave her to us. The son she will bear to the lord of creatures will kill Mahiṣa, the Daitya chief, and the demon Tāraka as well!"

Thus addressed by Menā, the mountain lord, accompanied by the mountains, said to his daughter, "O girl, I now give you to Śarva!" And he said to the sages, "My little daughter Kālā, O seers rich in *tapas* [asceticism], the bride of Śaṅkara, bows in devotion to do you honor!" And Arundhatī took Kālā on her lap and encouraged her with words made auspicious by the frequent mention of Hara's name.

The great lord Hara was delighted at this and honored the seers one by one, according to the rules, and Arundhatī as well. Thus worshiped, they went around to invite the gods. Brahmā, Viṣṇu and the Sun then came to see Hara. When they arrived, great seer; they made obeisance to Maheśvara. Then they entered his house, led by Nandin, where he received them all. Praising Hara in his presence, they sat down. Surrounded there by the hosts of gods, the lord of the mountain, with his unkept hair loose, shone forth like a mighty tree with sprouting shoots among the *arja* and *kadamba* trees in the forest.

When he saw that the gods had assembled, Nandin told his master, Śiva, who arose to give Hari a warm and affectionate embrace. Śaṅkara graciously received all the gods, bowing his head to Brahmā, greeting Indra of a hundred sacrifices and paying due attention to the host of gods. Crying, "Victory, O god!" the *gaṇas* led by Vīrabhadra; Śiva's followers, the Pāśupatas and others, ascended Mt. Mandara. And lord Śarva went to mighty Mt. Kailāsa with the gods to prepare for the marriage festival, where the blessed Aditi, mother of the gods, Surabhi, Surasā and other women were already busy with the decorations.

Hara [Śiva] was radiant, crowned with skulls, wearing a handsome saffron-colored *tilaka* [forehead mark], clothed in a lion-skin, decked out in earrings made of snakes that were black as bees, his bracelets bejeweled with cobras, adorned with necklaces; armlets and, anklets, his matted hair piled high, riding on a bull. Before him went his *gaṇas* astride their own mounts, while the gods, led by Fire, came behind. Mounted on Garuda, Janārdana went forth together with Lakṣmī, while the Grandfather rode alongside the god on his goose.

The thousand-eyed god Indra, together with Śacī, rode on his elephant, carrying an open parasol of white cloth. The lovely river Yamunā sat on a tortoise, holding a beautiful white yak-tail fan in her hand. Mounted on an elephant, holding a fine chowrie fan white as a goose, jasmine or the moon was the beautiful river Sarasvatī. The six seasons, roaming the world at will, came too, bringing fragrant flowers of five colors for the great lord. Riding an elephant in rut that thundered, along like Airāvata, Prthīdaka went there carrying unguents. Led by Tumbaru, Gandharvas followed after Mahādeva singing sweet songs, while Kinnaras made music, Apsarases danced, and seers praised the three-eyed lord of the gods with a trident in his hand.

There passed in the procession eleven crores [crore = 10,000,000] of Rudras, twelve crores of ādityas, sixty-seven crores of *gaṇas* and forty crores of superior celibate seers. Countless numbers of hurrying hosts of Yakṣas, Kinnaras and Rākṣasas followed the great lord to the wedding festival.

The lord of the gods soon reached the foot of the lord of the mountains where other mountains riding elephants were converging on all sides. Then the blessed three-eyed lord bowed down to the mountain king who bowed in turn to the lord, gratifying him greatly. In this way did the bull-marked god, along with the gods and his retinue, enter the great city of the mountain king on the path shown by Nandin.

"Jīmūtaketu, the cloud-crested god, has arrived!" cried the townswomen, abandoning their housework in their eagerness for a glimpse of the lord. One lovely woman approached Śaṅkara holding half a garland in one hand and her hair in the other. Another one, her eyes distraught, hurried to see Hara with one foot reddened by lac [resin], the other plain. Still another, having heard of the dread one's arrival, ran in his direction carrying a pigment pencil, only one eye darkened with collyrium [lamp black]. Another lovely woman, longing eagerly for the sight of Hara, went out naked like a fool, holding her robe and belt in her hand. Another young thin-waisted girl, slowed by the burden of her bosom, heard that the lord had already passed by and angrily cursed her youth. Causing confusion among the women of the town in this manner, Hara, mounted on a bull, went toward the heavenly palace of his father-in-law.

When they saw Śambhu enter the house of the mountain king, the women said, "Ambikā must have practiced difficult *tapas* [asceticism] indeed to win this mighty god Śambhu! It is he who rendered invisible the body of Kandarpa, whose weapon is flowers, who destroyed Dakṣa's sacrifice and the eye of Bhaga, who bears the trident and the bow Pināka. Glory, glory be to Śaṅkara, trident in hand, robed in tiger-skin, Time's destroyer! Praise, praise be to the beloved of Pārvatī, adorned with earrings, wearing a cobra necklace!"

Thus honored, Śambhu mounted the wedding altar which was covered with designs and enjoyed by Fire, under a parasol held by the king of the gods, praised by Siddhas and Yakṣas, wearing a bracelet made of a snake, his body smeared with fine ashes, preceded by Brahmā, the first-born of creation, who went before him with a happy heart, and followed by Viṣṇu in the rear.

During the arrival of the slayer of Tripura with his retinue, accompanied by the seven seers, the people in the house of the mountain king were occupied with the adornment of Kālī, while the mountain divinities who had arrived busied themselves with their own offerings. Friends who await the wedding ceremony of a daughter are usually in a state of confusion!

When the women had finished preparing the mountain-born goddess, the pillar of her body was dressed in fine white cloth. Her brother Sunābha, who had arranged the celebration, brought her into Śaṅkara's presence. While the gods who stood on the beautiful golden terrace witnessed the actions of Śaṅkara and Kālā, the god and the slender-waisted woman began the ceremony to the delight of the crowd. There were all kinds of entertainments amid flowering trees and fountains, while on the ground richly fragrant powders were heaped here and there. For the delight and amusement of the mountain daughter and Hara, others struck them freely with ropes of pearls while the two of them reddened the earth with copious clouds of vermilion.

After these sports, Hara and the little mountain maid went together to the massive southern altar that is revered by the sages, Then the holy Himavat approached dressed in white cloth, holding in his hand, the *pavitra* [stalk] of sacred grass and the *madhuparka* offering of milk and honey. The three-eyed god sat down facing the eastern region, which is presided over by Indra, while the king of the mountains was comfortably seated facing the north, the direction of the constellation of the seven seers.

The mountain, hands folded in greeting, spoke these fine words obedient to his Dharma, to Śarva who was seated on his fine seat, "Accept the offering of my daughter Kālā, blessed one, the granddaughter of Pulaha's elder brother, the daughter's daughter of the Fathers!" So speaking, the lord of the mountain joined their hands together and presented his daughter to Śiva, saying aloud, "Take her, O lord!"

"I have no mother and no father, no kin and no relations by marriage. I dwell on the mountain peaks without a home. I accept your daughter, O king of the mountains!" So saying, the groom pressed the hand of the little mountain girl with his own. When she felt Śambhu's touch, she became ecstatically happy, divine sage. Then the groom mounted the altar with the daughter of the mountain where together they offered white parched grain and ate the offering of milk and honey.

After this, Viriṇca Brahmā said to the mountain-born girl, "Look at your husband's face that shines like the moon, O Kālā! Look fixedly in the same direction and walk around the fire." When she saw Hara's face, a shudder went through Ambikā just as the ground heated by the sun's rays shimmers in the rain. When the Grandfather repeated once again, "Look at your husband's face!" she replied shyly and softly to Brahmā, "I have seen." And then the bride and groom circumambulated the fire three times, after which they threw into it the parched grain together with the oblation.

Then the bridesmaid Mālinī seized Hara's feet and asked for a nuptial gift, to which he replied, "I shall give you what you desire. Release me!" So Mālinī said to Śaṅkara, "Give to my friend the good fortune in love that runs in your family, Śaṅkara, and then I will let you go!" To this Mahādeva answered, "Release me, Mālinī! And listen while I tell you about my fabled way with women. Madhusādana, who wears a yellow garment and carries a conch, derives his luck in love from me; it comes from my family." When he said this, Mālinī, garlanded by the good conduct of her own family, let go of the bull-bannered god.

When Mālinī was clasping Hara's lustrous feet, Brahmā had been watching Kālā's face, which shone brighter than the moon. As he looked at her, he began to shake until he spilled his semen. In consternation, he rendered it powerless in the earth, whereupon Hara spoke out, "O Brahmā you are not to kill brahmins! There are great sages in your semen, Grandfather, the blessed Vālakhilyas!" After the great lord said this, 88,000 ascetics, known as the Vālakhilyas, were born from Brahmā's seed.

At the close of the wedding ceremony, Hara himself entered into the festivities. All night he made love with Ūmā, and he arose again at dawn. Śambhu was happy after he married the daughter of the mountain, and so were the gods, the Bhūtas [spirits] and his *gaṇas*. After being honored by the mountain king, he returned at once to Mt. Mandara. Bowing to the gods, who were led by Brahmā, Hari and Indra, and worshiping each according to his rank, the god of eight forms took his leave and, along with his Bhūtas, settled down to live on Mt. Mandara.

[Śiva Purāṇa, The Betrothal and Wedding of Śiva and Pārvatī, in *Classical Hindu Mythology: A Reader in the Sanskrit Purāṇas*, ed. and trans. Cornelia Dimmit and J. A. B. van Buitenen (Philadelphia: Temple University Press, 1978), pp. 164–171]

THE KARMA OF MARRIAGE: THE KING'S WIFE, THE BRAHMIN'S WIFE, AND THE OGRE

This ancient story is about the tangled lives of a king, a Brahmin, their wives, and an ogre; and three locales: palace, wilderness, and underworld. The king, Uttama, desperately loved his wife, who was indescribably beautiful, but she did not return his affection. In a moment of anger he banished her to the wilderness. Later, a Brahmin came to the king with the news that his own wife, who was ugly, has been kidnapped. Without her he could not perform sacrifices and was therefore useless. He begged the king to find her. The king then went into the wilderness and sought the help of another Brahmin, an ascetic living in the midst of the forest. The sage explained King Uttama that the Brahmin's wife had been taken by an ogre and sent him to rescue her. Furthermore, he told the king that his wife has been taken to the underworld, ruled over by a serpent king. The serpent king desired her, but his daughter protected her, an act of defiance that led the king to curse his daughter to be mute. The king returned the Brahmin's wife to him. He summoned the ogre to rescue his wife from the serpent king's home. His wife was returned, along with the serpent-king's daughter. The Brahmin performed a sacrifice to remove the curse on her. As the sage in the forest explained to the king, the cause of his wife's lack of affection was a crossing of the stars at the time of the wedding. Finally, the king and his wife were restored to mutual affection, leading him to rule justly. Sprinkled throughout the story are teachings about the *dharma* of marriage, the importance of loyalty, and the benefits of learning from one's mistakes. From the *Markandeya Puränna* Ch. 66.3–37, 43–69; 67.1–39; 68.1–29; 69.1–41 (ca. 300 CE).

Document 4–6

THE KARMA OF MARRIAGE: THE KING'S WIFE, THE BRAHMIN'S WIFE, AND THE OGRE

King Uttanapada had a son named Uttama ("Supreme"), the child of his queen Suruci, famous, powerful, and courageous. He was the very soul of *dharma*, noble, a king wealthy in aggressiveness, surpassing all creatures, like the sun in his valour. He was the same to an enemy and to a friend, to an opponent and to his own son, since he knew *dharma*; to an evil man he was like Yama, king of the dead, but to a good man he was like Soma. And, knowing *dharma*, that son of Uttanapada married a woman named Bahula, of the race of Babhru, just as the supreme Indra married Saci. His heart was always excessively affectionate toward her, just as the moon's heart always takes its place in the constellation Rohini. His mind did not become attached to any other object; the heart of that king depended upon her even in his dreams. Simply from looking at her lovely body his eyes made his body hot; and when he touched her body, he melted into her.

But the voice of the king, even though it was so loving, disturbed her hearing; and she regarded even his great respect for her as a humiliation. She disdained the garland that he gave her, and all the beautiful jewels. She would get up as if half-drunk when he was drinking the finest liquor; and when the king was eating and would hold her hand just for a moment, she would eat only a very little food and show that she was not very happy. Thus, though he was so loving toward her, she was not very loving toward him; but this simply made the excessive passion of the king grow even greater.

Then, one day, when the king was engaged in drinking, and all the other kings were looking on, and they were surrounded by courtesans and were being serenaded by sweet sounds, he very respectfully placed in the queen's hand a drinking goblet full of wine. But she did not wish to take that goblet, and she turned away, before the eyes of all the kings. That made the king furious; he summoned a door-keeper, hissing like a snake—for she whom he loved had repelled her unloved husband—and he said, "Door-keeper, take this hard-hearted woman to a deserted forest and leave her there right away; do not hesitate about this command of mine." Then the door-keeper, regarding the king's command as something about which there must be no hesitation, put the beautiful queen in a carriage and abandoned her in a forest. And when the king had had her abandoned in the forest in this way, and she didn't see him, she considered that he had done her a great favour. But the king, the son of Uttanapada, was tormented by his passion for her; his heart and soul ached, and he found no other wife. He remembered her, with her lovely body, day and night, ceaselessly. He carried on governing his kingdom, protecting his subjects with *dharma*, caring for his subjects as if he were a father and they were the sons sprung from his loins.

Then a certain Brahmin came there and with an aching heart said to the king, "Great king, I am very unhappy; listen while I tell you about it, for the cure for the sufferings of men comes from nowhere but the king. While I was asleep, during the night, someone stole my wife, without even breaking open the door of the house. You must bring her back." The king said, "Don't you know who stole her or where she was brought to? Who am I to fight with? Where am I to bring her back from?" The Brahmin said, "While I was sleeping in my house, with the door shut just as tight as could be, someone stole my wife—I've already told you that. You are our guardian, your majesty, whom we hire by giving you a sixth of our wealth. And therefore men sleep at night without worrying about your *dharma*."

The king said, "I've never seen your wife. What sort of looks does she have, what sort of body? How old is she, and how patient? Tell me, what sort of character does your Brahmin lady have?" The Brahmin said, "She has piercing eyes and is very tall; she has short arms, and a bony face. Her belly hangs down, and she has flat buttocks and small breasts. She is very ugly, your majesty; I am not blaming her, that's just the way she is. Her speech is coarse, too, your majesty, and her nature is not at all gentle. That is how I would describe my wife; she is hideous to look at. And she has ever so slightly passed her prime. That is what my wife looks like; I am telling you the truth."

The king said, "You've had enough of her, Brahmin; I will give you another wife. A pretty wife will bring you happiness; that sort is a source of misery. Lack of beauty may sometimes be a cause of a very good character; but a woman who lacks both beauty and character should be abandoned. Yours was carried off by someone else." The Brahmin said, "It is written in scripture, your majesty: 'Protect your wife.' When the wife is protected, the offspring are protected. For one's self is born in one's offspring; and when the offspring are protected, the self is protected. So she must be protected, your majesty. If she is not protected, the various classes will become commingled, and that will cause one's previous ancestors to fall from heaven, your majesty. Every day that I live without a wife, I lose *dharma*, because I have ceased to perform the obligatory rituals, and that, too, will cause me to fall. My future line of descendants is in her, your majesty; she is the one who will give you the sixth part (of our income); she is the cause of *dharma*. That is why I have described to you the wife that was stolen from me, my lord; bring her back, since you are the supreme authority for protection."

When the king heard this speech, he thought about it. Then he mounted his chariot, that was equipped with all the things that one might want. He wandered this way and that way over the earth in that chariot until he saw in a great forest a superb hermitage for ascetics; he dismounted and entered in, and there he saw a sage seated on a silk cushion, blazing with glory, as it were. When the sage saw that the king had arrived, he stood up hastily and welcomed him respectfully; then he said to his pupil, "Bring the water to greet the guest." But the pupil said to him, quietly, "Why should he be given the water of greeting, great sage? Think about it and command me, and I will do what you command." Then the Brahmin realised what had happened to the king, and he honoured him merely by giving him conversation and a place to sit. The sage said, "For what reason have you come here, and what do you wish to do? I know that you are King Uttama, the son of Uttanapada."

The king said, "Great sage, someone—I don't know who—stole a Brahmin's wife right out of the house, and I have come here in search of her. I have come to your house and bow before you; and I hope that out of your pity for me you will tell me what I ask of you." "Ask me, your majesty," said the sage, "and do not worry about what can be asked. If it is something that I can tell you, I will tell you truly." The king said, "When you first saw me arrive at your house, great sage, you were about to give me the water with which a guest is welcomed; why, then, was it withheld?" The sage said, "The minute I saw you, in my haste I gave a command to this pupil, but then he admonished me. By my grace, he knows what is to come in this universe, just as I know what has happened and is happening everywhere. When he said, 'Consider, and then command,' then I knew. That is why I did not give you the water for a guest. In truth, your majesty, you deserve the water, since you, Uttama, are born in the family of the self-created Manu; nevertheless, we think that you are not fit to receive the water."

The king said, "What did I do, Brahmin, knowingly or unknowingly, so that I do not deserve the water from you, though I have arrived from a great distance?" The sage said, "What, have you forgotten that you abandoned your wife in the forest? Your majesty, you abandoned your entire *dharma* along with her. A man whose ritual life has been ruined becomes untouchable for a fortnight; so you whose obligatory rituals have been ruined (are untouchable) for a year. Just as an affectionate wife must put up with a husband even if he lacks good character, so too, even if a wife has a bad character, she must be supported. The wife of that Brahmin, the one who was stolen, was unpleasant; but, nevertheless, because he wished for *dharma*, he has outshone you. You set other people straight when they deviate from their *dharma*, great king; but who else is there who will set you straight when you deviate from your own *dharma*?"

The king was truly embarrassed when that wise man talked to him like that. "Yes," he said. And then he asked the sage about the Brahmin's wife who had been stolen: "Sir, who stole the Brahmin's wife, and where did he take her? You know the past and the future in this universe, without any error." The sage said, "An ogre named Balaka, the son of Adri, took her. You will see her today in the Utpalavataka forest, your majesty. Go and reunite the Brahmin with his wife right away. Don't let him become a breeding ground for sin day after day, like you."

The king bowed before the great sage and mounted his chariot and went to the Utpalavataka wood that he had mentioned. And there the king saw the Brahmin's wife, who looked just as her husband had described her. She was eating bilva fruits. He asked her, "Good woman, how did you come to this forest? Tell me plainly: are you the wife of Susharman Vaishali?" The Brahmin lady said, "I am the daughter of Atiratra, a Brahmin who lives in the forest, and I am the wife of Vaishali, whose name you just uttered. I was stolen by a bad ogre named Balaka; while I slept inside my house, I was separated from my brothers and my mother. Someone should burn to ashes that ogre who separated me in this way from my mother and brothers, and from others; I am living here in great misery. He brought me into this very deep forest, but then he abandoned me; I don't know why it is that he enjoyed me neither carnally nor carnivorously, neither for the pleasures of the flesh nor for the pleasure of flesh."

The king said, "Do you happen to know where the ogre went when he had let you go? Your husband sent me here, O giver of joy to Brahmins." The Brahmin lady said, "The night-wandering ogre is staying inside this very forest. Go in and see—unless you're afraid." He entered on the path that she had indicated, and saw the ogre, who was surrounded by his troops. The moment that the ogre saw the king, he made haste from afar to touch his head to the earth, and then he approached the king's feet and said, "By coming here to my house you have done me a great favour. Command me; what can I do for you? For I live within your political domain. Please accept this welcoming water and take this seat. We are your servants; you are our master. Command me absolutely."

The king said, "You have done everything, and rendered me all recompense. But for what purpose did you bring the Brahmin's wife here, night-wanderer? She is not good-looking; there are other wives, if you stole her for that. And if you brought her here to eat her, why haven't you eaten her? Tell me that." The ogre said, "We don't eat people; those are other ogres, your majesty. But we eat the fruit of a good deed. And I will tell you about the fruit of a good deed: that is how I came to be reborn in the cruel and terrifying womb of an ogre. When we are dishonoured, we eat the very nature of men and women. But we do not eat flesh; we do not eat living creatures. When we eat the patience of men, they become angry; when we have eaten their evil nature, they become virtuous. We have gorgeous female ogres who are the equal of the celestial nymphs when it comes to beauty. While they are here, how could we take sexual pleasure in human females?"

The king said, "If you want her neither for your bed nor for your table, night-wanderer, then why did you enter the Brahmin's house and steal her?" The ogre said, "That Brahmin is outstanding when it comes to knowing mantras; as I went to sacrifice after sacrifice, he would recite the mantra that destroys ogres and prevent me from doing my job. We're starving because of the ritual of mantras that he uses to keep us from making our living. Where can we go? That Brahmin is the officiating priest in all the sacrifices. Therefore we brought this deficiency upon him: without a wife, a man is not fit to perform the rituals of sacrifice."

When he said the word "deficiency," referring to the Brahmin, the king became deeply depressed, thinking, "He is talking about the Brahmin's defi-ciency, but truly I am the one that he censures. And that excellent sage also said that I did not deserve the water for a guest. Since the ogre, too, spoke to me about the deficiency of that Brahmin, I must really be in a very tight spot as a result of not having a wife." As the king was thinking these thoughts, the ogre spoke to him again, bowing low to the king and cupping his hands in reverence: "Your majesty, do me the favour of giving me a command as I bow before you, your servant who lives in your realm." The king said, "Night-wanderer, since you did say, 'We eat the very nature. . . . ' , listen to what we would like you to do. Eat the evil nature of this Brahmin lady, right now. When you have eaten her evil nature, she may become nice. Then take her to the house of the man whose wife she is. When this is done, you will have done all that can be done for me as one who has come to your house."

Thereupon, by the king's command, the ogre used his own power of illusion to enter inside the woman and eat her evil nature. And when he had stripped the Brahmin's wife of her extremely fierce evil nature, she said to the king, "By the ripening of the fruits of my own karma, I was separated from my noble husband; this night-wanderer was merely the proximate cause of that. The fault was not his, nor that of my noble husband; the fault is mine, no one else's; one eats the fruit of what one has done oneself. In another life, I separated myself from some man; and that separation has now fallen upon me; what fault could there be in my noble husband?"

The ogre said, "My lord, I will take her to her husband's house, as you command. But command me to do whatever else can be done for you, your majesty." The king said, "When this is done, you have done everything for me, heroic night-wanderer. But come to me whenever I think of you, when the time comes for something to be done." "Yes!" said the ogre, and then he took the Brahmin's wife—who was purified and without her evil nature—and brought her quickly to her husband's house.

Now, when the king had sent the woman to her husband's house, he sighed and thought, "What good deed could there be in this? The noble sage said that I was wretched because I was unfit for the offering of water to a guest, and this night-wanderer spoke of deficiency, referring to the Brahmin. I abandoned my wife. How shall I act? I shall ask that incomparable sage, who has the eye of knowledge." Reasoning in this way, the king mounted his chariot and went to the dwelling of the great sage—the soul of *dharma*, knower of past, present and future. He dismounted from his chariot, approached the sage, bowed to him, and told him what had happened to him: how he had met the ogre, and seen the Brahmin woman, and how her evil nature had vanished, and how he had sent her to her husband's house, and the reason for his own return.

The sage said, "I already knew what you had done, your majesty, and your reason for coming back to me with an aching heart: you came to ask me, 'What am I to do about this?' Now that you have come, your majesty, listen to what you must do. A wife is a powerful cause of *dharma*, profit, and pleasure for men; in particular, a man who abandons a wife is abandoned by *dharma*. A man who has no wife, your majesty, is not fit to perform the obligatory rituals, whether he is a Brahmin, a Kshatriya, a Vaishya, or a Shudra. When you abandoned your wife, you didn't do a very good thing; for just as women should not abandon a husband, so too men should not abandon a wife."

The king said, "Sir, what shall I *do*? This was the ripening of my karmas, that made me abandon her because she was not affectionate to me when I was affectionate toward her. Whatever one does one endures with an aching heart and an inner soul that fears separation. But she was abandoned in the forest, and now I do not know where she has gone. Maybe she was eaten in the forest by lions or tigers or night-wandering ogres."

The sage said, "She has not been eaten, your majesty, by lions or tigers or night-wandering ogres. She is now in the subterranean watery world, but there is still no stain on her character." The king said, "Who took her to the subterranean world? And how did she come to remain unstained? This is most marvellous, Brahmin; you must tell me how it happened."

The sage said, "In the subterranean world there is a Naga king, the famous Kapotaka. He saw her when you had abandoned her and she was wandering around in the great forest. And since the young woman has both beauty and good character, he fell in love with her, declared his intentions to her, and carried her to the subterranean world. Now, the wise Naga king has a beautiful daughter named Nanda, your majesty; and he also has a charming wife. When the daughter saw your queen, more beautiful than her mother, she thought, 'This woman will become the rival co-wife of my mother,' and so she brought her to her own house and hid her in the inner apartments of the women there.

But when Nanda was asked (for the queen), she refused to give any answer; and so her father said to his daughter, 'You will become mute.' The daughter remained there, under this curse; and your wife, that was carried off by the Naga king, is still kept there by his daughter, and is still chaste."

The king, rejoicing, asked that outstanding Brahmin the cause of his own bad luck with regard to the woman he loved: "Sir," said the king, "everyone likes me very much, but my own wife is not very fond of me; what is the cause of this? I long for her excessively, even more than for my own vital breath, great sage; but she is badly disposed toward me. Tell me the reason for that, Brahmin." The sage said, "At the moment when you took her hand in the marriage ceremony, the sun, Mars, and Saturn looked down on you, and Venus and Jupiter looked down on your wife. At that moment, the moon was for you, and Mercury, the son of the moon, was for her. These two groups are inimical to one another, and very inimical to you, your majesty. Now, go and protect the earth according to your own *dharma*; with your wife as your assistant, perform all the rituals of *dharma*." When King Uttama heard this, he bowed to the sage, mounted his chariot, and went back to his own city. When he arrived at his own city, the king saw the Brahmin, now joyously united with his wife, who now had a good character. The Brahmin said, "Best of kings, I have achieved my aims, since you who know *dharma* have protected *dharma* and brought my wife back to me." The king said, "You have indeed achieved your aims, incomparable Brahmin, by protecting your own *dharma*. But we are in a tight spot, since we do not have a wife in the house." "Great king," said the Brahmin, "if she has been devoured by beasts of prey in the forest, you should not disregard *dharma* by allowing anger to overpower you. Enough of her; why don't you take the hand of another woman in marriage, your majesty? There are beautiful maidens in the houses of kings." The king said, "The woman I love was not eaten by beasts of prey; she is alive, and her character is still unstained. How shall I act in this matter?"

The Brahmin said, "If your wife is alive and has not gone astray in her virtue, why do you ruin your whole life by living without a wife?" The king said, "Because even if I brought her back, she is always unpleasant to me; she causes me misery, not happiness. Enough of her! She is no friend of mine. Whatever you did, Brahmin, to gain power over your beautiful wife, make the same effort to give me power over my wife." The Brahmin said, "There is a ritual called 'the desire of a lover' that will make her fond of you, and I will also perform the ritual of 'finding a friend,' which people use when they want friends. For it produces fondness between two people who are not fond of one another, and it generates the greatest affection between a wife and husband. I will do that sacrifice for you, your majesty. Wherever your lovely wife is, bring her here from there; she will become extremely fond of you, your majesty." When he heard this, the king collected all the things needed for the ritual, and the Brahmin performed the sacrifice. Seven times the Brahmin performed that sacrifice, again and again, in order to give the king his wife. And when the great Brahmin sage thought that he had made her friendly to her own husband, he said to the king, "Bring here, close to you, the woman you long for, your majesty. Enjoy all pleasures with her, and perform the sacrifices with reverence."

The king was amazed at the Brahmin's words, and then he remembered that most virile night-wanderer, who kept his promises. As soon as he thought of him, he came to the king immediately, bowed to him, and said, "What can I do for you?" Then the king told him, at great length; and the ogre went to the subterranean world, took the king's wife, and returned. As soon as she was brought back, she looked upon her husband with ecstatic joy and said, "Forgive me," over and over, overflowing with happiness. The king embraced her violently and said to the proud woman, "My darling, I *do* forgive you. Why do you keep saying that?" His wife said, "If your heart has truly forgiven me, then I want to ask you for a favour; do it to honour me." The king said, "Speak without hesitation and tell me what you desire from me. There is nothing you cannot get from me, my darling; I am entirely at your disposal."

His wife said, "My friend, the daughter of the Naga, was cursed by him for my sake: 'You will be mute,' he said, and she became mute. If, out of your fondness for me, you are able to find a cure for her and to remove the impediment to her speech, then there is nothing that you will not have done for me." The king said to the Brahmin, "What ritual is there for this, to dispel her muteness?" The Brahmin replied to the king, "Your majesty, I will perform a sacrifice to Sarasvati, the goddess of speech, by your command; and your wife here will pay her debt by restoring her friend's speech." Then that excellent Brahmin performed the sacrifice to Sarasvati on her behalf, muttering all the verses to Sarasvati with deep concentration.

In the underworld the girl regained her speech, and a sage there, named Garga, said to her, "This very difficult favour was done for you by your friend's husband." When she learned this, Nanda the Naga's daughter went quickly to the city and embraced the queen, her friend, and praised the king over and over again with sweet and auspicious words. Then the Naga woman sat down and said, "Great hero, you have just done me a favour, and so my heart goes out to you. Listen to what I say. You will have a son of great heroism; he will wield an unchallenged wheel of power upon the earth. He will truly know all the Shastras on politics and will be intent upon the practice of *dharma*; he will be a Manu, the wise ruler of this interval of Manu." And when she had given him this boon, the daughter of the Naga king embraced her friend again and went back to the underworld.

The noble king made love to his wife for a very long time, while he continued to rule his subjects, and then she bore him a son, like the lovely full-orbed moon that is born on full-moon day. When he was born, all the people rejoiced, together with the gods; the drums of heaven roared, and showers of flowers fell from heaven. Seeing that his form and character would be lovely, all the assembled sages called him Auttama ("The best"), saying, "The boy was born in the family of Uttama ('Supreme'), and he was born at the best time, and he has the best limbs; so he will be 'The Best.'" And so Uttama's son became famous under the name of Auttama; he was a Manu, with the power of a Manu.

Whoever listens constantly to the story of Uttama and to the life of Uttama will never be hated by the wives he loves or by his sons or relatives; nor will anyone who hears or recites this story ever experience separation from anyone.

[Markandeya Purāna, The Karma of Marriage: The King's Wife, the Brahmin's Wife, and the Ogre, in *Textual Sources for the Study of Hinduism*, ed. and trans. Wendy Doniger O'Flaherty (Totowa, NJ: Barnes and Noble, 1988), pp. 106–114]

A CONTEMPORARY HINDU MARRIAGE CEREMONY

The next selection is taken from a contemporary source that reflects the theology, social practices, and rituals among middle-class and upper-caste Hindus in north India. It is an example of a number of books and pamphlets written in English to instruct families—especially families living abroad where access to priests may be more intermittent and links to "home" traditions in India may be one or two generations removed—on the attitudes and procedures that should be followed in keeping with the Hindu tradition, broadly defined. This selection provides a moment-by-moment discussion of both the ritual aspects and the moods and responses that are appropriate for various members of the wedding party. It is important to keep in mind that many marriage practices reflect particular communities, regions, and language traditions. Because marriage is always local, an example from a particular tradition within the vast spectrum of Hinduism—in this selection, the Arya Samaj community—will give a better sense of what actually takes place that an attempt to construct a generalized summary. It is common practice among Hindus to refer to the bride and groom as the "girl" and "boy."

Document 4–7

HINDU MARRIAGE CEREMONY ACCORDING TO THE
ARYA SAMAJ TRADITION

Hindus strongly believe in the concept that the marriages are a continuation of a relationship between the two persons from previous births, between the two families that are expected to interact, develop the bondage and fulfill their responsibilities towards their parents and ancestors, by continuing the natural process of procreation, caring for their offspring, and continuing God's creation.

In spite of such an inherited preaching and belief, families on both sides, the boy's and the girl's, engage in the karma of selecting a suitable match for their child and their family. This effort involves the whole clan on both sides. Clan means the living adults, maternal and paternal grandparents (and great grandparents, if living), uncles, aunts, brothers, sister, brothers-in-law, and sister-in-law.

Making a Suitable Choice

The first step is taken by the parents of the girl or boy to discuss with their elders, to seek their blessings and to investigate and try to arrange the marriage of the grown up boy or girl. At this stage, the elders may suggest certain families that they know and consider suitable to establish the future relationship/kinship. Then the parents of the future bride/groom explore the availability of any suitable young person in any of those families. Suitability means age, health, height, education, behavior personality, character within the family and the society at large. Emphasis is placed upon the family heritage above all these factors. If no suitable person is located within those families, then they search for other families through the sources of friends, relatives, etc. Science of genetics was very well known, understood and practiced by Hindus from the ancient times of Vedas, as taught under Ayurveda. Breeders of thoroughbred horses are proud to raise them with their known hereditary traits. They try their best to produce future offspring with the desired inherited traits and then encourage growth and development of the same in the new generation. They thoroughly check the pedigree and pay a high price for it. Very little attention is given to these factors when it gets to selection of a mate for human beings in the "modern" time! Contact and the selection process takes the help of newspaper advertisements (with very little investigation of inheritance) and short and limited social contacts in school or club or on dance floors. Many times parents or other elders of the family are involved only as guests at the marriage ceremony with very little or silent participation or as a showpiece.

At the second step, while exploring different avenues, the parents of the boy and girl consult the boy and the girl as to their feelings and expectations. Maybe because of coeducation or other social opportunities, the girl or the boy may have thought of someone else to be their spouse. Parents, usually, are inclined to consider the situation favourably unless there is something that they feel is absolutely undesirable.

The third step, after initial consideration on either side, is that the parents seek help from some go-between relative or a friend who acts as a confidant to feel out the other side. If the response is encouraging, then the first step is taken by the father of the girl, to meet the father of the boy with the help of the same friend and present a proposal. If the boy's parents have already investigated on their own about the family of the girl, the father of the boy accepts the proposal subject to the condition that both sides should discuss it with the boy and girl and then make a commitment. Besides this, it is helpful to let an astrologer look into the horoscopes of the boy and the girl to check about the possible effects of the marriage. As a formal affair, the members of the boy's family and as many relative as they may like to involve visit the girl's home to get to know each other and also to have an opportunity to let the boy and the girl discuss with each other their own expectations and evaluate each other. This visit may take a few hours or a whole day. If everything goes well and both families develop a feeling of mutual agreement, the boy's mother puts a gold necklace around the neck of the girl. This necklace is usually old, previously used by the mother. This ceremony is also known as Vāg Dāna, a firm commitment by the boy's family to the family of the girl.

Except in big cities, marriages are normally planned at a reasonable distance (maybe fifty to one hundred miles) between the two families for several reasons like:

1. Families consider all girls of the town as their own daughters and the girls are respected and cared for as such. Old tradition families still treat them the same way.

2. Sociologically and psychologically, boys and girls grow up as brothers and sisters within the community and not as girl/boy friend. This reduces chances of abuse or other unwanted behavior patterns like unwed parenthood.

3. When the girl marries, she is not dependent upon her mother and other relatives, detachment of apron strings does happen.

4. Old traditions still prevail. According to these traditions, biological parents of the girl normally do not eat or drink in the town in which the girl is married. This automatically disciplines the attitude of detachment of the girl's parents and discourages any attempt to influence the girl's new family and directly or indirectly benefiting from it.

Engagement

The fourth step is more formal and it marks the beginning of the religious ceremonies, the day and time for which is usually fixed and planned by the religious priests on both sides, using the astrological signs. A priest, the father of the girl, an elder person of the community of the girl's side, and an elder brother of the girl, and sometimes a few friends, go to the boy's parents' home. There they are received with the appropriate mannerisms. From the boy's side, a priest, an elder person of the community, the father, and other adult men of the family are usually present for the occasion in the reception room. Of special notice at this time is the fact that they all sit on the floor, like any other religious ceremony. The girl's eldest brother does tilak [marking the forehead with red colored powder] to the boy—presenting a gold ring or some other ornament like a chain, a suit consisting of five or seven clothes, and some gifts for the family of the boy. The boy acknowledges and reciprocates in the same manner by doing tilak to his future brother-in-law and gives him a suit of five or seven clothes. The boy's father presents five dresses for the girl, a set of ornaments, a set of cosmetics, and a few gifts for the girl's siblings and other younger children within the family or friends, and some sweets for distribution in the community of the girl's home. The giving of a set of cosmetics by the parents of the boy is literally a permission to learn the proper use of cosmetics for her future married life. This set has to have mehandi (dried green leaves in ground form), scented oil, kājal [lamp-black], comb, hairbrush, etc. All of these are an important part of the set. Also, there are a few glass bangles of different colors, except black and blue.

During this entire ceremony, religious mantras are chanted by the priests, and some humorous songs full of blessing are sung by the group of females who usually sit separately from the men. At this time, a suitable auspicious date for marriage is figured out by the two priests and agreed to by both sets of parents.

Invitation for Marriage

The girl's parents send a formal invitation, hand written in a religious form by their priest, to the parents of the boy, to come and wed their daughter on the fixed date and time. This invitation usually lists the genealogy of the girl's side, going back at least four generations on the paternal and maternal side. Also, the genealogy of the boy likewise is described. This is to strengthen the point that the girl and the boy, both, are from well-established, unblemished families, socially or religiously, by any acts and they are supported by their extended families.

Invitation to the Maternal Grandparents of the Boy/Girl

Mothers of the boy and girl, accompanied by their husband, go to their parents' homes to invite them to participate in the marriage of their grandson/grand-daughter. On this occasion, the mother takes a few gifts for the younger children—a dry coconut, a supārī (a whole betel nut), some sweets, and a dress for each of the younger children in the family. Upon acceptance of the invitation, the eldest male member of the family, accepts all of the gifts or a few of them, especially the supārī, the coconut, and a tilak from their son-in-law and the daughter. [The] [e]ldest male member from the maternal grand parents' recip-rocates with tilak (along with some gifts of cash and clothes) to their son-in-law and daughter. Maṅgalagāna may be set up for the evening at their home, where ladies and children of the community are invited, and sweets are distributed.

Other Religious Ceremonies of the Marriage

In both of the homes, religious ceremonies are initiated about five days prior to the date of the marriage. One of the important events is maṅgalagāna. This is done by the ladies of the community in the evening and early part of the night. Maṅgalagāna includes music, playing of music, playing of musical in-struments, dances, skits, and a distribution of sweets at the end. This may con-tinue for all five days.

Ganeśa and Navagraha Pūjā [Worship]

Parents in both homes perform this pūjā for the blessings of Ganeśa and nine planets for fulfillment of the project with peace and without any obstacle.

Gaṅgā/Well Pūjana

At both homes, the mothers, accompanied by other women, the girls of the family, and maybe a few close friends go to the nearby river or the village well to fetch a pitcher or earthen pot full of water from there. [The] [m]other of the boy/girl carries the pitcher on her head. They go in procession, singing prayer songs in chorus. The priest or the wife of the priest accompanies them for the pūjā of the river or well. After the pūjā, the pitcher is filled with water and brought home to give a sacred bath to the boy or girl. This ceremony has two significant purposes. One is to strengthen feelings of importance of water in life and its sanctity (that no one may ever try to pollute the wells and rivers), and the other demonstrates the physical and spiritual cleansing of the boy or girl. The boy and the girl are given a massage and helped to clean their bodies by using a mixture of curd, powered sarson (yellow mustard), coconut or coconut oil, turmeric powder, chandan [sandalwood] saw dust, and gram flour. The women sing maṅgalagāna. After the bath, there is another ceremony called tel-charhana and tel-utarna to ward off evil spirits.

Reception of the Maternal Uncle and His Family at the Home of the Bride and Groom

This is another very important occasion. The parents of the boy or girl make arrangements at one of their friend's house for the maternal uncle and his family's short stay to relax, change clothes, etc., after a long journey. The host friend normally serves light refreshments to the guests. Then the mother of the girl or boy, accompanied by the father and other women and children of the family, go to that house to formally receive the family and bring them home in a procession while they continually sing welcoming songs. At home each one of the members of the family steps on a chowki [low stool]. Each takes a turn beginning with the eldest male member and his spouse. Other members of the family follow according to seniority of age or relationship. Each one is given a tilak by the mother and father of the boy or girl. The eldest male members give cash and other gifts from the maternal grandparents' family, to the mother and father of the boy or girl. This is called "Bhāta" from them. The amount of the cash and gifts varies greatly, depending upon the financial strength of the family, and perhaps the needs of the parents of the boy or girl on this great and expensive occasion.

Minimum essential constituents of Bhāta from the maternal uncle are clothes for the sister, brother-in-law, groom/bride. They are expected to wear these clothes during the marriage ceremony. Other items considered minimum essential for their auspiciousness are:

In case of the girl's marriage, *nath* (nose ring) and *tīkā* (ornament for the forehead) made of gold, anklet and *bicwas* (toe rings made of silver). Giving of *nath* signifies testimony by the maternal uncle to the fact that the girl is virgin and of sound character; *tīkā* signifies that she will uphold the good example set by her mother in her family (for the honour of her biological parents) and the extended family in the future; anklets and *bichwas* as a blessing for her future long-lived married life and a reminder to the girl that she has to observe the Sīmā-Bandhana of both families' tradition.

Normally a set of kitchen utensils and a bedroom set are also given by the maternal uncle. Gift giving varies in different communities and according to socio-economic condition of the two families. Under no circumstance this should cause any financial hardship for the sake of compliance to certain customs.

Usually the maternal uncle is given the active responsibility of looking after the *bhandāra* (a storage place for all the sweets in the case of the girl's side) and the handling of the money for all purposes, on different occasions. Often the maternal uncle is called Bhandari (treasurer). This was a very important role when all sweets were cooked by the professional cooks at the home of the girl and kept in the storage for a number of days (four to five). None of these sweets were eaten by any member of the family until the girl had been married and sent to her new home. In those days, actual cash was used for all transactions.

Kaṇgana Bandhana

Kaṇgana (amulet) is made of handspun and hand-dyed yarn, including many different colors except black and blue, with a number of attached items such as an iron ring, a supari, a conch-shaped sea shell, a copper ring, a whole turmeric, and mustard seeds on a red piece of cloth for tying around the wrist. This is usually done a day before the departure for the marriage ceremony at both of the homes. In addition Navagraha pūjā is performed. Both the boy and girl are kept at home after this, until the boy departs for the girl's home, and the girl is married.

Sehrā Bandhi and Ghur Charhi

This particular ceremony is done only at the boy's home. In the presence of all the members of the family, relatives and friends, the groom takes a vow that he has in the past always lived up to the traditions of the family and in the future will represent the cultural heritage of the family and the society. The priest of the family or the eldest male member of the family bestows his blessings and acts as sākṣī [witness] for the groom and the family by putting the turban (symbol of respect and honor) on the head of the groom and tying the sehrā [garland] on the turban. The groom, dressed up for marriage, rides on a well-decorated horse, escorted by two people carrying *ballama*s [mace or spear] and a man behind the horse carrying a big umbrella, followed by quite a few family members. On the way, women continue singing maṇgalagān in chorus. In the front all along the procession there is normally a big band playing. The boy and the party go to the nearest temple for worship. The procession ends at the home of a friend, or wherever the parents have planned for the overnight stay of the groom, if the marriage party is to depart the next day. Otherwise, from the temple, the party departs for the girl's home. Along with the groom, a young boy, usually from the maternal uncle's side, is made "sarbālā," (Vināyaka) a close associate of the groom. He too is dressed like the groom.

Sisters-in-law (bhābhies) put kājala in the eyes of the groom for cosmetic reasons, and to ward off the evil spirits, and as a sākṣī to the behavior of the groom towards the female members of the family. The groom seeks their blessings by touching their feet and giving each of them some ornament as a gift. Sister[s] of the groom tie or braid the long mane of the horse and feed the horse with pre-soaked gram dal. As a ritual, the brothers-in-law escort the horse for a little while. Sisters of the groom and brothers-in-law are presented with cash or other gifts. On this occasion, also called Sehrā Bandī, relatives and friends give cash gifts (called shagun in northern India) to the boy and also his young associate.

Reception of the Groom's Marriage Party in the Home Town of the Bride

Depending upon the mode of transportation used by the groom's party, a reception group is arranged to meet the party where they enter the city. The party is then taken to a place where they can stay for the night (if it is an overnight stay) or to some suitable place where they can relax, change clothes, etc. At this place, light snacks are served. This part of the reception is led by an elder brother of the girl. A few close relatives and friends form the group for the reception into the town.

After the party has had enough time to relax, the girl's father, an elder person of the community, a few other relatives, and some friends with a priest, come to this place for a formal reception. The girl's father does tilak to the groom and presents some gifts. The father of the boy presents some jewellery sets, five or more dresses, a cosmetic set for the girl, and a few gifts for the children of the family. These, are given to the father of the girl. Jewellery given for the girl is called strī-dhana, or personal property of the girl. In a very rare and difficult situation she may part with these for the protection of the family. This is exempt from bankruptcy under Indian law. The role of the two priests continues as usual with chanting of mantras.

Reception of the Groom and his Party at the Bride's Home

The groom rides on a well-decorated horse just as he did in his own hometown, sometimes in a horse buggy, a convertible car or on an elephant led by a band, a party of musicians on a separate open truck, a group of nafiri players and whatever the family chooses for pomp and show, followed by other members of the party to the girl's home. This walk, in a procession, is usually limited to less than a mile. The children and adults dance in groups or in solo dances, stopping at times along the way. It may take two or three hours to cover this short distance. Adequate security measures are provided by the girl's family so that no unwanted person might cause any problems.

When the party reaches the girl's home, men from the bride's side stand in two rows to leave a passage in between for the marriage party. The father of the girl and other close relatives of the girl stand at the gate for reception of the party. It has become customary to recite a poem on behalf of the groom's party. This is done by the groom's brother-in-law, stating the genealogical inheritance of the boy, along with the blessings of ancestors and wishes from all the living relatives and friends on this occasion. This poem is called Seharā and is printed on a quality paper. A framed copy is presented to the girl's father. [The] [b]oy's brothers-in-law bring perfumed rose water in silver sprinklers to sprinkle on the relatives from both families on this occasion. The girl's side arranges enough garlands made of fresh flowers, so that at least one can be offered to each member of the immediate family and also other members of the groom's party. Boy's side also arranges for enough garlands that are offered to the immediate relatives of the girl individually in reciprocation at the time of *milni* (introduction of equivalent status relatives) on this occasion. A big garland is arranged for the bride. The girl's parents and other close relatives offer some cash or gifts to the corresponding relative in the groom's party. This cash or gift is called *milni*. Many times this is also given to the close friends of the groom's family, depending on their closeness to the family. Other members of the party are also given some gifts. Gift or cash given is simply a recognition of the relatives.

The mother of the bride, or the eldest sister-in-law in the absence of the mother, does arati [circular waving of a lighted lamp] of the groom at the entrance of the home. This location may be shifted if the marriage ceremony is to be performed at some other place than the home of the bride. The groom stands, without shoes on a chauki, which is placed in front of the rangoli, made with different colored cereals, flour, flowers, etc. No one steps on the rangoli. The woman who does the āratī [clockwise waving a lighted lamp] has to be a suhagin, having a living husband. This is probably more of a tradition rather than a religious dictate. Other women sing songs of welcome in a chorus. After the āratī, the bride steps forward, assisted by her friends and sisters to welcome the groom. She first offers water to wash his feet. Then she puts a big garland made of fresh flowers around the groom's neck. Reciprocating the reception by the bride, the groom also puts a garland around the neck of the bride. Usual worship-service mantras are recited by the priest of the girl's side. All of this ceremony is to pray and wish blessings from God for good relationship between the families of the girl and the boy.

The Marriage Dinner

After this ceremony, the groom's party is led to the *vivāha mandapa* (place where the actual marriage ceremony takes place). Many times the dinner is arranged before going to the *vivāha mandapa* for the marriage ceremony. In this case, they all go to the well-decorated dining area. It is a very formal dinner. In old days the dinner was arranged on the roof of the house of the girl and the party was seated on the floor in groups. All serving on the table is done by the close relatives and friends of the bride's side. The cooks and other personnel are usually kept outside the dining area. [The] [r]eason for this is mutual affection, respect, care, and joy amongst the two families and friends (boy's and girl's). Elders used to say that any type of food and service (from hired help) can be obtained at any place. The feeling of joy and feeding your guests can be there only when the hosts themselves serve their guests. After everyone has been served, no one starts eating until the groom does. The father of the boy receives two complete trays of dinner—one for dedication to the *devatās* (gods) and the other for the future daughter-in-law. He then puts some cash in the tray and sends it with his blessings to the bride. Money is usually distributed to the cooks or servants of the family, and the boy's father gives enough cash by way of tip. The tray is carried by anyone of the bride's brothers. This ceremony, and the giving of clothes, is a religious testimony of the resolve of the girl's parents-in-law, that they take full responsibility of her future needs. This religious ceremony is literally a pledge in the presence of the whole community from both sides and the total acceptance of the girl's healthful living in her new family.

After this ceremony, everyone starts eating. The bride's relatives and friends eat after the marriage party has finished eating and have gone to the vivāha mandapa. The bride's parents and grandparents, of course, remain on fast throughout the day and do not eat until the next morning or maybe not until the girl has left with the marriage party. This is for very special reasons:

i. The Kanyā Dāna ceremony, the most important yagna of their life, has to be performed without having eaten anything on that day.

ii. Lest anyone on either side or any poor person of the community may have gone hungry on that day.

The vivāha mandapa

At the mandapa, the priest of the girl's side and her parents receive the priest of the groom's side, the groom's parents, and the groom, in order to perform the ceremony. The groom sits on the right side of the two seats placed on the west side of the Havana Kunda (facing east) with his parents behind him. The priest of the girl's side sits on the south side facing north, and the boy's priest sits on the east side facing west. The girl's parents sit on the north side facing south. In this seating arrangement, the father of the girl is sitting closest to her because he will play an active part in the ceremony. To his left or right sits the mother as his partner in the ceremony. The bride is escorted by her maternal uncle and elder brother to the mandapa. She takes her seat on the left of her future husband. Depending upon their educational upbringing, different scholars may have different seating arrangements. The maternal uncle sits just behind the girl. The girl's sisters and friends usually sit close to the bride and often play little jokes, like hiding the shoes of the groom.

Ganapati, Navagraha and Jala Pūjana

Like any other activity or religious ceremony, Ganapati, and Navagraha pūjana are an essential part of this yagna. Both priests and parents actively participate in this ceremony so that the following yagna may have the blessing of all grahas and the Ganapati and be completed without any mishap or obstacle. Besides, Jala pūjana is another part of this ceremony. This is for two reasons:

i. The water is the most important part of life and its sanctity should be observed.

ii. If for any reason any mishap takes place due to the yagna fire, it could be used to save the situation. Pitchers full of water with a coconut on top are kept in the four corners of the mandapa.

Jala (Water) Presentation to the Groom

The bride presents a small pitcher of water *(lotā)* to the groom to wash his feet and hands to make him feel relaxed. This is a common custom to be observed in every household when the husband returns home from work in the evening or any guest comes from a distance, and the lady of the house or the eldest member or host presents jala to the guest. For the same reason, Hindus are expected to wash their feet and hands before they enter the temple for worship service or eat in the kitchen.

Nāma Parivartana and Yagnopavīta Dhārana

If the bride/groom have not had *Yagnopavīta-dhārana* [*upanāyana*, sacred thread ceremony] earlier or are not wearing at this time, Yagnopavīta-dhārana should be done at this time. Besides the boy's parents should give a new name to the girl. This is the name she is known by in the future.

Yagnopavīta is worn by those who are known as twice-born, one physical natural birth and the other initiation by the teacher priest for education and learning about Self and God (omnipresent in Self). Before marriage a person wears six-threaded yagnopavīta and three-threaded after the marriage. Both husband and wife are to wear three-threaded, viz., two parts of the six-threaded yagnopavīta. After marriage they both share being jointly responsible for the religious vows. The three threads of the yagnopavīta are an indicator of link of continuity between the past, present and the future. The person takes a vow to learn from the samskrtika [refined] experiences of the past, live according to those in the present and be a guardian trustee of the same for the future generations. The three threads united by a knot at one spot indicate the unity of heart, mind *(citta)* and spirit *(manas —* soul) residing in the living person, who wears the sacred thread to remind him of his purpose in life on this earth and what has been learnt by him in the past.

Hātha Pīley Karanā

This samskāra is performed by the parents of the bride. Mild paste (liquid form) of turmeric powder is applied on both the palms and forefingers of the bride before Kanyā Dāna and Pāni Grahana Samskāra. This is important for the following reasons based on chemistry and medicinal values of turmeric:

1. All activities performed by the bride and with her inspirational strengths by her husband be immune from all infections, in the life of the couple.

2. All actions of the couple may be soothing and healing in their effects on any emotional or physical injuries caused in their family and social environment.

3. Yellow color of the turmeric is affected by its place amongst other natural colors of the rainbow—red and orange on one side and green and blue on the other. Red influences with its aggressive tendencies; orange with the inspiration for sacrifice; green for productivity and growth; and blue for its calmness. Such influences of both families are transmitted to form one yellow in the couple.

4. Couple's life may be peaceful and harmonious. Incidentally yellow ribbons are used in the West for similar reasons.

5. Family life may be prosperous and pleasant to all like the flowers of Sarson (Mustard) in spring season.

Kanyā Dāna and Pāni Grahana

This is the most important part of the whole ceremony. The parents of the bride jointly give the greatest of their well-nurtured daughter to the family of the groom through the matrimonial alliance with the groom. This is considered the greatest dāna (gift-cum-donation) in one's life for fulfillment of God's purpose in every living being. Any couple who does not have a daughter of their own, usually adopts a daughter from some other relative or anyone outside for the performance of this dāna . The word Kanyā also has a great significance. This indicates that the parents have successfully nurtured their daughter as a virgin and to be loyal physically, emotionally, and spiritually to her spouse and the family. When a couple adopts another girl for this yagna in their life, they bind themselves morally and ethically to fulfill the responsibilities of being her god parents in their lifetime, and their other children do the same.

According to the Hindu beliefs, this yagna bestows upon the girl's family quite a few responsibilities for seven generations, by way of due courtesy, reverence, and economic and emotional support to the family of their daughter.

In this particular ceremony, dhāna (unhusked rice) is considered an important part of the ceremony. The parents of the bride fill the hands (coupe) of their daughter with dhāna and then give the hands of their daughter to the groom. According to Manu's Dharma Śāstra and Hindu beliefs, no religious ceremony can be performed without equal participation by the wife. Rāmacandra got a gold statue of Sītā to participate in the Aśvamedha Yagna [Vedic horse sacrifice] because Sītā was not physically available.

Dhāna is used for very many reasons. Just like the rice inside the dhāna, their daughter is totally unaffected by outside influences, has never thought of any other person, and will merge herself into the soil of the new family in order to flourish and give prosperity to the family. The parents have taken care of her as *dharohara* (trust) of the new family. Just like the rice plants are sown in one field, grow up like paddy plants, and before the time of their flourishing, are transplanted in a new field, similarly, this girl, born and raised through her tender age of childhood *(brahmacarya)* in one family, is becoming part of the new family where she will grow and flourish and be known in the future as part of her new family.

Both families are responsible for other important factors in this ceremony. First, the family of the bride is morally obligated to select the most suitable young man and family for their daughter. In so doing, they must give consideration to the health, education, height, weight, and social, emotional, and spiritual temperaments of their daughter, and find a family and a groom that would provide the most conducive environment for the future growth and prosperity of their daughter. Similarity of virtues between the boy and girl is of great consideration on both sides. Maharsi Dayānanda Sarasvatī has quoted Ṛg Veda for different characteristics in his *Samskara Vidhi*. They are age, family, place of origin, physique, behavioral characteristics, education, intelligence and future aspirations (P. 267–268); and according to *Satyārtha Prakāśa* by Maharsi [Dayananda] (P. 53–55) other considerations are chastity of boy/girl, unrelated to each other for six generations, and whether either family lacks good actions in life, people of good character, religious minded persons or characteristically have very long hair on the body (except head). [Those who suffer] from hemorrhoids or tuberculosis or emphysema, chronic cough or asthma or stomach problems or epilepsy and leprosy [should not be selected]. Besides, the girl should be of smaller physique in height and body build than the boy. The girl should also not be a blabbermouth type or with eyes like a cat. Suggested differential of age of the boy over the girl is sixteen to twenty-four years in *Satyārtha Prakāśa*.

In modern times, some of these considerations of medical history or age difference may be difficult to follow. Thus, today an age-gap of two to five years is considered reasonable. Similarly, there could be an educational gap up to five classes. For instance, if a boy is a post-graduate and the girl he chooses to marry has completed eleven or twelve years of her education, it is considered all right. In the same way, one should do what is feasible in today's context in respect of checking of medical history and similarity between the professional-social-economic backgrounds of the boy's and girl's families. If for any reasons, these considerations or overlooked, the giving of a daughter to an undesirable family is considered "Kanyā haran" that is, the killing of the girl, the greatest sin a person could commit.

In the same ceremony, *jala* [sacred water] is poured by the parents of the bride, through the hands of their daughter into the hands of the groom, indicating the merging of Jamunā into Gaṇgā, to become a bigger Gaṇgā, and that the parents will be supportive of the new family and be a hidden part of the growth of the new family, just as water loses its own form and shape to provide nurturance to the living beings and flows through the arteries without creating new arteries or pathways. Lack of due diligence or intentional overlooking of the truths of the situation, can result in the destruction of the new family within three generations. *Mahābhārata* is an evidence of this. Satyavatī's children could not continue their progeny, and the family of Śāntanu vanished from this earth with the death of Bhīṣma.

The family of the groom and the groom are similarly under great obligation and moral and religious responsibility to give similar consideration to all the factors in accepting a kanyā in dāna. They should not be so carried away by greed or other ulterior motives or any consideration whatsoever providing [a] suitable environment to the girl for her entire life. If they knowingly do something undesirable, they cannot expect their family to flourish by making the new member part of their family. A person who accepts any kind of help, dāna, to the best of his knowledge, ability, and judgment should be deserving of it.

The bride's parents, at this time, give jewellery, gifts, and a cow through their daughter to the new family. They give according to the best of their socio-economic ability and their personal desires. The groom's parents, on the other hand, should not accept these gifts with any feelings or judgments according to their own expectations. They should accept whatever is given with utmost regard for and gratitude to the family of the girl and with thanksgiving to God. If, according to their feelings or considerations, they feel that the bride's parents could have done better or should have done better, that feeling should be set aside in thoughts and actions. They should never do anything that puts the girl's parents to any test or hardship. Dāna has to be at the goodwill of the donor and not according to the wishes of the donee.

After Kanyā dāna, the responsibility of the girl's parents is over. The maternal uncle of the girl, paternal uncles and brothers take over the responsibility of active participation in the rest of the ceremonies that follow Kanyā Dāna.

According to Ŗg Veda, book X, section 85 describing Sūryā Vivāha, Panikkar, *The Vedic Experience*, pp. 256–257, interprets as follows:

> I take your hand in mine for happiness,
> that you may reach old age with me as husband.
> Bhaga, Savitar, Aryaman, Purandhi,
> have given you to be my household's mistress. [10.85.36]
> Dwell in this home; never be parted!
> Enjoy the full duration of your days,
> with sons and grandsons playing to the end,
> rejoicing in your home to your heart's content. [10.85.42]
> To you they bring, first, in bridal procession
> this Sūryā, guiding her steps in circles.
> Return her now, O Agni, to her husband
> as rightful wife, and grant to her children. [10.85.38]
> Agni has now returned the bride
> endowed with splendors and length of life.
> May she live a lengthy span of days
> and may her husband live a hundred autumns! [10.85.39]
> May Prājāpati grant to us an issue,
> Aryaman keep us till death in holy marriage!
> Free from ill omens, enter the home of your husband
> Bring blessings to both humans and cattle. [10.85.43]
> Bless now this bride, O bounteous Lord,
> cheering her heart with the gift of brave sons.
> Grant her ten sons; her husband make the eleventh. [10.85.45]
> May all the divine Powers together with the Waters
> join our two hearts in one! May the Messenger,
> the Creator, and Holy Obedience unite us! [10.85.47]

Maṅgala Pherā

This ceremony consists of going around the fire. Havana Agni, four, five, or seven times. This varies according to local customs and the educational background of the priest who performs the ceremony. Four times around the fire is considered a minimum. Both the groom and the bride express the feelings that they are taking all the vows with [a] pure heart and soul participating in all parts of the ceremony with complete understanding of the meanings, responsibilities, and self-dedication for the rest of their lives. Yagna Agni is the witness to the whole ceremony. Going around the Agni four times is a reminder of the four stages of life—as taught and initiated by Manu of the Sanātana Samāja of India. These four stages are Brahmacarya (Celibate student life), Gṛhastha (Married life), Vānaprastha (Learning, self-study and preparation for Samnyāsa), and Samnyāsa (Renounced for service to mankind and worship of God).

According to Manohar and Kamalā Rathi, in Rājāsthan, seven mangala pherās are performed. First three pherās are on behalf of the maternal grandparents—specifically performed with the assistance and dedication by the maternal uncle of the girl. By doing so he vouches for the family and the virtues of the girl.

With the first circle around the fire, the bride and groom both convey that they have completed their first stage of life (from birth through the date of marriage—it used to be twenty-five years) with total celibacy, dedication to Sarasvatī, goddess of learning, having learned whatever they could to the best of their potentials and capabilities, and are now grown up to step into the second, third, and fourth stages of human life. Each of these stages was expected to last twenty-five years. This is why Vedika mantras say, one hundred years of life to continue the trust and responsibilities bestowed upon them by God, society, teachers, and their parents and repay the three debts (mas), Deva (God's) Ṛna, Ṛsi (Teacher's) Ṛna, and Pitṛ (Parent's) Ṛna.

In the first three mangala pherās, the girl leads the boy which signifies that women are more mature and grown up emotionally and physically, are capable of making greater sacrifices, and have put in more efforts to learn the responsibilities of the future family life, adjust to the new family (not just with the groom), to keep harmony among all, to bear and raise children, and to learn the family traditions including the following: internal management within the means of the family's earning ability, interpersonal relationships, and hosting the friends and guests. She also must learn the subtle ways of introducing modifications and improvements, if they are proven desirable and the new family is willing to accept them. In the family life she must keep the balance and harmony between the different temperaments of the members of the family.

The groom, on the other hand, has had little or lesser need to learn as much about the family environment because most of his responsibilities relate to being the major breadwinner and being in-charge of the external affairs. At home, the responsibilities are shared by other female members. The mother-in-law plays an important role in the education of the new family member.

The second phase of life, the Gṛhastha, is probably of greater importance because this involves many complex tasks, including, and not limited to, those in the following list:

i. Have mutual intimate relationships with due regard to the purpose of procreation and continuity of God's creation and the family progeny as the primary objective, and pleasure and fulfillment of physical needs as secondary;

ii. Care and nurturance of the future generation;

iii. Provide healthful living for the entire family;

iv. Enact responsibilities towards the elders, same-age relatives, and the younger relatives.

v. Manage finances so that needs and desires do not cause stress for the husband and other family members;

vi. Make the home a home—a place of warmth, respect, love, affection, a safe haven where all the family members and guests belong and feel loved; and

vii. Learn and live the life of trusteeship of God-gifted capabilities given to the couple and the family.

The list of such responsibilities goes on and on. All of these responsibilities belong more to the girl because the female sex is more capable of such big undertakings and adjustments. The life expectancy of the second phase of life is also twenty-five years and the girl leads the second mangala pherā.

The third phase of life, the Vānaprastha, is also of great importance and responsibility for both because this involves discipline of the mind and a growing desire to renounce worldly belongings and desires and transmit the trust holdings of cultural and physical manifestations to the future generation. The bride has the most difficult task in this phase because of her greater attachment to the family's internal affairs for the previous twenty-five years. She also has to be a strong support to her spouse and cater to his needs and lifelong habits. This [is] more stressful for the bride, and this is why the bride leads the third mangala pherā. Adjustment to the new environment and to the discipline should lead to the fourth stage of Samnyāsa.

The fourth mangala pherā signifies the period of samnyāsa, when the husband plays the leading role as a preacher for the society. The groom is expected to have acquired the required strength, emotionally and physically, to renounce attachment to all worldly possessions in order to undertake the difficult task of dedication to the society. He leads the fourth mangala pherā.

During the whole ceremony of the mangala pherā, the couple needs to concentrate on the physical, psychological, and spiritual feelings of the God-gifted life. These are strengthened by the chanting and recitation of Vedika mantras by the priest and the couple. They are given explanations of the mantras and reminded of the four basic principles of life that should continue to govern all their activities and thought processes. They are as follows:

Dharma: Leading a life with trust, sincerity, honesty, discipline, and the feeling of being a trustee of God-gifted talents and capabilities as a human being and with due reverence for the culture evolved by the society.

Artha: Earning their livelihood for the family by truthful and honest means with utmost care and reverence for maintenance of balance between the domains of motherhood and the social obligations, greater responsibility is on the groom to earn honestly and on the bride to manage within financial means without causing stress for the husband and the family.

Kāma: Pleasure. Desire to seek pleasure in life as heavenly a bliss inspires activity in life. Activity is a characteristic sign of all living beings. These activities may be Sāttvika [purity], Rājasa [energy] or Tāmasa [inertia], depending upon the prakrti of the living organism engaged in that activity. Any action goes through three stages: mana, vacana and actual karma (thought, verbal expression, and the activity for implementation of the thought). At all three stages, full attention should be paid to the intentions of self, perceptions of the society and others affected by the karma, and the effects on the society. A great sense of self-discipline is of utmost importance. It is a misnomer that we have "a personal, a private" life. That is negation of the basic principle of existence of God's creation and His omnipresence. The life of every individual is and should be an open book for the society to read.

Mokṣa: Renunciation, a feeling of trusteeship of the capabilities to perform the act, and keeping selfish interests away from the activities of life. This leads to Nirvāna, freedom from the cycles of physical birth and death in the life after death.

The couple promises to each other, to the great Sākṣi of yagna fire, their parents, the families on both sides and the society at large that they will, at all times, live life under the four well-founded and developed principles of life throughout the four stages of life. They will set an example for the younger generation and the society in the manner that is expected of them.

Māṇga Bharāī and Cunariyā

The groom puts *sindūra* [red colored powder] in the *māṇga* (a line of parting of hair on the head) of the bride indicating that she is suhāgin and his love and protection will always be with her. This protects her from other men for any of their desires. Use of Sindūra for māṇga and bindī has been described to have a scientific base for health reasons.

Cunriyā [shawl] is presented by the phūphā (paternal aunt's husband) of the groom, on behalf of the family, to the bride. This is a Sākṣī from the son-in-law of the groom's family, after having known the family for many years.

Saptapadī and Śilārohana Pūjana

This has different purposes—*pūjana* of different deities and goddesses and also to pledge that all seven days of the week, which are governed by the teachings of the seven Ṛṣis are different grahas and God's manifestations. The couple shall lead their life with their blessings according to the guiding principles set by them for those days. Every day of the week is influenced differently by *grahas*. Dietary control and behavioral attitudes are disciplined accordingly. An example would be to refrain from eating meat, eggs, onions or garlic on Tuesday, Ekādaśī, Amāvasyā, and Pūrnimā even by those who may normally be non-vegetarian. These are developed according to the understanding of the principles of healthful living and as perceived by different great teachers—ṛṣis and the society. As a symbolic gesture, seven steps are taken on a piece of rock which is moved with each step symbolizing steadfastness like rock. Brothers of the bride give emotional support by assisting the bride in this act. These two ceremonies may be done separately or in combination, according to the local customs and convictions of the priest. The reason that the bride goes through this ceremony is because she is the śakti (strength) behind her spouse. She is the one who has to play the most important role in her future, her spouse's and the family's future.

Another significant purpose of *saptapadī* ceremony is that the bride affirms the following seven feelings and promises, one with each step:

Hey Deva! Having been blessed by my good deeds in many previous lives, I got you as my Soubhāgya (husband).

I shall nurture all your relatives from infancy through old age. I shall be happily satisfied with whatever I shall get (for expenses) from you.

I shall obey you everyday and prepare sweet (with natural juices) food, vegetables, etc.

Using all the clean (and healthy) natural cosmetics, I shall with my heart, words, and body actions engage in physical activities with you.

With the (God-gifted) capabilities of forbearance in hard, difficult and painful times and of happiness in good times I shall share your feelings in happiness and sorrow, and never give company (in thoughts and actions perceived or otherwise) to another man.

I shall perform all your assignments with happiness; I shall serve my parents-in-law and pay due respects and be hospitable to all the relatives. I shall live wherever you live. I shall never cheat my beloved (husband), and I shall never be cheated by him.

Oh my lord! I shall assist you in all religious activities hawan-yagna etc. and in religious, economic, intimate-sex related activities. I shall live up to your expectations. In the presence of agni as sākṣī, brāhmana priest, my parents and members of the family. I have accepted you as my lord and I have surrendered myself (body) to you.

According to Ṛg Veda, while the bride takes seven steps to the north-east (the bridegroom sings the following verses) Panikkar, p 263:

> "First Step for Vigor,
> Second Step for Vitality,
> Third Step for Prosperity,
> Fourth Step for Happiness,
> Fifth Step for Worldly Wealth,
> Sixth Step for (six) Seasons,
> Seventh Step for Friendship.
> To me be devoted."

After the seventh step, he lets her remain on the *śilā* [stone] and says:

> "With seven steps we have become friends.
> Let me reach your friendship.
> Let me not be severed from your friendship.
> Let your friendship not be severed from me."

The priest greets the couple, sprinkling them with holy water, and chants blessings. Next, while standing to her left, the groom places his arm around the shoulders of his bride and touches her heart reciting, "Into my will I take thy heart; thy mind shall dwell in my mind. In my world, thou shall rejoice with all thy heart. May Umāpati, God Śiva, join thee to me."

Hṛdaya Sparśa

Sadhvī kanyā dedicates her heart only to her husband by letting him symbolically touch her heart. The groom promises with the sākṣī of all the people participating in the ceremony and the Agni that he will protect and respect her feelings by accepting the trust of the bride.

Besides, the husband affirms his faith that the śakti of the women is the source of the inspiration, growth and development, success and achievement in every family and the symbolic touch acts like a connection between the electrical wire and the generator. This connection is the source of light and warmth in the environment.

Sun or Pole Star/Darśana

Just as the sun and the pole star are perpetually set in their location, and actively performing their duties to guide the world, so the couple will be steadfast in their actions. The groom sees the sun/pole star and points it out to the bride so that her future life in her new family will be guided by the sun/pole star.

Another aspect of this ceremony is the reminder of Devī Arundhatī and Ṛṣi Vaśiṣṭha as a couple. Arundhatī devoted her śakti to support the Ṛṣi in the attainment of his worldly and spiritual strengths in her subtle and non-exhibitionistic ways. Ṛṣi Vaśiṣṭha obtained for her a place in the ever-existing sky as the pole star to be worshipped by couples in the marriage ceremony, this star has guided the world scouts for determining the direction at night. The groom remembers the role of Arundhatī in Vaśiṣṭha's life and says to the bride, "Oh Devī (incarnation of Arundhatī)! Like Vaśiṣṭha, I seek your strengths to support me in my endeavors in life." The pole star is a satellite planet that stays fixed at one place and seven other stars (the consortium of Milky Way) revolve around this in a twenty-four hour cycle like Earth facing the sun. This is a strong indication of existence of scientific knowledge of sending satellites into the solar system in ancient times.

Marriage is a beautiful union of man's creative ambitions and woman's inherent supportive strengths. Another simile is in the mixture of milk and sugar. Sugar dissolves in milk and makes it more tasty and acceptable for the consumer.

Agni Pernāhuti

The groom, the bride, and other members of the family offer three āhuties of sāmagrī (dhāna and ghee are important parts) to the yagna fire as a gesture of completion of the ceremony and of their Sākṣī to it with all the purity of their hearts and souls.

Pañcāmṛta, Madhuparka

A cup of perfect food-mixture of yogurt, milk, honey, kesar, and Tulsi leaves— is fed by the groom and the bride to each other as a symbolic gesture that they will provide for each other's physical and emotional needs and prosperity in future life until death and after death in thoughts and spirit.

Before they feed each other, the groom offers the food to all the four *dishas* (directions) east, west, north, and south, fifth *ākasa* (sky) and sixth Earth— Sarvamvai—God's total creation of living beings. This conveys the feelings that whatever he is provided by God (in the form of food, wealth, etc.) is to be shared with all the living beings before he or his immediate family would consume for themselves. According to the Hindu Śāstras, "A person who earns for himself (and family) only and consumes any food or other material wealth does so with sin toward God and all living beings."

Seeking Blessings from Priest and Relatives

The couple touches the feet of the priests and of the close relatives, who are elder to them in relationship, to seek their *āśīrvāda* (blessings) for strength to fulfill their responsibilities and duties as expected of them. All of these people bless the couple using different gestures—kisses—and verbal statements like *soubhāgyavatī bhava, cirāyu bhava*. Elders may kiss on the head or forehead of the groom/bride. Mothers, sisters, and brothers may kiss on the cheeks. Of particular mention is the fact that the bride and the groom do not engage in any act like kissing, holding hands (with passion or feeling of lust) or embracing each other during the whole ceremony or any time thereafter in public.

Pūjā

This ceremony at the bride's parents' home is called Ganapati and Iṣṭa Deva Pūjā. This is a thanksgiving by the elder ladies, gents and the couple together to Lord Ganapati for having helped the family to fulfill the Samskāra with peace, happiness and without obstacles.

Iṣṭa Devatās of the family are thanked for having helped the bride grow up in the family of her biological parents and making her worthy of Kanyā Dāna. Furthermore, the groom and the bride also pray that continued help and blessings will be bestowed upon them for their mutual happiness; family growth; prosperity, and their ability to fulfill all the responsibilities of the human life.

Another important part of this ceremony is searching for a ring in the big bowl or thali full of water. Both the groom and the bride try to outwit each other in a joyful mood. No matter who wins, the groom puts the ring on the finger of the bride. Kaṇganas of the bride and groom are exchanged.

Vidāī-Farewell

The first part of this ceremony consists of the couple sitting on the bed together, with almost all other married couples walking around the bed seven times and spraying puffed rice on the couple. This again is a symbolic gesture that the "Dhāna" used in the Kanyā Dāna Yagna, having transformed its identity during the performance of the yagna, will help the couple prosper and flourish like puffed rice. Similarly the bride, having been transplanted into the new family, may prosper and flourish. She literally and spiritually denounces her allegiance to the family of birth and steps forward to promote the prosperity of the new family—with her new name and Gotra [lineage] given by her in-laws.

The parents of the bride bless and give the last bit of advice that the bride's "real parents" and relatives are the people in their respective roles in her new family. She should merge herself and identify with the family in the same manner as she had previously done in the family of her birth. This is similar to the merging of Jamuna and Sarasvatī into the Gaṇgā in Allahabad Saṇgama [confluence] and becoming a bigger Gaṇgā. The father of the bride ritually hands over his daughter to the father of the groom with a ceremonial statement that knowingly or unknowingly there may have been some differences between the nurturance of the girl and the ideas of the family, but she will learn, adopt, and grow into the traditions of the new family to the best of her capabilities and according to the expectations of her elders. She may now be accepted as part of the in-laws family.

The parents of the bride and other relatives and friends give gifts and cash to the bride. These can include all articles necessary for the household, a number of dresses and jewellery for the girl, sweets for distribution in the community, and gifts for the members of the marriage party. Of great importance is the fact that a needle and thread is a must amongst these articles to indicate that the girl should make a concerted effort to keep the family together. A pair of scissors or a knife or a lock is never given as a gift to indicate that she will never be secretive from her parents/family and never be a cause of disruption. The value and quantity of gifts and cash is dependent upon the family and its socio-economic status.

The parents and other family members see the girl and the marriage party off to the city limits if they are going to another city. Otherwise they see them off to the end of their neighborhood community. Thereafter, ceremonies start at the home of the groom.

Reception of the Bride at the Home of the Groom

The first ceremony is the reception at the entrance of the home. In this, the mother of the groom does āratī of the couple. Panni Varna, and attempts to take a sip of the water three times. Of particular notice is the fact that the āratī is done by the mother (or elder Gṛha Laksmī of the family in the absence of the mother) without consideration of her being a suhāgin. This signifies that the mother vows three times to accept the bride as an integral part of the family, takes away all, if any, faults of the new member and ingests them without anyone else knowing them. The groom tries to prevent his mother from sipping the water for the first two attempts. This signifies the fact of life that as a human being the girl may make a mistake one, two or three times. The mother signifies that no matter what, she, as a mother of the groom has the capability to ingest all such situations and finally does take a sip on the third occasion.

The sisters of the groom try humorously to stop the couple's entry into the home. The brother, with the cash or other gifts, indicates that their sister-in-law has come to them with all the gifts of her personal virtues, and they should be happy to enlarge their family by accepting the bride as such.

According to Rg Veda, Panikkar, *The Vedic Experience*, p. 263, the groom says to the bride, "Enter with your right foot. Do not remain outside."

The couple then enters the house and goes to the place of the family's Iṣṭa Devatā to worship Ganapati and Iṣṭa Devatā for the acceptance of the bride as a new member of the family. Kaṇgana is taken off the bride and the groom and presented to the Lord Ganapati and the Iṣṭa Devatā.

Bride's Mukh Dikhāī and Goda Bharāī

Women and children of the community visit the bride to see her and give her a shagun (gift) as a gesture welcoming her into the family/community. The bride touches the feet of the elders and the sisters of the groom as an indication of her respect to them. The mother of the groom brings some money or clothes to the bride to be given to the elder/sisters as a token of recognition and mutual goodwill. This may also be an indication of the feelings that her joining of the family/community will always be for the pleasure and betterment of the family/community. Younger brothers and nephews of the groom touch the feet of the bride and seek her āśirvāda.

Other ceremonies are performed according to the customs, family traditions, and economic status of the family without extending themselves beyond their means. Expenses by the girl's parents are limited to a level that they feel that they should give to the girl as gifts for their own and the girl's pleasure.

Old Indian traditions and religious beliefs do not give the bride any rights to the property inheritance from her biological parents. They do entitle her full rights in her parents-in-law's property. Thus, the parents and other members of the family from the girl's side try to go overboard at the time of her marriage in giving her cash, jewellery, and other gifts. This religious custom later developed into bargaining and the evil practice of contracting a dowry.

The second part of this ceremony is Goda Bharāī. A male child of the family, either a younger brother or a cousin or a nephew, is given by the mother-in-law to the bride (literally put in her lap). This implies two auspicious thoughts:

i. The new Gṛha-Lakṣmī adopts all the younger children of the new family as her own children.

ii. May God bless the bride with a son as her first child.

The bride gives a gift of cash or some other most wanted gift to the child.

[Hindu Marriage Ceremony According to the Ārya Samāj Tradition, in Hindu Marriage Samskara, Prem Sahai (Allahabad: Wheeler, 1993), pp. 20–50]

"COUNTING THE FLOWERS," A SHORT STORY BY CHUDAMANI RAGHAVAN, TRANSLATED FROM THE TAMIL BY THE AUTHOR

Chudamani Raghavan's story takes the reader into the setting of a marriage negotiation between the impoverished parents of young Brinda, the bride, and those of her potential husband who are better off financially. While her parents anxiously discuss the possible terms of the marriage, and its costs, the focus shifts to Brinda's thoughts and feelings as she gazes at the blossoms of the nagalinga tree. Its flowers, both in their beauty and fleeting fragility, become a metaphor for Brinda's own place and destiny as her future is bartered away. Set against the background of Hindu marriage, the story is a poignant evocation of the inner dimensions of marriage traditions from a perspective of a bride-to-be in present-day South India.

Document 4–8

CHUDAMANI RAGHAVAN, "COUNTING THE FLOWERS"

"Brinda! Bring the coffee, child." Brinda brought the coffee.

"This is Brinda." Take a good look, the tone of his voice added. And the visitors did. The girl was not fair skinned, only wheat colored. But a wheat colored vision! Her face and figure vied for supremacy. Of more than average height, she had a luminous air of easy, natural grace about her that brushed aside poverty as one might shake off a fly.

"Prostrate before visitors." It was another command from the girl's father. Brinda prostrated before the visitors.

"Sit down, child," said the boy's father. Brinda sat down and fixed her eyes on the nagalinga tree visible through the window in front of her.

The boy's mother glared at her husband. Was it not for *her* to invite the girl to sit down? And the girl, too, had sat down at once. Really!

"Please drink your coffee," the girl's father urged, doing the honors.

"Oh, yes!" The boy's mother turned to the girl, "How far have you been educated?"

The girl's father gave a start. Had the marriage broker not apprised the bridegroom's party of these details?

"We had to stop her schooling with the Eighth Standard."

"Not good at studies, I suppose?"

Brinda looked intently at the tree. On top, at a great height, the dense green foliage fanned out against the sky. Clusters of thin offshoots sprouting from the lower branches hung down, heavy with flowers. Flowers resembling serpents' heads, each with a lingam inside, as if crying out to be christened nagalinga. Petals of pink and pale yellow all around. In the center, the snake's raised hood over the tiny knob of the lingam. These flowers certainly had a beauty all of their own.

"Actually, she was very good at her studies and wanted to continue, but we didn't have the facility."

"Why talk of facility? Schooling is free."

"I meant the circumstances at home. My wife does not keep well. And I am often away on duty, being a traveling medical salesman. So Brinda had to give up school and stay home to look after her mother and the family, and run the house."

"It does not matter," said the boy. "Going to school isn't all that important."

This was totally unexpected. All eyes, except Brindas, turned toward him. His mother's face went red with anger. Even his father gave him an embarrassed look that plainly bemoaned his naivete, as he said, "Isn't it surprising for a girl not to have completed her school education these days, when even a B.A. is so common?"

The girl's father voiced his anxiety, "I had asked the broker to tell you everything about us. Didn't he do so?"

"Oh yes, he did."

Then why the questions, the girl's mother seemed to ask silently as she raised her head for the first time to look at the boy's mother. Just for the pleasure of saying, "Not good at studies?"

"Your coffee is getting cold," said the girl's father. The visitors drained their tumblers.

"Good coffee," commented the boy's father, mentally adding that these people must have prepared it specially for this day.

"Brinda made it. The bondas gloss and sojji gloss were also made by her. A very competent girl, our Brinda. Adept at all household arts." The girl's father spoke with the pride of a salesman advertising his wares. The girl's mother sat with her eyes carefully averted from her daughter, afraid that she might break down if she looked at her.

My, my, how many flowers there were on that tree! Brinda counted them as far as her eyes could reach: One, two, three, four, five. . . . Before she had counted up to a dozen, the flowers got mixed up. Had she counted the one on the upper branch or not? She guessed that there would be about three dozen flowers in all. A wealth of delicately hued blossoms, silken in their softness. There must be many more strewn at the foot of the tree. The strip of wall below the window obstructed the view. She would be able to see better if she stood up.

"Why is the girl so quiet?" asked the boy's mother and turned to Brinda with the question. "What are you looking at so intently out there?"

"At the nagalinga tree," Brinda said without lifting her gaze. "What's the idea? Turn round and talk to us."

"Talk about what?" Brinda's eyes had still not budged from the tree. Suddenly she began to talk. "Do you know about this tree? It has its autumn at least four times a year. For days on end you see it shedding its brown leaves in the wind. They pile up thick and high on the ground. You have a tough time sweeping out the place. And then, in just a few days, right in front of your eyes, the green leaves appear again, fast and fresh, and cover the entire tree in no time! You wouldn't believe it was the same tree that had been bare such a short while ago. Even as the dead leaves are falling off, the tiny new green ones are sprouting alongside—what an enchanting sight! Almost as if the old tree has sloughed off its skin and a new one was appearing from within."

The boy was looking happily at the girl, a fact noted both by his mother and the girl's father.

His mother seethed inwardly. Did the wretched boy have no pride, for God's sake? His eyes were going to pop right out of his head. . . . She controlled her temper and, wanting to distract him, turned back hastily to the girl to say, "Your father said you made the tiffin. Can you cook meals also?"

No, there weren't three dozen flowers. Perhaps four or five short. The petals were spread out wide and had created the illusion of there being many more than there actually were. Nothing more.

"Brinda, didn't you hear Aunty?" rebuked her father. "Why don't you speak? Turn round and answer her."

Brinda turned toward the lady, "What did you say, Aunty?"

"I wanted to know if you can cook."

"I can."

"What did I tell you! Our Brinda is very capable," said Brinda's father.

"Hm."

"The eldest of our sons, Seenu, is also a capable, brilliant boy. If put through college he will do very well and come up in life. Perhaps you would consider helping us with this. . . . " The girl's father smiled ingratiatingly, remembering what the marriage broker had advised: "There's no harm in your asking them, anyway."

The boy's parents took some time to get over their shock. Then: "Well, I like that!" the boy's mother exploded: "We have been generous enough in making a concession to your circumstances and agreeing to accept only ten thousand rupees from you for the marriage, including dowry and everything, and now you want us to educate your son as well! Has anyone heard the like of this?"

"Calm down," the boy's father said to his wife. "Let him ask what he likes. We are not going to agree, after all. He is only expressing a wish."

"Wish? But this is greed! One doesn't snoot off one's mouth like that. . . . "

"I didn't say anything improper, madam," said the girl's father. "I was only asking for help. And it is not as though we are going to be strangers to you, we'll become your kinsmen through this marriage. . . . "

"There are many parents who demand even half a lakh [lakh = 100,000] of rupees from the bride's family, while we made you a concession by settling for only ten thousand. Did you think of that? No! And on top of it you have the gall to make this outrageous proposal!"

"That ten thousand is fifty thousand for us, madam! We are poor people, as you know. Yet we incur this expense because we do not wish to deny our girl entirely. If you will only think of that and be kind enough to help us with our son. . . . "

"You are only doing your duty for your daughter. How are you justified in making that an excuse to profit from us? If you get back all your money's worth from us like this, what do we have left—we, the bridegroom's people?"

Brinda began to look at the nagalinga tree again.

"Don't you have anything left?" asked the girl's father. "What about the girl herself? And such a girl, too!"

"Uneducated," said the boy's mother. "You ought to give us three thousand rupees more for that reason alone."

"But what about her efficient household work? You should cut down a couple of thousand for that."

"Efficient, my foot! The bondas were too hot. The coffee smelled of raw powder. What is a marriage without the boy's people getting at least twenty thousand rupees? But we, in our broadmindedness, have agreed to a mere. . . ."

"A beautiful girl is worth more than twenty thousand rupees."

"That's a laugh. What effrontery! It was only because the broker had said the girl wasn't too bad-looking that we agreed to this small sum. Normally a boy's parents would expect not less than thirty thousand rupees. . . . "

The girl's father glanced at the boy, "For *this* boy?" He did not voice the question, but the boy flushed and instantly pulled in his right leg under his dhoti. His parents, too, fell abruptly silent.

The girl's father chuckled softly, "Why should we bandy these arguments? The broker has informed both our parties of how matters stand, hasn't he?"

"Then let us finalize things. Why bring up a new issue like your son's education?" asked the boy's father.

"That isn't such an objectionable suggestion. . . . "

"Has anyone heard of the boy's people educating the girl's brother? It is just not done. What game are you playing, mister?"

"The broker happened to mention that quite a few earlier marriage proposals for your son have fallen through," the girl's father said in a smooth voice.

The boy's father mopped the beads of perspiration that broke out on his brow. The boy's mother paused a while, then said, "All right. Make it fifteen thousand and we'll help with your son's education."

"If I were that well-off, wouldn't I help him myself?"

"Then forget it."

"Wouldn't you like to earn credit for educating a deserving poor boy? After all I am giving you a good-looking girl and ten thousand rupees. Just a small favor in return. . . . "

"Do you want this marriage to come through or not?"

Sensing their anger, the girl's mother's eyes lit up for a moment in sudden hope. She made bold to turn round and glance at her daughter.

. . . sixteen, seventeen, eighteen . . . Brinda had been mentally counting the nagalinga flowers over and over from the beginning. Now, counting for the umpteenth time; her mind stopped at eighteen.

"Oh please, what sort of talk is that? If we hadn't been keen about this alliance would we have proceeded in the matter at all? Please don't misunderstand what I said. . . . " The girl's father smiled anxiously. "If you don't wish to help our son, let's say no more about it. Let us not break off the marriage negotiations for that reason."

. . . eighteen, nineteen, twenty, twenty-one, twenty-two. No, not that one. That was just a bud. The next now. Twenty-two, twenty-three, twenty-four, twenty-five . . .

"Good. *Now* you are talking sense. After all, why should we educate your son?"

"I have already said we'll drop the matter."

"Then everything is settled."

"Yes, settled. Only. . . . "

"What now?"

"I have made no secret of my circumstances. So . . . it would be a great help if you would come forward in your generosity to cut down a bit . . . say, some five thousand rupees . . . from the agreed sum. . . . "

"You have a nerve, I must say! Are you crazy? Even ten thousand is a pittance. Don't forget, we are the boy's party. We could demand so much more from a girl's people just to cover what our son's education cost us. . . . "

"True enough. Still, five thousand isn't much to forgo in view of the girl's good looks."

"I've seen better looks."

"Didn't you admit that she was good-looking?"

"Not bad-looking. But certainly no beauty. Her skin is brown."

"Is complexion everything? The Mahabharata describes Draupadi as incomparably beautiful. And what was her complexion? Dark, if you please! Dark! Skin color isn't important. Look at our Brinda's features—every one of them perfect, as if chiseled! Couldn't you cut down at least four thousand. . . . "

"Do you know how absolutely beautiful these nagalinga flowers are?" Brinda's voice cut into the exchange. "People walk down the street gazing at this house. And every one in ten is sure to come in to ask for a few of them to be used in worship. I believe these flowers are especially suited for the worship of Shiva—no wonder! This itself is a lingam, isn't it, and may even be worshipped as such. My mother worships God daily, did you know that? Isn't that so, Amma? Not only Shiva, she worships all the gods with these flowers. And it makes the whole room smell so sweet, so sweet. Perhaps the fragrance from the tree reached you as you entered the gate? But the next day, when they wilt, they have a strong unpleasant odor. And the petals will come loose and drop off, just like that, if you so much as touch them. But when they are fresh, what lovely, lovely flowers they are! Worthy to be offered in worship. To be sought after by people passing by who come in and ask for them for Shiva. After all, there are many other flowers that can be offered to the gods—jasmines, roses, champaks—but no! This nagalinga is superior to them all."

The girl's mother never raised her eyes.

"Look at her eyes and her hair!" exclaimed the girl's father. "You'll never have your fill! A girl so lovely, so good and competent and intelligent—one might accept such a bride without demanding any money at all but I do not ask for that, do I? I am only requesting you to reduce the total amount by just four thousand . . . or even three. . . . "

The girl's father glanced at the boy's leg. The boy was not paying any attention to what was going on. His eyes were glued to the girl.

And the girl's eyes were glued to the nagalinga tree. Clusters of buds, green like raw fruit, were visible on the tips of branches. Blossoms in embryo. Future flowers. The boy's mother spoke sharply, "All said and done, he is a man. What does a man's appearance matter? Is he not educated? Is he not employed? And yet we took everything into consideration and settled for a mere ten thousand rupees instead of demanding thirty or forty thousand. How can you haggle over *that?*"

The girl's father turned to his daughter, "Brinda, my dear, why are you in this heavy Chinnalampat sari? Go, change into the georgette that your friend Minakshi gave you last week. Don't you want to show it to Aunty? Get up."

Brinda did not stir.

"Get up and go in now, will you?"

Brinda shut her eyes for a moment, tight, then opened them again. She got up and went into an inner room.

"There is a Chettiar girl named Minakshi who is a close friend of our Brinda's. Very close indeed, the two of them, since their childhood. Whenever Minakshi goes to Singapore or some other place, she never fails to bring back a present for her dear friend. Any number of georgette and nylex saris. Her father is an affluent man. . . . "

Brinda came back, clad in the georgette sari. The thin material clung to her body and clearly underlined her physical charms. The boy's eyes widened. The girl's father watched him from the corner of his eye and addressed his parents. "Don't you think it is a pretty sari? Minakshi just dotes on Brinda. Presses gifts on her. Won't take no for an answer. A good girl, that."

Brinda was about to sit down.

"Just a minute, Brinda," called her father. "I left a little packet of Sovereign betel powder on the table over there. Would you mind bringing it to me?"

Brinda walked up to the table at the other end of the room and walked back. The boy's eyes followed her all the way.

"There isn't any betel powder there."

"Oh dear, I must have already finished it. How forgetful of me! That's all right, sit down now."

Brinda sat down and the boy's eyes sat down with her.

The girl's mother got up abruptly and left the room.

"Yes, my daughter has a rich friend but I am a poor man all the same," said the girl's father. "I have proceeded in this matter purely out of the desire to see my daughter married. My family is large. My wife is sick. Ten thousand rupees is a sum quite beyond my means. I'll have to borrow the money. How am I going to repay it? The very thought makes me shudder. . . . Couldn't raise the amount even by selling myself. . . . I appeal to your kindness. I promise to perform the marriage with religious rites and not scrimp on the essentials. A concession of just three thousand rupees would be a great help. . . . "

"Out of the paltry ten thousand agreed on? If that is the way you feel, let us call off the whole. . . . "

Even before the boy's mother, finished speaking, the boy spoke up, "So what's wrong with cutting down on the amount, Amma? It is all right, sir. We'll accept seven thousand."

His parents, aghast, swung around and glowered at him. Brinda began to study the nagalinga tree again.

"What are you blabbing, you fellow?"

"I am not, Amma. The poor gentleman is pleading so hard. Can we remain unmoved?"

"A lordly benefactor, aren't you?" his father snapped at him. "You fool. . . ."

The boy held up his hand. "It is my marriage, after all. If I have no objection to this, why should you bother?"

The boy's father was dumbfounded.

Brinda counted the nagalinga flowers feverishly. One, two, three, four. . . .

The manner in which the three thousand rupees were to be slashed from the budget was decided between the parties by mutual agreement. The boy's party then took their leave, asking the girl's father to have an auspicious date set for the wedding.

The girl's mother had come out again at the last minute for the formality of seeing the visitors off. When they left, she raised her head and looked straight into her husband's eyes.

He turned away. "Don't look at me like that. I know my place is reserved in the blackest hell. I'm going to the park for a stroll." He thrust his feet into his slippers and rushed out of the house and down the street, as if fleeing from himself.

The girl's mother turned toward her daughter. Then she looked away, tee-tered, and sat down.

"There are quite a lot of flowers on the nagalinga tree today, Amma. Plenty of them high up and many strewn on the ground too. I am going to count the whole lot. There must be at least four dozen flowers in all, if not six." Brinda looked hard at the tree. She must count the flowers. Must count the flowers. That was all. Count the flowers. She must observe the flowers with care and count them correctly . . . nine, ten, eleven, twelve, thirteen, fourteen . . . There were sure to be four dozen flowers, no doubt about that . . . twenty-five, twenty-six, twenty-seven, twenty-eight . . . And even as she was counting, suddenly the flowers seemed to vanish and she saw on the tree four dozen lame legs.

["Counting the Flowers," Chudamani Raghaven, in *The Slate of Life: More Contemporary Stories by Women Writers in India*, ed. Kali for Women (New York: Feminist, 1990), pp. 79–86]

Chapter 5

BUDDHISM

Alan Cole

INTRODUCTION

BUDDHISM'S ORIENTATION TO THE FAMILY

To reckon the place of family and sexuality in Buddhism, three particularities of the Buddhist tradition need to be kept in view. First, Buddhism, like Christianity, grew out of the matrix of another religion. Consequently, Buddhism's ethical system emerged resting squarely on a body of preestablished forms of family practice, and supported by a fairly codified sociolegal system that had already taken form under the aegis of the Brahmanical tradition, sometime before the sixth-century BCE. Thus, as a relatively late arriver, Buddhism accepted, tacitly, many of the given forms of social praxis in India. And, even when Buddhism sought to redefine religious goals and family values, these efforts were manifested vis-à-vis patterns that had already been in place for centuries. In short, whatever the exact historical reasons, one will look in vain for Buddhist spokespersons seeking to redo marriage law in India or in other Asian countries. Similarly, Buddhist authors did not launch campaigns to redefine procreative norms or sexual practices, and, thus, Buddhist authors seem to have been generally content to let much of family life proceed as it had. When they did address the family, it was usually regarding topics more germane to maintaining a symbiotic relationship between the family and the emerging Buddhist community of ascetic renunciants, be they in the monasteries or less organized wanderers. With this situation in view, we ought to be ready to accept that there will always be much that goes unaddressed in Buddhist discussions of the family, and this is simply because the niche on the social landscape that Buddhism occupied was much smaller than that commanded by many other religions.

Second, Buddhism preserved, to some degree, its identity as a "religion of choice" that one participated in willfully and not through the givenness of birth and/or ethnicity. In particular, on the level of being professionally Buddhist— that is, as a monk or nun—one chose to leave a prior realm of family norms to participate in another zone of legality that in many ways stood against the prior religious and legal structures found in the home. Hence there are good reasons to think of Buddhism as a kind of hyper-religion—one predicated on a doubling of religious law and the establishment of a secondary form of religiosity that, though reliant on the former level, still rests at some remove from the daily life of the family. Of course, it is not unusual that religions have differing legal and/ or ethical structures for specialists and nonspecialists. It is just that in the case of Buddhism this divide is more marked and results in notably different ethical injunctions. In considering this cultivated separation, the point is not that Buddhism avoided forging deep and lasting symbiotic ties with family and government. Rather, it is that these ties were constructed across the divide created by Buddhism's basic orientation to set itself apart in a monastic zone that prided itself on defining its own code of conduct. Making sense of this self-chosen distance helps explain why Buddhism never developed anything like canon law in medieval Europe, where all sorts of familial concerns were aggressively adjudicated and enforced.

Third, and in concert with the two above points, Buddhism has very infrequently enjoyed the kind of hegemony that is the norm in many other religious situations. In practice this means that Buddhism maintained a fairly flexible posture vis-à-vis competing religions and never sought to require laity to identify themselves exclusively as Buddhist or to rely singularly on the Buddhist clergy for all their spiritual needs. Given this basic flexibility and open-endedness, it is not surprising that Buddhism has, in different times and places, morphed into a variety of forms as it negotiated different arrangements for sharing religious power and privilege. Thus, in line with the first point, this simply means that there are many zones of family praxis and law that Buddhist thinkers were happy to let others legislate and oversee. Summing up these points, we simply need to keep in mind the specific purview within which Buddhist thought and practice were intended and the resulting structural configurations that would inform much of what was said about Buddhism and the family.

FAMILIES, MONASTERIES, AND THE
"PATRON-PRIEST" EXCHANGE

Keeping the above three particularities of the Buddhist tradition in view, we would do well to conceptualize Buddhism's position vis-à-vis the family in terms of a basic system of exchange, rightfully categorized as "patron-priest" relations. Buddhism works within this structure insofar as Buddhism was organized around the exchange of two very different types of goods, goods that were produced on either side of the line dividing monastics from laity. Some of these exchanges are fairly straightforward with the laity offering visible items, such as food and material goods, to the clergy in return for merit *(punya)*, which was reckoned as a kind of cosmic power that could be put to a variety of uses including health, wealth, and good fortune along with care for the dead. In this exchange the stuff of life—food, resources, produced goods, etc.—is transacted for a higher kind of currency (merit), which is believed to be reliably powerful and productive at a more sublime level from which the stuff of life can then be recuperated and, ultimately, controlled in predictable ways. That is, Buddhist patrons were instructed that the very resources that they were donating could and would be regathered through this cycle of merit that was both the effect of their donations and then the cause of their future fecundity.

On another level of exchange, there is evidence that the wall between family and monastery often functioned as a mirror of sorts, with both sides looking across the divide to find images of their own identity. This angle of interpretation becomes particularly important when we recognize that the monastic space was regularly organized as something like a patriarchal family that employed the language of fathers and sons to structure discipline, identity, and authority in a way that rendered monastic identity not all that different from those templates constructed within the sphere of the lay family. With the importance of the religious family *inside* the monastery in view, it may even be worth hypothesizing that the monastic version of the patriarchal family functioned as a perfected version of the at-home patriarchal family in a way that simultaneously confirmed the monastic family as "natural" and familiar even as it proved the deepest claims of patriarchy—that life and abundance could be harnessed and managed without the direct assistance of women. Presumably, the promotion of the monastic Buddhist "family" as the final cause and source of cosmic power made similar patriarchal patterns at home appear anchored in deeper universal structures. While these are difficult perspectives to extract from scarce historical remains, at the very least we can say that though Buddhism is regularly thought of as a religion of renunciation, its institutional forms show steady and close ties with the family that range from standard patron-priest relations up to much more interesting patterns of mutual recognition and legitimization that seem to involve the exchange and verification of symbolic logic.

FOUR TYPES OF FAMILY RHETORIC IN BUDDHIST DISCOURSE: AN OVERVIEW

To sharpen our analysis of the interplay between family and Buddhism, we would do well to shape our discussion around four types of familial issues that appear in the Buddhist tradition. Naturally this typology will not cover all relevant matters, but it will organize our reflections and clarify a significant body of Buddhist concerns. First, there is a discourse on the negative aspects of family life, *the language of renunciation*, which appears throughout the Buddhist tradition and is designed to generate distrust of at-home life and to urge the listener/reader to search for truth and value in the extrafamilial space of the monastery. Second, there is a metaphoric language in which identity within the monastic setting is understood as a kind of replicate of the patriarchal family—a kind of *corporate familialism* in which the Buddha is designated as a master-father of sorts, with the clergy and the faithful understood to be his filial progeny. Third, there evolved a variety of narrower lineage claims made within the monastery that sought to establish an elite Buddhist family within the monastic family. That is, while all monks or nuns might be offered a kind of fictive kinship with the Buddha, there emerged a much more narrow kind of *elite monastic descent group* that identified specific monks as the unique inheritors of the Buddha's legacy. In short, as in the case of tantric Buddhism or Chan and Zen, there was a privileged family set within the Buddhist family that worked to define more tightly authority and legitimacy within the Buddhist clergy. Fourth, there are guidelines for correct conduct at home—*pastoral advice* from the Buddhist establishment that tends to focus on proscribing harmful behavior and encouraging the cultivation of a positive and generous attitude toward the Buddhist clergy.

Before exploring these four types of familial rhetoric, and then introducing primary documents that demonstrate these styles of speaking and writing, several important caveats need to be in place. First, as is probably already obvious, there is no one singular form of the Buddhist tradition or even one Buddhism. Buddhism, even in the early period before the common era, was geographically widely dispersed and riven with doctrinal differences. As the centuries passed and Buddhism spread to more distant locales, and even to lands outside of the Indian subcontinent, it continued to adapt and develop, thereby further expanding and enlarging its range of doctrinal positions and notions of orthopraxy. The upshot of this is simply that one should always hesitate before saying anything like "the Buddhist position on topic X is simply Y." Against this kind of reification, it is always better to couch assessments in more defined zones of time and space. Similarly, though many early occidental Buddhist scholars saw fit to do so, it is not at all productive to go back over historical examples of Buddhism to point out what is and is not truly Buddhist about particular practices or positions. For instance, it is quite clear that though most Buddhists held

to the ethics of nonviolence and human dignity, various forms of slavery and/
or serfdom were, on and off, practiced by a number of monastic centers in Asia.
While this might appear in the eyes of a modern thinker as an undeniable fall
from Buddhist ethics, in fact, many Buddhists at the time seem to have con-
doned such practices and not to have seen a contradiction. In short, let's agree
that Buddhism is as Buddhism does.

Sensitivity to this problem of pluralistic Buddhism is all the more important
when we explore the development of Buddhism in East Asia. As it turns out,
once Buddhism began to take root in China in the first and second century
CE, it gradually shifted in noticeable ways. Largely through engaging Chinese
ethics, and working at building a stable relationship with the powerful bureaucratic Chinese government, Buddhist discourse on family and society in China
took forms that often seem quite at odds with Indian precedents. Though some
have been tempted to see East Asian Buddhism as a rather distant cousin of
Indian Buddhism, in fact there is much continuity and many of the more
notable differences are best considered in terms of emphasis. Nevertheless,
there are developments in East Asian Buddhism which do not have clear precedents in India—such as a singular preoccupation with filial piety, an unusually involved relationship with the state, and a growing notion that life production is fundamentally sinful and that mothers can expect to go to hell for their
involvement in the life cycle. Certainly these trends and developments warrant
inclusion in the history of Buddhism's relationship to the family, even if purists
would prefer to discount them as "local" aberrations.

The question of evaluating developments in Buddhist thought and practice
also requires reflecting on the nature of the evidence that will be presented
here. As it turns out, textual statements are, at this point in our study of
Buddhism, the most useful evidence for reconstructing the role of family in
Buddhism in medieval and premodern periods. This means that our evidence
will, for the most part, be drawn from works produced by Buddhist authors,
and this ushers in a body of hermeneutical concerns since our statements will
be drawn from those authors most deeply involved in the symbolic system. As
is well known, textual statements regarding religious practices, especially statements formally made by committed participants, are not necessarily descriptive of either social praxis or belief. Instead, they are best taken as signposts
for how groups went about formulating their notions of identity, proper behavior, and the general scope of good and bad ways of being in the world. As
long as we approach these various types of documents within the sense that
they simply represent what the Buddhists wrote and talked about when these
matters came up, we won't commit the error of thinking that texts directly
reflect thinking or acting. To develop a perspective on the role of family
Buddhist tradition that is sensitive to these issues, I'll briefly explore the four
types of familial discourse mentioned above and then support them with primary source-documents.

FOUR MODES OF FAMILY RHETORIC IN BUDDHIST DISCOURSE: A BRIEF EXPLORATION

1. As for the language of *renouncing the family*, examples of Buddhist rhetoric attacking and undermining the sanctity and finality of the family are truly legion in the surviving sources. They range from the content of the Buddha's biographies to more tailored comments defining what humans ought to be doing with their allotted time on earth. Thus, though the flavor may vary considerably, it is regularly said throughout the Buddhist world that by continuing to reside at home one can expect to become further ensnared in the cycle of life and death (*samara*). According to the logic of karma and rebirth, which is amply played out in the various accounts of the Buddha's own escape from the confines of family, life at home is a site fraught with distracting desires, petty concerns, a lack of free time, and an overall tendency to forget the bigger issues of life, death, and enlightenment that Buddhist thinkers insist are the true concerns of human beings. Consequently, family life is not only judged detrimental to spiritual development, it also is condemned as a deleterious environment that can only encourage negative patterns of conduct and thinking that will bind one in the cycle of birth and death and keep one from making progress toward nirvana. More topically, among these statements about the generic risks of family life, one can also find statements about the physical dangers that women court as they follow the prescribed life cycle within the family, the risks of childbirth being paramount.

In brief, though the Buddhists will in other contexts have much to say about the correct modes of participating in family life, in the end, family life is something that needs to be overcome and left behind, since it does not have intrinsic value and, in fact, inhibits access to the goals that Buddhists posit as the real end of human being. In this sphere of discourse the Buddhists are encouraging everyone to reflect on the benefits of leaving the encumbering and dangerous domain of family life in order to pursue higher spiritual goals, even if it is well understood that only a small fraction of any population will actually do so. On another level, one could also say that, even in the earliest statements, Buddhist rhetoric has a tendency to see life as essentially negative, but not in some Manichaean sense of being evil, simply rather as something to avoid. In fact, the most well-known Buddhist myth of origins explains that the formation of human sexuality, the family, and patterns of ownership and government all result from grand cosmic errors. In sum, family as the zone of reproduction and sexuality is opposed to the final destination of human identity (*nirvana*) and, moreover, the family is held to be fundamentally flawed in a cosmic way, thereby rendering it ultimately valueless, at least within the terms of this type of Buddhist discourse.

2. The second form of Buddhist family rhetoric, what might be best described as a kind of *corporate familialism*, appears in the historical record when the

Buddhists began to settle down into land-owning religious groups, approximately two or three centuries before the beginning of the common era. At this point, even as the evils of family life were still espoused, monastic relations appear to have been explained with an appeal to a kind of patriarchal familialism. Though we do not know when, or why, exactly, it is clear the Buddhists began to construct an ulterior family of monastics, actually a purer form of patriarchy, that was to solidify and legitimize Buddhist identity within the perimeter of the monastic walls. Thus, in formally gaining the identity of a monk or nun one joined the Buddha in a kind of fictive kinship that sealed one's Buddhist identity with a kind of "naturalness" that was expected to facilitate harmony within the monasteries. In fact, the ritual for becoming a monk or nun seems to have been considered as a kind of rebirth back into one's "original" family; one was thereafter called "a son of the Buddha." This motif of rebirth is clear, too, in the way that one's seniority within the monastery was, and still is, determined not by real age but by the number of years that have passed since one's ordination. In effect, with this development, the Buddhist world appears to be made up of two kinds of patriarchal families, with the lay side defined as a procreative family that fully takes up the task of making bodies and food, while the other appears dedicated to maintaining truth and higher ethics in the rarified realm of the monastery, which, though essentially nonproductive, nonetheless has some of the trappings of a reproductive patriarchal family made of fathers, sons, and lasting legacies.

Only slightly later, with the emergence of what is called Mahāyāna Buddhism, this language of belonging to a patriarchal family defined by sonship to the Buddha became more pronounced and extensive in works such as the *Lotus Sutra* and the *Tathāgatagarbha Sutra*. In these works a form of Buddhist sonship was conceived as an ontological reality found at the base of every individual, whether monastics or laity. At this rather crucial juncture in the evolution of Buddhist rhetoric, it seems that patriarchal family nomenclature, besides being useful for defining social life in the monasteries, expanded to define any devotee's relationship to truth and truth-beings, like the Buddha. Thus, in the very act of accepting the new constellation of Mahāyāna truth claims and the texts that housed them, readers and listeners were tempted with the idea to leave even prior monastic forms of Buddhist family-identity in order to step into the identity of the *bodhisattva* (buddha-to-be) and thereby reclaim one's deepest heritage.

In this evolution in Buddhist familial language, it seems that though Buddhist authors so regularly insisted on the ineffability of truth and meditation, on the plane of seducing readers into their various literary projects the Mahāyāna language of family was often relied upon to give the reader the sense of deep belonging to the Buddha's legacy, beyond institutional arrangements, and confidence in being able to forge lasting relations with Buddhist realties of truth and purity.[1]

3. As for the third category of familial rhetoric—*elite monastic descent groups*—at different times in Buddhist history there appeared mystical genealogies, even more refined than those offered in the Mahāyāna texts, in which a higher Buddhist family was established within the already domesticized space of the Buddhist establishment. Thus, in tantric Buddhism in India and Tibet, as well as in Chan and Zen Buddhism in East Asia, it was claimed that certain monks were more directly related to the Buddha than other Buddhist monks or nuns. In both cases the language of fathers and sons was relied upon to explain why certain monks should be taken to be living representatives of the tradition, with truth, authority, and legitimacy flowing directly down the lineage from the Buddha to the present masters. Less noticed in modern accounts of these forms of Buddhist rhetoric are the intricate logics that emerged to explain how these elite "sons of the Buddha" were put in charge of guiding other less connected Buddhists back to their true familial relationship to the Buddha. In essence, even though these spiritual lineages seem dedicated to further privatizing Buddhist legitimacy, it turns out that this gesture was actually always part of a dialectic that was turned outward toward the public in the hope of eliciting more support and devotion. Consequently, these special lineages of privilege ought to be seen as refined forms of the basic patron-priest pattern, but arranged in a more exclusive and captivating manner. In sum, creating these private Buddhist lineages that supposedly descended directly from the Buddha allowed Buddhist leaders to overcome the basic tension in most forms of religious legitimacy: how to posit a perfect origin of truth and legitimacy in the distant past and yet maintain that perfection in the present. Or, more to the point, how to monopolize religious power and legitimacy while continuing to elicit support and good will from those excluded.[2]

4. The fourth sphere of family discourse in Buddhism, *pastoral advice*, appears in the way that Buddhists, likely from the earliest phases of the religion, prescribed proper conduct for those who remained in the family. These moral guidelines define the lifestyle to be maintained at home: one is to be obedient to seniors and considerate of others' needs, while also adhering to the generic set of Buddhist precepts—not murdering, stealing, lying, drinking, or committing adultery. The logic at work in promoting these ethics for the family was that householders, by maintaining this baseline of moral conduct, could collect quantities of merit and avoid deeds that likely would, after death, cast them into eons of suffering in hell or in some other unsavory rebirth. Little was said about actual conduct between family members, other than mutual respect and the avoidance of aggressive or divisive behavior. Buddhist authors also seem to have had no interest in legislating particular sexual codes. When the topic was broached, the norm seems to have been to advocate mutual satisfaction without concern for particular styles of sexual activity.

Given the overall tenor of Buddhist family values, and particularly those that urge filial submission to one's parents and seniors, one can see that Buddhist discourse was, and still is, intent on stabilizing and even bolstering the traditional family structures. The reasons for Buddhism's advocacy of traditional family practice are complex, but one very important reason is that the Buddhist monasteries relied on the families to support them financially. That is, without perhaps directly realizing or admitting it, it must have been apparent on some level that the monastic form of Buddhism, as found throughout Asia, with its extensive landholding and deep involvement in economic enterprises, could only be sustained in a social setting of relative order and status quo.

Within thinking about Buddhism's placement of itself as a quiet advocate for the traditional family, we should not overlook the many stories in which the Buddha or a leading Buddhist figure are presented as fertility figures of sorts who, when properly beseeched, can bring rain, good harvests, pregnancies, and continuity in the at-home patrilines. In short, male Buddhist figures of stature were regularly advertised as sources for exactly what the family needed to reproduce itself and its way of life. In fact, looking at the framing of these stories, there are probably good reasons for speaking of a certain erotic asceticism that runs through Buddhism, as much as it does through Brahmanical beliefs, as Wendy Doniger (O'Flaherty) has argued. Thus, somewhat ironically, it was the very success of world-renunciants that was taken as the mark of their command over the forces of fertility and well-being *in* the world.

In a less obvious way the Buddhist attempt to appear in control of fertility and well-being hinges on their effort to institute a Buddhist form of care for the dead. Throughout Asia, Buddhist care for the deceased ancestors of the laity often figures prominently in structuring and defining the role of Buddhism in society. In this configuration there is something like a triangle of exchange established between the family, the deceased ancestors, and the Buddhist monastery. Within this triangle material goods are given to the Buddhists who, upon receiving them, transfer merit to the ancestors of the donors, thereby saving the ancestors from untoward fates and fostering fertility-producing chains of exchange between the living and the dead. On this level it seems altogether fair to say that the Buddhist institution came to see itself as providing an invaluable service to lay families who otherwise wouldn't have such direct means for succoring their deceased relatives and managing the ever important contacts between generations that were widely believed to define success or failure in food production and sexual reproduction.

The symbiosis between monasteries and the life cycles of the family has another angle as well. It seems that even when men and women joined the Buddhist order they often continued to pay tribute to their parents, dedicating gifts, art, and architecture specifically to win merit for the well-being of their parents, deceased or living. Thus though becoming a Buddhist cleric formally required the breaking of familial bonds, and accepting a new name and a new set of authority structures, there is a wide body of evidence to show that well-trained professional Buddhists were still intent on maintaining connections, symbolic and otherwise, with their parents (as Gregory Schopen has shown). In fact, even in their most religious and public activities, it was normal for clerics to dedicate their Buddhist deeds to the well-being of their parents. Thus, we ought to see that besides simply caring for the laity's ancestors, Buddhism appears to have been an item of transaction *between* parents and children such that though children might exit the family to practice Buddhism, even their Buddhist pursuits might be publicly construed as gifts back to their parents. In this perspective even the family-renouncing aspects of Buddhism seem to fit closely within familial systems of emotion, indebtedness, and continuity.

In East Asian Buddhism this tendency to underwrite traditional patriarchal forms of authority and reproduction expanded, and there appeared a variety of arguments and myths designed to facilitate exchanges between the family and the monastery. In fact, in a development that further emphasized the porous wall dividing monasteries from families, Buddhist discourse in East Asia often emphasized that one is only a good, filial son at home if one patronizes the Buddhist monasteries. Playing off the construction of what was called "greater filial piety" *(daxiao)*, Buddhists argued that Buddhist ethics, including support for the monasteries, were essentially both the same and better than traditional Confucian ethics, even when these Buddhist ethics in many ways undercut and subverted Confucian agendas. Certainly encouraging funds to flow from the family out into the public sphere of the Buddhist monasteries, which were generally seen by Confucians as fundamentally parasitic, ran counter to many basic Confucian suppositions regarding the scope and logic of family values, and yet this is exactly what the Buddhist re-creation of filial piety sought to encourage.

Within this context of Buddhist reconstructions of filial piety in East Asia two notable phenomena appear. First, it is said that the only way one can truly be a filial son at home is to patronize the Buddhists, since the Buddhists will, in the end, be in charge of the destinies of the ancestors. Thus, in essence, the Buddhists argued that the only way really to practice Confucianism was to practice Buddhism, since, after all, Buddhism alone could succeed in ancestor care. Second, and in a somewhat counterintuitive development, it is quite clear that the Buddhist monastic ideal of the self-effacing, submissive, and restrained monk was exported back to the family. In this unexpected turn of events, the model of the Buddhist monk became merged with the filial son at home such that good sons, though needing to reproduce to continue the family line, might otherwise be expected to conduct themselves with the calm detached chastity of a monastic, thereby avoiding indulging in destructive pursuits of pleasure and sensuality. Here, in effect, Buddhism appears co-opted by Confucian agendas insofar as the discipline and docility of Buddhist monks seems to have been "mined" from the monastic setting and reminted back in the zone of the family for purposes altogether antithetical to monastic pursuits.

METASTATIC PATRIARCHY AND THE
RELATIONSHIP BETWEEN BUDDHIST FAMILIES
AND BUDDHIST MONASTERIES

In trying to make sense of these rather dense and intertwined forms of speaking familially and creating a variety of family identities and practices within Buddhism, I believe we would do well to step back from the details to recognize that patriarchal forms of family seem to be metastatic in some sense, regularly generating "higher" forms of themselves, be they in monastic or esoteric forms. Thus, to explain the more or less mystical reason why children belong in the father's lineage at home, and not in their mother's, there is often recourse to a "higher," religious patriarchal model, Buddhist or otherwise, that reproduces in a similarly immaculate manner, that is, without the direct input of women. And, yet, this higher form of patriarchy as found in the Buddhist monastery never ends its ambivalent relationship to the primary family: On one level it buttresses the logic of the patriarchal family, and yet it is also degrades the at-home patriarchy with its own pretension to be above the travails of sexuality, pregnancy, and child-rearing. That is, in its implicit claim to do patriarchy better than at-home patriarchy, it never ceases to be an implicit criticism of its founding template. It is also worth wondering on a more sociological level if the patriarchal family structure is always delicate and forever in need of a sort of *überpater* that can direct and legislate this form of human reproduction.

Of course, in thinking about how stacks of variously defined families develop and forge working relations with one another, we should not overlook a theme that Hegel and Freud developed: More complex and universal forms of social arrangement, such as "a people" or a nation, seem to grow out of the more basic family structure and mimic family structures, even as they seek to place themselves above that primary family structure, both as its caretaker and governor. If we take this supposition as a starting place, then we may have good reason to see that once patriarchal claims to own truth and the right to legislate identity have been complicated by reproducing *themselves* in this sequence of ever more rarefied versions of patriarchy that move away from the at-home template, it shouldn't surprise us that there is an equally prominent discourse explaining something close to "the sin of life" in which truth, purity, and legitimate identity are defined as masculine and ethereal and certainly far from the zones of materiality, women, and sensuality that are inevitably a part of at-home patriarchy. Buddhism, in short, takes its place among many religions that both cares deeply about the family but denigrates it in its effort to establish itself as the site of ultimate authority and value.

THE BEGINNING OF THE WORLD

Though it is widely said, and correctly so, that Buddhism lacks a definitive creation story, it is also true that the following selection is a widely known account of how our world came to be. This story, apparently already present in rather early strata of Buddhist literature, perhaps as early as the second century BCE, explains that within the wider cycles of the creation and destruction of our universe, the particularities of human existence derive from altogether dubious actions. In particular, this narrative of the genesis of our world shows, in a gnostic sort of way, that humans descended from beings made of light that only slowly took physical form as the result of desire and greed. In depicting this gradual "fall of man," the narrative offers an etiology of the major problematic elements of human life, including the body, family, sexuality, ownership, and political order. Above all, the story offers the reader the viewpoint that though s/he may currently be rather involved in the material world, it is still the case that all humans have their true origins in a more ethereal, noncorporeal condition, thereby implying that life as we know it is but an ad hoc condition that can be overcome in favor of the ease and finality of nirvana.

Document 5–1

AGGAÑÑA SUTTA

O monks, eventually there comes a time when, after a long period, this world starts to wind down. And as the world is winding down, beings for the most part are reborn out of it, in the Realm of the Radiant Gods. Eventually, after another long period, it happens that this world that has ended begins to reevolve. And as it is reevolving, settling, and becoming established, certain beings, in order to work out their karma, fall from the Realm of the Radiant Gods and come to be once again in this world. These beings by nature are self-luminescent and move through the air. They are made of mind, feed on joy, dwell in bliss, and go where they will.

When at first they reappear, there is no knowledge in the world of the sun and the moon. And likewise there is no knowledge of the forms of the stars, of the paths of the constellations, of night and day, month and fortnight, seasons and years. . . .

Eventually, this Great Earth appears; it is like a pool of water. It is pretty and savory and tastes just like pure sweet honey, and in physical appearance it is like the scum on milk or ghee.

Now, monks, it happens that a certain being, fickle and greedy by nature, tastes some of this earth-essence with his finger. He enjoys its color, its smell, and its savor. Then other beings, seeing what he has done, imitate him. They also taste some of the earth-essence with their fingers, and they too take pleasure in its color, its smell, its savor.

Then, on another occasion, that being takes a morsel of earth-essence and eats it, and the other beings too, seeing what he has done, imitate him. . . . And because they take morsels of earth-essence and eat them, in due course their bodies become heavy, solid, and hard, and their former qualities—of being self-luminescent, of moving through the air, being made of mind, feeding on joy, dwelling in bliss, and going where they will—disappear. And when this happens, the sun and the moon and likewise the forms of the stars, the paths of the constellations, night and day, month and fortnight, seasons and years come to be known in the world.

Now, monks, for a very long time these beings continue to consume this earth-essence. It is their food, what they eat, and it shapes them. Those who eat a lot of it take on an ugly appearance, whereas those who consume only a little of it become good looking. And the ones who are good looking become contemptuous of those who are ugly. "We are handsome," they declare, "and you look bad." While they go on in this way, convinced of their own superior beauty, proud and arrogant, the earth-essence disappears. And there appear instead "earth-puffs," which are like mushrooms. They are pretty and sweet smelling and taste just like pure honey. . . .

Now, monks, for a very long time, these beings continue to consume this creeper. . . . And those who eat a lot of it take on an ugly appearance, whereas those who consume only a little of it become good looking. And the ones who are good looking become contemptuous of those who are ugly. "We are handsome," they declare, "and you look bad." While they go on in this way, convinced of their own superior beauty, proud and arrogant, the creeper disappears. And there appears instead a rice that is huskless, polished, and sweet smelling. If it is reaped in the evening, by daybreak it has grown back, sprouted, and ripened, as though it had never been cut. If it is reaped in the morning, by evening it has grown back, sprouted, and ripened, as though it had never been cut. [. . .]

Now monks, when those beings eat the rice that is huskless, polished, and sweet smelling, bodily features of femininity appear in those who are women, and bodily features of masculinity appear in those who are men. Then, overflowing thoughts of passion for each other arise in their minds; they are pleased with each other, consumed by passion for each other, and have illicit sex together.

Then, other beings see them having illicit sex together and throw sticks and clods of dirt and dust at them. . . . Nowadays, when a girl is carried off to be married, people throw sticks and clods of dirt. In this way, they repeat an ancient primeval custom without realizing the meaning of it. In former times, it was thought to be immoral, profane, and undisciplined, but nowadays it is deemed moral, sacred, and disciplined. . . .Then, it occurs to a certain being who has gone out to gather rice that he is needlessly wearying himself. "Why," he reflects, "should I go on tiring myself by getting rice for supper in the evening and rice for breakfast in the morning, when I could be gathering it for both evening and morning meals just once a day?" And that is what he begins to do.

Then, one evening, some other being says to him: "Come, my friend, let's go get some rice."

But the first being replies: "You go, friend. I already brought back rice for both evening and morning meals."

Then it occurs to that second being: "This is a wonderful way of doing things! Why, I could be gathering rice all at once for two or three days!" And that is what he begins to do.

Then, monks, it happens that a third being says to him: "Come, my friend, let's go get some rice."

And he replies: "You go, my friend. I already brought back rice for two or three days."

Then it occurs to that third being: "Now this is a wonderful way of doing things! Why, I could be gathering rice all at once for four or five days!" And that is what he begins to do.

But because these beings are now hoarding and consuming that rice that is huskless, polished, and sweet smelling, husks and reddish coatings begin to appear on it. And if it is reaped in the evening, by daybreak it has not sprouted, ripened, or grown back, and it is clear that it has been cut.

Then, those beings quickly assemble together and take counsel with one another: . . . "Now what if we were to divide the rice fields and draw boundaries between them?"

And that, monks, is what those beings do, declaring, "This field is yours, and this field is mine."

Then it occurs to one of those beings who has gone to gather rice: "How will I get my livelihood if my allotment of rice is destroyed? Why don't I now go and steal someone else's rice?"

And so that being, while guarding his own share of rice, goes and steals somebody else's portion. But another being happens to see him stealing that other person's portion, and he goes up to him and says, "Ho, my friend, you have taken someone else's rice!"

To which he replies: "Yes, my friend, but it will not happen again." Nonetheless, it occurs a second time . . . and a third time. He goes and steals somebody else's portion, and another being sees him. But this time, that other being goes up to him and beats him with a stick, and says: "This is the third time, friend, that you have taken someone else's rice!"

Then that being holds up his arms, wails, and cries out: "Friends, immorality has appeared in the world! Irreligion has appeared in the world, for the taking up of sticks is now known!" But, the first being throws his stick on the ground, holds up his arms, wails, and cries out: "Friends, immorality and irreligion have appeared in the world, because stealing and lying are now known!"

In this way, monks, these three evil and demeritorious things first come to be known in the world: theft, lying, and violence. . . .

[The myth then goes on to recount the origins of kingship and the taxation system. The beings get together and decide they need to elect someone to maintain order in their world and mete out punishment where punishment is due. That person becomes the first "king," known as the Great Elected One (Mahāsammata), and is compensated for his role by being assigned a share of the crops of each of the beings in the world.]

[Translated in John S. Strong, *The Experience of Buddhism* (Belmont, CA: Wadsworth, 1995) , pp. 101–104]

THE JOYS OF ASCETICISM

In this short description of the wandering ascetic, often considered to belong to one of the oldest, if not the oldest, strata of Buddhist discourse, we see a stripped-down eulogy of the life of renunciation. The wandering mendicant is portrayed as one who has cast aside all attachments, including his family, friends, and his belongings. Equally important, he has cast away desire for these items, and instead delights in the free and easy life of the wanderer, totally released from social obligations and the searing pain of desire and longing. Nonetheless, the narrative seems to speak knowingly of the charms of family life, though these pleasures are quickly denounced as truly threatening distractions from the life of the lone ascetic who is glamorized as elephantlike in his presumably regal and important travels. Presumably the metaphor of the rhinoceros horn is to evoke the solitude, firmness, and force of the mendicant.

Document 5–2

THE RHINOCEROS HORN

Laying aside violence in respect of all beings, not harming even one of them, one should not wish for a son, let alone a companion. One should wander solitary as a rhinoceros horn. Affection comes into being for one who has associations; following on affection, this misery arises. Seeing the peril (which is) born from affection, one should wander solitary as a rhinoceros horn. Sympathising with friends (and) companions [one misses one's goal, being shackled in mind. Seeing the danger in acquaintance (with friends),] one should wander solitary as a rhinoceros horn.

[The consideration which (exists) for sons and wives is like a very widespreading bamboo tree entangled (with others). Like a (young) bamboo shoot not caught up (with others)], one should wander solitary as a rhinoceros horn.

As a deer which is not tied up goes wherever it wishes in the forest for pasture, an understanding man, having regard for his independence, should wander solitary as a rhinoceros horn.

In the midst of companions, whether one is resting, standing, going (or) wandering, there are requests (from others). Having regard for the independence (which is) not coveted (by others), one should wander solitary as a rhinoceros horn.

In the midst of companions there are sport, enjoyment, and great love for sons. (Although) loathing separation from what is dear, one should wander solitary as a rhinoceros horn.

One is a man of the four quarters and not hostile, being pleased with whatever comes one's way. A fearless bearer of dangers, one should wander solitary as a rhinoceros horn.

[Even some wanderers are not kindly disposed], and also (some) householders dwelling in a house. Having little concern for the children of others, one should wander solitary as a rhinoceros horn.

Having removed the marks of a householder, like a Koviḷāra tree whose leaves have fallen, a hero, having cut the householder's bonds, should wander solitary as a rhinoceros horn.

If one can obtain a zealous companion, an associate of good disposition, (who is) resolute, overcoming all [dangers] one should wander with him, with elated mind, mindful. If one cannot obtain a zealous companion, an associate of good disposition, (who is) resolute, (then) like a king quitting the kingdom (which he has) conquered, one should wander solitary as a rhinoceros horn.

Assuredly let us praise the good fortune of (having) a companion; [friends better (than oneself) or equal (to oneself) are to be associated with. If one does not obtain these, (then) enjoying (only) blameless things], one should wander solitary as a rhinoceros horn.

Seeing shining (bracelets) of gold, well-made by a smith, clashing together (when) two are on (one) arm, one should wander solitary as a rhinoceros horn.

["In the same way, with a companion there would be objectionable talk or abuse for me." Seeing this danger for the future], one should wander solitary as a rhinoceros horn.

For sensual pleasures, variegated, sweet (and) delightful, disturb the mind with their manifold form. Seeing peril in [the strands of sensual pleasure], one should wander solitary as a rhinoceros horn.

"This for me is a calamity, and a tumor, and a misfortune, and a disease, and a barb, and a danger." Seeing this danger in [the strands of sensual pleasure], one should wander solitary as a rhinoceros horn.

Cold and heat, hunger (and) thirst, wind and the heat (of the sun), gadflies and snakes, having endured all these, one should wander solitary as a rhinoceros horn.

As an elephant with massive shoulders, [spotted], noble, may leave the herds and live as it pleases in the forest, one should wander solitary as a rhinoceros horn.

It is an impossibility for one who delights in company to obtain (even) temporary release. Having heard the voice of the sun's kinsman, one should wander solitary as a rhinoceros horn.

Gone beyond the contortions of wrong view, arrived at [the fixed Course (to salvation)], having gained the way, (thinking) "I have knowledge arisen (in me); I am not to be led by others," one should wander solitary as a rhinoceros horn.

Having become without covetousness, without deceit, without thirst, without hypocrisy, with delusion and faults blown away, without any inclination (to evil) in the whole world, one should wander solitary as a rhinoceros horn.

One should avoid an evil companion, [who does not see the goal, (who has) entered upon bad conduct. One should not oneself associate with one who is intent (upon wrong views, and is) negligent.] One should wander solitary as a rhinoceros horn.

One should cultivate one of great learning, expert in the doctrine, a noble friend possessed of intelligence. [Knowing one's goals, having dispelled doubt], one should wander solitary as a rhinoceros horn.

Not finding satisfaction in sport and enjoyment, nor in the happiness (which comes) from sensual pleasures in the world, (and) paying no attention (to them), abstaining from adornment, speaking the truth, one should wander solitary as a rhinoceros horn.

Leaving behind son and wife, and father and mother, and wealth and grain, and relatives, and sensual pleasures to the full extent, one should wander solitary as a rhinoceros horn.

"This is an attachment; here there is little happiness, (and) little satisfaction; here there is very much misery; this is a hook." Knowing this, a thoughtful man should wander solitary as a rhinoceros horn.

Having torn one's fetters asunder, like a fish breaking a net in the water, not returning, like a fire (not going back) to what is (already) burned, one should wander solitary as a rhinoceros horn.

With downcast eye and not foot-loose, with sense-faculties guarded, with mind protected, [not overflowing (with defilement)], not burning, one should wander solitary as a rhinoceros horn.

Having discarded the marks of a householder, like a coral tree whose leaves have fallen, having gone out (from the house) wearing the saffron robe, one should wander solitary as a rhinoceros horn.

[Showing no greed for flavours, not wanton, not supporting others, going on an uninterrupted begging round, not shackled in mind to this family or that], one should wander solitary as a rhinoceros horn.

Having left behind the five hindrances of the mind, having thrust away all defilements, not dependent, having cut off [affection and hate], one should wander solitary as a rhinoceros horn.

Having put happiness and misery behind oneself, [and joy and dejection already, having gained equanimity (which is) purified calmness], one should wander solitary as a rhinoceros horn.

Resolute for the attainment of the supreme goal, with intrepid mind, [not indolent, of firm exertion, furnished with strength and power], one should wander solitary as a rhinoceros horn.

Not giving up seclusion (and) meditation, constantly [living in accordance with the doctrine in the world of phenomena], understanding the peril (which is) in existences, one should wander solitary as a rhinoceros horn.

Desiring the destruction of craving, not negligent, not foolish, learned, possessing mindfulness, [having considered the doctrine, restrained], energetic, one should wander solitary as a rhinoceros horn.

Not trembling, as a lion (does not tremble) at sounds, not caught up (with others), as the wind (is not caught up) in a net, not defiled (by passion), as a lotus (is not defiled) by water, one should wander solitary as a rhinoceros horn.

Wandering victorious, having overcome like a strong-toothed lion, the king of beasts, one should resort to secluded lodgings, one should wander solitary as a rhinoceros horn.

Cultivating at the right time loving-kindness, equanimity, [pity,] release, and (sympathetic) joy, [unimpeded by the whole world], one should wander solitary as a rhinoceros horn.

Leaving behind passion, hatred, and delusion, having torn the fetters apart, not trembling at (the time of) the complete destruction of life, one should wander solitary as a rhinoceros horn.

(People) associate with and resort to (others) for some motive; nowadays friends without a motive are hard to find. Wise as to their own advantage, men are impure. One should wander solitary as a rhinoceros horn.

[Translated in *The Rhinoceros Horn and Other Early Buddhist Poems*, trans. K. R. Norman (London: Pali Text Society, 1985), pp. 7–11]

MARRIED LIFE VERSUS THE LIFE
OF THE ASCETIC

This short narrative, also likely from the earliest strata of Buddhist discourse, is interesting because it explicitly develops a dialogue between the Buddha and a successful herder, both of whom are anticipating a mighty rain. As a discourse ploy, the story works up a set of parallels that work to identify the Buddha's life as a remarkable makeover of the life of the herder Dhaniya. Of course, more than a comparison, this is a steady celebration of the superior value of the Buddha's life of renunciation. What is curious is that the comparison comes to closure by having the herder and his wife convert to Buddhism—actually to celibacy *(brahmacariya)*—and thus the story seems to finish by suggesting that the productive life of the family can be brought to a happy end in a newfound commitment to renunciation. Of course, it is not happenstance that the story stops at the point of their conversion, for certainly it would have been hard to explain how the herdsman family would hold together once it had adopted Buddhist goals of renunciation.

There is, too, another interesting element to point out in this story. The Buddha is metaphorized as a bull and an elephant, a trope found in many Buddhist stories, and thus there is implicitly a claim that power, and perhaps even a kind of fertility, are not strangers to the Buddha's identity. This connection is made all the clearer when the mighty rain arrives just as the Buddha is finishing his discourse, likely implying the Buddha's power over such forces of nature, a possibility supported by the accompanying claim by the herder that "the gains indeed are not small for us who have seen the Blessed One."

Document 5–3

THE DHANIYA DISCOURSE IN THE SUTTA-NIPĀTA

"I have boiled my rice and done my milking, said [Dhaniya the herdsman.] "I dwell with my family near the bank of the Mahī. My hut is thatched, my fire is heaped up (with fuel). [So rain, sky(-deva), if you wish."]

"I am free from anger, my (mental) barrenness has gone," said the Blessed One. "I am staying for one night near the bank of the Mahī. My hut is uncovered, my fire is quenched. [So rain, sky(deva-), if you wish."]

"No gadflies or mosquitoes are found (here)," said Dhaniya the herdsman. "The cows pasture in the water-meadow where the grass grows lush. They could tolerate even the rain if it came. [So rain, sky(-deva), if you wish."]

"A well-made float is indeed tied together," said the Blessed One. "(I have) crossed over, gone to the far shore, having overcome the flood. There is no need of a float. [So rain, sky(-deva), if you wish."]

"My wife is attentive, not wanton," said Dhaniya the herdsman. "She has lived with me for a long time (and) is pleasant. I hear no evil of her at all. [So rain, sky(-deva) if you wish."]

["My mind is attentive, completely released," said the Blessed One. "(It has been) developed for a long time (and) is well controlled. Moreover no evil is found in me. [So rain, sky(-deva), if you wish."]

"I am supported by my own earnings," said Dhaniya the herdsman, "and my sons are living with me in good health. I hear no evil of them at all. [So rain, sky(-deva), if you wish."]

"I am no one's hireling," said the Blessed One. "I wander throughout the whole world by means of my earnings. There is no need of wages. [So rain, sky(-deva) if you wish."]

"There are cows, bullocks, cows in calf, and breeding cows too," said Dhaniya the herdsman. "There is a bull too here, the leader of the cows. [So rain, sky(-deva), if you wish."]

"There are no cows, no bullocks, nor are there cows in calf or breeding cows either," said the Blessed One. "There is not even a bull here, the leader of the cows. [So rain, sky(-deva), if you wish."]

"The stakes are dug-in, unshakable," said Dhaniya the herdsman. "(There are) new halters made of munja grass, of good quality. Even the bullocks will not be able to break them. [So rain, sky(-deva), if you wish."]

"Having broken my bonds like a bull," said the Blessed One, "like an elephant [tearing a pūti-creeper asunder], I shall not come to lie again in a womb. [So rain, sky (-deva), if you wish."]

Straightway the great cloud rained forth, filling the low land and the high. Hearing the sky(-deva) raining, Dhaniya said this:

"The gains indeed are not small for us who have seen the Blessed One. We come to you as a refuge, one with vision. Be our teacher, great sage.

My wife and I are attentive. Let us practice the holy life in the presence of the Well-farer. Gone to the far shore of birth and death, let us put an end to misery."

"One with sons rejoices because of (his) sons," said Māra the evil one. "Similarly the cattle-owner rejoices because of (his) cows. For acquisitions are joy for a man. Whoever is without acquisitions does not rejoice."

"One with sons grieves because of (his) sons," said the Blessed One. "Similarly the cattle-owner grieves because of (his) cows. For acquisitions are grief for a man. Whoever is without acquisitions does not grieve."

[Translated in *The Rhinoceros Horn*, pp. 4–6, with minor cosmetic changes in presentation of the text]

SONGS BY BUDDHIST WOMEN

For as androcentric as Buddhism seems to have been, there is nonetheless a fascinating collection of hymns (Therīgāthā) that purport to have been composed by early Buddhist women shortly before the common era. Though it is clear that the hymns are highly stylized and reflect, in part, the form, content, and even wording of a parallel collection of hymns by Buddhist men, the Therīgāthā still is our best source for imagining the lives and motivations of early Buddhist women. In the following selection Sumedhā, as a princess betrothed and on the verge of marriage, makes a long plea to her parents to cancel the marriage. In the course of this involved speech she beseeches her parents to allow her to renounce normal life and become a wandering ascetic. This hymn is interesting for addressing, in a rather uncompromising fashion, the conflict between the ongoing reproduction of normal social life—as symbolized by the royal marriage—and Sumedhā's religious goals, which are dedicated to avoiding sensuality, desire, and the normalcy of life in the palace of her fiancé. The hymn is also notable for its relentless attack on the body, with ample discussion of the perilous fate that awaits those who would pursue pleasure.

Document 5–4

SUMEDHĀ'S SONGS FROM SONGS BY BUDDHIST WOMEN (THERIGATHA)

In the city of Mantāvatī there was Sumedhā, a daughter of King Konca's chief queen; (she was) converted by those who comply with the teaching. Virtuous, a brilliant speaker, having great learning, trained in the Buddha's teaching, going up to her mother and father she said, "Listen, both of you. I delight in quenching; existence is non-eternal, even if it is as a deva; how much more (non-eternal) are empty sensual pleasures, giving little enjoyment (and) much distress. Sensual pleasures, in which fools are bemused, (are) bitter, like a snake's poison. Consigned to hell for a long time, they (fools) are beaten, pained. Because of evil action they grieve in a downward transition, being evil-minded, without faith; fools (are) unrestrained in body, speech, and mind.

Those fools, unwise, senseless, hindered by the uprising of pain, not knowing, do not understand the noble truths, when someone is teaching them. They, the majority, not knowing the truths taught by the excellent Buddha, rejoice in existence[, mother]; they long for rebirth among the devas. Even rebirth among the devas is non-eternal; (it is) in the impermanent existence; but fools are not afraid of being reborn again and again. Four downward transitions and two (upward) transitions are obtained somehow or other; but for those who have gone to a downward transition there is no going-forth in the hells.

Permit me, both of you, to go forth in the teaching of the ten-powered ones; having little greed I shall strive for the elimination of birth and death. What (have I to do) with existence, with delight, with this unsubstantial worst of bodies? For the sake of the cessation of craving for existence, permit me, I shall go forth.

There is a rising of Buddhas; the inopportune moment has been avoided; the opportune moment has been seized. As long as life lasts I would not infringe the rules of virtuous conduct and (the living of) the holy life."

So Sumedhā speaks to her mother and father; "Meanwhile I shall not take food as a householder; (if I do not go forth) I shall indeed have gone into the influence of death."

Pained, her mother laments; and her father, smitten (by grief), strives to reconcile her (as she lies) fallen to the ground on the roof of the palace. "Stand up, child; what (do you want) with grieving? You are bestowed. In Vāranavatī is King Anīkaratta, (who is) handsome; you are bestowed upon him. You will be the chief queen, the wife of King Anīkaratta. The rules of virtuous conduct, the living of the holy life, going-forth, are difficult to perform, child. In kingship there are (giving of) orders, wealth, authority, happy enjoyments; you are young; enjoy the enjoyments of sensual pleasures; let your marriage take place, child."

Then Sumedhā spoke to them, " May such, things not be; existence is unsubstantial. Either there will be going-forth for me or death; not marriage. Why should I cling to this foul body, impure, smelling of urine, a frightful water-bag of corpses, always flowing, full of impure things? What (do) I know it to be like? A body is repulsive, smeared with flesh and blood, food for worms, vultures, and (other) birds. Why is it given (to us)? The body is soon carried out to the cemetery, devoid of consciousness; it is thrown away like a log by disgusted relatives. Having thrown it away in the cemetery as food for others, one's own mother and father wash themselves, disgusted; how much more do common people? They are attached to the unsubstantial body, an aggregate of bones and sinews, to the foul body, full of saliva, tears, excrement, and urine. If anyone, dissecting it, were to make the inside outside (= turn it inside out), even one's own mother, being unable to bear the smell of it, would be disgusted.

Reflecting in a reasoned manner that the elements of existence, the elements, the sense-bases are compounded, have rebirth as their root, (and) are painful, why should I wish for marriage? Let 300 new(-ly sharpened) swords fall on my body every day; even if the striking lasted 100 years it would be better, if thus there were destruction of pain. He should submit to this striking who thus knows the teacher's utterance, 'Journeying-on is long for you, being killed again and again.' Among devas and among men, in the womb of animals, and in the body of an asura, among petas and in hells, unmeasured (= unlimited) strikings are seen. There are many strikings in hells for a defiled one who has gone to a downward transition. Even among the devas there is no protection; there is nothing superior to the happiness of quenching. Those who are intent upon the teaching of the ten-powered one have attained quenching; having little greed they strive for the elimination of birth and death. This very day, father, I shall renounce (the world); what (have I to do) with unsubstantial enjoyments? I am disgusted with sensual pleasures; they are like vomit, made groundless like a palm-tree."

Thus she spoke to her father, and at the same time Anīkaratta, to whom she was betrothed, surrounded by young men, came to the marriage at the appointed time. Then Sumedhā, having cut her black, thick, soft hair with a knife, having closed the palace(-door), entered on the first meditation. Just as she entered on it, Anīkaratta arrived at the city; in that very palace Sumedhā developed the notion of impermanence. Just as she was pondering, Anīkaratta mounted (the palace) quickly. With his body adorned with jewels and gold, with cupped hands, he begged Sumedhā, "In kingship there are (giving of) orders, wealth, authority, happy enjoyments; you are young; enjoy the enjoyments of sensual pleasures; happiness(es) from sensual pleasures are hard to obtain in the world. (My) kingship has been bestowed upon you; enjoy enjoyments; give gifts; do not be depressed; your mother and father are pained."

Then Sumedhā, not being concerned with sensual pleasures, being without delusion, said this: "Do not rejoice in sensual pleasures; see the peril in sensual pleasures. Mandhātar, king of the four continents, was the foremost of those having enjoyment of sensual pleasures. He died unsatisfied, nor were his wishes fulfilled. Let the rainy one rain the seven jewels all around in the ten directions; but there is no satisfaction with sensual pleasures; men die unsatisfied indeed. Sensual pleasures are like a butcher's knife and chopping block; sensual pleasures are like a snake's head; they burn like a fire-brand; they are like a bony skeleton. Sensual pleasures are impermanent, unstable; they have much pain, they are great poisons; (they are) like a heated ball of iron, the root of evil, having pain as the fruit. Sensual pleasures are like the fruits of a tree, like lumps of flesh, pain(ful); (they are) like dreams, delusive; sensual pleasures are like borrowed goods. Sensual pleasures are like swords and stakes, a. disease, a tumor, evil destruction, like a pit of coals, the root of evil, fear, slaughter. Thus sensual pleasures have been said to have much pain, to be hindrances. Go! I myself have no confidence in existence. What will another do for me when his own head is burning? When old age and death are following closely one must strive for their destruction."

Having opened the door, and having seen her mother and father and Anī-karatta seated on the ground lamenting, she said this:

"Journeying-on is long for fools and for those who lament again and again at that which is without beginning and end, at the death of a father, the slaughter of a brother, and their own slaughter. Remember the tears, the milk, the blood, the journeying-on as being without beginning and end; remember the heap of bones of beings who are journeying-on. Remember the four oceans compared with the tears, milk, and blood; remember the heap of bones, (of one man) for one eon, equal (in size) to Mt. Vipula. (Remember) the great earth, Jambudīpa, compared with that which is without beginning and end for one who is journeying-on. Little balls the size of jujube kernels are not equal to his mother's mothers (i.e., the earth split up into little balls . . .). Remember the leaves, twigs, and grass compared with his fathers as being without beginning and end. (Split up into) pieces four inches long (they) are not equal to his father's fathers indeed. Remember the blind turtle in the sea in former times, and the hole in the yoke floating (there); remember the putting on of it (= the yoke) as a comparison with the obtaining of human birth. Remember the form of this worst of bodies, unsubstantial, like a lump of foam. See the elements of existence as impermanent; remember the hells, giving much distress. Remember those filling up the cemetery again and again in this birth and that. Remember the fears from the crocodile; remember the four truths.

When the undying exists, what do you want with drinking the five bitter things? For all delights in sensual pleasure are more bitter than the five bitter things. When the undying exists, what do you want with sensual pleasures which are burning fevers? For all delights in sensual pleasures are on fire, aglow, seething. When there is non-enmity, what do you want with sensual pleasures which have much enmity? Being similar to kings, fire, thieves, water, and unfriendly people, they have much enmity.

When release exists, what do you want with sensual pleasures, in which are slaughter and bonds? For in sensual pleasures, unwilling, people suffer the pains of slaughter and bonds. A grass fire-brand, when kindled, burns one who holds it and does not let go; sensual pleasures are truly like firebrands; they burn those who do not let go. Do not abandon extensive happiness for the sake of a little happiness from sensual pleasures; do not suffer afterwards, like the puthuloma fish having swallowed the hook. Willingly just control yourself among sensual pleasures. (You are) like a dog bound by a chain; assuredly sensual pleasures will treat you as hungry outcasts treat a dog. Intent upon sensual pleasures you will suffer both unlimited pain and very many distresses of the mind; give up unstable sensual pleasures.

When the unageing exists, what do you want with sensual pleasures, in which are old age and death? All births everywhere are bound up with death and sickness. This is unageing, this is undying, this is the unageing, undying state; without grieving, without enmity, unobstructed, without stumbling, without fear, without burning. This undying has been attained by many, and this is to be obtained even today (by one) who rightly applies himself ; but it cannot (be attained) by one who does not strive."

So Sumedhā spoke, not obtaining delight in the constituent elements. Conciliating Anīkaratta, Sumedhā simply threw her hair on the ground. Standing up (that same) Anīkaratta with cupped hands requested her father, "Let Sumedhā go, in order to go forth; (she will be) one with insight into the truths of complete release." Allowed to go by her mother and father, she went forth, frightened by grief and fear; the six supernormal powers were realized by her while (still) undergoing training, (and also) the foremost fruit.

Marvelous, amazing was that quenching of the king's daughter; as she explained at the final time (= last moment) the activities in her former habitations. "In the time of the blessed one Konāgamana, in the Order's pleasure park, in a new residence, we three friends, women, gave a gift of a vihāra. Ten times, one hundred times, ten hundred times, one hundred hundred times we were reborn among the devas. But what (need of) talk (about rebirth) among men? We had great supernormal powers among the devas. But what (need of) talk (about powers) among mankind? I was the queen of a seven-jewelled (king); I was his wife-jewel. That was the cause, that the origin, that the root; that very delight in the teaching, that first meeting, that was quenching for one delighting in the doctrine."

So they say who have faith in the utterance of the one who has perfect wisdom; they are disgusted with existence; being disgusted with it they are disinterested (in it).

[Translated in *Elders' Verses*, trans. K. R. Norman, 2 vols. (London: Luzac, 1971), vol. 2, pp. 45–51]

THE CONVERSION OF THE NUN, PAṬĀCĀRĀ

This narrative depicts the harrowing pathway that led a woman, Paṭācārā, to become a celebrated Buddhist nun. Though the story likely derives from an era well after the death of the Buddha, the narrative portrays a luckless women coming to realize that the Buddhist criticisms of the family, and human life in general, are accurate and can only lead to the firm decision to renounce involvement in mundane desires. While the above story presents the princess Sumedhā's conversion from a position of strength and wisdom, the conversion of Paṭācārā works by showing the reader how she, in time, came to be convinced of the Buddhist position through a series of devastating events that leave her completely bereft and alone in the world.

Document 5–5

THE CONVERSION OF PAṬĀCĀRĀ

At the time of the birth of the Buddha, a certain girl was born in Śrāvastī in the household of a guild master. When she had come of age, she secretly became sexually intimate with a workman in her household. In due time, however, her parents decided that she was to marry into a family of the same caste as her own. In desperation, she said to her lover: "Starting tomorrow, a hundred guards will prevent you from seeing me; if you are up to the task, take me away with you right now!"

"All right," he replied, and taking a certain amount of movable wealth, he went with her three or four leagues from the city, where they took up residence in a village. In time, she became pregnant, and when she was about to give birth, she said: "Husband, we are without resources in this place, let us go back and have this child in my family's home."

But he only said: "Shall we go today? Shall we go tomorrow?" Unable to decide, he let time pass. Seeing him procrastinate in this way, she thought, "This fool will never take me." So, when he was out of the house, she set off on her own, thinking, "I will return home by myself!"

When her husband got back to the house, he did not find her anywhere. He asked the neighbors where she was, and they told him she had gone home. "Because of me, this daughter of a good family has become destitute," he thought, and he set out after her and caught up with her. There on the road, she went into labor and gave birth. Thus, the very purpose for which they had set out had become accomplished in mid-journey. And thinking, "Why do we now need to go on?" they returned to the village.

Once again, she became pregnant, and everything repeated itself just as it had happened before. This time, however, when she went into labor and gave birth in the middle of the road, great clouds arose in all four directions. She said to her husband: "Husband, unseasonably, storm clouds have arisen all around; try to make me a shelter from the rain."

"I will do so," he replied, and built a hut out of sticks. Then, thinking he would get some grass for the roof, he went off to cut some at the foot of an anthill. But a black snake who lived in the anthill bit him on the foot, and he fell to the ground in that very place. She spent the whole night, thinking: "He will come back now! He will come back now!" Then she thought: "Surely, he thinks I am a destitute woman, so he has abandoned me on the road and gone away." But when it became light the next day, she followed his tracks and saw him fallen, dead, at the foot of the anthill.

"My man has perished because of me!" she lamented, and taking her younger child on her hip and holding the elder by the hand, she went along the road until she came to a river flowing across her path. "Now I cannot carry both children across at once," she reflected. "I will leave the elder on this bank, carry the younger one across to the other bank, put him down on a piece of cloth, come back again to get this one, and go on." So she entered the river and carried the baby across. But when, on her way back, she reached the middle of the stream, a hawk, thinking, "Here is a piece of meat," arrived to peck at the infant left on the bank. She waved her hand in order to scare the bird away. Seeing her gesture, the elder boy thought, "She is calling me" and went down into the river. He fell into the stream and was carried away by it. The hawk then carried off the infant, just before she could reach it. Overwhelmed by great sorrow, she went down the middle of the road, wailing this song of lament:

> Both my sons are gone
> and my husband is dead upon the road!

Thus lamenting, she arrived in Śrāvastī and went to the well-to-do neighborhood where she had lived, but . . . she was not able to find her own home. "In this place, there is a family of such and such a name," she said. "Which one is their house?"

"Why do you ask about that family? The house where they dwelt was blown down by a great gust of wind, and all of them lost their lives. They are now, young and old, being burned right there, on a single funeral pyre. Look, you can still see the smoke." Hearing this, she cried: "What are you saying?" And unable to bear even the clothes her body was dressed in, she stripped them off and, crying with outstretched arms the way she had at birth, she went to her family's funeral pyre and gave voice to this lament of total grief:

> Both my sons are gone
> and my husband is dead upon the road!
> And my mother and father and brother
> burn on a single pyre!

Again and again she tore off the garments that people gave her and threw them away. . . .

One day, when the Buddha was preaching the Dharma to a great crowd of people, she entered the monastery and stood at the edge of the assembly. The Master, spreading out his pervasive loving-kindness, said to her: "Sister, regain awareness, acquire mindfulness."

As soon as she heard the words of the Master, she became profoundly ashamed and fearful, and she sat down right there on the ground. A man standing nearby threw her his outer garment. She put it on and listened to the

Dharma. With reference to her conduct, the Master then recited this verse from the *Dhammapada:*

> Neither sons, nor parents, nor kinfolk are a refuge.
> Relatives offer no shelter for one seized by Death.
> Knowing this situation, the wise, exercising moral restraint,
> can quickly clear the way that leads to nirvāṇa.

At the end of the verse, even as she stood there, she became a stream-winner. She approached the Master, venerated him, and asked to be ordained. He agreed to her ordination, telling her to go to the home of the nuns and wander forth there. She was ordained, and it was not long before she obtained arhatship, and grasping the word of the Buddha, she became a master of the book of the discipline (Vinaya). Subsequently, when the Master was seated at the Jetavana and assigning statuses to each of the nuns, he established Paṭācārā as the foremost of those knowing the Vinaya.

[Translated in Strong, *The Experience of Buddhism*, pp. 56–58]

THE BUDDHA ACCEPTS HIS AUNT, GOTAMĪ, AS A NUN

While the above two stories display women unrelated to Buddha accepting the Buddhist appraisal of the stupendous pitfalls encumbent on householders, the surviving literary tradition also includes several narratives about the Buddha's mother, Māyā, and his aunt Mahāprajāpatī (also known as Gautamī; or Gotamī), who was believed to have raised him after his mother died some seven days after his birth. In the case of his mother, Māyā, it was widely held in several genre of early Buddhist literature that the Buddha, during one particular rainy season retreat, rose up magically to heaven, where she was abiding, in order to spend three months teaching her the dharma so that she could gain enlightenment and escape from samsara. The logic of this story rests on the assumption that the Buddha made this decision to care for his deceased mother based on recognizing that he owed her a debt for her role in bringing him into the world. Thus, in a way that runs somewhat counter to modern popular interpretations of the Buddha, the story sought to present the Buddha as a careful and diligent filial son who managed all his affairs perfectly, and can't rest until his dear mother is rescued from samsara. The story is also telling in so far as it presents an intersection of family and ascetic values since the Buddha, though now enlightened, is shown working to save from rebirth the very woman who gave him birth, thereby clearly suggesting that his transcendence didn't exactly annul his previous relations, a trope that we will see played out in various ways in the stories below.

An equally telling story regarding the importance of the Buddha's female relatives is the account of Mahāprajāpatī, his aunt and wet-nurse. Again working from his "milk-debt" to her, this story depicts the Buddha's reluctance to accept women into the ascetic order being finally convinced when Mahāprajāpatī reminds him that she breast-fed him in his infancy. Unlike the sparse narratives of the joys of ascetic isolation, this story seems rather sophisticated in its effort to explain the advent of Buddhist nuns, even as it casts that invention in a decidedly unflattering light since we learn that the Buddhist religion will, supposedly, flourish for half as long now that the Buddha has acquiesced to Mahāprajāpatī's request to join the monastic order. Like the story of the Buddha saving his mother in heaven, this narrative works to negotiate, in some measure, the Buddha's trailing familial obligations and to both allow a place for women in the order, even as their presence is explained as the primary cause for the precocious demise of Buddhism.

Document 5–6

THE BUDDHA ACCEPTS HIS AUNT, GOTAMĪ, AS A NUN

Then Mahāprajāpatī Gautamī, together with her four companions and five hundred other Śākyan women, approached the Blessed One and, after paying obeisance to him, sat down to one side. And Mahāprajāpatī Gautamī said this to the Buddha:

"Blessed One, the appearance of Buddhas in the world is rare; instruction in the True Dharma is difficult to obtain. But now the Blessed One . . . has appeared, and the Dharma whose preaching is conducive to tranquillity and parinirāvna is being expounded by him and is causing the realization of ambrosial nirvāna. It would be good if the Blessed One were to allow women to be initiated into his order and ordained as nuns."

The Blessed One said: "Gautamī, do not long for the initiation of women into the order, or for their ordination as nuns."

Now Mahāprajāpatī Gautamī, thinking that the Buddha would not give women a chance to become initiated and ordained, paid obeisance to the Blessed One and took her leave. Then, together with her companions she approached the Śākyan women and said: "The Blessed One will not allow honorable women to be initiated and ordained as nuns. However, let us honorable women cut our own hair, acquire our own monastic robes, and attach ourselves to the Blessed One's party and follow after him, . . . wandering where he wanders throughout the land of Kośala. And if the Blessed One allows it, we will be initiated, and if he does not allow it, we will lead a chaste life in the presence of the Holy Buddha. . . . "

Now the Blessed One, after dwelling as long as he wished in the city of Kapilavastu, set forth to travel through the land of Kośala. And Mahāprajāpatī Gautamī, together with her companions, cut their own hair, acquired their own robes, attached themselves to the Blessed One's party, and followed after him. . . . Wandering through Kośala in the company of a large group of monks, the Blessed One arrived at the city of Śrāvastī. There he dwelt in the Jetavana, Anāthapiṇḍada's park.

Then Mahāprajāpatī Gautamī approached the Blessed One, paid obeisance to him, and sat down to one side. And she said: "Blessed One, the appearance of Buddhas in the world is rare, instruction in the True Dharma is difficult to obtain, but now the Blessed One . . . has appeared, and the Dharma whose preaching is conducive to tranquillity and parinirvāṇa is being expounded by him and causing the realization of ambrosial nirvāṇa. It would be good if the Blessed One were to allow women to be initiated into his order and ordained as nuns."

The Blessed One said: "Gautamī, do not long for the initiation of women into the order or for their ordination as nuns."

And again, Mahāprajāpatī Gautamī, thinking that the Buddha would not give women a chance to become initiated and ordained, paid obeisance to the Blessed One and withdrew to the gateway of the Jetavana. There, she stood crying and scuffing her toes on the ground.

Now a certain monk, seeing her there, went to the Venerable ānanda, and said: "Venerable Ānanda, Mahāprajāpatī Gautamī is standing crying in the gateway of the Jetavana, scuffing the dirt with her toes. You should go, Ānanda, and find out why she is crying."

Ānanda therefore approached Mahāprajāpatī Gautamī and said to her: "Why are you crying, Gautamī?"

"Indeed, I am crying, Noble Ānanda, because truly the appearance of Buddhas in the world is rare, instruction in the True Dharma is difficult to obtain, and now the Blessed One . . . has appeared, and the Dharma whose preaching is conducive to tranquillity and parinirvāṇa is being expounded by him and causing the realization of ambrosial nirvāṇa, but the Blessed One will not give women a chance to be initiated and ordained into his order and to become nuns. It would be good, Ānanda, if you were to go to the Blessed One so as to obtain permission for women to be initiated and ordained."

"That would be good, Gautamī," agreed the Venerable Ānanda. So, approaching the Buddha, he paid obeisance to him and sat down to one side. Sitting there, he said: "The appearance of Buddhas in the world is rare, instruction in the True Dharma is difficult to obtain, and now the Blessed One . . . has appeared, and the Dharma . . . is being expounded by him and causing the realization of ambrosial nirvāṇa. It would be good if the Blessed One were to allow women to be initiated into his order and ordained as nuns."

Thus addressed, the Blessed One replied to the Venerable Ānanda: "Mother Gautamī should not long for the initiation of women into the order or for their ordination."

Then the Venerable Ānanda . . . after taking leave of the Buddha, went to Mahāprajāpatī Gautamī and told her what had happened.

Upon hearing this, Mahāprajāpatī Gautamī replied: "It would be good, Ānanda, if you were to go to the Blessed One and ask him a second time. . . ."

[So Ānanda went and repeated his request a second time, and] the Blessed One again replied: "Mother Gautamī should not long for the initiation of women into the order or for their ordination as nuns. Such a thing, Ānanda, would be just as though the disease known as kāraṇḍava were to fall upon a ripe field of grain and make it turn to chaff. Just as that would be a great defilement to the field of grain, so it would be a great defilement to the teaching of the Buddha were Mother Gautamī allowed to be initiated into his order and become a nun. Indeed, Ānanda, it would be just as though the disease known as 'red rust' were to fall on a ripe field of sugar cane. Just as that would be a great defilement to the field of sugar cane, so it would be a great defilement to the teaching of the Buddha were Mother Gautamī allowed to be initiated into his order and become a nun. Indeed, Ānanda, it would be just as though a great storm were to fall on a ripe field of rice in such a way as to bring about the destruction and utter ruin beyond hope of recovery of the rice crop. Just as that would be a great defilement to the field of rice, so it would be a great defilement to the teaching of the Buddha, were Mother Gautamī allowed to be initiated into his order and become a nun."

Then the Venerable Ānanda . . . returned to Mahāprajāpatī Gautamī and said to her: "Gautamī, the Blessed One will not give women a chance to be initiated and ordained into his order and to become nuns."

Upon hearing this, Mahāprajāpatī Gautamī replied: "It would be good, Ānanda, if you were to go to the Blessed One and ask him a third time. . . . "

"That would be good, Gautamī," agreed the Venerable Ānanda, and, he went a third time, and paid obeisance to the Buddha and sat down to one side. Sitting there, he said: "Blessed One, how many assemblies of disciples did enlightened Buddhas of the past have?"

The Blessed One replied: "Previous Buddhas, Ānanda, had four assemblies of disciples, to wit, monks, nuns, laymen, and laywomen."

Then the Venerable Ānanda said to the Blessed One: "Blessed One, the four fruits of monastic life—namely, the fruit of a stream-winner, the fruit of a once-returner, the fruit of a nonreturner, and the highest fruit of arhatship—can a woman who is earnest and zealous and who dwells in seclusion realize any of these?"

The Buddha replied: "Yes, Ānanda, a woman who is earnest and zealous and who dwells in seclusion can realize any of these four fruits of the monastic life."

"Well, then," the Venerable Ānanda said to the Blessed One, "since, Blessed One, enlightened Buddhas of the past had four assemblies—namely, monks, nuns, laymen, and laywomen—and since women who are earnest and zealous, and who dwell in seclusion are able to realize the four fruits of the monastic life—namely, the fruit of stream-winnner up to the highest fruit of arhatship—it would be good if the Blessed One were to allow women to be initiated into his order and to be ordained as nuns. Moreover, Mahāprajāpatī Gautamī performed some difficult tasks for the Blessed One; she nourished, fed, and suckled him after his mother had passed away. And for this the Blessed One is grateful and recognizant."

Hearing this, the Blessed One said to Ānanda: "This is true, Ānanda, Mahāprajāpatī Gautamī did perform difficult tasks for the Tathāgata; and she did nourish, feed, and suckle him after his mother passed away. And for this the Tathāgata is grateful and recognizant. But, Ānanda, the Tathāgata, too, performed some difficult tasks for Mahāprajāpatī Gautamī. Thanks to him, she took refuge in the Buddha, she took refuge in the Dharma, and she took refuge in the Sangha. . . . "

Then the Blessed One reflected: "If I oppose the request of Ānanda a third time, this will cause him mental distress, and the teachings which I have revealed and entrusted to him would become utterly confused in his mind. I would like my true Dharma to last a thousand years, but it is preferable that ānanda not become mentally distressed and that the revealed teachings not become utterly confused, even though, this way, my true Dharma will abide but five hundred years."

[Translated in Strong, *Experience of Buddhism*, pp. 52–56]

THE BUDDHA'S RENUNCIATION OF HIS FAMILY

An especially interesting attempt to fuse family values with Buddhist renunciation is found in a version of the Buddha's biography that recounts his exit from his family in a decidedly innovative manner. This narrative is found within the Mūlasarvāstivādin monastic rules (the Vinaya), and thus presumably was regarded as copacetic with other monastic ideals. (Establishing a date for the composition of this narrative, and the entire Vinaya in which it is found, remains controversial, though we could provisionally argue for a period slightly after the common era, though it is also likely that this Vinaya, like the others, grew incrementally.)

In this version of the Buddha's exit from family life, his ties to his family are played up in a remarkable manner. First, we are told that before leaving his wife and harem he purposefully slept with his wife Yaśodharā in order to deflect the expected charges that he wasn't a man or that he didn't fulfill his familial obligations. She becomes pregnant, presumably from this encounter, but this added emphasis on the Buddha's concern for upholding familial expectations opens the door for a much more interesting turn of events. In developing a long split-screen narrative, the Buddha's six years of ascetic practice are mirrored by his wife's equally extended pregnancy with their son. Thus the Buddha's travails as an ascetic seeking enlightenment and total freedom from the family are ironically doubled by his wife's six-year-long wait to give birth to their son, an event that would presumably count as the fulfillment of the Buddha's familial role. This trope is further emphasized when the narrative has the Buddha's enlightenment arrive simultaneously with his wife's final delivery of their son, Rāhula. In effect, then, the Buddha's spiritual quest is presented as the cause for finally achieving his familial goals of reproducing a son for his at-home family. Arguably, this explicit linkage, and others like it, suggest a Buddhist version of the "erotic-ascetic," to borrow the term that Wendy Doniger coined to describe Śiva's virile asceticism.

Document 5–7

MULASARVĀSTIVĀDIN VINAYA

THE NIGHT OF THE GREAT DEPARTURE

Then King Śuddhodana met with his brothers, Droṇodana, Śuklodana, and Amṛtodana, and said to them: "The brahmin soothsayers and fortune tellers have predicted that my son . . . will become a cakravartin king if he does not leave home to become a wandering ascetic. Therefore we should watch the bodhisattva carefully . . . and keep the city well guarded."

So they encircled the city of Kapilavastu with seven walls and seven moats, and iron doors were put in each city gate. Very loud bells were attached to the doors, so that whenever the doors were opened, they could be heard up to a distance of a league around. They saw to it that the bodhisattva, in his palace, was constantly attended to by entrancingly beautiful women who danced, sang, and played instruments. Royal ministers, commanding armed men and riders, were posted outside on the walls, and they patrolled everywhere, keeping watch all around. Five hundred men were likewise stationed at the door to the bodhisattva's harem and ordered to sound the alarm in King Śuddhodana's quarters were that door to be opened. [. . .]

Now when the bodhisattva was in his harem, in the absence of other men, the women sought to amuse, delight, and seduce him by playing instruments. And it occurred to him: "Lest others say that the Prince Śakyamuni was not a man, and that he wandered forth without 'paying attention' to Yaśodharā, Gopikā, Mṛgajā, and his other sixty thousand wives, let me now make love to Yaśodharā." He did so, and Yaśodharā became pregnant.

That night, in her sleep, Yaśodharā had eight dreams: she saw her own maternal line cut off, her marvelous couch broken, her bracelets broken, her teeth falling out, the braid of her hair undone, happiness departed from her house, the moon eclipsed by Rāhu, and the sun rising in the east and then setting there again.

And the bodhisattva, going to sleep, had five dreams: he saw himself lying on the great earth, with Mount Meru, the king of mountains, as his pillow, his left arm resting in the great Eastern Ocean, his right arm in the great Western Ocean, and his feet in the great Southern Ocean. He saw an upright grass reed grow out of his navel and reach up as far as the sky. He saw large śakunaka birds, all white with black heads, standing at his feet and up as far as his knees. He saw other birds of various colors (varṇa) coming from the four directions and then becoming one color in front of him. He saw himself walking back and forth over a mountain of feces.

Seeing all this, he was pleased and thought: "From what I have seen in my dreams, it will not be long now before I attain highest knowledge."

Then Yaśodharā told the bodhisattva about her eight dreams . . . and the bodhisattva reflected: "The dreams Yaśodharā has seen are surely related to her worries about my going away today; thus I will speak so as to make light of them." And in order to explain them away, he interpreted them as follows: "You say your maternal line was cut off, but is it not established? You say your couch was broken, but it is not broken; it is right here. You say your bracelets were broken, but see for yourself, they are not. You say your teeth fell out, but you yourself know they have not. You say the braid of your hair was undone, but it is itself; look, it is not undone. You say that 'happiness has left my house,' but for a woman, a husband is happiness, and I am right here. You say the moon was eclipsed by Rāhu, but is that not the moon over there? You say the sun rose in the east and then set there again, but it is now midnight and the sun has not yet risen, so how can it have set?"

At this explanation, Yaśodhara remained quiet. But then she said: "Lord, wherever you go, take me there with you." And the bodhisattva, thinking he was going to nirvāna [and would show her the way there], said, "So be it; where I am going, I will take you."

Now Indra, Brahmā, and the other gods, knowing the thoughts of the bodhisattva, approached him and said: . . . "Get up, get up, well-minded one! Leave this place and set out into the world! Upon reaching omniscience, you will save all beings."

The bodhisattva replied: "Do you not see, Indra? I am trapped in a net like the king of beasts. The city of Kapila is completely surrounded by a great many troops, with lots of horses, elephants, chariots, and very capable men bearing bows, swords, and scimitars . . . "

Indra said: "Good sir, recall your former vow, and the past Buddha Dīpaṃkara's prediction, that having abandoned this world that is afflicted by suffering, you would wander forth from your home. We gods will arrange it so that you will be able to dwell in the forest this very day, free from all hindrances."

Hearing this, the bodhisattva was very pleased. Then Indra, Lord of the gods and causer of sleepiness, gave orders to Pāñcika, the great yaksa general: "My friend, bring on sleep, and the bodhisattva will come down from his palace!" So he brought on sleep, and the bodhisattva came out.

Then, as had been prearranged by Indra, the bodhisattva came across his attendant Chandaka, and saw that Chandaka had succumbed to a deep sleep. With some effort, he managed to rouse him and spoke to him this verse:

"Ho! Chanda! Get up, and from the stable, quickly fetch me Kanthaka, that jewel of a horse; I am determined to set out for the forest of asceticism which previous Buddhas enjoyed and which brings satisfaction to sages. . . . "

Then the bodhisattva, seeing that the king of horses, Kanthaka, stood ready, . . . mounted him, and with Chandaka holding on behind, he flew up into the air. This was out of the bodhisattva's bodhisattva-power, as well as out of the divine power of the gods.

And because of the departure of the bodhisattva, the divinities who inhabited the harem of the palace began to cry, and the tears of those crying divinities began to fall onto the earth. And Chandaka said: "Prince, drops of water are falling. Why is the god making it rain?" The bodhisattva replied: "The god is not raining, but, because of my departure, the deities who dwell in the harem of the palace are crying; their tears are falling down everywhere." And Chandaka, his own eyes filled with tears, heaved a long emotional sigh, and remained silent.

Then the bodhisattva, turning his whole body around to the right like an elephant, considered the following matter: "This for me is the last night on which I will have lain with a woman." And he further reflected: "I will depart through the eastern gate; were I to go out through another gate, my father, the king, would be upset that I, as prince, did not come to see him and take my leave at this final moment." Therefore he went and gazed upon King Śuddhodana, who was sleeping soundly. He circumambulated him and said: "Father, I am leaving not out of lack of respect, not out of lack of reverence, but for no other reason than that I wish to liberate the world, which is afflicted by old age and death, from the fear of the suffering that comes with old age and death. . . . "

Then, surrounded by several hundreds of thousands of deities headed by Indra and Brahmā, the bodhisattva crossed over to the other side. . . . And, unsheathing his sword, which was like a blue lotus, he cut off his hairknot and threw it very high into the air. It was taken by Indra, king of the gods, and received with great honor by the deities in his heaven, who instituted a Festival of the Hairknot. Also, the faithful brahmin householders in that place established a caitya called the Keśagrahaṇa [Receiving of the Hair] Shrine, which the monks still venerate today. . . .

RECEIPT OF THE ROBES

[After he had sent Chandaka back to Kapilavastu, together with the horse Kanthaka], there arose the matter of obtaining the bodhisattva's robes. Long ago, in that peerless city, there lived a certain householder who was rich, the possessor of great fortune and felicity, the owner of vast estates, as wealthy and well endowed as the god Vaiśravaṇa. He had married a woman from a family of equal status. They dallied, embraced, and made love, and a son was born.

Similarly, in time, ten sons were born, and all of them, wandering forth from the householder's life, became enlightened on their own as pratyekabuddhas. Their mother was then old; she offered to them some robes of hemp, but they said: "Mother, we are go ing to attain parinirvāna. We have no use for these, but King Śuddhodana will have a son named Śākyamuni who will attain unsurpassed complete enlightenment. You should pass these robes on to him. In that way, you will obtain great meritorious rewards."

After saying this, they performed the miracle of simultaneously glittering with both fire and rain showers, and passed away into complete final nirvāna. The old woman, at the time of her death, gave the robes to her daughter, telling her everything that had happened. In time, that daughter too became sick, and she, about to succumb to death, placed the robes on a tree, requesting the deity who dwelt in that tree to give them to the son of King Śuddhodana.

Now Indra, king of the gods, sees everything that happens down below. Thus, he went down and took the robes, and then, taking on the form of a hunter ravaged by old age, he dressed himself in those robes and went and stood on the bodhisattva's path, holding a bow and some arrows. And in due time, the bodhisattva came along that path and saw the hunter dressed in the monastic robe, . . . and he said to the man: "Ho! fellow! Those hempen clothes are fit for one who has wandered forth. Take these garments of Benares silk, and give me those in exchange."

The hunter replied: "Prince, I cannot give you these robes, because if I do, there may be others who will say that I deprived a royal prince of his life in order to steal his garments of Benares silk"

The bodhisattva said: "Ho, fellow! The whole world knows me and the kind of power that I have. Who is able to deprive me of life? Who would believe that you could kill me? Give without fear."

Thereupon, Indra fell at the feet of the bodhisattva and presented to him the hempen robes, and he received the bodhisattva's silken robes in exchange, . . . and taking them, he established among the gods in his heaven the Festival of the Benares Silk Robes. And the faithful brahmin householders in that place built a caitya called the Reception of the Monastic Robes Shrine, and the monks still venerate it to this day. . . .

Now the robes of hemp did not fit the bodhisattva's body, so he said: "Oh! May my hempen robes fit my body!" And just as soon as he had uttered those words, the hempen robes became the right size. This also was due to the bodhisattva's bodhisattva-power and to the divine power of the deities. . . .

MEETING WITH KING BIMBISĀRA

Then the bodhisattva reflected: "The city of Kapilavastu is still near. It would be best not to stay here; the Śākya men could cause a commotion. Therefore, let me cross the Ganges."

So he crossed the Ganges and, walking along, reached the city of Rājagṛha. Being skilled in all the arts and crafts, the bodhisattva then made a begging bowl of oleander leaves and . . . entered Rājagṛha to go questing for alms. At that time, King Bimbisāra was walking on the terrace of his palace. He saw the bodhisattva and, impressed by his demeanor, had his bowl filled with food. . . . [He then later went to visit him on nearby Mount Pāṇḍava.]

"I want to give you, for your enjoyment," he declared, "a bevy of women, unsurpassed riches. . . . "

"O, King," replied the bodhisattva, "I am a kṣatriya, a Śākya, I belong to the solar clan, descendant of Ikṣvāku. I come from Kosala, a kingdom near the Himālayas. It is filled with riches and grain; I do not long for sensual pleasures."

"Sir," Bimbisāra then asked him, "for what purpose did you wander forth?"

The bodhisattva answered: "For unsurpassed complete enlightenment."

The king said: "Sir, when you attain unsurpassed complete enlightenment, then please turn your thoughts to me."

"I will do so," the bodhisattva replied, and he departed from Rājagṛha.

STUDY WITH VARIOUS TEACHERS

Not far from there, near Vulture's Peak, there was a hermitage of ascetics, and that is where the bodhisattva now went. He stayed there and meditated, engaging in those ascetics' practices. If they stood on one foot for a portion of the day, the bodhisattva did so for two portions. If they engaged in the painful practice of sitting between four fires with the sun shining overhead for one portion of the day, the bodhisattva did so for two. In this way they were amazed, and began to call him the great quester. . . .

The bodhisattva asked them: "Sirs, what is the purpose of your practice?"

And some said, "We want to gain the status of the god Indra"; and others said, "We want to gain the status of Brahmā"; and still others said, "We want to gain the status of Māra."

And the bodhisattva thought, "Indeed, these ascetics are caught in a whirlpool, practicing a wrong path."

So, finding that path inadequate, he went to the hermitage of Ārāḍa Kālāma. . . . He asked Ārāḍa what sorts of dharmas he had realized.

"O, Gautama," answered Ārāḍa, "every thing up to the stage of nothingness."

The bodhisattva then declared: "The faith of Ārāḍa Kālāma is also my faith. The determination, the mindfulness, the concentration, the wisdom of Ārāḍa Kālāma are also my determination, mindfulness, concentration, and wisdom. The dharmas that Ārāḍa Kālāma has realized, up to the stage of nothingness, I will realize." . . .

[The bodhisattva then followed and completed all of ārāda's practices, but he was not fulfilled by them.] "This path," he declared, "is not adequate for knowledge, not adequate for seeing, not adequate for unsurpassed total enlightenment."

And having thus determined Āarāḍa's path to be insufficient, the bodhisattva went to Udraka Rāmaputra. . . . He asked Udraka what sorts of dharmas he had realized.

"O, Gautama," Udraka replied, "everything up to the stage of neither perception nor nonperception."

The bodhisattva then declared: "The faith of Udraka Rāmaputra is also my faith. The determination, mindfulness, concentration, and wisdom of Udraka Rāmaputra are also my determination, mindfulness, concentration and wisdom. The dharmas that Udraka Rāmaputra has realized, up to the stage of neither perception nor non-perception, I will realize." . . .

[The bodhisattva then followed and completed all of Udraka's practices, but he was not fulfilled by them either.] "This path too," he declared, "is not adequate for knowledge, not adequate for seeing, not adequate for unsurpassed total enlightenment."

And having thus determined that path to be insufficient, the bodhisattva went on.

THE PRACTICE OF AUSTERITIES

Now King Śuddhodana, overcome by sorrow for his son, constantly sent out messengers to search for the bodhisattva. In this way, he learned that the bodhisattva had left Udraka Rāmaputra, departed Rājagrha, and was wandering around without any attendants. Having heard that, he sent three hundred servants to attend to him. And in the same royal city, the Śākya Suprabuddha, Queen Māyā's father, heard the same news, and he sent two hundred servants. So the bodhisattva, surrounded by five hundred attendants, wandered in the forest of asceticism.

Soon, he reflected: "Dwelling in crowds is no good for discipline in ascetic practices and is antithetical to the search for the deathless state. Therefore I will retain five servants only and send the others away." So he kept two from the maternal side and three from the paternal side, and they attended to his needs.

Now, with his entourage of five attendants, he went on a journey to the south of Gayā, to Urubilvā, the village of Senāpati. There he found a lovely spot, a grove of trees near the Nairañjanā River. . . . And he sat himself firmly down at the base of a tree, clenched his teeth, placed the tip of his tongue on his palate, and grabbed, gathered, and pressed hard his thoughts with his mind. . . . [And he began to fast] As he gradually took smaller and smaller amounts of food, his backbone became like a string of beads, and his buttocks became like the foot of a camel. Taking hold of his body from the front, he found he held it at the back. Taking hold of it from the back, he found he held it in front. He rubbed and stroked his body with his hands, and where he did so his hairs readily fell off. [. . .]

In the meantime, King Śuddhodana heard that the bodhisattva was practicing austerities, and he sent 250 spies to report on his activities. And Suprabuddha as well sent 250 spies. And they, every day, sent various reports back to Kapilavastu: "The bodhisattva is carrying out such and such an austerity." "He is eating a meal of one sesame seed, one grain of rice, one jujube, one pulse pod, one bean . . . " "He is sleeping on darbha grass."

Learning all this, King Śuddhodana became very worried about his son, and, his eyes clouded with tears, his heart and mind in torment, he suffered himself and began to make his own bed on darbha grass.

And the bodhisattva's wife, Princess Yaśodharā, . . . learning the news about her husband, was overcome with sorrow for him, and, her face wet with tears, her ornaments and garlands cast aside, despondent, she too undertook austerities. She too began to eat meals of one sesame seed, one grain of rice, one jujube, one pulse pod, one bean, and she slept on a bed of straw. As a result, the child in her womb wasted away.

King Śuddhodana heard of her condition and reflected: "If Yaśodharā continues every day to receive news of the bodhisattva, and thereby to be stricken with sorrow for her husband, and to persist miserably in her asceticism, she will not be able to bear this fetus, and it will perish."

Therefore he undertook measures to ensure that no more news of the bodhisattva be told to Yaśodharā. . . . The spies were instructed to communicate any information about the bodhisattva only to Śuddhodana. And keeping what he heard secret, and hiding his own distress from Yaśodharā, he deceived the whole harem, and Yaśodharā regained her health. . . .

Meanwhile, the bodhisattva, who was practicing bodily austerities, thought: "No one engaged in the discipline of great ascetic striving has ever transcended suffering; therefore this path as well is not adequate for knowledge, not adequate for seeing, not adequate for unsurpassed total enlightenment." And he began to relax his strenuousness; and his body, which had been suppressed, became calm, . . . and his mind, which had been repressed, became one-pointed.

And he reflected: "What is the way that is adequate for knowledge, for seeing, for unsurpassed total enlightenment?" Then it occurred to him: "I remember when, as a boy, I sat down in the shade of the jambu tree while attending a festival at the place of my father Śuddhodana; at that time, I attained a trance state that was free from sensual desires, free from sinful and demeritorious things, thoughtful, reflective, arising from discrimination, and blissful. That must be the way, that must be the path that is adequate for knowledge, for seeing, for unsurpassed total enlightenment. . . . "

So the bodhisattva began to take substantial food, porridge and gruel, and he rubbed his limbs with ghee and oil, and he took a warm bath. . . . And gradually he regained his bodily strength, his vigor and energy, and, in time, he went to the village of Senāyani. There, lived a villager named Sena. He had two daughters, Nandā and Nandabalā. They had heard that the bodhisattva was the prince of the Śākyas, who had been born in the foothills of the Himālayas on the banks of the Bhāgīratha River, not far from the hermitage of the sage Kapila, and that brahmin soothsayers had predicted he would become a cakravartin king. . . . So they prepared for him, in a crystal bowl, some sweetened milk-rice condensed sixteen times. . . .

Then the bodhisattva consumed the milk-rice, and, after washing the bowl, he threw it into the Nairañjanā River. There the nāgas took hold of it. But the gods are aware of what happens down below, and Indra, king of the gods, took on the form of a garuda bird, stirred up the waters of the Nairanjanā, terrified the nagas, took away the bowl, and instituted a Festival of the Bowl among the gods in his heaven.

Then the bodhisattva asked Nandā and Nandabalā: "What did you seek by virtue of your gift?"

They replied: "Blessed One, as a result of the merit of our gift and of our resolution, we would like to have you, the Prince of the Śākyas, as our husband . . . you who, the soothsayers predicted, would become a cakravartin king."

The bodhisattva replied: "This is not possible; I am one who has wandered forth and have no desire for sensual pleasures."

They said: "Blessed One, if that is the case, let the meritorious fruit of this act of giving be your highest enlightenment." [. . .]

ENLIGHTENMENT OBTAINED

Then, having received some grass from the grass-cutter Svastika, the bodhisattva approached the foot of the Bodhi Tree, by the road pointed out to him by the gods. Getting there, he prepared a broad, nicely arranged, firmly established seat of grass. . . . And mounting this adamantine throne, he sat down with his legs crossed like a sleeping snake-king's coils. Holding his body upright and fixing his mind in front of him, he resolved: "I will not uncross my legs until the destruction of defilements has been attained." [. . .]

And in the first watch of the night, he inclined his mind toward achieving firsthand knowledge of the field of supernatural powers, . . . and he set himself to the task of remembering, in a firsthand way, his former births. . . . He recalled his many various previous existences: one birth, two, three, four, . . . ten, twenty, thirty, forty, fifty, a thousand, . . . many thousands, . . . many hundreds of thousands. . . .

And in the second watch of the night, he inclined his mind to achieving firsthand knowledge of the transmigration of beings from one existence to another. With his pure divine eye transcending human sight, he saw beings dying and being reborn, of good caste and bad, low and high, in good rebirths, in unfortunate ones. . . . They were wandering in samsāra according to the evil inclinations of their sensual desires, birth, and ignorance. . . .

Then in the third watch of the night, he declared his intention to achieve direct perception of the destruction of evil inclinations, and disciplining himself and persevering, he meditated on the dharmas that are conducive to enlightenment. . . . And he truly realized: "This is the Noble Truth of Suffering; this is the Origination of Suffering; this is the Cessation of Suffering; this is the Noble Truth of the Way leading to the Cessation of Suffering." Knowing that and seeing that, he was then released from thoughts inclined to sensual desire, he was released from thoughts inclined to rebirth, he was released from thoughts inclined to ignorance. And released, he had a realization of his liberation: "Destroyed is my birth; consumed is my striving; done is what had to be done; I will not be born into another existence!" Thus the Blessed One attained to the highest enlightenment. . . .

BIRTH OF RĀHULA

When the Buddha attained highest enlightenment, Māra, . . . the evil-minded One, was angry. Making himself invisible, he spitefully had his godlings announce to the city of Kapilavastu: "The bodhisattva Śākyamuni, after practicing austerities and mounting the adamantine throne, has died on his seat of grass."

Hearing this, King Śuddhodana, together with his harem, the princes, and his ministers, was stricken with great sorrow, as was the whole population of Kapilavastu. And . . . Yaśodharā, remembering the qualities of her husband, fainted and fell on the ground. Recovering her senses when some water was sprinkled on her face, she lamented incessantly, her face ever filled with tears, her words choked with sobs, the women of the harem trying to console her.

Soon, however, seeing that her behavior was in response to a deception, some divinities who had faith in the Buddha declared, "The bodhisattva is not dead, but he has attained highest knowledge."

Hearing this, King Śuddhodana, together with his entourage and the population of Kapilavastu, was transported with great joy.

Now when the Blessed One attained highest knowledge, Yaśodharā gave birth to a son. . . . And King Śuddhodana, seeing this good fortune, was pleased, happy, delighted, filled with highest joy. He arranged for a great celebration in the city of Kapilavastu. . . . And because, at the time of the boy's birth, Rāhu had caused an eclipse of the moon, the bodhisattva's son was given the name Rāhula.

[Translated in Strong, *Experience of Buddhism*, pp. 10–18]

CONFUSION OVER THE BUDDHA AS A FERTILITY GOD

In the famous story of Sujātā, supposedly the first female to convert to Buddhism, the linkage between the Buddha's spiritual success is again linked to family concerns, and fertility in particular. On the night of his enlightenment, Sujātā offers him a bowl of rice-milk and it is due to this rich meal that the

Buddha is able to achieve enlightenment. However, around this simple act the story develops several layers of complexity. First, Sujātā is said to make her offering to the Buddha through misrecognizing him as a tree-spirit whom she thinks responsible for granting her the birth of her son, Yasa. This error in no way ruins her offering, either for her own karmic account, or for the Buddha's enlightenment that follows. In fact, this erroneous offering opens the door to another cycle of action that more closely links the Buddha's enlightenment to Sujātā's family since, once Yasa has grown up, he, just as the Buddha supposedly had done, one day finds his harem disgusting and leaves. Thus the son that Sujātā "mistakenly" thanked the Buddha for turns out to behave just like the Buddha. And, since the story offers no explanation for this odd parallel, one might be tempted to read Yasa's action as proof that in some way the Buddha's identity was passed on to him because of his mother's gift to the Buddha. However one chooses to read that section of the narrative, the connection between this family and the Buddha are more amply developed when Yasa's father comes to the Buddha to find out what happened to his son — presumably a point of conflict that the story wants to negotiate — and the Buddha magically hides Yasa while he gives the father a dharma lesson. This lesson results in both Yasa and his father awakening to the status of arhants, free forever from samsara. However, the story is not over until Yasa, as a monk, returns one day to beg from his homestead only to use the opportunity to preach dharma to his mother who, too, achieves arhant status.

Thus, in a cleverly wrought narrative, the story mediates the conflict between family and Buddhist renunciation and even suggests that dharma can, in reverse, work its way back into the family, in this case via Yasa's renunciation, so that his mother and father are indirectly saved as the result of their son's exit. Better still, all this is implicitly effected through the mother's unwitting gift to the Buddha that aided him at the crucial final moment before achieving enlightenment and also set in motion the cycle of events that would result in her entire family finding Buddhist salvation.

Document 5–8

THE STORY OF SUJĀTĀ

Long ago, at the time of the past Buddha Padumuttara, a woman was born into a good family in Haṃsavatī. One day, after listening to the Master preach the Dharma and witnessing his establishment of a laywoman as "foremost of those taking refuge," she made a formal resolution, aspiring to attain that same status herself.

For one hundred thousand aeons, she was repeatedly reborn in saṃsāra, in the realms of gods and humans, until just before our own Master Gotama's birth, she was reborn in the house of the landlord Senāni in the village of Senāni in Uruvelā. Once she had come of age, she made this promise to the god of a banyan tree: "If, once I am married to someone of the same caste, my first child is a son, I will, every year, make a food offering to you."

Her wish was successful and a son, Yasa, was born to her. Then, on the full moon day of the month of Visākha, when coincidentally the six years of the bodhisatta's practice of extreme asceticism were just about over, she got up early in the morning and milked her cow before dawn, thinking, "Today, I will make that food offering!" The cow's calves had not yet suckled, but as soon as a new pot was put under the udder, the milk flowed out of its own accord. Marveling at this, Sujātā took the milk in her own hand and directed it into the new pot, and she herself put it on the fire to cook. And when that milk-rice started to boil, great bubbles appeared, and auspiciously turned to the right. So that in bursting they would not splash over the sides, the god Brahmā held an umbrella [as a lid over the pot], . . . while Indra regulated the fire, and the gods of the four directions added a divine nutritive essence to the milk-rice.

Beholding all these marvels, Sujātā said to her servant Puṇṇa: "It has been a long time since I have seen so many good omens; go quickly and prepare the place of the god!"

"Yes, mistress," she answered, and as told, she hurried to the foot of the banyan tree.

Now the bodhisatta had gotten up early, and waiting for the time of the begging round, he was sitting under that tree. And Puṇṇa, arriving at that pure place, mistook him for the tree god. She went back to Sujātā and said: "The divinity himself is seated at the foot of the tree!"

Sujātā replied, "Ah! If what you say is true, then it was he who gave me my son!" And putting on all of her ornaments, she piled the milk-rice on a golden plate worth a hundred thousand pieces of gold, enclosed it in another golden bowl, wrapped it in a white cloth, added wreaths of sweet-smelling garlands, picked it up, and set forth. When she saw the Great Man, there arose in her an overpowering gladness, and she bowed down very low in front of him, touching her head to the ground. Uncovering the dish of milk-rice, she offered it to the Blessed One with her own hand, saying, "Just as my wish has been fulfilled, so may yours be accomplished." Then she went away.

The bodhisatta went to the bank of the Nerañjanā River and put the golden dish down there on the shore; he bathed, got out, fashioned the milk-rice into four balls, and ate it. He then washed the dish in the river, and in due course he went to the seat of enlightenment, attained omniscience, spent seven times seven days contemplating his enlightenment, and set in motion the excellent wheel of the Dharma at the Deer Park of Isipatana.

In the meantime, Sujātā's son, Yasa, had grown, and the Buddha, realizing that he had within him the conditions necessary for enlightenment, went and sat down under another tree planning to encounter him. Young Yasa, finding the door to his harem open at midnight, was suddenly full of restlessness. Muttering: "How depressing! How distressing [is this life of sensual pleasure]!" he left his house, went out of the city, happened across the Blessed One, heard from him the teaching of the Dharma, and attained the first three fruits of the path.

Then his father, searching for him, followed his tracks until he too came to the Blessed One. He asked what had happened to his son. The Master, however, concealed young Yasa by making him invisible and preached the Dharma to his father. At the end of the sermon, Yasa's father attained the fruit of entering the stream, and Yasa [who, though invisible, had been listening], became an arhat. The Blessed One then ordained Yasa simply by saying, "Come, monk," and as soon as he heard those words, the characteristics of a layman in him disappeared and he became like a great elder, bearing a begging bowl and all the requisites of a monk, which had been magically created.

Yasa's father invited the Buddha to their home. The Blessed One, taking young Yasa as his novice disciple, went to their house, ate a meal, and preached the Dharma. At the end of the sermon, Yasa's mother, Sujātā . . . also attained the fruit of entering the stream . . . and at the same time uttered the formula of the threefold refuge. Subsequently, when the Master was assigning statuses to the laywomen, he established her as the foremost laywoman among those taking refuge.

[Translated in Strong, *Experience of Buddhism*, pp. 48–49]

BUDDHISM AS A THREAT TO THE INDIAN FAMILY

While the above stories leave little doubt about the care given to finessing a mutually productive pattern of exchange between Buddhism and the family, one can also find explicit stories admitting the dread with which families might have regarded the Buddhists, since they threatened to draw their beloved and much needed sons away from them. In the following story the Buddha's imminent arrival, with a group of twelve hundred monks, prompts the villagers to go on the offensive, hoping physically to persuade the Buddha to leave them and theirs alone. The story, though articulating a rather vivid antipathy toward the Buddhist ascetics—they are likened to a hailstorm that decimates crops— still manages to present a calming point of closure, since the rampaging mob is quickly overcome by a complex trick. In this ruse a Buddhist sympathizer in the village knowingly sets fire to the village once the mob has gone out to "rough up" the Buddha. The mob learns that their village is being destroyed, even as they take action to save it by heading off the Buddha's arrival, and yet the Buddha magically quenches the fires and proceeds to preach them dharma, presumably quelling the other metaphoric fires that ravage their home-focused lives.

Document 5–9

THE LYNCH MOB STORY

At that time, the Blessed One was traveling in the country of Kosala and was headed for a brahmin village. The non-Buddhist heretical masters there, learning of the coming of the wanderer Gautama, hastened to visit the families of the brahmin householders.

"May your happiness increase!" they declared to them. "We are leaving!"

"Reverend sirs," the householders responded, "why are you going?"

The heretics replied: "Having seen you rich, we hate to see you ruined. That is why we are leaving!"

"What do you mean, reverend sirs?" the others asked. "Why do you say we shall be ruined?"

"You should know that the wanderer Gautama is coming, at the head of twelve hundred disciples. His band is like a hailstorm that decimates the crops. Countless parents among you will doubtless be deprived of your sons."

The householders said: "But, reverend sirs, if that is the case, we must remain united and support each other. . . . "

The heretics said: "Let us make an agreement, then. We promise to stay here, but you must go and ill-treat the wanderer Gautama."

"We will rough him up!" the brahmin householders declared, and taking swords, sticks, bows, and arrows . . . they headed down the road.

Now, there was in that town an old man who was inclined toward Buddhism. He saw those men and asked them, "Where are you going?"

"We're going to get someone!" they replied.

"Whom are you mad at?" the old man asked.

"The wanderer Gautama!" they answered.

"Go home," the old man told them. "The Blessed One is a great teacher; if you are angry with him, whom would you consider to be a friend?"

But they refused to go back.

The old man then reflected: "People of this sort—it is not possible to convert them by preaching the Dharma. They can only be tamed by the performance of some kind of magical display."

So he went back to the village and set fire to it. The fire rose up on every side, and those who had stayed in the village started screaming. Those who wanted to assault the Buddha heard their cries and were afraid.

"The wanderer Gautama is still far from here," they said to one another, "and already a horrible thing has happened: the village is on fire! We must go back and put out the blaze." They tried to do so, but found they could not.

Soon, however, the Blessed One arrived. "Why are you afraid?" he asked.

The villagers replied: "Our houses are being consumed by the flames, and we can't do anything about it!"

The Buddha then said to them: "I will put the fire out for you. . . . "

And then, just as soon as the Tathāgata had finished speaking, the fire was extinguished by his supernatural powers, and faith was engendered in the hearts of all those brahmin householders.

"Blessed One," they said to the Buddha, "what did we do to merit your coming?"

"It is for your sake that I have come," the Blessed One said to them. And understanding their character and knowing their roots of merit, he preached the Dharma to them, and instructed them in the Four Noble Truths. . . .

[Translated in Strong, *Experience of Buddhism*, pp. 59–61]

THE BUDDHA'S ADVICE FOR LAITY

In this important text that appears to have been well known in Southeast Asia and East Asia, the Buddha is shown supplementing a father's advice to his son. At the moment of the discussion, the son is, in accordance with his deceased father's instructions, performing prostrations in the six directions—the four cardinal directions plus up and down—without assigning any particular meaning to this daily gesture. The Buddha intervenes and explains to the boy, in detail, how to organize these ritual observances so that they function to articulate and reaffirm all his familial and social obligations, even as the Buddha explains how to set all these responsibilities within a wider Buddhist context. In the first section of the document, which is unrelated to our topic and has been omitted here, the Buddha explains lists of four and six items relevant to Buddhist ethics and practice that presumably could be correlated with the four and six directions. In the second half of the work, duplicated below, the Buddha takes up the more germane topic of mapping the bowing in the six directions onto the boy's social world. Thus, beginning with a bow to the east, he is to honor his mother and father, followed by a bow to the south representing his teachers, then to the west for his wife and children, to the north for his friends, with the nadir reserved for his servants, and the zenith position, not surprisingly, held by ascetics. By supposedly advocating this handy ritual design, the Buddha is shown both fulfilling what the boy's biological father had failed to transmit to him, and giving the boy (and the reader) the structure and content to create a hiearachized, and yet integrated, map of familial, social, and religious obligation.[3]

Document 5–10

SIGĀLAKA SUTTA: ADVICE OF LAITY IN THE DĪGHANIKĀYA

Thus have I heard. Once the Lord was staying at Rājagaha, at the Squirrels' Feeding Place in the Bamboo Grove. And at that time Sigālaka the householder's son, having got up early and gone out of Rājagaha, was paying homage, with wet clothes and hair and with joined palms, to the different directions: to the east, the south, the west, the north, the nadir and the zenith.

And the Lord, having risen early and dressed, took his robe and bowl and went to Rājagaha for alms. And seeing Sigālaka paying homage to the different directions, he said: "Householder's son, why have you got up early to pay homage to the different directions?' "Lord, my father, when he was dying, told me to do so. And so, Lord, out of respect for my father's words, which I revere, honor and hold sacred, I have got up thus early to pay homage in this way to the six directions." "But, householder's son, that is not the right way to pay homage to the six directions according to the Ariyan discipline." "Well, Lord, how should one pay homage to the six directions according to the Ariyan discipline? It would be good if the Blessed Lord were to teach me the proper way to pay homage to the six directions according to the Ariyan discipline." "Then listen carefully, pay attention, and I will speak." "Yes, Lord," said Sigālaka, and the Lord said: . . .

"And how, householder's son, does the Ariyan disciple protect the six directions? These six things are to be regarded as the six directions. The east denotes mother and father. The south denotes teachers, The west denotes wife and children. The north denotes friends and companions. The nadir denotes servants, workers and helpers. The zenith denotes ascetics and Brahmins.

"There are five ways in which a son should minister to his mother and father as the eastern direction. [He should think] 'Having been supported by them, I will support them. I will perform their duties for them. I will keep up the family tradition. I will be worthy of my heritage. After my parents' deaths I will distribute gifts on their behalf.' And there are five ways in which the parents, so ministered to by their son as the eastern direction, will reciprocate: they will restrain him from evil, support him in doing good, teach him some skill, find him a suitable wife and, in due time, hand over his inheritance to him. In this way the eastern direction is covered, making it at peace and free from fear.

"There are five ways in which pupils should minister to their teachers as the southern direction: by rising to greet them, by waiting on them, by being attentive, by serving them, by mastering the skills they teach. And there are five ways in which their teachers, thus ministered to by their pupils as the southern direction, will reciprocate: they will give thorough instruction, make sure they have grasped what they should have duly grasped, give them a thorough grounding in all skills, recommend them to their friends and colleagues, and provide them with security in all directions. In this way the southern direction is covered, making it at peace and free from fear.

"There are five ways in which a husband should minister to his wife as the western direction: by honoring her, by not disparaging her, by not being unfaithful to her, by giving authority to her, by providing her with adornments. And there are five ways in which a wife, thus ministered to by her husband as the western direction, will reciprocate: by properly organizing her work, by being kind to the servants, by not being unfaithful, by protecting stores, and by being skilful and diligent in all she has to do. In this way the western direction is covered, making it at peace and free from fear.

"There are five ways in which a man should minister to his friends and companions as the northern direction: by gifts, by kindly words, by looking after their welfare, by treating them like himself, and by keeping his word. And there are five ways in which friends and companions, thus ministered to by a man as the northern direction, will reciprocate: by looking after him when he is inattentive, by looking after his property when he is inattentive, by being a refuge when he is afraid, by not deserting him when he is in trouble, and by showing concern for his children. In this way the northern direction is covered, making it at peace and free from fear.

"There are five ways in which a master should minister to his servants and workpeople as the nadir: by arranging their work according to their strength, by supplying them with food and wages, by looking after them when they are ill, by sharing special delicacies with them, and by letting them off work at the right time. And there are five ways in which servants and workpeople, thus ministered to by their master as the nadir, will reciprocate: they will get up before him, go to bed after him, take only what they are given, do their work properly, and be bearers of his praise and good repute. In this way the nadir is covered, making it at peace and free from fear.

"There are five ways in which a man should minister to ascetics and Brahmins as the zenith: by kindness in bodily deed, speech and thought, by keeping open house for them, by supplying their bodily needs. And the ascetics and Brahmins, thus ministered to by him as the zenith, will reciprocate in six ways: they will restrain him from evil, encourage him to do good, be benevolently compassionate towards him, teach him what he has not heard, and point out to him the way to heaven. In this way the zenith is covered, making it at peace and free from fear." Thus the Lord spoke.

And the Well-Farer having spoken, the Teacher added:

> "Mother, father are the east,
> Teachers are the southward point,
> Wife and children are the west,
> Friends and colleagues are the north.
> Servants and workers are below,
> Ascetics, Brahmins are above.
> These directions all should be
> Honoured by a clansman true.
> He who's wise and disciplined,
> Kindly and intelligent,
> Humble, free from pride,
> Such a one may honour gain.
> Early rising, scorning sloth,
> Unshaken by adversity,
> Of faultless conduct, ready wit,
> Such a one may honour gain.
> Making friends, and keeping them,
> Welcoming, no stingy host,

> A guide, philosopher and friend,
> Such a one may honour gain.
> Giving gifts and kindly speech,
> A life well-spent for others' good,
> Even-handed in all things,
> Impartial as each case demands:
> These things make the world go round
> Like the chariot's axle-pin.
> If such things did not exist,
> No mother from her son would get
> Any honour and respect,
> Nor father either, as their due.
> But since these qualities are held
> By the wise in high esteem,
> They are given prominence
> And are rightly praised by all."

At these words Sigālaka said to the Lord: "Excellent, Reverend Gotama, excellent! It is as if someone were to set up what had been knocked down, or to point out the way to one who had got lost, or to bring an oil-lamp into a dark place, so that those with eyes could see what was there. Just so the Reverend Gotama has expounded the Dhamma in various ways, May the Reverend Gotama accept me as a lay-follower from this day forth as long as life shall last!"

[Translated in *The Long Discourses of the Buddha: A Translation of the Dīghanikāya*, trans. Maurice Walshe (Boston: Wisdom, 1987), pp. 461–469]

AN EARLY BUDDHA LINEAGE

This is a fascinating narrative explaining the identity of Buddha Śakyamuni, the Buddha of our era. To explain and legitimize the Buddha, this narrative creates a chain of parallel figures who stretch back in time, and, rather remarkably, all have the identical biographic details as the Buddha Śakyamuni, save for a couple name changes. Here we see the articulation of a fundamental problem in Buddhist cosomology—the single knower of the final mode of reality in the universe must in turn be verified by other equally exalted figures. In short, the rule seems to be that it takes a Buddha to know a Buddha, and thus there were presumably several structural reasons for creating multiple buddhas and hooking them together in mutually confirming ways. Moreover, as the title of this work suggests, "The Great Lineage," to make this chain of buddhas appear logical and coherent it is fashioned as kind of patriline that, though producing in some unseen manner without women or sex, still shares with the reproductive family the image of legitimacy, continuity, and what we might call a "conservation of identity." Hence, though the Buddha, in line with all his predecessors, is shown breaking with his natal family, this rupture is only explainable by creating a kind of "over-family" to which the Buddha belongs as a rightful successor. More exactly, to create the image of the Buddha as an universal subject, completely free of the particulars of his birth in a certain age, to certain parents. etc., he is ironically given another family, albeit a universal family. Interest in building these sorts of "buddha-families" was not unique to this text and both pre-Mahāyāna and Mahāyāna authors would give considerable attention to constructing and purveying this sort of "over-family" often with the implication that, as in the Gospels, one could gain entrance to this family simply by recognizing the legitimacy of its principle participants.

Equally worth noting is the emphasis on the family particulars given for each buddha. Thus, their father's and mother's names and status are listed, their places of residence and so on. Again there seems to be an interesting tension between these mundane details and the grandiosity of the figure who is to be associated with these details. Perhaps it is best simply to say that the image of universality must, ironically, be built with the most familiar of items.

Document 5–11

MAHĀPANADĀNA IN DĪGHANIKĀYA

Soon after the Lord had gone, another discussion arose among the monks: "It is marvellous, friends, it is wonderful, the Tathāgata's great power and ability— the way he recalls past Buddhas who have gained Parinibbāna, having cut away the hindrances, cut off the road [of craving], put an end to the round of becoming, overcome all suffering. He recalls their birth, their name, their clan, their life-span, the disciples and assemblies connected with him: 'Being born thus, these Blessed Lords were such-and-such, such were their names, their clans, their discipline, their Dhamma, their wisdom, their liberation.' Well now, friends, how did the Tathāgata come by the penetrative knowledge through which he remembers all this . . . ? Did some deva reveal this knowledge to him?" This was the conversation of those monks which came to be interrupted.

Then the Lord, rising from the seclusion of the rest-period, went to the Kareri pavilion and sat down on the prepared seat. He said: "Monks, what was your conversation as you sat together? What discussion did I interrupt?" And the monks told him.

"The Tathāgata understands these things . . . by his own penetration of the principles of Dhamma; and devas, too, have told him. Well, monks, do you wish to hear still more about past lives?" "Lord, it is time for that! Well-Farer, it is time for that! If the Lord were to give a proper discourse on past lives, the monks would listen and remember it" "Well then, monks, listen, pay close attention, and I will speak." "Yes, Lord," the monks replied, and the Lord said:

"Monks, ninety-one aeons ago the Lord, the Arahant, the fully-enlightened Buddha Vipassī arose in the world. He was born of Khattiya race, and arose in a Khattiya family. He was of the Koṇḍañña clan. The span of his life was eighty thousand years. He gained his full enlightenment at the foot of a trumpet-flower tree. He had the pair of noble disciples Khaṇḍa and Tissa as his chief followers. He had three assemblies of disciples: one of six million eight hundred thousand, one of a hundred thousand, and one of eighty thousand monks, all Arahants. His chief personal attendant was the monk Asoka. His father was King Bandhumā, his mother was Queen Bandhumatī. The king's capital was Bandhumatī.

And so, monks, the Bodhisatta Vipassī descended from the Tusita heaven, mindful and clearly aware, into his mother's womb. This, monks, is the rule. It is the rule, monks, that when a Bodhisatta descends from the Tusita heaven into his mother's womb, there appears in this world with its devas, māras and Brahmās, its ascetics and Brahmins, princes and people an immeasurable, splendid light surpassing the glory of the most powerful devas. And whatever dark spaces lie beyond the world's end, chaotic, blind and black, such that they are not even reached by the mighty rays of sun and moon, are yet illumined by this immeasurable splendid light surpassing the glory of the most powerful devas. And those beings that have been reborn there recognise each other by this light and know: 'Other beings, too, have been born here!' And this ten-thousandfold world-system trembles and quakes and is convulsed. And this immeasurable light shines forth. That is the rule.

It is the rule that when a Bodhisatta has entered his mother's womb, four devas come to protect him from the four quarters, saying: 'Let no man, no non-human being, no thing whatever harm this Bodhisatta or this Bodhisatta's mother!' That is the rule.

It is the rule that when a Bodhisatta has entered his mother's womb, his mother becomes by nature virtuous, refraining from taking life, from taking what is not given, from sexual misconduct, from lying speech, or from strong drink and sloth-producing drugs. That is the rule.

It is the rule that when a Bodhisatta has entered his mother's womb, she has no sensual thoughts connected with a man, and she cannot be overcome by any man with lustful thoughts. That is the rule.

It is the rule that when a Bodhisatta has entered his mother's womb, she enjoys the fivefold pleasures of the senses and takes delight, being endowed and possessed of them. That is the rule.

It is the rule that when a Bodhisatta has entered his mother's womb, she has no sickness of any kind, she is at ease and without fatigue of body, and she can see the Bodhisatta inside her womb, complete with all his members and faculties. Monks, it is as if a gem, a beryl, pure, excellent, well cut into eight facets, clear, bright, flawless and perfect in every respect, were strung on a blue, yellow, red, white or orange cord. And a man with good eyesight, taking it in his hand, would describe it as such. Thus does the Bodhisatta's mother, with no sickness, see him, complete with all his members and faculties. That is the rule.

It is the rule that the Bodhisatta's mother dies seven days after his birth and is reborn in the Tusita heaven. That is the rule.

It is the rule that whereas other women carry the child in their womb for nine or ten months before giving birth, it is not so with the Bodhisatta's mother, who carries him for exactly ten months before giving birth. That is the rule.

It is the rule that whereas other women' give birth sitting or lying down, it is not so with the Bodhisatta's mother, who gives birth standing up. That is the rule.

It is the rule that when the Bodhisatta issues from his mother's womb, devas welcome him first, and then humans. That is the rule.

It is the rule that when the Bodhisatta issues from his mother's womb, he does not touch the earth. Four devas receive him and place him before his mother, saying: 'Rejoice, Your Majesty, a mighty son has been born to you!' That is the rule.

It is the rule that when the Bodhisatta issues from his mother's womb he issues forth stainless, not defiled by water, mucus, blood or any impurity, pure and spotless. Just as when a jewel is laid on muslin from Kāsī, the jewel does not stain the muslin, or the muslin the jewel. Why not? Because of the purity of both. In the same way the Bodhisatta issues forth stainless. . . . That is the rule.

It is the rule that when the Bodhisatta issues forth from his mother's womb, two streams of water appear from the sky, one cold, the other warm, with which they ritually wash the Bodhisatta and his mother. That is the rule.

It is the rule that as soon as he is born the Bodhisatta takes a firm stance on both feet facing north, then takes seven strides and, under a white sunshade, he scans the four quarters and then declares with a bull-like voice: 'I am chief in the world, supreme in the world, eldest in the world. This is my last birth, there will be no more re-becoming.' That is the rule.

It is the rule that when the Bodhisatta issues from his mother's womb there appears in this world . . . an immeasurable, splendid light. . . . This is the rule.

Monks, when Prince Vipassī was born, they showed him to King Bandhumā and said: 'Your Majesty, a son has been born to you. Deign, Sire, to look at him.' The king looked at the prince and then said to the Brahmins skilled in signs: 'You gentlemen are skilled in signs, examine the prince.' The Brahmins examined the prince, and said to King Bandhumā: 'Sire, rejoice, for a mighty son has been born to you. It is a gain for you, Sire, it is a great profit for you, Sire, that such a son has been born into your family. Sire, this prince is endowed with the thirty-two marks of a Great Man. To such, only two courses are open. If he lives the household life he will become a ruler, a wheel-turning righteous monarch of the law, conqueror of the four quarters, who has established the security of his realm and is possessed of the seven treasures. These are: the Wheel Treasure, the Elephant Treasure, the Horse Treasure, the Jewel Treasure, the Woman Treasure, the Householder Treasure, and, as seventh, the Counsellor Treasure. He has more than a thousand sons who are heroes, of heroic stature, conquerors of the hostile army. He dwells having conquered this sea-girt land without stick or sword, by the law. But if he goes forth from the household life into homelessness, then he will become an Arahant, a fully-enlightened Buddha, one who draws back the veil from the world.'

'And what, Sire, are these thirty-two marks . . . ? (1) He has feet with level tread. (2) On the soles of his feet are wheels with a thousand spokes. (3) He has projecting heels. (4) He has long fingers and toes. (5) He has soft and tender hands and feet. (6) His hands and feet are net-like. (7) He has high-raised ankles. (8) His legs are like an antelope's. (9) Standing and without bending, he can touch and rub his knees with either hand. (10) His male organs are enclosed in a sheath. (11) His complexion is bright, the colour of gold. (12) His skin is delicate and so smooth that no dust adheres to it. (13) His body-hairs are separate, one to each pore. (14) They grow upwards, bluish-black like collyrium, growing in rings to the right. (15) His body is divinely straight. (16) He has the seven convex surfaces. (17) The front part of his body is like a lion's. (18) There is no hollow between his shoulders. (19) He is proportioned like a banyan-tree: his height is as the span of his arms. (20) His bust is evenly rounded. (21) He has a perfect sense of taste. (22) He has jaws like a lion's. (23) He has forty teeth. (24) His teeth are even. (25) There are no spaces between his teeth. (26) His canine teeth are very bright. (27) His tongue is very long. (28) He has a Brahmā-like voice, like that of the bird. (29) His eyes are deep blue. (30) He has eyelashes like a cow's. (31) The hair between his eyebrows is white, and soft like cotton-down. (32) His head is like a royal turban.'

'Sire, this prince is endowed with the thirty-two marks of a Great Man. To such, only two courses are open. If he lives the household life he will become a ruler, a wheel-turning righteous monarch of the law. . . . But if he goes forth from the household life into homelessness, then he will become an Arahant, a fully-enlightened Buddha, one who draws back the veil from the world.'

Then King Bandhumā, having clothed those Brahmins in fresh clothes, satisfied all their wishes.

And King Bandhumā appointed nurses for Prince Vipassī. Some suckled him, some bathed him, some carried him, some dandled him. A white umbrella was held over him night and day, that he might not be harmed by cold or heat or grass or dust. And Prince Vipassī was much beloved of the people. Just as everybody loves a blue, yellow or white lotus, so they all loved Prince Vipassī. Thus he was borne from lap to lap.

And Prince Vipassī had a sweet voice, a beautiful voice, charming and delightful. Just as in the Himālaya mountains the *karavīka*-bird has a voice sweeter, more beautiful, charming and delightful than all other birds, so too was Prince Vipassī's voice the finest of all.

And owing to the results of past kamma, the divine eye was present to Prince Vipassī, with which he could see for a league day and night alike.

And Prince Vipassī was unblinkingly watchful, like the Thirty-Three Gods.

And because it was said that he was unblinkingly watchful, the prince came to be called "Vipassī". When King Bandhumā was trying a case, he took Prince Vipassī on his knee and instructed him in the case. Then, putting him down from his knee, his father would carefully explain the issues to him. And for this reason he was all the more called Vipassī.

Then King Bandhumā caused three palaces to be built for Prince Vipassī, one for the rainy season, one for the cold season, and one for the hot season, to cater for all the fivefold sense-pleasures. There Prince Vipassī stayed in the rainy-season palace for the four months of the rainy season, with no male attendants, surrounded by female musicians, and he never left that palace.

[Translated in *Long Discourses*, pp. 199–207]

EAST ASIAN BUDDHISM: AN OVERVIEW

All the above selections are found in Indian sources in Sanskrit, Pali, and other Indic languages. These narratives were translated into Chinese, often more than once, and in various permutations, during the slow migration of Buddhism to China, which began in the first century and more or less ceased in the ninth or tenth century, though the bulk of the translation work was done before the eighth century. While most of the above narratives seem to have been known, and to have circulated in China, they were in many ways displaced, and in some cases, surpassed, by a crop of indigenous Buddhist texts, written by the Chinese in the borrowed form of the Indian sutra-format, and circulated widely as though they were translations deriving from Indian sources. These home-grown sutras were terribly important for defining the emerging content and contours of Chinese Buddhism. In the selections that follow, I have selected writings related to family mores that we know to have been important and which clearly also gave rise to other works that picked up these themes and developed them in further directions. In fact, though these works were all written in the medieval period, with the earliest probably dating to fifth century, they are still in circulation in Taiwan. While I can't prove that each of these works has enjoyed an uninterrupted history of circulation since its inception, I do have some confidence in identifying them as being regularly in circulation and often pointed to as "proof-texts" for Buddhist family values in China.

This work, *The Sutra on the Difficulty of Repaying the Kindness of Parents*, is probably one of the oldest statements of Buddhist family values in Chinese sources and is first mentioned in an encyclopedia dated to 518. Pieces of this text seem to have been drawn from works translated from Indic texts, but nothing resembling this text has been found in Indic sources, and with the Confucian-styled rhetoric framing the intro and conclusion there is good reason to see it as a Chinese construction. For the purpose of thinking about the evolution of Buddhist mores in China, the text offers three important elements. First, it explains that simply caring for parents in a physical manner—as demonstrated by the trope of carrying them around on one's shoulders—is not enough, and this explanation is presumably tendered to persuade readers that Confucian-styled filial piety is insufficient, a charge that will be made in many other period pieces. According to this text, real filial piety is to be understood as converting one's parents to Buddhism and thereby leading them to what is called "a safe and secure place," an ambiguous phrase which nonetheless has post-mortem overtones. The third trope is already present in the second point but warrants singling out: Buddhism is being identified as an element that is to be transacted within the family, and between generations. Thus the text is premised on the understanding that children, sons in particular, need to reciprocate their parent's kindness as explained by Confucian forms of filial repayment, and yet this repayment imperative is now to be fulfilled by converting them to Buddhism. In short, this text works to tuck Buddhism into the normal, at-home flow of life production by borrowing the form of Confucianism and inserting Buddhist-styled concerns as the content. This clever engineering is made all the clearer with the final play on words in which the monk *qua* son is invited to see himself as one with two children: his mother and father.

Document 5–12

FUMO EN NANBAO JING: THE SUTRA ON THE DIFFICULTY OF REPAYING THE KINDNESS OF PARENTS

Thus I heard. Once, when the Buddha was at Śrāvastī in Anāthapiṇḍaka grove he said to the monks, "Father and mother have been of immense benefit to their sons *(zi)* by breastfeeding them and long nurturing them and educating them in accordance with their development. So when the four elements have become complete [in the son's person], if he were to carry his father on his right shoulder and his mother on his left shoulder for 1,000 years without any resentment, even if he was urinated on for this time, then he still would not have done enough to repay the kindness *(en)* of his father and mother."

[Therefore,] if father and mother do not believe [in Buddhism], make them believe so that they may achieve a safe and secure stele. If they are without the [Buddhist] precepts, make them accept them so that they may achieve a safe and secure state. If they do not listen [to the dharma], make them listen so that they may achieve a safe and secure state. If they are stingy and greedy, make them love to give and encourage them to be happy so that they may achieve a safe and secure state. If they are without wisdom, make them light [the fire of] wisdom and encourage them to be happy so that they may achieve a safe and secure state.

Thus [they should] believe in the Tathāgata who achieved true reality and complete enlightenment, practicing the good and renouncing the world and achieving peerless liberation, the great master, the instructor of heaven and earth called Buddha, the World Honored One.

If they do not believe in the dharma, make them believe so that they may achieve a safe and secure state. The various dharmas are ever so profound. The import of receiving the karmic effect of this present body is ever so profound. Those that have awakened to this know well this practice, so make [your parents] believe in the holy [Buddhist] community. The Tathāgata and the holy community practice in complete purity, are upright, unperverted and in harmony. Numerous dharmas they have achieved, samadhis [too] they have achieved, wisdom [also] they have achieved, liberation they have achieved, liberation and seeing wisdom they also have achieved and that is why they are called the "holy community." Multiply this by two, by four, by eight and that is what is called the "holy community of Tathāgatas" who are the most worthy of respect and the most precious. [Therefore,] everyone should respect, honor, and trust in this merit field *(futian)* which is without peer in the world.

Thus all must teach their fathers and mothers to practice compassion. [Actually,] all monks have two children/disciples *(zi)*: the child/ disciple that produced *(sheng)* them [refers to the father] and the child/disciple that nurtured them [the mother], therefore they are called "monks who have two children/ disciples." Hence every monk must imitate *(xue)* those who produced *(sheng)* him by speaking of the dharma essence [in order to turn them into Buddhist "adults"]. It is in this way that all monks should consider [Buddhist] practice.

At this time all the monks, having heard what the Buddha taught, were happy and made prostrations.

[*Taishō shinshū daizōkyō*, translated by Alan Cole][4]

THE SUTRA ON THE FILIAL SON

While the above sutra on the theme of "profound kindness of parents" is gentle and unassuming in its presentation, the following selection is pitched in a much more aggressive tone. Too, the scope of this version of Buddhist family values is much wider and clearly sets out to explain the value of Buddhist filial piety in a manner that situates it squarely in the midst of family life. Building on the trope that physical care for parents, presumably in accord with Confucian dictates, is insufficient, the text launches into a harangue about the lengths to which a son should go to get his parents to convert to Buddhism, including taking them to execution grounds to show them a facsimile of their hellish future should they fail to convert. Of particular interest in the second major section of the text is the explanation that converting parents to Buddhism will lead to the strengthening of the family lineage. In brief, the text makes no qualms about advertising Buddhism, or more exactly, its own version of Buddhism, as that which fortifies and increases the well-being and security of the family. Ironically, then, Buddhism as a supposedly transcendental effort to escape the family is here being redirected back to the family sphere to secure and promote it. The text also, in the later sections, seems to be focusing on "milk-debt" as the primary element in motivating a son to lead his parents to Buddhism. This theme, developed in other works presented below, has led me to conclude that part of the evolving content of Chinese Buddhism involved generating a new form of filial piety defined by focusing on what sons owed their mothers, with the normal items including a debt for the pain caused during birth and then this "milk-debt," though the list grew in other directions as well. Key to note is that though the Buddhists seemed to have given a lot of thought toward generating this sense of indebtedness to one's mother, this new form of filial responsibility in no way disrupted the standard forms of patriarchal family reproduction. In fact, I would argue that by emphasizing what Margery Wolf would call "uterine family" connections, the Buddhists found a way to strengthen the patriarchal family, even as they found a more vigorous and presumably enticing way to draw a son and his resources out into the public sphere of things Buddhist.

Two final points to make: first, the *Sutra on the Filial Son* is really unusually direct in pointing out the dangers of sexual desire in the home sphere and seems intent on applying Buddhist models of discipline to men at home, presumably in the hopes of maintaining stability and fiscal solvency. Thus, it could be argued that the familial sphere is, after a fashion, harvesting the enviable levels of discipline generated in the monastic space, and bringing them back within the purview of the reproductive family. In several of the selections to follow we will again see evidence of a kind of "at-home-monk," who nonetheless is expected to play his role in the normal reproductive family. Second, this text, much more than any other translated here, is written in a rough style, with odd vocabulary and twisted syntax. I've left question marks in the more difficult passages, but I want to signal to the reader that several passages of this text may not ever be fully resolved.

Document 5–13

XIAOZI JING: THE SUTRA ON THE FILIAL SON

The Buddha said to the monks, "When your parents gave birth to you, [your mother] was pregnant for ten months, her body was as though it had a severe sickness. On the day of your birth, she was scared and your father was terrified. These emotions are hard to describe. After you were born she put you in the dry places and slept in the damp ones.[5] She was so completely sincere [in her caring for you], that she even turned her blood into milk [for you]. [Then] you were petted, fed, bathed, and given clothes, food, and instruction [on the need] to pay respect to teachers and friends, and to offer support to the worthy and the elderly (*junzhang*).

When the son's face was happy his parents were happy. When the son was sad, his parents' heart burned. When you went out, they missed you. And when you returned they asked where you had been. They were so concerned that you not do something bad. With your parents giving you so much *(en)* how are you going to repay it?"

All the śramaṇas (renunciants) replied, "We must with total politeness *(li)* and with complete compassion care for them *(gongyang)* to completely match the kindness *(en)* of our parents."

The World Honored One said, "If sons offer *(yang)* to their parents ambrosia *(ganlu)* of a hundred flavors for them to eat, heavenly orchestras for them to listen to, and first-rate clothes that make their bodies resplendent, or again, if a son carried his parents around on his shoulders throughout the world until the end of his life—to match the benevolence and nurturing [they showed him]—could that be called filiality?"

All the śramaṇas said, "Great filiality could not surpass this."

The Buddha said, "It is not to be considered filial piety. As long as one's parents are ignorant and do not worship *(feng)* the Three Jewels *(zun)* and are cruel and vicious, deceitful and dishonest, lecherous and adulterous, lying, drunken and rowdy, with their backs turned against the Way in this manner, then a son must do everything possible to enlighten them, as they are so deluded. In order to convert them, you should present them with a similitude [of their fate] by showing them the emperor's prisons. [Explain to them that] all the prisoners' punishments are due to their own waywardness. Their bodies covered with various poisons, they summon their own deaths. At the end of their lives, their spirits *(shen)* are tethered to Mt. Tai. There they are scalded and burned, suffering thousands of tortures, and one is alone with no way to escape. [Tell them] it is because of their evil ways that they will meet this awful fate. If after this instruction, they still do not reform [their evil ways], then you must cry and lament and go on a hunger strike. Your parents, even though they are stupid, will, from the pain of love *(aien zhi tong)* and fearing that their son will die, fully admit their [errors], get control over their minds and worship the Way *(chongdao).*"

"If your parents will make a resolution to uphold the five Buddhist precepts to 1. be benevolent and do not kill, 2. be pure and yielding and not steal, 3. be chaste and not lascivious *(yin)*, 4. be trustworthy, do not lie or cheat, 5. be filial, do not get drunk—then in the lineage *(zong)* parents will be benevolent and children/sons will be filial.[6] The husband will be upright and the mother will be chaste, and the nine generations[7] of the clan will be harmonious and the servants will be obedient. The benefit will spread far and wide, and [all] those who have blood[8] will be grateful *(shouen).* And, among all the Buddhas of the ten directions, along with the heavenly nagas, the ghosts and gods, the upright princes, the loyal officials and the vast commoners, there will be none who do not respect and cherish [your family] or protect it and make it peaceful. Even if there are perverted [government] policies, with the machinations of deceitful concubines and wicked sons, and witchy wives [making] everything weird and depraved, there is nothing they could do [to this household]. And thus both your parents would, while alive always be at ease, and at death their spirit *(guiling)* would be reborn in heaven [where] they would be with all the Buddhas and get to hear the dharma and achieve the Way, and thereby transcend this world and be forever free of suffering."

Then the Buddha said to the *śramaṇas*, "When I look at the world, I do not see any who are filial. Only this kind of [practice] can be considered [real] filialness, which is causing your parents to leave evil and turn toward the good: to uphold the five precepts, to maintain the three refuges continually to the end of their lives. The profound kindness *(en)* of parents [shown in] the nurturing of breastfeeding *(rubu)* is [a case of] limitless benevolence. So if you are unable to, with the three honorables [Buddha, Dharma, Sangha], convert *(hua)* your parents, then though you take care of them *(xiaoyang)* with filialness it still is as though you are unfilial."

"You must not fall under the spell of your wife/wives who might cause you to separate from wise men and avoid them, and you must not [indulge] in your desire for girls which might be so intense and indefatigable that it breaches filialness even to the point of killing your parents and making a mess of the national government and causing the masses to flee for their lives. . . . So when all those polluted wives get together, or those sexy women, crazed with desire and intent on bewitching, or those goblin [women] with numberless provocative poses, then men short on wisdom and officials short on insight who see such things, will not see signs [of trouble] and will gradually be seduced and led away until their intention [to follow the Way] is lost. Thus, by the evil magical words of these goblinesses, [these men] may endanger their relatives, and may [even] kill lords. With a poker face [on the outside] but with roiling emotions [on the inside], they are angry and arrogant, minds a mess, and blind—their actions resemble beasts. (. . .)

"Thus, *śramaṇas* be single and do not pair. To be pure in this intention [to study] the Way, that is your responsibility. Only those who uphold wisdom, and the precepts should serve as ministers *(jun)* and protect the four oceans, or be officials loyal [in their efforts to] nurture the people with benevolence *(ren)*. Only when the father understands dharma, will the son be filial and benevolent. Only when the husband is trustworthy will the wife be chaste. When male and female householders are able to maintain practice like this, then lifetime after lifetime they will meet the Buddha, see the Dharma and attain the Way. The Buddha taught it thus, and the disciples were overjoyed.

[*Taishō shinshū daizōkyō*, translated by Alan Cole][9]

THE GHOST FESTIVAL SUTRA

This text, which was probably composed in China in the sixth century, pulls together previous narrative elements from other works, some forged in China, some of Indian provenance, and makes the complex argument that normal family reproduction necessitates the intermediary powers of the Buddhist monastic system. The text, though clumsy in many ways, still moves rather effectively from a narrative account of Mulian learning to rescue his mother from hell, where she apparently is suffering for her profound sins, into a ritual prescription that details how all men are to respond similarly and save their mothers with offerings presented to the Buddhists on the fifteenth day of the seventh lunar month. What is crucial to note is that the story works to show that direct attempts to feed the dead, something widely practiced in pre-Buddhist China, not only fail but literally enflame the situation. Thus, this form of Buddhist family values is breaking into the hallowed pattern of exchange between the living and their ancestors to articulate a triangular arrangement in which, as in India, the Buddhist institution takes over as the mediator for the family's calendrical efforts to care for the dead. This text is, like those above, also notable for its construction of "milk-debts" which, in terms of the narrative at least, drive the entire sequence. Thus, the author has taken the natural sequences of life-production and folded them into an ideological package in which not only is there no free-lunch, but the reception of mother's milk and her kindness seem to impel her into hell and hunger. The implication that Mulian's mother is in hell simply for reproducing is made all the clearer since no one else but her progeny are apparently required to act on her behalf. Thus though her sins are left unexplained the structure of the narrative and the way the second half of the text universalizes the problem to all mothers, implies that at this early stage we have something like a Buddhist "sin of life" taking form. The more developed versions of this story, such as *The Blood Bowl Sutra* (see below) that would appear in the following centuries, make Mulian's mother's sins explicitly related to her sexuality and reproductive powers.

Note: The phrase *yulan bowl* that appears in the title and several times in the final section of the sutra simply means the bowl of offerings, whatever their content, made on this festival date that goes by the formal title *yulan*.

Document 5–14

YULAN PEN JING: THE GHOST FESTIVAL SUTRA

Thus have I heard. Once, the Buddha resided in the kingdom of Śrāvastī, among the Jetavana trees in the garden of Anāthapiṇḍika. The Great Mu Qian Lian [Mulian] first obtained the six penetrations and then, desiring to save his parents to repay the kindness of breast-feeding, he used his divine eye to search the worlds. He saw that his departed mother had been reborn among the hungry ghosts where she never saw food or drink—[it was so bad] that her skin hung off her bones. Mulian took pity, filled his bowl with rice, and sent it to his mother. When his mother received the bowl of rice, she used her left hand to guard the bowl and her right hand to gather up the rice, but before the food entered her mouth it changed into flaming coals, so in the end she could not eat. Mulian cried out in grief and wept tears. He rushed back to tell the Buddha and explained everything as it had happened.

The Buddha said, "The roots of your mother's sins are deep and tenacious. It is not within your power as a single individual to do anything about it. Even though the fame of your filial devotion moves heaven and earth, still [all] the spirits of heaven and the spirits of earth, harmful demons and masters of the heterodox paths—the Daoist priests, and the four spirit kings of heaven, cannot do anything about it. You must rely on the mighty spiritual power of the assembled monks of the ten directions in order to obtain her deliverance. I shall now preach for you the method of salvation, so that all beings in dire straights may leave sadness and suffering, and have their sinful impediments swept wiped way. "

The Buddha told Mulian, "On the fifteenth day of the seventh month, when the assembled monks of the ten directions release themselves, you should, for the sake of seven generations of ancestors, up to and including your current parents—those in dire straights—gather food of the one hundred flavors and five kinds of fruit, basins for washing and rinsing, incense, oil lamps and candles, and mattresses and bedding. Then place these, the sweetest, prettiest things in the world, in a bowl and offer it to the assembled monks, those of great virtue of the ten directions. On this day, the entire assembly of saints—those in the mountains practicing meditation and concentration; those who have attained the fruit of the four paths; those who practice *(jinxing)* under trees; those with the six penetrations, and composure *(zizai)* who convert others, the Hearers, and the Solitary Realizers, and the great men, those bodhisattvas of the ten stages who provisionally manifest the form of a monk—all of those who are part of the great assembly shall with one mind receive the bowl of rice. The assembly of saints possess fully the purity of the precepts and the Way—their virtue is vast indeed. When you make offerings to these kinds of monks as they release themselves, then your current parents, your seven generations of ancestors, and your six kinds of relatives will obtain release from the suffering of the three evil paths of rebirth and will be liberated and clothed and fed naturally. If one's parents are still living, then they will have one hundred years of joy and happiness [from this offering]. If they are already deceased, then [they and] the seven generations of ancestors will be reborn in the heavens; born freely through magical transformation, they will enter into the light of heavenly flowers and receive unlimited joy."

Then the Buddha decreed that the assembled monks of the ten directions should first chant prayers on behalf of the family of the donor for the seven generations of ancestors and practice meditation and concentrate their thoughts before receiving the food. In receiving the bowls, they should first place them in front of the Buddha's stupa, and when the assembled monks have finished chanting prayers, they may then individually partake of the food.

At this time the monk Mulian and the assembly of great bodhisattvas rejoiced. Mulian's sorrowful tears ended and the sound of his crying died out.

Then, on that very day, Mulian's mother gained release from an eon of suffering as a hungry ghost.

Then Mulian told the Buddha, "The parents who gave birth to me, your disciple, are able to receive the power of the merit of the Three Jewels because of the mighty spiritual power of the assembly of monks. But all of the future disciples of the Buddha, those who practice filial devotion, may they or may they not also present *yulan* bowls as required to save their parents and their seven generations of ancestors?"

The Buddha said, "Excellent! This question pleases me very much. It is just what I would like to preach, so listen well! My good sons, if there are monks, or nuns, kings of states, princes, sons of kings, great ministers, counselors, dignitaries of the three ranks, any government officials, or the tens of thousands of common people who practice filial compassion, then on behalf of their current parents and the past seven generations of ancestors, on the fifteenth day of the seventh month, the day of which the Buddha is happy, the day on which the monks release themselves, they must all place food and drink of the one hundred flavors inside the *yulan* bowl and donate it to monks of the ten directions who are releasing themselves. When the prayers are finished, one's present parents will attain long life, passing one hundred years without sickness and without any of the torments of sufferings of hungry ghosthood, attaining rebirth among gods and humans, and blessings without limit."

The Buddha told all of the good sons and good daughters, "Those disciples of the Buddha who practice filial devotion must in every moment of consciousness think of and care for their parents and their seven generations of ancestors. Each year on the fifteen day of the seventh month, out of filial devotion and compassionate consideration for the parents who gave birth to them and for the seven generations of ancestors, they should always make a *yulan* bowl and donate it to the Buddha and Sangha to repay the kindness bestowed by parents in nurturing and caring (*zhangyang ciai zhi en*) for them. All disciples of the Buddha must carry out this law."

Upon hearing what the Buddha preached, the monk Mulian and the four classes of disciples rejoiced and put it into practice.

[*Taishō shinshū daizōkyō*, translated by Alan Cole based, in part, on Stephen F. Teiser's translation in his *The Ghost Festival in Medieval China* (Princeton: Princeton University Press, 1988), pp. 49–54]

THE SUTRA ON THE PROFOUND KINDNESS OF PARENTS

This text appears to have been very popular in the Tang period (618–907) and continues to be a favorite in modern Taiwan. Coming slightly later than the two above selections, this text is distinctive for its more elaborate depiction of the loving nostalgia that a son should feel toward his mother, who is presented as a wonderful and solicitous caretaker during the son's baby days. Again the trope of replacing Confucian filial piety with Buddhist filial piety appears early in the work, but this text is really unique for the middle section that begins to chronicle the deep pathos apparently expected at the heart of the typical Chinese family. In this section we are taken behind closed doors to witness what the author assumes the reader to know about already—the kind of deadly animosity that erupts in Chinese families as the live-in son takes a wife. More exactly, the text shows that the author wants to give voice to some fundamental angst haunting standard modes of reproducing the Chinese family and, by implications, seems to be offering Buddhist filial piety as solution to these frightful episodes. As I argued in *Mothers and Sons in Chinese Buddhism,* "By inserting an extensive complaint about unfilial adult sons into the budding form of Buddhist mother-son filial piety . . . *The Sutra on the Profound Kindness of Parents* presents Buddhist filial piety as the stabilizing force that can overcome the inevitable tension surrounding the act of wife-taking. Perhaps this text reveals an equitable solution to the problem of Buddhism in China. On the one hand, Buddhism was to be granted high status and its institutions were to be patronized. On the other hand, the concerns of family were to be offered the power of the new Buddhist filial piety, which would assist in solving a long-standing problem in Chinese family life."[10]

Document 5–15

FUMU EN ZHONG JING: THE SUTRA ON THE PROFOUND KINDNESS OF PARENTS

Thus I heard. Buddha was once Gṛdhrakuta Moutain with great Bodhisattvas and Śravakas assembled together along with monks, nuns, laymen, and laywomen, as well as heavenly humans *(tian fenmin)*, heavenly nagas *(tianlong)*, and ghosts and gods, all of whom had come together to single-mindedly listen to the Buddha. When they stared at his face they could not take their eyes off him for an instant.

The Buddha said, "People are born into the world with father and mother as parents. Without the father there would be no birth *(sheng)*, and without the mother there would be no rearing *(yang)*. Therefore it depends *(jituo)* on the mother who carries [the baby] in her womb for ten months until the time when it is fully formed, and she gives birth, and the child drops on the grass [mat?]. [Then after the baby is born,] the father and mother nurture him *(yangyu)*. When he is lying [asleep] they put him in a crib or otherwise, they hold him and make harmonious noises for him; he smiles, not yet able to speak. Now, when he is hungry he needs food, and without the mother he could not eat. When he is thirsty, he needs drink, and without the mother he could not suckle.

Mothers swallow the sour food and give[11] the sweet things to him when he is hungry, and [in bed] she puts him in the dry places and accepts the wet places. Without [fulfilling] this responsibility *(yi)* they would not be parents. Without the mother, the child could not be raised. The loving mother raises the son *(er)* and when she takes him out of the crib there is food between his ten fingers and the child is unclean. Each [child] requires eighty-four pecks [of milk]. This is what is reckoned and spoken of as the kindness of the mother *(muen)* and it is as vast as the horizon of heaven *(hao tian wang ji)*. Exclaiming about the loving mother, the Buddha asked, "How can we repay [her]?"

Ānanda said to the Buddha, "The World Honored One has asked, 'How can we repay this debt?' but this is just what I want [you] to explain."

Then the Buddha said to Ānanda, "You listen well and think hard about this while I analyze and explain it for you. The kindness of our parents is as vast as the horizon of heaven. It can be repaid by a filial, obedient, and loving son *(zi)* who is able, for the sake of his parents, to make merit, produce sutras or perform the ghost festival offering *(yulan pen)* on the fifteenth of the seventh month. By offering [in this manner] to the Buddha and the sangha, the results you gain are limitless and you are able to repay your parents. Or again, if there is someone who is able to copy this sutra and distribute it among the people [making them] accept it, praise it, and recite it, then this person is known to have repaid his debt to his parents even though his parents [might] say 'How is it repaid?'"

When parents leave to go somewhere in the neighborhood, to the well, or stove, or to grind [some grain] and do not come back for a while, my son *(woer)* cries at home because he wants me to return to the house right away. As I come back, my son watches me from a distance. Or, [if we go out] if he is the stroller, I cuddle his head, and tickle him as we go along.[12] If he is calling out for his mother, the mother, for the sake of the son, bends over for a long time extending her arms to wipe up the "dust." Cooing sweetly with her mouth, she opens her blouse and takes out her breasts and gives them to him.

When the mother sees the son, she is happy. When the son sees the mother, he is happy. The two feel kindness *(en)*, compassion, intimacy and love [for each other]. There is nothing stronger than this kind of love *(ci)*. At about two or three years the boy starts to think and begins to walk . . . When the mother returns from being out, she goes immediately to where he is seated, and sometimes she has gotten cakes or meat which she does not eat or suck the flavor from. Instead nine times out of ten she brings them back for him, which always makes him happy, otherwise he would cry and sob. Children who cry are not filial. They must have the five obediences.[13] Filial children do not cry, rather they are loving and obedient.

In time the child grows up, and makes friends with whom he goes about. He combs his head and rubs his hair and wishes to get nice clothes to cover his body. Low quality cloth will not do, so the father and mother take whatever nice cloth they have and give it to the child. With regard to his coming and going, they are publicly and privately worried sick. They look north and south and follow the son east and west [trying to keep] abreast of his lead. Then they find him a wife who will be a woman to their son. Then the parents turn and separate [from the son] and live happily, talking to each other. When the parents get older their strength weakens and they age. From morning to night he does not come to ask how they [the parents] are doing. Or again, the father or mother might be lonely, having lost their spouse and living by themselves in an empty room, like a traveler stopping at someone else's place [and not feeling at home in their own house.] Always without dutiful love *(enai)* and without soft blankets, they are cold. Suffering, they meet with danger and misfortune. When they are really old, they loose their color and have lots of lice. They cannot sleep at night and are always sighing, "What crime or past error [have we committed] to have produced this unfilial son?" Sometimes [they] call out [for him], and glare with surprising anger, but wife[14] and son scold them, lowering their heads and smirking. His wife is also unfilial. They [the young couple] pervert the five obediences and jointly engage in the five wayward deeds *(wu ni)*.[15] Sometimes the parents call for him when they are very sick and could use his help, but they will call ten times and he will disobey nine times.[16] He simply is not obedient. Scolding and swearing at them wrathfully, he says, "It would better if you died early and were already in the ground." When his parents hear this, they cry miserably and are deeply disturbed. Tears pour forth from their eyes, and they cry until their eyes are swollen. [They say to him,] "When you were small, if it had not been for us you would not have grown, but it would have been better if we had never given birth to you at all."

The Buddha said to Ānanda, "If there are good men and women who, for the sake of their parents are able to receive, recite, copy the line or one verse of the *Mahāyāna Perfection of Wisdom Sutra on the Profound Kindness of Parents* [even if they should] hear or see only one line, they will have all of their five heinous crimes and serious sins wiped away, forever removed without a trace remaining. They will always see the Buddhas and hear dharma, and quickly attain liberation." Then ānanda got up from where he was sitting and with his robe on his right shoulder, long knelt with his hands clasped, and then asked the Buddha, "World Honored One, what should we call this sutra? How shall we keep this sutra?"

The Buddha said, "Ānanda, this sutra is to be called *The Sutra on the Profound Kindness of Parents*. All sentient beings, if they are able to, for the sake of their parents, make merit *(zuofu)*, reproduce this sutra, burn incense, petition the Buddha, worship and make offerings to the Three Jewels, or give food and drink to the sangha, then let it be known that this person has repaid his debt to his father and mother." Then the heavenly Buddhist Indra and all the other gods and people who had heard this together were delighted, gave rise to *bodhi* mind, wept to such an extent that the ground shook while their tears ran down like rain as they did full body prostrations [to the Buddha], faithfully paying homage to the Buddha's feet. Then [still] delighted, they rose and left.

[*Taishō shinshū daizōkyō* 85.1403, translated by Alan Cole]

THE BLOOD BOWL SUTRA

This sutra, composed in China, probably in circulation by the thirteenth century and still widely available in China and Japan, retells the Mulian-saves-his-mother motif, as seen above in *The Ghost Festival Sutra*, but develops the problematic of that narrative in several ways. First, it explicitly creates a women-only hell to which, apparently, all women are doomed for simple biological realities, such as menstruation and blood-letting during child-birthing. Second, by explaining that the cause of this hell is due to vaginal blood being accidentally offered to the Buddha—in a cup of tea—the text articulates a clear divide and antipathy between the "pure one" (the buddhas, presumably) and women, and perhaps humans in general. In this light the text represents an almost Manichaean divide between ethereal buddhas and earth-bound humans. Third, though this sutra clearly draws on the Mulian story, here Mulian's task of rescuing his mother has broken free of the Ghost Festival offering on the fifteenth of the seventh lunar month, as explained above in *The Ghost Festival Sutra*; now the offering is focused on a funeral sequence initiated by her death and lasting for three years. In short, parallel with *The Ghost Festival Sutra*, this text articulates a kind of "sin of life" dogma, but in a much clearer and undeniable manner. Too, it's evident that this doctrine treats the sin of life not as a failure of morality, or an Augustinian perversion of the will, but rather as a purity problem deriving exclusively from female reproductive fluids. In effect, in this text morality has disappeared to be replaced by a hard-hitting demonization of female biology, which, nonetheless, has implications for the son who has to adapt his cosmology to this point of view and marshal resources to offer to the Buddhist in order to ensure his mother's postmortem well-being. Though this rescue effort is understood as the son's duty in the text, I should draw readers' attention to that line near the end that recommends that women can repay their debt to their mothers by copying and circulating this text, a development that suggests a growing willingness to include women as active participants in this form of Buddhist family values.

Document 5–16

XUEPEN JING: THE BLOOD BOWL SUTRA

Once, some time ago, Venerable Mulian was traveling in Yu Zhou looking for Yang Province when he saw a blood bowl/pool hell (*xuepen chi di yu*) that was 84,000 leagues (*yojanas*) wide. In the pool were 120 implements of steel beams, steel pillars, steel yokes, and steel chains. He saw Yama,[17] with a pitchfork in his hand, leading many women *(nufen)* by the hair on their heads, which was all asunder. In this hell the ghost in charge of the punishments three times a day takes blood and makes the sinners *(zuifen)* drink it. If the sinners are not willing to submit to him and drink, then he takes his steel rod and beats them as they scream.

When Mulian saw this, he sadly asked the hell warden, "I do not see any men from earth here suffering these torments. [Why] do I only see women here receiving this cruel retribution?" The warder answers him, "Teacher, it is not something that involves *(gan)* men. It only has to do with women who every month leak menses, or release blood in childbirth, which soaks the ground even to the gods' realm. And, more, they take their filthy garments to the river to wash, thereby polluting the river water. Later, an unsuspecting good man or woman draws some water from the river, boils it for tea and then offers *(gon-gyang)* it to the holy ones *(zhu sheng)*, causing them to be impure. The great general of heaven takes note of this and marks it in his book of good and evil. After a hundred years when their lives are over, [the sinful women] undergo this retribution of suffering [that you see before you].

When Mulian heard this he was very sad and asked the warden, "How can we repay *(baoda)* our moms *(aniang)* for the kindness of giving birth to us *(chansheng zhi en)* in order that they may leave the blood pool hell?"[18] The hell warden answered, "Teacher, you only need to carefully be a filial son or daughter, respect the Three Jewels, and for the sake of your mom, hold Blood Bowl Feasts for three years, including organizing Blood Bowl Victory Meetings *(xuepen shenghui)* for which you invite monks to recite this sutra for a full day and have confessions *(chanhui)*. Then there will be a paramita vessel to carry the mother across the river to the other side, and they will see the blood pool turn into a five-colored lotus pond, and the sinners will come out happy and contrite, and they will be able to take rebirth *(chaosheng)* in a Buddha Land [to live] with great bodhisattvas.

Mulian [returned] and began to tell the good sons and daughters of the world to awaken at once, to practice and uphold the great discrimination, and, in the future, not to lose grip of it, as it could mean 10,000 kalpas of hardship.

The Buddha again told women, saying, "As for the *Blood Pool Sutra*, if you, with a believing mind, copy and keep this sutra then you will be causing, as far as possible, the mothers of the three worlds to gain rebirth in heaven, where they will receive pleasures, clothes, and food naturally; their lives will be long, and they will be rich aristocrats."

Then the nagas of the eight quarters, the humans and nonhumans, etc., were all very happy, believed and accepted the teaching, paid obeisances and left.

The Great Canonical Blood Bowl Sutra Taught by the Buddha

[Translated by Alan Cole, based on a version of the text edited and published by Tairyo Makita in his *Gikyō kenkyū* (Tokyo: Kyoto daigaku jinbun kagaku kenkyūjo, 1976), pp. 79–80]

NOTES

1. In the selections below I have opted not to include examples of this form of Buddhist family rhetoric because of the length of Mahāyāna narratives; interested readers can refer to my *Text as Father: Paternal Seductions in Early Mahāyāna Buddhist Literature* (Berkeley and Los Angeles: University of California Press, 2005).

2. Because these genealogical texts are often long and convoluted, I have not included any examples in the following selections; I am currently working on a study of Buddhist patrilines in China, tentatively titled "Patriarchs on Paper: The Gradual Birth of Chinese Buddhas in Tang-Era Literature."

3. For a discussion of this text in its Chinese reformulation, see my "Homestyle Vinaya and Docile Boys in Medieval China," in *Positions: East Asia Cultures Critique* (Durham: Duke University Press, 1998), pp. 27–31.

4. See the discussion in Alan Cole, *Mothers and Sons in Chinese Buddhism* (Palo Alto: Stanford University Press, 1998), pp. 42–46. A modern edited version of the text can be found in the *Taishō shinshū daizōkyō*, hereafter referred to as "T," which is the modern Japanese edition of the Chinese Buddhist canon that is the standard reference for canonical texts. I cite it by volume number, page number, folio, and line, when this is appropriate. Thus T.54.328a.5 refers to Taishō volume 54, page 328, folio "a" (the first out of three), and the fifth line in from the right.

5. This phrase was used in pre-Buddhist literature to evoke a mother's selfless compassion.

6. This list of the five Buddhist precepts for the laity is interesting for the way it interjects Confucian values around Buddhist ethics—the most notable addition being filial piety, tucked in rather incongruously after the injunction against drinking.

7. Counting six or seven generations back is the more normal arrangement.

8. This is a traditional pre-Buddhist term for sentient beings.

9. See Cole *Mothers and Sons*, pp. 68–79.

10. See ibid., pp. 142–143.

11. Literally, "spit out the sweet," which presumably refers to the practice of mothers partially chewing food and then transferring it to the baby's mouth in order to aid their digestion and to remove spices.

12. My rendering of this passage is tentative.

13. This may refer to the "five constants" *(wuchang)* in Confucian ethics: benevolence, uprightness, propriety, wisdom, and trust.

14. Based on Zong Mi's citation of this passage, I am switching a radical to read *fu* (wife) for *gui* (return). See T.39.508b.29.

15. The term *wuni* refers to the five most heinous crimes in Buddhism: 1. killing one's father, 2. killing one's mother, 3. killing an arhant, 4. drawing the blood of a buddha, 5. disrupting the sangha. The rather exaggerated charge that the younger couple is involved in the most serious of Buddhist crimes is interesting because it suggests that the author wants to link their unfilial conduct, the most heinous of crimes from the Confucian point of view, with charges of equal atrocity from the Buddhist code of ethics; presumably, there is also an implied threat since it was well known that committing any of these five Buddhist sins resulted in direct rebirth in the worst of hells.

16. Repeating this phrase, "nine times out of ten," from the opening section on

mother-son love highlights the disjunction between the time when the infant son received the total attention of his mother and his adult failure to replicate a facsimile of that relationship in caring for his now needy and childlike parents.

17. Yama is the king of death, known throughout Indian mythology.

18. Though the passage does not use the word *we* in phrase, "how can we repay our moms," I see every reason to translate as I have. First, by using the family term *a niang* for mother, we know that Mulian is saying, "How can we, those who refer to this woman in the familiar, make this repayment?" The later passages make clear too that this is a repayment to be made by the children of this mother.

CONFUCIANISM

Patricia Ebrey

INTRODUCTION

Confucianism is a Western term, not a translation of a Chinese term. The history of the term is closely tied to the efforts of centuries of Christian missionaries to understand the doctrines and beliefs of the Chinese elite and associate them with a founding figure. When used broadly it encompasses the teachings of Confucius, the ancient texts now conventionally called the Confucian Classics, the traditions of commentary and interpretation surrounding those texts, and the learning associated with the political elite in China and tested in the civil service examinations. In China, a term as broad and encompassing as *Confucianism* was not in common usage until the twentieth century, when social critics wanted people to reject Confucian teachings. Early in the twentieth century Chinese reformers, influenced by Western liberal ideologies, decried the deleterious effects of Confucian teachings on Chinese behavior. The New Culture reading of Confucianism was that it sacrificed individuals for the sake of families and fell particularly hard on young people and women, who were given very little autonomy.

Intellectual historians are generally uncomfortable with these broad understandings of Confucianism. They tend to use Confucianism more narrowly to refer to the core ideas of the founders and leading thinkers of Confucianism. These thinkers would by no means have wanted their ideas to be equated with the conventional ways of thinking of the educated class of their day, which they generally criticized.

Although it is important to keep these wider and narrower understandings of Confucianism in mind, when the issue is teachings on sex, marriage, and the family there is little controversy about what constituted the Confucian position. Confucian authors over the centuries celebrated the patrilineal, patriarchal, patrilocal family system and urged men and women alike to be filial to their parents and elders, serious in their obligations to their ancestors and kin, and willing to put the interests of their family before their personal interests. The ideas that underlay the daily practice of the Chinese family system can thus with some justice be labeled *Confucian*, even though many of them predated Confucius or were not elaborated until centuries after his death.

The canonical core of Confucian teachings on the family go back to the Han dynasty (202 BCE — 220 CE), when the Five Classics were completed and texts like the *Analects* in wide circulation. By then the early Zhou period (1045–256 BCE) was identified as the ideal age, and the family system of the aristocracy in the early Zhou period as described in the Classics was the model for all to aspire toward. A central feature of this family system was that descent was patrilineal and a matter of great importance. The connections from ancestor to descendant were maintained through regular performance of ancestral rites, which consisted of offerings of food and wine accompanied by prayers.

Marriage within a patrilineal descent group was forbidden, so marriage served to link descent groups. Since family names were passed down patrilineally, this came to mean in practice that one should marry someone of a different family name. The ritual Classics describe a system in which men of high rank had both a wife and concubines, the higher the man's rank the larger the number of concubines. Much of the ritual of marriage as described in the Classics thus concerned the ritual elevation of wives over concubines. Marriage was viewed as obligatory for men because of the need to provide heirs to continue the ancestral rites. Part of a man's obligations to his ancestors was to see to it that wives were found for his sons, and the authority of the family head in decisions about marriage was largely taken for granted.

The most elaborate of the family rituals described in the Classics were the long series of ceremonies associated with death, burial, and mourning. The *Record of Ritual* discusses aspects of them in several chapters and treats them as a matter of utmost seriousness, central to the fulfillment of filial piety. Immediately after the death the survivors called back the soul, washed and dressed the body, and set out a representation of the dead that could receive offerings. Within a few days they had to perform two laying out ceremonies in which the body is placed in the coffin and the coffin is packed with clothes and shrouds. At this point the mourners put on mourning garments appropriate to their degree of kinship and began ritualized wailing. They were also expected to send out announcements of the death and receive condolence visits. After preparing the grave they would arrange a procession to the grave. After the burial they would bring back the spirit tablet and perform the first of a long series of post-burial funerary sacrifices. Not until the last was completed would the ancestral tablet be incorporated into the regular ancestral rites more than two years after the death.

The concept of the five grades of mourning governed how each individual performed his obligations to deceased relatives. The grade varied by the coarseness of the required garments and how long they were worn (three years, one year, nine months, five months, three months). Within a family, when a man died, his sons owed him three years of mourning wearing "untrimmed" hemp garments; his brothers and unmarried sisters, his sons's wives, and his daughters owed him one year of trimmed hemp garments; his father's sisters, his married sisters, his first cousins, and his grandchildren owed him nine months; his brothers' grandchildren and his second cousins owed him five months; third cousins and his daughter's husband and children and his mother's brother's sons were supposed to wear relatively fine clothes for three months. The mourning grades codified the primacy of patrilineal kinship connections: one owed a heavier degree of mourning to a cousin though one's father's brother than through one's father's sister or one's mother's brother.

The Confucian literature on mourning gives fullest detail on the behavior expected of those in mourning for their parents. They were to abstain from comforts, including tasty food and soft beds, and withdraw from many activities, including political office and making offerings at the ancestral altar. They could not marry or officiate at a marriage and were expected to abstain from sexual relations and from drinking wine.

Over time, as funerary practices not documented in the Classics gained hold, Confucian scholars debated at length which ones could be considered minor variations of canonical practices, which were harmless elaborations, and which were pernicious violations of the spirit of the Classics that had to be opposed. In Song times (960–1276) Zhu Xi and other leading Confucian scholars wrote against such practices as cremation instead of burial, playing music at funerals, calling in monks to perform Buddhist services, and leaving bodies unburied for long periods of time, often because the descendants were not yet able to secure a grave that would be favorable according to geomancy.

Although many Confucian scholars became specialists in ritual, an equally important strand of Confucianism stressed the moral dimensions of family life. Particularly important here was the concept of filial piety, understood as the feelings of love and obligation a child should have toward his parents and the ways he should act on them. Even though filial piety was strongly associated with the followers of Confucius, other religions and schools of thought did not attack it. Buddhists, in adapting to China, did not challenge the weight placed on filial piety; rather they argued that their teachings allowed a child to fulfill his filial duties to the utmost, for instance by aiding the salvation of deceased ancestors. Daoists of the Song and later regularly promoted filial piety in their moral tracts.

The exaltation of filial piety was carried to extreme heights in the Han period. In the *Record of Ritual* Zengzi asserts that true goodness, propriety, righteousness, and sincerity all lay in reverent, persistent service to parents and cautious behavior that avoids bringing shame on them. The *Classic of Filial Piety* attributed to Confucius the statement that "filial piety is the root of all virtue and the source of all teachings." The Han government made filial piety a criterion for selecting men to office and rewarded extreme acts of filial piety. Depictions of paragons of filial piety were a common theme in Han art. Religious passion often seems to have underlay the more extreme forms of filial piety. Truly devoted children, for instance, would cut off a piece of their flesh to feed an ill parent, confident that it would cure them. Stories of such self-sacrificing filial exemplars were eventually collected into the widely circulated *Twenty-Four Filial Sons*.

The moral weight assigned to filial piety had pervasive effects on Chinese culture and social organization. Proverbs and popular literature show the contempt people had for those who flouted or ignored the demands of filial piety. Law codes treated violations of filial piety, such as cursing parents or accidentally causing them bodily harm, as major crimes. The opinion of Mencius that the worst of unfilial acts was to fail to have descendents, often quoted in later ages, not only shaped Chinese family dynamics but also Chinese population growth.

Much more space is given in the core Confucian texts to filial piety, ancestral rites, and the proper way to bury and mourn parents than to sex and husband-wife relations. The *Record of Ritual* includes instructions on wedding rituals and the proper behavior of daughters-in-law, but says much more about how a married woman should treat her parents-in-law than how she should treat her husband (and even less on how a man should treat his wife). Within the tradition of Confucian scholarship every effort was made to avoid direct discussion of sexual acts. Thus, to refer to the need to abstain from sexual intercourse as part of the purification necessary before making offerings to ancestors, the phrase "does not enter the inner quarters" was used. Girls not yet married are referred to as "girls living at home," which implied that they had not yet had sexual relations but not nearly as explicitly as the term *virgin* does in English.

SELECTION OF TEXTS

For this sourcebook texts were selected to illustrate the several ways Confucianism has been associated with sex, marriage, and the family in China. The texts are arranged chronologically, with the first six illustrating what is found in the Classics. Even fragmentary statements in the Classics on subjects such as marriage were frequently quoted by later authors as authoritative. Besides passages that assert the desirability of certain behaviors, I have also included passages that describe but do not comment on sexual matters. Songs in the *Book of Poetry* touch on issues of sexual attraction and courtship. The *Zuo zhuan* includes matter-of-fact references to nonstandard sexual behavior—from incest and rape to rulers who took over the wives of their subordinates and women who schemed to supplant rivals or advance their children over the children of other wives.

The Classics may have been the authoritative source for correct family behavior, but they were not easy to read. To reach children and those with less education, Confucian teachers over the centuries wrote didactic works of all kinds. Here we have selections from seven, ranging from the Han (202 BCE–220 CE) through the Song periods (960–1276). The first one included here, the *Classic of Filial Piety*, was eventually classed as a Confucian Classic, but it was probably originally written as a primer aimed at young people. Some didactic literature was aimed specifically at women and girls, three examples of which are given here. Although some didactic works extol extreme cases of self-sacrifice, there was also a tradition of offering more practical advice. Selections from two such works are included here, one by Yan Zhitui of the sixth century, the other by Yuan Cai of the twelfth.

Confucianism underwent a major transformation during the eleventh and twelfth centuries, a movement variously called Neo-Confucianism or the Learning of the Way. Neo-Confucianism reiterated basic Confucian teachings on the family and marriage, tried to purify them of contamination by Buddhism (and to a lesser extent Daoism), and made new efforts to bring the Confucian message to ordinary people. In terms of teachings about sex, marriage, and the family, the Neo-Confucian tradition, especially as it was elaborated in later centuries, tended to be more conservative than earlier teachings. It put more emphasis on the purity of women and the chastity of widows. Here I have included several selections from the writings of the major master Zhu Xi (1130–1200).

Confucian teachings on sex, marriage, and the family had never been conveyed solely in texts written by Confucian scholars. Once Confucianism became the ideology of the state, the state played a role in defining and elaborating these principles, especially in its law codes. Unlike societies in which religious professionals preside at weddings and decide what is or is not a legal marriage, in China weddings were largely a matter that families arranged on their own. The legality of a union was, however, a matter of concern to the state as it has implications with regard to property rights. The law codes of the successive dynasties reinforced Confucian teachings in many of their provisions. For instance, Confucian family ethics also entered into the gradation of crimes. Injuring one's father or uncle was more serious crime than injuring one's son or nephew, for instance. Chinese law codes also set limits on acceptable sexual activity, defining the equivalent of adultery, incest, and rape and distinguishing degrees of seriousness. For this sourcebook the laws on illicit sexual activity of the Qing dynasty (1644–1911) code are coupled with actual rulings and advice from an experienced official on how to apply the law.

This chapter on Confucianism ends with two twentieth-century pieces that give some sense of the questioning of Confucian teachings on marriage and the family that occurred in the twentieth century, one by Chen Duxiu, a representative of the New Culture movement, ready to throw out most Confucian strictures, the other by Feng Youlan, a philosopher who saw much worth retaining.

Confucianism is still a vital force today, but its association with teachings about family behavior is now rather attenuated. None of those who identify themselves as Confucians today argue that the separation of the sexes should be reinstated, that parents should have control over their children's marriages, that wives or children should endure mistreatment out of devotion to fidelity or filiality, or that widows should renounce remarriage. Confucians today want Confucianism to evolve in a way that accommodates all the changes that have occurred in the family system as well as ideas about the equality of males and females introduced by feminism. The one traditional virtue that does still get praised is filial piety, reinterpreted as respect for elders and support for elderly parents. Some contemporary Confucians hold up the persistence of filial piety in East Asia as evidence of the superiority of Confucianism over modern Western ways of thinking. Others lament its decline among the young.

Although all of the texts selected here originated in China, Confucian teachings on the family had influence throughout East Asia, especially in Korea and to a lesser degree in Japan. Confucian scholars in Korea and Japan recognized the same texts as Confucian Classics and also read the works of great Confucian teachers such as Zhu Xi. Some of the Chinese didactic works also circulated outside China, but Korean and Japanese Confucian teachers also wrote their own, drawing examples from their own societies. The selections here from the legal tradition are more particular to China, though parallels could be found in the other East Asian countries. Similarly, although Chen Duxiu and Feng Youlan would not be household names in Korea or Japan, the issues they struggled with were common ones in the early twentieth century.

THE BOOK OF POETRY (SHI JING)

The 305 poems preserved in the *Book of Poetry* (*Shi jing*) mostly date to the Western Zhou period (1045–771 BCE). Over half of the poems are thought to have originated in folk songs. The remainder are songs or hymns sung at court, some for use in sacrificial ceremonies, others in praise of the founders of the dynasty. Confucius referred to the *Book of Poetry* respectfully, and other early sources, such as the Zuo zhuan, show that those who spoke at court frequently quoted from it. Because it came to be recognized as one of the Five Classics revered by Confucians, for centuries students studied these poems closely.

Tradition allowed for the allegorical reading of these poems, so that poems that seem on the surface to be complaints of neglected lovers could be read as the complaints of officials not properly appreciated by their lords. Nevertheless, many readers over the centuries recognized that some poems in this collection describe sexual attraction, love, and pleasure. Of the four poems given below, the first three concern love between young men and women; the last is included for its depiction of differences in the way boys and girls should be treated. In the original the poems do not have titles; here they are referred to by the traditional numbers assigned to them (the Mao numbers).

Document 6–1

POEM 1

"*Guan, guan*" [cry] the ospreys
on the isle in the river.
The reclusive, modest girl
is a good mate for the noble man.

Long and short is the duckweed
To the left and to the right we look for it.
The reclusive, modest girl—
waking and sleeping he seeks her.
He seeks her and does not obtain her.
Waking and sleeping he pines and yearns for her.
Oh, anxious! Oh, anxious!
He tosses and twists and turns onto his side.

Long and short is the duckweed.
To the left and to the right we gather it.
The reclusive, modest girl—
among lutes and citherns, he shows her his friendship.
Long and short is the duckweed.
To the left and to the right we pick it.
The reclusive, modest girl—
as a bell to a drum, he delights in her.

Document 6–2

POEM 23

In the field there is a dead roe.
With white grass we wrap it.
There is a girl who longs for spring.
A fine fellow seduces her.

In the forest there is the *pusu* tree.
In the field there is a dead deer.
With white grass we bind it.
There is a girl like jade.

Oh, undress me slowly.
Oh, do not upset my kerchief.
Do not make the shaggy dog bark.

Document 6–3

POEM 159

The fish in the nine-meshed net
are rudd and bream.
I see this young man
in regal robes and embroidered skirt.

The wild geese fly along the sandbar.
When the Duke goes back, there will be no place [for us].
I will stay with you one more time.

The wild geese fly along the hill.
The Duke is going back and will not return.
I will lodge with you one more time.

Oh, here we had the regal robes.
Oh, do not go back with our Duke.
Oh, do not make my heart grieve.

Document 6–4

POEM 189

A male child is born.
He is made to sleep on a bed.
He is made to wear a skirt.
He is made to play with a scepter.
His crying is loud.
His red knee-covers are august.
He is the hall and household's lord and king.

A female child is born.
She is made to sleep on the floor.

She is made to wear a wrap-cloth.
She is made to play with pottery.
She has no wrong and right.
Only wine and food are for her to talk about.
May she not send her father and mother any troubles.

[From Paul Rakita Goldin, The Culture of Sex in Ancient China
(Honolulu: University of Hawaii Press, 2002), pp. 12, 22–25]

THE *ANALECTS (LUNYU)* OF CONFUCIUS

Confucius (traditional dates, 551–479 BCE) was China's earliest moral philosopher. China in the period was divided into larger and small states that often fought with each other. As a young man Confucius served in the court of his home state of Lu without gaining much influence. After leaving Lu he wandered through neighboring states with a small group of students, searching for a ruler who would take his advice. Although he yearned for a ruler to serve devotedly, he spent most of his life teaching young men who shared his aspirations for political service.

Confucius's ideas are known to us primarily through the sayings recorded by his disciples in the *Analects (Lunyu)*. This book does not provide carefully organized or argued philosophical discourses, and the sayings seem to have been haphazardly arranged. Yet the *Analects* became a sacred book, memorized by beginning students and known to all educated people in China.

Confucius spoke of filial piety *(xiao)* as an important virtue. The word *xiao* had occurred in earlier texts primarily with reference to the ancestral cult—it referred to the obligation of sons to make offerings to their deceased parents and earlier ancestors. Confucius, however, gave it much broader meanings of obligation toward living as well as deceased parents.

Document 6–5

ANALECTS OF CONFUCIUS

1:2 Master You said, "It is rare for a person who is filial to his parents and respectful to his older brothers to go against his superiors, and unheard of for those who do not go against their superiors to rebel against them. The gentleman devotes his efforts to the roots, for it is on the basis of them that the Way develops. Filial piety and fraternal respect are the root of goodness." . . .

1:11 The Master said, "When your father is alive observe his intentions. When he is deceased, model yourself on the memory of his behavior. If in three years after his death you have not deviated from your father's ways, then you may be considered a filial child."

2:5 Meng Yizi inquired about filial piety. Confucius said, "Do not offend your parents."

Fan Zhi was giving Confucius a ride in a wagon, and Confucius told him, "Meng Sun questioned me about filial piety and I told him, 'Do not offend your parents.'"

Fan Zhi said, "What are you driving at?"

Confucius replied, "When your parents are alive, serve them according to the rules of ritual. When they are deceased, give them a funeral and offer sacrifices to them according to the rules of ritual." . . .

2:7 Ziyou inquired about filial piety. Confucius said, "Nowadays, filial piety is considered to be the ability to nourish one's parents. But this obligation to nourish even extends down to the dogs and horses. Unless we have reverence for our parents, what makes us any different?"

4:18 The Master said, "You can be of service to your father and mother by remonstrating with them tactfully. If you perceive that they do not wish to follow your advice, then continue to be reverent toward them without offending or disobeying them; work hard and do not murmur against them."

4:19 The Master said, "When your father and mother are alive, do not go rambling around far away. If you must travel, make sure you have a set destination." . . .

4:21 The Master said, "It is unacceptable not to be aware of your parents' ages. Their advancing years are a cause for joy and at the same time a cause for sorrow."

9:18 The Master said, "I have never seen anyone who loves virtue as much as sex."

13:18 The Duke of She said to Confucius, "In my land there is an upright man. His father stole a sheep, and the man turned him in to the authorities."

Confucius replied, "The upright men of my land are different. The father will shelter the son and the son will shelter the father. Righteousness lies precisely in this."

16:7 Confucius said, "There are three things a gentleman should guard against. In his youth, when his blood and *qi* are not yet settled, he should guard against lust. In his prime, when his blood and *qi* have stiffened, he should guard against anger. In his old age, when his blood and *qi* are in decline, he should guard against greed.

17:21 Zai Wo asked about the three-year mourning, saying "Even one year is long. If a gentleman gives up performing rituals for three years, the rites will suffer. If he gives up practicing music for three years, his music will deteriorate. A year is enough for the old grain to be used up and the new grain to ripen and for the fire to be renewed.

The Master said, "Would you at that point be comfortable eating rice and wearing brocades."

"I would."

"If you are comfortable, then do it. The Gentleman in mourning finds no pleasure in food or music and no comfort in his home, which is why he refrains from them. Since you enjoy them, you can do them."

After Zai Wo left, the Master said, "Yü has no compassion. For the first three years of a child's life he is held by his parents. Three years of mourning is the common practice everywhere under Heaven. Didn't Yü receive three years' love from his parents?" . . .

¹⁷:²⁵ The Master said, "Only women and inferior men are difficult to take care of. If you treat them on familiar terms, they become insubordinate. If you keep your distance, they complain."

¹⁸:⁴ The people of Qi sent some female musicians. Ji Huanzi accepted them and for three days did not hold audiences. Confucius left.

¹⁹:¹⁸ Zengzi said, "I have heard from Confucius that the filial piety of Meng Zhuangzi is such that it could also be attained by others, but his not changing his father's ministers and his father's government is a virtue difficult indeed to match."

[Translated by Patricia Ebrey]

MENCIUS ON FILIAL PIETY

The most influential of Confucius's early followers was Mencius (ca. 370–ca. 300 BCE). After studying with a grandson of Confucius, Mencius taught disciples and offered advice to rulers he visited. Mencius's thought is known from the book named after him (Mengzi), which includes conversations between Mencius and rulers, other philosophers, and disciples. In many of these conversations Mencius advises rulers to rule through virtue rather than force. Like all Confucians, he accepted the high value placed on filial piety and occasionally discussed it. The passages below are all from the fourth chapter of his six-chapter work. The most often cited of them is 4A:26 on the overriding need for heirs.

Document 6–6

MENCIUS' MENGZI

4A:9 Mencius said, "The Way lies in what is near and yet people seek it far away. Service lies in what is easy, and yet people seek it in what is difficult. If everyone would be loving to his parents and treat elders with proper respect, the world would be at peace." . . .

4A:19 Mencius said, "Of all forms of service, which is the greatest? It is the service of one's parents. Of all kinds of vigilance, which is greatest? It is vigilance over one's own body. I have heard of cases of people who by not losing their own bodies were able to serve their parents, but I have never heard of people who had lost their own bodies but were able to serve their parents. There are many who should be served, but serving one's parents is the root of them all. There are many things one should be vigilant about, but vigilance over one's body is the root of them all.

"When Zengzi took care of [his father] Zeng Xi, he regularly supplied wine and meat. Before clearing it away, he would always ask to whom leftovers should be given. When asked if there was extra he always said that there was. After Zeng Xi died, when Zeng Yuan was taking care of Zengzi, he regularly supplied wine and meat, but when he cleared it away he did not ask whom to give it to, and if asked if there was extra, would say that there was none, planning to serve it again. This is what is called "taking care of the mouth and body." Zengzi's approach can be called "taking care of the intentions." In serving one's parents, one should follow Zengzi's model." . . .

4A:26 Mencius said, "There are three things which are unfilial, and the worst of them is to have no heirs. It was because he had not heirs that Shun married without informing his parents. The superior person considered this equivalent to informing them."

4A:27 Mencius said, "The core of humaneness is serving one's parents. The core of duty is obeying one's elder brother. The core of wisdom is recognizing these two truths and not departing from them. The core of ritual is regulating and adorning these two truths. The core of music is taking joy in these two. When there is joy, they grow. When they grow, how can they be stopped? Once they cannot be stopped, unconsciously the feet begin to dance and the hands to move."

[Translated by Patricia Ebrey]

HISTORICAL INCIDENTS FROM THE ZUO ZHUAN

Below are three episodes from the *Zuo zhuan*, a late Zhou chronicle traditionally treated as a commentary to the *Spring and Autumn Annals*, the laconic chronicle of the state of Lu considered one of the Five Classics. The rulers whose activities are narrated in this source sometimes engaged in irregular sexual activity and suffered the consequences. These historical cases, thus, were treated as evidence of the human frailties of jealousy and lust, as well as the power of sexual attraction and ambition. An implicit theme is that men's attraction to women leads them to do things not in the interests of their state or family line. Women, for their part, are depicted as manipulative, as often to benefit their children as themselves.

Document 6–7

ZUO ZHUAN

DUKE HUAN 16TH YEAR (696 BC)

Earlier, Duke Xuan of Wei committed incest with his father's concubine Yi Jiang, and from this union was born Jizi. He was entrusted to the Ducal Son of the Right. A bride was brought for him from the state of Qi, but because she was beautiful, Duke Xuan took her for himself. From this union were born

Shouzi and Shuo. Shouzi was entrusted to the Ducal Son of the Left. Yi Jiang committed suicide by strangling herself.

Duke Xuan's bride from Qi plotted with her son Shuo to do away with Jizi. As part of the plot, Duke Xuan ordered Jizi to go on a mission to Qi and arranged for robbers to lie in wait at Xin and kill him.

Shouzi informed his half brother Jizi of the plot and urged him to flee, but Jizi refused, saying, "Who would have any use for a son who disobeys his father's orders? In a country where there are no fathers, such behavior might be acceptable."

When the time for departure came, Shouzi gave Jizi wine to drink and then, placing Jizi's banner on his own carriage, he set out ahead of Jizi. The robbers accordingly killed him.

When Jizi arrived, he said, "I'm the one you want—what fault has he committed? Please kill me!" The robbers killed him as well.

DUKE ZHUANG 28TH YEAR (666 BC)

Duke Xian of Jin took a bride from the state of Jia but she bore no sons. He had a clandestine affair with Lady Jiang of Qi, the concubine of his father, Duke Wu, and from this liaison were born the daughter who later became the wife of Duke Mu of Chin and the son, Shensheng, who became Duke Xian's designated heir. He also took two brides from the Rong people, Huji or Lady Hu of the Greater Rong, who bore him Chonger, and a daughter of the Lesser Rong, who bore him Yiwu.[1] When the state of Jin attacked the Rong people of Li, the ruler of the Li Rong gave his daughter Liji or Lady Li to the duke. The duke took her home with him and she bore him a son named Xiqi. Her younger sister, who accompanied her, bore him a son named Zhuozi.

Lady Li enjoyed great favor with the duke and hoped to have her son Xiqi appointed heir. She accordingly bribed two ministers who also enjoyed the duke's favor, Liang Wu and Dongguan Wu, and had them speak to the duke as follows: "Quwo is the site of our lord's ancestral temple, while Pu and Qu are on the frontier of our lord's realm. They must not be left without proper overseers. If the city of the ancestral temple lacks an overseer, the people will not view it with awe; and if the frontier stations lack overseers, the Rong tribes will be tempted to harbor ambitions. If the Rong harbor ambitions and the people of Jin look with contempt on their government, the state will suffer injury. We suggest that the heir apparent, Shensheng, be appointed overseer of Quwo, and Chonger and Yiwu be made overseers of Pu and Qu respectively. Then you can awe the people, put fear into the Rong, and at the same time make a display of the ruler's merit."

The two men were further instructed to say: "Since the lands of the barbarians are so broad and vast, Jin should make Pu and Qu into cities of importance. Jin will thus be broadening its territory—would that not be wise?"

Duke Xian was pleased.

In the summer he ordered the heir to take up residence in Quwo, Chonger to reside in the city of Pu, and Yiwu to reside in Qu. The remainder of his sons were all sent to outlying areas. Only the two sons of Lady Li and her younger sister remained in the capital city of Chiang. Thus the two ministers Liang Wu and Dongguan Wu joined with Lady Li in slandering the other sons of the duke and working to have Xiqi set up as heir. The men of Jin referred to this as "the teamwork of the two Wus."

DUKE XANG 25TH YEAR (548 BC)

The wife of the lord of Tang in Qi was an older sister of Dongguo Yan, a retainer of Cui Shu. When the lord of Tang died, Dongguo Yan drove Cui Shu to the lord's residence so he could offer condolences. Cui Shu observed the lord's wife, Lady Jiang, and admired her beauty. He instructed Dongguo Yan to arrange a marriage.

Dongguo Yan said, "Man and wife must be of different surnames. But you, my lord, are descended from Duke Ding of Qi, and I am descended from Duke Huan. It is out of the question!"

Cui Shu divined by the milfoil stalks and arrived at the hexagram *kun* or "adversity," which changed into the hexagram *daguo* or "excess."

The historians who conducted the divination all declared the response to be auspicious. But when Cui Shu showed the results to the Qi minister Chen Wenzi, he said, "Husband gives way to wind, wind blows the wife away. Such a match will never do! Moreover, the interpretation reads: 'Troubled by rocks, thorns and briers to rest on, the man enters his house but does not see his wife—misfortune!' 'Troubled by rocks' means he cannot cross over. 'Thorns and briers to rest on' means that what he leans on injures him. 'He enters his house but does not see his wife—misfortune!' means he has no place to turn to."

Cui Shu said, "She's a widow, so what does all that matter? Her former husband has already suffered the misfortune!" Thus in the end he married Lady Jiang.

Duke Zhuang of Qi carried on an adulterous affair with Lady Jiang, paying frequent visits to Cui Shu's house. At one time he took Cui Shu's hat and presented it to someone else. His attendant said, "That will not do!" But the duke replied, "Is Cui the only person who deserves a hat?"

For these reasons, Cui came to hate the duke. Also, when Duke Zhuang took advantage of the trouble in Jin to launch an attack on that state, Cui said, "Jin is certain to pay us back for this!" He therefore resolved to assassinate the duke in order to ingratiate himself with Jin, but could find no opportunity to do so. However, the duke thrashed one of his attendants named Jia Ju and then later allowed the man to wait on him again. This man spied on the duke for Cui Shu.

In the summer, the fifth month, the ruler of the state of Ju came to pay a court visit to Qi because of the military action carried out by Ju at Juyu.

On the day *jiaxu* a banquet was held for the ruler of Ju at the northern outer wall of the capital. Cui Shu, pleading illness, played no part in the affair.

On the day *yihai* Duke Zhuang went to Cui Shu's house to inquire how he was. While there, he sought out Cui Shu's wife, Lady Jiang. She led him into a chamber, but then she and Cui Shu slipped out by a side door. The duke began rapping on a pillar and singing.

Meanwhile, the duke's attendant Jia Ju instructed the party of men who had accompanied the duke to remain outside while he went in the house. Then he shut the gate on them. At that point Cui Shu's soldiers made their appearance.

The duke clambered up to the upper terrace, where he begged to be allowed to go free. His request was refused. He begged to be allowed to conclude an alliance with Cui Shu, but his request was refused. He begged to be allowed to take his own life in the ancestral temple, but his request was refused.

The soldiers all said, "The ruler's minister Cui Shu is sick and cannot inquire of the ruler's orders. Since this house is close to the ducal palace, we retainers of the Cui family have been assigned to patrol the area at night. If there are trespassers, the only orders we have are to attack!"

The duke tried to climb over the wall, whereupon someone shot at him with an arrow and hit him in the thigh. He fell backward from the wall, and in this way was finally assassinated.

Jia Ju, Zhou Chuo, Bing Shi, the ducal son Ao, Feng Ju, Duo Fu, Xiang Yi, and Lü Yin all died in the fighting.

[From *The Tso Chuan: Selections from China's Oldest Narrative History*, trans. Burton Watson, modified (New York: Columbia University Press, 1989), pp. 13–14, 21–22, 143–145]

RECORD OF RITUAL

The *Li ji*, translated in the nineteenth century by James Legge as *Record of Ritual*, was compiled in the second or first century BCE from earlier texts. From early times it was early considered one of the Confucian Classics, and it became the authoritative source for issues relating to family, marriage, and such key family rituals as funerals and ancestral rites. The text is quite long, and because it was created by collecting independent texts, there is much repetition from one section to another. The passages selected here come from several different sections, and were chosen to illustrate both specific ideas about family rituals and more general attitudes toward the moral basis of family relations.

In this translation the Master refers to Confucius. Legge's numbering of paragraphs has been retained, for the convenience of those who want to read the entire chapter.

Document 6–8

LI JI

The Pattern of the Family

3. Sons' wives should serve their parents-in-law as they served their own. At the first crowing of the cock, they should wash their hands and rinse their mouths; comb their hair, draw over it the covering of silk, fix this with the hairpin, and tie the hair at the roots with the fillet. They should then put on the jacket and over it the sash. On the left side they should hang the duster and handkerchief, the knife and whetstone, the small spike, and the metal speculum to get fire with; and on the right, the needle-case, thread, and floss, all bestowed in the satchel, the great spike, and the borer to get fire with from wood. They will also fasten on their necklaces and adjust their shoestrings.

4. Thus dressed, they should go to their parents and parents-in-law. On getting to where they are, with bated breath and gentle voice, they should ask if their clothes are too warm or too cold, whether they are ill or pained, or uncomfortable in any part; and if they be so, they should proceed reverently to stroke and scratch the place. They should in the same way, going before or following after, help and support their parents in quitting or entering the apartment. In bringing in the basin for them to wash, the younger will carry the stand and the elder the water; they will beg to be allowed to pour out the water, and when the washing is concluded, they will hand over the towel. They will ask whether they want anything, and then respectfully bring it. All this they will do with an appearance of pleasure to make their parents feel at ease. They should bring gruel, thick or thin, spirits or must, soup with vegetables, beans, wheat, spinach, rice, millet, maize, and glutinous millet, whatever they wish, in fact; with dates, chestnuts, sugar and honey, to sweeten their dishes; with the ordinary or the large-leaved violets, leaves of elm-trees, fresh or dry, and the most soothing rice-water to lubricate them; and with fat and oil to enrich them. The parents will be sure to taste them, and when they have done so, the young people should withdraw. . . .

6. All charged with the care of the inner and outer parts of the house, at the first crowing of the cock, should wash their hands and mouths, gather up their pillows and fine mats, sprinkle and sweep out the apartments, hall, and courtyard, and spread the mats, each doing his proper work. The children go earlier to bed, and get up later, according to their pleasure. There is no fixed time for their meals. . . .

16. If parents have a boy born to the father by a handmaid, or the son or grandson of one of his concubines, of whom they are very fond, their sons should after their death not allow their regard for him to diminish so long as they live.

If a son have two concubines, one of whom is loved by his parents, while he himself loves the other, yet he should not dare to make this one equal to the former whom his parents love in dress, or food, or the duties which she discharges, nor should he lessen his attentions to her after their death. If he very much approves of his wife, and his parents do not like her, he should divorce her. If he does not approve of his wife, but his parents say, "she serves us well," he should behave to her in all respects as his wife without fail even to the end of her life. . . .

18. When her father-in-law is dead, her mother-in-law [retires and]takes the place of the old lady; but the wife of the eldest son, on occasions of sacrificing and receiving guests, must ask her directions in everything, while the other sons' wives must ask directions from her. When her parents-in-law employ the eldest son's wife, she should not be dilatory, unfriendly, or impolite to the wives of his brothers (for their not helping her). When the parents-in-law employ any of them, they should not presume to consider themselves as equal to the other; walking side by side with her, or giving their orders in the same way, or sitting in the same position as she.

19. No daughter-in-law, without being told to go to her own apartment, should venture to withdraw from that of her parents-in-law. Whatever she is about to do, she should ask leave from them. A son and his wife should have no private goods, animals, or vessels; they should not presume to borrow from or give anything to another person. If anyone give the wife an article of food or dress, a piece of cloth or silk, a handkerchief for her girdle, an iris or orchid, she should receive it and offer it to her parents-in-law. If they accept it, she will be glad as if she were receiving it afresh. If they return it to her, she should decline it, and if they do not allow her to do so, she will take it as if it were a second gift, and lay it by to wait till they may want it. If she wants to give it to some of her own cousins, she must ask leave to do so, and that being granted, she will give it. . . .

SECTION II

13. The observances of propriety commence with a careful attention to the relations between husband and wife. The outer and inner parts of houses were distinguished. The men occupied the exterior; the women the interior. The mansion was deep and the doors were strong, guarded by porter and eunuch. The men did not enter the interior; the women did not come out into the outer section.

14. Males and females did not use the same stand or rack for their clothes. The wife did not presume to hang up anything on the pegs or stand of her husband; nor to put anything in his boxes or satchels; nor to share his bathing-house. When her husband had gone out from their apartment, she put his pillow in its case, rolled up his upper and under mats, put them in their covers, and laid them away in their proper receptacles. The young served the old and the low served the noble also in this way.

15. Between husband and wife, it was not until they were seventy that they deposited these things in the same place without separation. Hence though a concubine were old, until she had completed her fiftieth year, it was the rule that she should be with the husband once in five days. When she was to do so, she purified herself, rinsed her mouth and washed, carefully adjusted her dress, combed her hair, drew over it the covering of silk, fixed her hair-pins, tied up the hair in the shape of a horn, brushed the dust from the rest of her hair, put on her necklace, and adjusted her shoe-strings. Even a favorite concubine was required in dress and food to come after those ranked above her. If the wife were not with the husband, a concubine waiting on him would not venture to remain the whole night.

16. When a wife was about to have a child, and the month of her confinement had arrived, she occupied one of the side apartments, where her husband sent twice a day to ask about her. If he were moved and came himself to ask about her, she did not presume to see him but made her governess dress herself and reply to him.

When the child was born, the husband again sent twice a day to inquire of her. He fasted now, and did not enter the door of the side apartment. If the child were a boy, a bow was placed on the left of the door; and if a girl, a handkerchief on the right of it. After three days the child began to be carried, and some archery was practiced for a boy, but not for a girl . . .

23. When an heir-son has been born, the ruler washed his head and whole body, and put on his court robes. His wife did the same, and then they both took their station at the top of the stairs on the east with their faces towards the west. One of the ladies of quality, with the child in her arms, ascended by the steps on the west. The ruler then named the child; and (the lady) went down with it.

26. When a concubine was about to have a child, and the month of her confinement had arrived, the husband sent once a day to ask for her. When the son was born, at the end of three months, she washed her mouth and feet, adjusted herself early in the morning and appeared in the inner chamber (belonging to the wife proper). There she was received with the ceremonies of her first entrance into the harem. When the husband had eaten, a special portion of what was left was given to her by herself; and forthwith she entered on her duties of attendance.

27. When the child of an inferior member of the ruler's harem was about to be born, the mother went to one of the side apartments, and at the end of three months, having washed her head and person, and put on her court robes, she appeared before the ruler. One of her waiting women appeared with the child in her arms. If the mother was one to whom the ruler had given special favors, he himself named the son. In the case of other such children, an officer was employed to name them.

28. Among the common people who had no side chambers, when the month of confinement arrived, the husband left his bed-chamber, and occupied a

common apartment. In his inquiries for his wife, however, and on his son's being presented to him, there was no difference (from the observances that have been detailed).

29. In all cases though the father is alive, the grandson is presented to the grandfather, who also names him. The ceremonies are the same as when the son is presented to the father; but there is no interchange of words between the mother and him.

30. The wetnurse of the ruler's boy left the palace after three years, and, when she appeared before the ruler, was rewarded for her toilsome work.

The son of a Great Officer had a wetnurse. The wife of an ordinary officer nursed her child herself. . . .

THE MEANING OF SACRIFICES

4. Thus the filial piety taught by the ancient kings required that the eyes of the son should not forget the looks of his parents, nor his ears their voices; and that he should retain the memory of their aims, likings, and wishes. As he gave full play to his love, they seemed to live again; and to his reverence, they seemed to stand out before him. So seeming to live and stand out, so unforgotten by him, how could his sacrifices be without the accompaniment of reverence? . . .

6. It is only the sage who can sacrifice to God, and only the filial son who can sacrifice to his parents. Sacrificing means directing one's self to. The son directs his thoughts to his parents and then he can offer his sacrifice. Hence the filial son approaches the personator of the departed without having occasion to blush; the ruler leads the victim forward, while his wife puts down the bowls; the ruler presents the offerings to the personator, while his wife sets forth the various dishes; his ministers and great officers assist the ruler, while their acknowledged wives assist his wife. How well sustained was their reverence! How complete was the expression of their loyal devotion! How earnest was their wish that the departed should enjoy the service! . . .

11. What the sacrifice of a filial son should be can be known. While he is standing (waiting for the service to commence), he should be reverent, with his body somewhat bent; while he is engaged in carrying forward the service, he should be reverent, with an. expression of pleasure; when he is presenting the offerings, he should be reverent, with an expression of desire. He should then retire and stand, as if he were about to receive orders; when he has removed the offerings and (finally) retires, the expression of reverent gravity should continue to be worn on his face. Such is the sacrifice of a filial son.

To stand without any inclination of the body would show insensibility; to carry the service forward without an expression of pleasure would show indifference; to present the offerings without an expression of desire (that they may be enjoyed) would show a want of love; to retire and stand without seeming to expect to receive orders, would show pride; to retire and stand, after the removal of the offerings, without an expression of reverent gravity would show a forgetfulness of the parent to whom he owes his being. A sacrifice so conducted would be wanting in its proper characteristics. . . .

11. Zengzi said, 'The body is that which has been transmitted to us by our parents; dare anyone allow himself to be irreverent in the employment of their legacy? If a man in his own house and privacy be not grave, he is not filial; if in serving his ruler, he be not loyal, he is not filial; if in discharging the duties of office, he be not reverent, he is not filial; if with friends he be not sincere, he is not filial; if on the field of battle he be not brave, he is not filial. If he fail in these five things, the evil (of the disgrace) will reach his parents. Dare he but reverently attend to them?'

To prepare the fragrant flesh and grain which he has cooked, tasting and then presenting them before his parents, is not filial piety; it is only nourishing them. He whom the superior man pronounces filial is he whom the people of his state praise, saying with admiration, 'Happy are the parents who have such a son as this!'—that indeed is what can be called being filial. . . .

14. The disciple Youzheng Chun injured his foot in descending from his hall, and for some months was not able to go out. Even after this he still wore a look of sorrow, and one of the disciples of the school said to him, 'Your foot, master, is better; and though for some months you could not go out, why should you still wear a look of sorrow?' Youzheng Chun replied, 'It is a good question which you ask! It is a good question which you ask! I heard from Zengzi what he had heard the Master say, that of all that Heaven produces and Earth nourishes, there is none so great as man. His parents give birth to his person all complete, and to return it to them all complete may be called filial duty. When no member has been mutilated and no disgrace done to any part of the person, it may be called complete; and hence a superior man does not dare to take the slightest step in forgetfulness of his filial duty. But now I forgot the way of that, and therefore I wear the look of sorrow. A son should not forget his parents in a single lifting up of his feet, nor in the utterance of a single word. He should not forget his parents in a single lifting up of his feet, and therefore he will walk in the highway and not take a by-path, he will use a boat and not attempt to wade through a stream;—not daring, with the body left him by his parents, to go in the way of peril. He should not forget his parents in the utterance of a single word, and therefore an evil word will not issue from his mouth, and an angry word will not come back to his person. Not to disgrace his person and not to cause shame to his parents may be called filial duty.

RECORD OF THE DIKES

33. The Master said, 'The ceremonial usages serve as dikes to the people against bad excesses (to which they are prone). They display the separation which

should be maintained (between the sexes), that there may be no occasion for suspicion, and the relations of the people be well defined. It is said in the *Book of Poetry* (Mao 101),

> "How do we proceed in hewing an axe-handle?
> Without another axe it cannot be done.
> How do we proceed in taking a wife?
> Without a go-between it cannot be done.
> How do we proceed in planting hemp?
> The acres must be dressed length-wise and cross wise.
> How do we proceed in taking a wife?
> Announcement must first be made to our parents."

In this way it was intended to guard the people (against doing wrong), and still there are some (women) among them, who offer themselves (to the male).

34. The Master said, "A man in taking a wife does not take one of the same surname with himself, to show broadly the distinction (to be maintained between man and wife). Hence, when a man is buying a concubine, if he does not know her surname, he consults the tortoise-shell about it. In this way it was intended to preserve the people (from going wrong in the matter). . . .

35. The Master said, "According to the rules, male and female do not give the cup to one another, excepting at sacrifice. This was intended to guard the people against (undue freedom of intercourse); and yet the marquis of Yang killed the marquis of Mo, and stole away his wife. Therefore the presence of the wife at the grand entertainments was disallowed."

36. The Master said, "With the son of a widow one does not have interviews—this would seem to be an obstacle to friendship, but a superior man will keep apart from intercourse in such a case, in order to avoid (suspicion). Hence, in the intercourse of friends, if the master of the house be not in, a visitor, unless there is some great cause, does not enter the door. This was intended to preserve the people (from all appearance of evil); and yet there are those who pay more regard to beauty than to virtue."

37. The Master said, "The love of virtue should be like the love of beauty (from an inward constraint). Princes of states should not be like fishers for beauty (in the families) below them. Hence the superior man keeps aloof from beauty, in order to constitute a rule for the people. Thus male and female, in giving and receiving, do not allow their hands to touch; in driving his wife in a carriage, a husband advances his left hand; when a young aunt, a sister, or a daughter has been married, and returns (to her father's house), no male can sit on the same mat with her; a widow should not wail at night; when a wife is ill, in asking for her, the nature of her illness should not be mentioned—in this way it was sought to keep the people (from irregular connections); and yet there

are those who become licentious and introduce disorder and confusion among their kindred."

38. The Master said, "According to the rules of marriage, the son-in-law should go in person to meet the bride. When he is introduced to her father and mother, they bring her forward and give her to him—being afraid things should go contrary to what is right. In this way a dyke is raised in the interest of the people; and yet there are cases in which the wife will not go (to her husband's).

RECORD ON EXAMPLES

29. "Here now is the affection of a father for his sons; he loves the worthy among them and places on a lower level those who do not show ability; but that of a mother for them is such, that while she loves the worthy, she pities those who do not show ability. The mother deals with them on the ground of affection and not of showing them honor; the father, on the ground of showing them honor and not of affection.

THE MEANING OF THE MARRIAGE CEREMONY

1. The ceremony of marriage was intended to be a bond of love between two families of different surnames, with a view, in its retrospective character, to secure the services in the ancestral temple, and in its prospective character, to secure the continuance of the family line. Therefore the superior men, (the ancient rulers), set a great value upon it. Hence, in regard to the various introductory ceremonies—the proposal with its accompanying gift; the inquiries about the lady's name; the intimation of the approving divination; the receiving the special offerings; and the request to fix the days—these all were received by the principal party on the lady's side, as he rested on his mat or leaning stool in the ancestral temple. When they arrived, he met the messenger and greeted him outside the gate, giving place to him as he entered, after which they ascended to the hall. Thus were the instructions received in the ancestral temple, and in this way was the ceremony respected, and watched over, while its importance was exhibited and care taken that all its details should be correct.

2. The father gave himself the special cup to his son and ordered him to go and meet the bride, it being proper that the male should take the first step in all the arrangements. The son, having received the order, proceeded to meet his bride. Her father, who had been resting on his mat and leaning stool in the temple, met him outside the gate and received him with a bow, and then the son-in-law entered, carrying a wild goose. After the bows and yieldings of precedence, they went up to the hall, when the bridegroom bowed twice and put down the wild goose. Then and in this way he received the bride from her parents.

After this they went down, and he went out and took the reins of the horses of her carriage, which he drove for three revolutions of the wheels, having handed the strap to assist her in mounting. He then went before, and waited outside his gate. When she arrived, he bowed to her as she entered. They ate together of the same animal and joined in sipping from the cups made of the same gourd, thus showing that they now formed one body, were of equal rank, and pledged to mutual affection.

3. The respect, the caution, the importance, the attention to secure correctness in all the details, and then the pledge of mutual affection—these were the great points in the ceremony, and served to establish the distinction to be observed between man and woman, and the righteousness to be maintained between husband and wife. From the distinction between man and woman came the righteousness between husband and wife. From that righteousness came the affection between father and son; and from that affection, the rectitude between ruler and minister. Whence it is said, "The ceremony of marriage is the root of the other ceremonial observances."

4. Ceremonies might be said to commence with the capping; to have their root in marriage; to be most important in the rites of mourning and sacrifice; to confer the greatest honor in audiences at the royal court and in the interchange of visits at the feudal courts; and to most promote harmony in the country festivals and celebrations of archery. These were the greatest occasions of ceremony and the principal points in them.

5. Rising early the morning after marriage, the young wife washed her head and bathed her person, and waited to be presented to her husband's parents, which was done by the directrix as soon as it was bright day. She appeared before them, bearing a basket with dates, chestnuts, and slices of dried spiced meat. The directrix set before her a cup of sweet liquor, and she offered in sacrifice some of the dried meat and also the liquor, thus performing the ceremony which declared her their son's wife.

6. The father and mother-in-law then entered their apartment, where she set before them a single dressed pig, thus showing the obedient duty of their son's wife.

7. Next day, the parents united in entertaining the young wife, and when the ceremonies of their severally pledging her in a single cup and her pledging them in return had been performed, they descended by the steps on the west, and she by those on the east, thus showing that she would take the mother's place in the family.

8. Thus the ceremony establishing the young wife in her position; followed by that showing her obedient service to her husband's parents; and both succeeded by that showing how she now occupied the position of continuing the family line: all served to impress her with a sense of the deferential duty proper to her. When she was thus deferential, she was obedient to her parents-in-law and harmonious with all the occupants of the women's apartments; she was the

fitting partner of her husband and could carry on all the work in silk and linen, making cloth and silken fabrics, and maintaining a watchful care over the various stores and depositories of the household.

9. In this way when the deferential obedience of the wife was complete, the internal harmony was secured; and when the internal harmony was secured, the long continuance of the family could be counted on. Therefore the ancient kings attached such importance to the marriage ceremonies.

10. Therefore, anciently, for three months before the marriage of a young lady, if the temple of the high ancestor of her family were still standing, she was taught in it, as the public hall; if it were no longer standing, she was taught in the public hall of the head of that branch of the surname to which she belonged; she was taught there the virtue, the speech, the carriage, and the work of a wife. When the teaching was accomplished, she offered a sacrifice to the ancestor, using fish for the victim and soups made of duckweed and pond-weed. So was she trained to the obedience of a wife.

11. Anciently, the queen of the Son of Heaven divided the harem into six palace halls, occupied by the three ladies called *furen*, the nine called *pin*, the 27 called *shifu*, and the 81 called *yuqi*. These were instructed in the domestic and private rule which should prevail throughout the kingdom, and how the deferential obedience of the wife should be illustrated; and thus internal harmony was everywhere secured, and families were regulated. In the same way the Son of Heaven established six official departments, in which were distributed the 3 gong, the 9 qing, the 27 dafu, and the 81 shi of the highest grade. These were instructed in all that concerned the public and external government of the kingdom, and how the lessons for the man should be illustrated; and thus harmony was secured in all external affairs, and the states were properly governed.

It is therefore said, "from the Son of Heaven there were learned the lessons for men; and from the queen, the obedience proper to women." The Son of Heaven directed the course to be pursued by the masculine energies, and the queen regulated the virtues to be cultivated by the feminine receptivities. The Son of Heaven guided in all that affected the external administration (of affairs); and the queen, in all that concerned the internal regulation of the family. The teachings of the one and the obedience inculcated by the other perfected the manners and ways of the people; abroad and at home harmony and natural order prevailed; the states and the families were ruled according to their requirements: this was what is called the condition of complete virtue.

12. Therefore when the lessons for men are not cultivated, the masculine phenomena in nature do not proceed regularly; as seen in the heavens, we have the sun eclipsed. When the obedience proper to women is not cultivated, the feminine phenomena in nature do not proceed regularly; as seen in the heavens, we have the moon eclipsed. Hence on an eclipse of the sun, the Son of Heaven put on plain white robes and proceeded to repair what was wrong in the duties of the six official departments, purifying everything that belonged to

the masculine sphere throughout the kingdom; and on an eclipse of the moon, the queen dressed herself in plain white robes and proceeded to repair what was wrong in the duties of the six palace halls, purifying everything that belonged to the feminine sphere throughout the kingdom. The Son of Heaven is to the queen what the sun is to the moon, or the masculine energy of nature to the feminine. They are necessary to each other, and by their interdependence they fulfill their functions.

13. The Son of Heaven attends to the lessons for men—that is the function of the father. The queen attends to the obedience proper to women—that is the function of the mother. Therefore it is said, "The Son of Heaven and the queen are (to the people) what father and mother are." Hence for him who is the Heaven-appointed king, they wear the sackcloth with the jagged edges, as for a father; and for the queen they wear the sackcloth with the even edges, as for a mother.

TANG GONG

4. When Zishang's mother died, and he did not perform any mourning rites for her, the disciples of his father Zisi[2] asked him, saying, "Did your predecessor, the superior man, observe mourning for his divorced mother?" "Yes," was the reply. And the disciples went on, "Why do you not make Bai also observe the mourning rites for his mother?" Zisi said, "My progenitor, a superior man, never failed in pursuing the right path. When a generous course was possible, he took it and behaved generously; and when it was proper to restrain his generosity, he restrained it. But how can I attain to that? While she was my wife, she was Bai's mother; but when she ceased to be my wife, she was no longer his mother." It was in this way that the Kong family came not to observe mourning for a divorced mother; the practice began from Zisi. . . .

6. When Confucius had succeeded in burying his mother in the same grave with his father at Fang, he said, "I have heard that the ancients made graves only, and did not raise mounds over them. But I am a man who will be traveling east, west, south, and north. I cannot do without something by which I can remember the place." On this he resolved to raise a mound four feet high. He then first returned, leaving the disciples behind. A great rain came on; and when they rejoined him, he asked them what had made them so late. "The earth slipped," they said, "from the grave at Fang." They told him this thrice without his giving them any answer. He then wept freely, and said, "I have heard that the ancients did not need to repair their graves." . . .

10. Confucius, being quite young when he was left fatherless, did not know the location of his father's grave. Afterwards he had (his mother's) body coffined in the street of Wufu. Those who saw it all thought that it was to be interred there, so carefully was everything done, but it was (only) the coffining. By inquiring of the mother of Manfu of Zou, he succeeded in burying it in the same grave with his father at Fang. . . .

14. When the mother of Duke Mu of Lu died, he sent to ask Zengzi what ceremonies he should observe. Zengzi said, "I have heard from my father that the sorrow declared in the weeping and wailing, the feelings expressed in the robe of sackcloth with even or with frayed edges, and the food of rice made thick or in congee, extend from the Son of Heaven to all. But the tent-like covering for the coffin is of linen cloth in Wei, and of silk in Lu." . . .

20. The practice in Zhulou of calling the (spirits of the dead) back with arrows took its rise from the battle of Shengxing. That in Lu of the women making their visits of condolence simply with a band of sackcloth round their hair took its rise from the defeat at Taitai.

21. At the mourning for her mother-in-law, the Master instructed his niece, the wife of Nangong Tao, about the way in which she should tie up her hair with sackcloth, saying, "Do not make it very high, nor very broad. Have a hairpin of hazel-wood, and the hairknots (hanging down) eight inches." . . .

26. When Zilu might have ended his mourning for his eldest sister, he still did not do so. Confucius said to him, "Why do you not leave off your mourning?" He replied, "I have but few brothers, and I cannot bear to do so." Confucius said, "When the ancient kings framed their rules, (they might have said that) they could not bear (to cease mourning) even for (ordinary) men on the roads." When Zilu heard this, he forthwith left off his mourning. . . .

28. When the mother of Boyu died, he kept on wailing for her after the year. Confucius heard him, and said, "Who is it that is thus wailing? The disciples said, "It is Li." The Master said, "Ah! That is excessive!" When Boyu heard it, he forthwith gave up wailing.

29. Shun[3] was buried in the wilderness of Cangwu, and it would thus appear that the three ladies of his harem were not buried in the same grave with him. Ji Wuzi said, "Burying (husband and wife) in the same grave appears to have originated with the Duke of Zhou." . . .

34. When the mother of Ziliu died, (his younger brother) Zishi asked for the means (to provide what was necessary for the mourning rites). Ziliu said, "How shall we get them?" "Let us sell (the concubines), the mothers of our half-brothers," said the other. "How can we sell the mothers of other men to bury our mother?" was the reply, "that cannot be done."

After the burial, Zishi wished to take what remained of the money and other things contributed towards their expenses, to provide sacrificial vessels; but Ziliu said, " Neither can that be done. I have heard that a superior man will not enrich his family by means of his mourning. Let us distribute it among the poor of our brethren." . . .

37. There was a man of Bian who wept like a child at the death of his mother. Confucius said, "This is grief indeed, but it would be difficult to continue it. Now the rules of ceremony require to be handed down, and to be perpetuated. Hence the wailing and leaping are subject to fixed regulations." . . .

43. The mourning worn for the son of a brother should be the same as for one's own son: the object being to bring him still nearer to one's self. An elder brother's wife and his younger brother do not wear mourning for each other: the object being to maintain the distance between them. Slight mourning is worn for an aunt, and an elder or younger sister (when they have been married); the reason being that there are those who received them from us, and will render to them the full measure of observance.

[From *The Li Ki,* in *The Sacred Books of the East,* trans. James Legge (Oxford: Oxford University Press, 1885), vol. 27, pp. 122–147, 450–476; vol. 28, pp. 211–229, 297–299, 341, 428–434, modified and with many deletions]

THE RECORD OF RITUAL OF THE ELDER DAI

Besides the early texts incorporated in the *Record of Ritual,* early ritual texts assembled in the first century BCE by Dai De have been preserved under the title *Record of Ritual of the Elder Dai (Da Dai Liji).* This work is the earliest source on the grounds for divorce and several other often quoted teachings on marriage and gender.

Document 6–9

DA DAI LIJI

The word "male" means responsible; the word "child" means offspring. The term male-child refers to their responsibility for taking care of all under heaven or on earth, their duty to aid the growth of all living things. Therefore they are called "senior supports." Senior means old, support means giving assistance, which refers to their role in the growth of all living things. They know what should be done and what should not be done; they know what should be said and what should not be said; they know what should be practiced and what should not be practiced. For this reason, they examine the ethical principles and understand the separation of the sexes. This is the virtue of the proper man.

The world "female" means similar; the word "child" means offspring. The term female-child refers to their being educated in a way similar to boys to develop their moral understanding. Therefore they are called "wife-persons." A wife is someone who submits to a person. For this reason she does not have to take charge herself. She has the Way of the three submissions: at her home, she submits to her father; after marriage she submits to her husband; after her husband dies, she submits to her son, never daring to proceed alone. Orders do not issue from the women's quarters. A woman concentrates her efforts on food preparation. Therefore women stay in the inner quarters all day, and do not travel to a funeral more than 100 li away. Their Way does not include taking initiative or acting alone. They act after consultation, speak after giving consideration. When walking at night they carry a candle. They take charge of the silkworms and domestic animals. This is how they are trustworthy; this is the virtue of the proper wife.

There are five types of women who should not be taken in marriage. The daughter of an insubordinate family should not be taken; the daughter of a wild family should not be taken; the daughter of a family with criminals in prior generations should not be taken, the daughter of a family that in prior generations had noxious diseases should not be taken, and the daughter who grew up in a family where the wife has died should not be taken. The daughter of an insubordinate family will oppose virtue; the daughter of a wild family will cause confusion to ethical principles. Families that have criminals have been abandoned by society; families with noxious diseases have been abandoned by heaven. A girl who grew up without a mother will have no one to instruct her in her proper role.

There are seven grounds for divorcing a wife. If she is not obedient to [her husband's] parents, send her away. If she has no children, send her away. If she commits adultery, send her away. If she is jealous, send her away. If she has a noxious disease, send her away. If she talks a lot, send her away. If she steals, send her away. The reason for sending her away if she disobeys the parents is that this violates virtue; when she has no children, it is because it cuts off the family line; when she is adulterous, it is because this confuses kinship connections; when she is jealous, it is because this brings disorder to the household; when she has a noxious disease, it is because she cannot participate in making offerings of food to the ancestors; when she speaks too much, it is because this causes estrangement among relatives; and when she steals, because it is counter to morality.

There are three situations in which wives cannot be divorced. She cannot be sent away when she was taken from a home but there is no longer a home to which she can return. She cannot be sent away when she has mourned [a parent-in-law] for three years. She cannot be sent away if when first married [her husband] was poor and lowly but now he is rich and high ranking.

[Translated by Patricia Ebrey from *Kao Ming, Da Dai li ji jin zhu jin yi* (Taibei: Commercial, 1975), pp. 466–469]

THE *CLASSIC OF FILIAL PIETY*

The brief *Classic of Filial Piety* (*Xiao jing*) was probably written early in the Han dynasty (202 BCE-220 CE). It purports to record the conversations between Confucius's disciple Zengzi and Confucius. The Han was a period when filial piety was greatly extolled, and in this text filial piety was presented as a political virtue, tied to loyalty to political superiors. From Han times on this text was used as a basic primer in the education of children.

Document 6–10

OPENING THE DISCUSSION AND EXPLAINING THE PRINCIPLES

Confucius was at home and Zengzi was attending him. Confucius said, "The former kings had the highest virtue and the essential Way. By using them they kept the world ordered and the people in harmony, and neither superiors nor inferiors resented each other. Is this something you know about?"

Zengzi rose from his mat and replied, "Since I am not clever, how can I know about this?"

Confucius said: "Filial piety is the root of virtue and the source of civilization. Sit down again and I will explain it to you. Since we receive our body, hair, and skin from our parents, we do not dare let it be injured in any way. This is the beginning of filial piety. We establish ourselves and practice the Way, thereby perpetuating our name for future generations and bringing glory to our parents. This is the fulfillment of filial piety. Thus filial piety begins with serving our parents, continues with serving the ruler, and is completed by establishing one's character."

In the Daya [section of the *Book of Poetry*], it says, "Think of your ancestors and maintain the practice of their virtues."[4]

THE FEUDAL LORDS

"Although in superior positions, they are not arrogant and thus can hold lofty positions without peril. By exercising restraint and caution they can have plenty without going overboard. Holding a lofty position without peril is the way to preserve high rank for a long time. Having plenty without going overboard is the way to preserve wealth for a long time. If they retain their wealth and rank they will later be able to protect their heritage and keep their people in peace. This is the filial piety of the feudal lords."

In the *Book of Poetry*, it says: "Be as cautious as if you were standing on the edge of a chasm or treading on thin ice."[5]

THE MINISTERS AND HIGH OFFICERS

"They do not dare wear garments not prescribed by the former kings; they do not dare use words not approved by the former kings; they do not dare to behave in any ways outside the virtuous ways of the former kings. Thus, they will not speak improper words and will not follow anything against the Way. Their words are not arbitrary, nor their actions capricious. Their words reach all in the world, yet offend no one. Their actions fill the world, yet give no one cause for complaint. Those who fulfill these three conditions are able to preserve their ancestral altars. This is the filial piety of the ministers and high officers."

The *Book of Poetry* says: "Never negligent morning or night in the service of the One Man."[6]

THE COMMON PEOPLE

"They follow the laws of nature to utilize the earth to the best advantage. They take care of themselves and are cautious in expenditures in order to support their parents. This is the filial piety of the common people. Thus from the Son of heaven to the common people, unless filial piety is pursued from beginning to end, calamities will surely result."

THE THREE POWERS

Zengzi said, "How exceedingly great is filial piety!"

Confucius responded, "Filial piety is the pattern of heaven, the standard of the earth, the norm of conduct for the people. When people follow the pattern of heaven and earth, they model themselves on the brilliance of heaven and make use of the resources of the earth and through these means comply with all under heaven. Thus, [a ruler's] instruction succeeds without being stringent, and his policies are effective without being severe. The former kings, realizing that their instruction could transform the people, showed them an example of universal love. As a consequence, men did not neglect their parents. These kings set an example of rectitude and virtue, and as a consequence the people enthusiastically copied them. The kings showed an example of respectful yielding, and the people did not contend with each other. They taught through ritual and music, and the people lived in concord. They made clear to them the difference between good and evil, and as a consequence the people knew restraint."

The *Book of Poetry* says: "How dignified is Master Yin! The common people all look on him with reverence."[7]

BRINGING ORDER THROUGH FILIAL PIETY

Confucius said, "Formerly the illustrious kings brought order to the world through filial piety. They did not dare neglect the ministers of small states—not to mention their own dukes, marquises, earls, counts, and barons. Therefore they gained the support of all the states, making them better able to serve the former kings. The rulers did not dare insult the widows and widowers—not to mention the upper class or the common people. Therefore they gained the support of all the people, making them better able to serve their former rulers. The heads of families did not dare mistreat their servants and concubines—not to mention their wives and children. Therefore they gained their support, making them better able to serve their parents. Accordingly, while living, parents were well taken care of; after their death, their ghosts received sacrifices. In this way the world was kept in peace and harmony. Calamities did not occur nor was disorder created. Such was the way the former illustrious kings brought order to the world through filial piety."

The *Book of Poetry* says: "The states in the four directions will follow the one whose conduct is truly virtuous."[8]

THE RULE OF THE SAGES

Zengzi said, "May I ask if there isn't anything in the virtue of the sages that surpasses filial piety?"

Confucius replied, "Of all the creatures in heaven and earth, man is the most important. Of all man's acts, none is greater than filial piety. In the practice of filial piety, nothing is greater than respecting one's father. For respecting one's father, nothing is greater than placing him on the level with heaven.

"The person who did all this was the Duke of Zhou. In former times the Duke of Zhou sacrificed to the Spirit of Agriculture, placing him on a level with heaven. He sacrificed to his father King Wen, in the Bright Hall, placing him on a level with the Supreme Lord. Therefore, within the four seas all of the lords, according to their stations, came to sacrifice. Thus, how can there be anything in the virtue of the sages that surpasses filial piety? From infancy a child's desire to care for his parents daily grows more respectful. The sages used this natural reverence for parents to teach respect and used this natural affection to teach love. Thus, the teachings of the sages were effective though not severe and their rule was orderly though not harsh. This was because they relied on what was basic to human nature.

"The proper relation between father and son is a part of nature and forms the principles which regulate the conduct of rulers and ministers. Parents give life—no tie is stronger than this. Rulers personally watch over the people—no care is greater than this. Therefore to love others without first loving one's parents is to reject virtue. To reverence other men without first reverencing one's parents is to reject the rules of ritual. If one copies such perversity, the people will have no model to follow. Although a person who does not do good but only evil may gain a high position, a man of honor will not esteem him. The practice of a man of honor is different: his speech is praiseworthy, his behavior is pleasing, his standards are respected, his management of affairs can be taken as a model, his department is pleasant to observe, his movements are deliberate. When a man of honor deals with his people they look on him with awe and affection; they imitate and seek to resemble him. Thus he can carry out his moral instruction and put into effect his political directives."

The *Book of Poetry* says: "The good man, the true gentleman, his deportment is impeccable."[9]

FILIAL CONDUCT

Confucius said, "Let me comment on the way a filial son serves his parents. While at home he renders the utmost reverence to them. In supporting them he maximizes their pleasure. When they are sick he takes every care. At their death he expresses all his grief. Then he sacrifices to them with full solemnity.

"Only a son who has fulfilled these five requirements is truly able to serve his parents. He who really loves his parents will not be proud in high position. He will not be insubordinate in an inferior position. And among equals he will not be quarrelsome. If he were proud in high station he might be ruined. If he were insubordinate in an inferior position he might incur punishment. If he were quarrelsome among his equals, he might end up fighting. Thus, unless these three evils are eliminated, a son cannot be called filial—even if every day he supplies his parents the three choice meats."

THE FIVE PUNISHMENTS

Confucius said, "There are three thousand offenses subject to the five punishments, but of these the most heinous is lack of filial piety. To use force against the ruler is to defy authority. To deny the sages is to be unprincipled. And to decry filial piety is to renounce kinship ties. These are the roads to chaos."

ELABORATING "THE HIGHEST VIRTUE"

Confucius said, "A man of honor in teaching the duties of filial piety does not need to go daily to the people's homes to observe them. He merely teaches the principles of filial piety and all the fathers in the world receive the filial respect due to them. He teaches the principles of fraternal love and all the elder brothers receive the respect due to them. He teaches the duties of subjects and all the rulers of the world receive the reverence due to them. The *Book of Poetry* says: 'Affectionate the man of honor, a father and mother to the people.'[10] Unless he possessed the highest virtue, who could educate the people to such an extent?"

ELABORATING "PERPETUATING ONE'S NAME"

Confucius said, "The man of honor's service to his parents is filial; the fidelity involved in it can be transferred to his ruler. His service to his elder brothers is deferential; the obedience involved in it can be transferred to his superiors. Self-disciplined at home, he can transfer his good management to official life. Through these means when his conduct is perfected at home his name will be perpetuated to later generations."

ADMONISHING

Zengzi remarked, "I understand your teachings concerning kind affection, loving respect, comforting one's parents, and bringing glory to one's name. May I ask if a son who obeys all of his father's commands can be called filial?"

Confucius replied, "What kind of talk is this? What kind of talk is this? In ancient times if the Son of Heaven had seven ministers to point out his errors, he would not lose his empire, even if he were imperfect. If a feudal lord had five good ministers to point out his errors, he would not lose his state, even if he were imperfect. If a high officer had three officials to point out his errors, he would not lose his patrimony, even if he were imperfect. If a gentleman had a friend to point out his errors, he would not lose his good name. And if a father had a son to point out his errors, he would not fall into doing wrong. Thus, when he might do something wrong, a son must not fail to warn his father against it, nor a minister fail to warn his ruler. In short, when it is a question of doing wrong, one must admonish. How can following a father's orders be considered fulfilling filial piety?"

MUTUAL INTERACTION

Confucius said, "In ancient times the illustrious kings, because they were filial to their fathers were able to serve heaven intelligently. Because they were filial to their mothers they were able to serve earth with circumspection. Superiors could govern inferiors because the young obeyed their elders. Thus, because heaven and earth were served with intelligence and care the spirits manifested themselves brilliantly. Even the Son of Heaven had someone he paid reverence to, that is to say, his father. He had someone he deferred to, that is to say, his elder brothers. At the ancestral temple he was reverential, not forgetting his parents. He cultivated his character and acted prudently, for fear of disgracing his ancestors. When he paid reverence at the ancestral temple, the ghosts and spirits sent blessings. When his filial piety and fraternity were perfected, his influence reached the spirits. He illuminated the four seas; there was no place his virtue did not penetrate."

The *Book of Poetry* says: "West, east, south, north, no one fails to submit to him."[11]

SERVING THE RULER

Confucius said, "In serving his superior the man of honor makes every effort to be faithful when he is in office. In retirement he tries to make up for his shortcomings. He encourages his superior in his good inclinations and tries to keep him from doing wrong. In this way, the relations between superiors and inferiors can be cordial."

The *Book of Poetry* says: "In his heart is love. Why not admit it? He stores it in his heart. When could he forget it?"[12]

MOURNING FOR PARENTS

Confucius said, "When mourning a parent a filial son weeps without wailing loudly, he performs the rites without attention to his appearance, he speaks without attention to the beauty of his words, he feels uncomfortable in elegant clothes, he gets no joy from hearing music, he does not relish good food—all of this is the emotion of grief. After three days he eats again to show men that the dead should not hurt the living and that the suffering should not lead to the destruction of life. This was the regulation of the sages. The period of mourning is not allowed to exceed three years, thus showing the people that everything ends. [The filial son] prepares a double coffin and grave clothes. When he sets out the sacrificial vessels, he grieves. Beating the breast, jumping up and down, and crying, he bids a last sad farewell. He divines to choose the burial place where the body can be placed to rest. He prepares an ancestral altar, so that the ghost can receive sacrifices. Spring and autumn he offers sacrifices thus thinking of the dead one every season. When his parents were alive he served them with love and reverence; in death he grieves.

"With the man's fundamental duty fulfilled, relations between the living and the dead are complete, and the filial son's service to his parents is finished."

[Translated by Patricia Ebrey from *Under Confucian Eyes: Writings on Gender in Chinese History*, ed. Susan Mann and Yu-yin Cheng (Berkeley: University of California Press, 2001), pp. 49–69, with many omissions]

LIVES OF MODEL WOMEN

One of the most influential texts used for the education of girls was written by Liu Xiang (79–8 BCE) in the Han dynasty. This *Lives of Model Women (Lienü zhuan)* is a collection of brief biographies of 125 women of earlier times, most selected because they exemplified a virtue such as wisdom, loyalty, or constancy, though a few were cautionary stories of women who led men astray. The moral exemplars often were willing to sacrifice themselves to aid a parent or husband. The biography given below is of the mother of the Confucian scholar Mencius.

Document 6–11

LIENÜ ZHUAN

THE MOTHER OF MENCIUS

The mother of Mencius lived in Zou in a house near a cemetery. When Mencius was a little boy he liked to play burial rituals in the cemetery, happily building tombs and grave mounds. His mother said to herself, "This is no place to bring up my son."

She moved near the marketplace in town. Mencius then played merchant games of buying and selling. His mother again said, "This is no place to bring up my son."

So once again she moved, this time next to a school house. Mencius then played games of ancestor sacrifices and practiced the common courtesies between students and teachers. His mother said, "At last, this is the right place for my son!" There they remained.

When Mencius grew up he studied the six arts of propriety, music, archery, charioteering, writing, and mathematics. Later he became a famous Confucian scholar. Superior men commented that Mencius' mother knew the right influences for her sons. The Book of Songs says, "That admirable lady, what will she do for them!"

When Mencius was young, he came home from school one day and found his mother was weaving at the loom. She asked him, "Is school out already?" He replied, "I left because I felt like it." His mother took her knife and cut the finished cloth on her loom. Mencius was startled and asked why. She replied, "Your neglecting your studies is very much like my cutting the cloth. The superior person studies to establish a reputation and gain wide knowledge. He is calm and poised and tries to do no wrong. If you do not study now, you will surely end up as a menial servant and will never be free from troubles. It would be just like a woman who supports herself by weaving to give it up. How long could such a person depend on her husband and son to stave off hunger? If a woman neglects her work or a man gives up the cultivation of his character, they may end up as common thieves if not slaves!"

Shaken, from then on Mencius studied hard from morning to night. He studied the philosophy of the master and eventually became a famous Confucian scholar. Superior men observed that Mencius' mother understood the way of motherhood. The *Book of Poetry* says, "That admirable lady, what will she tell them!"

After Mencius was married, one day as he was going into his private quarters, he encountered his wife not fully dressed. Displeased, Mencius stopped going into his wife's room. She then went to his mother, begged to be sent home, and said, "I have heard that the etiquette between a man and a woman does not apply in their private room. But lately I have been too casual, and when my husband saw me improperly dressed, he was displeased. He is treating me like a stranger. It is not right for a woman to live as a guest; therefore, please send me back to my parents."

Mencius' mother called him to her and said, "It is polite to inquire before you enter a room. You should make some loud noise to warn anyone inside, and as you enter, you should keep your eyes low so that you will not embarrass anyone. Now, you have not behaved properly, yet you are quick to blame others for their impropriety. Isn't that going a little too far?" Mencius apologized and took back his wife. Superior men said that his mother understood the way to be a mother-in-law.

When Mencius was living in Qi, he was feeling very depressed. His mother saw this and asked him, "Why are you looking so low?" "It's nothing," he replied. On another occasion when Mencius was not working, he leaned against the door and sighed. His mother saw him and said, "The other day I saw that you were troubled, but you answered that it was nothing. But why are you leaning against the door sighing?" Mencius answered, "I have heard that the superior man judges his capabilities and then accepts a position. He neither seeks illicit gains nor covets glory or high salary. If the dukes and princes do not listen to his advice, then he does not talk to them. If they listen to him but do not use his ideas, then he no longer frequents their courts. Today my ideas are not being used in Qi, so I wish to go somewhere else. But I am worried because you are getting too old to travel about the country." His mother answered, "A woman's duties are to cook the five grains, heat the wine, look after her parents-in-law, make clothes, and that is all! Therefore, she cultivates the skills required in the women's quarters and has no ambition to manage affairs outside of the house. The *Book of Changes* says, 'In her central place, she attends to the preparation of the food.' The *Book of Poetry* says, 'It will be theirs neither to do wrong nor to do good; only about the spirits and the food will they have to think.' This means that a woman's duty is not to control or to take charge. Instead she must follow the 'three submissions.' When she is young, she must submit to her parents. After her marriage, she must submit to her husband. When she is widowed, she must submit to her son. These are the rules of propriety. Now you are an adult and I am old; therefore, whether you go depends on what you consider right, whether I follow depends on the rules of propriety."

Superior men observed that Mencius' mother knew the proper course for women. The *Book of Poetry* says, "Serenely she looks and smiles, / Without any impatience she delivers her instructions."

[From *Chinese Civilization: A Sourcebook*, ed. Patricia Buckley Ebrey
(New York: Free Press, 1993), pp. 72–74]

ADMONITIONS FOR WOMEN

Ban Zhao was a member of one of the most eminent families of the first century CE. One brother was a general, the other a historian. She was widowed early, and when her brother died in 92, the emperor called on Ban Zhao to finish the history he had been working on. She came to the palace where she not only worked on the history but also became a teacher of the women of the palace. According to the *History of the Later Han*, she taught them the Classics, history, astronomy, and mathematics. In 106 an infant succeeded to the throne and Empress Deng became regent. The empress frequently turned to Ban Zhao for advice on government policies. In her *Admonitions for Women (Nüjie)* Ban Zhao complained that many families taught their sons but not their daughters. She did not claim they should have the same education—after all "just as yin and yang differ, men and women have different characteristics." In subsequent centuries Ban Zhao's *Admonitions* became one of the most commonly used texts for the education of girls. The two excerpts below show the sorts of virtues she encouraged and the types of arguments she made.

Document 6–12

NÜJIE

HUMILITY

In ancient times, on the third day after a girl was born, people placed her at the base of the bed, gave her a pot shard to play with, and made a sacrifice to announce her birth. She was put below the bed to show that she was lowly and weak and should concentrate on humbling herself before others. Playing with a shard showed that she should get accustomed to hard work and concentrate on being diligent. Announcing her birth to the ancestors showed that she should focus on continuing the sacrifices. These three customs convey the unchanging path for women and the ritual traditions.

Humility means yielding and acting respectful, putting others first and oneself last, never mentioning one's own good deeds or denying one's own faults, enduring insults and bearing with mistreatment, all with due trepidation. Industriousness means going to bed late, getting up early, never shirking work morning or night, never refusing to take on domestic work, and completing everything that needs to be done neatly and carefully. Continuing the sacrifices means serving one's husband-master with appropriate demeanor, keeping oneself clean and pure, never joking or laughing, and preparing pure wine and food to offer to the ancestors.

There has never been a woman who had these three traits and yet ruined her reputation or fell into disgrace. If a woman loses these three traits, she will have no name to preserve and will not be able to avoid shame.

DEVOTION

According to the rites, a man is obligated to take a second wife but nothing is written about a woman marrying twice. Hence the saying, "A husband is one's Heaven: one cannot flee Heaven; one cannot leave a husband." Heaven punishes those whose actions offend the spirits; a husband looks down on a wife who violates the rites and proprieties. Thus the Model for Women says, "To please one man is her goal; to displease one man ends her goal." It follows from this that a woman must seek her husband's love not through such means as flattery, flirting, or false intimacy, but rather through devotion.

Devotion and proper demeanor entail propriety and purity, hearing nothing licentious, seeing nothing depraved, doing nothing likely to draw notice when outside the home; never neglecting one's appearance when at home; never gathering in groups or watching at the doorway. By contrast, those incapable of devotion and proper demeanor are careless in their actions, look at and listen to whatever they like, let their hair get messy when at home, put on an act of delicacy when away, speak of things they should not mention and watch what they should not see.

[From Ebrey, *Chinese Civilization*, pp. 75–76]

FILIAL SONS

From the Han period on, stories of sons who exemplified filial piety circulated widely and became common themes for pictorial art, such as the decoration of tombs. A group of these tales eventually circulated as the *Twenty-Four Filial Sons (Ershisi xiaozi)*, one of the most popular didactic tracts in later centuries. The stories below are some of those that decorated the funerary shrine of a low official dated to 151 CE. The texts are drawn from several early compilations, none as old as the shrine, however.

Document 6–13

ERSHISI XIAOZI

Min Ziqian had a younger brother. After their mother died, their father remarried and had two other sons. Ziqian drove a chariot for his father and dropped the bridle. His father held his hands and [found] that he wore only thin clothing. The father then went home and called the sons of the stepmother. He held their hands and [found] that they were wearing thick, warm clothing. He blamed his wife, saying, "The reason that I married you was for my sons. Now you are cheating me and I cannot keep you here!" Ziqian went forth and said, "When mother is here, only one son is wearing thin clothing; if mother leaves, four sons will be in the cold." His father became silent. Therefore people say that Min Ziqian kept his mother home by one word and made three sons warm by a second word.

Elder Laizi was a native of Chu. When he was seventy years old, his parents were both still alive. With the ultimate filial piety, he often wore multicolored clothes to serve his parents food in the main hall. Once he hurt his feet. Afraid to sadden his parents, he made himself tumble stiffly to the ground and bawled like an infant. Confucius remarked: "One does not use the word 'old' when one's parents are getting old, because one fears this will make them grieve about their elderliness. A person like Elder Laizi can be called one who does not lose a child's heart."

Zhu Ming was from the Eastern Capital, and he had a brother. After their parents passed away, the two brothers divided up the family property; each obtained a million cash. The younger brother was arrogant and willful, and soon spent all his money. He then went to his older brother to beg, and his older brother always provided. This happened several times, and Zhu Ming's wife became angry [about this] and cursed and beat her brother-in-law. Zhu Ming heard this and said to his wife: "You are a daughter of a different family, but [my brother] is related to my own flesh and blood. Since there are so many women in the world, I can have another wife, but it is impossible to have another brother." Then he divorced his wife and never saw her again.

Yan Wu was a native of Dongyang. After his father died, he buried the deceased and carried soil on his back to build the tumulus without others' help. The work was hard, and his plan was difficult to accomplish. His spirit, however, moved Heaven. A crowd of crows flew over, carrying bits of earth in their bills to help him. Their bills were hurt [from the work], and their blood colored the soil. Therefore, that county was named Wuyang ["Crow Hill"]. Later, Wang Mang changed the name of the county to Wuzhe ["the Crow"].

Zhao Xun had a filial nature even in childhood. When he was five or six years old, whenever he had some delicacy, he would never eat it himself, but would first offer it to his father. When his father went out, he would wait for him to return and only then have his meal. If his father did not return on time, he would stand at the door and cry until his father came home. Several years later his father died. Xun longed for his father and became wan and sallow and worn to a mere shadow. He cried and lived beside his father's tomb mound. The people of his clan all praised him; his name became well known, and his reputation spread far. His official rank reached the palace attendant level during Emperor An's reign (107–26 CE).

The origin of Yuan Gu is unknown. When his grandfather was old, his parents detested the old man and wanted to abandon him. Gu, who was fifteen years old, entreated them piteously with tears, but his parents did not listen to him. They made a carriage and carried the grandfather away and abandoned him. Gu brought the carriage back. His father asked him, What are you going to do with this inauspicious thing?" Gu replied: "I am afraid that when you get old, I will not be able to make a new carriage, and so I have brought it back." His father was moved and ashamed and carried the grandfather back and cared for him. He overcame his selfishness and criticized himself. He finally became a "purely filial [son]" and Gu became a "purely [filial] grandson."

[From Wu Hung, *The Wu Liang Shrine: The Ideology of Early Chinese Pictorial Art* (Palo Alto: Stanford University Press, 1989), pp. 178, 280, 294, 303–05, slightly modified]

MR. YAN'S FAMILY INSTRUCTIONS

Mr. Yan's Family Instructions (Yanshi jiafan) was written by Yan Zhitui (531–591) for his sons. It draws on Confucian teachings but does not exclude Buddhism and takes into consideration such issues as personality differences and political realities. Yan himself lived through highly unstable times and appreciated family solidarity. His book was widely appreciated not only for the advice it offered but also for its wit and insight.

Document 6–14

YANSHI JIAFAN

INSTRUCTING CHILDREN

Those of the highest intelligence will develop without being taught; those of great stupidity, even if taught, will amount to nothing; those of medium ability will be ignorant unless taught. The ancient sage kings had rules for prenatal training. Women when pregnant for three months moved from their living quarters to a detached palace where they would not see unwholesome sights nor hear reckless words, and where the tone of music and the flavor of food were controlled by the rules of decorum [rites]. These rules were written on jade tablets and kept in a golden box. After the child was born, imperial tutors firmly made clear filial piety, humaneness, the rites, and rightness to guide and train him.

The common people are indulgent and are unable to do this. But as soon as a baby can recognize facial expressions and understand approval and disapproval, training should be begun so that he will do what he is told to do and stop when so ordered. After a few years of this, punishment with the bamboo can be minimized, as parental strictness and dignity mingled with parental love will lead the boys and girls to a feeling of respect and caution and give rise to filial piety. I have noticed about me that where there is merely love without training this result is never achieved. Children eat, drink, speak, and act as they please. Instead of needed prohibitions they receive praise; instead of urgent reprimands they receive smiles. Even when children are old enough to learn, such treatment is still regarded as the proper method. Only after the child has formed proud and arrogant habits do they try to control him. But one may whip the child to death and he will still not be respectful, while the growing anger of the parents only increases his resentment. After he grows up, such a child becomes at last nothing but a scoundrel. Confucius was right in saying, "What is acquired in infancy is like original nature; what has been formed into habits is equal to instinct." A common proverb says, "Train a wife from her first arrival; teach a son in his infancy." How true such sayings are!

Generally parents' inability to instruct their own children comes not from any inclination just to let them fall into evil ways but only from parents' being unable to endure the children's looks [of unhappiness] from repeated scoldings, or to bear beating them, lest it do damage to the children's physical being. We should, however, take illness by way of illustration: how can we not use drugs, medicines, acupuncture, or cautery to cure it? Should we then view strictness of reproof and punishment as a form of cruelty to one's own kith and kin? Truly there is no other way to deal with it. . . .

As for maintaining proper respect between father and son, one cannot allow too much familiarity; in the love among kin, one cannot tolerate impoliteness.

If there is impoliteness, then parental solicitude is not matched by filial respect; if there is too much familiarity, it gives rise to indifference and rudeness.

Someone has asked why Chen Kang [a disciple of Confucius] was pleased to hear that gentlemen kept their distance from their sons, and the answer is that this was indeed the case; gentlemen did not personally teach their children [because, as Yan goes on to show, there are passages in the Classics of a sexual kind, which it would not be proper for a father to teach his sons] . . .

In the love of parents for children, it is rare that one succeeds in treating them equally. From antiquity to the present there are many cases of this failing. It is only natural to love those who are wise and talented, but those who are wayward and dull also deserve sympathy. Partiality in treatment, even when done out of generous motives, turns out badly. . . .

BROTHERS

After the appearance of humankind, there followed the conjugal relationship; the conjugal relationship was followed by the parental; the parental was followed by the fraternal. Within the family, these three are the intimate relationships. The other degrees of kinship all develop out of these three. Therefore among human relationships one cannot but take these [three] most seriously. . . .

When brothers are at odds with each other, then sons and nephews will not love each other, and this in turn will lead to the cousins drifting apart, resulting finally in their servants treating one another as enemies. When this happens then strangers can step on their faces and trample upon their breasts and there will be no one to come to their aid. There are men who are able to make friends with distinguished men of the empire, winning their affection, and yet are unable to show proper respect toward their own elder brothers. How strange that they should succeed with the many and fail with the few! There are others who are able to command troops in the thousands and inspire such loyalty in them that they will die willingly for them and yet are unable to show kindness toward their own younger brothers. How strange that they should succeed with strangers and fail with their own flesh and blood! . . .

FAMILY GOVERNANCE

Beneficial influences are transmitted from superiors to inferiors and bequeathed by earlier to later generations. So if a father is not loving, the son will not be filial; if an elder brother is not friendly, the younger will not be respectful; if a husband is not just, the wife will not be obedient. When a father is kind but the son refractory, when an elder brother is friendly but the younger arrogant, when a husband is just but a wife overbearing, then indeed they are the bad people of the world; they must be controlled by punishments; teaching and guidance will not change them. If rod and wrath are not used in family discipline, the faults of the son will immediately appear. If punishments are not properly awarded, the people will not know how to act. The use of clemency and severity in governing a family is the same as in a state. . . .

A wife in presiding over household supplies should use wine, food, and clothing only as the rites specify. Just as in the state, where women are not allowed to participate in setting policies, so in the family, they should not be permitted to assume responsibility for affairs. If they are wise, talented, and versed in the ancient and modern writings, they ought to help their husbands by supplementing the latter's deficiency. No hen should herald the dawn lest misfortune follow. . . .

The burden of daughters on the family is heavy indeed. Yet how else can Heaven give life to the teeming people and ancestors pass on their bodily existence to posterity? Many people today dislike having daughters and mistreat their own flesh and blood. How can they be like this and still hope for Heaven's blessing? . . .

It is common for women to dote on a son-in-law and to maltreat a daughter-in-law. Doting on a son-in-law gives rise to hatred from brothers; maltreating a daughter-in-law brings on slander from sisters. Thus when these women, whether they act or remain silent, draw criticism from the members of the family, it is the mother who is the real cause of it. . . .

A simple marriage arrangement irrespective of social position was the established rule of our ancestor Qing Hou. Nowadays there are those who sell their daughters for money or buy a woman with a payment of silk. They compare the rank of fathers and grandfathers, and calculate in ounces and drams, demanding more and offering less, just as if bargaining in the market. Under such conditions a boorish son-in-law might appear in the family or an arrogant woman assume power in the household. Coveting honor and seeking for gain, on the contrary, incur shame and disgrace; how can one not be careful?

[From *Sources of Chinese Tradition*, ed. W. Theodore De Bary and Irene Bloom, rev. ed. (New York: Columbia University Press, 1999), pp. 542–546]

THE *CLASSIC OF FILIAL PIETY FOR WOMEN*

The original *Classic of Filial Piety* was written in gender neutral language, as though addressed to both males and females, but many of the situations it discusses clearly were more relevant to men's lives. During the Tang dynasty an official's wife, Miss Zheng, tried to remedy this by writing a separate *Classic of Filial Piety for Women (Nü xiao jing)*. She describes the greatest offense as jealousy, adds a section on prenatal education and instead of the section "serving the ruler," has a section on "maternal properties." In the place of the dialogue between Confucius and his disciple Zengzi, Ban Zhao is made to play the role of authority figure and responds to her students' questions.

In Song times (960–1279) several sets of paintings were made to illustrate this didactic text.

Document 6–15

NÜ XIAO JING

OPENING THE DISCUSSION AND EXPLAINING THE PRINCIPLES

Lady Ban was at home at leisure and the girls were sitting in attendance. Lady Ban said, "In antiquity, the two daughters of the Sage Emperor [Yao] had the filial way and went to the bend of the Gui River [to marry Shun]. They were humble, yielding, respectful, and frugal; they concentrated their thoughts on the way to be a wife. Wise and well-informed, they avoided problems with others. Have you heard about this?"

The girls rose from their seats and apologized, "We girls are ignorant and have not yet received all of your teachings. Could you tell us about it?"

Lady Ban said, "Study involves gathering information, questioning and evaluating it, and discarding the doubtful. In this way one can become a model for others. If you are willing to listen to my words and put them into practice, I will explain the principles to you.

"Filial piety expands heaven and earth, deepens human relationships, stimulates the ghosts and spirits, and moves the birds and beasts. It involves being respectful and conforming to ritual, acting only after repeated thought, making no effort to broadcast one's accomplishments or good deeds, being agreeable, gentle, pure, obedient, kind, intelligent, filial, and compassionate. When such virtuous conduct is perfected, no one will reproach you."

This is what is meant by the passage in the *Book of Documents*, "Filial piety is simply being filial and friendly to one's brothers."[13]

NOBLE LADIES

"Although occupying honored positions, they are able to show restraint and thus they can hold their positions without relying on partiality. They observe the diligent toil [of others] and understand their viewpoints. They can recite the *Poetry* and *Documents*; they can perform the *Rituals* and *Music*. As a consequence, they consider it a misfortune to be well-known but unworthy and a calamity to be great in status but little in virtue, and in fact take a warning from such cases. By first ensuring that their persons, at rest or in movement, conform to propriety, they are able to get along well with their children and grandchildren and preserve the ancestral temple. This is the filial piety of the noble ladies."

The *Classic of Changes* says; "When one removes the false and preserves one's integrity, the virtue will spread and transform others."[14]

THE WIVES OF OFFICIALS

"They do not dare wear garments not prescribed by the ritual codes; they do not dare use words not modeled on the *Poetry* and *Documents*; they do not dare to behave in any way outside the virtuous ways based on honesty and moral principle. There is nothing better than not saying what one wishes others would not hear, not doing what one wishes other would not know, and not performing what one wishes others would not pass on. Those who fulfill these three conditions are able to preserve their ancestral altars. This is the filial piety of the wives of officials."

The *Book of Poetry* says: "She picks the artemisia by the pond and on the islands for use in service to the lords."[15]

THE COMMON PEOPLE

"They follow the way of the wife and utilize moral principle to the best advantage. They put others first and themselves last in order to serve their parents-in-law. They spin and weave and sew clothes; they prepare the sacrificial foods. This is the filial piety of the wife of a common person."

The *Book of Poetry* says: "Women do not have public affairs [for if they did] they would stop their weaving."[16]

SERVING PARENTS-IN-LAW

"With regard to a woman's service to her parents-in-law, she is as reverent as to her own father, as loving as to her own mother. Maintaining this attitude is a matter of duty, and adhering to it is a matter of ritual. When the cock first crows, she washes her hands, rinses her mouth, and gets dressed to make her morning call. In the winter she checks that [her parents-in-law] are warm enough, in the summer cool enough. In the evening she checks that they are settled, in the morning that they are getting up. She is reverent in correcting inside matters, principled in her dealings with the outside. She establishes herself as a person of principle and decorum and then acts on them."

The *Book of Poetry* says: "When a girl departs, she distances herself from her parents and brothers."[17]

THE THREE POWERS

The girls said, "How exceedingly great is the husband."

Lady Ban responded, "The husband is heaven. Can one not be devoted to him? In antiquity, when a girl went to be married she was said to be going home. She transfers her heaven to serve her husband. The principle in this is vast. It is the pattern of heaven, the standard of the earth, the norm of conduct for the people. When women follow the nature of heaven and earth, model themselves on the brilliance of heaven, make use of the resources of the earth, and guard against idleness and adhere to ritual, then they can bring success to their families. On this basis, a wife acts first to extend her love broadly, then her husband will not forget to be filial to his parents. She sets an example of rectitude and virtue, and her husband enthusiastically copies it. She takes the initiative in being reverent and yielding, and her husband will not be competitive. If she follows the path of ritual and music, her husband will join in harmoniously. If she indicates the difference between good and evil, her husband will know restraint."

The *Book of Poetry* says: "Intelligent and wise in order to protect her person."[18]

BRINGING ORDER THROUGH FILIAL PIETY

Lady Ban said, "In ancient times, virtuous women brought order to their nine relations through filial piety. They did not dare neglect the lowest ranking concubine, not to mention their sisters-in-law. Therefore they gained the support of their six relatives, making them better able to serve their parents-in-law. Those placed in charge of family business did not dare insult the chickens and dogs—not to mention the lower-ranking family members. Therefore they gained the support of their superiors and inferiors, making them better able to serve their husbands. Those in charge of the women's quarters did not dare mistreat the servants—not to mention the master. Therefore they gained the support of the people, making them better able to serve their parents. Accordingly, while living, parents were well taken care of; after their death, their ghosts received sacrifices. In this way the nine relations were kept in peace and harmony. Pettiness did not occur nor disorder arise. Such was the way virtuous women brought order to superiors and inferiors through filial piety."

The *Book of Poetry* says: "Not erring, not forgetting, conforming in all matters to the old rules."[19]

WISDOM

The girls said, "May we ask of there isn't anything in the virtue of a wife that surpasses wisdom?"

Lady Ban replied, "Humankind is patterned on heaven and earth; yin and yang are interdependent. Making use of one's intelligence is always beneficial, especially when done in a purposeful manner.

"In former times, King Zhuang of Chu was holding court in the evening. Lady Fan entered and said, 'Why don't you end this court session? It is so late. Aren't you tired?' The king said, 'Today I have been talking with a wise person and have been so happy I have not noticed the time.' When Lady Fan asked the identity of the wise person, the king said Yu Qiuzi. Lady Fan covered her mouth and laughed. The king, perplexed, asked her what made her laugh. She answered, 'Yu Qiuzi may be wise but he is not loyal. For eleven years I have had the favor of occupying a place in your rear chambers, where I still attend to you with wash basin, towel, and comb and clean up. During this time I have introduced nine other women. Today two of them are wiser than me and the other seven are my peers. Even thought I know how to safeguard your love for me and snatch your favor, I would not dare keep you in the dark [about other women] for selfish reasons. Rather I wish that you be broadly informed. Now, Yu Qiuzi has been prime minister for ten years but the only people he has recommended are his descendants or his collateral relatives. I have never heard of him recommending someone wise or demoting someone unworthy. Can he be called wise?'

"When the king repeated this to him, Yu Qiuzi, in his confusion, he abandoned his home and slept outside. The king sent someone to invite Sun Shuao, and on his arrival made him prime minister. Thus because of the wisdom of a single person's advice, the feudal lords did not dare attack, and in the end King Zhuang became the paramount leader of the states. All this was due to the efforts of Lady Fan."[20]

The *Book of Poetry* says: "Those who obtain the right men prosper; those who lose them are defeated." and "When language is harmonious, the people will be united."[21]

VIRTUOUS CONDUCT

Lady Ban said, "Let me comment on the way a woman serves her husband. From the time her hair is arranged and she meets him [during the wedding ceremony], she maintains the formality appropriate between an official and the ruler. When helping him wash or serving him food, she maintains the reverence appropriate between father and child. When reporting her comings and goings, she preserves the manner appropriate between siblings. She always keeps agreements, thus maintaining the trust appropriate among friends. Her words and actions are unblemished, giving her the capacity to manage the family.

"Only a woman who has fulfilled these five requirements is truly able to serve her husband. Such a woman will not be proud in a high position. She will not be insubordinate in an inferior position. And among equals she will not be quarrelsome. If she were proud in a high station, she might be ruined. If she were insubordinate in an inferior position, she might incur punishment. If she were quarrelsome among her equals, she might end up fighting. Thus, unless these three evils are eliminated, a woman cannot be called wifely—even if she harmonizes with her husband as well as the lute and the zither."

THE FIVE PUNISHMENTS

Lady Ban said, "There are three thousand offenses subject to the five punishments, but of these the most heinous is jealousy. It is the first among the seven grounds for divorce. The teachings of the sages are encompassed in purity, obedience, rectitude, straightforwardness, gentleness, absence of jealousy, being orderly in the inner quarters, having no contact with the outside, and an ability not to be so stimulated by sights and sounds that desires are pursued recklessly. You girls should put this into practice."

The *Book of Poetry* says: "Fine his deportment and appearance. He models himself on the ancient rules and applies himself to attaining dignity."[22]

ELABORATING "PRESERVING TRUST"

"The way of establishing heaven is called yin and yang; the way of establishing earth is called gentle and tough. Yin and yang, gentle and tough, these are the beginnings of heaven and earth. Men and women, husbands and wives, these are the beginnings of human relationships. *Qian* and *kun* are interconnected and pervasive, with no space between them. The wife is earth, the husband is heaven; neither can be dispensed with. But the husband has a hundred actions, the wife has a single purpose. For men there is the principle of successive marriages, but there is no text authorizing women to take a second dip.

"Formerly, King Zhao of Chu took a trip and left [his wife] Miss Jiang at Qian pavilion. The river flooded and the king sent someone to get the lady, but because he should have had a tally, she would not go with him. Miss Jiang said, 'I have heard that a chaste woman, as a matter of principle, does not break an agreement, just as a brave soldier does not fear dying. Now I know that I will surely die if I do not leave. But without a tally I do not dare break the agreement. Although if I leave I will surely live, to live without faith is not as good as dying to preserve principle.' It happened that when the messenger returned to get the tally, the water rose above the pavilion and she drowned. Such was the way she preserved faith. You should strive to emulate it."

The *Book of Changes* says: "The crying magpie resides in yin; its child joins it in harmony."[23]

PRENATAL EDUCATION

Lady Ban said, "With regard to the way people receive the five constant virtues, at birth they have an intrinsic nature, but much is also learned. If they are exposed to good, then they will be good; if exposed to evil, they will be evil. Even while they are in the womb, how can they not be given education! In ancient times, when women were with child, they did not lie on their side while sleeping, nor sit to one side, nor stand on one foot? Nor eat anything with a strange taste, nor walk on the left side of the road, nor eat anything not cut straight, nor sit on a mat that was not laid straight, nor look at or listen to any evil sights or sounds, nor utter any wild words, nor touch any deviant objects. At night they would recite the classical texts; in the morning they would discuss ritual and music. When they gave birth to children, their form was correct and their talent and virtue surpassed that of others. Such was their prenatal education."

REMOVING EVILS

The girls said, "We have reverently heard your instructions on the way of the wife. Even though we children are not clever, we wish to devote our lives to putting your teachings into practice."

"May we ask, were there also any bad women in antiquity?"

Lady Ban responded, "The rise of the Xia dynasty was because of [the wife of the founder] Tushan. Its fall was due to [the concubine of the last king] Moxi. The rise of the Yin dynasty was because of [the wife of the founder] Youxin; its fall was due to [the concubine of its last king] Danji. The rise of the [Western] Zhou dynasty was because of [the mother of the founder] Tairen; its demise was due to [the concubine of the last king] Baosi. It was because of women that the kings of these three dynasties lost the realm, their lives, and their states. This is even more true at the level of feudal lords, greater officers, and common people. Thus the calamity that befell [the crown prince of Jin] Shensheng resulted from [the slander of his father's concubine] Linu. The demise of [the last heir of the Liang dynasty] Minhuai began with [the Jin empress] Nanfeng.

"When viewed in this way, there are women who deserve credit for founding their families and others who destroyed their families. Then there is the case of the Miss Xia, the wife of Chen Yushu who brought about the deaths of three husbands, a son, and a ruler, chased away two ministers, and brought on the destruction of a state — this must be the most extreme case of evil. It is appalling to think a single woman could destroy the patrimony of six families.

"If, however, you practice the way of goodness, you will never reach such an extremity."

[Translated by Patricia Ebrey from *Under Confucian Eyes: Writings on Gender in Chinese History*, ed. Susan Mann and Yu-yin Cheng (Berkeley: University of California Press, 2001), pp. 49–60, with many omissions]

YUAN CAI ON CONCUBINES

Yuan Cai (ca. 1140-ca. 1195) wrote a book of advice, called *Mr. Yuan's Models for the World (Yuanshi shifan)* in the tradition of Yan Zhitui's *Family Instructions*. It too considers what can go wrong in a family and how family heads can try to avoid problems. The items given here concern a matter that Yan said little about: the issues that arise because the family head or other men in the family have one or more concubines in addition to a wife. Concubines were recognized as legal mates in Chinese law and their sons were considered full heirs, with rights to a share of the family property. Both maids and concubines were normally purchased and the distinction between maid and concubine was often blurry, as a maid could be promoted to concubine if the master began a sexual relationship with her.

Document 6–16

YUANSHI SHIFAN

PRECAUTIONS FOR MAIDS AND CONCUBINES

Maids come into close contact with their masters, and some make use of this to form an illicit relationship. When the servant class bear children, they attribute them to the master. As a result people often raise stupid and vulgar off-spring who end up ruining the family.

The general rule with maids and concubines is to be careful of what is begun and to take precautions concerning how things may end.

RESTRICTING THE MOVEMENTS OF MAIDS

When men do not prohibit their maids and concubines from freely coming and going, sometimes a woman may have relations with an outsider and get pregnant. If the master simply drives the woman away without clearly establishing her guilt, often after he has died she claims that the child was his and tries to get the boy accepted into the family. This easily gives rise to lawsuits.

Take warning from this so as not to burden your descendants with trouble.

SETTING UP MAIDS AND CONCUBINES

Some men with jealous wives set up maids or concubines in separate houses. Some even support prostitutes as their concubines, ordering them to stop seeing anyone else. Such men set up very tight precautions and arrange for very thorough supervision. Yet the man entrusted with the task of supervising may be bribed to turn around and serve as the lookout for some outsider who wants to come and go without the master's knowledge. This can reach the point where the master rears the outsider's son as his own heir.

Another problem occurs when the woman gives birth while the master is away. She then can discard the girl she bore and substitute someone else's boy. The master then rears him without knowing he is not his own son. How naive and stupid these men are!

TAKING CONCUBINES LATE IN LIFE

Most women are jealous, so men with wives seldom keep concubines, and those who do keep them usually are without wives.

If you keep maids and concubines, precautions and restrictions are needed both with regard to your sons and younger brothers within the family and with regard to servants outside it. Even when you have a wife to act as mistress there is sometimes trouble, so naturally there is more when no one is in charge.

If only one person is keeping an eye out, deception will be easy. Therefore, doing this late in life is especially unsuitable. What would you do if an unexpected disaster happened?

GUARDING CONCUBINES

Families that keep concubines sometimes are so foolish as to house them in side rooms no one else ever passes or rooms with side doors to the outside. Sometimes the toilet is next to the kitchen and a man manages the kitchen.

Sometimes at night there is drinking in an inner room and male servants help in the service.

Some of the deceptions are beyond anyone's ability to prevent because concubines plan carefully to keep the master from getting suspicious. Since they will take turns keeping a lookout for each other, the master has no means of learning what is going on.

ATTRACTIVE CONCUBINES

For the amusement of their guests, some men teach their maids and concubines to sing and dance or to serve food and wine. In such cases do not select women of striking beauty or superior intelligence, for there is the danger that such a woman will arouse feelings of lust in some evil guest. On seeing such beauty he will want to get a hold of it and will chase after it with such singlemindedness that he ignores all obstacles. If the guest has authority over you, anything can happen. The affair of Lüzhu is an example from antiquity,[24] but there are also plenty in recent times that I'd prefer not to mention by name.

> [From *Family and Property in Sung China: Yuan Ts'ai's Precepts for Social Life*, trans. Patricia Buckley Ebrey (Princeton: Princeton University Press, 1984), pp. 286–288, slightly modified]

ZHU XI ON FAMILY AND MARRIAGE

During the Song period (960–1279) Confucian teachings were reinvigorated by a series of major teachers and thinkers, among whom Zhu Xi (1130–1200) stands out for his prodigious output and his influence on the development of Confucian thought in subsequent centuries. Zhu Xi was the first great synthesizer of what has been called the Learning of the Way or Neo-Confucianism. He wrote, compiled, or edited almost a hundred books, corresponded with dozens of other scholars, and met regularly with groups of adult students.

Marriage and the family were never Zhu Xi's main concerns, but he wrote a guide to the practice of family rituals (weddings, funerals, and ancestral rites above all) that became the standard work for the next several centuries. He viewed issues related to family and marriage as issues particularly relevant to ordinary people, and during his brief terms as a local official he tried to reform the practices of the people in his district. In his conversations with disciples he discussed the sorts of issues that were more relevant among the educated class, such as what to do when a parent wanted to follow a disapproved practice.

The excerpts below come from three books. The first is from a chapter devoted to regulating the family in *Reflections on Things at Hand (Jinsi lu)*, a book that he compiled jointly with Lü Zuqian (1137–81). This chapter, like the rest of Reflections, is made up of selections from earlier Song period Confucian scholars, especially the Cheng brothers, Cheng Hao (1032–85) and Cheng Yi (1033–1107). It includes Cheng Yi's famous statement that it would be better for a widow to die than marry again. After it is a proclamation issued by Zhu Xi in

1190, when he was prefect of Zhangzhou. It would have been posted for people to read or have read to them. The third section is drawn from his *Classified Conversations (Zhuzi yulei)*.

Document 6–17

JINSI LU

2. Mencius said, "It will be all right to serve one's parents as Zengzi served his."[25] Mencius never considered Zengzi's filial piety to be excessive. For whatever a son can personally do should be done.

3. "In dealing with the troubles caused by one's mother, one should not be too firm."[26] In dealing with his mother, the son should help her with mildness and gentleness so she will be in accord with righteousness. If he disobeys her and the matter fails, it will be his fault.

Is there not a way to obey with ease? If one goes forward with his strength and abruptly resists or defies her, the kindness and love between mother and son will be hurt. That will be great harm indeed. How can he get into her heart and change her? The way lies in going backward, bending his will to obey-, and following his mother so that her personal life will be correct and matters well managed. The way strong ministers serve weak rulers is similar to this. . . .

6. In family relationships, parents and children usually overcome correct principles with affection and supplant righteousness with kindness. Only strong and resolute people can avoid sacrificing correct principles for the sake of personal affection. Therefore in the hexagram *jiaren* [family], essentially speaking, strength is considered good. . . .

8. The text of the second lowest, undivided line of the *guimei* [marriage of a maiden] hexagram says that correctness and tranquility should be maintained. This principle is not out of accord with the normal and correct relationship between husband and wife. People today consider indecent liberties and improper intimacies as normal and therefore consider correctness and tranquility as abnormal, without realizing that these are the normal and lasting ways of the relationship between husband and wife.

9. Most people today are careful in choosing sons-in-law but careless in selecting daughters-in-law. Actually the character of sons-in-law is easy to see but that of daughters-in-law is difficult to know. The choice of a daughter-in-law is very important. Why should it be neglected?

10. When one's parents have passed away, he should be doubly sorrowful on their birthdays. How can he have the heart to give a banquet and amuse himself with musical entertainment? If both parents are still living, that will be all right. . . .

12. QUESTION: Diwu Lun had a different attitude toward his son's sickness from that toward his nephew's sickness, and he confessed that it was selfishness.[27] Why?

ANSWER: It does not matter whether he slept peacefully or not. The fact that he did not get up in one case but got up ten times in the other shows selfishness. Love between father and son is essentially a matter of impartiality. To attach any personal idea to it is selfish.

FURTHER QUESTION: Should there be any difference between one's treatment of his own son and his treatment of his brother's son?

ANSWER: When the Sage instituted social regulations, he said, "The sons of brothers are the same." That means one should treat his brother's son as his own.

FURTHER QUESTION: By nature one attaches more importance to his own son and less importance to his brother's son. It seems there should be some difference. Is that right?

ANSWER: It seems so because people today look at the matter from the selfish point of view. Confucius said, "The relation between father and son is rooted in nature."[28] This was said only in relation to filial piety and therefore he said that the relation between father and son is rooted in nature. But are the relations between ruler and minister, elder and younger brothers, guest and host, and friends not rooted in nature also? Simply because people today take these relations too lightly they have not traced their source and therefore they think there should be a difference. How much difference is there between one's own son and his brother's son? They are both the offspring of one's parents. Brothers are called hand and foot simply because they have separate bodies. Because of this fact, most people love their own sons differently from their brother's sons. This is a great mistake.

FURTHER QUESTION: Confucius regarded Gongye Chang as inferior to Nan Rong and therefore gave his brother's daughter to Nan Rong in marriage and his own daughter to Gongye Chang.[29] Why?

ANSWER: This is to judge the Sage by one's own selfish mind. Anyone who avoids suspicion is internally deficient. The Sage was perfectly impartial. Why should he have to avoid suspicion? In giving one's daughter in marriage, one seeks a match according to her qualifications. If, as we may suppose, one's brother's daughter is not very beautiful, one must select a young man of corresponding quality to match her, and if one's own daughter is beautiful, he must select a young man of good talents to match her. Why should one avoid any suspicion? In the case of Confucius, it may have been that the ages of the daughters and the pupils did not match or that the marriages took place at different times. We do not know any of these facts. To think that Confucius did what he did in order to avoid suspicion is greatly mistaken. Even a worthy does not do things in order to avoid suspicion. How much less does a sage!

13. QUESTION: According to principle, it seems that one should not marry a widow. What do you think?

ANSWER: Correct. Marriage is a match. If one takes someone who has lost her integrity to be his own match, it means he himself has lost his integrity.

FURTHER QUESTION: In some cases the widows are all alone, poor, and with no one to depend on. May they remarry?

ANSWER: This theory has come about only because people of later generations are afraid of starving to death. But to starve to death is a very small matter. To lose one's integrity, however, is a very serious matter."

14. [CHENG HAO] To leave parents or children who are sick in bed to a quack doctor is tantamount to having no parental affection or filial piety. In serving parents, one should know something about medicine.

15. [CHENG YI] At his father's funeral, Master Cheng asked Zhou Gongshu to take charge of receiving the guests. A guest wanted wine. When Gongshu told the Teacher, the Teacher said, "Do not lead people to do wrong."

16. In most cases employing a wet-nurse is unavoidable. If the mother is unable to feed her child, someone must be employed. However, it is wrong to kill another mother's child as a result of feeding one's own child.[30] If a wet-nurse is absolutely necessary, employ two so that the milk for two babies can be used to feed three. In that case, any eventuality can be taken care of. If one of the wet-nurses becomes sick or even dies, there will be no harm to one's own child and one will not be killing another person's child as a result of feeding one's own. The only thing is that it is expensive to employ two. [But if only one is employed and she dies] and something should happen to her child, what greater harm can there be?

[From *Reflections on Things at Hand*, trans. Wing-tsit Chan (New York: Columbia University Press, 1967), pp. 171–182, modified and with deletions]

Document 6–18

PROCLAMATION POSTED AT ZHANGZHOU

Following are items of instructions to be observed:

1. Instructions to members of community units *(baowu)* on matters about which they should encourage and remind each other:

All members should encourage and remind each other to be filial to parents, respectful to elders, cordial to clansmen and relatives, and helpful to neighbors. Each should perform his assigned duty and engage in his primary occupation. None should commit vicious acts or thefts, or indulge in drinking or gambling. They should not fight with or sue each other.

If there are filial sons or grandsons, or righteous husbands and virtuous wives, and their deeds are noteworthy, they should be reported. The government, in accordance with provisions of the statutes, will reward them and honor them with banners. Those who do not follow instructions should be reported, examined, and punished in accordance with the law.

2. Injunctions to members of community units on matters of which they should mutually watch and investigate each other:

People should always be alert to save water, prevent fire, investigate thefts and robberies, and prevent infighting.[31] Do not sell salt that is privately produced,[32] or kill plow oxen. They should not gamble with their properties. Nor should they spread or practice demon religion *(mojiao)*.[33] People in the same community unit should watch each other. Anyone who is aware of a crime but fails to report it will share in the punishment.

3. Instructions to gentlemen *(shi)* and commoners *(min)*:

People should understand that our body originates from our parents and that brothers come from the same source. Thus, we are endowed by nature with a feeling of obligation to parents and brothers, most profound and grave. What makes us love our parents or respect our elder brothers is not forced but comes spontaneously from the original mind-and-heart. And this love is inexhaustible.

Now some people are unfilial to parents and disrespectful to brothers. They often violate their parents' instructions and commands and even fail to provide for them; they easily become angry and fight with their brothers and even refuse to help them out. They defy Heaven and violate all principles. I deeply lament and feel sorry for them. They should urgently reform their conduct, otherwise they will invite immediate disaster.

4. Instructions to gentlemen and commoners:

It should be understood that the marital relationship between husband and wife is chief among the human moral relationships.[34] The rites and laws regarding betrothal and engagements are very strict. However, the customs of this region include what is called "looking after someone," that is, living openly with a woman who is neither a wife nor a concubine. Another is called "elopement," when two people who are not betrothed seduce each other and flee in secrecy. No violating of the rites and breaking of the law is more serious. The offenders should urgently reform so as to avoid punishment.

5. Instructions to gentlemen and commoners:

People should be kind and cordial toward villagers, neighbors, clansmen, and relatives. If sometimes a minor quarrel occurs, both parties should reflect deeply and make every effort to negotiate and reach a reconciliation. They should not lightly bring suit. Even if one is right, one's property will become diminished and one's work and livelihood may be cut off. How much worse is it if one is not right? In that case one cannot avoid imprisonment and punishment. It will end in calamity. All should earnestly take this as a serious warning.

6. Instructions to official households *(guanhu)*:

Since these are known as "households of public servants," and they thus differ from the common people, they should be especially content with their status and obey the law. They should devote themselves to "controlling oneself" and benefiting others. Moreover, villagers and neighbors are, in fact, all relatives and friends. How can one rely on his strength to bully the weak, or his wealth to appropriate the property of the poor? Prosperity and decline come in cycles. This calls for deep reflection.

7. Instructions when there has been a death in the family:

There should be timely burial of the dead. It is not permissible to keep the coffin at home or in a temple. If coffins or ashes have been temporarily stored in a temple, they should be buried within one month. Never should one employ Buddhist monks to make offerings to the Buddha, nor engage in extravagant display at funerals. The ceremony should be on a scale in keeping with one's resources. What matters is only that the dead should be returned to the soil soon. Anyone violating this should be flogged a hundred strokes with a heavy rod in accordance with the law. In addition, officials [violating this] should not be eligible for appointment, nor should scholars be allowed to take the civil examinations. Villagers, relatives, and friends who come to console may assist by making contributions. They should not oblige the family to provide food and drink for them.

8. Instructions to men and women:

They should not establish hermitages on their own under the pretext of engaging in religious practice. If there are such people, they should be expected to marry before long.

9. Restrictions on temples and people:

They are prohibited from holding mixed gatherings of men and women during the day or evening under the pretext of worshiping the Buddha or transmitting the sutras.

10. Restrictions on town and village:

They are prohibited from collecting money or donations, or making and parading figurines under the pretext of averting disasters or gaining good fortune.

With respect to the instructions above, I only wish that everyone understand what is right and be a good person. Everyone should realize that if he does not offend the authorities, there is no reason why he should be subject to punishment. All should earnestly follow these instructions so that peace and harmony will be with them. If anyone does not follow them and dares to be defiant, the law of the state is clear and officials must be impartial [in enforcing the law].

Everyone should deeply reflect on this so he will have no cause for regret later.

[Translated by Ron Guey Chu from *Sources of Chinese Tradition*, pp. 749–751]

Document 6–19

ZHUZI YULEI

1. A student asked, "Girls also should be taught. What if, besides teaching them the *Classic of Filial Piety*, they are taught the readily understandable passages in books like the *Analects*?"

Zhu Xi said, "That would be fine. Ban Zhao's *Exhortations for Women* and Sima Guang's *Family Models* are both good."

2. A student asked, "On which day should the bride be introduced in the ancestral shrine?"

Zhu Xi said, "The ancients waited three days before introducing her."

"Why is it necessary to wait three months?"

Zhu Xi said, "Until then one does not know what the wife's character or behavior are like. After three months, her performance of the role of wife will be clear. Only then does she become a wife. However, today one cannot wait till the third month. One can only make the gesture [of waiting till the third day]."

3. The student asked, "After the ancients presented the gift of silk, they presented the results of the divination. What did they do if the divination showed that [the marriage] was inauspicious?"

Zhu Xi said, "Then they stopped it."

"The ancients presented a betrothal gift of five bolts of cloth. This seems too slight. Wouldn't it be hard to adopt?"

Zhu Xi answered, "To describe it as elaborate or simple is to discuss it in terms of financial advantage [and therefore inappropriate]. However, if there is no hope for people of our sort to restore the ancient system, are we going to be able to change anyone else's customs through education?"

4. Yaoqing asked about the position of the husband and wife when they are buried together. Zhu Xi responded, "When I buried my late wife, I saved the eastern space, but I had not checked what the ritual texts specify."

Anqing said, "On earth, the right side is the more honored one, so I suppose the man should be on the right."

Zhu Xi said, "In sacrifices, the west is the superior position, so it ought to be the same in burials."

5. A student asked, "What if one's mother dies and one's father is still alive and the father wants to follow customary practices with regard to mourning garments, employ Buddhist monks for services, and have the body cremated?"

Zhu Xi responded, "What do you think?"

The student responded, "One could not obey."

Zhu Xi said, "The first two are superficial matters. If it is as you say, obeying would be all right. But cremation cannot be practiced."

Yong said, "Cremation destroys the parents' remains."

Zhu Xi added, "Discussing it along with mourning garments and Buddhist services shows an inability to recognize degrees of importance."

6. With bows to one's parents, they both accept the bow seated. The same is true for bows to one's paternal uncles and their wives. As for a sister-in-law and her husband's younger brother who live in the same household, they must bow, but they should respond with a bow. Husbands and wives also respond with a bow to the other's bow.

In Jianyang there was a wife whose husband had no means of supporting her, so her parents wanted to take her home [thus ending the marriage]. When the matter was reported to the officials, the recorded ruled that they could be separated. Zhidao [Zhu Xi's disciple Zhao Shixia] thought that that was very wrong, saying, "How can the moral obligations of husband and wife be discarded because of poverty? How can the authorities follow the request?"

Zhu Xi responded, "This sort of case should not be viewed from one side only. If the husband is incompetent and unable to support his wife, and the wife has no way to supply herself, what else can be done? In this sort of case one should not stick to high principles. But you must investigate carefully to make sure it is not a case that has been twisted because the wife wants to leave her husband.

[Translated by Patricia Ebrey from *Zhuzi yülei*, 7.127, 89.2273, 89.2281, 89.2286, 91.2332, 106.2644 (Beijing: Zhonghua shuju, 1986)]

SEXUAL OFFENSES IN THE CODE OF THE QING DYNASTY

Each Chinese dynasty issued a legal code, and these codes survive from the Tang period (618–907) on. The main laws tended to be carried over from one code to the next, though over time more substatutes were added. For the last of the dynasties, the Qing dynasty (1644–1911), we have not only the code but discussions of it and cases where it is cited and interpreted.

Chinese law drew from several traditions, including Confucian notions of the hierarchical basis of family relations and the obligations of family members. Legal marriage was defined and regulated by the code, as claims to property and punishment for offenses depended on precise kinship relations between the parties involved.

The section given below deals with rape and other types of illegal sexual activity. The English distinction between adultery and fornication is not relevant to the Chinese code, which does not treat illicit sexual intercourse differently when one or both of the accused were married to someone else. However, because most women married soon after puberty, the general assumption in the statutes translated below is that the woman is married.

It should be noted in reading the sections of the code below that death sentences were often commuted or reduced to a lesser form of the death penalty through the judicial review process.

The parenthetical passages below are from the commentaries to the code, not the code itself.

Document 6–20

COMMENTARIES ON THE CODE OF THE QING DYNASTY

ARTICLE 366: OFFENSES OF ILLICIT SEXUAL INTERCOURSE

1. In the case of illicit sexual intercourse by mutual consent, the punishment is 80 strokes of the heavy bamboo. If the woman has a husband, the punishment

is 90 strokes of the heavy bamboo. For illicit sexual intercourse brought about by intrigue, (whether or not she has a husband), the punishment is 100 strokes of the heavy bamboo.

2. In the case of forcible rape, the punishment is strangulation (with delay). If the act is not consummated, the punishment is 100 strokes of the heavy bamboo and exile to 3000 li. *(For a finding of forcible rape, it is necessary that there be such force that the woman could not break away, also that others have known [of the act] or heard [a cry], or that there be injuries to the skin or the body, or a tearing of the clothes.*

Only then can [the man] be sentenced to strangulation. If there is force and then agreement, and on the basis of the agreement [the sexual act] is consummated, then this is not a case of [rape with] force. If one man uses force and seizes [the woman] and another rapes her, the one who engages in illicit sexual intercourse will be tried [and sentenced to] strangulation. The one who forcibly seized [the woman] will be punished for [rape which] is not consummated; he is punished with exile. Again, if someone sees a woman engaging in illicit sexual intercourse, and the one who sees her uses force to rape her, since she is already a woman who engages in illicit sexual intercourse, this cannot be viewed as rape with force. [Rather,] sentence on the basis of the law of illicit sexual intercourse brought about by intrigue [seduction].)

3. If someone engages in illicit sexual intercourse with a young girl of twelve or below, then, although there is agreement, it is the same as rape.

4. As for consensual illicit sexual intercourse, or illicit sexual intercourse by use of intrigue [seduction], the man and the woman receive the same punishment. If the illicit sexual intercourse causes the birth of a boy or a girl, it will be the responsibility of the man to bring it up. The adulterous wife will be sold or married [to another] as her husband wishes. If he wishes to keep her, he may. If she is married or sold to the adulterous lover, the adulterous lover and the real husband will both receive 80 strokes of the heavy bamboo. The woman will have to leave the new home and return to her own clan. The property will be forfeit to the government.

5. In the case of rape, the woman is not punished.

6. If there is a broker or one who accepts *(individuals into his house)* to engage in illicit sexual intercourse, his punishment will be reduced one degree from that of those who *(by means of agreement or craftiness)* engage in illicit sexual intercourse.

7. *(If a person is guilty of illicit sexual intercourse which has already been discovered, the one who acted for him)* in privately making an agreement in regard to illicit sexual intercourse [e.g. by giving money to the husband] will in each case [have his punishment] reduced two degrees *(from the penalty for illicit sexual intercourse with consent, intrigue [seduction], or force).*

8. If [the guilty pair] have not been seized in a place where the illicit sexual intercourse took place [but were apprehended somewhere else], or someone

pointed them out as guilty [but offered no proof], they will not be punished. If the adulterous wife becomes pregnant *(then although there is proof as to the woman, there is no proof as to the man)*, the punishment is inflicted on the woman alone.

ARTICLE 367: FACILITATING AND TOLERATING THE WIFE'S OR CONCUBINE'S ILLICIT SEXUAL INTERCOURSE

1. In the case of anyone who facilitates and tolerates his wife or concubine engaging in illicit sexual intercourse with another, the husband, the adulterous lover, and the adulterous wife will each receive 90 strokes of the heavy bamboo. If someone forces his wife, concubine, or adopted daughter to engage in illicit sexual intercourse with another, the husband or the adoptive father will each receive 100 strokes of the heavy bamboo. The adulterous man will receive 80 strokes of the heavy bamboo. The wife or the daughter will not be punished. Moreover, her relationship [with the husband or father] is terminated. She is returned to her clan.

2. If someone facilitates and tolerates or forces his own daughters, or the wives or concubines of sons and son's sons, to engage in illicit sexual intercourse, the punishment will be the same.

3. If consideration is used to buy a divorce or to sell a divorce [i.e. someone gives the husband money to cause him to get rid of his wife] (in order) that [the one giving it] may marry another man's wife (by agreement), the husband and the wife and the one who is buying the divorce, will each be punished with 100 strokes of the heavy bamboo. The wife will be divorced and returned to her own clan, and the wedding gifts will be forfeit to the government. If the one buying the divorce and the wife use tricks to put pressure on the husband to divorce her, and if otherwise the husband would not have sold the divorce, he is not punished. The one who buys the divorce and the wife are each given 60 strokes of the heavy bamboo and penal servitude of one year. Redemption will be received for the remainder of the wife's penalty. She will be returned to her husband, who may marry her off or sell her. If it is a concubine, reduce the punishment one degree. If there is a broker, his penalty will be reduced from that of the offender *(the one who purchases the divorce or uses force to induce the sale of the divorce)* one degree. *(If [the husband] does not denounce [the woman] because of her adultery, but marries her off and sells [her] to the adulterer, the husband receives 100 strokes of the heavy bamboo and the adulterous lover and the adulterous wife will each get the full punishment of the law [applicable to each, Art. 366].)*

ARTICLE 368: ILLICIT SEXUAL INTERCOURSE BETWEEN RELATIVES

1. Everyone who has sexual relations with a member of the same clan who is not within the degrees of mourning,[35] or with the wife of a relative beyond the

degrees of mourning, will receive 100 strokes of the heavy bamboo. *(If there is force, the offender will be beheaded with delay.)*

2. If one engages in illicit sexual intercourse with *(a paternal or maternal)* relative of the fifth degree and above, with the wife of a relative of the fifth degree or above, or with the daughter of the wife's former husband, or with his sisters of the same mother [as himself but] a different father, the punishment is 100 strokes of the heavy bamboo and three years of penal servitude. If there is force, *(the male offender)* will be beheaded *(with delay)*. If there is illicit sexual intercourse with the paternal grandmother's father's brother's son's wife, or the paternal grandfather's sister, or the wife of the paternal grandfather's father's father's brother's son's son, or a daughter of the paternal grandfather's father's father's brother's son, or daughters of the father's brothers, or the mother's sisters, or wives of brothers, or the wives of the brother's sons *(the offending man and woman)* will each be sentenced to strangulation *(with [im-mediate] execution)*. It is only in the case of illicit sexual intercourse with a paternal grandfather's sister or the daughter of a paternal grandfather's father's father's brother's son who have left the family by marriage that there is execution with delay. If there is force, *(then the offending man is)* sentenced to beheading *(with [immediate] execution. It is only in the case of rape of the daughter of the paternal grandfather's father's brother's son's son or father's brother's son's daughter or brother's son's daughter who have been married, and thus reduced the degree of the mourning relationship, that there will be beheading with delay. If there is illicit sexual intercourse with the natural mother of the wife, then to award [the penalty] as for a relative of the fifth degree is too light, so sentence as for the sisters of his own mother.)*

3. If someone engages in illicit sexual intercourse with the concubine of his father or paternal grandfather, or with the wife of the elder or younger brother of the father, or with a sister of his father, or with his own sisters, or with the wife of a son or son's son, or with the daughter of a brother, the *(male and female offenders)* will be beheaded *(immediately)*. If it is rape, the rapist will be immediately beheaded.

4. Everyone who engages in illicit sexual intercourse with a concubine *(of one of the formerly mentioned [male] relatives)* will receive a punishment re-duced one degree *(from that for engaging in illicit sexual intercourse with a wife)*. In the case of rape, he will be strangled *(with delay. The question of whether the wife or the daughter receives the same penalty or not, as well as whether or not the act was consummated, whether there was a broker, whether there were those who tolerated and facilitated the act, will be decided according to the article on illicit sexual intercourse [Art. 366]. However, sons or daughters born of illicit sexual intercourse in the same clan are not to be entered in the clan register. It is permitted to register them in any other part of the register [presum-ably parts reserved for base persons]).*

[From *The Great Qing Code*, trans. William C. Jones (Oxford: Clarendon, 1994), pp. 347–350, modified]

ADVICE TO LOCAL OFFICIALS ON HANDLING SEXUAL OFFENSES

Huang Liuhong (b. 1633) passed the provincial level civil service examination in 1651 and in 1670 received his first appointment as a county magistrate. He had a long and successful career, and by the 1690s he was serving in the capital. While ill in 1696 he dictated a manual for local officials, titled *A Complete Book Concerning Happiness and Benevolence (Fuhui quanshu)*. It offered practical advice on everything a new degree holder would need to know when taking up office, from collecting taxes to handling lawsuits, performing ceremonies, and providing famine relief. The book served a real need and quickly gained wide circulation. Below Huang discusses how to handle sexual offenses, interpreting the statutes for his readers and offering the benefit of his experience.

Document 6–21

FUHUI QUANSHU

ILLICIT SEXUAL INTERCOURSE: GENERAL DISCUSSION

Illicit sexual intercourse is the result of unsuppressed passion between man and woman. When it is rampant among the people, good social customs suffer. When it is unsuppressed, society's moral principles deteriorate.

Licentious customs are easily developed through the maintenance of intimate contact between the sexes. The enforcement of strict separation between males and females is the foundation of the cultivation of proper conduct. It is important therefore for those who rule over others to teach them that men and women should be segregated and that marriages should take place at proper times. A girl ten years old should not eat at the same table even with her brothers. Boys and girls must sit on separate benches. Male and female relatives should not mingle and dwellers of inner and outer apartments should never meet except on ceremonial occasions. Male servants young and old should not enter the inner gate unless summoned. Female go-betweens, mediums, quacks, or procuresses should be banned from the home so that they will have no chance to swindle and seduce the womenfolk. Young women should not be permitted to visit temples on the pretext of burning incense or to indulge in outings and wanderings in springtime. Local elders and village headmen should be instructed to oust licentious women or prostitutes in their localities when they are found, and, with the parents' assistance, to teach frivolous and dissipated youths to mend their ways and perform useful work. If these steps are taken the avoidance of contacts between sexes can be expected to help reduce the chances for lewd dalliance and suppress the spread of licentious habits.

Members of rich and prosperous families develop lascivious habits because they have leisure time on hand, while those of indigent families are oblivious to a sense of shame because they are ignorant and have to strive for a living.

Many iniquitous and vicious individuals develop lustful desires as soon as they see a pretty face, and some dissipated and unstable youths forget to conduct themselves properly when they have a glance of an attractive woman.

When men flirt with females and use lewd expressions and clever language to consummate illicit liaison, their actions are called illicit sexual intercourse by consent. When individuals use stratagems and deception to achieve their lustful purpose and thus ruin the reputation of faithful wives, these crimes are called illicit sexual intercourse by intrigue. When wicked persons carrying weapons forcibly violate the bodies of females by breaking into their dwellings, their actions are called rape. The most shameless situation is the one in which a husband knowingly allows a man to commit adultery with his wife and he himself becomes a spectator of his cuckoldry. There are also cases in which because of poverty or jealousy a woman seduces a man and later accuses him of rape in order to cover up her guilt. Such cases start with illicit sexual intercourse and end with false accusation of rape.

Although there are all kinds of illicit sexual intercourse cases, they can be largely divided into illicit sexual intercourse by mutual consent and rape. Despite this simple difference, the nature of the crime varies according to the relationship between the culprits and the victims—whether the crime is committed between relatives, between people of different social standing, or between government officials and common people. In each case the punishment is different. . . .

ILLICIT SEXUAL INTERCOURSE BY MUTUAL CONSENT

Under the Penal Code on illicit intercourse by mutual consent between a man and an unmarried woman, both parties shall be punished with seventy blows; between a man and a married woman, both parties shall be punished with eighty blows. In illicit intercourse between a man and a female under twelve years of age, the man shall be punished as a rapist in all cases.

Persons abetting or conniving at meetings of parties guilty of illicit intercourse shall suffer the punishment next in degree, as usual in the case of accessories.

For illicit intercourse between relatives, the offenders shall be punished with 100 blows, three years of penal servitude, or even with strangulation, depending upon the relationships of the offenders and the circumstances under which the crimes were committed. For illicit intercourse with someone's concubine, the offenders shall receive a punishment reduced by one degree.

A slave or an indentured servant who has illicit intercourse with his master's wife or daughter shall suffer decapitation and so shall the woman. If a slave or an indentured servant is guilty of illicit intercourse with his master's relative within the fourth degree, he shall suffer strangulation and the dissolute woman shall be punished one degree less.

For civil or military officers of government and their official clerks and attendants guilty of illicit intercourse with the wives or daughters of the inhabitants under their jurisdiction, the punishment shall be two degrees more severe than in ordinary cases between equals; they shall also be deprived of their offices and employment. The woman, if consenting, shall be punished for such consent only as in ordinary cases.

In the case of an official who commits illicit intercourse with a woman prisoner, since he has used his power of office to achieve his purpose he is subject to the penalty of three years penal servitude. The female prisoner may be left with no choice but to submit; therefore, she shall not be subject to any aggravation of the punishment to which she was previously liable. But the crime is not considered a rape on the part of the offending official, because only female criminals who have committed murder or other serious crimes are condemned to death and confined in prison. They are not ordinary free citizens, hence illicit intercourse with them cannot be considered rape.

A slave who is guilty of illicit intercourse with the wife or daughter of a freeman shall be punished one degree more severely than a freeman would be under the same circumstances. On the other hand, the punishment of a freeman for having illicit intercourse with a female slave shall be one degree less than in ordinary cases.

RAPE

Among all sexual crime cases, only the crime of rape is punishable by death. The trial of rape cases should, therefore, be carried out with utmost care for fear of condemning innocent people to death. Rapes are accomplished by the use of force, either by threatening with knife or ax when the victims have no way to resist, or by using ropes to tie up the victims, leaving signs of struggle such as wounds on the body or torn clothes. Only under such circumstances are the criminals convicted of rape and subject to the death penalty.

If illicit intercourse is committed by the use of force at the beginning, but the woman acquiesces at the end, or if during the commission of the crime she yells and struggles at first but accedes to the will of her violator when the act is successfully carried out, the crime cannot be considered rape.

If a woman commits illicit sexual intercourse by consent with a person and is discovered by another who then uses force to have illicit intercourse with her, the crime cannot be considered rape, since she is a dissolute woman in the first place. The case should be considered as a case of illicit sexual intercourse by intrigue.

There are cases in which vicious individuals, admiring the beauty of certain women, satisfy their carnal desires by bribing lewd procuresses or immoral nuns to induce the woman to attend festivals or go to the temple to burn incense, and by putting drugs secretly into their drinks rendering these women unconscious so the ravishers can satiate their lust. Such crimes may not involve the actual use of force or physical restraint on the victims, yet they are consummated by the use of tricks and drugs and cannot be considered anything but rape. The principals of these crimes should be punished as rapists, while the procuresses or nuns who connived with them must be punished as accessories of rapists. If the rape is unconsummated, the offender shall receive 100 blows and exile to a distance of 3000 li, the punishments commensurate to the crime.

There are also cases in which a husband at first consents to the illicit sexual intercourse of his wife or concubine and then orders her to accuse the man of rape afterward. In some instances the woman yells loudly for help in the room and the man flees, leaving his clothes behind. On other occasions the husband waits for the man outside and ambushes him with weapons before he has a chance to escape. When such cases are brought to the court, can the magistrate declare that they are all rape cases indiscriminately?

In such cases it is quite possible that the husband accuses the adulterer of rape because he wants to stop the liaison between his wife and the man and to cover up his past permissiveness. The woman pleads the same because she is afraid of her husband and, incidentally, can maintain her innocence and preserve her reputation of fidelity. The clothes left behind by the adulterer may represent either a trick played by the woman or a struggle, and the ambush may be a clever maneuver to entrap an unwary person. There will be grave injustice if all such cases are considered rape.

As to the proof of illicit sexual intercourse, the statute provides that there shall be no conviction for illicit intercourse unless the participants are caught in the act; conviction cannot be obtained simply because someone states that it has taken place. Since the statement of a third party is not valid proof, conviction cannot result from it.

Someone may ask whether a couple could be considered as committing illicit sexual intercourse when they are caught indulging in an obscene embrace and voluptuous kissing, just short of actual intercourse. The statute on killing a man who has engaged in illicit sexual intercourse provides that when a woman is discovered by her husband in the act of illicit sexual intercourse, if the husband kills the adulterer, the adulterous wife, or both in the act, he shall not be subject to punishment. A note attached to this statute provides that if the guilty parties are not caught in the act, the husband who kills either of them shall not be protected by this statute. This means that under such circumstances the law concerning killing the adulterer in the act does not apply. Indulgence in obscene embraces and voluptuous kissing, short of actual intercourse, is a crime punishable under the statute covering lewd dalliance. Whether the husband wants to prosecute the pair or not remains his choice.

Someone may inquire whether, since the husband must be the one to catch the adulterer in the act, the woman's father- or mother-in-law, her husband's uncles, or brothers are ineligible to expose such a crime. Suppose the husband has to leave home for a long time, who is there to restrain a adulterous wife from indulging in shameless and licentious conduct? A note attached to the statute provides that the husband's brothers, relative with mourning obligations, people living in the same household, and people having the responsibility for performing such duties are all eligible to catch the adulterers. If anyone among the woman's parents, uncles, aunts, brothers, sisters, or even maternal grandparents wounds or kills the adulterer on the spot, he or she enjoys the same immunity the husband would have. The only injunction is that a junior relative should not kill a senior relative; if that happens, the culprit should be punished according to the statute on killing by intent. On the other hand, if a senior relative kills a junior relative under the same circumstances, he shall be punished according to the degree of closeness of their relationship. Therefore the husband is by no means the only one eligible to catch his wife's adulterer. . . .

Someone may pose the following question: Suppose there is a woman who has no senior relative and whose husband leaves home for a distant place; the woman lives in an isolated dwelling and her paramour comes and leaves without inhibition; she may have sons or nephews, but being junior relatives they cannot take action. Under such circumstances should the law permit such licentiousness to continue, affronting decent social custom?

The answer is that there must be neighbors and villagers who, detesting the woman's open debauchery, could catch the adulterer on the spot with the village headman and the local elders as witnesses. Fired by righteous indignation, they might even kill the adulterers on the spot. In such a case it would be inappropriate to treat them as a third party and punish them according to the statute on killing in an affray. Since the village headman and local elders have the responsibility of advising and controlling the local population, they cannot be considered outsiders, but "persons having the responsibility to perform such duties." From this we can conclude that the law on illicit sexual intercourse is very stern toward the offenders.

Some say that because the statute on illicit sexual intercourse by mutual consent punishes the offenders with flogging only it is too lenient and fails to inhibit violations. I am of the opinion that the statute on illicit sexual intercourse by mutual consent is by no means too lenient. We must admit that sexual desire is universal and no one is immune from it. Only by observing the principles of propriety can a cultivated person refrain from indulging in it. There are occasions when mixed company is traditionally permitted; these are the occasions when flirtations between men and women get started. Many social gatherings where large numbers are present provide opportunities for licentious couples to arrange appointments for trysts. Secluded pavilions and deserted corridors where privacy can be expected become places for practicing carnal knowledge. If Draconian laws are applied to such offenders, many young and beautiful lovers will have to forfeit their lives. Therefore when the ancients enacted the law, they considered human feelings. The principle of propriety is used to govern the conduct of gentlemen and gentlewomen, while the law is used to control the behavior of the common people. Lustful behavior and shameless conduct are manifestations of the animal instinct. The fact that the penalty for illicit sexual intercourse by consent is limited to flogging is based on the idea that lowly people, like animals, are so stupid that they are unworthy of reprimand.

As to the sexual crimes that violate the order of consanguinity or good social custom, such as the crime of incest between close relatives, the offenders shall be subject to strangulation. Even if the crime is unconsummated, the offenders shall be subject to flogging and exile. In the case of a slave having illicit intercourse with his master's wife or daughter, even by mutual consent, the slave shall be beheaded and the woman strangled. This shows that not all offenders in illicit sexual intercourse cases can get away with merely being flogged.

Why does the statute provide a heavier penalty for rapists than any other sex offenders? When a sexual act is forced on a woman, an innocent and chaste person suffers violence and dishonor under duress. The death penalty imposed on the rapist is a means of acclaiming the virtue of chastity and discouraging debauchery of womanhood. The heavy penalty is not designed simply to punish those who use force to satisfy their animal desire.

Among relatives there is a difference between the senior and junior relatives in the order of consanguinity. If incest is committed by the use of force, the offender shall be beheaded; if the victim is a concubine, the offender shall be strangled. The same severe penalties are also applied to cases in which the offender is a slave or an indentured servant, since the crime is considered more serious than that committed by an ordinary person. If an official rapes the wife or daughter of a subordinate, the offender shall be beheaded because he has used his influence or power in committing the crime. Likewise, a father-in-law who rapes a daughter-in-law, or an elder brother-in-law who rapes a younger sister-in-law shall also suffer decapitation because the offender has used his position to coerce his junior relative into submission. . . .

ILLICIT SEXUAL INTERCOURSE BY INTRIGUE

There are two kinds of illicit sexual intercourse by intrigue. In one kind a woman is enticed by flattery and sweet talk of someone in the service of the adulterer to forsake her husband and leave her home to consort with the adulterer. Another kind occurs when the adulterer uses his influence to intimidate a woman into succumbing to his demand. Although in both cases the illicit sexual intercourse is committed by consent, they are essentially different from those cases in which the parties indulge in carnal knowledge as a result of mutual admiration.

In enticing by sweet talk, the go-between may trick the woman by comparing the poverty of her husband with the wealth of the other man; another may emphasize the old age and ugliness of her husband as against the youthful and handsome appearance of her admirer; still another may say that her husband is rough and uncouth while her admirer is considerate and tender. By nature all women are fickle and only a few can resist such temptations. To be sure, there are virtuous and chaste women who resolutely reject such proposals with stern language as soon as they are offered, and the go-between then has to retreat in shame. But if the woman listens attentively and becomes interested, she will not be able to restrain herself from falling into the trap.

When a go-between induces a woman to commit illicit sexual intercourse, there must be an adulterer behind the scheme. The magistrate must investigate thoroughly who the go-between was and where the illicit sexual intercourse took place. The penalties should go beyond the administering of the usual number of blows to each of the guilty parties; the go-between should be punished also. As to the case in which the adulterer uses his influence to intimidate the woman into illicit sexual intercourse, if she fails to reject his proposal with stern language as a virtuous woman should, and instead succumbs to his proposal, the statute governing cases of illicit intercourse by mutual consent or by intrigue provides that the man and the woman should be deemed equally guilty.

Nevertheless, if the crime of illicit sexual intercourse is committed under intimidation, it is essentially different from the illicit sexual intercourse committed as a result of mutual admiration. The woman who loses her chastity through intimidation is really a victim of the scheme initiated by the man. Although the law does not provide a heavier punishment for the man in such a case, his behavior is contemptible when human feelings are taken into consideration. I myself feel that the man should be punished by analogy under the statute on illicit intercourse between an official and females under his jurisdiction, that punishment being two degrees more severe than an ordinary case of illicit sexual intercourse between equals. The woman should be punished as in an ordinary case of illicit sexual intercourse because she was under intimidation of the man when the crime was committed. Thus the punishment will fit the crime. This, however, is my personal opinion. I mention it here in the hope that it will serve as a deterrent to those who may attempt to commit illicit sexual intercourse by intrigue.

TRIAL OF ILLICIT SEXUAL INTERCOURSE CASES

When a husband brings a complaint of illicit sexual intercourse to the court, he usually pleads that it was a case of rape. The magistrate must therefore carefully compare the statements made by the parties with the contents of the original written plea. He should observe the demeanor of husband and wife to see if they are really full of righteous indignation. He further observes the appearance of the accused to determine if he is really a knavish and wicked fellow and whether his testimony is over casual or evasive. The witnesses are then questioned minutely.

If it is a case of rape, the statements in the plea will be straightforward and coincide with the oral testimony. If it is a case of illicit sexual intercourse by consent misrepresented as a case of rape, the statements in the plea will be twisted and their oral accounts ambiguous. The demeanor of the husband will not show true indignation. He will pretend indignation and will keep glancing fleetingly at his wife for fear she may say something inappropriate. The woman's appearance will give no sign of wrath or mortification and her statement will be incoherent. During cross-examination she will contradict herself frequently. When confronted with the accused, she will bow her head and become speechless. This proves that the woman is still under the spell of the accused and is not entirely unmindful of their past friendship. If the appearance of the accused does not indicate a malignant personality and his answers to questions appear to be forthright and honest, and if the statements of the witnesses do not provide conclusive evidence of the use of force, it would be imprudent to decide that it is a case of rape. The witnesses are bound to have some knowledge of the affair if it was an illicit sexual intercourse by consent, and in the atmosphere of a public trial, even though they are compelled to tell the truth, they are not disposed to state arbitrarily that it was a case of rape.

Rape often occurs in isolated dwellings or lonely mountain passes where it is opportune to commit such a crime. Anticipating resistance, the offender usually brings with him a knife or other weapon to threaten the victim. During the struggle both parties are apt to have wounds on their faces or wrists. The woman's underclothes will be torn during her resistance as the offender forces her in haste. How could an intruder burst into a village dwelling in broad daylight without a weapon, rape a woman, and leave her with no marks or wounds and no torn clothes?

There are instances when a fierce desperado commits flagrant rape by sheer brute force; the victim cannot resist his overwhelming strength or is tied up and gagged by the intruder. But if the woman is chaste and decisive and prefers to die rather than be ravished, she will yell in spite of gagging. Would no one in the neighborhood come to her rescue when they heard her yelling for help? Those who come to help would see the scene and bear witness. Under such circumstances the verdict of rape can be passed without hesitation and no fear of miscarriage of justice should bother the magistrate.

However, if there is yelling at the beginning, but the noise suddenly stops as the neighbors begin to wonder about the commotion, this is probably a case of rape at the beginning, but the woman then acquiesces. After the man leaves the scene, the woman regrets what has happened, or as the neighbors gather to inquire about the commotion she cannot keep silent and is obliged to tell her husband tearfully that she has been raped. The husband, without knowing of the woman's acquiescence, insists on vengeance and prosecution of the man as a rapist. This puts the magistrate in a dilemma, since he cannot put extremely intimate questions to the parties in public and the witnesses may be unwilling to mention in a trial that there was noise at the beginning and silence at the end. In this situation should the magistrate declare that it is a case of rape?

Under the statute, a rape which is not resisted to the end should not be considered a rape and the offender should not be subject to strangulation. The rationale of the ancient lawmakers for inserting this provision in the statute was the desire to judge a case by the offender's intentions. For instance, when a woman is confronted with a rapist and her reputation is at stake, she will disregard her safety and yell for help. When she is under duress, her hope of rescue constantly occupies her mind. Even after the rapist departs, her yelling and wailing will continue without interruption. Despite the physical abuse, her intention of keeping her chastity prevails. On the other hand, if a woman who is forced to perform a sexual act by an intruder protests with a loud noise, but after the act is successfully consummated changes her mind and acquiesces to the violence, it means that the woman has given her tacit consent to the rapist, and the case must be considered as illicit sexual intercourse by mutual consent rather than rape. The sitting magistrate should pronounce it a case of illicit sexual intercourse by consent or a doubtful case in which the culprits are punished with reduced penalties.

There are also cases in which a woman screams rape in her room in the daytime or at night and the husband turns up suddenly to catch the rapist. This is probably a trick to frame an enemy by using one's wife as bait. It is just too coincidental for the husband to turn up at just the right moment. The sitting magistrate confronted with such a case should investigate most carefully to determine the authenticity of the complaint and avoid passing a death sentence on an innocent person.

It is most important for the magistrate to maintain a solemn attitude in the court during illicit sexual intercourse trials. He will be well advised to avoid the use of imprudent expressions or scornful language simply because these cases involve licentious matters. The magisterial court is the focal point of attention of the whole district and illicit sexual intercourse cases have a bearing on the customs of society. The slightest flippancy by the sitting magistrate, who is supposed always to promote morality, will undermine decent social custom.

When interrogating a woman offender, the magistrate should never order her to go near the dais or talk to her in a hushed voice, and should avoid staring at her, lest people laugh at him behind his back and create a scandal. When preparing the statement of decision, the summary of depositions, and so on, frivolous expressions and playful words should be avoided. Otherwise the local gentry will consider the magistrate lacking in seriousness and his superiors will deem him untrustworthy.

In trials of illicit sexual intercourse cases, only the women directly involved are interrogated. Care should be taken to avoid the unnecessary involvement of other women because it would create situations detrimental to the normalcy and tranquility of society.

[From Huang Liu-hung, *A Complete Book Concerning Happiness and Benevolence*, trans. Djang Chu (Tucson: University of Arizona Press, 1984), pp. 431–43, modified]

QING LEGAL CASES CONCERNING SEXUAL OFFENSES

To see how judges interpreted the statutes on illicit sexual intercourse, below are eight cases, classed under three statutes. They are from the *Conspectus of Legal Cases* (*Xing'an huilan*), compiled by Zhu Qingqi and Bao Shuyun in 1834. The work contains over 5,650 cases, most of them from the period 1784–1834. Both compilers served for years in the Board of Punishments and put together this work to provide officials with a handy body of precedents.

Document 6–22

XING'AN HUILAN

SEXUAL VIOLATIONS

The governor-general of Zhili has reported a case in which Fan Youquan tried unsuccessfully to rape a girl of fourteen, Li Erjie. In view of the girl's youth and immaturity, Fan feared the rape would be difficult to carry out. He therefore started by thrusting his finger into her vagina, causing flow of blood.

The girl and her father both maintain that the rape was unachieved, and a midwife who has examined the girl likewise attests her still to be a virgin. The governor-general has accordingly sentenced Fan Youquan to exile [at a distance of 3,000 li] under the statute on attempted but unsuccessful rape. This sentence being in accord with the facts, it is appropriate to request a confirmatory reply.

The governor-general of Zhili has memorialized concerning a case in which Zhang Wentong, perceiving the clear white countenance of Zhao Daoqi, a boy of twelve, decided with Shi Jincai to commit successive sodomies upon the boy. The act was achieved.

By analogy to the sub-statute on successive consummated rapes by more than one man of a respectable woman, Zhang Wentong, as ringleader, is now sentenced to immediate decapitation, and Shi Jincai, as accomplice, to strangulation after the assizes.

TOLERATION BY A HUSBAND OF A WIFE'S OR CONCUBINE'S INFIDELITY

The governor of Henan has reported a case in which Wang Heigou sold his wife to Li Cunjing to become the latter's wife.

Investigation shows that Wang's act was prompted by poverty and illness, which gave him no alternative. Thus, it differs from the selling of a wife done without due cause. His wife, moreover, has no natal family to which to go, so that were her marriage dissolved as provided by statute, this would be detrimental to feminine morality.

After careful consideration of the circumstances, this Board finds that the wife should be permitted to remain with the second husband Li Cunjing, and that Wang Heigou should not be required to surrender the gift-money paid to him.

The general commandant of the gendarmerie of Beijing reported and transferred to this Department a case in which Qu Da seized and had sexual relations with the wife of Chen Wu. In this case, Qu Da has accordingly been sentenced to life exile for forcible seizure of a woman.

Remaining for consideration is the fact that the husband, Chen Wu, tolerated the relationship of his wife with Qu Da, which according to the relevant sub-statute, properly means that her marriage with Chen ought to be dissolved. It also appears, however, that Chen's toleration of the affair sprang from fear of Qu Da's strength and fierceness and was thus dictated by coercion. Moreover, according to what Chen Wu himself says, were his children to remain solely in his care after dissolution of the marriage, his straitened circumstances would make it impossible for him to care for them alone, so that the consequences would be disastrous.

Consideration of the basic circumstances leads us to the decision that both Mrs. Chen and the children should return to her husband and resume living with him.

The Censorate of the North City of Beijing has transferred to this Department a case involving Qiu Gui, who was originally the wife of Wang Bao. Wang, because of poverty, arranged with his wife's father to fabricate a report that he, Wang, had died, so that he might in this way sell his wife as a concubine to Pan Shoulin. Later, however, when Fan learned the facts, Pan's own wife reviled and beat Qiu Gui, who ran away.

Under the statute concerning the buying or selling of a woman, Wang Bao, Pan Shoulin, and Qiu Gui are each to receive 100 blows of the heavy bamboo.

The Censorate of the North City of Beijing has transferred to this Department a case in which Yang Jingrong sold his wife through a go-between to Li Tingzhi, who took her as his wife in ignorance of the fact that she already had a husband.

In accordance with the statute on selling women, the first husband, Yang, and his wife are both to receive 100 blows of the heavy bamboo. His wife, however, is to continue living with her new husband, Li.

ILLICIT SEXUAL INTERCOURSE BETWEEN RELATIVES

The governor of Shandong has reported a case in which Zhang Yongbao had sexual relations with the daughter of his fifth-degree younger cousin, Zhang Yongchao. When the affair was discovered, the girl committed suicide.

Zhang Yongbao is now sentenced to 100 blows of the heavy bamboo and three years penal servitude, this being the penalty provided by sub-statute for a man whose fornication with a consenting woman, on being discovered, leads to her committing suicide out of shame. Furthermore, he is to wear the cangue for 40 days, as specified in the sub-statute which adds this punishment to the basic penalty for fornication, when such occurs between members of the same clan whose relationship to each other lies beyond the five degrees of mourning.

The governor of Shanxi has memorialized concerning a case in which Mrs. Li nee Zhang, after having been widowed for many years, happened to hear of someone getting married in her neighborhood, which so aroused licentious thoughts in her that she enticed Li Mingze, a son of her deceased husband through a former marriage, to have sexual relations with her.

Li had been reared by Mrs. Li during his childhood, and in allowing himself nonetheless to be enticed by her, he showed complete disregard for her status as a stepmother. Both persons are thus equally guilty of a licentious behavior destructive of the primary human relationships. The Code, however, [rather surprisingly] contains no article dealing with sexual relations between a son and his stepmother. Therefore Mrs. Li and Li Mingze, subject to final approval from the throne, are both now sentenced to immediate decapitation by analogy to the statute providing this penalty for illicit sexual relations between a man and the wife of his paternal uncle.

[From Derk Bodde and Clarence Morris, *Law in Imperial China Exemplified by 190 Ch'ing Dynasty Cases* (Cambridge: Harvard University Press, 1967), pp. 427–433, modified]

CHEN DUXIU ON THE WAY OF CONFUCIUS AND MODERN LIFE

Chen Duxiu (1879–1942) was a founder of and frequent contributor to *New Youth*, the magazine that launched the New Culture movement in 1915. Chen had studied in both Japan and France and on his return advocated that the young take history into their own hands. They should break with stagnant old ideas that stood in the way of modern life, with its principles of equality and human rights. In 1917 Chen became dean of the College of Letters at Peking University. The article below appeared in December 1916.

Document 6–23

CHEN DUXIU

The pulse of modern life is economic, and the fundamental principle of economic production is individual independence. Its effect has penetrated ethics. Consequently, the independence of the individual in the ethical field and the independence of property in the economic field bear witness to each other, thus reaffirming the theory [of such interaction]. Because of this [interaction], social mores and material culture have taken a great step forward.

In China, the Confucians have based their teachings on their ethical norms. Sons and wives possess neither personal individuality nor personal property. Fathers and elder brothers bring up their sons and younger brothers and are in turn supported by them. It is said in chapter 30 of the *Record of Ritual*: "While parents are living, the son dares not regard his person or property as his own" [27:14]. This is absolutely not the way to personal independence. . . .

In all modern constitutional states, whether monarchies or republics, there are political parties. Those who engage in party activities all express their spirit of independent conviction. They go their own way and need not agree with their fathers or husbands. When people are bound by the Confucian teachings of filial piety and obedience to the point of the son not deviating from the father's way even three years after his death[36] and the woman not only obeying her father and husband but also her son,[37] how can they form their own political party and make their own choice? The movement of women's participation in politics is also an aspect of women's life in modern civilization. When they are bound by the Confucian teaching that "To be a woman means to submit,"[38] that "The wife's words should not travel beyond her own apartment," and that "A woman does not discuss affairs outside the home,"[39] would it not be unusual if they participated in politics?

In the West some widows choose to remain single because they are strongly attached to their late husbands and sometimes because they prefer a single life; they have nothing to do with what is called the chastity of widowhood. Widows who remarry are not despised by society at all. On the other hand, in the Chinese teaching of decorum, there is the doctrine of "no remarriage after the husband's death."[40] It is considered to be extremely shameful and unchaste for a woman to serve two husbands or a roan to serve two rulers. The *Record of Ritual* also prohibits widows from wailing at night [27:21] and people from being friends with sons of widows. For the sake of their family reputation, people have forced their daughters-in-law to remain widows. These women have had no freedom and have endured a most miserable life. Year after year these many promising young women have lived a physically and spiritually abnormal life. All this is the result of Confucian teachings of ritual decorum.

In today's civilized society, social intercourse between men and women is a common practice. Some even say that because women have a tender nature and can temper the crudeness of man, they are necessary in public or private gatherings. It is not considered improper even for strangers to sit or dance together once they have been introduced by the host. In the way of Confucian teaching, however, "Men and women do not sit on the same mat," "Brothers- and sisters-in-law do not exchange inquiries about each other," "Married sisters do not sit on the wine neat with brothers or eat from the same dish," "Men and women do not know each other's name except through a matchmaker and should have no social relations or show affection until after marriage presents have been exchanged,"[41] "Women must cover their faces when they go out,"[42] "Boys and girls seven years or older do not sit or eat together," "Men and women have no social relations except through a matchmaker and do not meet until after marriage presents have been exchanged,"[43] and "Except in religious sacrifices, men and women do not exchange wine cups."[44] Such rules of decorum are not only inconsistent with the mode of life in Western society; they cannot even be observed in today's China.

Western women make their own living in various professions such as that of lawyer, physician, and store employee. But in the Confucian Way, "In giving or receiving anything, a man or woman should not touch the other's hand,"[45] "A man does not talk about affairs inside [the household]," and a woman does not talk about Affairs outside [the household] and "They do not exchange cups except in sacrificial rites arid funerals."[46] "A married woman is to obey" and the husband is the mainstay of the wife.[47] Thus the wife is naturally supported by the husband and needs no independent livelihood.

A married woman is at first a stranger to her parents-in-law. She has only affection but no obligation toward them. In the West, parents and children usually do not live together, and daughters-in-law, particularly, have no obligation to serve parents-in-law. But in the way of Confucius, a woman is to "revere and respect them and never to disobey day or night,"[48] "A woman obeys, that is, obeys her parents-in-law,"[49] "A woman serves her parents-in-law as she serves her own parents,"[50] she "never should disobey or be lazy in carrying out the orders of parents and parents-in-law." "If a man is very fond of his wife, but his parents do not like her, she should be divorced."[51] (In ancient times there were many such cases, like that of Lu You [1125-1210].) "Unless told to retire to her own apartment, a woman does not do so, and if she has an errand to do, she must get permission from her parents-in-law."[52] This is the reason why cruelty to daughters-in-law has never ceased in Chinese society.

According to Western customs, fathers do not discipline grown-up sons but leave them to the law of the country and the control of society. But in the Way of Confucius "When one's parents are angry and not pleased and beat him until he bleeds, he does not complain but instead arouses in himself the feelings of reverence and filial piety."[53] This is the reason why in China there is the saying, "One has to die if his father wants him to, and the minister has to perish if his ruler wants him to." . . .

Confucius lived in a feudal age. The ethics he promoted is the ethics of the feudal age. The social mores he taught and even his own mode of living were teachings and modes of a feudal age. The objectives, ethics, social norms, mode of living, and political institutions did not go beyond the privilege and prestige of a few rulers and aristocrats and had nothing to do with the happiness of the great masses. How can this be shown? In the teachings of Confucius, the most important elements in social ethics and social life are the rules of decorum, and the most serious thing in government is punishment. In chapter 1 of the *Record of Ritual*, it is said, "The rules of decorum do not go down to the common people and the penal statues do not go up to great officers" [1:35]. Is this not solid proof of the [true] spirit of the Way of Confucius and the spirit of the feudal age?

[From Chen Duxiu, "Kongzi zhi dao yu xiandai shenghuo," pp. 3–5, trans. Wingtsit Chan, in *Sources of Chinese Tradition*, ed. W. Theodore De Bary and Richard Lufrano, rev. ed. (New York: Columbia University Press, 2000), vol. 2, pp. 353–356]

FENG YOULAN ON THE PHILOSOPHY AT THE BASIS OF TRADITIONAL CHINESE SOCIETY

Feng Youlan (1895–1990) studied philosophy at Columbia University from 1920 to 1923, then returned to China to teach philosophy and the history of philosophy, from 1928 at Qinghua University in Beijing. By the 1930s he was a dominant figure in Chinese philosophy circles. In 1949, when many intellectuals left China, Feng decided to stay. He became professor at Peking University in 1952. He strongly believed that traditional Chinese thought, especially Confucian thought, could provide a basis for a modernized China, a view which at times led to strong attacks on him. The essay below was published in English in 1949 and later translated into Chinese for his collected works.

Document 6–24

FENG YOULAN

Traditional Chinese society originated at a time long before the Christian era, and continued to exist, without fundamental change, until the latter part of the last century, when it began to break down with what is usually called the invasion of the East by the West but which is really an invasion of medieval by modern society. The basic factor in modern society is its industrialized economy. The use of machines revolutionized the preindustrial economy which might be agrarian like that of China or commercial like that of Greece and England. . . .

Modern industrialism is destroying the traditional Chinese family system and thereby the traditional Chinese society. People leave their land to work in the factories, together with other people who are neither their brothers nor their cousins. Formerly they were attached to the land but now they are more mobile. Formerly they cultivated their lands collectively with their fathers and brothers, so that there were no products they could claim as their own. Now they have their own income in the form of wages received in the factory. Formerly they usually lived with their parents and perhaps grandparents but now they live by themselves or with their wives and children. Ideologically, this is known in China as the "emancipation of the individual from the family."

With this change of social structure, it is natural that filial piety, which was the ideological basis of the traditional society, should receive the most severe attacks. That is exactly what has happened in China. The attacks reached a climax during the earlier period of the Republic which was established in 1912 when the abolition of *zhong* or loyalty to the sovereign as a moral principle took place. As we shall see, in traditional Chinese society, *zhong* and *xiao*, or filial piety, were parallel moral principles. *Xiao*, once considered the foundation of all moral good, is now regarded by some critics as the source of all social evil. In one popular book of the Taoist religion it is said: "Among all the evils, adultery is the first; among all the virtues, filial piety is the first." In the earlier period of the Republic one writer paraphrased this statement by saying that among all the evils filial piety is the first, although he did not go so far as to say that among all virtues adultery is the first.

During recent years there have been fewer attacks on filial piety and the traditional family system. This fact does not mean that they have recovered much of their lost influence but rather indicates that they have almost completely lost their traditional position in Chinese society. They are dead tigers, to use a Chinese expression, and attacking dead tigers is no evidence of courage. I remember quite clearly that during my youth I often heard people arguing over the advantage or disadvantage of the traditional family system. But now it ceases to be a question of argument. People realize that they simply cannot keep it, even if they want to.

The attacks on the traditional family system have been mostly polemic in character; as a consequence some of the criticisms have failed to do justice to it. For instance, among the many criticisms a major one is that, in the traditional family system, an individual completely loses his individuality. His duties and responsibilities for the family are so many that it seems he can be only the son and grandson of his parents and ancestors, but never himself.

In answer to this criticism it may be said that an individual, in so far as he is a member of a society, must assume some responsibility for the society. The assumption of responsibility is not the same as the abolition of one's personality. Moreover, it is questionable whether an individual's burden of responsibility toward his family and society in the traditional Chinese scheme is really greater than that of an individual in the modern industrial order.

A society under the industrial system is organized on a basis broader than blood relationship. In this system the individual has less responsibility for the family but more for society as a whole. In modern industrialism the individual has less obligation to obey his parents but more of a duty to obey his government. He is less bound to support his brothers and cousins but is under greater pressure to give, in the form of income tax and community chest, to support the needy in society at large.

In modern industrialized society the family is just one of many institutions. But in traditional China the family, in the wider sense, was actually a society.

In traditional China the duties and responsibilities of an individual toward his greater family were really those of an individual toward his family in the modern sense, plus those toward his state or society. It is due to this combination that the duties and responsibilities of an individual toward his family looked heavy.

So far as the traditional Chinese social philosophy is concerned, the emphasis is upon the individual. It is the individual who is a father or a son, a husband or a wife. It is by becoming a father or a son, a husband or wife, that an individual enlists himself as a member of society, and it is by this enlistment that a man differentiates himself from the beasts. In serving his father and sovereign a man is not giving up his personality. On the contrary, it is only in these services that his personality has its fullest development. . . .

According to traditional social theory each individual is a center from which relationships radiate in four directions: upward being his relationship with his father and ancestors, downward being that with his sons and descendants, to the right and left being that with his brothers and cousins. In James Legge's translation of the *Record of Ritual*[54] there are several tables [of mourning obligations] illustrating this point. Within the radius there are different degrees of greater and lesser affections and responsibilities. Persons outside the limit of the radius are considered by the person at the center as "affection ended" and are to be treated by him on the basis of the relationship of friends.

Thus according to traditional social theory every individual is the center of a social circle which is constituted of various social relationships. He is a person and is to be treated as a person. Whatever may be the merit or demerit of traditional Chinese society and its family system, it is quite wrong to say that there was no place for the personality of the individual.

I mention these arguments only to show that, although traditional Chinese society is radically different from a modern one, it is not so irrational as some of its critics may suppose. In saying this I have no intention of supporting it as a working social system in present-day China. In order to live in the modern world in a position worthy of her past China must be industrialized. When there is industrialization, there is no place for the traditional family system and the traditional social structure. But this does not mean that we should not try to have a sympathetic understanding of them and their underlying ideas.

I shall try to give a brief account of these ideas as expounded in the Classics and accepted by most of the educated people in traditional China.

THE IDEA OF XIAO OR FILIAL PIETY

The central philosophical idea at the basis of traditional Chinese society was that of filial piety. "Filial piety" is the common translation of the Chinese word *xiao*, which in Chinese traditional literature has a very comprehensive meaning. In the book *Xiao jing*, or the *Classic of Filial Piety*, translated by Ivan Chen under the title, *The Book of Filial Piety*,[55] it is said that there is a "perfect virtue and essential principle, with which the ancient kings made the world peaceful, and the people in harmony with one another." This perfect virtue is *xiao*, and this essential principle is also *xiao*, which was considered as "the foundation of all virtues, and the fountain of human culture." . . . In Book XIV of the *Lüshi chunqiu*, which is a work of [the third] century [BC] and a product of the eclectic school, it is said: "If there is one principle by holding which one can possess all the virtues and avoid all the evils, and have a following of the whole world, it is filial piety." All the social and moral philosophers of later times agreed with this statement. Even the emperors of the following dynasties in Chinese history used to say proudly with the *Classic of Filial Piety*: "Our dynasty rules the world with the principle of filial piety."[56]

Such is the very comprehensive implication of the word *xiao*, which the simple English phrase filial piety can hardly suggest. To those who are not familiar with its Chinese equivalent, filial piety may mean simply taking care of one's parents. But as the *Record of Ritual* says: "To prepare fragrant flesh and grain which one has cooked, tasting and then presenting before one's parents, is not filial piety; it is only nourishing them."[57] This is no doubt an over-statement, but from the above quotations we can see that taking care of one's parents is certainly only a very small part of the comprehensive implication of the word *xiao*.

One would not be surprised to find that the virtue of *xiao* was so much emphasized in the traditional Chinese social philosophy if one realized that traditional Chinese society is founded on a family system and that *xiao* is the virtue that holds the family together. . . .

THE IDEA OF ZHONG OR LOYALTY TO THE SOVEREIGN

The relationship between sovereign and subject can be conceived in terms either of that between father and son or of that between husband and wife. That is why I say that in ancient times the royal family of the ruling dynasty was considered in one respect as a family over and above the other ones but in another respect as theoretically only one of the many families.

It was quite common to consider the Son of Heaven as the father of the people. It was a common saying that "the serving of the sovereign by the subject was analogous to the serving of the parents by the son." In the *Classic of Filial Piety* it is said: "From the way in which one serves one's father, one learns how to serve one's mother. The love toward them is the same. From the way in which one serves one's father, one learns how to serve one's sovereign. The respect shown to them is the same. To one's mother, one shows love, to one's father both love and respect."[58] In these sayings the relationship between sovereign and subject is conceived in terms of that between father and son. If this relationship is considered in this way, then the royal family of the ruling dynasty must be considered as a superfamily over and above all other families.

But it was also very common for the relationship between sovereign and subject to be conceived in terms of that between husband and wife. One of the similarities between the two relationships is that the tie between sovereign and subject, like that between husband and wife, is, as the Chinese philosophers said, a "social or moral" one, not a "natural" one. That is to say, the tie is not one of blood. That is why, as it is said in the above quotation, one shows one's father both respect and love but to one's sovereign only respect, which is also, according to the Chinese philosophers, what husband and wife should show to each other.

One does not have a chance to choose one's father. That is something determined by fate. But one can choose one's sovereign, just as a girl, before her marriage, can have a choice as to who should be her husband. It was a common saying that "the wise bird chooses the right tree to build its nest; the wise minister chooses the right sovereign to offer his service." It is true that traditionally all the people of the Chinese Empire were theoretically the subjects of the emperor. But it is also true that traditionally the common people had not the same obligation of allegiance toward the emperor as those who entered the official ranks of the government. It was to the officials that the relationship between sovereign and subjects was especially relevant. So even in the time of unification when there was only one sovereign, one still could choose whether to join the official ranks or not, just as a girl might choose to remain single, even though there were only one man whom she could marry. In Chinese history, if a scholar chose to remain outside the official ranks, he was a man, as a traditional saying puts it, "whom the Son of Heaven could not take as his minister, nor the princes take as their friend." He was a great free man, without any obligation to the emperor except the paying of taxes.

Traditionally the analogy between the relationship of sovereign and subject and that of husband and wife was carried further in the common saying that "a good minister will not serve two sovereigns, nor a good wife, two husbands." Before a man decided whether to join the official rank or not, he was quite free to make the choice, but once it was made the choice was final and irrevocable. In the same way, traditionally, a girl before getting married was free to choose her husband, but after marriage her choice was made once and for all.

Traditionally, a marriage was a transference of a girl from the family of her parents to that of her husband. Before marriage she was the daughter of her parents; after it she became the wife of her husband. With this transformation she had new duties and obligations, and above all she had to be absolutely faithful to her husband.' This faithfulness is called *zhen* or *jie* and was considered the most important virtue for a wife.

Traditionally, when a man joined the official ranks, he was in a sense "married" to the sovereign. He transferred himself from his own family to the royal family, which in this sense was but one of the many families. Before this transference he was the son of his parents, but after it he became the minister of the sovereign. With this transformation he had new duties and new obligations, and above all he had to be absolutely loyal to the sovereign. This loyalty was called *zhong* and was considered the most important virtue of a minister.

When a man "married" himself to the royal family, he should devote himself completely to his new duties and obligations, just as, after marriage, a woman should devote herself completely to the management of the household of her husband. Such a change in a man's status was called in olden times the "transformation of filial piety into loyalty to the sovereign."

In traditional Chinese society *zhong* and *xiao* were considered the two major moral values in social relations. A loyal minister and a filial son both commanded universal respect. But this does not mean that *xiao* is not the basic moral principle underlying traditional Chinese society. In the transformation mentioned above a filial son does not cease to be a filial son. On the contrary, in his new circumstances, this is the only way in which he can continue to be a filial son. . . .

THE CONTINUATION OF THE FAMILY

According to traditional Chinese social theory, of the five social relationships that between father and son is the first in importance but that between husband and wife is the first in origin. In the *Book of Changes* it is said: "Following the existence of Heaven and Earth there is the existence of all things. Following the existence of all things, there is the distinction of male and female. Following this distinction, there is the relationship between father and son. Following this, there is the relationship between sovereign and subjects."[59]

Before the establishment of the relationship between husband and wife, "people only knew that there were mothers, but not that there were fathers." In this situation men were the same as the beasts. The establishment of the relationship between husband and wife was the first step in the development of the distinction whereby men distinguish themselves from the beasts. . . .

The marriage of man and woman becoming husband and wife is the beginning of the family. Once there is the family, the marriage of its younger members is needed to continue its existence. In the continuance of one's family one enjoys an immortality that is both biological and ideal. In this continuance one has both the remembrance of the past and the hope of the future.

An individual must die, but death is not necessarily the absolute end of his life. If he has descendants, they are actually portions of his body that are perpetuated. So he who has descendants does not actually die. He enjoys a biological immortality which is possible for all living creatures. This is a fact of nature, but it is only with the social organization of the family system that this fact is brought into bold relief.

With the social organization of the family system, one who has descendants enjoys not only a biological immortality through their bodies but also an ideal immortality through their works and their memories. In their works one's own work is continued, and in their memories one continues to be known in the world. Thus in the family system one is kept both from physical extinction and spiritual oblivion.

Traditionally, marriage was considered in this light. It is said in the *Record of Ritual* that the purpose of marriage is "to secure the service of the ancestral temple for the past, and to secure the continuance of the family for the future."[60] Marriage provides a means for the transference of the life of the ancestors in the past to the children in the future. Traditionally, it was a great duty of a son to become a father. If he failed to do this, not only would his own life face extinction, but what is more important, the life of his ancestors, carried on by him, would also be terminated. So Mencius said: "There are three things (meaning many things) that are unfilial, and to have no posterity is the greatest of them."[61]

In traditional Chinese society, to have a son or sons was the greatest blessing of human life and to have none the greatest curse. The proverb says: "If only one has a son, he should be satisfied with everything." "To play with the grandchildren" was considered the greatest happiness that an old man could have. In traditional Chinese society, when a man had sons and grandsons, he could look on them as extensions of his own life. Hence in his old age he could regard his existence and that of his ancestors as already having been entrusted to others and so could await death calmly, without further care as to whether his soul after death would continue to exist or not. Why should he be anxious about an immortality that was extremely doubtful when he already had one that was assured?

ANCESTOR WORSHIP

Here we see the essential meaning of the practice of ancestor worship. In traditional Chinese society, the function of this practice was both social and spiritual. Socially it served as a means for achieving the solidarity of the family. Since the traditional Chinese family was a very complex organization, its solidarity depended upon some symbol of unity, and the ancestors of the family were the natural symbol.

In traditional China, in places where the family system was carried out in strict accordance with the ideal pattern, the people of the same surname living in one place used to have a clan temple. The temple had its own land and income, which were considered the common property of the clan. The income of the temple was to be used for preparing sacrifices to the ancestors, for helping the widows, orphans, and needy of the clan to live, and also for offering scholarships to the promising youth of the clan to study or take state examinations in the capital. Thus the temple functioned actually as a social work center for the clan.

In the practice of ancestor worship, according to the theory of the Chinese philosophers, the dead are called back by the living descendants, not as ghosts coming from a supernatural world, but as forms cherished in the minds of the descendants. This is the spiritual or emotional, personal side of the practice, as it comforts the individual and strengthens his morale, in addition to fostering the solidarity of society. . . .

Thus the filial piety taught by the ancient kings required that the eyes of the son should not forget the looks (of his parents), nor his ears their voices; and that he should retain the memory of their aims, likings, and wishes. As he gave full play to his love, they seemed to live again; and to his reverence, they seemed to stand out before him. So seeming to live and standing out, so unforgotten by him, how could sacrifices be without the accompaniment of reverence?

Thus in the practice of ancestor worship the departed, no matter whether they are good or bad, great or insignificant, become familiar once more in the living world. They are not in the world of oblivion but in the living memory of those who are actually the perpetuation of their own flesh and blood. He who practices the worship has the feeling that he will be known to his descendants in the same way also. In such circumstances, he feels that his life is one of the links in a series of an indefinite number of lives, and this fact is at once the insignificance and the significance of his living.

So, in theory there is nothing superstitious in the practice of ancestor worship as conceived by the Chinese philosophers. The fundamental idea of this practice, as they conceived it, is quite scientific. Westerners used to call the practice "religion." I do not wish to argue about terms, especially about such an ambiguous term as religion. But I wish to point out that, if this practice can be called religion, it is one without dogma or supernaturalism. It takes life and death as biological facts. Yet the psychological effect is that a man is "saved" from the momentariness of his life and gains a genuine feeling of a life beyond. Through ancestor worship a man can have salvation without a God or divine savior.

[From *Ideological Differences and World Order: Studies in the Philosophy and Science of the World's Cultures*, ed. F. S. C. Northrop (New Haven: Yale University Press, 1949), pp. 18–34, modified with deletions]

NOTES

1. The Rong were non-Chinese peoples living along the northern and western borders of the Chinese states at this time. Jin, situated on the northern border in the area of present-day Shanxi, was frequently troubled by incursions of the Rong. The Greater Rong used the Chinese surname Ji, claiming descent from Dangshu, the founder of the ruling family of Jin. The Li Rong, mentioned in the next sentence, also bore the surname Ji, and their ruler held the title of nan or baron.

2. Zisi was a grandson of Confucius.

3. Shun was a legendary predynastic sage ruler.

4. Mao 235.

5. Mao 195.

6. Mao 260.

7. Mao 191.

8. Mao 256.

9. Mao 152.

10. Mao 251.

11. Mao 244.

12. Mao 228.

13. *Shi jing* 49 (Zhoushu, Junchen); cf. e.g., James Legge, *The Chinese Classics* (Oxford: Clarendon, 1893–95), 3:535.

14. *Yijing* hexagram 1; cf. Lynn, *Classic of Changes*, 133.

15. *Shi jing*, Mao 13; cf. Legge, *The Chinese Classics*, 4:333.

16. *Shi jing*, Mao 264; cf. Legge, *The Chinese Classics*, 4:562.

17. *Shi jing*, Mao 39; cf. Legge, *The Chinese Classics*, 4:63.

18. *Shi jing*, Mao 260; cf. Legge, *The Chinese Classics*, 4:543.

19. *Shi jing*, Mao 249; cf. Legge, *The Chinese Classics*, 4:482.

20. This story and most of the others cited here are from the *Lienü zhuan*. See Albert R. O'Hara, *The Position of Woman in Early China According to the Lieh nü chuan* (Washington, DC:. Catholic University of America, 1945).

21. *Shi jing*, Mao 254; cf. Legge, *The Chinese Classics*, 4:500. The first quotation is not found in the *Book of Poetry*.

22. *Shi jing*, Mao 260; cf. Legge, *The Chinese Classics*, 4:542.

23. *Yijing* hexagram 61.

24. Lüzhu was a favored concubine of Shih Chong (d. 300). When the prince Sun Hsiu saw her, he wanted her; when he couldn't get her easily, he arranged to have Shih executed. Lüzhu committed suicide rather than be taken. In the end Shih's whole family, fifteen people in all, lost their lives.

25. According to the *Book of Mencius*, 4A:19, Zengzi always served his father with wine and meat. If any was left, he would ask to whom it should be given. If his father asked if there was any more, he would always answer, "There is." The point is that he always wanted to carry out his father's will.

26. *Book of Changes*, text of hexagram no. 18, *gu* [trouble]. The lower trigram is *sun* [yielding], symbolic of obedience. Cf. James Legge, trans., *Yi King*, in *The Sacred Books of China: The Texts of Confucianism* (New York: Scriberner's, 1899), p. 95.

27. According to the *Hou Han shu*, 71:9a, someone asked Diwu Lun if he had any selfishness. He answered, "Once my brother's son was sick. I got up ten times during the night to see him. Then I retired and slept peacefully. When my son was sick, although I did not get up to see him, I could not sleep at all during the night. Can this be called unselfishness?"

28. *Classic of Filial Piety*, chapter 9.

29. Both were Confucius's pupils. See the *Analects*, 5:1.

30. Assuming that the wet-nurse had only enough milk for her employer's child and therefore neglected her own child.

31. The people of Zhangzhou were said to he much given to feuding.

32. Trading salt outside the salt monopoly was prohibited.

33. Although *mofa* sometimes refers to Manichaeanism, it is more likely that the term here means unorthodox, folk religion.

34. Refers to the *Classic of Changes*, "Providing the Sequence of the Hexagrams" ("Xu gua"): "When there arc husband and wife, then there are parent and child. When there are parent and child, then there are ruler and minister *Zhouyi zhengyi (SBBY)* 9:71.

35. Among patrilineal relatives those who were second cousins or closer had mourning obligations to each other. Among relatives of other surnames (through one's mother, father's sisters, and so on), only a much smaller circle were mourning relatives.

36. Referring to *Analects*, 1:11.

37. *Record of Ritual*, 9:24.

38. Ibid.

39. Ibid., 1:24.

40. Ibid., 9:24.

41. Ibid., 1:24.

42. Ibid., 10:12.

43. Ibid., 10:51.

44. Ibid., 27:17.

45. Ibid., 27:20.

46. Ibid., 10:12.

47. Ibid., 9:24.

48. *Yili*, chapter 2; John Steele, trans., *The I-li, or Book of Etiquette and Ceremonial* (London: Probsthain, 1917), 1:39.

49. *Record of Ritual*, 41:6.

50. Ibid., 10:3.

51. Ibid., 10:12.

52. Ibid., 10:13.

53. Ibid., 10:12.

54. Legge, *Record of Ritual*, 2:209.

55. *Xiao Ching*, trans. by Ivan Chen (London, Murray, 1908).

56. Ibid., chap. viii.

57. Legge, *Record of Ritual*, 2:226–227.

58. *Xiao Ching*, chapter 5.

59. *Book of Changes*, appendix 6.

60. Legge, *Record of Ritual*, 2:428.

61. *Mencius*, IVA.26.

INDEX